MAKING CIVIL RIGHTS LAW

MAKING CIVIL RIGHTS LAW

Thurgood Marshall and the Supreme Court, 1936–1961

MARK V. TUSHNET

New York   Oxford
OXFORD UNIVERSITY PRESS

Oxford University Press

Oxford   New York
Athens   Auckland   Bangkok   Bombay
Calcutta   Cape Town   Dar es Salaam   Delhi
Florence   Hong Kong   Istanbul   Karachi
Kuala Lumpur   Madras   Madrid   Melbourne
Mexico City   Nairobi   Paris   Singapore
Taipei   Tokyo   Toronto

and associated companies in
Berlin   Ibadan

First published in 1994 by Oxford University Press, Inc.,
198 Madison Avenue, New York, New York 10016

First issued as an Oxford University Press paperback, 1996

Oxford is a registered trademark of Oxford University Press

Library of Congress Cataloging-in-Publication Data
Tushnet, Mark V., 1945–
Making civil rights law: Thurgood Marshall
and the Supreme Court, 1936–1961 /
Mark V. Tushnet.
p. cm. Includes bibliographical references and index.
ISBN 0-19-508412-8
ISBN 0-19-510468-4 (pbk.)
1. Civil rights—United States—History.
2. Marshall, Thurgood, 1908–1993.
3. Judges—United States—Biography.   I. Title.
KF4755.T87   1994   342.73'085'09—dc20
[3028509]   93-397

9 8 7 6 5 4 3 2 1

Printed in the United States of America
on acid-free paper

To EA, in the tradition of TM

Preface

The movement for civil rights from the 1930s to the early 1960s had many forms. Some were cultural: the African-American experience in World War II, the accelerating migration of African-Americans from the South, Jackie Robinson's performance in desegregating major league baseball. Others were political: Harry Truman's order desegregating the armed forces, the NAACP's efforts to secure antilynching legislation, Lyndon Johnson's support for a civil rights statute in 1957 to strengthen his chances for the Democratic presidential nomination in 1960. Still others were extrapolitical: A. Philip Randolph's threatened march on Washington in 1941, the Montgomery bus boycott of 1955–56. This book examines the most sustained and arguably the most successful of the civil rights efforts in this period: the effort to secure civil rights through litigation. Thurgood Marshall's work as a civil rights lawyer provides the main line of my discussion, but I also deal with litigation that did not involve Marshall directly. Marshall's career, though, shows what the work of civil rights litigation was, and the length and depth of his involvement in civil rights litigation provides an opportunity to explore the ambiguities that characterized the effort to transform civil rights through litigation. Marshall's departure from the National Association for the Advancement of Colored People (NAACP) Legal Defense and Educational Fund in 1961 serves as a fitting close to the study. By the late 1950s and continuing into the 1960s civil rights activity was moving out of the courts and into the streets and the halls of Congress.

Still, Marshall and his colleagues painstakingly constructed the foundations for modern civil rights law. Because this work was *legal* to the core, I show how Marshall, a skilled trial lawyer and appellate advocate, went about the job of making civil rights law. Marshall's trial work was rarely the thrust-and-parry dramatized in film; much more often it was the patient compiling of facts to present to hostile juries and judges. His oral advocacy was commonsense and down to earth, capturing the heart of the moral case for transforming civil rights law.

Yet, although Marshall serves as the focus of the book, the story of how civil rights law was made must include more than Marshall alone. As the head of a law firm engaged in long-term litigation, Marshall helped the lawyers he worked with structure their attacks on public and private discrimination. Marshall's story is therefore also the story of those lawyers and their clients, who were essential to the execution of the litigation plans that Marshall and his colleagues developed; many of the cases that Marshall handled personally were only part of a larger series of cases that his law firm handled. To demonstrate the difficulty of the legal issues Marshall confronted, the book presents a fair amount of detail about the technical legal doctrines that Marshall had to reshape.

Finally, there was another set of actors: the justices of the Supreme Court. The way the justices responded to each case the NAACP presented affected what Marshall and his colleagues could do in the next case. The book therefore goes inside the Supreme Court to describe what the justices were worried about in the NAACP's cases.

Three preliminary notes are necessary. First, I was a law clerk for Justice Marshall in the 1972 Term of the Court, and undoubtedly some of my impressions of him from that time have affected my presentation. I have tried to find sources other than my recollection for statements about Marshall's career and work, in part because I am not confident about the accuracy of my memory. I should note as well that I did not stay in close touch with Justice Marshall after the conclusion of my clerkship, and that I have done my best to avoid relying on the privileged access I had to him for information about his relations with other members of the Court. Finally, as I try to make clear in the body of this book, Marshall has generated intense loyalty in many of those who worked for him, because of the way he gave them responsibility for doing important work and because of their appreciation for his place in the history of the United States.

Second, except in quotations from other sources, I have used the term "African-American" to describe Marshall's race and that of the members of his community. Over the course of his career, standard usages changed dramatically, as did the usages preferred by Marshall and the members of his community. Before 1985–86, Justice Marshall used the term "Negro" in his opinions; from that time to 1989 he used the term "blacks"; then in 1989 he stated that he intended to use "Afro-American," saying that "I spent most of my life fighting to get Negro spelled with a capital N. Then people started saying 'black' and I never liked it." He told an interviewer, "It's everyone on his own. It's like what the old lady said when she kissed the cow—everyone to his own liking" (New York *Times,* Oct. 17, 1989, p. A21, col. 2). Deletions of single letters or word endings, to achieve verb-subject agreement and the like, are indicated with empty brackets ("[ ]").

Finally, during the course of my research for this book, some of the NAACP's papers in the Library of Congress were refiled into boxes different from the ones I found them in. To assist others in locating documents I cite, I have tried to provide as much detail on their location as possible, to the point where the citations may contain a fair amount of redundant information. The detail has the advantage, however, of reducing the possibility that documents cannot be located because of the inevitable mistranscriptions or typographical errors that plague all scholars. In quoting Supreme Court cases, I have ordinarily given only the standard citation to the case, omitting citations indicating the precise pages on which quotations are found.

I would like to thank former Dean Robert Pitofsky and Dean Judith Areen of the Georgetown University Law Center, the staff of the Law Center library, especially Joan Marshall, and the Woodrow Wilson International Center for Scholars for their support of this project. Presentations at the law schools of the University of Southern California, the University of Chicago, the University of Miami, the University of Toledo, and the University of Akron helped me to clarify various chapters. In addition, conversations with Lincoln Caplan, Robert Ferguson, and James Hutson led me to lines of inquiry that I might otherwise have overlooked. Tom Krattenmaker read drafts of nearly every chapter, and made extremely useful suggestions. Katya Lezin and Nicole Tapay gave me crucial research assistance at the late stages of the project.

Washington, D.C.   M.V.T.
May 1993

Contents

Prologue: "You'll Never Find a Better Constitution"   3

1. Setting the Stage: Baltimore and the NAACP   6

2. "No Star Performance": The Office in the 1940s   20

3. "You Did All You Could . . .": Routine Work in the 1940s   42

4. "A Negro on Trial for His Life": Criminal Law and Race Discrimination   56

5. The "Increasing Power" of Private Discrimination   67

6. "A Carefully Planned Program": Attacking Restrictive Covenants   81

7. "Interference with the Effective Choice of the Voters": Challenging the White Primary   99

8. "Passing Through a Transition": Education Cases, 1939–1945   116

9. To "Determine the Future Course of Litigation": Making the Record on Segregated Universities   126

10. "Replete with Road Markings": The Supreme Court Deals with Segregated Universities   137

11. "A Direct Challenge of the Segregation Statutes": Making the Record in *Brown*   150

12. "Behind This Are Certain Facts of Life": The Law in *Brown*   168

13. "Boldness Is Essential But Wisdom Indispensable": Inside the Supreme Court   187

14. "Quietly Ignoring Facts": Examining History   196

15. "When They Produce Reasons for Delay": Devising the Remedy   217

(on "balancing equities" (222-23))

16. To "Open the Doors of All Schools": Passive Resistance to *Brown*, 1955–
    1961   232

17. "Civil Rights . . . Civil Wrongs": Massive Resistance to *Brown*, 1955–
    1961   247

18. The "Battle Between the Sovereigns": Violent Resistance to *Brown*, 1955–
    1961   257

19. "An Act to Make It Difficult . . . to Assert the Constitutional Rights of
    Negroes": The Attack on the Lawyers, 1955–1961   272

20. "A Mortal Blow from Which They Will Never Recover": The Attack on the
    NAACP, 1955–1961   283

21. "I'd Kind of Outlived My Usefulness": The Changing Context of Civil Rights
    Litigation   301

Epilogue: "Power, not Reason"   314

Notes   317

Bibliography   371

Table of Cases   381

Index   385

MAKING CIVIL RIGHTS LAW

Prologue:
"You'll Never Find a Better Constitution"

The course of civil rights litigation in the 1940s and 1950s was not smooth. It was a version of the duality that W.E.B. Du Bois said described the lives of all African-Americans: "an American, a Negro; two souls, two thoughts, two unreconciled strivings; two warring ideals in one dark body."[1] For civil rights lawyers like Thurgood Marshall, this duality went to the heart of their work. They were committed to enforcing a Constitution whose promises had been repeatedly betrayed. In speeches and anecdotes, Marshall often expressed the ambiguities of civil rights litigation and the Constitution that ran through civil rights lawyers' work.

Marshall, a great raconteur, used his stories to convey a sense of the ambiguity of a successful career devoted to securing civil rights through litigation. Many, like those in the repertoire of all good storytellers, are variants on the Trickster theme in the African-American oral tradition, and they capture some of the ironies of working within a racist system to combat racism. For example, Marshall described a church that decided to make a charitable donation "to help . . . 'the poor little Negroes of New York.'" They decided to give a major African-American church some land for a cemetery, but the whites in the neighborhood objected to using the land for a cemetery for African-Americans. "They went to the zoning board, the city council, and even to the mayor's office." The minister and other church officials repeatedly persuaded the officials that their project was a worthy one, but each time the white neighbors would find another objection. Eventually, the whites got an injunction against the use of the land for a cemetery. The church still retained the land, and "one day a white man came to the Negro church to talk about the land. Thinking that the white community had finally come to its senses, the minister welcomed the caller," who "quickly made it clear that . . . he was the representative for a major developer who wanted to buy the church's land. After some brief negotiations, the church agreed to sell the land at a price that not only would allow it to purchase land for a cemetery anywhere in the city, but also would pay off the mortgage, repair the building, and generally do just about

3

anything else that it wanted." Marshall concluded this story with its moral: "Thank God for prejudice!"[2]

Another story dealt with the period during which Marshall had a recess appointment to the Second Circuit. The court was to meet in the chambers of Judge Charles Clark to have its picture taken. While setting up his equipment, though, the photographer blew some fuses in the offices, and Judge Clark's secretary called for the building's electrician. Marshall arrived at the chambers for the picture. After the picture was taken, Marshall returned to his own chambers and told his law clerk, "There's a crazy lady down in Judge Clark's chambers." When asked what he meant, Marshall replied, "When I went in, the lady there said, 'You must be the electrician to fix the fuses.' [Pause] She'd have to be crazy to think that *I* could be a member of the electricians' union in New York!"[3]

A final story deals with Marshall's first years on the Supreme Court. By the traditions of the Court, the conferences of the justices are completely closed to outsiders. When a justice needs to send a message out—for example, to ask a law clerk to get an opinion that the justice wants to refer to, or to get some briefs in cases being discussed—the justice who has been appointed most recently takes the message from the conference room to an antechamber, and, if some material is to be delivered into the conference room, takes the material in. Marshall described how this worked in his case: "Here I am, born in the ghetto, worked my way up to be Special Counsel for the NAACP, a judge on the Second Circuit, Solicitor General, and now, what do I hear? 'You boy, open that door!'"[4]

Irony and triumph are intertwined in Marshall's stories about racism and about himself. He presents himself as a successful lawyer, a federal judge, and a Justice of the Supreme Court whose recollections are of general public interest. Yet, integral to each story of success is a statement about the way in which being an African-American qualified Marshall's success. He is marked by segregation, mistaken for an electrician when anyone should know that no African-American could be an electrician in New York—much less, the message is, a federal judge.

Marshall's public speeches, rarely given after his appointment to the Supreme Court, reveal some of the duality that characterized his commitment to the Constitution. To students at Howard Law School in 1979, Marshall reminisced about his legal education, his mentor Dean Charles Hamilton Houston, and the attack on segregation. The talk began, though, with Marshall's criticism of the view that African-Americans had come a long way. "I am also amazed," he said, "by people who say, 'You ought to go around the country and show yourself to Negroes and give them inspiration.' For what? These Negro kids are not fools. They know when you tell them there is a possibility that someday you'll have a chance to be the O-N-L-Y Negro on the Supreme Court, that those odds aren't too good." He said that he was trying to tell the students "there's a lot more to be done." Then, after talking about his career, he returned to the theme of what was to be done. "[W]e have also got to look to the future. They are still laying traps for us. . . . When I say *they*, I think we all know who *they* would include." He urged the students "to continue [the] basic method of practice" that Houston had developed, and to "be careful of these people who say, 'You have made it. Take it easy; you don't need any more help.'"[5]

Perhaps Marshall's most celebrated public statement about the Constitution, aside from his opinions, was an address provoked by the celebration of the bicentennial of the United States Constitution. Marshall was troubled by "the tendency for the celebration to oversimplify," and he refused to "find the wisdom, foresight, and sense of justice exhibited by the Framers particularly profound," because "the government they devised was defective from the start." The difficulty for Marshall was that the framers intentionally perpetuated the system of African-American slavery, "to trade moral principles for self-interest." Marshall pointed out that "while the Union survived the Civil War, the Constitution did not," because it was replaced by "a new, more promising basis for justice and equality, the fourteenth amendment, ensuring protection of the life, liberty, and property of *all* persons . . . ," including African-Americans. Marshall found "striking" the "role legal principles have played throughout America's history in determining the condition of Negroes. They were enslaved by law, emancipated by law, disenfranchised and segregated by law; and, finally, they have begun to win equality by law." This progress was "dramatic," he said, and "it will continue." He concluded by "seek[ing] a sensitive understanding of the Constitution's defects, and its promising evolution," so that "we will see that the true miracle was not the birth of the Constitution, but its life, a life nurtured through two turbulent centuries of our own making, and a life embodying much good fortune that was not."[6] In its statement of the ambiguous success of the struggle for equality through constitutional law, the speech was more subdued than speeches by justices ordinarily are.

In retrospect, the claims made on behalf of African-Americans may seem like "simple justice," to quote the title of Richard Kluger's superb study of school desegregation litigation. Marshall and his colleagues had a better understanding of the Constitution's complexity and ambiguity in practice, which shaped their overall view of the Constitution. Marshall concluded a 1979 speech about affirmative action: "the goal of a true democracy such as ours . . . is that any baby born in the United States, even if he is born to the blackest, most illiterate, most unprivileged Negro in Mississippi, is, merely by being born and drawing his first breath in this democracy, endowed with the exact same rights as a child born to a Rockefeller. Of course it's not true. Of course it never will be true. But I challenge anybody to tell me that it isn't the type of goal we should try to get to as fast as we can." And, in a 1987 broadcast interview, Marshall responded to Carl Rowan's question about "the constitutional perils of the future" by saying, "Oh, we're going to have our setbacks, we're bound to have them, but it'll work. You'll never find a better Constitution than this one, I know."[7]

1

Setting the Stage:
Baltimore and the NAACP

In the late 1920s, Charles Hamilton Houston implemented a plan to transform the law school at Howard University, Washington's university for African-Americans, into a place where the African-American community could find leaders to fight the racial discrimination embedded in the law. Until 1930, Howard's law school had been a typical municipal law school, operating in the evening so that working students could obtain law degrees. Most instructors were practicing attorneys who took their affiliation with the law school as a distinctly secondary part of their work. Houston was a 1922 graduate of Harvard Law School, where he had been the first African-American chosen, on the basis of his grades, for membership on the prestigious Law Review. His academic work attracted the attention of Felix Frankfurter of Harvard's faculty, who sponsored him for an overseas fellowship and supervised his post-graduate work at Harvard. Houston joined Howard's faculty in 1924, while he practiced law with his father in Washington, and he became its academic dean at the end of the decade.[1]

Houston absorbed the lessons of American legal realism from Frankfurter. He described law as "social engineering." As social engineers, lawyers had to decide what sort of society they wished to construct, and then they had to use the legal rules at hand as tools. But, Houston understood, the lawyers' toolbox included more than the rules that the courts stated. It also included an appreciation of the social setting in which the law operated. Lawyers therefore had to be able to explain to lawmakers how rules actually operated in society, and to do that they had to draw on the information that sociologists, historians, and other students of social life made available.

From the beginning, Houston wanted to train lawyers who could attack race discrimination. As Marshall put it, Houston was "hell bent on establishing a cadre of Negro lawyers, dedicated to fighting for equal rights . . . [both] to do something for Negroes as such, and . . . to raise the image of the Negro lawyers." In 1927 and 1928 Houston conducted a study of African-American lawyers. As he saw it, the lawyers fell into younger and older groups, with the younger having "a higher conception of the privileges and responsibilities of the lawyer" than the older. He was particularly critical of older African-American lawyers "who have depended chiefly on Negro practice," writing that "they tend to regard the profession as a trade for exploitation" and did not respond to "civic or racial matters which do not touch directly upon their own personal interests." Community activists complained that "the lawyers have isolated themselves from other forces and agencies working for racial advancement." Houston did note that the older lawyers' "struggle for existence has been so hard and bitter" that they had little time for other activities. In contrast, the younger lawyers showed "a distinct responsiveness to the ideals of the profession," and were "alive to curre[n]t community and national problems and their possible effects on the Negro group."[2]

Houston's vision of the possibilities for the African-American bar coincided with the desire on the part of Howard's president Mordecai Johnson to upgrade the law school. In his first years at Howard, Houston began to redesign the curriculum, and he took charge of the law school when he was appointed academic dean in 1929. He phased out the evening division and secured accreditation of the law school from the Association of American Law Schools. Houston was an inspiring figure, perhaps because he was "a very hard man," a "perfectionist," who demanded that his students become "highly skilled professionals," because, if they were to transform the law of race discrimination, they would have to "meet the best out there." According to Marshall, Houston taught his students that "the secret was hard work and digging out the facts and the law." Houston introduced students to examples of professional achievement by drawing on his connections with Harvard to bring eminent lawyers and scholars like Clarence Darrow and Roscoe Pound to address them. He began to build a library sufficient to help train lawyers to fight discrimination.[3]

The rigor that Houston required made Howard a new kind of law school. Rather than produce lawyers who would provide ordinary legal services to African-Americans, Houston produced lawyers who wanted to change society. That, of course, affected students in different ways. Some found the new course too challenging; only about one-quarter of the class that entered with Marshall graduated with him in 1933. Those who remained were strongly motivated by Houston's vision. They sat around the law library discussing how they could attack race discrimination after they graduated and, Marshall said, there was scarcely an issue that the Supreme Court dealt with over the next decades that Houston's students had not thrashed out in the early 1930s.[4]

Thurgood Marshall always described himself as "a Southerner . . . [b]orn and brought up down there." In the 1940s he told people that "about three-fourths of my work is down below the Smith and Wesson line." But he was an African-American Southerner, and his experiences shaped his interpretation of the United States and its Constitution. In an interview in 1989, when he was eighty years old, Marshall described his hometown of Baltimore as "the most segregated city in the United States." In 1987, Marshall responded to a suggestion that African-Americans are too "sensitive" about discrimination by describing how he had rushed from downtown Baltimore, where no store would let African-Americans use their bathrooms, to use the toilet at home. As Marshall said,

"That is a little more than an inconvenience. And guess what? I remembered it!"[5]

Marshall was born in Baltimore on July 2, 1908, the second boy in the family. His parents William and Norma Arica named him Thoroughgood after his paternal grandfather, a modest invocation of the African-American tradition of giving children unique names. (Marshall's mother was named after Bellini's opera, which her father heard in the South American seaport Arica. Among her sisters and brothers were Avonia Delicia and Fearless Mentor.) As a boy, Marshall found his name too long, and shortened it to Thurgood.[6]

Marshall's family lived on Druid Hill Avenue, a "respectable street" in west Baltimore. Druid Hill was the center of the African-American middle class community, though Marshall later said that he hung out in the "back alleys where the roughnecks and the tough kids" were. Marshall's father was a dining-car waiter on the Baltimore and Ohio Railroad, and through Marshall's childhood was a steward at the elite white Gibson Island club, running the club's service operations as a sort of "maitre d'." His mother taught kindergarten.[7]

The image of the strong African-American was part of the Marshall family's lore. As Marshall told the story, a "rich man from Maryland went to the Congo on a hunting expedition." A young boy followed him to his boat, and the man brought him back to America, "thinking he was getting a free slave." The boy grew up "into one mean man," and his master told him, "You're too ornery to keep and too ornery to sell to a white man." But, he said, he would set him free "if you'll get out of the town and county and state." Marshall's great-grandfather replied, "I ain't going nowhere," and "settled down a couple of miles away . . . and nobody ever laid a hand on him." That, Marshall concluded, "is what I call ornery."[8]

Marshall's mother wanted him to be a dentist, but his father led him in the direction of law by orchestrating arguments about politics at the dinner table. Will Marshall, fair-skinned and blue-eyed, could have passed for white; he used phrases like "That's right black of you" as a form of praise and "That's the white man in the wood pile" as a criticism. He told his sons, "If anyone calls you nigger, you not only got my permission to fight him—you got my orders to fight him."[9]

Marshall brought this view about race relations to his study of the Constitution, which he said he first encountered as a result of classroom misbehavior. As punishment, his grammar school principal required Marshall to learn a section of the Constitution. Marshall was punished so often that "[b]efore I left that school . . . I knew the whole thing by heart." Like Marshall's story about his ornery great-grandfather, this one is more significant as an indication of Marshall's attitudes than of events in his life. His law school classmate Oliver Hill recounts a similar story about reading the Constitution: When a relative died, Hill inherited a copy of the United States Code; after reading the Fourteenth Amendment, Hill concluded that no reasonable person could believe that segregation was consistent with the Constitution. Similar stories about reading the text of the Constitution and being inspired by it pervade accounts of the early lives of African-American lawyers, but appear less often in accounts of the lives of white lawyers. It is hard to avoid the feeling that the Constitution and its text resonated in the lives of these African-American lawyers in the way that, and perhaps because, the Bible resonated in the life of the African-American community. When, in later life, a magazine writer referred to "Marshall's feeling of love and awe for the Constitution," and another mentioned Marshall's "profound, almost religious, respect for the law," the undercurrents are brought to the surface.[10] And, as with religious texts, the tension between the Constitution's words and segregation's reality provided the impetus for these lawyers to reconcile reality with the words.

Until the first decade of the twentieth century, Maryland had a vigorous two-party system in which African-Americans participated actively as members of the Republican party. Republicans took control of the Baltimore government in 1895, but the Democrats returned to power in 1899 in a campaign whose slogan was "This Is a White Man's City." Over the next decade the Democrats conducted a sustained struggle to disfranchise African-Americans and consolidate their own power. Although some restrictions on voting were imposed in 1904, opposition from Republicans and the "intense political involvement" of African-Americans defeated the effort to enact more significant restrictions in 1905 and 1909. Although African-Americans were able to protect their formal voting power, the circumstances of their lives changed. Heightened racial tension led to "numerous incidents" in which African-American women were "accosted sexually" by white men during this period. Jim Crow laws, new to Maryland, were adopted, and there was a "sharp increase" in "informal segregation."[11]

Marshall attended Baltimore's segregated high school for African-Americans. He did well enough in the school's strong academic program, though he was not an outstanding student. After graduation in 1925 he went to Lincoln University in Pennsylvania, sixty miles from Baltimore. Lincoln was, as its name suggested, a school for African-Americans, but its faculty was all white. Marshall began as a pre-medical student, intending to satisfy his mother and become a dentist. However, he had persistent run-ins with a biology professor, which contributed to his decision to change his career plans.[12]

Marshall graduated with honors from Lincoln. Barred by Maryland's segregation laws from attending the state university's law school in Baltimore, Marshall began law school in 1930 at Howard. To save money, he and his wife Buster, whom he had married in September 1929, lived with his family. Marshall commuted to Washington each day by train, getting up at five in the morning and returning to Baltimore on the last train of the evening. Despite his academic achievements at Lincoln, Marshall had not spent much time on his studies there. Howard, though, was different, and Marshall said that he really studied "for the first time in my life" at Howard.[13]

Marshall graduated in 1933 and opened a law practice in Baltimore. It was not an auspicious time. The city's African-American community, always heavily concentrated in domestic service and common labor, suffered severely from the effects of the Depression. More than 40 percent of the community was on relief in 1934, compared with 13 percent of the white community. The city administration in Baltimore was slow in developing relief programs, and was particularly uninterested in ensuring that African-Americans participated fairly in relief efforts.[14]

These economic conditions made starting a legal career hazardous. When

Marshall's friend Oliver Hill opened his practice in Roanoke, Virginia, he found that most of his work consisted of garnishing the wages of workers on behalf of the Norfolk and Western Railroad; this was so dispiriting that he gave up the practice and returned to Washington, where he worked for several years as a waiter. Marshall had somewhat greater success. The African-American bar in Baltimore was the only one that Houston praised in his 1928 survey. Houston found that "no Negro lawyer in Baltimore has ever had any considerable white practice." The older lawyers "consider the lawyer as a defender of rights," and they had routinely taken cases of "discrimination or oppression . . . with or without fee." One of these lawyers, Warner McGuinn, had been one of the first African-Americans to graduate from Yale Law School, where he had received financial assistance from Mark Twain. McGuinn allowed Marshall to operate out of an office next to his, though they never became partners. According to Marshall, McGuinn "bailed [him] out a couple of times," by keeping Marshall from making mistakes in his lawyering.[15]

Marshall began to develop the usual practice of a new lawyer on his own. He handled tenant-landlord disputes, some misdemeanor cases, and various other small claims. A typical case saw him accepting a $15 fee to investigate a client's claim that she was entitled to a divorce based on adultery; Marshall obtained the criminal record of his client's husband, but then, after a brief investigation indicated that his client had no case, offered to refund the $15. The lawyer who took over much of Marshall's practice when he left Baltimore accurately described Marshall's cases: "You have the happy faculty of securing some of the damnedest cases of any young lawyer on record." A secretary later said, "He had a genius for ignoring cases that might earn him any money." In his first year, Marshall lost $1,000 on his practice. Gradually, Marshall began to attract more substantial clients, including a large laundry, the association of African-American funeral directors, and, perhaps more important, Carl Murphy, the publisher of the Baltimore *Afro-American*. Even so, Marshall had to take a job at a city health clinic, where he worked as a file clerk two nights a week and on Saturdays, finding that the job paid reasonably well and, perhaps more important, gave him an assured salary.[16]

Marshall's practice developed slowly because he was deeply involved in the affairs of the Baltimore branch of the National Association for the Advancement of Colored People (NAACP). Founded in 1909, the NAACP was the largest organization devoted to transforming the system of race relations in the United States through public education and legal action. The NAACP had branches throughout the country, though its policy was set by a national staff and board of directors in New York. The Baltimore branch had been moribund in the late 1920s, but Marshall and civic leader Lillie Jackson devoted enormous efforts to getting the branch active again. They held meetings at which Marshall spoke, conveying to NAACP members Houston's ideas about using the law to change society. Marshall's activities brought his name to the attention of potential clients like Carl Murphy (and to a group who asked whether he was interested in running for Congress), but his devotion to the community meant that he was frequently called upon to represent people who could not pay him. One judge told a woman from

South Carolina that she needed a lawyer and should "go down to this lawyer Marshall. He's a freebie." That was when, Marshall said, he "realized that that wasn't a good way to make a living."[17]

Marshall could not make a living in Baltimore during the Depression if he counted only on the routine work that the African-American community could give him—nor did he want to. His NAACP work was what he cared about. Inspired by Houston, Marshall wanted to change the law. "My first idea," he said, "was to get even with Maryland for not letting me go to its law school."[18] So he did.

In December 1933, barely six months after he opened his practice in Baltimore, Marshall became interested in suing the University of Maryland. He wrote Conrad Pearson, who had graduated from Howard in 1932, for the papers from a lawsuit that Pearson had filed on behalf of Thomas Hocutt, an applicant to the University of North Carolina's pharmacy program. Hocutt's lawsuit failed because he had graduated from the North Carolina State College for Negroes, whose president James Shepard, believing that the successful operation of his college required that he refrain from challenging segregation, refused to provide Hocutt with an official transcript and recommendations. Marshall was in a happier situation in Maryland. Finding "things . . . very slow just now," Marshall was anxious to begin a legal challenge in January 1934, but it was not until March 1935 that he and a client got together.[19]

Marshall's client was Donald Murray, a graduate of Amherst College from a prominent Baltimore family, who wanted to attend the University of Maryland law school. In December 1934 Murray applied for admission and, of course, was rejected. William Gosnell, counsel for the Alpha Phi Alpha fraternity to which Marshall belonged, brought Murray's case to Houston's attention. The university's president pointed out that the state did have a statute saying that the board of regents could award scholarships for attending out-of-state schools, though the legislature had appropriated only $600 for the scholarships in 1933. Once the correspondence had finished, Marshall consulted with Houston and they filed a petition in state court on April 8, 1935, asking that the board of regents be directed to admit Murray to the law school.[20]

Marshall's interest in suing the university stemmed from his experience and, perhaps more important, from plans that Houston had been developing to challenge the Jim Crow system in court. From its founding through the 1920s the NAACP supported litigation against segregation, but until the 1930s it did so catch-as-catch-can, dealing with cases of injustice that had attracted national attention or with cases that individual litigants and their lawyers wanted to pursue. In the late 1920s the NAACP developed a working relationship with the American Fund for Public Service, a left-wing foundation also known as the Garland Fund because it received its money from Charles Garland. Garland set up the fund with an inheritance he refused to live on because, in his view, it was founded on the exploitation of the working class. Roger Baldwin, who also founded and directed the American Civil Liberties Union, ran the Garland Fund. Garland and Baldwin combined interest in mobilizing the working class with an interest in civil liberties and civil rights, mainly because they believed that agitation to secure civil rights was a useful organizing technique.[21]

James Weldon Johnson, the executive secretary of the NAACP in the 1920s, was also a director of the Garland Fund. He proposed that the fund give the NAACP money "to finance a large-scale, widespread, dramatic campaign to give the Southern Negro his constitutional rights" and thereby "a self-consciousness and self-respect, which would inevitably tend to effect a revolution in the economic life of this country." Despite Johnson's effort to cast the proposal in revolutionary terms, Baldwin and Garland were skeptical about its radical credentials. Anticipating that litigation successes would be highly qualified, Baldwin wrote a friend that the proposal "amaze[d]" him, because "such a legalistic approach will fail of its object because the forces that keep the Negro under subjection will find some way of accomplishing their purposes, law or no law." By a closely divided vote, the Garland Fund board decided to offer the NAACP about $100,000 to support a coordinated campaign of litigation against Jim Crow laws in transportation, education, voting, and jury service.[22]

The law of race relations in the 1930s took as its starting point the Supreme Court's 1896 decision in *Plessy v. Ferguson,* which established that states could impose segregation by law. Although *Plessy* did not explicitly say so, it rapidly became clear that states could impose segregation under the Constitution only if they provided "separate but equal" facilities for African-Americans. The proposed campaign was designed to make it so expensive to maintain a segregated system, by enforcing the requirement of separate equality, that the South would abolish the Jim Crow system.

The first step in the plan was to hire a lawyer to "map[ ] out" a litigation strategy by figuring out which defendants to sue, what sort of lawsuit to bring, and, where the implications of the separate but equal doctrine might be unclear, what proper legal theories to apply. Houston endorsed the candidacy of Nathan Margold for the job. Margold, a white lawyer who had recently graduated from Harvard Law School, began working in October 1930. He hoped to produce the litigation plan within six months, but it took until May 1931 before he delivered it. The primary reason for the delay was that the Garland Fund money trickled in to the NAACP, and never was enough to enable Margold to work on the plan full time. Eventually the Garland Fund provided the NAACP with a little more than $20,000, over a three-year period.[23]

Margold gave the NAACP a 218-page report, divided almost evenly between a discussion of legal challenges to segregated education and a discussion of challenges to residential segregation. Johnson's proposal to the Garland Fund had suggested using taxpayer suits to force Southern legislatures to spend equal amounts on both parts of the dual school systems. Margold, in contrast, argued in favor of a direct attack on segregation rather than an attempt to enforce the "equal" part of separate but equal. In his view, it would be extraordinarily difficult to devise lawsuits to enforce equality; the precise language of the South's segregation laws meant, as Margold interpreted the law, that there would be serious procedural problems in figuring out whom to sue and what relief to ask for. He suggested that the NAACP's lawsuits focus on the facts that state law required

separate schools, that expenditures were unequal, and that there were no mecha-
nisms under state law to make expenditures equal. "We have," Margold wrote, "a
case of segregation irremediably coupled with discrimination." He believed that, in
these circumstances, the courts could be persuaded to declare that segregation
itself was unconstitutional.[24]

Because the Garland Fund did not come through with all the money it had
promised, the NAACP did not immediately begin to implement Margold's suggestions. The fund did give the NAACP a final grant of $10,000 in 1933. By then
Margold had started working for the federal government. The NAACP hired
Houston to coordinate the litigation campaign, and Houston left Howard for the
NAACP's New York headquarters in 1935. Even while he had been in Washington, though, Houston had consulted closely with the national office, and he had
been developing his own ideas about how to attack segregation. As an educator,
Houston found himself drawn to segregated schools, rather than segregation in
housing or transportation, as the key to the problem. He prepared a film for the
Garland Fund on the conditions of segregated schools, and his notes for the sound
track indicate that he believed that "education is a preparation for life." He
believed that "[e]conomically inferior education makes [African-Americans] less
able to stand competition with whites for jobs," and that students who were denied
"real educational opportunity" were a "drag" on the entire state. As the work he
had done to transform Howard Law School showed, he also believed that it was
essential to develop a talented leadership class in the African-American community. These interests converged in the plan that Houston implemented at the
NAACP.[25]

Houston returned to the original idea of making it too expensive for the South
to maintain segregated schools. At the level of tactics, he focused on two targets.
He wanted to bring lawsuits to make the salaries of African-American teachers
equal to those of white teachers, and he wanted to force Southern universities to
admit African-Americans to their graduate and professional programs. The equalization suits were attractive because, Houston believed, establishing inequality
would be relatively easy: the lawyers just had to produce evidence about salaries,
rather than examine in detail the many different components that made African-
American schools as a whole inferior to white schools. The equalization suits also
were attractive, because if they were successful they would provide an immediate
financial benefit to African-American teachers. This would bring credit to the
NAACP as an organization, and it would bring more money into the community as
a whole. The university suits were attractive for similar reasons. If the suits
succeeded, there would be more African-American professionals to serve as leaders of the community. And the legal theory in the university cases was straightforward in the 1930s. Southern states provided graduate programs for whites, but,
although they had undergraduate institutions for African-Americans, they had no
graduate programs for them. Some states provided scholarships to support attendance by African-Americans at out-of-state universities, but it seemed to Houston
that even such schemes could not overcome the obvious argument that the states,
rather than providing separate but equal graduate programs, were providing none
at all.[26]

A hearing on the Murray case was scheduled for June, and throughout May Marshall sent memos to Houston almost daily on Murray's case and others he was handling. Houston had Marshall find out how many foreign students attended the university, the number of students at Howard who were from Maryland, the number of scholarships the state had awarded under its program for African-Americans—all in an effort to show that denying admission to Murray was unreasonable. Concerned about public reaction, Houston suggested that they issue a press release pointing out that African-Americans had attended the University of Maryland in the past; indeed, two had graduated from the law school in 1889. They had little to fear, as it turned out. The June hearing was held before Judge Eugene O'Dunne, a popular and colorful judge who "ha[d] a genius . . . for publicity." After O'Dunne heard testimony from Murray, the university president, the law school dean, and a few other witnesses, the state's lawyers moved to adjourn the hearing to give Judge O'Dunne time to make a decision. O'Dunne told Marshall to object, and then ruled from the bench that Murray had to be admitted to the law school in September.[27]

The state appeals court denied the university's request to accelerate the schedule for hearing its appeal so that the university would not have to admit Murray in September. Marshall asked the Alpha Phi Alpha fraternity to give Murray money for books and tuition, and Murray registered and attended the law school without incident. Through the summer and early fall Marshall worked intensively on his response to the state's appeal, which proceeded despite Murray's enrollment. He asked Houston whether he should take two weeks off from his other work to prepare summaries of every case related to *Murray* "so that we may have a brief which may be used in all subsequent cases." Houston agreed that "it is much more important to have the Murray case in good shape." Marshall wondered whether the brief should try to distinguish law schools from undergraduate programs where there might be concern about contact between African-American men and white women. Houston thought not: "From a standpoint of organization tactics, that would be to convict us of chiseling a principle just to acquire a technical victory." In October Marshall sent Houston a draft brief that consisted mainly of a compilation of quotations from other cases. Houston told Marshall that it "needs to be thoroughly re-worked," and within a few weeks Marshall produced a substantially improved draft, in which the arguments were made more clearly and more argumentatively. With Houston's guidance, Marshall was maturing as a lawyer.[28]

In its most substantial argument, the university contended that the scholarship program satisfied the state's obligation under the separate but equal doctrine. Marshall and Houston responded that sending students elsewhere could not satisfy the state's *own* duty to provide separate schools for African-Americans. At the oral argument before the court of appeals, Houston, the more experienced advocate, was more polished in his presentation, but Marshall got to the heart of the case when he said, "What's at stake here is more than the rights of my clients; it's the moral commitment stated in our country's creed." Marshall said that the state "confuse[d] the issue of segregation and exclusion. . . . Donald Murray was not sent to a separate school of the University of Maryland. . . . Donald Murray was excluded from the University of Maryland entirely." The court of appeals appreciated the point; it affirmed Judge O'Dunne's decision. The core of its opinion was that the state could not balance a complete exclusion from the law school by making scholarships available to attend some other school: equal treatment meant equality "in respect to any one facility or opportunity furnished to citizens, rather than of a balance in state bounty to be struck from the expenditures and provisions for each race generally."[29]

Houston's close supervision of Marshall's work in *Murray* was Marshall's real introduction to the careful practice of law. Marshall quickly appreciated the importance of attention to detail, as he pursued his task of summarizing all the relevant cases and the investigations that Houston asked for on matters that might seem quite peripheral to the case, like identifying the law schools the judges attended. *Murray* was Marshall's first great success, but he also learned about how to be a lawyer in a second, unsuccessful challenge to segregation.

Houston's plan to attack segregation did not include an immediate attack on inequality in facilities. His film for the Garland Fund was part of a plan for "public exposure" to "appeal to the conscience of the better minded whites" rather than preparation for litigation. Houston was reluctant to get into cases involving facilities because he believed that establishing inequality—as distinct from exclusion, as in *Murray*—would be quite difficult. The factual investigations that had to precede filing a lawsuit were relatively well defined in the first university cases. Investigating inequality in facilities, in contrast, meant going around to all the schools in a district, examining how recently they were built, how well they were maintained, whether they had laboratories and how well equipped those were, and much more. Finally, even a victory in one school district might have little impact on segregation elsewhere, if the district's response were merely to increase its expenditures on a few schools. Eventually, of course, paying for equal facilities would become too expensive, as Johnson's proposal to the Garland Fund said. But, at the early stages of the litigation campaign, it did not make much sense, in Houston's eyes, for the national office to devote many of its limited resources to attacks on unequal facilities.[30]

The picture was different in Maryland, where Marshall had a lot of energy and time on his hands. In mid-1935, even before the trial court's decision in *Murray*, Marshall spent days travelling on Maryland's Eastern Shore and around Baltimore, inspecting the schools, giving speeches on behalf of the NAACP, and taking pictures of classrooms and laboratories. Marshall found the case he wanted close to home, though, and it was more like an exclusion case than a facilities one. Baltimore County, wrapped around the city, had no high schools for African-Americans. Students who wanted to continue their education had to attend the segregated schools in the city of Baltimore. The city charged tuition to nonresidents, but the county would pay the tuition through the eleventh grade for African-American students who passed an entrance examination. The legal theory for a challenge to the county's system was simple. It had a high school for whites and none for African-Americans. If anything more was needed to show that here separate was not equal, it should have been enough to point out that whites did not have to pass a special entrance examination to attend high school, while African-Americans did.[31]

Carl Murphy located some students who were willing to become plaintiffs in an NAACP challenge. Marshall and Houston consulted regularly about the suit. First they had to decide what sort of remedy to ask for. Having been imbued by Houston with the idea of law as social engineering, Marshall believed that the case gave them a chance to "experiment, try out the different remedies and discover which is the best to be used" in cases to be brought elsewhere. Houston suggested that Marshall prepare two lawsuits, one against the city, to force admission to the segregated schools there without an entrance examination, and one against the county, to insist on desegregation of its schools. The suit against the city would reduce adverse reaction by whites who feared desegregation. The suit against the county was more important. Houston believed that it would force the county to choose between providing a high school for African-Americans and desegregating the existing schools; he knew that actually providing separate but equal schools would probably be too expensive.[32]

Marshall began by meeting with the county's parent-teachers' association. After he told them that a young woman named Margaret Williams was prepared to apply for admission to the city high school without having passed the examination, the meeting "turned toward the left and resulted in a drive for N.A.A.C.P. membership." Over the next months Marshall prepared a thorough factual case about the schools in the city and the county. He calculated the distance from various neighborhoods to the city high schools and took pictures of the schools. He wanted to show that the county's segregated schools were so bad that the courts should disregard the fact that graduates often failed the entrance examination they had to take; Margaret Williams, for example, received a grade of 244 on her second try at the test, when 250 was a passing grade. In some ways Marshall's preparation may have been *too* thorough, because it may have obscured the simple legal theory on which the case rested. But, as Marshall knew, they were "in for a real battle" because the judge was strongly opposed to the NAACP's position. At a hearing in July 1936, "the main sore point with the other side was our statement . . . that they were not willing to face the facts and were trying to dodge the issues and, in so many words, 'just couldn't take it.'"[33]

Houston gave Marshall a detailed outline of what to do at the trial. Although one of Houston's colleagues at Howard called Marshall's work before and during the trial "a thing of beauty," the trial judge followed through on his inclinations and ruled against Marshall, finding that the central issue in the case was not whether students should be allowed to skip the entrance examination but was, instead, whether the plaintiff had passed it, which everyone knew she had not. Marshall appealed this decision, and again his concentration on the inadequacies of the county's schools may have misled the appeals court. First it said that he had sought the wrong remedy. If the entrance examination did not actually test the applicant's true ability because of defects in the county's schools, the remedy should have been to develop a new test, not to admit her without a test. Then the court said that requiring an examination of African-American applicants but not of whites was not discrimination, because the city's entrance examination was the equivalent of the final exams that white students took. It acknowledged that the white students' final examinations were geared to what they had been taught in each class, while the entrance examination was general and was not designed with what the African-American applicants had studied in mind. But, the court said, these were mere details, "incidental differences" to handle "practical problems."[34] More than a decade passed before Marshall and the NAACP took up the challenge of desegregating high schools.

Houston understood that in Marshall he had a student who had the potential to surpass him. Houston nurtured Marshall's career in many ways. He was always available to answer Marshall's questions, and their correspondence reveals Marshall gradually growing as a trial lawyer under Houston's supervision. Marshall learned that the events in the courtroom were only a small part of the trial lawyer's work. Far more important, he had to develop the facts through intensive investigation. Once the facts were in hand, Marshall learned, the trial lawyer had to be sure that they were admitted into evidence. Even if the trial judge ruled against him, as would frequently happen in civil rights cases, Marshall had to be sure that he developed a record that would allow an appellate court to reverse the trial judge. There was nothing flashy about this part of the job; getting the facts and getting them admitted are essential, but they are not exciting tasks. Fortunately, Marshall found that he could make speeches for the NAACP and meet with people wherever he went to dig up the facts, and the personal contacts he had invigorated him. Marshall was a charismatic speaker, "lean, hard, and Hollywood-handsome, a black Ronald Colman," who easily drew his audience along with him.[35]

Houston sponsored Marshall in other ways, as well. Clients came to Marshall because he was, as he put it, Houston's "Baltimore associate." In January 1935, when Houston sent Marshall a check for $25 to repay some litigation expenses, Marshall told him that Houston "cannot imagine how much I needed" the check: "I have had a terrible month and everything has been in a jam." Another check, Marshall told Houston later that year, "will keep the wolf away from my door."[36]

Houston also helped Marshall inside the NAACP. In 1935 he asked Walter White, the NAACP's chief executive, to give Marshall money to travel to the national conference of the NAACP "to acquaint him with the work and to let the Conference and public see more young Negro lawyers who are working for the Association." He encouraged White to give Marshall a call because "the psychological effect on him will be good." When the Alpha Phi Alpha fraternity asked Houston to speak to it on the Murray case, Houston suggested Marshall as a substitute because he was "the real counsel" there, with Houston simply giving it "the weight of greater experience." Recognizing Marshall by inviting him to speak would, Houston wrote, encourage others "that if they go out and achieve, they will receive recognition and acclaim."[37]

Houston may have thought that Marshall's work for the NAACP would help him gain clients in Baltimore, but he knew that Marshall should not "drop everything for N.A.A.C.P. work." He told Marshall to "keep a finger on your office practice whatever you do. You can get all the publicity from the N.A.A.C.P. work but you have to keep your eye out for cashing in." That, though, was not something Marshall found easy to do. He just could not see collecting debts or handling divorces as part of the social engineering that Houston had convinced him the law was. By May 1936, Marshall wrote Houston that "things are getting worse and worse" financially. He asked for help: "Personally, I would not give up these cases here in Maryland for the world, but at the same time there is no opportunity to get down to really hustling for business." Marshall had already begun to explore the possibility of leaving law practice in Baltimore, and applied for a job on the Howard faculty.[38]

Before anything came of that application, Houston solved Marshall's problem. In September 1936 Marshall proposed that he receive a monthly retainer of $150 from the NAACP for his work. Houston knew that he needed help with the legal program. He described himself as an "outside man" who broke down "under too much routine"; he preferred to "keep free to hit and fight wherever circumstances call for action." Houston saw a real opportunity in Marshall's letter, for he knew that Marshall's strengths complemented his own. Marshall's joviality made him extremely adept at the tasks of negotiating and conciliating that office politics required. It also made him superb at what Houston and Marshall came to call "chambers practice," the informal negotiations that are associated with trial work. And, Houston knew, Marshall was getting better and better as a trial and appellate lawyer.[39]

Houston answered by return mail that Marshall should leave Baltimore and join the NAACP's national staff in New York. Houston told Marshall that the NAACP "would consider regular monthly payments" only for members of the staff. And, he wrote, Marshall could not really expect to combine his NAACP work with a regular practice. "The very time your clients wanted you you would be out of the office. The time you had a private case on the docket, that day the Association would require your services." The NAACP needed Marshall in New York, not Baltimore, because of "access, consultation, incidental work, and general utility." And Houston needed Marshall too. "I am not only lawyer but evangelist and stump speaker," necessary work that took him "out of the office for long stretches of time, and slow[ed] down the legal work in New York." He said that he would ask White to hire Marshall "for six months if that interests you." He ended by cautioning Marshall to give the proposal "careful thought"; if he left Baltimore even for six months it would mean "almost a total loss of business" and if he returned he would have to "start[] over again."[40]

Marshall did not hesitate. As soon as he received Houston's letter, he wrote back agreeing to the move. Giving up his Baltimore practice "would mean a loss of practically no profit" because he had been "more or less specializing in the N.A.A.C.P. cases and under those circumstances would much rather do that." He had some ideas for expanding the challenge to segregation, and, he wrote, Houston's idea meant that they had "a chance to do double work to actually carry on a fight, and with a correlation of membership drives to establish strong branches."[41] Houston then went to work to get Marshall the job. He had to persuade White and Arthur Spingarn, the NAACP's president, that the NAACP could afford to hire another lawyer and that Marshall was the right one for the job.

Houston told them that they could "generally depend on [Marshall's] judgment, backed up by [Spingarn] until he has seasoned; and you can absolutely depend on his research." He strengthened his case by making a note on a letter Lillie Jackson had sent indicating that the branch had paid Marshall about $200 in 1936. "[N]ot much," Houston noted, "for a year or half year's work. . . . You've always got to remember that Thurgood's practice had vanished and all he had was his NAACP work. Figure out also the moral effect on the Negro bar in general from rewarding one of our young lawyers who stripped himself for us. May lead others to work harder." White did not need much persuading, for he was already "disturbed about Thurgood's situation, both for his personal sake and because he can contribute so much." White had Houston prepare a letter urging the Garland Fund to approve an appropriation to hire Marshall. Houston then told Marshall to start winding things up in Baltimore. On October 6, 1936, Marshall thanked White for the new job. "I have an opportunity now," he wrote, "to do what I have always dreamed of doing! That is, to actually concentrate on the type of work the Association is doing."[42]

Marshall arrived in New York in October 1936, with a commitment from the NAACP to pay him for six months. "Step by step," his stay extended, first to a year, and then to 25 years at the NAACP.[43]

2

"No Star Performance"
The Office in the 1940s

Around the time Marshall was hired, Houston learned that NAACP members in Tennessee were concerned because, they believed, he had withdrawn from a university desegregation case there. Houston told his colleagues in Tennessee, "This is no star performance." He was "primarily the administrator" of the legal campaign against discrimination, and he wanted to make sure that it would become "self-perpetuating so that the loss of the head or any set of members will not hamper progress." One way to do that, he pointed out, was to ensure that "Negroes not only have a few lawyers but dozens who can push the program through." Even more, "switching and changing" made the campaign more effective because it demonstrated to opponents that they could not derail the challenges merely by harassing Houston with "personal reprisals." Houston understood a central feature of civil rights litigation: that lawyers operated under constraints that limited their success. As Jeremy Bentham put it, "The law is not made by judge alone, but by Judge and Company." Opposing lawyers, unsympathetic judges, clients, the NAACP as an organization, other interest groups—all were part of the "company" with which the NAACP's lawyers had to deal.[1]

The teachers' salary cases were almost perfect vehicles that Marshall and Houston used to show that Houston was not the NAACP's only lawyer. The legal theory was simple, and teachers had a direct financial interest at stake. Indeed, the NAACP insisted that it would support these cases financially only if the teachers and the local NAACP branch provided some litigation funds. Joint efforts meant that there would be many public meetings, and Marshall's powerful public speeches, which captured the urgent moral core of the NAACP's appeal, established close links between the national office and the local branches.

Teachers' salary cases were attractive to the NAACP for many reasons. Teachers were part of the NAACP's strong middle-class constituency. Making their salaries equal to those of white teachers would, as Marshall put it, give "a material benefit to Negroes in general," as the teachers spent their money buying goods and services from African-American "physicians, dentists, lawyers and other

20

professional and business men." There were teachers everywhere, and they could continue teaching—unless they were fired—while their lawsuits proceeded, unlike students attending universities or public schools, who had to get on with their educational plans. Maryland actually had a tenure statute that insulated long-term public school teachers from retaliation, and Baltimore had more African-American teachers than any other city. Further, salary disparities were dramatic. In 1930, African-American elementary school teachers in Maryland received 57 percent of white teachers' salaries. From a litigator's point of view, the salary differences almost spoke for themselves. There were essentially no differences between the formal qualifications of African-American and white teachers that might justify the disparities; in Maryland more than 90 percent of the African-American teachers had regular state teaching certificates, which compared favorably with the rate for white teachers. Finally, seeking to equalize salaries did not challenge, and indeed could be seen as attempting to enforce, the separate but equal doctrine. Its only threat to school boards was financial. Once the NAACP's lawyers proved the differences in salaries, school boards had few legal defenses available.[2]

Marshall began to explore the possibility of a salary suit while still in Baltimore. In late 1935 a teacher who lived there and commuted to his job in Anne Arundel County agreed to let Marshall represent him in a salary suit. Unfortunately, in 1936 the teacher took a job elsewhere, and Marshall could not locate another potential plaintiff quickly. After he moved to New York, Marshall used his Maryland connections to develop salary cases. His office had been in the same building as the offices of the state Commission on Higher Education for Negroes, chaired by federal judge Morris Soper, a liberal on issues of race. Marshall tried to find out whether Soper would be sympathetic to a salary suit, but Soper told him that he should at least refrain from filing in federal court until the commission reported in January 1937. Marshall agreed because he thought "it will be more advantageous to have him on the bench when and if such a case is brought."[3]

Throughout October 1936, in the midst of his relocation, Carl Murphy and Enolia Pettigen McMillan, the head of the state's association of African-American teachers, urged Marshall to start a salary suit. Though neither Marshall nor Pettigen was able to find a plaintiff, the NAACP's publicity paid off when William Gibbs, the principal of a small school in Montgomery County, volunteered to be a plaintiff. Following the procedure Marshall developed, Gibbs asked his school board to equalize salaries in the system; when his request was denied as expected, Gibbs appealed to the state board of education. Marshall's familiarity with Maryland politics allowed him to persuade the state superintendent of schools to have the board rule on Gibbs's appeal immediately. As a result, Marshall filed the case while the state legislature was in session, placing pressure on it to equalize salaries.[4]

Marshall spent most of December 1936 in Maryland preparing the lawsuit, which was filed in state court on the last day of the year. The school board moved to dismiss the complaint, and then for several months nothing happened. Experience would show that this delay was hardly unusual, but Marshall and, more important, the teachers became impatient. After Marshall asked for an early hearing on the board's motion, it was held on July 9. Within two weeks the judge denied the board's motion, and the board immediately proposed to settle the lawsuit on terms Marshall regarded as favorable; the board would equalize salaries over a two-year period, rather than immediately, because the board would have to raise the money by a bond issue that could not take place right away.[5]

By September Marshall wrote Enolia McMillan that it was time to "map plans" for salary suits throughout the state. Over the next year Marshall traveled to counties all over the state to drum up support for salary suits. His work on the Eastern Shore of Maryland was especially important. There had been lynchings there in 1931 and 1933, and African-Americans lived in conditions of "poverty and occasional terror." Marshall later wrote Lillie Jackson, "I, personally, would be in favor of any case in which there was a possibility of striking back at the Eastern Shore of Maryland and everything it represents."[6]

A memorandum Marshall prepared describing one of his trips in Maryland suggests how active he was: He spent April 4, 1938, in Cecil County and divided the next day between Kent County and Queen Anne's County on the Eastern Shore. He was supposed to appear before the school board in Anne Arundel County on April 6, but the board adjourned its meeting before he arrived, and Marshall said that he would not put up with that sort of evasion any longer. Then he returned to the Eastern Shore, taking a hard negotiating stance on a settlement, rushing to Prince George's County near Washington at the end of the day. Some counties did reach agreements with the NAACP to equalize salaries, and the state's Republican governor Harry Nice, as well as the platform of the state Democratic party, supported salary equalization. When legislators responded by introducing bills to raise the salaries of white teachers, Marshall told the committee supporting the lawsuits to write the governor that the bill was unconstitutional, but not to urge that the governor veto the bill; as Marshall pointed out, once salaries were equalized, the higher salaries the bill provided for whites would spread to African-American teachers.[7]

The only real difficulty in the initial stages of the salary cases in Maryland arose when some superintendents tried to retaliate against the teachers. Gibbs, the first to come forward, lost his job in Montgomery County because, it turned out, he did not have a principal's certificate and did not apply for a teacher's job soon enough. The board in Prince George's County, bound by the teacher tenure law, nonetheless refused to renew the contracts of all the probationary African-American teachers. When a principal was fired because he supported the salary campaign too actively, Marshall told McMillan to keep the information confidential: "If the idea gets around that a teacher has been fired as a result of these cases, it will do much to take away the fighting spirit that the teachers are now showing." As Marshall knew, the campaign could "move no faster than the teachers" in each county.[8]

The boards had other tactics to delay the salary adjustments that they probably knew were inevitable. The board in Prince George's County, for example, rejected the teachers' request for equalization in January 1938, and responded to Marshall's lawsuit, filed in March, by resisting his request to inspect the board's records so that he could compile information about individual salaries. Marshall had to sue to get access to the records. The board also engaged in protracted negotiations over a settlement. The basic outlines were agreed on in October 1938, but it took until January 1940 for the board to agree to equalize salaries at the start of the next academic year. These tactics made the teachers "anxious," and Marshall had to spend time reassuring them, "to prevent them from accepting a compromise which will endanger the entire fight."[9]

Marshall got his first precedent in a salary case in November 1939, when federal judge Calvin Chesnut ruled in favor of teachers in Anne Arundel County. The case had been simple from the beginning. Initially, Marshall tried out an ingenious theory that would have brought the state board of education into the case, arguing that because the state provided some money for the county boards, it was implicated in their salary discrimination. If the argument succeeded, Marshall would have been able to cut short his efforts in each county; the state legislature would have to equalize salaries in each county. Judge Chesnut, though, disagreed with Marshall's theory, holding that the state's role in providing funds to the counties was too limited to justify drawing it into the suit. Marshall then returned to the "very simple" and "very clear" position that the county board could not discriminate, and this time Judge Chesnut agreed. He praised the board for its recent actions in reducing salary differentials but, he held, there was no justification, either in different qualifications or different responsibilities, for continuing to pay African-American teachers less than white ones.[10]

Marshall wanted to expand the teachers' salary litigation throughout the South. From the time he joined the staff in New York, Marshall encouraged correspondents to bring salary challenges. In February 1938, he wrote a Virginia teacher that the campaign was "progressing nicely" and that Maryland would be "cleaned up sometime in the near future and [he] will immediately go into Virginia." He viewed the lawsuits as an example of "Heaven helps them who help themselves," and prepared a pamphlet explaining the constitutional issues in terms nonlawyers could understand. He concluded that the teachers could use the lawsuit to "make [whites] glad to give you your rights."[11]

Despite Marshall's best efforts, teachers found it difficult to organize themselves. Marshall understood that the ethics governing lawyers prevented him from "look[ing] for a teacher" to be a plaintiff; someone else had to do that. In July 1938 Marshall received a letter from S. D. McGill, a lawyer in Florida who was interested in bringing a salary suit. The teachers in Brevard County paid the lawyer $500 and asked the national office to chip in. Marshall asked Houston what to do. He believed that, because they had already won some cases in Maryland, "it would be well to jump from there to Florida at the bottom of the southern states, so that the boys in between would know that we mean business." Houston replied that the case seemed "fine if it's soundly planted." He told Marshall that they would "have to go very carefully here and be sure of each step" before they moved. But he advised Marshall against "skipping about in this fight," saying that they should "clean up" Maryland first, then go on to states in the upper South, "where the apple is ripe . . . [and] where the public won't be afraid to support us." Continuing to act as Marshall's mentor, Houston concluded by telling Marshall to "get the preliminaries over by correspondence, but be sure to protect yourself when you write. Always figure in writing this type of letter, that you may have to meet and explain it some future day."[12]

Marshall tried to guide McGill from New York, but McGill, an older lawyer outside Houston's circle of influence, resisted direction. The Florida courts rejected McGill's lawsuit, and Marshall criticized him for failing to prepare the case well enough. After several teachers were fired, Marshall wrote in disgust that the procedures McGill followed "just will not work in those states where they fire the teachers without cause or refuse to give them new contracts. It is not our fault that they do these underhand things but it ruins the cases. Our only hope is in the Federal courts to seek injunctive relief."[13]

Marshall tried again in the deep South in 1938. He met with the head of the Alabama association of African-American teachers, and worked out a detailed litigation plan with Arthur Shores, an African-American attorney from Alabama, but again nothing came of Marshall's efforts. Later in the year Marshall went to Alabama and Florida. He spoke on salary equalization to the convention of the national association of African-American teachers, and found that "enthusiasm . . . is growing much faster than we realize." The teachers supported the program, and the group agreed to increase its dues and send a portion of the increase to the NAACP. However, out of concern for public reaction, Marshall advised that the arrangement be kept confidential. Marshall met privately with teachers from West Virginia, North Carolina, Georgia, Alabama, Louisiana, Texas, and Florida, and expected that they would begin to work on developing salary suits. Marshall thought that teachers in Montgomery might file a lawsuit within a few months. Perhaps displaying his own enthusiasm as yet undampened by the difficulties he faced, Marshall described another trip to Florida as "really worth making." He spoke to small and large groups and believed that the teachers were "ready to go." The "spirit" they were showing was, Marshall thought, "perfect. I am sure we will be able to organize the state around them." Though Marshall carefully refrained from actively seeking plaintiffs for salary suits, his meetings with teachers and his public speeches were designed to encourage the teachers themselves to locate plaintiffs.[14]

Marshall was much more successful in Virginia. In August 1937, after getting the Montgomery County, Maryland, school board to agree to salary increases, Marshall wrote teachers in Virginia that he "would like to get something started" there. In October and again in November he met with leaders of the state teachers' association, who decided to establish a committee to support a lawsuit. Virginia teachers, unlike Maryland's, were not protected by tenure, and the committee planned to raise $5,000 to replace the salary of any plaintiff who might be fired. Teachers were understandably reluctant to draw attention to themselves by suing, and although Marshall's efforts had strong support from P. B. Young, the publisher of the leading African-American newspaper in Virginia, no one came forward to act as plaintiff until October 1938. Then, suddenly, Marshall had two. Melvin Alston, the president of the Norfolk teachers' association, was prodded into volunteering by his members' impatience at the lack of progress. However, Marshall believed that Aline Black, a teacher in Norfolk, was "by far the better plaintiff" because her personal presence made it likely that she would be a better witness. African-American teachers in Norfolk were paid between 60 percent and 70 percent of what whites with equivalent training and responsibilities received. As soon as Marshall filed a petition with the school board asking for equal salaries, the board began to "check up" on Black. When her contract came up for renewal in 1939, the board refused to offer her a contract. She no longer was a suitable plaintiff because she could not benefit from future increases in salaries for African-American teachers in Norfolk, which is all that the equalization suits asked for. The committee overseeing the litigation paid her one year's salary, and she left Virginia to pursue a graduate degree in New York. [15]

The Norfolk African-American community demonstrated to support Black, but Alston had second thoughts. Still, after meeting Marshall in September 1939, Alston agreed to act as a plaintiff, and a new lawsuit was filed at the end of the month. The teachers in Virginia were disappointed with the progress of the cases, and Black complained that Marshall had not given her enough information about why her lawsuit had been dropped. [16]

Marshall went to Virginia in October to explain the situation to the teachers. He told them that "the confusion is based upon a failure to understand our position." The first difficulty, he said, was that the cases were *"new* to the law. There are no precedents." Therefore, the cases were "to an extent experiments," and the lawyers had to find the way to present the complaints "with the least risk and the greatest possibility of success." He explained that the NAACP had tried to compel the boards to raise salaries through actions in state court. But, he continued, the lawyers had begun to realize that "there were several possible ways for school board to defeat [these] actions on technical grounds." The lawyers had not expected that the judge in Black's case would "grant postponement after postponement," to the point when the board was able to fire Black. As a result of this sort of difficulty, the lawyers had developed a theory that allowed them to seek injunctions from the federal courts. Unfortunately, when they first began work on that theory, it seemed to them that the relevant statutes meant that they could use the theory only if some teacher would get a raise of more than $3,000 when equalization occurred, which was almost never going to happen. (Alston's salary, for example, was $921, while that of white teachers with equivalent experience and duties was $1,200, a difference of only $280 per year.) But in June 1939, Marshall said, the Supreme Court held that, in cases like the ones the NAACP wanted to bring, the plaintiffs did not have to show that they would gain any particular amount. The lawyers "immediately started work" on a suit for an injunction in the federal court, and as soon as Alston decided to pursue the litigation, the case was filed. [17]

Alston's case was heard in Norfolk by Judge Luther Way. As Marshall remembered it, he knew he was in trouble when he pointed out that the judge had scheduled the case for Lincoln's Birthday, a federal holiday, and the judge replied, "Well, you follow Lincoln's Birthday up your way—down here, we follow Jeff Davis day." At the hearing the judge "ripped at everything I said," and rejected Alston's complaint on the ground that Alston, by signing a contract setting his salary, waived any objections he might have to the fact that other teachers got higher salaries. Marshall appealed, and in June 1940 the court of appeals agreed with him, saying that the waiver argument was irrelevant because Alston wanted a salary increase for the future, not an increase in his current pay. The court of appeals was impressed by the dramatic differences shown by the school board's salary schedule: In the city's high schools, newly hired African-American women teachers received $271 less than white ones, and African-American men received $416 less than whites. Achieving equal salaries was harder than Marshall and the teachers had expected. The board promised to equalize salaries, but wanted the teachers to dismiss their lawsuit, which would have left them without a legal basis for enforcing the board's promise. Marshall's threat to withdraw from representing the teachers if they accepted the board's offer derailed the agreement, and negotiations continued.[18]

According to Marshall, at one point he had to go back to Judge Way to seek an order holding the school superintendent in contempt of court for refusing, in the superintendent's words, to "pay[ ] a nigger the same money I pay a white person." The judge asked Marshall whether he wanted a criminal contempt order or a civil contempt order. Marshall said that he replied that he saw "nothing to be gained by putting a man in jail," and that he was "perfectly willing to go with civil, if it's all right with you." The judge replied, "Did you know that that's my best friend?" When Marshall said that he did not, the judge said, "Well, despite that, I'm going to go with you." Marshall pointed out, "that's the same man. He was getting ready to put his best friend in jail. Because, you see, in his mind, the law had changed. . . . When the Court of Appeals tells him the law is the other way, that's the way he goes." Marshall took the incident to illustrate that his deference even to hostile judges, reflected in the phrase "if it's all right with you," was justified in the end by his and their commitment to "the law." Eventually the board and the teachers agreed that salaries would be equalized over a three-year period, and that the agreement could be enforced in court.[19]

Marshall's work on the teachers' salary cases placed him at the heart of the NAACP's legal activities. He expanded his acquaintance with NAACP activists beyond Maryland. He gave speeches everywhere. He was so involved in his work that he took no vacation in 1937 and postponed his summer vacation in 1938 to travel to Tennessee to investigate complaints about discrimination by the Tennessee Valley Authority. Within two years of Marshall's arrival in New York, Houston knew that his pupil could take the teacher's place.[20]

According to Marshall, Houston never planned to make a career out of working in civil rights law. His father insisted that Houston return to Washington to help maintain the family law practice; Houston found the strains of the work for the NAACP hard on his health; and, most important, Houston believed that eventually the job of attacking race discrimination through law would be completed, and wanted to be sure that he had some other kind of legal practice to fall back on when the fight against discrimination ended. Houston left New York in 1938, and Marshall formally took over his position as Special Counsel in May 1939. White decided to list both men as Special Counsel, and Houston had no objection because "Thurgood has been doing all the work and I have felt uncomfortable," and because "even if we were both in the office I would endorse Thurgood's being special counsel because we were on a parity at the end."[21]

Another change occurred in 1939. One of the NAACP's major activities in the 1920s and 1930s was lobbying for a federal law against lynching. Under the federal tax laws, the NAACP's lobbying meant that it was not a tax-exempt organization. In 1938, after some regular donors told the NAACP's fund raisers that they would stop contributing unless their donations were tax-deductible, the NAACP tried to get the Internal Revenue Service to change its position. When that effort failed, Marshall picked up on a suggestion made by IRS officials during the negotiations that the NAACP could set up a separate arm for lobbying. Donations to the lobbying group would not be exempt, but donations to the other parts of the organization would be. The idea of setting up a separate organization made sense, but the NAACP's board realized that it would be easier to get large donors to give money for legal and educational activities than for lobbying, while the NAACP's members were a sure source of funds for lobbying. The result was to switch the proposal around—to establish a separate organization to carry on the legal work: the NAACP Legal Defense and Educational Fund, Inc., known later as the LDF or the "Inc Fund." To assure donors that the legal work would be coordinated with the NAACP's overall program, the boards of the two groups overlapped: Marshall served as Director-Counsel of the Inc Fund and as Special Counsel to the NAACP, and part of Walter White's salary was paid by the Inc Fund.[22]

With Houston's departure from New York in 1938, Marshall took charge of the NAACP's legal activities. Houston continued to advise Marshall when asked, but he held firm to his position that Marshall was now in charge, and never sought to interject himself into Marshall's work. Over the course of the next decade, Marshall constructed the job of civil rights lawyer. The job description, later familiar to other public interest attorneys, required Marshall to combine activity in court with managerial and public relations duties. Conducting litigation and arguing cases in the Supreme Court, the activities for which Marshall became famous, were only a small part of his work.

Shortly after Houston left the national office, Marshall told him that "I didn't know anything about money matters," but Marshall rapidly became deeply involved in fund raising and the NAACP's financial affairs. He began to understand that he was a fund raiser as well as a lawyer, writing Walter White at one point, "I am slipping. Hoped to get $1,000 for N.A.A.C.P. but only got $400" at a teachers' meeting. He also became an executive. He advised the NAACP regarding appointments to its legal committee. For example, in 1943 he suggested that James Marshall be appointed: He "controls the Marshall trust fund involving several million dollars—'nuff said."[23]

Marshall, working from New York, also had to coordinate the work of local lawyers. Because the legal work had to be parceled out to lawyers working away from New York, conflicts sometimes arose among lawyers in the field, and Marshall had to pacify the contesting parties. Finally, as a manager, Marshall organized the work inside the LDF office and coordinated its actions with those of the NAACP.

The everyday life of the civil rights lawyer was dominated by the routine of the work. Each day, letters poured in to the NAACP complaining about acts of discrimination in employment, housing, transportation, and all other aspects of people's lives. People sought the aid of the NAACP in rectifying these injustices. The organization lacked the resources to respond favorably to many of them, and in any event the law as it existed, or as it could be changed in the short run, provided few avenues of relief for most of the problems. Even so, the NAACP had to respond to the complaints, if only to show its constituency that it paid attention to their difficulties. Letters to the NAACP office were sorted and the ones having some connection to legal difficulties were channeled to Marshall.[24]

There were so many letters that answering the daily mail necessarily occupied a significant amount of time. A typical letter during the Second World War recounted the circumstances of a soldier whose wife and baby were forced to move out of their basement apartment because they could not pay the rent. Although the soldier's discharge had been approved, and his former employer promised to give him his job back, his discharge was held up because of the outbreak of the war. "The Chaplan made a loan so my wife could buy food and clothing for her and the baby it is snowing and cold up where she is staying," the soldier wrote. Nothing in this letter even referred to the writer's race, much less to racial discrimination as the cause of his difficulties. Responding to the obvious human suffering described in the letter, Marshall had the letter answered and sent it along to William Hastie, then serving as civilian assistant to the Secretary of War with primary responsibility for racial matters, with a request for an investigation. Marshall himself sometimes reviewed the letters in detail, making notes on them and going over transcripts to see if there was anything the NAACP could do.[25]

At the outset, Marshall was the only legal staff member. Over the next few years he hired a few part-time legal assistants, and the secretarial staff picked up some of the legal skills needed for routine office work. Until 1945, though, Marshall was the only lawyer with substantial courtroom duties. The modest staff growth could not fully alleviate the demands of routine letters on staff time. The staff expanded because the NAACP's legal work had itself grown; in growing, it had attracted the kind of attention that generated still more routine letters of complaint. Marshall, and later his staff, ordinarily required that the complaint be based on racial discrimination of a sort that legal action could rectify, and, even more stringently, discrimination whose elimination promised general benefits to African-Americans in the country. As they repeatedly said, the NAACP could not act as a legal aid bureau to assist every victim of discrimination; rather, they sought to take cases involving "the establishment of a precedent which will benefit Negroes in general." In criminal cases, the staff said that it would assist only defendants who were innocent of the crimes for which they were charged or convicted.[26]

Implementing these guidelines was more difficult than it might seem, however. With limited resources, the staff had to be selective, but when a letter arrived in the office, the staff could not always tell whether it presented a mere "legal aid" complaint or offered the opportunity for a broader challenge to discrimination. The initial letters tended to be thin on detail, requiring the staff first to decipher the complaint and then to ask for additional information—again increasing the time devoted to dealing with routine and, usually, unproductive matters.

Restricting criminal representation to innocent defendants was even more difficult to implement. As a general guideline it too was sensible. In declining to act in one case, a staff lawyer wrote that because of "the very large number" of criminal cases, the NAACP required that a case present a "clear question" of discrimination, and that there were "a large number of other more outrageous cases" than the complainant's. There were enough innocent African-Americans convicted of crimes to occupy the staff, and it would have impaired the public image of the NAACP to work on behalf of guilty defendants. Edward Dudley, a staff lawyer, wrote in 1944 that the organization did not generally enter rape cases despite the general belief that the penalties in such cases were too heavy, because there was enough work that did "fall within our rules." Marshall described another rape case as "borderline" because it involved "illicit relations [and] this type of case does not receive much support from many sections of our membership," and declined to participate in another, where a sixteen-year-old was charged with rape and received a death sentence, because the defendant, who had participated in a jail break, "is not the type of person to justify our intervention." Yet, located in New York, the staff was rarely in a position to evaluate the innocence or guilt of defendants. It had to rely on reports from lawyers and NAACP branches where the trials took place, and sometimes these reports were not entirely unbiased themselves.[27]

As the 1940s progressed, and particularly as a result of the large number of courts-martial of African-Americans during World War II, the standards for intervening in criminal and similar cases gradually relaxed. At the outset, the NAACP acted "only in those relatively few cases where it is apparent on the face of the record that the defendant was denied a fair trial because of his race or color." With courts-martial, the policy changed somewhat. According to Franklin Williams, the staff lawyer concerned primarily with military matters, the "court-martial boards have been smart enough to see that such evidence [of discrimination] is not obvious in the records." A policy requiring that racial discrimination be apparent led to strains when there was patent unfairness in the proceedings that nevertheless could not be linked in any clear way to race. This led to efforts to infer racial discrimination from unfairness, as in William Hastie's statement about a case in which the legal issues were unrelated to race: "the obviously improper attitude and conduct of those conducting the trial colors the entire procedure." Under this sort of pressure, the new policy became "more lenient." The office would try to help when "the sentence was grossly disproportionate to the crime charged or the sentence generally meted out in such cases, or where the case involved racial conflict, e.g., rape of a white woman, mutiny of Negroes against white officers, and where in such cases the evidence in our opinion has not established the guilt of the Negro serviceman beyond a reasonable doubt." Marshall and the staff came to understand that the impact of a successful appeal in a criminal case, where the defendant might have been guilty, was often more significant in changing ongoing practices than simply freeing the innocent would be.[28]

What Marshall described as the increased "leniency" in these cases, though, posed new problems. Replacing rigid rules with flexible standards necessarily increased the number of cases that had to receive serious attention, and Marshall continued to caution against getting "too far out on the limb . . . in view of the lack of evidence on our side." Perhaps more important, the new guidelines meant that in more cases the NAACP's action would be a "gesture" aimed at showing that the organization would "go through the motions . . . wherever possible" in capital or other serious cases. These cases did present situations of desperate need, to which the branches sometimes responded inappropriately. On several occasions Marshall had to advise his correspondents to be "careful." When a fugitive from Southern justice came to the NAACP, Marshall said, "we have an unbreakable rule that we will not do anything for them *officially*, while they are fugitives. In this type of organization there is always the possibility of having some trumped-up charge of obstructing justice, etc., and it is always best to be careful." Going through the motions, losing more cases, and investing more time in cases that eventually were failures cost the lawyers both professionally and psychologically.[29]

Marshall and his staff developed canned replies to many of the letters the office received. If no racial discrimination appeared at all on the face of the letter, the writer was told that the NAACP did not handle such cases. If an individual case of racial discrimination seemed to be involved, but no issue of broader significance, the NAACP's replies often referred the writer to a lawyer in his or her city or state, or to the local NAACP branch, which might be in a position to provide some assistance.

Even routine letters about discrimination received relatively personal attention. The letters were often handwritten; once the lawyer figured out the implications of a letter, a response consisting of a modest personalized variation on standard themes did not take much more time to produce. Further, the lawyers, particularly new ones on the staff, naturally responded to the real stories of human difficulties recounted in these letters as compassionately as they could, and resisted becoming "case-hardened." Finally, the African-American lawyers on the staff shared in the experiences of discrimination, and wanted to give personal responses to complaints about discrimination similar to what they had experienced.[30]

Another aspect of the lawyers' routine work affected Marshall in particular. He was an imposing figure who inspired confidence and was able to rouse audiences to enthusiastic support of the NAACP. As a result, he was in high demand as a speaker. When he visited a community to check on the progress of litigation, he almost always spoke at a mass meeting sponsored by the local NAACP branch. According to his secretary and office manager, people treated him like "the Messiah come to town," and were thrilled just to shake hands with him. On occasion he appears to have been brought to town nominally to work on pending litigation but actually to rally the troops. Traveling around the country to make these speeches, while essential to the organizational and legal work of the NAACP, was tiring, and it sometimes limited Marshall's ability to participate actively in litigation. Testifying before President Harry Truman's Committee on Civil Rights in 1947, Marshall said that he spent more than two-thirds of his time in the South. His mileage accounts show an impressive amount of travel: 26,000 miles in the first seven months of 1941, 24,000 miles in the first five months of 1942, 30,000 miles in 1943.[31]

Snapshots of Marshall's travels in the 1940s give some indication of what the job entailed for him and the range of cases he was involved in—teachers' salary cases, challenges to the white primary, labor union discrimination, and more. In November 1941, he sent the office a memorandum he called "Saving the Race." Noting that he had left New York on October 31 for two days in Washington "with enough clothes for one day and a tooth brush," he said wryly that he was "still on the road" nearly three weeks later. When he arrived in Dallas on November 5 to discuss the pending challenge to Texas's white primary, he found that some local supporters had made "some rather bad statements about 'messing up' the case," and Marshall had to explain to them how difficult the case was. "All agreed that if we did not get another case started all of us would have to leave the U.S. and go live with Hitler or some other peace loving individual who would be less difficult th[a]n the Negroes in Texas who had put up the money for the case." Finding that there was no available plaintiff in Dallas to begin a new challenge to the primary, Marshall went to Houston "still not anxious to go live with Hitler." There he located Dr. L. E. Smith, who was prepared to be the plaintiff, and started drafting the complaint. He could not, however, find a stenographer "who specialized in typing—no such animal available." After being frustrated in his attempt to learn at the county courthouse the names of the various election officials who would have to be named as defendants, Marshall posed as a reporter to obtain the names from the only official he had been able to identify. When the complaint was filed two days later, Marshall concluded that "departure from the United States was thereby delayed at least." He then went to New Orleans, where he worked on a brief in a teachers' salary case. "One of our leaders here was told by a leader of the other race Saturday that the powers that be here cannot afford to let a 'northern nigger' win a case against them so they want to settle. Will you please respect the fact that I am now a *northern* nigger."[32]

Writing from New Orleans again on January 18, 1943, Marshall reported on six meetings he had attended on the day before: he met with New Orleans teachers who wanted to contribute money to the NAACP, with officials of the state teachers' association to develop plans for spreading the salary litigation statewide, with citizens who might organize a support committee for the same litigation, with representatives of NAACP branches who wanted to establish a state conference of branches, and with two groups of teachers about their cases. He also addressed the branch meeting, giving the "usual baloney" speech. The day ended with a "very important meeting at one of the bars in town for the purpose of forgetting about the other meetings—this meeting was a great success." He ended his report with a note that it was "hot as the devil down here." Another letter mentioned that he left Louisville on Derby Day; Marshall noted, "I bet if I had stayed I would have made enough money to pay off the deficit in the legal defense fund or maybe I would have walked to Texas."[33]

These trips, as Marshall said, were sometimes "rather hard," but they put him in contact with the NAACP's members and gave him a sense of what his constituency wanted of him. Reporting on a trip to Birmingham, for example, Marshall said that he discovered that African-Americans there "are *not* afraid. They still have courage." The exchanges, though, were mutual. Marshall's speeches could push the members along a path he wanted them to follow, while their responses suggested some limits to the pace and direction of the litigation.[34]

At the end of 1943, Marshall became involved in an important labor dispute. The boilermakers' union in California, representing workers in an industry that had expanded substantially during the war, refused to accept African-Americans as members, although it had a separate auxiliary for African-American workers. The union negotiated a closed-shop agreement, so that African-Americans who were not members of the union or its segregated auxiliary could not work at the shipyard. As a result, 450 African-Americans were barred from work. The situation came to Marshall's attention on Tuesday, November 30, and he flew to California on Wednesday. On Friday he presented the African-American workers' case for a preliminary injunction against their discharge—which was granted two weeks later—and on Saturday he spoke to a radio audience about the situation. As much as his legal ability, the simple fact of Marshall's presence counted here. As a correspondent put it two weeks later in connection with a similar case on the East Coast, "What could be better" than Marshall's presence at a trial? Another branch leader told Marshall, in connection with a different matter, "Your charging personality made quite a hit with the Iowa people when you were here last year." And, after a visit to Detroit, the executive secretary of the Detroit branch of the NAACP wrote Marshall, we "were marvelling at the tremendous amount of verbal 'bull' that you flout about, and yet when the occasion demands you are able to articulate intelligently."[35]

Marshall's presence carried weight, as well, when he attended a court-martial arising out of an incident at Port Chicago near San Francisco. Three weeks after an ammunition ship blew up while being loaded, killing 320 men—including more than 200 African-American ammunition handlers—large numbers of African-American seamen refused to continue to load ammunition. In a mass court-martial, fifty were charged with mutiny. The African-American community in northern California regarded these charges as grossly excessive because the seamen were only protesting unsafe working conditions. To the community, the charges reflected deep-rooted racism in the Navy, particularly in light of the fact that jobs were segregated at Port Chicago, with African-Americans handling ammunition and whites giving the orders.[36]

The court-martial took six weeks, and Marshall attended for twelve days. He helped the military defense attorneys with their investigation, but he did not take part in the trial itself, saying that, although the NAACP "should have been here from the beginning," at that point "this is no place to inject civilian counsel." Marshall also addressed community meetings about the case. The president of the Alameda County NAACP branch described the effects of Marshall's presence: "We are proud that Thurgood Marshall was able to come out because I think his presence is going to have its effect. As a matter of fact his presence caused the San Francisco Chronicle to give the hearings about three or four times as much space this morning as they have been giving it before." After the seamen were convicted, Marshall made a personal appearance before the military appeals board, a departure from the board's usual practice, seeking to overturn the convictions.[37]

The expansion of the NAACP legal staff during the 1940s alleviated some of the problems of routine legal practice (though not the burdens of travel), but it also introduced new difficulties. Marshall hired Frank Reeves as his assistant in 1940. Reeves, a native of Canada, received his law degree from Howard in 1939, but because he did not become a citizen of the United States until 1943, he was unable to join the bar while he worked at the NAACP.

Marshall's action in hiring Reeves occasioned the first of numerous disputes over Marshall's role in personnel decisions. Roy Wilkins, with primary responsibility for running the NAACP office and protective of his prerogatives, objected to Marshall's decision because it had not gone through proper channels. Marshall responded, "Knowing Roy Wilkins as I do I will join the hundreds of others and ignore the sarcastic tone he so often uses." Marshall preferred a much more unstructured style of management than Wilkins did. According to one staff member, Marshall was not "neatly laid out or scheduled," and did not like to be at his desk. Marshall hired people he believed were qualified, attempted to inspire them with the importance of the work, and then left them essentially free to do their work on their own. According to Robert Carter, "Marshall had great confidence in the staff he had chosen, and he did not believe that a senior lawyer was needed to monitor a younger colleague's first trial. In his view, a competent lawyer could— and should—plunge in and learn to swim unassisted."[38]

As Wilkins understood, this management style could sometimes lead to difficulties. For example, during the war Marshall hired Prentice Thomas, an African-American pacifist from Kentucky, to work in the office. Thomas was not up to the job, though; he could not produce legal research fast enough to be useful, and his recommendations about what should be done had "a certain vagueness" that was unhelpful. Ultimately Thomas was eased out of the national office and returned to Kentucky to practice law.[39]

Though Marshall's relations with Wilkins were not untroubled, the two did develop a relatively easy working relationship, revealed, for example, in an exchange of notes about hiring a part-time secretary in 1942. Marshall responded to Wilkins's suggestion that they try to hire one "if your schedule is such that you will be in the city for a few days," by scrawling, "What about Miss Universe?" Wilkins returned the note with his own: "Oh yeah—would you insult Miss Universe by calling her a part-time secretary? Now I *knows* you can't have her, you vile schemer, you!"[40]

Marshall's relations with Walter White were more strained. Both he and Wilkins came to see White as less interested in developing a concrete program than in public relations and, as part of public relations, in putting himself in the public eye. From Marshall's point of view, White too often took positions on legal matters about which he was uninformed. White seemed to be uncomfortable with Marshall's rise to prominence, continuing to see him as a young lawyer from Baltimore. Marshall insisted that the NAACP's stance on legal issues be "cleared" with him. Otherwise, the NAACP would "go[] so far out on the 'limb' that no one could save them." It would be better to get the lawyers' advice before "all hell had broken loose."[41]

By 1943 Marshall found it necessary to develop a legal staff that could handle cases directly. Here too his unstructured managerial style came into play. Rather than engaging in an extensive search for new lawyers, or calling the many professors he knew at Howard and other law schools for their recommendations, Marshall tended to hire people who let him know they were interested in a job when he happened to have money available. As a result, Marshall paid little attention himself to such matters as the applicant's race or gender. The NAACP staff had two parts. Some staff members had to have a great deal of direct contact with the branches and members, while others, including many of the lawyers, were engaged in more purely technical work. According to one white staff member, the NAACP had a "completely interracial environment" in the technical jobs.[42]

Marshall hired Milton Konvitz in May 1943 and Edward Dudley in October. Konvitz, a graduate of the New York University Law School, abandoned graduate school because the job prospects for a Jew in higher education were bleak during the Depression, and opened his own law practice in Newark. After working as general counsel to the Newark Housing Authority, Konvitz began to teach in an adjunct capacity at NYU Law School. At the same time he began his work at the NAACP. He was to be responsible primarily for writing briefs, and, in a "special arrangement," could largely determine the times when he would be in the NAACP office. This arrangement too led to a clash with Wilkins, who wanted the NAACP staff to be in the office more regularly and predictably; Wilkins thought that Konvitz had informed Wilkins of the special arrangement in a "disagreeable" manner.[43]

According to Marshall, he hired Dudley to handle correspondence and "to relieve [me] and Mr. Konvitz of as much other routine work as possible." Dudley, an African-American born in Virginia, graduated from St. John's Law School in New York in 1941. As a member of the New York bar, Dudley could handle cases as well. He took charge of the office when Marshall was away, thereby allowing Konvitz "to concentrate on research and the preparation of briefs." Dudley left the office in 1948, when he was appointed ambassador to Liberia, and returned in 1953.[44]

The organization of the legal office remained somewhat haphazard. Marshall's extensive travels meant that the office frequently had no one close to the leadership of the NAACP with whom White or Wilkins could deal. The situation threatened to deteriorate further in 1945, when Konvitz, overworked in the several jobs he held simultaneously, left New York to teach at Cornell University.

Fortunately, the end of the war made more money available for the legal program. Convinced that "we will have to spend more money on regular defense cases because these teachers' salaries cases and university cases will not continue to keep our name going[, n]or can we raise much money on them," Marshall requested a doubling of his budget in 1941, from $4,000 to $9,000. He argued that the NAACP had been "reaping the reward upon a number of legal victories for which it has not paid a great deal of its own treasury," including the education cases. Over the next few years, the legal budget increased to around $20,000, but the real breakthrough occurred in 1944, when the budget went to $63,000. At the same time, the NAACP began a fund-raising effort aimed at large donors to its legal activities, to be conducted by a professional fund raiser through a select "Committee of 100." In light of Marshall's position in the NAACP's legal work, he began to solicit contributions actively.[45]

The new resources allowed Marshall to expand the staff, which reached a total of five in 1949. The most important new staff member was Robert Carter. Born in Florida but raised in New Jersey, Carter, like Marshall, graduated from Lincoln University and Howard Law School, where he heard Houston prepare for his arguments at the Supreme Court. Then he received a master's degree in law at Columbia University. After serving in the Air Force until 1944, Carter joined the NAACP staff. Although Carter had no experience in law practice when he began working for Marshall, he rapidly became Marshall's primary assistant, and brought what he called a "Northern urban" perspective to the office, to complement Marshall's Southern perspective. Carter later wrote that "Marshall expected me to be responsible for the day-to-day running of the office and to resolve all internal office disputes without his participation." Marshall regarded Carter as a sort of "gadfly," who would develop a strategy that sometimes seemed "out in left field." Carter described himself as a lawyer who "like[d] to write and to do research." Marshall appreciated the contribution Carter's sometimes abstract theorizing made, and protected Carter from criticism and from involvement in office politics. Partly because Marshall was away from the office so often, Carter was a somewhat officious manager. In addition, in the summer of 1946, after Carter had established his place at the NAACP, Marshall became seriously ill and took no substantial part in the office's legal activities for several months. During that time, the initial steps were taken in several important education cases, and Carter appears to have taken a proprietary interest in them; as a result, he seems to have resented somewhat the fact that Marshall took the cases over once he recovered from his illness. One of the NAACP's cooperating lawyers later said that Carter was "always looking for some praise for himself," which may have reflected Carter's uncertain sense that his contributions to the office were properly acknowledged.[46]

Two other lawyers joined the staff in 1945. Marian Wynn Perry, a 1943 graduate of the Brooklyn Law School, had worked in the Wage and Hour Division of the U.S. Department of Labor, but "derived the greatest satisfaction out of [her] work" as secretary of the Constitutional Liberties Committee of the New York chapter of the National Lawyers' Guild. As her activism in the left-wing Guild indicates, Perry had concluded "during the early days of the depression that if progressive causes were ever to achieve a strong foothold in America they would have to do so within the framework of our legal system." Because, as she put it, good-looking young women with Anglo-Saxon names were "as scarce as hen's teeth" in the New York left, she rapidly became prominent in the Lawyers' Guild. Her work with the Guild involved lobbying for fair employment legislation in New York, and during that effort she met and worked with Marshall and Dudley. Perry was hired to work on employment and housing discrimination issues and sustained contacts with leftist legal organizations in the New York region until she resigned from the legal staff in 1949 to accompany her husband to his new job in upstate New York.[47]

Franklin Williams was also hired in late 1945, to replace Dudley. Williams was a native of Flushing, New York; he had attended Lincoln University and had just received his law degree from Fordham Law School, where he was an editor of the law review. He approached Marshall through a lawyer for whom Williams had done some clerking, and who lived at 409 Edgecombe Avenue, where Marshall lived too. Initially Williams handled cases involving complaints about the treatment of African-Americans in the military forces, but eventually his work expanded to cover the range of NAACP cases. Williams was an urbane and self-confident man: Shortly after the Supreme Court ordered that railroad dining cars be desegregated, Williams went for dinner on a train. He found himself seated exactly where he would have been if segregation had existed; although the railroad had taken down the curtain separating the areas, the signs of the partition remained. Knowing that the railroads were extremely sensitive to criticism for mistreating foreign diplomats, Williams asked the headwaiter, "Pour-quoi?," and was immediately given a seat in the main dining area. Whenever the headwaiter passed by during dinner, Williams continued the charade by talking in French to his companion.[48]

Constance Baker Motley, while a student at Columbia Law School, worked as a volunteer at the NAACP in the summer of 1945, dealing with court-martial cases. That fall Marshall offered her a job as a "legal research assistant" when she graduated the next year. Motley continued in that capacity until 1949. She became dissatisfied, though, suffering from staff members' perception that, having started at the NAACP as a law clerk and research assistant, she could not be a full-fledged member of the legal staff. At a staff conference in 1949, Marshall defined her duties as legal research, writing briefs, answering miscellaneous correspondence, dealing with people who walked in to the national office for legal advice, and maintaining the files and reports of the legal department. When Robert Carter told Motley to attend the New Jersey State Conference of NAACP Branches, she objected that she should not "be given the same assignments which are given to the assistant special counsel when I am neither classified as such nor paid the salary of an assistant special counsel." Marshall immediately came up with the money to pay Motley the appropriate salary, and she became an assistant special counsel in mid-1949.[49]

The core staff was completed with the addition of Jack Greenberg in 1949. Greenberg had grown up in Brooklyn and attended Columbia Law School where, as a student, he had participated in a seminar led by Professor Walter Gellhorn in which the students did legal research and wrote memoranda for civil liberties organizations.* Unable to find a job with such a group when he graduated, Greenberg went to work for the New York State Law Revision Commission, but asked Gellhorn to let him know if the kind of job he wanted became available. When Marshall called and said that he was looking for another staff attorney, Gellhorn told Marshall, "If you weren't racially biased I could suggest a good person to you,"

---

*The prevalence of the Northerners on the NAACP legal staff resulted in large part from the office's New York location. Marshall and the other executives of the NAACP had numerous dealings with New York lawyers and when positions became available on the legal staff, it was naturally easier for them to hire people with whom they had worked, like Carter, Perry, and Motley.

to which Marshall laughingly responded, "I'll try to overcome my prejudice if you want to send someone to me to be interviewed."[50]

The personality differences between Carter and Marshall, and Carter's treatment of Motley, were perhaps minor, but they symbolize one of the difficulties caused by staff expansion. Further, as the staff grew, the sheer fact that the lawyers were crowded together created new problems. As early as 1944 Marshall had tried to get more space for the legal staff. Throughout 1947, Marshall complained to White about crowding. He noted that during his entire time at the NAACP he was the only member of the core staff who had to share offices, first with Houston, then with Reeves, Konvitz, Dudley, and Motley, all the while "doing highly technical legal work needing concentration." Carter, Perry, and Williams also shared a single office, and, Marshall said, "I don't see how they make it as is." He told White that he had "reached the end of his rope." The period early in 1947 was crucial for the research and planning of cases involving white primaries, transportation, restrictive covenants, education, and the like. "I am expected to come up with the answers," he wrote, and "can not do this type of concentration and research in an office shared with two other people also working on these and other problems." When White did not respond favorably to his request for more space, Marshall violated the conventions of the NAACP and, without White's approval, asked the board of directors for more space. A board committee told him to work something out with White, and eventually a satisfactory accommodation was reached.[51]

This incident reveals Marshall's role as a manager. Whatever personal tensions might sometimes arise within the legal staff, the staff members could be sure that Marshall would advance their interests as professionals devoted to doing the best job possible. When Gloster Current, the director of the branch department, tried to pull rank on Marian Perry, Marshall sent Current a strong memorandum criticizing him for trying to give the branches legal advice on the housing issues Perry dealt with. Important, too, was the way Marshall treated the staff's work. The secretaries in the office put in extremely long hours when necessary, sometimes working through the night. The secretaries "never thought of saying no" to his requests because Marshall always looked out for them: directing Alice Stovall, his office manager, to send a secretary home when he noticed that she had a cold, inviting them to fund-raising events and then asking the audience to acknowledge the contributions the secretaries made to the LDF, and generally demonstrating his respect for them as people and for the work they did.[52]

Once Marshall had a legal staff for essential legal research and brief writing, he began to approach the task of being a lawyer differently. Drawing on his experience at Howard, he relied heavily on staff meetings in which the staff would tell him what the research had disclosed. According to Carter, Marshall "gave his staff considerable freedom and encouraged innovative thinking." He looked at trial records to get a feel for what was involved, then talked through the legal issues with the staff lawyer who had developed the case. From the outset, he convened meetings of cooperating attorneys and advisers like Houston and Hastie to discuss procedures and novel lines of argument that the LDF needed to develop. These conferences gave Marshall the information and analysis he needed to "straighten out" the problems he and his staff faced. In these meetings, the lawyers laid out possible lines of argument for Marshall to consider. By the late 1940s, Marshall's experience in civil rights litigation had made him an extremely sensitive judge of what arguments would be persuasive and what would not. As he saw it, "if we once get the theory straight, I have a suspicion that the rest will be comparatively easy." He was not as flashy at developing lines of argument as some of the advisers were, and in part because of that he had enormous respect for them. As one staff lawyer put it, he was "a genius at getting from others the best they had to offer, all the while making believe he wasn't serious" about the work. Marshall was a superb listener, and he probably was pleased that, when it came to making a decision, these able lawyers deferred to Marshall's judgment.[53]

In preparing to argue cases before the Supreme Court, Marshall continued a practice Houston began. Before the argument he held a moot court at Howard Law School, where he and his colleagues faced a panel of academics who peppered them with questions they expected some justices to raise. These dry runs did more than help Marshall pin down the legal arguments he had to make. They also helped him develop a style that would appeal to all the justices. As one of his advisers told him, he had to make sure to get his argument "down to the level" of some of the justices.[54]

In addition to instructing Marshall, the meetings solidified good relations between Marshall and the lawyers who worked with the NAACP throughout the country. Often Marshall was familiar with the technical details, but he would ask for help anyway. After Marshall had been in practice for nearly two decades, he wrote to an older lawyer to request "some more lessons in pleading." Marshall routinely sent personal letters praising lawyers for their work, especially when the NAACP or Marshall had received publicity. Probably recalling his own difficulties in establishing his private practice in Baltimore, Marshall wrote one young attorney in Buffalo, "It is quite evident that you did a splendid job and I only hope that the people in that neighborhood appreciate it. At any rate, you are getting some good experience. I know you can't pay your rent on experience, and I have never been able to pay the grocer on newspaper publicity, but you can try, if you want to. However, a case of this type will do much to help build up your name and in the long run you will win more than you lose in the matter of time and energy." To Raymond Pace Alexander, a prominent African-American lawyer in Philadelphia, Marshall wrote about a case in which the NAACP resisted the extradition of an African-American charged with assaulting a white man, "I am sure you realize, however, that we realize that the responsibility for obtaining this decision rests with you and for that reason you are the one who is really to be commended." Alexander replied, "Thanks *sooo much* for your fine letter. Only one like you who has been thru the test of terribly hard work required in the handling of such a case can appreciate what counsel has to do and the part he plays. He however is *generally* ignored in the press comment and in messages of congratulations. *You* are an exception."[55]

Marshall's personality was an important element in making the office operate effectively. Marshall never gave the staff a sense that he was somehow "above" them, and few if any resented the prominence he gained. His personality made the office work. He "made everybody feel important and happy." Because he was "unassuming and never . . . put on airs," he did not press the staff to meet artificial deadlines. After completing some difficult job, he made sure that the staff relaxed with drinks while he regaled them with his stories. By unwinding with the staff and the other lawyers he worked with, Marshall relaxed "on the job," and recovered his energy without taking vacations. His devotion to the path-breaking work of the office led the lawyers to do their best work without feeling pushed around. He never minimized his own importance, though, and was a proud man who understood his unique contribution to the LDF's activities. His ego satisfaction derived from his altruism.[56]

Marshall was responsive to his staff when they did raise questions about his role. Franklin Williams, who was somewhat brash and, according to another attorney in the office, arrogant, became frustrated at developing cases that got to the Supreme Court, only to find that Marshall would take over the argument or let one of his friends from Howard argue the case. When the Court decided to hear one of Williams's cases, he asked Marshall to let him argue the case. The Court had agreed to review two questions, one about the methods the police used to extract a confession and the other dealing with the way in which the grand jury that indicted the defendant had been selected. Marshall did not respond immediately, but shortly before the day of argument he told Williams that he could argue the confession issue. Later Carter said that Marshall's decision to let Williams argue was essential for the morale of the staff, but at the time Williams thought that Marshall had been a little unfair. Not only was time short, but Williams believed that he had much more experience in dealing with grand jury claims. Marshall may have had other considerations in mind, though, because the Court ruled in favor of the NAACP's client on the confession issue that Williams argued.[57]

Marshall's method of learning from his staff drew on his experience and his ability to select good arguments from the mix that people generated in free-wheeling discussions. His style was to respond skeptically to a lawyer's claim that some particular legal position should be asserted by the NAACP. For example, he corresponded with Loren Miller, a cooperating attorney in California, about a case involving a fugitive from a Georgia chain gang. The prisoner had been located in California, and the Georgia authorities sought his return to serve out his time. As in many similar extradition cases, the fugitive claimed, and the NAACP's lawyers agreed, that he had been convicted unconstitutionally. The problem was to develop a legal theory that would bar the fugitive's return to the state in which he was convicted. The principal difficulty was that the Constitution itself provides that states shall return fugitives from justice. When this case arose, though, there was some chance that the federal courts outside the South would be so repelled by Southern justice that they would provide some relief to the fugitive. Marshall prodded Miller on the question of what that relief would be, asserting that the only thing the courts could possibly do would be to return the fugitive to Georgia for a new trial; that, of course, was not what the fugitive wanted most. Marshall acted as the "devil's advocate" in challenging Miller's claim that the proper course was to let the defendant go free rather than send him back for a new, fair trial. "Frankly," Marshall wrote, "I do not believe the courts would go along with you." He encouraged Miller to persist, though, because the issue was worth pursuing.[58]

Marshall's objections were rarely to the technical details of the argument.* Instead, he would say that this position was simply not one that the NAACP should adopt. In criminal cases, he asked, "How can we justify taking hard-earned nickels and dimes to defend a vicious killer?" By giving his staff a hard time in this way, Marshall accomplished a number of things. First, particularly in the 1940s, he balanced the inexperience of the staff. Although they were dedicated to the NAACP, the younger members of the staff did not have a good sense of what reasonably could be done with the cases that came into the office. For example, when Jack Greenberg waxed indignant about the conviction of an African-American in Virginia for stealing some peanuts, Marshall told him to check the facts carefully, whereupon Greenberg discovered that the defendant had stolen several large and valuable sacks of peanuts—and the truck carrying them as well.[59]

Second, Marshall learned by listening to people argue. When he responded skeptically to an argument that his staff expected him to find immediately appealing, Marshall spurred the lawyers on to greater efforts to defend the position. When he told them, "You have to convince me," they began what one called "an unsentimental attack on the law books." When Marshall went along in the end, he had been given the strongest case possible to present. Third, Marshall was more sensitive to the way in which the NAACP's arguments would work in Southern courtrooms because he was from the South himself, while the staff consisted of Northerners.[60]

Finally, and perhaps most important, because Marshall did not focus on the technical details, his skepticism captured the core of the opposing position, the aspects of the position that made it morally credible to his opponents. By presenting the staff with that core position, Marshall overcame the natural inclination of inexperienced advocates, particularly advocates devoted to a cause, to take the position they are asserting as the only morally responsible one and therefore to underestimate the importance of developing powerful technical arguments to counter the opponents' moral appeal.

Houston was right when he said that the NAACP's legal activities were "no star performance." He groomed Marshall as his successor. But Marshall surpassed

---

* Sometimes Marshall made mistakes. Saying that he had been wrong before but insisting that he and the staff had gone over the matter "backwards and forwards," Marshall strongly urged an Ohio lawyer not to appeal a judgment upholding segregation at a swimming pool because the facts, as they appeared to Marshall, indicated that the pool had been operated for veterans only and therefore excluded many whites as well as all African-Americans. When the appeal actually succeeded, the graciousness of Marshall's initial letter ensured that the Ohio lawyer would not resent Marshall's position. Similarly, when the Supreme Court reversed a judgment in a case that the NAACP had not entered because of Marshall's opposition, he apologized to Marian Perry, saying, "I am afraid I was wrong on my original decision not to get into" the case. (TM to W. M. Howard, Feb. 6, 1948; Howard to Perry, July 27, 1948, both in NAACP Papers, Box II-B-66, file: Discrimination, Swimming Pool, Warren, Ohio, Correspondence 1947–49; TM to Perry, May 27, 1947, NAACP Papers, Box II-B-109, file: O, 1940–49.)

Houston because they had different personalities. Marshall inspired confidence and motivated people on the legal staff and in the NAACP's branches, as Houston had. Yet Marshall was more a man of his people, who developed personal ties that deepened their affection for him. And, in the end, Marshall became the central figure in the NAACP's legal activities because he knew what to do, and everyone else knew he knew it.

3

"You Did All You Could. . . ."
Routine Work in the 1940s

The NAACP's legal work was directed at eliminating segregation, and its lawyers understood that ending segregation required a mobilized African-American community. Overstating his views a bit to conciliate a branch official who had been offended by correspondence with Marian Perry, Marshall wrote, "We are here to serve the branches—this is our only responsibility." Marshall even used criminal cases as vehicles for organization, in part because of the requirement that defendants whom the NAACP aided had to be (or had to be believed to be) innocent. In connection with one criminal case, Marshall urged Hastie and Leon Ransom, another adviser, to hold mass meetings, "to further demonstrate to the community the work being done by the NAACP and its D.C. branch. We cannot do this too often nor can we solicit the cooperation of churches too often. It seems to me that effective work can be done to further the name of the NAACP in Washington because this [is] the type of case which will attract a tremendous amount of attention." He praised one branch president for her work on a criminal case, saying that "[s]ome of our branches sit back and permit other organizations to take the lead in work that we should be doing. Others miss the important cases and important issues. Even others fail to handle the cases in the proper manner. However, the majority of our branches, like your branch, operate in such a fashion as to do credit to themselves, our Association and our program." At national conventions of the NAACP, Marshall attentively listened to sometimes inarticulate statements made on the floor and sought out the speakers to determine whether he and his staff could help them. Attention to the branches and the membership was essential, in Marshall's view, because it was "dangerous" for the legal work to outpace the development of "whole-hearted" support in the branches.[1]

Yet, though Marshall believed that the NAACP's resources should be used to benefit large numbers of African-Americans, he never lost sight of the fact that in each case, particularly in criminal cases, there was an individual defendant whose interests were involved. So, when a branch president suggested that a defendant who had been released on bail was willing to tell his story "for propaganda purposes," Marshall cautioned that "we should be very careful about this case for the sake of the defendant," whose bail could be revoked in retaliation for NAACP activities.[2]

Marshall's concern for the organization and its legal campaign, as well as his personality, enabled him to mediate disputes within the NAACP branches, between the branches and the local cooperating attorneys, and between staff and cooperating lawyers. For example, Marshall responded soothingly to Lillie Jackson's charge that Franklin Williams, in what Jackson called a "typical example" of the legal staff's inattention to the branches, had failed to see her when he was in Baltimore. Marshall said that "it was just a question of not having time enough to come by and see the officers of the Branch" in a quick visit squeezed between two other trips.[3]

In Louisiana, A. P. Tureaud had been handling almost all of the NAACP's work in Louisiana until, in 1950, another African-American lawyer started accepting NAACP cases. Tureaud's friends learned that the new lawyer was saying that "as a law school professor, he knew all of the law and Tureaud knew none." Marshall assured people in Louisiana that both lawyers were able and that, "as to courage, I know of places that Tureaud has gone into in upper Louisiana and Mississippi where few other people would have gone." He told the NAACP's supporters in Louisiana that, although the national office would cooperate with whichever lawyer they chose, he regarded Tureaud as the national office's representative in Louisiana. "I know most of the people in our work in Louisiana," he concluded, "and I know their proclivity for running off half cocked. I also know that they have a terrific job to do. . . . I shall expect that we can now work within these rules with a spirit of cooperation rather than a spirit of distrust."[4]

Disputes over fees to lawyers arose because the lawyers who represented African-Americans in the South often had fairly marginal practices, and saw the national NAACP as a possible source for more substantial income. Marshall's dealings with cooperating attorneys were sometimes complicated by the interventions of other officers of the NAACP, particularly White and Wilkins. Willie Francis's case illustrates the problems. Francis was a young African-American convicted in Louisiana of murder. His case became a cause célèbre when the electric chair malfunctioned, subjecting him to intense pain but failing to kill him. The prison authorities were uncertain about whether they could try to execute him again, and while they deliberated attorneys for Francis filed a constitutional challenge to a second attempt to execute him, on the ground that to do so would subject Francis to "cruel and unusual punishment" in violation of the Eighth Amendment to the Constitution.[5]

Although the NAACP was not deeply involved in the legal maneuvers to save Francis's life, after the United States Supreme Court denied Francis's claims by a five-to-four vote, Francis's attorney Bertrand LeBlanc telegraphed the NAACP national office: "As attorneys for Willie my associate and I wish to ask for rehearing. Normally our fee would be $5,000. Your organization is reputed to help the unfortunate of your race. Do you wish to contribute all or part of this amount to help this boy?" Walter White was outraged by this telegram, which he thought an "impudent" demand for $5,000. With the approval of Carter, White issued a press release stating that the NAACP had been "barred" from the case by LeBlanc, who had "demand[ed] that he be given a large sum of money to file a further appeal." Marshall was troubled by this press release, because, "in the first place, I think this is the type of publicity that will certainly do harm to Willie Francis, who, after all, is the person involved in the matter." In addition, he said, "I don't see how we can construe his telegram as demanding anything. It is rather a request." Marshall told White that the press release "does more harm than good." White responded that he did not "propose ever to pass on any legal question," but that "as a matter of sound public relations, it seemed to be necessary that the public know that whatever faults in the legal handling of this case, if there were any such, were not the Association's which some persons implied. . . . I did not want any person believing that Willie Francis may have to go to the electric chair a second time through any failure or error on the part of the NAACP."[6]

The legal staff operated within an organizational environment that included other liberal and leftist organizations as well as the NAACP branches. Roger Baldwin of the ACLU, for example, developed an "unwritten rule" to refer all "negro cases" to the NAACP. In 1944 Marshall met with Baldwin to divide the work and, it seems, to ensure that the ACLU would not interfere with the NAACP's strategy. They agreed that the ACLU would assist in the attack on segregation and would concentrate its efforts on housing, but the ACLU was cautioned that it was not useful to attack laws prohibiting interracial marriages "because they are commonly circumvented and do not constitute a practical issue." Marshall also called on the ACLU for political support in the Port Chicago mutiny case, and thought that the organization might be able to provide him legal briefs on questions of conspiracy law that arose in the prosecution.[7]

The NAACP was most concerned about interventions by groups related to the Communist Party. In the 1930s, the NAACP and a party-related group, the International Labor Defense, struggled over control of the defense and appeals in the famous Scottsboro cases, in which nine African-American men were charged with raping two white women and received grossly unfair trials. Communists charged that the NAACP was not sufficiently militant, even in its legal defense, to vindicate African-American interests, and they competed with the NAACP for financial support from the African-American community and from left-leaning whites. Within the NAACP, Communists were seen as attempting to use criminal cases "for other purposes than the effective defense" of the accused. Yet, when a 65-year-old African-American man was accused of rape in San Francisco and the NAACP was peppered with letters, even Walter White, who believed that "the defense committee is largely made up of left-wingers," thought that if the accused was innocent, "we should be interested and should give help in the most effective way we can without becoming involved in entangling alliances."[8]

Marshall was less hostile to Communist involvement in legal cases than were other leaders of the NAACP. Conventionally liberal on issues other than race, Marshall did not support Communist activities—he removed a picture of Paul Robeson from his office when Robeson took the Soviet side during the early years of the Cold War, and he resigned from the National Lawyers' Guild when it severely criticized the conduct of Judge Harold Medina during the sedition trials of Communist leaders in 1949, but he had no objections to Marian Perry's continued association with the Lawyers' Guild and other leftist groups. He filed an *amicus* brief in a case handled by the Southern Tenant Farmers Union and the Workers Defense League, both more left-wing than the NAACP.[9]

When the International Labor Defense took charge of a case in 1942 challenging the extradition to South Carolina of David Williams, an African-American who had escaped from peonage, Marshall urged that the NAACP participate in the case, which was a "natural" for the organization. Not only was Williams's life and "the economic status of his family" at stake; even more, the NAACP could use the case to attack South Carolina's system of "keeping thousands of Negroes in peonage. If we can have this statute thrown out, we will have done a tremendous job of bettering the economic condition of a large number of Negroes." In addition, the extradition case would let the NAACP develop procedures for using the federal courts in extradition cases, which it had been "trying repeatedly" to do. The interaction of the personal benefits to Williams with the organizational benefits to the NAACP left Marshall puzzled about what to do in light of Walter White's objection to working with the ILD. He agreed with "the established rule that we may cooperate with organizations on individual cases but never on complete programs," and sometimes was quicker than White or Wilkins to conclude that the benefits to individual defendants, and to the NAACP's program, outweighed the costs of cooperating with Communist-affiliated organizations. As Marshall put it, "I, for one, have no antagonism at all concerning Communists or any other group other than Dixiecrats," though he agreed that it might be "injurious" to participate in a case where the Communists appeared to be in control.[10]

Even at the end of the decade, when anti-Communist feeling was extremely strong, Marshall remained open to cooperation with groups widely viewed as dominated by Communists. Marshall was lukewarm about the matter when he interpreted the NAACP's anti-Communist resolution, adopted in 1950, as a statement about discrimination: "I do not believe a Negro as a Negro has any more or any less of a right to join the Communist Party as any other person. I also do not believe a Negro as a Negro has any more or any less of a responsibility to suffer the consequences of such affiliation." He did not dismiss out of hand the Communists' suggestion that the NAACP file an *amicus* brief in support of Eugene Dennis, a party leader. Instead of endorsing the party's legal position, though, Marshall referred the request to Houston, who agreed that the legal theory proposed by the Communists was a good one but thought that the party's lawyers, not the NAACP, should present it.[11]

Marshall understood that he had to walk a tightrope in deciding how to respond to cases presented to the NAACP by other organizations. In 1943, an agent for the Federal Bureau of Investigation reported that Marshall had told an audience in Savannah, Georgia, that the Communists were less active in the African-American community than they had been, because "the colored people have found that Communism does not give them what they expect to get." He testily rejected efforts to involve the NAACP in cases of African-Americans who were fired from the government because they refused to take loyalty oaths, criticizing the efforts as attempts to "blackjack[] the N.A.A.C.P. into fighting" other groups' battles. As he

saw it, the organizations were not "interested in either the N.A.A.C.P. or Negroes or our problems but are more interested in their own selfish aims which in
many instances are directly contrary to our own purposes."[12]

But, where the interests of African-Americans and the NAACP were involved,
Marshall was not reluctant to cooperate with other groups despite the possibility of
being tarred by association, or of losing credit for whatever was accomplished. His
response to the Progressive Party illustrates his approach. The party ran former
Vice-President and Secretary of Agriculture Henry Wallace for president in 1948.
After Wallace failed to receive a significant number of votes, the party came
increasingly under the control of Communists. Still, when the party sponsored an
attempt to integrate tennis courts in Baltimore in 1948, Marshall said that "we
nevertheless cannot close our eyes to the fact that it is an attack on segregation,"
even though he believed that the real motive for prosecuting the Progressives for
violating the city's segregation law was political and not racial. He recommended
full cooperation "in whatever way possible, such as brief amicus curiae [or] research." Marshall advised one correspondent in 1950 that he should accept a small
contribution from the Progressives to support a case, even though the party would
use the contribution to take credit for the case. For Marshall, "a mere contribution
does not in any manner signify a control of the Association."[13] Communist organizations, though sometimes important in the African-American community at
large, touched the NAACP's legal activities only lightly, and Marshall paid attention to them only to ensure that their work did not interfere with his.

The national office's location in New York also affected the legal staff's activities.
Marshall met Marian Wynn Perry in the course of lobbying the New York state
legislature to adopt fair employment laws. After the laws were adopted, Marshall
allowed Perry to pursue litigation challenging employment discrimination in the
construction of the Brooklyn Battery Tunnel, believing that it was important to
ensure that the first cases brought under the new statute were effectively prosecuted. He was skeptical, though, about the importance of these cases for the
overall program of the NAACP. He thought that only individual workers would
benefit from the cases, and did not see how they would generate substantial
precedent that could benefit African-Americans throughout the country. As he put
it, all you could do after winning one employment discrimination case was "take
another case." Marshall probably would not have devoted similar resources to
employment discrimination cases elsewhere in the country, but pressure from the
New York branch and the relative ease of doing the litigation led him to support
it.[14]

Being in New York, then, had some special effects on the lawyers' work.
People who complained about discrimination in New York could simply walk into
the office to present their complaints. These rarely fit the NAACP's criteria for
cases in which the organization would take an active role, but they had to be dealt
with. Further, African-Americans in New York were somewhat more willing to
pursue racial discrimination claims than those elsewhere, in part because they
could call on the resources of the relatively active branches of the NAACP to get
the national office's attention. In addition, the New York location meant that

servicing the nearby branches in New York, New Jersey, and Connecticut was easier for the staff. Instead of setting aside a day or two for a trip to address a branch meeting, for example, staff members could attend evening meetings and still be in the office the next day.

Moreover, the NAACP and its legal staff found themselves part of a network of liberal activist organizations in New York. That network had two consequences for the NAACP. Its members encouraged the NAACP's lawyers, acting as a source of moral and emotional support in difficult times. But each organization, with its own agenda, pressed the NAACP's legal staff to take on cases in which its agenda overlapped to some extent with the NAACP's; action by the NAACP might lend credibility and legitimacy to the other organization's activities, and it would distribute the financial burden more broadly. Finally, the New York environment skewed the NAACP's activities because, as in a few other instances, the political arena was more receptive to the NAACP's claims than were politics in the South and in Washington, D.C. Because winning was important in sustaining morale, the relatively receptive political climate was valuable even if the problems facing the organization's members were more serious elsewhere.

Marshall and the staff found that some parts of the political system were more open to influence than others. Exercising that influence provided the staff with the important psychological boost that comes with winning; it also sometimes improved the lives of some of the NAACP's constituents.

In the 1940s there were relatively few enforceable legal limitations on many types of discrimination. The NAACP had been attempting to secure the enactment of a federal antilynching law, for example, precisely to provide a legal tool to control that practice. Many NAACP cases in the 1940s were aimed at *developing* legal remedies for racial discrimination by private employers, the owners of bars, hotels, and restaurants, and the like. But even in Northern states where there were some laws against private discrimination, enforcing them was difficult. When the secretary of the York, Pennsylvania, branch of the NAACP brought a case of private discrimination to Marshall's attention, he replied, "The only way to handle such cases is to require the local District Attorney to prosecute. Very often the District Attorney refuses to prosecute such cases because Negroes in the community do not have sufficient political strength to require him to do so. . . . [I]t is the job of the N.A.A.C.P. to do everything in its power to require the District Attorney to prosecute such violations of the law with the same vigor as is used in the prosecution of Negro criminals." He enclosed a memorandum the office had prepared, describing what branches should do to put pressure on local officials by careful investigations of the facts and publicity.[15]

The NAACP's focus on securing benefits for African-Americans throughout the country meant that a substantial amount of time was spent on pressing the Roosevelt and Truman administrations to act. NAACP officials had reasonably good access to some in the administration, who in turn were sometimes readily responsive. The NAACP lawyers had notable success, of a certain sort, in getting the armed forces to reduce court-martial sentences. In one six-month period, the NAACP staff reviewed fifty-one records and identified twenty-six cases of racial discrimination and obtained a total of 883 years of reductions in sentence. The military authorities in the field routinely assessed extremely heavy penalties, and the authorities away from the field routinely reduced those penalties. As Franklin Williams noted in 1948, "the armed services seem to have adopted a policy of commuting all post-war sentences of death to life imprisonment upon review by the Board of Review and thereafter at various annual intervals reducing sentences until eventually they remain at a period of approximately twelve years' imprisonment." For publicity purposes, and in generating good feeling in the branches, the NAACP's actions in these cases were quite valuable. Yet, as Williams suggested, the reductions after NAACP intervention "would probably have been granted" anyway, as Williams showed by comparing NAACP cases with others in which the NAACP had not acted.[16]

In other areas the armed forces were not nearly as receptive to objections to discrimination. In the Port Chicago case as well as in others, Secretary of the Navy James Forrestal was completely resistant to Marshall's efforts. The Air Force refused to allow four injured African-Americans to recuperate at its facility in Plattsburg, New York, on the ground that they would be "'unhappy' in the northern climate." Marshall wrote a strong letter of protest to Secretary of War Henry Stimson, calling this excuse "unbelievable" and saying that "there is no doubt that many of the white patients from homes in lower Florida, Louisiana, Texas and California might be 'unhappy' in the winter climate of Plattsburg. This is the same type of reasoning used in an unsuccessful effort to justify segregation."[17]

In 1943 and 1944, Marshall and White engaged in substantial correspondence and meetings with James Bennett, the head of the federal Bureau of Prisons, attempting to eliminate segregated facilities in the prisons. Bennett was always accommodating, acknowledging that segregation sometimes occurred but denying that the federal prisons had a policy of segregation. After Marshall became frustrated at the lack of progress in actually eliminating segregation, he asked White to approach the attorney general on the issue. Segregation was soon eliminated at one facility, but continued elsewhere. White then went to President Truman. Stung by these efforts, Bennett wrote a plaintive letter to White referring to his correspondence with Marshall and asking them to call him or stop by for a meeting, and within a month the problem was resolved.[18]

Lobbying with the federal housing authorities was more difficult. Marshall found the Federal Housing Authority "thoroughly unreliable." In addition, sometimes lobbying strategy was unclear. When NAACP members in Newport, Rhode Island, tried to get the federal authorities to support a housing project, Marshall told Roy Wilkins, "I can't see why they should ask for a 'Negro project' when they can just as easily ask for a 'project.'"[19]

Perhaps more troublesome, the legal staff could not engage in serious lobbying without endangering the tax-exempt status of the Legal Defense Fund. Marshall was extremely sensitive to this concern, and did his best to confine his lawyers' contacts with public officials to situations in which litigation was planned or pending. When Walter White suggested to the LDF board of directors that there would be tax advantages if the LDF bought the building the NAACP was renting in Washington and then leased it to the NAACP, Marshall responded with an anxious memorandum. He wondered how the LDF could own a building in Washington "and at the same time maintain that it is not interested in influencing legislation." Marshall believed that the organizations had to be "more than careful" in protecting the LDF's tax exemption.[20]

The lawyers' most frustrating contacts were, perhaps ironically, with the Department of Justice. As attorney general in 1939, Frank Murphy established a special Civil Liberties Unit, later called the Civil Rights Section, in the Department of Justice, whose charge was to protect "fundamental rights." Murphy, a committed liberal and supporter of African-American interests, set up the section partly for political reasons, to recover some ground among liberals after his defeat in a race for governor of Michigan. As Murphy noted, the section's ability to protect those rights was "somewhat limited" by the Constitution, which, as then interpreted, placed rather few restraints on law enforcement. The Supreme Court had held that beating prisoners to extract confessions violated the due process clause of the Fourteenth Amendment, and officials who participated in lynchings could be prosecuted for depriving defendants of their constitutional right to a jury trial. In general, however, federal officials believed that prosecuting crimes committed against African-Americans, even by state police officers, had to be left to state authorities because of constitutional limitations on the national government's power.[21]

Raymond Carr's case dramatically illustrates the conception the Department of Justice had of its proper role. Carr was a soldier assigned to patrol in Alexandria, Louisiana. A white police officer ordered him to leave his position and, when Carr refused, drew his gun. Carr attempted to defend himself but was killed by the police officer. Marshall wrote Attorney General Francis Biddle seeking the police officer's prosecution. Instead, the case was presented to a "high type" state grand jury, with the assistance of a federal agent. After the grand jury failed to indict the police officer, the Department of Justice decided to take no further federal action. Marshall called this decision a "distinct shock" in view of the many similar incidents of police abuse of African-American soldiers, and disagreed with the Department's assertion that the simple killing of a soldier was not a federal offense.[22]

The Department of Justice position in the Carr case was not entirely unfounded in existing law, but it was quite cautious; an aggressive prosecutor could easily have developed an argument that it was indeed a federal offense to kill a soldier. The department's caution, however, may have been justified by what the Supreme Court did when the department acted more forcefully. In 1940 the Civil Liberties Unit instructed federal prosecutors that a federal statute, section 51 of the federal criminal code, made it a criminal offense for state officials to deprive African-Americans of federal rights, including the right to vote and rights in criminal cases. The statute, however, required that the deprivation be "willful." The unit instructed the prosecutors that, "because of the obvious impropriety of prosecuting an officer merely for his joyful acquiescence in the policy of a statute he may be enforcing, any practical construction of 'willfull' should include not only the element of 'evil intent' but also the element of 'without justifiable excuse.'"[23]

When the unit obtained a conviction of Sheriff Claude Screws of Baker County, Georgia, for killing a prisoner in the course of a brutal beating, thereby denying the prisoner's right to a trial, Screws appealed to the Supreme Court. The Court gutted the effectiveness of prosecutions under section 51 by defining "willfulness" even more stringently. To avoid finding the statute unconstitutionally vague, the Court construed it to mean that a state official willfully deprived someone of constitutional rights only if the official acted with specific intent to deprive the victim of a right that had itself been made specific by the Constitution or Supreme Court decisions. In the *Screws* case, for example, the Court's interpretation meant that Sheriff Screws would be liable only if the reason he beat the victim to death was to make sure that no trial ever occurred. The impact of the Court's decision can be seen in the fact that Screws, who had been convicted by a Georgia jury at his first trial, was acquitted at his retrial.[24]

The Department of Justice routinely cited *Screws* in letters rejecting NAACP complaints about police brutality, leading Marian Perry to refer to the letters as the "usual brush-off from the Department." The Civil Rights Section declined to attempt to prosecute a sheriff who blinded Isaac Woodard, an African-American veteran, in a beating, because the blinding resulted from only one or two blows, not the kind of "prolonged assault" that would show the sheriff's willfulness under *Screws*. Meb Vines, another discharged veteran, was killed in Farmville, North Carolina, shortly after midnight one evening after two police officers overheard him say to a friend, "To hell with the law." When Vines and one of the officers began fighting, the other drew his gun and shot Vines five times. Here too the department declined to prosecute; in support of its conclusion that a jury was unlikely to find that the officer intended to deprive Vines of his constitutional right to a trial, it cited Vines's "belligerent attitude" and the officer's duty to protect his partner. As this incident suggests, the department was concerned about potential prejudice against the victims of criminal assaults by police officers, as well as the possibility that Southern juries would be prejudiced against the federal government itself. Although the NAACP's legal staff was frustrated by its inability to secure action by the Department of Justice, the head of the Civil Rights Section believed that he had "good relationships" with the NAACP, which "usually understood the limitations of the Civil Rights Section program and the legal and administrative difficulties restricting its activities." Indeed, Marshall's response in the Vines case was simply to note that "we should keep such cases in Dept. of Justice files for use when bill introduced in Congress," suggesting that Marshall agreed with the Department's assessment of its prospects and abilities under existing law.[25]

Overall, then, the NAACP's legal staff often failed to obtain what they believed justice required. Even the successes were sometimes less significant than they appeared to be. In 1939 and 1940 NAACP lawyers persuaded the Supreme Court to reverse three convictions on the ground that confessions had been coerced. The cases involved confessions that had been produced by severe beatings extending over several days. One, from Florida, produced an opinion written by Justice Hugo Black, who used the occasion to denounce "third degree" police methods as reminiscent of Nazi Germany:

Today, as in ages past, we are not without tragic proof that the exalted power of some governments to punish manufactured crime dictatorially is the handmaid of tyranny. Under our constitutional system, courts stand against any winds that blow as havens of refuge for those who might otherwise suffer because they are helpless, weak, outnumbered, or because they are the non-conforming victims of prejudice and public excitement.

A month later, the Court reversed a conviction from Alabama without hearing oral argument; two weeks later, it reopened a case in which it had earlier denied review and here too summarily reversed a Texas conviction for rape. Lawyers associated with the NAACP participated in all three cases, and were pleased with the results. Leon Ransom, who had argued the Florida case in the Supreme Court, wrote Marshall after the Alabama decision that "[s]o far as I know the action of the Court is unprecedented," and suggested jokingly that, with the NAACP's record of fourteen victories in fifteen cases presented to the Court, "Are we crowding our luck?"[26]

Three years later Ransom received "a peculiar and significant" request from the Supreme Court. The Court's librarian asked him to find out what had happened in nine criminal cases where the Court had reversed convictions and remanded for new trials in the state courts. Ransom believed that "the Court may be making an independent inquiry into the question of whether real justice is accomplished by merely remanding." Konvitz examined the NAACP's files and came up with information about the ultimate outcome in five of the cases. In one, the indictment was dismissed. In another, the three defendants, who had been originally convicted of murder, pleaded guilty to manslaughter and received sentences of 6 months, 2 ½ years, and 7 ½ years. In a third case the defendant pleaded guilty and received a life sentence, while in the fourth the defendant was retried and received a death sentence for the second time. The final case was the Florida case in which Justice Black had written. There the defendants had been released from custody, but two of them were in insane asylums, apparently having become "unbalanced" at learning of the Supreme Court's action in their case. In the Texas rape case that the Court had reversed summarily, the defendant was on his way to court for a new trial when he was shot to death by the victim's husband; the killer was tried within the week for murder and was acquitted after two minutes of jury deliberation. The NAACP later learned that in yet another case about which the Court had enquired, the defendant had been reindicted and convicted, again receiving a death sentence.[27]

Even the NAACP's successes in criminal cases, then, were equivocal, particularly in view of the fact that the NAACP lawyers entered these cases believing that the defendants were innocent of all charges. In other cases the lawyers were unable to do much from the outset. In 1946 Marshall asked a Mississippi attorney to look into the case of a fifteen-year-old who had been sentenced to death, because, Marshall said, "I, for one, am opposed to the electrocution of fifteen-year-old boys for crimes." Nothing came of his inquiry, though, because the case had been badly handled at the trial, and there was nothing the NAACP could do to salvage it on appeal. The case of Eugene Burnam is more poignant. Burnam was charged with rape, a capital crime, when he was fifteen years old. He was convicted, but the conviction was reversed by the Kentucky appellate court. At his second trial, Burnam was defended by Prentice Thomas and state Senator Charles Anderson, and was again convicted. This conviction too was reversed on the ground that the trial judge had erred in giving the jury a forceful charge designed to lead them to come to agreement prematurely. At Burnam's third trial the jury deliberated for 72 hours before reporting that it was unable to reach a unanimous verdict; five jurors wanted to acquit Burnam. A fourth trial was held, and Burnam was convicted and sentenced to death. This time his appeals failed, and he was executed in 1942. After the execution Burnam's mother wrote "to all of the lawyers who helped me in my troubles":

> You did all you could for Eugene, and I appreciate it from the bottom of my heart. Don't feel bad because things didn't turn out like we wanted them to. We always don't understand the work of the Lord. He does everything for the best. Just because Eugene is gone don't give up because there are other boys to be saved. . . . Of course one hates to see their children died but I am satisfied that he has gone to rest. I would rather have him gone than have him spend the rest of his life in that place. . . . P.S. Keep your chin up and smile, that is what Eugene said for us to do.[28]

Marshall's work was stressful not only because he cared about the lives of his clients, but also because he, like other NAACP lawyers, ran real risks of physical danger. Ransom had just left a courtroom hearing in Nashville about the exclusion of African-Americans from juries—a hearing conducted with a "friendly attitude" on all sides—when he was attacked in the hallway by a former deputy sheriff, who said, "We are going to teach these Northern Negroes not to come down here raising fancy court questions." A grand jury refused to indict Ransom's assailant; its foreman had attacked African-Americans in the same courthouse the day after the assault on Ransom. In 1950, Arthur Shores, an African-American lawyer from Alabama, reminded Marshall of a recent trip they had taken from Montgomery to Birmingham, during which they had passed a posse that was looking for "a tall yellow Negro, with a gold tooth, who had raped a white woman and murdered her four year old son. . . . Lucky for us we did not stop, with your fitting the description of the accused." Marshall replied that he was glad that Shores had not taken his suggestion to slow down: "I am sure what would have happen[e]d if they had first charged me with being the one they wanted and I had told them 'I am not him, I am Thurgood Marshall from New York and this is Arthur Shores from Birmingham.' I think we would then have had quite a time. At any rate such is life when you go about doing the Master's business in Alabama."[29]

Marshall's major encounter with violence occurred in November 1946. On February 25, 1946, Mrs. Gladys Stephenson and her son James, a nineteen-year-old who had just completed three years of service in the Navy, complained to a radio repair store owner in Columbia, Tennessee, that she was being overcharged for faulty repairs on her radio. The repairman got indignant and slapped Mrs. Stephenson, and James struck back. A crowd of whites gathered, and the police arrested the Stephensons. Rumors flew through the white community about the incident, and a lynch mob gathered. The sheriff took the Stephensons out of the jail without alerting the crowd, which disbanded. The African-American community, which resided in an area of Columbia called Mink Slide, feared a general attack, and its leaders spread word to keep off the streets and to turn out the lights. Responding to white fears that the African-Americans were preparing some sort of insurrection, the state patrol and national guard surrounded Mink Slide, and at 6 A.M. on the morning of February 27, mounted an assault on Mink Slide. When the police entered the area, someone cried out, "Here they come," and shots were fired. The police shot out windows, rampaged through offices, and destroyed houses. Over one hundred of the African-American residents of Mink Slide were arrested, and two were shot to death in jail.[30]

Immediately after the riot, the Civil Rights Section of the Department of Justice began an investigation to see whether the civil rights of Mink Slide's residents had been violated. A grand jury was convened, and three attorneys from Washington went to Tennessee to supervise the presentation of evidence. After FBI agents had asked provocative questions that led the residents to conclude that "they were being investigated rather than the state officers," local African-American lawyers advised them not to cooperate with the investigation "to guard against the chance of a complete breakdown on the part of the less stalwart." In addition, the United States attorney in Tennessee was unenthusiastic about the investigation, and most of the grand jury's attention was directed at white supporters of civil rights. The grand jury report in June found that civil rights had not been violated, that the police had used reasonable force throughout the incident, and that the two prisoners who had been killed in jail had grabbed some guns that had been left in the room with them. The grand jury criticized "inflammatory articles" in Communist newspapers.[31]

Even before the federal investigation was concluded, Tennessee charged more than thirty African-Americans with various offenses, including attempted murder. Marshall, who had planned to lead the defense team, became seriously ill with viral pneumonia in May 1946. Walter White said that Marshall's "overwork caught up with him." Marshall felt the mental and physical strain of preparing for the Columbia cases; the temperature in Columbia had been 103°F and Marshall was extremely sensitive to heat. Marshall was suddenly hospitalized and there was some concern for his life, though on the day of his hospitalization he told White to "give them the bad news that I'll live." Marshall left the hospital at the beginning of July under strict orders to rest until September, and in early September he went to the Virgin Islands as the guest of Hastie, then the governor of the territory, where he tried to keep from working. The extended period of rest was so unusual that, as he wrote White, "I will have a difficult job persuading Buster to leave."[32]

Having filed preliminary challenges to the composition of the grand jury that indicted the African-American defendants, Marshall sought to have the trial postponed while he recovered. The NAACP's lawyers in Tennessee were somewhat annoyed at Marshall's attempt to delay the trial. White wrote Buster to tell him, "when [he] is both well enough and in a good enough mood to stand a little annoyance," that Ransom's feelings were "badly hurt."[33]

The trial went forward without Marshall. The cases of six defendants were set apart from the rest, to be tried later, one defendant died before trial, and twenty-five went to trial. To obtain a relatively unbiased jury, the trial was shifted from Columbia to Lawrenceburg. Three lawyers conducted the defense: Ransom, Z. Alexander Looby, an African-American lawyer from Nashville who had worked with the national NAACP office in the past, and Maurice Weaver, a young white lawyer from Chattanooga. Because African-Americans had no place to sleep overnight in Lawrenceburg, the lawyers had to drive more than one hundred miles daily from Nashville to conduct the trials.[34]

The second trial began on August 13, 1946. The atmosphere was tense. One witness, the state commissioner of public safety, answered one of Weaver's questions, "I have many friends among the colored people, and I have more respect for any one of them than I have for you." Walter White began to interfere with the local lawyers because he did not have much confidence in their ability, especially when he received reports from the lawyers that "so far they ha[ve] failed to win a single argument." White was also upset at the trial's expense, and urged Robert Carter to take part in the trial. Carter, although reluctant at first, agreed, in part to "gain necessary experience so that in the future the National Office will not be met with a similar situation." Not surprisingly, Ransom, Looby, and Weaver resented the national office's lack of confidence, and opposed Carter's participation. At this point Carter called upon Marshall, who was still recuperating, to mediate the dispute. Marshall said that at first he wanted Carter at the trial, "but in view of the fact that you first asked [the local lawyers] about it and they gave you their advice I think it best not to do it at this time."[35]

On October 4, 1946, the Lawrenceburg jury, apparently resenting the burden that had been placed on their town by Columbia, or, as a reporter from New York suggested, convinced that no one should be punished "for what everybody realizes was the reflex of their woeful terror," convicted only two of the defendants and acquitted the remaining twenty-three. The prosecutor later recommended that the two convictions be vacated, and dismissed the indictments against most of the other defendants. Two defendants, Lloyd Kennedy and William Pillow, went to trial on November 18, 1948, in Columbia. Having recovered from his illness, Marshall went to Columbia to take part in the trial. Pillow was acquitted of attempted murder, and Kennedy was convicted of attempted second-degree murder and was sentenced to up to five years in prison, later commuted to one year.[36]

After the sentence was handed down, Marshall and Looby left Columbia, with Marshall driving. After a few minutes they heard police sirens behind them and pulled over. Three carloads of police officers emptied and ordered Marshall and Looby out of the car, so that, the officers said, they could search for liquor. Marshall and Looby observed the search closely, to ensure that the police did not plant liquor in the car. When the search turned up nothing, they were allowed to leave. Looby told Marshall that Looby should take over the driving. When the police noticed the change in drivers, they asked to see the driver's licenses and "called out the names." When Marshall's was called, someone in the crowd said, "That's the one." Marshall was arrested for driving while drunk, even though he was no longer driving the car. He told them that he had not had a drink in two days—the length of the trial.

The officers took Marshall in one police car and began to drive down a side road. Looby followed in his car, and, when the officers failed to persuade Looby to stop following them, the cars went into Columbia. According to Marshall, the town was empty, because "everybody was down at the Duck River waiting for the party." The police told him to get out of the car and go to the justice of the peace office down the block. Marshall asked whether he was still under arrest, and when he was told that he was, he said, "I go where you go, you ain't going to shoot me in the back while escaping." The justice of the peace, a teetotaler, gave Marshall his "special" test, smelling Marshall's breath. Finding that, as Marshall put it, "I was extremely sober," the justice of the peace told the police, "That man is not drunk, he hasn't even had a drink." The police left the room, and Marshall was told that he was free to go. He ran out and jumped into Looby's car, and they went to Mink Slide. Sol Blair, a community leader who had been acquitted in the first round of trials, gave Looby and Marshall his car to use, "and three cars went three different ways just as they came down the street." Looby's car was followed, and the young man driving it was beaten up, but Marshall and Looby got safely back to Nashville. He immediately called United States Attorney General Tom Clark to tell his story. Marshall's voice got "more and more Southern" as he talked. When Clark asked Marshall whether he had been drunk, Marshall said, "No, but exactly five minutes after I hang up this phone I'm going to be drunk."[37]

4

"A Negro on Trial for His Life"
Criminal Law and Race Discrimination

Fascism's rise in Europe, which Justice Black alluded to in his *Chambers* opinion, brought third-degree methods and discrimination in jury selection to the center of the Supreme Court's concern about racial equality. The African-American community pressed civil rights lawyers to pursue cases raising these issues. Those were truly pressing cases of sheer human need, and they appealed to Marshall's instincts as a trial lawyer. During the 1940s "Judge and Company" laid the foundations of the law of criminal procedure that eventually came into full flower under Chief Justice Earl Warren.

The Supreme Court limited what the NAACP's lawyers could do in criminal cases. Before the 1940s, the Court placed few limits on state criminal procedures. In 1937 the Supreme Court rejected the argument that the states had to comply with everything in the Bill of Rights, and it reiterated that position, though over a strong dissent, in 1947. The Court had imposed some limitations on states in criminal cases, though, relying on the general phrases in the Fourteenth Amendment guaranteeing that defendants must receive "due process of law" and that everyone must receive "the equal protection of the laws." Soon after the amendment was adopted in 1868, the Court held that African-Americans could not be intentionally excluded from grand juries or trial juries. The Court's first cases involved exclusions resulting from state statutes explicitly denying African-Americans the right to serve, but the Court extended its holding to cases in which African-Americans were in fact intentionally excluded. The Court also held that convictions resulting from "kangaroo courts" dominated by mobs were invalid, and that convictions resulting from the introduction of coerced confessions could not stand.[1]

These holdings provided some opportunities for NAACP lawyers, but the legal and social setting in which criminal procedure cases arose constrained their ability to exploit those opportunities. Grand jury challenges were particularly important to the organization, because exclusions from grand juries not only affected the rights of criminal defendants but also reflected the white community's judgment that even law-abiding African-Americans were not fit to participate in an important government function. Once Southern states realized that the Supreme Court would not let them enforce statutes barring African-Americans from service, the issue became one of fact: Were African-Americans intentionally excluded from service even without a statute? Long-standing procedural rules in many states required that criminal defendants bring challenges to the composition of grand juries almost immediately after their indictment, on the theory that an immediate challenge allowed the state to rectify the problem and reindict the defendant quickly. Defense lawyers, particularly white ones, often were reluctant to raise these challenges in a timely manner, in part because they did not want to disrupt local patterns of race relations. Yet trying to raise the issue of exclusion from grand juries after the time limit on filing the challenges had expired was "practically useless."[2]

The passage of time also caused difficulty in kangaroo court cases. The whole point of kangaroo courts was to provide a quick decision to give a facade of legality to what was in effect a mob lynching. Typically, local African-Americans were able to notify the national NAACP in New York only after the trial had been completed. By then, as Marshall put it, "usually the record is in such bad shape that we are unable to do anything legally."[3]

The difficulties caused by records "in bad shape" were compounded in the coerced-confession cases. The problem the NAACP faced was caused by the response of the police to Supreme Court decisions condemning third-degree tactics. The police did not stop using those tactics; instead, having been told that they could not use the third degree, the police began to deny that the confessions they obtained resulted from improper tactics. The police developed two lines of argument. First, if they acknowledged that third-degree tactics had been used, prosecutors refrained from introducing confessions obtained immediately after the defendant was beaten, and instead introduced confessions made at a later time, contending that the coercive effects of the beatings had dissipated. Second, they often simply denied that they had used coercive tactics, and the state courts usually found as a matter of fact that no beatings had occurred. The Supreme Court was not in a good position to evaluate the competing factual accounts, although it is reasonably clear that sometimes the justices were suspicious of the police stories. As a result, the Court began to focus not on direct physical coercion but on the psychological dimensions of being held in police custody for extended periods, cut off from family and friends, and the like.

The shift from a focus on physical coercion to psychological pressure made the lawyers' task more difficult. It weakened the connection between the coerced-confession cases and questions of racial oppression. Justice Black had properly stressed in *Chambers v. Florida* that the police often used physical coercion in cases involving despised minorities. But the police used psychological pressure to secure confessions in a much broader range of cases. Because the new psychological focus meant that a much larger number of criminal defendants could raise coerced-confession claims, the Court began to be more concerned about the impact of its decisions on the administration of criminal justice generally. In short, the Court became less receptive to coerced-confession claims because, as a result of the

Court's inability to resolve factual disputes, its doctrine had shifted the focus away from the kinds of police misconduct most closely related to racial oppression.[4]

Some of the lawyers' difficulties could have been alleviated if the national staff had been able to rely on local attorneys to develop proper records. The staff did distribute a general outline of procedure that NAACP branches should follow, which included a short statement on criminal cases. It also made available to the branches, and through them to cooperating local attorneys, a six-page memorandum by Leon Ransom on procedures for challenging the exclusion of African-Americans from juries. Few lawyers in the South wanted to handle these cases, though. African-American lawyers could not specialize in criminal defense, which was costly and unremunerative for lawyers who often found it difficult to make a living from their practices anyway. Handling unpopular cases was difficult under any circumstances, but was particularly difficult for lawyers defending African-Americans in the South. In one case, "the lawyer in South Carolina who handles our cases is unable to handle them on a voluntary basis because as soon as he began defending Negroes he lost his paying practice and cannot afford to take any cases on a purely voluntary basis." The lawyer, Joseph Murray, had to relocate his practice from McCormick to Columbia in 1940 because he defended an African-American who had been prosecuted for murdering a policeman in 1925 and whose home had been burned down the next day, forcing him to flee the state. The reference to "the" lawyer in South Carolina is of course significant, for it demonstrates how few lawyers there were to help the NAACP. As late as 1947, Robert Carter wrote that there were no lawyers in Florida on whom the NAACP could rely. As historian Neil McMillen suggests, describing the situation in Mississippi, pursuing an activist legal career there "would have been, quite simply, suicidal."[5]

In criminal cases, then, the NAACP had to rely on lawyers with whom it had relatively few contacts. As in other cases, the local lawyers believed that the NAACP could provide them with the kind of fees that their clients could not, and as in other cases, this regularly produced problems between the national office and the local lawyers. The problems were most severe at the beginning of the 1940s, when the budget for the NAACP's legal department was quite small. The situation in South Carolina suggests the dimensions of the problem. Joseph Murray handled a number of criminal cases for the NAACP in early 1940. When he asked for $200, Marshall thought that this was "very reasonable" and should be sent to Murray because "he has always been more than cooperative." After learning from Roy Wilkins that the budget would not support a fee even of that amount, Marshall asked the branches in South Carolina to raise money.[6]

Marshall continued to be plagued by cases in which the NAACP had to support lawyers the national staff believed to be inadequate. In one South Carolina case, where a young African-American had killed a local farmer, the NAACP branch had done a great deal of fund raising and helped pay the fee for a defense conducted by the son of the incoming governor. Marshall was incredulous: "I am perfectly frank in saying that it is almost impossible that the son of the Governor of South Carolina would have the same outlook on these cases as we have. There are, of course, exceptions to every rule, but I think the odds are that this type of an attorney might not be wholly satisfactory. Our lawyers always have to be in a position where they are above pressure. The Governor of South Carolina is subject to all types of pressure from the 'other side'. This pressure would quite naturally carry over to the son." Assured by James Hinton, an NAACP leader in South Carolina, that the lawyer was sincere, Marshall agreed to send $100, noting that "we have been forced to put up quite a bit of money on legal cases in South Carolina because of the fact that the situation is so bad in that State."[7]

Similar questions about the sincerity and ability of local lawyers arose repeatedly. The national office tried to solve this problem by attempting to learn the facts of criminal cases "well in advance" so that it could negotiate with the local lawyers for reasonable fees, but the circumstances of the cases made that quite difficult.[8]

Marshall knew that criminal cases could be used to raise money for the NAACP's general program. Once, in the case of a sharecropper who killed his landlord in an argument over his proper share, the NAACP cooperated with the Workers Defense League, a leftist group; Marshall ruefully noted, "I wish we could raise money on our cases as easy as they have on this case." Yet, even fundraising activities could cause difficulties with the cooperating attorneys. The elder Sidney Redmond once complained to Marshall that he was annoyed at Walter White's efforts to "tell me how best to handle [fee] matters . . . in Mississippi, indicating to a degree that advertisement of the NAACP was a large part of the matter." Marshall told Redmond that the national office would pay his expenses even though it had understood that the local branch would pay.[9]

Relations with local attorneys were not always strained, of course. Willie Carter received a death sentence for killing a police officer in Mississippi. Marshall learned of Carter's case in the late summer of 1944, when he received a letter dated August 22 that was forwarded to him from the Pittsburgh *Courier,* saying that Carter's execution was set for September 24. Marshall immediately wrote Forrest Jackson, Carter's lawyer, to find out what could be done, although, he said, the facts as he knew them led him to "seriously doubt that anything can be done legally" to help Carter. Jackson replied that he could file an appeal for a fee of $1,500. Marshall countered by offering $250, which Jackson accepted as a fee for obtaining a stay of execution. The NAACP attempted to raise the full $1,500, and Jackson agreed to accept whatever the organization could provide. When Carter's conviction was reversed, Jackson and Marshall agreed on a $1,000 fee for representation at the second trial. Although Carter was convicted and again received a death sentence, and despite the protracted dealings with regard to Jackson's fee, Marshall praised Jackson for doing a "splendid job" on the case—which, given the underlying offense, almost certainly could not have resulted in any other outcome anyway.[10]

The Supreme Court began to examine grand jury discrimination more closely in 1942. *Hill v. Texas* involved an African-American convicted of rape in Dallas. Marshall did not trust the lawyer handling the case and, after examining the record, decided not to participate. Although Hill's lawyers had shown that no African-Americans had served on Dallas grand juries for at least sixteen years and that the grand jury commissioners did not attempt to identify African-Americans who satisfied the state's statutory qualifications for grand jury service, the Texas appeals court had rejected Hill's challenge because they had not shown how many qualified African-Americans there were in Dallas. Marshall believed that the Supreme Court might have ignored the failure to prove how many qualified African-Americans there were, except that the grand jury commissioners had testified that they were not prejudiced against African-Americans. In addition, he noted that Hill had confessed to the crime, and that the case therefore fell outside the NAACP's rule of representing only innocent defendants.[11]

Marshall was mistaken about the Court. It unanimously reversed the conviction, on the ground that Hill did not have to do more to support his claim than he had. Noting as Marshall had that Hill's guilt was clear, Justice Robert Jackson prepared a dissent saying, "I can think of no assumption more discreditable to the negro race, or more harmful to it in its struggle for its rights, than that negroes . . . would have given this person immunity from indictment," and concluding, "I would affirm this conviction and right race wrongs in a cause more representative of the race grievance." However, he withheld the dissent to avoid having "a bad effect on race relations" during the war. Justice Harlan Fiske Stone's colleagues praised his opinion for the Court as "restrained and correct" and "clean and lean, as it should be." After the decision was announced, Marshall responded a bit testily to a lawyer who wrote saying that he did not want to "rub [the reversal] in." Marshall defended his decision, calling the record in the case "lousy" and noting that "it is necessary that we at all times look out for the reputation of the Association. It is not a question of just trying to win cases."[12]

The NAACP was also involved in a sequel to *Hill*. L. C. Akins attempted to board a street car in Dallas before all the white women passengers had boarded. An off-duty police officer tried to stop Akins, and when Akins drew a knife there was a scuffle during which Akins grabbed the officer's gun and shot him. Akins was charged with murder. His lawyer wrote Marshall asking for information about challenging the grand jury's composition, and an officer of the Dallas branch wanted Marshall to recommend that Akins refuse to take part in the trial so as to preserve the grand jury claim in its cleanest form. Marshall rejected the latter suggestion, saying that, in a capital case, the lawyers could not take "short cuts" but had to go to trial and raise issues that might occur during trial. Akins was convicted and received a life sentence. His conviction was reversed because of *Hill*. A new grand jury was convened, which had eleven whites and one African-American, and Akins was again indicted. He was retried and, upon his reconviction, received a death sentence, which was later commuted to life. The Dallas branch actively supported Akins's case, but "did not seek headline publicity for the organization because it was felt that such publicity would not help Akins during the last stages of the appeal for executive clemency." The International Labor Defense, though, did publicize the case, and, according to a Texas NAACP official, "caused a storm of protest" against outside meddling in Texas affairs.[13]

Akins appealed his conviction to the United States Supreme Court, again raising a challenge to the composition of the grand jury. The Supreme Court, in an opinion by Justice Stanley Reed, affirmed the conviction. Akins claimed that the grand jury commissioners had responded to *Hill* by deliberately limiting the number of African-American grand jurors to one per panel. Much of Justice Reed's opinion was devoted to the proposition that the Constitution was not violated if

African-Americans were not proportionally represented on grand juries, which was not in dispute. The real issue, as the chief justice asked at the Court's conference, was, "[H]ow can they determine on any [number] of colored people without discrimination?"[14]

As Reed analyzed the facts, proportional representation of African-Americans on grand juries in Dallas would produce just under two African-Americans, on average, per grand jury. Noting that one African-American had served on both of the grand juries that had been convened after *Hill* and before Akins's indictment, Reed said that "we cannot say that the omission from each of the two lists of all but one of the members of a race which composed some fifteen per cent of the popula- tion alone proved racial discrimination." And, despite statements by the commis- sioners that "we had no intention of placing more than one negro on the panel," and that "our intentions were to get just one negro on the grand jury," Reed was "unconvinced that the commissioners deliberately and intentionally limited the number of Negroes on the grand jury list," because "the law of their state, the instructions of the judge, their oath of office required them to choose prospective jurors . . . without regard to their color or the number of representatives of various races who might appear upon the list. We cannot say the commissioners violated these obligations." Justice Frank Murphy focused on the commissioners' testimony to support his dissent, saying that "clearer proof of intentional and deliberate limitation on the basis of color would be difficult to produce." As he read the record, the commissioners "refused . . . to disregard the factor of color in selecting the jury personnel. To that extent they have disregarded [Akins's] right to the equal protection of the laws. To that extent they have ignored the ideals of the jury system."[15]

When cases came to the office before trials occurred, the legal staff could help shape the record and ensure a decent presentation of the issues the organization was interested in. At the same time, Marshall came to have personal contact with the defendants, and often became rather close to them.

In *Lyons v. Oklahoma,* Marshall was one of the defendant's trial lawyers be- cause the state, faced with a politically embarrassing case, delayed the trial for nearly a year. Mr. and Mrs. Elmer Rogers and their four-year-old son were murdered on New Year's Eve, 1939, in their home in Choctaw County, Oklahoma. W. D. Lyons was arrested on January 11, 1940, and, he testified later, was severely beaten, leaving him bruised and scarred, by a special investigator from the gover- nor's office. He did not then admit anything. Eleven days later he was questioned again, starting at the county prosecutor's office at about 6:30 in the evening and ending early the next morning at about 2:30. Lyons testified that he had been beaten again, and, as before, his testimony was supported by other witnesses. During the evening Lyons was taken to the Rogers's home, and a pan of the victims' bones was placed in his lap. Lyons then confessed. He was returned to the jail and, in the early afternoon, was taken to the state penitentiary in McAlester, where, between 8 and 11 at night, he signed a second confession.[16]

In March 1940, after Lyons's confession but well before his trial, Roscoe Dunjee, a prominent African-American lawyer and newspaper publisher in Oklahoma, wrote Walter White asking for a contribution to Lyons's defense, which, Dunjee wrote, presented "a case better than" *Chambers* for the NAACP. Marshall looked into the facts and became convinced that Lyons was innocent. He learned that a convict at a state prison camp had confessed to the murders immediately after they occurred, which led to an investigation of the camp and the firing of the warden. As Marshall saw it, the governor's special investigator had participated in Lyons's interrogation in order to defuse the political fallout that would have occurred if the murders had been attributed to wardens who let a prisoner commit murder. Marshall's confidence in Lyons's innocence was bolstered because the state delayed bringing Lyons to trial, contrary to the usual practice of having extremely prompt trials in cases where African-Americans were accused of murdering whites.[17]

Lyons was initially represented by Stanley Belden, a liberal white lawyer. Dunjee noted that there was no ill feeling against Lyons in the community and that, indeed, the officers who had beaten him had been defeated in a recent election. When Lyons's trial began on Monday, January 27, 1941, Marshall actively participated in the defense. He wrote the office that the courtroom was extremely crowded, but that the sentiment was "good," with "no evidence of mob spirit." He said that "several white people have complimented us on the type of defense," and later notified the office that the white mayor of Chickasha, Oklahoma, had started a defense fund with a contribution of $100. He was annoyed, though, that the judge referred to the trial as a "gala day": "Imagine it—a Negro on trial for his life being called a 'gala Day.'" However, Marshall was pleased that students from several white schools attending the trial were "given a lesson in constitutional law and rights of Negroes that they wouldn't get in their schools." As Marshall entered the courtroom "word went around that 'a nigger lawyer from New York' was on the case." He said that the court personnel were "very nice and explained that this was their first experience in seeing a Negro lawyer try a case— first time they had seen such an animal." Before Lyons's case was called, there were some motions in another case in which the police chief had been jailed for conspiracy to sell whiskey, which led Marshall to comment, no doubt referring as well to Lyons's beating, "a model law enforcement community." Everyone in the courtroom, including the judge, was very informal.[18]

When Lyons's case was called, Marshall was introduced to the court and "the building did not fall and the world did not come to an end." The first day of trial was consumed with selection of the jury and preliminary testimony, with Belden handling the defense. On Tuesday the prosecution sought to introduce Lyons's confessions. Marshall cross-examined the police witnesses "because we figured they would resent being questioned by a Negro and would get angry and this would help us. It worked perfect," Marshall wrote. "They all became angry at the idea of a Negro pushing them into tight corners and making their lies so obvious. Boy, did I like that—and did the Negroes in the Court-room like it. You can't imagine what it means to those people down there who have been pushed around for years to know that there is an organization that will help them." The prosecutor too became angry and admitted that he himself had seen Lyons being beaten, notwithstanding the denials made by some of the police officers. After the governor's special investigator denied from the stand that he had struck Lyons, Marshall called several white witnesses who testified that the investigator had told them that he had beaten Lyons for seven hours. "There are some good white people in this world," Marshall noted. At the conclusion of the presentation, the judge ruled that Lyons's initial confession, immediately after the "pan of bones" incident, could not be used but that the second confession, given at the McAlester penitentiary, was voluntary and could be admitted. The trial concluded on Thursday, with the prosecutors asking for the death penalty. The jury, after five hours of deliberation, returned a guilty verdict but imposed only a life sentence. To Marshall, given the brutality of the crime, this "show[ed] clearly that they believed him innocent."[19]

Marshall thought that the case was "in a perfect position" for an appeal, and was clearly suitable for a major fund-raising effort. "We could use another good defense fund and this case has more appeal tha[n] any up to this time. The beating plus the use of the bones of dead people will raise money." Two months after the trial, though, Belden, who had told Roger Baldwin that he "certainly appreciated having Mr. Marshall associated in the case with me," informed Marshall that representatives of the governor were soliciting money to give the governor in exchange for Lyons's freedom. Belden was unsure what to do:

> I am fully aware of our duty to our client but I am also aware of our duty to expose and not cover up the things that make possible such travesty of justice as took place in the Lyons case, and I feel it is our duty to the colored race, to the state and all concerned that we file the appeal and expose the corruption in this state even though in so doing we risk the liberty of our client and make sure that for some months to come he must stay in prison; but after all this thing is bigger th[a]n just the question of the immediate liberty of W. D. Lyons or any other individual.

Marshall told Belden to file the appeal, perhaps because the impropriety of the use of a bribe to secure Lyons's freedom meant that, for Marshall, there was no real conflict between appealing and serving Lyons's immediate interest.[20]

A month later Belden informed Marshall that he was leaving the state because his practice "has been ruined." Marshall responded that he was sorry about Belden's decision, and that someday officials would learn what civil rights and civil liberties really meant. "You won't see this day and I won't but at least you can be satisfied with the feeling that you have made your contribution."[21]

Marshall asked Belden to prepare the petition for appeal to the Oklahoma Supreme Court because Marshall did not completely understand some of Oklahoma's local procedures. During the preparations for the appeal, Belden was drafted, and Dunjee had to find new local counsel. His task was complicated by the fact that "the local attorneys always have been a little hostile (Negro) since I hired Belden and had you come to the state." Dunjee also spoke with the chief judge of Oklahoma's court to secure extensions of time and, at one point, to gain an indication of when the court's decision would be issued. After the state court affirmed the conviction, Marshall prepared to seek review in the United States Supreme Court. William Hastie wrote the Supreme Court brief, with some additions by Dudley and Konvitz, and Marshall edited it.[22]

The Supreme Court affirmed Lyons's conviction, in an opinion by Justice Reed. Reed stated the facts almost half-heartedly, writing that the evidence of some of the beatings was "conflicting" but that "disinterested witnesses" supported Lyons's version. The legal issue was whether the McAlester confession was "vitiated" by the continuing influence of the prior coerced confession. During the Court's conference, Justice Owen Roberts said that the police action was not "such a flouting of decencies as to violate due process," and a majority of his colleagues agreed. To Reed, the earlier events "do not lead unescapably to the conclusion that the [second] confession was brought about by the earlier mistreatments." The second confession occurred twelve hours later, after Lyons had been transferred from the control of the sheriff's office to the control of the prison warden, and, although one of the officers who had been present during the first "interrogation" was present when Lyons made his second confession, that officer was not one of those who had beaten Lyons. Lyons confessed soon after arriving at McAlester and after being told that he did not have to make a statement unless he wanted to. As in *Akins,* Justice Murphy dissented, saying that "this flagrant abuse . . . ought not to be approved." To him it was "inconceivable that the second confession was free from the coercive atmosphere that admittedly impregnated the first one." The entire set of events was "one single, continuing transaction. To conclude that the brutality inflicted at the time of the first confession suddenly lost all of its effect in the short space of twelve hours is to close one's eyes to the realities of human nature. An individual does not that easily forget the type of torture that accompanied [Lyons's] previous refusal to confess."[23]

Over the next decade Marshall corresponded with Lyons in the state prison, and in 1952 wrote a personal letter to the state attorney who had argued the case in the Supreme Court to see if it was time yet to seek clemency or parole for Lyons; the attorney responded that Lyons had to serve still more time before he was eligible for parole.[24]

Marshall called another trial significant nationally because it involved African-American soldiers charged with rape during the massive increase in African-American enlistment in the armed forces during the Second World War. Sergeant John Bordenave and privates Richard Adams and Lawrence Mitchell were serving at Camp Claiborne in Louisiana when the incident occurred. According to Sergeant Bordenave, he was on guard duty when he came upon private George Schuler and Mrs. Anna Mae Mason having intercourse "on the Negro side of the camp." He ordered them up and, he said, had Adams and Mitchell escort them to the white side. Several days later Mason reported that she had been raped. Another version of the events, offered in statements by the African-American soldiers, was that they had engaged in voluntary intercourse with Mason, who had left her husband in Ohio to follow Schuler to Louisiana. Marshall had some difficulty in coming to a conclusion, for himself, about what had happened. Eventually he became convinced that at least Bordenave had not had intercourse with Mason, but that Mitchell might have raped her and then exerted influence over Bordenave and Adams, who was moderately retarded, to concoct the story of voluntary intercourse. Marshall found the medical evidence most compelling; the evidence, developed by the Army, showed that Mason was so severely infected with gonorrhea that it was impossible for three men to have intercourse with her without at least one becoming infected, and that none of the defendants was infected.[25]

Bordenave, Adams, and Mitchell were prosecuted for rape under a provision of the United State Code making it a federal crime, to be prosecuted in the federal courts and not in army courts-martial, to commit rape on federal land, including army bases. Three local white attorneys were appointed to defend them, but, according to A. P. Tureaud, who looked into the case for the NAACP, the lawyers "manifested no interest" in the defense; one even attempted to get out of the case because he was a candidate for local district attorney and "would not risk the loss of his election by a vigorous defense of Bordenave." The soldiers were convicted and sentenced to death. The trial judge in the case approached Tureaud and asked if he was interested in the case. Eventually NAACP branches in Alexandria and New Orleans became interested in the case, and some conflict over publicity developed between them. Marshall counselled them that "all we have to do is to bear in mind that the important thing at this stage is to see that the men get justice."[26]

After first pursuing the thought that Adams could get a new trial based on newly discovered evidence that he was retarded, Marshall found himself "on the track of a perfect break" in the case. In 1940, before the United States acquired the land for Camp Claiborne, Congress passed a law providing that United States authorities could accept jurisdiction over land they acquired by filing a notice with the governor of the state in which the land was located, and that until the United States had acquired jurisdiction by filing a notice, "it shall be conclusively presumed that no such jurisdiction has been accepted." During the post-trial investigation, Marshall discovered that the United States had never filed such a notice with the governor of Louisiana, something that had been overlooked, he said, in "rushing [these] Negroes to trial." Marshall presented this legal argument to the court of appeals, which asked the Supreme Court to decide whether the federal courts could try the defendants for rape. The solicitor general, appearing for the United States, agreed that the federal courts could not exercise jurisdiction, and the Supreme Court directed that the convictions be reversed.[27]

In some ways, the reversal left Bordenave and the other soldiers in almost a worse position. If they had not committed the rape on federal territory, they had committed it in Louisiana, which was therefore in a position to prosecute them. Further, they had been dishonorably discharged from the Army as soon as they had been convicted. Thus, they faced immediate reprosecution in the courts of Louisiana, which they hardly welcomed. To avoid that, Marshall worked to get them back into the Army, on the ground that—no valid conviction ever having been rendered—they had been illegally discharged. Once they waived any claims to the pay that they would have earned, they were again enrolled in the army. The next step was a court-martial. Marshall traveled to Texas, where the soldiers were held, and participated in the trial. He cross-examined Schuler, asking why he had left Mason with the defendants on the evening of the incident, and why the rape had not been immediately reported. He also led Mitchell, probably the most culpable of the defendants, through direct examination. In addition, Marshall gave the first closing statement for the defendants, a somewhat rambling argument whose main point was to discredit the defendants' statements about voluntary intercourse by reminding the court of the general atmosphere in Louisiana, in which, even without specific threats, African-American defendants could reasonably fear mob violence and give false confessions because of that fear. The defendants were again convicted and sentenced to death. The sentences were commuted to life the next year, and reduced further to twelve years in 1946; the defendants were paroled in 1947.[28]

Most lawyers who saw Marshall in trial called him a master at examination and particularly cross-examination. His ability to understand the essence of a witness's testimony and to develop questions in response to a witness's unanticipated responses made him especially impressive. His cross-examinations in the Lyons and Camp Claiborne cases were typical. The prosecution witnesses gave testimony that Marshall showed to be incredible. Yet, in Southern courtrooms, no matter how incredible the testimony was, juries and judges accepted it. The audience for Marshall's trial work, then, was not primarily the jury or the trial judge.[29]

One audience was the Supreme Court: If the cases were appealed, Marshall had to build a record that showed why his opponent's witnesses should not be believed. Perhaps more important, his audience was the African-American community observing the trial. Outside the courtroom, the community knew Marshall as "high spirited, gregarious, jovial, flippant and full of zest for such of life's pleasures as late nights of poker with bourbon on the side, Western movies, [and] baseball. . . ." He was fully a member of the community that he served. Inside the courtroom, he was "an entirely different person." His intensity and seriousness, and his ability to show that the witnesses on the other side could not be believed, demonstrated to the African-American community that their cause was completely justified. Marshall's ability to change his demeanor was sometimes disconcerting to people who had seen him only inside the courtroom, or who projected on to him their own views about what the nation's leading civil rights lawyer should be like. But, by changing from the serious courtroom lawyer to the congenial man of the people, Marshall developed strong supporters in every forum that he worked in: Judges who saw him in court respected his talents as a trial lawyer and appellate advocate; clients who saw him outside of court respected his commitment to their individual cases; and the rest of the African-American community understood that he was one of them.[30]

The Lyons and Camp Claiborne cases were typical in another way. In both Marshall was convinced, with some reason, that the defendants were innocent; in both he ensured that the defendants were not executed; yet in both he did not secure their release. Civil rights successes were, as always, ambiguous.

5

The "Increasing Power" of Private Discrimination

During the 1940s Marshall and his staff mounted a comprehensive attack on racial discrimination and its consequences. They challenged discrimination in employment, in housing, in criminal procedure, in transportation, and in education. The precise issues the lawyers raised changed as the law developed in directions no one had foreseen, but the project of attacking racial discrimination comprehensively remained the same.

Lawyers, clients, and interest groups were part of the "Company" that, according to Bentham, made the law, but of course so were judges. The program the lawyers followed was shaped by their predictions about what the Supreme Court would do once it was faced with NAACP cases. Because Marshall believed that judges in lower courts would follow or even anticipate the Supreme Court, because the forces that influenced the Supreme Court affected lower courts as well, and because no one could predict at the outset which cases would reach the Supreme Court, the Court was the focus of the lawyers' thinking.

By 1940 the Supreme Court had been reshaped by President Franklin Roosevelt. Early in Roosevelt's first term the Supreme Court appeared to stand in the way of his New Deal programs; it invalidated the National Industrial Recovery Act and other efforts, sometimes misguided, to restructure the economy in response to the Depression. In 1936 Roosevelt asked his advisers to develop plans to deal with the Supreme Court. After his massive reelection victory, Roosevelt proposed what came to be known as the "Court-packing plan," which would have allowed him to appoint six new justices to the Court. Although it was widely perceived as an unjustified assault on the Court, the plan was almost adopted, but it failed for a number of reasons: it was packaged ineptly; civil libertarians were concerned about attacking the Court; one of the New Deal's opponents on the Court announced his retirement; and a decision by the Supreme Court upholding a state minimum-wage statute suggested that the Court had gotten the message and would no longer be quite as recalcitrant about Roosevelt's programs.[1]

Starting in 1937, Roosevelt began to reshape the Supreme Court directly. His first appointee, Hugo Black, replaced one of the Court's conservatives. Black, the senior senator from Alabama, had been an active supporter of the New Deal and a leader in the Court-packing fight. Shortly after the Senate confirmed his appointment, the press broadcast the fact that Black had been a member of the Ku Klux Klan in Alabama for two years in the 1920s. Black allayed concern in a national radio address, and his early opinion in *Chambers v. Florida*, attacking third-degree police methods as totalitarian, confirmed his place among the Court's liberals on questions of race. Roosevelt's next appointee, Stanley Reed, had been solicitor general in the Department of Justice, and had argued many of the cases involving New Deal legislation. A native of Kentucky, Reed reflected the views of Southern progressives; he was uncomfortable with what he saw as the excesses of the Southern system of segregation, but also believed that the South should be left alone to work out its problems gradually.

In 1939 Roosevelt made two important appointments. An expert on corporate law whose brilliance was legendary, William O. Douglas had been a law professor and was chair of the Securities and Exchange Commission when he was appointed. Firmly committed to liberal policies, Douglas was untroubled about using the Supreme Court's power to alter race relations.

Felix Frankfurter, also appointed in 1939, had a quite different view. When he was appointed, Frankfurter was probably the nation's leading scholar of the Supreme Court. He had been an informal advisor to Roosevelt, supporting the Court-packing plan behind the scenes while maintaining a public posture of neutrality that most observers took to signal his opposition to the plan. Frankfurter was an incorrigible note-writer and lobbyist for his views within the Court, to the point where, at one time or another, virtually every one of his colleagues found him an annoyance.

During his time on the Supreme Court, Frankfurter regularly recalled to his colleagues that he had been on the NAACP's National Legal Committee, a group of prominent lawyers who were occasionally consulted on legal questions. Yet he mentioned his work with the NAACP usually when he was cautioning against precipitate action. Suggesting that one of his colleagues tone down the language of a draft opinion, for example, Frankfurter wrote, "Before coming down here, when I was of counsel for the Association for the Advancement of Colored People, considerable practical experience with problems of race relations led me to the conclusion that the ugly practices of racial discrimination should be dealt with by the eloquence of action, but with austerity of speech."[2] Frankfurter's caution derived from a number of sources. He purported to adhere to a general theory of judicial restraint, though in fact his adherence to such a theory was irregular. He often mentioned that as a law professor at Harvard, he had taught a number of prominent moderate younger Southern lawyers, and he believed that he and the Supreme Court could influence the climate of informed opinion in the South by exercising constant pressure on the system of segregation without directly attacking any of its central pillars.

Late in the decade Frankfurter explained his position to his colleagues in *Lee v. Mississippi*, a challenge to a coerced confession used to convict a seventeen-year-old African-American of rape. The Mississippi Supreme Court affirmed the conviction without reaching the question of whether the confession had been coerced because, it said, Lee was barred from raising that question when he testified that he had in fact never confessed at all. Some of the justices wanted to reverse this decision without having the case argued, but Frankfurter objected, saying that "the case involves the susceptibilities of the States on the one hand and the feelings of the most sensitive minority group on the other." After the case was argued, Justice Frank Murphy circulated an opinion reversing the Mississippi Supreme Court. The draft said that the confession was coerced, and did not deal with the state supreme court's theory that Lee could not raise that claim.[3]

Justice Reed, apparently offended by the tone of Murphy's opinion, circulated an opinion concurring in the reversal. Frankfurter joined Reed's opinion, somewhat excessively regarding Murphy's opinion as "a characteristic harangue, full of sophomoric rhetoric." Frankfurter also sent Murphy a letter explaining that he joined Reed because Reed's opinion was "mild, . . . being strongly of opinion in a domain where feelings are deeply rooted and easily stirred, a strong conclusion is reenforced by mildness of expression." Somewhat self-righteously and perhaps with sensitivity to Murphy's view of himself as a strong defender of civil rights, Frankfurter said that while

> long experience . . . has left me with the conviction that while we should deal with these ugly practices of racial discrimination with fearless decency, it does not help toward harmonious race relations to stir our colored fellow citizens to resentment, however unwittingly, by needless detail or even sturdy expression of sentiment, nor do we thereby wean whites from what is so often . . . merely the unanalysed irrational tradition of the past.

Murphy redrafted his opinion to eliminate detailed references to the facts about Lee's confession, whereupon Reed withdrew his separate opinion. As published, the toned-down opinion said that, because the jury believed that Lee had confessed, the issue of coercion should indeed be considered by the state supreme court.[4]

Roosevelt appointed four more Justices in the 1940s. James F. Byrnes served only briefly, resigning to assist the coordination of the war effort. Wiley Rutledge and Frank Murphy were devoted liberals, consistently among the strongest supporters of the positions Marshall urged. When Charles Evans Hughes resigned as chief justice in 1941, Roosevelt promoted Harlan Fiske Stone to chief justice and appointed Robert Jackson to Stone's seat. Stone, a progressive Republican, had been appointed to the Court in 1925 by President Calvin Coolidge. He had consistently voted to uphold the constitutionality of New Deal programs.

Jackson, from upstate New York, was solicitor general and attorney general for Roosevelt. Widely regarded as a brilliant stylist and advocate, Jackson drifted in the direction of judicial restraint, influenced in part by deep personal conflicts with Justices Black and Douglas. Roosevelt promised to make Jackson chief justice when he could, but died before the position opened up. The vacancy occurred in 1946, when Chief Justice Stone had a massive stroke while he was reading an opinion from the bench. At the time, Jackson was serving as chief prosecutor in the war crimes trials at Nuremberg. Jackson thought that President Harry Truman should have honored Roosevelt's promise. When Truman appointed his former

Senate colleague Fred Vinson instead, Jackson believed that Truman had been swayed by Black.[5]

Most of the justices who served on the Court in the early 1940s were personally sympathetic, to varying degrees, to the legal positions asserted by the NAACP, and none had strong objections based in constitutional theory to acting in a manner consistent with their inclinations. In addition, as Justice Black's opinion in *Chambers* indicated, the justices were acutely aware of the relation between racism and totalitarianism, represented by the Nazi government in Germany. Finally, the history of the Supreme Court shows it repeatedly developing new constituencies of support, constituencies that simultaneously were important in the political coalition governing the other branches. As Roosevelt gained support among African-Americans, the Court began to take that community as one of its constituencies as well.

The NAACP's first Supreme Court victory in the coordinated attack on segregation occurred in 1938. Following Marshall's victory in the Murray case in 1935, Houston corresponded with Sidney R. Redmond, the leading African-American attorney in St. Louis, to see if they could develop a similar suit against the University of Missouri. Redmond found that Lloyd Gaines, the president of the senior class at Missouri's Lincoln University, wanted to attend law school and was interested in pursuing a suit like Murray's. When Gaines applied for admission, the university authorities said that he should apply to Lincoln even though Lincoln did not have a law school, because Lincoln would create a law school if he applied. Regarding that as acceptable—the as-yet-nonexistent law school could hardly be "equal though separate" as soon as it was created—Houston went to Missouri for the trial of Gaines's case. To no one's surprise, the state courts rejected his claims.[6]

Houston took the case to the Supreme Court, which ruled in his favor in December 1938. According to the opinion for the Court by Chief Justice Charles Evans Hughes, Missouri's intention to open a law school if Gaines asked for one was insufficient. Nor did an out-of-state scholarship program satisfy the "separate but equal" doctrine. The state, according to the Supreme Court, had to provide its African-American citizens the same opportunities it provided its white citizens; because whites had the opportunity to attend a law school in the state, so must African-Americans. Missouri attempted to comply with the Court's decision by opening a law school at Lincoln in time for Gaines to attend. In one sense the state's attempt was successful; it did open a law school in September 1939, which, the lower courts held, satisfied its obligation under the Supreme Court's decision. Gaines never attended the school, however; he simply disappeared and, despite strenuous efforts by the NAACP, he was never located. Despite this ambiguous ending to the litigation itself, the *Gaines* decision was the Court's first substantial inroad on the "separate but equal" doctrine, and it suggested to the NAACP's lawyers, and to lower courts, that the NAACP's legal program had to be taken seriously.[7]

The original proposal to the Garland Fund said that the NAACP planned to challenge Jim Crow transportation, but the NAACP lawyers were caught in a dilemma in dealing with that issue. In the South segregated transportation was required by law, yet the segregation statutes were identical to the one upheld in *Plessy v. Ferguson,* which was, after all, a transportation case. The NAACP could not attack segregated transportation in the South without taking on *Plessy* directly, and it had chosen to make that attack through education litigation. What was left, then, was a series of challenges to discrimination in interstate transportation. That sort of discrimination was not trivial, particularly during and after the Second World War, when large numbers of African-Americans traveled on interstate trains and buses to get to army training camps and to visit their families after they had migrated to the North. Devising appropriate legal theories to attack that type of discrimination was not easy, though, because it resulted from the interaction of local laws, federal regulation of interstate transportation, and the internal decisions of interstate carriers in making and enforcing rules for their own lines. The NAACP's lawyers were familiar with arguments about discrimination as a violation of the equal protection clause of the Fourteenth Amendment; they were much less at ease in dealing with the technicalities of the Interstate Commerce Act and the commerce clause of the Constitution.[8]

After *Plessy,* the Supreme Court had indicated that it meant to enforce the requirement of equality in separate transportation facilities. In 1914 it held unconstitutional a statute that required separate coach facilities for African-American and white travelers but explicitly allowed railroads to maintain sleeping and dining cars only for whites, with no similar cars for African-Americans; a majority of the Court found it irrelevant that so few African-Americans used sleeping and dining cars that it was unprofitable to include them on trains.[9]

The Court applied the principle underlying that decision in a 1941 case involving Congressman Arthur Mitchell of Chicago. Mitchell was traveling from Chicago to Hot Springs, Arkansas, on a ticket that allowed him to use a Pullman or a sleeping car. When his train left Memphis, Tennessee, for Hot Springs, however, the railroad conductor refused to allow him to use the Pullman seat because of the Arkansas separate but equal law. The conductor moved Mitchell to the coach car reserved for African-Americans, offering to refund the excess of the Pullman fare over the coach fare. Mitchell challenged the railroad's action as a violation of the Interstate Commerce Act, which made it unlawful for any interstate carrier to "subject any particular person . . . to any undue or unreasonable prejudice or disadvantage in any respect whatsoever." The Interstate Commerce Commission, the administrative agency that initially considered Mitchell's complaint, agreed that the coach for African-Americans was not equal to the Pullman car, but held that the resulting discrimination was not "undue or unreasonable" because the railroad was simply complying with state law in attempting to segregate its passengers. When the case reached the Supreme Court, the Department of Justice took Mitchell's side, as did the Court, in a unanimous opinion by Chief Justice Hughes. Hughes called the prohibition of discrimination in the Interstate Commerce Act "sweeping," and, as in the 1914 case, the Court saw no reason to refuse to apply the equality branch of separate but equal to Mitchell's claim.[10]

Mitchell gave the NAACP an additional legal basis for challenging segregation in interstate transportation, but it was in some ways a narrow precedent. It rested on the Interstate Commerce Act and therefore applied only to interstate carriers. More important from the point of view of the NAACP's litigators, it involved a clear-cut denial of equal facilities: whites could ride on Pullman cars and African-Americans could not. If the coach cars for African-Americans were in worse shape than the coach cars for whites, the *Mitchell* principle would in theory be violated, but to establish the violation the lawyers would have to convince the ICC to accept their version of the facts. Throughout the 1940s, Marshall believed that the ICC was "packed" with members who were hostile to African-Americans; as a result, using *Mitchell* was not terribly promising. At the same time, though, the increased traffic on Southern rail lines of Northern African-Americans in the armed forces meant that the NAACP received increasing numbers of complaints about segregation in interstate transportation. Marshall "expressed the view that he would like to see a hundred or more cases filed a month," and wrote in 1945 that the NAACP was "maintaining a steady stream of cases seeking to break down" segregated transportation.[11]

Devising an appropriate legal strategy was difficult, however. In part the difficulties resulted from Marshall's unwillingness to pursue the idea of seeking equality in separate facilities; to do so, he believed, would amount to stating that the NAACP accepted the idea of segregation if it really did involve equality, and Marshall would not make such a statement. Cases like *Mitchell* were different from cases involving coach cars precisely because everyone knew that if they were faced with the decision the railroads would not maintain an expensive system of separate Pullman cars for African-Americans, but would allow African-Americans and whites to ride on the same cars, albeit in separate parts of the cars.[12]

Spottswood Robinson graduated from Howard Law School in 1939 and began to teach there immediately. He became ill shortly before he was due to take the bar examination for the first time, and then found himself psychologically blocked about taking it over the next several years. Oliver Hill and Robinson's father, a member of the Virginia bar who spent most of his time as a real estate agent, devised a plan that would force Robinson to take the bar examination. They created a partnership between Hill and the younger Robinson, requiring Robinson to commute between Richmond and Washington until, under the pressure of increasing work and Hill's departure for military service, Robinson had to become a member of the bar. Robinson had a regular commuting schedule, which allowed him to travel on first-class cars between Richmond and Washington. The first-class cars were not segregated, but Robinson observed that the Jim Crow cars were in terrible condition because of the wartime overcrowding. Robinson was intensely involved with the intellectual dimensions of the law, and he was compulsive about the use of his time. Finding some extra time on his hands while he rode the train, he began to examine the possible legal challenges to the segregated conditions he observed. He developed a memorandum laying out the proposition that segregation on interstate facilities violated the constitutional rule that states cannot enact laws that interfere with the flow of interstate commerce.[13]

Once that argument was in hand, the NAACP had to find an appropriate plaintiff. The NAACP and Robinson's own practice were flooded with complaints about discrimination in interstate transportation, but most were not suitable cases for a legal attack on the Jim Crow statutes. Most of the complaints came from people who were charged with disorderly conduct after refusing to move when ordered to comply with the Jim Crow statutes. To show that the statutes interfered with interstate commerce, the NAACP needed a litigant who had been charged with violating the segregation laws. Robinson was surprised but pleased when Irene Morgan simply walked into his office saying that she wanted to hire him to defend her against a charge of violating the Jim Crow statutes. She had been taking a bus from Virginia to Baltimore and refused to move to the back so that her seat could be taken by white passengers. She was arrested for violating Virginia's segregation statute. Robinson knew that this case was the one he needed. [14]

Robinson brought Morgan's appeal. Ironically, when the case was argued he had not been a member of the bar long enough to qualify for admission to the Supreme Court bar and, though he was the NAACP's "specialist in transportation," he could not argue the case. Instead, he sat at counsel table and passed notes to Marshall and Hastie, who presented Morgan's case despite their unfamiliarity with the underlying commerce clause theory. [15]

Their difficulties were compounded by the fact that the justices were in the midst of a protracted struggle over what the constitutional doctrine in such cases should be. The commerce clause of the Constitution says simply that Congress has the power to regulate interstate commerce, but early decisions of the Supreme Court held that the commerce clause barred states from enforcing laws that interfered unjustifiably with interstate commerce. The Court had articulated several different bases for the rule that a constitutional provision referring solely to Congress's power actually limited state power as well, but by the 1940s most of the justices had come to believe that none of the Court's theories seemed to work very well.

Justice Harlan Fiske Stone had developed a theory that explained why state laws that treated out-of-state commerce differently from in-state commerce should be invalidated: because the out-of-state commerce, which bore the burden of the regulation, was not represented in the state legislature. That theory, however, did not account for decisions invalidating state statutes, like the Jim Crow laws, that applied even-handedly to out-of-state and in-state commerce. Further, when states adopted rules that affected both local and interstate commerce, they usually did so to promote important local interests like health or safety. One aspect of the Court's New Deal transformation was to refrain almost entirely from assessing the strength of such interests. The Court said, in essence, that courts did not have the ability to assess the importance of competing public policies embodied in social and economic legislation. This left quite obscure the constitutional status of state laws that regulated in-state and out-of-state commerce equally but which were said to interfere with interstate commerce by putting undue burdens on it.

By the mid-1940s the Court had taken the position that it had to balance the burden on interstate commerce against the importance of the state interest being pursued. Justice Black, however, vigorously protested that balancing tests left too much discretion to judges, and he would have preferred a doctrine that invalidated all discriminatory statutes—those that treated in-state and out-of-state commerce differently—and upheld all nondiscriminatory statutes.

Unfortunately for the NAACP, when Virginia's Jim Crow statute was considered within the doctrinal setting of the interstate commerce cases, it was one of the "even-handed" regulations of commerce that were giving the Court the most trouble. Of course, the statute did not treat African-Americans and whites evenhandedly, but that kind of discrimination was unimportant under commerce clause doctrine; what mattered was whether the statute treated in-state and out-of-state commerce the same, and the Virginia statute did.

When *Morgan* reached the Supreme Court, Justice Black told his colleagues in the Court's private discussion of the case that he "still thinks this Court should not decide questions of burden." Although Chief Justice Stone thought that the "interference with commerce [was] not very great," Justice Reed disagreed. To him, the "constant rearrangement of seating [was] disruptive"; he noted that "people's feelings were aroused" by the Jim Crow laws. Frankfurter responded to Black's concern about balancing burdens by pointing out that "nice lines have to be drawn," and he said that Hastie's brief "proves to the hilt that this would result in a crazy quilt."[16]

Justice Reed wrote the Court's opinion ruling in favor of Morgan.[17] He relied on the "recognized abstract principle" that state laws are invalid if they "unduly burden[] . . . commerce in matters where uniformity is necessary . . . in the constitutional sense of useful in accomplishing a permitted purpose." His opinion noted that Virginia's statute imposed a burden on interstate passengers who might be called upon to change their seats, as Morgan had, and that eighteen states prohibited and ten states required segregation on buses. Reed relied primarily on an 1878 case invalidating a Louisiana segregation statute that prohibited segregation on interstate carriers because, the 1878 Court said, the ban interfered with commerce. If a state could not *prohibit* segregation without interfering with commerce, Reed said, neither could it *require* segregation. He concluded that national uniformity in regulating seating on interstate carriers was necessary "to promote and protect national travel." As Justice Frankfurter put it in a concurring opinion, "the imposition upon national systems of transportation of a crazy-quilt of State laws would operate to burden commerce unreasonably, whether such contradictory and confusing State laws concern racial commingling or racial segregation."

By the time the decision was announced, Stone had died, and only Justice Harold Burton, normally a rather strong supporter of civil rights, dissented. He said that the commerce clause did not invalidate Virginia's statute but stressed that the Court did not address whether the Fourteenth Amendment made the statute invalid. He noted that the Court's analysis apparently invalidated state *anti*-discrimination laws in this area as well, which would "leave the regulation of the subject to the respective carriers," and might lead to an "increased lack of uniformity" concerning the treatment of interstate as compared with local passengers on the same bus. For Burton, the Court needed a detailed factual record indicating what exactly the burdens and benefits of the challenged statute were before it invalidated a statute on commerce clause grounds.[18]

The NAACP was not in a good position to provide that kind of factual record, which would deal primarily with commerce and only incidentally with segregation. The Morgan decision left the NAACP in an awkward position. Many NAACP members erroneously believed that *Morgan* invalidated all segregation on interstate carriers, in part because the precise meaning of Justice Reed's opinion was obscure. The legal staff had to urge Walter White to make it clear how limited the victory was, which did not endear the legal staff to White. In addition, as Justice Burton said, *Morgan* cast doubt on Northern antidiscrimination statutes, which the NAACP surely could not have welcomed. And, by apparently leaving decisions about passenger seating to the carriers themselves, *Morgan* drew the NAACP in the direction of attempting to devise a constitutional challenge to decisions by private operators of buses rather than decisions by state legislatures. Marshall and Hastie agreed that the NAACP was "not yet in a position to contest the [private] rules and regulations."[19]

In dealing with private discrimination, Marshall and the NAACP's lawyers were faced with problems arising from the Supreme Court's understanding of the Fourteenth Amendment, which provides that no *State* shall deny the equal protection of the law. In 1875 Congress passed a civil rights act prohibiting discrimination in privately owned inns, theaters, and other places of public accommodation. In 1883 the Supreme Court held that, in attempting to regulate private discrimination, Congress had gone beyond the power the Fourteenth Amendment gave it. To the Court, the amendment prohibited only discriminatory state action, such as the enactment of laws that denied equal protection. When the owners of private property simply exercised ordinary property rights, the Court said, they were not engaged in state action and were therefore not covered by the Fourteenth Amendment. The state-action doctrine posed a severe problem for the NAACP in a wide range of cases. In the area of transportation, it seemed to mean that when railroad owners decided to use Jim Crow seating arrangements because their customers wanted it, not because state law required it, the Constitution had nothing to say.

Marshall convened a meeting of lawyers to "find some basis for attacking the carrier which continues to enforce segregation on its own." The lawyers went back and forth. Some suggested that lawsuits might challenge what they thought could be called the delegation of authority to discriminate from the federal government to the carriers, or from the carriers to their drivers. They agreed that a challenge using the notion of "unreasonable discrimination" under the Interstate Commerce Act was promising, because they believed that they could show how discrimination increased the costs to railroads. But the discussion of the constitutional issues was inconclusive and diffuse. Robert Carter thought that they might argue that when carriers called the police, they drew the government into supporting their own discrimination, but another lawyer called that position an invitation to "anarchy" because it would convert every private action into action by the government. Although the meeting yielded some tentative approaches, it "did not give birth to any sure-fire legal techniques." According to Carter, "Frankly, we really don't know just how to proceed in this type of situation." Marshall and Hastie concluded that the NAACP's "immediate efforts" should be devoted to securing legislation and to placing "extra legal . . . pressures to get the carriers to abolish their private rules and regulations requiring segregation of the races."[20]

With *Morgan*, the challenge to segregated transportation seemed to peter out in doctrinal confusion. Marshall was "unwilling to make any further tests of the transportation problem" until the NAACP had worked out a direct challenge to *Plessy*. A few years later, the school segregation cases were joined with a transportation case in which the NAACP did challenge *Plessy*, but for the moment the transportation problem had led the NAACP into a direct confrontation with the state-action doctrine.[21]

Employment discrimination posed another problem of state action. The growth of labor unions during the New Deal and the fact that unions began to receive some degree of government encouragement gave the NAACP the opportunity and the need to challenge union discrimination. The NAACP and the labor movement often cooperated, and by the end of the 1940s the NAACP had created a labor department "to work toward the fullest coordination of our membership with organized labor in order to raise the standards of the workers in this country." Yet some important unions discriminated against African-Americans, and the lawyers associated with the NAACP attempted to develop legal strategies to attack those practices. According to Marshall, the NAACP challenged the practices of only two unions. The Boilermakers union, he wrote, has "never made any effort to do anything for Negroes, but has repeatedly insisted on relegating Negroes to the status of auxiliary members when it has been impossible to fill all of the jobs with white members. The auxiliary members were denied every right of a union member other than the right to pay dues to a small autocratic group in control of the union." Houston also sued the railroad brotherhoods, which negotiated contracts that effectively deprived African-Americans of seniority, so that "practically every Negro fireman was either displaced or given shorter runs solely because of his race or color."[22]

At least at first glance, unions were private associations of individual workers. In the 1940s there were no federal fair-employment laws. The NAACP lawyers relied on the judge-made common law of labor relations, the New Deal's statutes dealing with unions, and the Constitution.

Over the course of the labor movement, state courts had developed an approach to unions that the NAACP lawyers could use against discrimination. By the 1940s courts universally agreed that labor unions were proper forms of worker organization because, as the common law decisions put it, they pursued lawful purposes. Implicit in that analysis was the proposition that unions could be barred from pursuing unlawful purposes. In addition, the contracts unions negotiated with employers were, in legal terms, ordinary contracts which would not be enforced by the courts if they violated important public policies.

The NAACP used these common law arguments against the Boilermakers' Union in Rhode Island and California. Marshall conducted the trial in Rhode Island. There the local union had voted to allow African-American workers to join, only to be blocked by the officers of the international union, who sought an injunction against integrating the local. Marshall responded by obtaining an injunction against discrimination.[23]

The California Supreme Court accepted the NAACP's position in an important opinion in early 1945. The Boilermakers had negotiated a closed-shop contract that required Marinship Corporation, a shipbuilder, to employ only members of the union or its segregated auxiliary. Chief Justice Phil Gibson began his opinion for the court by noting that recent decisions by the United States Supreme Court dealing with the First Amendment rights of unions to engage in peaceful picketing did not "deny a state the power to protect against abuses of the rights." As Gibson analyzed the cases, "abuses" arose when unions sought goals that were "not permissible under state law and public policy." The question in the Marinship case, therefore, was "whether a closed union coupled with a closed shop is a legitimate objective of organized labor."

Gibson said no. "[A]n arbitrarily closed or partially closed union is incompatible with a closed shop. Where a union has . . . attained a monopoly of the supply of labor by means of closed shop agreements . . . . , such a union occupies a quasi public position similar to that of a public service business and it has certain corresponding obligations." The union's monopoly power meant that it could no longer freely exercise the right of other private associations to define its membership, because that power "affects the fundamental right to work for a living." Gibson then rejected the union's position that it had merely segregated African-Americans into an auxiliary, rather than denying them membership. More than segregation was involved, he said, because the white union completely controlled the activities of the auxiliary even though it did not allow the members of the auxiliary to participate in the governance of the white union. The racial discrimination practiced by the union was contrary to state and national public policy, state statutes prohibiting racial discrimination in restaurants, and President Roosevelt's declaration in 1943 that it was the policy of the United States to oppose racial discrimination in employment in war industries. More than a year after the California decision, the Boilermakers abolished their auxiliary locals, but Marshall remained suspicious of the union and encouraged the local lawyer for the African-American workers to file damage actions against the union for its past discrimination.[24]

Chief Justice Gibson's reference to the quasi-public status of unions indicates the other lines of argument Houston and the NAACP lawyers developed. The Fourteenth Amendment meant that public agencies could not engage in racial discrimination. The NAACP's problem was to apply that prohibition to labor unions. If the courts were persuaded that unions were quasi-public, they might agree that the Fourteenth Amendment applied to unions themselves even though the unions were in some sense private associations. In addition, the support the government gave to unions—by making it lawful for them to negotiate collectively, for example—might implicate the government in the contracts that resulted from such negotiations, so that the contracts should be treated as *government* actions.

Houston developed these arguments in detail. When he returned to Washington to resume his private practice, the African-American railroad workers organizations became his clients. African-American trainmen had been objecting to contracts white unions negotiated with the railroads, under which whites were given favorable work assignments and promotion before African-Americans with greater seniority. In *Steele v. Louisville & Nashville Railroad,* for example, the

union negotiated a contract dealing with the assignment of firemen, white and
African-American, on the Louisville and Nashville Railroad. Under the terms of
the contract, African-Americans, ineligible for union membership, were limited to
50 percent of the fireman positions in each district. When the railroad's passenger
runs were reduced, all the jobs were declared vacant, and all five African-
American firemen who had previously served on these runs were replaced by
whites who had less seniority.[25]

Houston and Marshall agreed that Houston should handle these cases because
the African-American trainmen could afford to pay their attorney. Although the
cases were nominally not NAACP cases, Houston saw them as a way to establish a
good working relationship between the NAACP and an organization of African-
American workers. As he explained, the African-American trainmen could serve
as "watch dogs" over the practices of the railroads. "This is a specialized field. The
Railway workers need the N.A.A.C.P.'s general support and prestige; the
N.A.A.C.P. needs the support of the railway workers."[26]

Houston developed a statutory and a constitutional challenge to the discriminatory contracts negotiated by the white unions and the railroads. The constitutional
argument was that Congress, in its labor law, had given the union the power to act
as exclusive bargaining agent. This power was essentially legislative; as Chief
Justice Stone summarized the constitutional argument, the union was "clothed
with power not unlike that of a legislature which is subject to constitutional
limitations on its power to deny, restrict, destroy or discriminate against the rights
of those for whom it legislates." Houston's point was that unions were sufficiently
powerful—almost like legislatures with respect to their control over such an important aspect of life as employment—that they were subject to constitutional
limitations as well.[27]

Houston argued, in addition, that if Congress had given the exclusive bargaining agent "unbridled and absolute power" to disregard the interests of African-
American workers, Congress's action would itself be unconstitutional. The constitutional concern that unions were like legislatures was reshaped in Houston's
argument about the proper interpretation of the federal labor laws. Here he argued
that unions were like legislatures because they had to represent all their constituents, not just their members. The analogy is to a legislator who is a member of one
party but who has a duty to represent everyone in the district, including those who
voted for the other party. Houston drew on the language of the statutes, which
referred to the exclusive bargaining agents as the "representatives" of the workers.
Working out the analogy in detail might prove troublesome, because legislators
typically do take the interests of their supporters more seriously than those of their
opponents, but the rhetorical appeal of the idea of fair representation was surely
powerful, particularly when read against the background of the constitutional
concerns Houston had raised.

The Supreme Court accepted Houston's statutory argument in *Steele*. The
United States filed a brief in a companion case supporting Houston, which Chief
Justice Stone found "persuasive." Stone, who regarded the case as presenting a
"gross wrong," wrote the Court's opinion. According to him, "unless the labor
union representing a craft owes some duty to represent non-union members of the

craft, at least to the extent of not discriminating against them . . . in the contracts which it makes . . . , the minority would be left with no means of protecting their interests or, indeed, their right to earn a livelihood by pursuing the occupation in which they are employed." Again drawing on Houston's analogy, Stone found the measure of that duty to be "at least as exacting" as the one "the Constitution imposes upon a legislature to give equal protection to the interests of those for whom it legislates." The union had to "exercise fairly the power conferred upon it in behalf of all those for whom it acts, without hostile discrimination against them." Stone concluded the central part of his opinion by saying, "Congress plainly did not undertake to authorize the bargaining representative to make such discrimination."[28]

This sentence, though, bothered Justice Murphy, who thought that it might suggest that Congress *could* authorize such discrimination, and he criticized Stone for relying "solely upon . . . legal niceties, while remaining mute and placid as to the obvious and oppressive deprivation of constitutional guarantees." For Murphy, although the union was a private association, "its power to represent and bind all members of a class or craft is derived solely from Congress," which meant that the union could not be authorized by Congress to do what Congress itself could not do.[29]

Immediately after the decisions in the railway and boilermakers' cases, Marshall wrote to the presidents of twenty-five unions that he believed discriminated against African-Americans, pointing out that the decisions meant that excluding African-Americans from membership or maintaining segregated locals was incompatible with having a closed shop and the basic right of representation. He expressed his hope that the unions would eliminate their exclusionary practices quickly so that labor would play a constructive part in the emerging system of race relations.[30]

Morgan and the labor cases left one important issue open. If federal law required uniform treatment of passenger assignment regulations in interstate transportation, and if federal law similarly regulated labor unions, what was the status of state antidiscrimination laws?

Two years after *Morgan*, the Court held that Michigan could apply its local antidiscrimination law to the operator of an amusement park located on an island in the Canadian portion of the Detroit River. The operator refused to transport African-Americans to the park from Detroit, and was prosecuted when it denied passage to a young African-American woman who was going on a class trip to the amusement park. After toning down his statement of the facts to assuage Frankfurter's concern that "even pertinent rhetoric or . . . a needless recital of details which are irrelevant to the legal issue" would "stir our colored fellow citizens," Justice Wiley Rutledge wrote the Court's opinion acknowledging that foreign commerce was involved but stressing the unique geographical circumstances of the case, which involved a trip that was only nominally "international."[31]

The Court had even less difficulty upholding the application of New York's antidiscrimination law to bar unions from denying membership to African-Americans. The case involved railway employees who handled federal mail, and the only remotely serious challenge to the state law was that states could not regulate the activities of people associated with the delivery of the mail. The Court dismissed the challenge on the ground that, although Congress might have regulated the clerks' union, it had not done so and enforcing the state law would not interfere with any policies Congress did seek to advance.

The NAACP filed *amicus* briefs in both the Detroit and New York cases, and the brief in the latter case, which was coordinated with the state's defense of its statutes, suggests the line of argument that the NAACP wanted most to pursue. The NAACP brief described in some detail the social and economic effects of discrimination in union membership, a theme that had been advanced in the Boilermakers' litigation as well. The material was included in the brief to demonstrate that "during recent years labor unions have been granted increasing power yet this power is limited by the courts whenever it has been used against the interest of the people."[32]

The NAACP'S complaints about discrimination in transportation and employment received a sympathetic hearing by the Supreme Court in the 1940s. Yet the lawyers continued to struggle with the state-action doctrine. They managed to work around the central difficulties with that doctrine by persuading the Court that federal statutes made discrimination unlawful. When the lawyers turned to the problem of housing discrimination, they were forced to develop a more comprehensive theory of state action.

6

"A Carefully Planned Program"
Attacking Restrictive Covenants

The NAACP'S litigation during the 1940s centered on restructuring the law so that courts could rely on the social and economic consequences of discrimination as a basis for invalidating state laws. This approach reached its first peak in the attack on racially restrictive covenants, and then was pursued even more fully in the education litigation that ended with *Brown v. Board of Education*. At the deepest intellectual level, the NAACP's lawyers were convinced that social and economic consequences were relevant to the law; they accepted the arguments of the American Legal Realists, expressed in the transformation of the Howard Law School, that constitutional law was a form of policy making and that understanding the consequences of legal rules was essential to developing sound constitutional law. This conviction led them to inject sociological evidence into the school segregation cases. The immediate source of attention to those consequences, however, was a problem of litigation strategy that the Supreme Court's rulings on racial discrimination in housing forced on the NAACP.[1]

The state-action doctrine shaped the overall outlines of the attack on discrimination. States initially used government power to support racial discrimination. For example, Oklahoma adopted a "grandfather clause" restricting voting to those who passed a literacy test or who were descendants of people entitled to vote on January 1, 1866, and Louisville adopted an ordinance barring whites from occupying a house in a block where the majority of houses were occupied by African-Americans, and vice versa. In two of the earliest cases handled by the NAACP, the Supreme Court had little difficulty finding these government actions unconstitutional.[2]

Advocates of racial discrimination then turned to other techniques of exclusion. Essentially the same residential patterns that the Louisville ordinance imposed could be achieved by agreements among white home owners not to sell their houses to African-Americans. These agreements were embedded in provisions, called covenants, in the deeds and contracts made when a house was sold. Restrictive covenants were permanent restrictions on the ability of anyone who bought the property later to sell to African-Americans. Similarly, in the area of voting, whites could organize political parties that, as a matter of internal party regulation, excluded African-Americans from participation.

Yet private agreements were less effective than public statutes. What could keep a white home owner from disregarding the covenant and selling a house to an African-American who offered a better price than any white buyer? And what could keep a faction in the political party from attempting to preserve its power, once its leaders had taken party office, by altering the party rules to allow African-Americans to participate? Racism and other ideological pressures provided some constraints on self-interested defections from these private agreements, but it was much easier to use the power of government to enforce those agreements, for example, by having the courts enjoin the sale to an African-American of a house subject to a racially restrictive covenant.

Once private parties called on the courts to enforce their private agreements, the way was open to challenge the arrangements under the Fourteenth and Fifteenth Amendments. The NAACP's legal activities in the 1940s dealing with private discrimination tracked this doctrinal course in the areas of housing and voting. Yet, although the NAACP's lawyers repeatedly obtained rulings that the discrimination they challenged was illegal, substantial opportunities for continued private racial discrimination remained.

The state-action doctrine was not the only doctrinal problem the NAACP lawyers faced, and in some ways it obscured the other major doctrinal difficulty. State laws can discriminate against African-Americans in several different ways. First, and most obvious, the laws can say explicitly that African-Americans are subject to certain rules that do not apply to whites. For example, a state might define its qualifications for voting to require African-Americans, but not whites, to pass a literacy test. Soon after the adoption of the Reconstruction amendments the Supreme Court held unconstitutional state laws drawing explicit racial lines of this sort. Second, and closely related, state laws can use terms whose effect is to distinguish African-Americans and whites. That was the problem with the Oklahoma grandfather clause. It did not say that all African-Americans but no whites had to pass a literacy test, but it defined the class exempted from the literacy test in a way that had exactly that effect. The Court treated these racial gerrymanders just like statutes explicitly using racial terms.

Third, state laws can use neutral terms, that is, not refer to race at all or even have racial gerrymanders, but still be administered in ways that produce discrimination. *Yick Wo v. Hopkins,* an 1886 decision, involved a San Francisco ordinance requiring owners of hand laundries to obtain a permit to operate, supposedly to ensure the safety of the operation.[3] Even though the ordinance did not refer to race at all, and even though the aim of promoting safety was clearly important, the Supreme Court invalidated the ordinance because it turned out that the city authorities granted permits to almost every non-Chinese applicant and denied permits to every Chinese one. Under *Yick Wo,* discrimination in administering neutral laws was unconstitutional. So, for example, if a state had a literacy test but allowed voting registrars to administer it one way to whites and another to African-Americans, the administration of the literacy test, though not the test itself, might be unconstitutional.

A litigator could use *Yick Wo* in one of two ways. The actual pattern of results might demonstrate unconstitutional discrimination; showing that, however, required substantial factual presentations by lawyers who were pressed by other concerns as well. Alternatively, the literacy test might itself be attacked not because requiring literacy was somehow discriminatory but rather because the statute creating the literacy requirement was so vague that it lent itself to racial discrimination in administration.

The Louisville housing segregation ordinance illustrates a fourth type of discrimination. Like statutes in the first category of discriminatory laws, that ordinance used racial terms—barring people who would be a racial minority on a block from purchasing a home there—but imposed its disabilities on both African-Americans and whites. In doctrinal terms, *Plessy v. Ferguson* fell into the same category. As the Court there had said, the statute treated African-Americans and whites equally in the sense that neither was allowed to ride on cars reserved for the other race. In dealing with this category of discrimination, the Court drew upon concepts that were in wide use when the Reconstruction amendments were adopted, and held that this sort of statute was constitutional where it affected "social" rights, such as the right to associate with other people, but was unconstitutional where it affected "civil" rights, such as the right to own property. The Louisville ordinance, because it affected property rights, was unconstitutional; the statute in *Plessy*, because it affected only social rights, was not.

The final category of discrimination involves statutes that do not use racial terms but that, even when administered even-handedly, impose disadvantages on African-Americans more frequently than on whites. Poll taxes provide a good example. Poor whites as well as poor African-Americans may be unable to vote because they cannot afford to pay the poll tax, but because in practice there were proportionately more poor African-Americans than poor whites, an even-handed poll tax excluded more African-Americans from voting than whites.

A long memorandum to Justice Reed from one of his law clerks in connection with a voting discrimination case explained, better than any other document within the Court, how the state-action doctrine was related to the substantive law of equal protection.[4] The clerk began by arguing that there was a difference between a state's denying permission for African-Americans to use its land and its deciding to provide "sanctions to a landowner's discriminatory refusal" to do so. These "sanctions," the clerk wrote, could be "negative," if the landowner simply threw the African-Americans off his property and then asserted his right to discriminate as a defense to a suit by the African-Americans for assault. Or, more important, the owner "could call upon courts, sheriff and police to carry out his intended discrimination" by having them throw the African-Americans off the land and enjoining them from reentering.

On this analysis, the Constitution was "not intended to affect the legal rights of private individuals themselves," at least as long as those rights were provided to all without regard to race. The law of trespass that the landowner invoked was precisely one of these generally available and nondiscriminatory rights. But, the clerk continued, if the Constitution did not affect those legal rights, "state judicial enforcement of a private citizen's discrimination in the exercise of his legal rights is not . . . state action," because the two statements of right—a private right to discriminate, and state judicial enforcement of that right—were "equivalent." The conclusion was that if "private citizens [have] a legal right, those private citizens may exert that right in a discriminatory way, and the state may lend the sanctions of its force to their discrimination without committing state action of the kind proscribed" by the Constitution.

The relation between state action and equality was posed most dramatically in the NAACP's challenge to restrictive covenants. The NAACP's lawyers had confronted housing discrimination at the outset of the organization's existence. In 1917 Moorfield Story, a prominent Boston lawyer who did legal work for the NAACP before it had its own legal staff, successfully challenged the Louisville segregation ordinance. Justice William Day, appointed to the Court by Theodore Roosevelt, wrote the opinion for a unanimous Supreme Court in *Buchanan v. Warley*.[5] Calling the ordinance a "drastic measure," Day emphasized property owners' right to dispose of their property as they saw fit, subject only to regulations seeking to advance goals like health and safety. The Court's cases applying the Fourteenth Amendment led Day to conclude that they "entitle a colored man to acquire property without state legislation discriminating against him solely because of color." Finally, Day said, neither the principle of separate but equal nor the state interest in promoting racial harmony could be promoted "by depriving citizens of their constitutional rights and privileges."

Housing segregation ordinances remained on the books in many areas, but with their unconstitutionality established, the NAACP's attention turned to other methods of maintaining residential segregation. The Court's emphasis in *Buchanan* on the rights of property owners suggested the restrictive covenant as an alternative method of achieving residential segregation. If two neighbors agreed that neither's property could be used as a business, they could draft a covenant stating that restriction, and have it inserted into the appropriate land title records. Once recorded, the covenant would bar any later purchaser from using the property as a business. After the Court's decision in *Buchanan*, white owners began to use covenants that restricted the transfer of their property to African-American purchasers. Typically they created a racially restrictive covenant covering a number of houses in a neighborhood; interlocking covenants had the same effect as a municipal ordinance requiring residential segregation. To the extent that the Supreme Court had been concerned about the property rights of buyers and sellers, however, covenants were more acceptable than ordinances. Covenants were contracts among private parties who agreed to limit their own property rights, while ordinances were imposed on owners who might be willing to sell to African-American purchasers for the right price.

Precisely because covenants were private arrangements, the NAACP's ability to mount a legal challenge diminished. The state-action doctrine meant that constitutional limits applied only to actions by governments, such as Louisville, but not to actions by individuals, such as the property owners who inserted racially restrictive covenants into their deeds. Still, the Court's decision in *Buchanan* had suggested that the ordinance was unconstitutional because it restricted the constitutional rights of African-American purchasers as well as the property rights of white sellers. A constitutional attack on restrictive covenants was not out of the question. The first challenge failed, however.

Corrigan v. Buckley involved property in the District of Columbia covered by a racially restrictive covenant. Irene Corrigan, the owner of a house covered by a covenant, signed a contract to sell her house to an African-American purchaser. John Buckley, who owned another house in the neighborhood covered by the same interlocking covenant, sued Corrigan to bar her from allowing the sale to be completed. Corrigan filed a motion to have the lawsuit dismissed on the ground that the racially restrictive covenant was void because it was unconstitutional and because it violated public policy. The District of Columbia courts rejected Corrigan's motion, and enjoined her from selling the property. Corrigan then asked the Supreme Court to review the decision. The procedure she invoked was technically known as an appeal, and appeals to the Supreme Court, in this technical sense, were limited by statute to cases in which the "construction or application" of the Constitution was "drawn in question." In addition, the constitutional question had to be "substantial in character and properly raised below" for the Supreme Court to have jurisdiction over an appeal.[6]

In *Corrigan v. Buckley*, Justice Edward Sanford wrote for a unanimous Court that because Corrigan had not presented a substantial constitutional question, the Court lacked jurisdiction to hear her case. As the case was presented to the Court, he said, the only constitutional question presented by Corrigan in the lower courts was whether the covenant was contrary to the Constitution. Sanford said that this contention was "entirely lacking in substance" because the Constitution applied only to state action. "None of [the] Amendments prohibited private individuals from entering into contracts respecting the control and disposition of their own property." Sanford noted that Corrigan had argued in the Supreme Court that the judgments of the lower courts enforcing the covenants themselves violated the Constitution. That issue, he said, had not been raised earlier in the proceedings. In addition, he wrote, "it is . . . lacking in substance." Corrigan, Sanford wrote, had been given a full hearing, so she was not denied procedural fairness, and the injunction was not arbitrary, so her property was not "taken" by the judgment of the lower courts.

Corrigan obviously placed obstacles in the way of later challenges to restrictive covenants. Its holding that the covenants themselves were not unconstitutional posed no difficulties, because the mere existence of the covenants could not affect sales to African-Americans. What mattered was whether a court could enjoin the sale of property subject to a racially restrictive covenant. If *Corrigan* were read to hold only that the issue of state action in the enforcement of covenants was not before the Supreme Court because it had not been raised in the lower courts, the issue of court judgments as state action was left open. However, if Justice Sanford's statements about the insubstantiality of that issue (had it been raised) were taken seriously, the legal problems were obvious. Somehow *Corrigan* had to be distinguished.

The Margold Report contained a long discussion of restrictive covenants and *Corrigan* in particular. Margold suggested that the most troublesome statements in *Corrigan* could be treated as mere dicta. He also suggested a different line of attack. Instead of arguing about equal protection, he said, the lawyers should argue that African-Americans had a property right to make purchases, which racial covenants denied.[7]

The most promising line of attack on restrictive covenants was the argument that racially discriminatory contracts could not be enforced by the courts, because the courts' actions would themselves amount to state action. This attack lent itself to an easily understood phrase—"Is judicial action state action?"—to which the answer seemed obvious. Of course judicial action is state action, but the real problem is whether judicial action is unconstitutional when it takes the form of enforcing ordinary private contracts whose terms would be unconstitutional were they part of a statute or ordinance. Nearly everyone involved in the litigation campaign, lawyers and judges alike, persistently blurred the differences between the state-action and equal-protection questions.

If judicial enforcement of such contracts is unconstitutional state action, the concept of state action as a limitation on the scope of the Constitution would disappear entirely. For, just as *Corrigan* showed that the mere existence of racially restrictive covenants is meaningless unless the courts stand ready to enforce them, so too with every other private arrangement, as Reed's law clerk pointed out. If judicial action is state action, every private arrangement becomes subject to constitutional limitations at the point where some court is called upon to enforce the arrangement. That conclusion seems so at odds with the point of the state-action doctrine that some technique of limiting the scope of the legal challenge to racially restrictive covenants was probably essential.[8]

Defining equal-protection law in a limiting way would have been one technique. The NAACP, though, fastened on an essentially factual technique. NAACP lawyers argued that, if courts examined the actual impact of racially restrictive covenants, they would discover that interlocking covenants had the same effects as segregation ordinances like the one invalidated in *Buchanan*. By looking at overall effects, the NAACP lawyers proposed to limit the scope of their state-action concept to situations in which the effects of private action were as socially significant as the effects of government action.

The lawyers developed this argument in two arenas during the 1940s. The first involved placing pressure on the Federal Housing Administration and other national housing authorities to eliminate subsidies for segregated housing systems. The second involved a complex litigation campaign culminating in the Supreme Court's decision in *Shelley v. Kraemer* in 1948 that judicial enforcement of racially restrictive covenants was unconstitutional state action.

The FHA provided support for housing development in the states. It sent a manual to its field agents describing the kinds of projects they should approve, which listed suggested covenants designed to ensure that the projects would be socially valuable. Among the suggested covenants was a racial restriction, and Marshall conducted what Walter White called a "one-man campaign against the F.H.A." to get the suggestion removed. After he won that battle, Marshall attempted to get the FHA to refuse projects with restrictive covenants. That effort, though, was a complete failure, and through the 1940s the FHA continued to accept housing projects with restrictive covenants.[9]

The challenges to the enforcement of restrictive covenants were more successful. In 1940, the Supreme Court had a chance to address the issue in *Hansberry v. Lee*.[10] The covenant there was to go into effect when 95 percent of the affected owners signed it. After Hansberry, an African-American, bought a house in the area and moved in, his neighbors sued to force his family to move out. Hansberry's lawyers discovered that the covenant had been signed by only about 55 percent of the owners, and asked that the suit be dismissed. In a prior lawsuit, though, the validity of the covenant had been challenged on the ground that neighborhood conditions had changed so much that the agreement could no longer be enforced. In that lawsuit the parties stipulated that 95 percent of the owners *had* signed, and the court upheld the covenant. In *Hansberry,* the Illinois Supreme Court held that, although the finding that 95 percent had signed was false, Hansberry could not challenge the prior judgment.

Hansberry's lawyers had cooperated with the NAACP in other cases, but the organization simply monitored this one. When the case reached the Supreme Court, Hansberry's lawyers raised the general point about the unconstitutionality of enforcing restrictive covenants, and the more specific one that it was grossly unfair to bind Hansberry by the prior judgment. As Marshall had feared after listening to the oral argument, the Supreme Court ruled in Hansberry's favor "on the narrow ground . . . and [did] not touch the important question of the validity of the restrictive covenants." Justice Stone's opinion invoked the general rule that people cannot be bound by judgments issued in cases they did not participate in, and held that the fact that Illinois called the prior proceeding a class action did not change the application of the rule. Hansberry could be bound, Stone said, only if he had been adequately represented by parties who were in the first lawsuit. Because Hansberry and others had interests against enforcing the covenant that conflicted with the interests of the parties in the first lawsuit, he could not have been adequately represented.[11]

After *Hansberry,* the NAACP mounted its attack on restrictive covenants in two stages. Because *Corrigan* presented serious analytic problems, Marshall insisted on having a fully developed legal theory in place before a full-scale challenge to restrictive covenants could begin. As a student at Howard Law School in 1938–39, Spottswood Robinson had participated in a research seminar on civil rights taught by James Nabrit. He chose the legality of restrictive covenants as his research topic and investigated the problem for the year-long course. In 1944, as the restrictive-covenant challenge began to develop, Marshall commissioned Robinson to write a comprehensive report on the issue. Robinson found it difficult to complete the report, telling Marshall that he could not tell how long his "complete reexamination" of the cases would take, for "I merely keep at it until I am satisfied that a good job has been done." Shortly before the study was due in October,

Robinson wrote Marshall that the study was not "progressing as rapidly as I had hoped," because "the feature which consumes time is the necessity of thinking out some aspects of the problem which before have received no treatment whatsoever." Although Marshall expressed some impatience at Robinson's compulsiveness, he did find the fact that the study was pending a useful foil to defer those who urged quick action. As he wrote to a branch officer, "We are holding up many cases on restrictive covenants because it is better to meet this problem by a carefully planned program than by scattered cases."[12]

Restrictive-covenant cases were percolating throughout the country. Some difficulties arose in developing records with which the NAACP was comfortable, given the legal theories its lawyers were developing, and in selecting appropriate cases for review. In addition, African-American purchasers of houses covered by restrictive covenants tended to be reasonably well-off within the community, and therefore had access to lawyers independent of the NAACP.

Lawyers loosely associated with the NAACP began challenges to restrictive covenants throughout the country, but the very looseness of the association made coordinating the challenges difficult. Marshall was afraid that the cases would come to the Supreme Court too quickly, before the lawyers had clarified the underlying legal theory. Marshall was convinced that the lawyers had to develop a powerful case demonstrating that the social harms of restrictive covenants were the same as the social harms of housing segregation ordinances. To ride herd on the lawyers dealing with these cases, Marshall convened a lawyers' conference in Chicago, in July 1945, to discuss the lawsuits. Thirty-three lawyers attended. Houston argued that the litigation should be used as a forum for public education, and so should "broaden the issues just as much as possible on every single base," including something that particularly bothered him, the necessity—and fundamental silliness—of making racial determinations as the predicate of legal action. The lawyers discussed where they should concentrate their efforts, with Irving Mollison, the Hansberrys' lawyer, arguing against focusing on the District of Columbia because too much property was covered by restrictive covenants there, including houses owned or rented by some of the Justices of the Supreme Court. Mollison thought that the extent of the covenants in Washington would make the decision's significance too apparent to the justices.* Marshall and Hastie understood that a Supreme Court decision on the issue would have nationwide impact no matter where the case came from, and so the origin could not really matter to the justices.[13]

The Chicago conference also brought sociological studies of the consequences of housing segregation to the attention of the lawyers. Robert Weaver, an African-American housing expert, showed that restrictive covenants led to overcrowding in the African-American community and urged the lawyers to give the courts statistics showing the relation between overcrowding and crime. Similarly, Marian Wynn Perry's husband, Dr. Alfred Yankauer, health officer at the East Harlem hospital, developed evidence showing that infant mortality was higher in over-

---

* Mollison may have been motivated as well by an understandable desire to achieve prominence by litigating the principal challenge to restrictive covenants, and so may have been trying to exclude competition.

crowded African-American neighborhoods; this evidence too could be presented in the litigation. The NAACP legal department hired Annette Peyser, a social scientist, to compile and distribute factual material about the conditions of African-American housing, for use in the restrictive covenant litigation. [14]

The possibility of coordinating the lawsuits to develop the strongest possible records disappeared over the next few years, as the local lawyers pursued their own cases. In California, Loren Miller became the expert in the field, and attempted to develop the records on which the lawyers' conference had focused. In the District of Columbia, a case with the right kind of record was litigated, but, when the Supreme Court refused to review the local court's decision upholding restrictive covenants, Marshall and the other lawyers associated in the campaign had to reassess their position. Marshall convened a second conference in January 1947 to attempt to select the best case to bring to the Supreme Court, because he did not want to "build up a record of many applications for certiorari denied." [15]

At that point there were cases pending in California, where Miller had followed the Chicago conference suggestions most closely, and in Michigan, the District of Columbia, and Missouri. The Michigan case that was farthest along, *Sipes v. McGee,* had a weak record on the sociological evidence, presented to the state courts mainly in an NAACP *amicus* brief. Marshall believed that better cases from Michigan could be pursued. [16]

Houston had litigated the case in the District of Columbia. The moving figure behind the African-American litigants, though, was Raphael Urciolo, whose business consisted largely of "block-busting" by attempting simultaneously to move African-Americans into and whites out of neighborhoods covered by overlapping restrictive covenants. Houston's litigation strategy, as he had hinted in Chicago, involved a series of challenges to covenants. He raised questions about the racial identifications of the plaintiffs and the defendants, presented expert testimony on racial characteristics, and moved to disqualify the trial judge because he lived in a rental unit subject to a restrictive covenant. In addition, Houston challenged the covenant on nonconstitutional grounds: he argued that it had become outdated by changing circumstances in the neighborhood, and that it violated public policy. These aspects of Houston's litigation strategy made his case less attractive as the central vehicle for the constitutional challenge to restrictive covenants. [17]

Miller's California case was probably the most attractive to the NAACP, both because of its record and because Miller had already worked closely with the national office in developing the case. Unfortunately, until the California Supreme Court issued its ruling Miller could not take his case to the United States Supreme Court. None of the NAACP's cases seemed to have everything in them that Marshall wanted, and he preferred to delay presenting the issue to the Supreme Court until a case was developed, perhaps from Chicago, in which the full evidence about housing conditions would be in the trial record. [18]

Marshall's strategy was thwarted by the pending case from Missouri. J. D. Shelley and his wife Ethel Lee had been living with their six children in rented housing in St. Louis during the war. Mr. Shelley was a construction worker, and Mrs. Shelley had been working in a munitions plant. They managed to save money during the war, and by 1945 wanted to buy a house. Mrs. Shelley spoke to Robert

Bishop, her church pastor, who also sold real estate, and he knew of a house for sale. The house was covered by a restrictive covenant signed in 1911 and lasting fifty years. A few days after the Shelleys bought the house they were sued by Louis and Fern Kraemer, who lived ten blocks away on the same street and whose property was covered by the same covenant. Mrs. Shelley went to Bishop, who sent her to his own lawyer, George Vaughn, an African-American lawyer active both in the local NAACP and in the St. Louis Democratic party.[19]

Vaughn had participated in the Chicago restrictive covenant conference, which had been held two months before the Shelleys came to him, and he saw their case as a good vehicle for the constitutional challenge. Vaughn squarely presented the constitutional question, but he referred to the material about housing conditions only in passing, to show that restrictive covenants limited the supply of housing for African-Americans and made African-American neighborhoods "a menace to health, morals, and general decency of cities." The trial judge ruled in favor of the Shelleys, saying that the covenant was intended to be effective only if all the owners in the area signed it, and nine had not. A year later, though, in December 1946, the Missouri Supreme Court reversed the trial judge, holding that the covenant was intended to be effective against anyone who signed it or bought from one of the signers.[20]

The second lawyers' conference took place the next month, but Vaughn did not attend. Instead, he asked the Supreme Court to review the Shelleys' case. Marshall believed that the Michigan and District of Columbia cases, though not perfect, were better than Vaughn's, and immediately arranged to have them brought to the Supreme Court as well. The Court agreed to hear all these cases, and Marshall began to plan a coordinated presentation. His strategy had two facets. First, he had to deal with the lawyers in the cases, which proved to be difficult. He did not have a great deal of confidence in Vaughn, and was somewhat annoyed at Vaughn's failure to cooperate with the NAACP. In addition, there was some pressure from the nonlawyers associated with the NAACP, transmitted through Walter White, to "have some 'big shot' in the cases," but, Marshall said, "I am not for having a person simply because he is reputed to be a 'big shot.'" He told Miller, "There is a tremendous amount of 'fast footwork around second base' going on and these cases are too important to tolerate any shenanigans."[21]

To get some control over the cases, Marshall convened a third conference in New York on September 6, 1947. He wanted the conference to address the way the NAACP's legal arguments could be presented to the Court. Vaughn, who attended this conference, was somewhat obstructionist in his objections to the lines of argument Marshall wanted developed. The lawyers worried mainly about the scope of the state-action doctrine they were urging on the Court. The difficulty, as they saw it, was that the Court was likely to be reluctant to accept a broad rule that judicial enforcement of private arrangements was always state action subject to the Constitution. Shad Polier of the American Jewish Committee brought up the same problem Justice Reed's clerk had posed: would it be state action to enforce a state's general laws against trespassing on private property when the underlying trespass occurred because African-Americans went on the property of a white person who did not want them there? Phineas Indritz, a federal employee moonlighting at the

American Veterans Committee, tried to limit the scope of the argument by confining it to situations in which the courts enforced a covenant against a buyer who wanted to sell to an African-American, but Bob Ming of Chicago pointed out that, as a matter of doctrine, that would not work: if judicial action was state action, it was state action even if an African-American tried to compel a white to sell and the court upheld the white's refusal on the ground that the property was covered by a covenant. Vaughn was impatient with all the technical arguments about the implications of the state-action doctrine, but when he said that he was concerned only about this case, Houston chastised him, saying, "You will be questioned further than that. We must answer these questions in our own minds here."[22]

No entirely satisfactory resolution of the doctrinal question came out of the New York conference. Once again, though, the lawyers appeared to believe that the sociological material was important in defining the scope of what they were asking the Court to do. Louis Wirth of the University of Chicago and Robert Weaver prepared a long memorandum on the social impact of restrictive covenants, which was then widely circulated among the lawyers associated with the cases.[23]

The second aspect of Marshall's strategy involved attempting to coordinate presentations to the Supreme Court by other interested groups. The American Jewish Committee wanted to participate "in a big way" by contributing money to support the litigation and by preparing a substantial brief dealing with the sociological material. A large number of other groups also participated as *amici* in the Supreme Court, but in the end, Marshall and Hastie were not able to secure much coordination. They wanted to avoid repeating arguments so that "each brief can present a new angle of the case," particularly by "providing the arguments that will salvage the judges' consciences or square with their prepossessions should they lean toward holding for us." The briefs, though, ended up being rather repetitious.[24]

The most important new participant in the litigation was certainly the Department of Justice. President Harry Truman appointed a Committee on Civil Rights in December 1946, and its report, *To Secure These Rights,* issued in October 1947, urged that the government intervene in the pending litigation. Indritz and Philip Elman of the solicitor general's office persuaded Oscar Chapman, undersecretary in the Interior Department, to tell the Justice Department that Interior opposed restrictive covenants because they adversely affected the Native Americans who came under Interior's jurisdiction. In addition, the NAACP and other groups pressed the Justice Department to intervene. Elman examined these requests and concluded that "there would be substantial justification for Government participation" despite the office's usual policy of staying out of private cases even if they involved important constitutional questions. Citing the interests of the Interior Department and other government agencies, Elman said that the government could intervene to protect the government's interests in the "social and economic problems which would be affected by the Court's decision," and not "merely because of our interest as lawyers in the questions of law presented." The Civil Rights Section of the Justice Department asked ten federal agencies to describe the way in which restrictive covenants affected their operations. With this material in hand, Solicitor General Philip Perlman spoke with Attorney General Tom Clark.

Clark then told Truman of Clark's personal belief that restrictive covenants were unconstitutional, and of the social problems associated with the use of such covenants. On the day after *To Secure These Rights* was released, Perlman announced that the government would file an *amicus* brief. The government's brief, in addition to referring to the purely legal arguments, stressed in its opening pages the social harms caused by restrictive covenants.[25]

In January 1948, ten lawyers presented oral argument to the Supreme Court in four consolidated cases, including two from the District of Columbia along with the St. Louis and Michigan cases. Perlman opened the argument with a one-hour presentation, "virtually unbroken by questions from the bench," in which he said that restrictive covenants "should be relegated to the limbo of other things as dead as slavery." He quoted *To Secure These Rights* on the impact of restrictive covenants "in the present serious housing shortage," and stated that the enforcement of restrictive covenants hindered the government in the fields of public health and housing and in the conduct of foreign affairs. He was referring to the position stated in *To Secure These Rights* that discrimination was a "serious obstacle" to making the United States a "positive influence for peace and progress" in a world where "those with competing philosophies have stressed—and shamelessly distorted—our shortcomings" as "a consistent oppressor of underprivileged people." According to Elman, Perlman found the experience of arguing "in a courtroom full of blacks" transforming.[26]

Vaughn opened the litigants' argument against covenants. He said that "the evil tendency, not actual injury, is the true test of public policy." In "the most moving plea in the Court" Elman ever heard, Vaughn closed by saying that "as the Negro knocks at America's door, he cries: 'Let me come in and sit by the fire. I helped build the house.'" "All of a sudden," Elman later recalled, "there was drama in the courtroom, a sense of what the case was really all about rather than the technical legal arguments."[27]

The basic constitutional argument was made first by Vaughn's associate from St. Louis, Herman Willer, who characterized restrictive covenants as the delegation of authority from the government to private citizens and judicial enforcement of the covenants as ratifying discrimination. He described covenants as "pressure by one group of the community against another group and . . . therefore 'in purpose and effect, racial zoning ordinances.'"

The Kraemers' lawyer, Gerald Seegers, was the nephew of the founder of a neighborhood "improvement association," founded in 1910 to promote the adoption of restrictive covenants. Aware that the justices might not have been sympathetic to his case, Seegers began by agreeing that the case would affect "millions of citizens," including whites, and tried to deflect the Court's attention from the sociological material by pointing out that "however deplorable" a situation was, the Shelleys had to show that restrictive covenants violated the Constitution. He stressed that his clients were simply exercising their rights as private property owners, and that the Missouri courts, rather than discriminating against African-Americans, merely enforced "its established rule equally applicable to any contract, whether black or white." When Justice Frankfurter asked him if Missouri could allow citizens to restrict transfers of property on grounds of race, Seegers said that it could, because the state would be allowing rather than requiring discrimination. Seegers closed by saying that "the problem of racial discrimination can not be solved by judicial decrees and the current housing problem is no justification for a judicial amendment of the Constitution."[28]

Loren Miller and Marshall prepared for their presentations in a moot court held before the students at Howard Law School. (Reportedly, a second-year student asked "a long, rambling question" that Justice Frankfurter actually raised during the argument.) They presented the Michigan case. *Buchanan,* Miller argued, established that the rights of African-Americans involved here were not mere property rights but were more important civil rights, and the enforcement of restrictive covenants, even if not intentionally designed to impair a civil right, did have that result.[29]

Marshall then continued the argument, in what one of Chief Justice Vinson's law clerks called his "typically elegant and articulate" way. After citing a long line of cases in which the Court had reviewed judicial action to see if it complied with the Constitution, Marshall made a crucial point by citing cases in which the Supreme Court had found judicially developed rules of law to be unconstitutional. The cases involved common-law prohibitions on picketing, which the Court held to be violations of the First Amendment. They established, Marshall said, that judicial action could be outlawed "on substantive considerations," and therefore, by inference, that judicial enforcement of restrictive covenants, which certainly was state action, could be unconstitutional.[30]

A central analytic issue arose here. In the picketing cases, the judically developed rule was that certain types of picketing were unlawful, and the Court held that such a rule violated the First Amendment; in the restrictive-covenant cases, the state courts were applying the rule that they would enforce all covenants, no matter what their content, and, as Seegers had argued, it is almost certainly true that *that* rule is perfectly constitutional. No one on the Court pursued this issue, though, and Marshall turned to the sociological material. Frankfurter asked him why it was relevant. Marshall, apparently taken aback, said both that the material was "legally significant" and "essential" to his argument, *and* that he did not have to rely on it.

The lawyers for the white homeowners in the Michigan case said that all that was involved was the right of people to choose their associates by making private contracts, and that the state court, in enforcing the covenant, was not enforcing discrimination but was rather "enforcing the private rights of citizens." James Crooks, one of the lawyers, did agree with Frankfurter's rather damaging formulation of the question: the private citizens "need the full strength of the state's judicial power to enforce something which the state could not itself declare as state policy."

Marshall presented a brief rebuttal, and in response to a question from Chief Justice Fred Vinson he seized upon Crooks's concession to specify "just where the state steps in." The covenant, Marshall said, "comes about because the parties . . . believe that the agreement is enforceable by the state. The essence of the contract is its ability to be enforced. Mr. Crooks admits that the state moves in at the time of judgment. We say that the state moves in when the contract or agreement is made in reliance upon the legislative or judicial sanctions that will be enforced. . . . The parties cannot enforce the agreement against a recalcitrant promissor without state aid." Marshall's rhetorically powerful argument cut away most of the analytic complexities in the cases.

Houston and Indritz concluded by presenting the District of Columbia cases, where the legal issues were somewhat different. The Fourteenth Amendment, aimed specifically at racial discrimination, applies only to "states," not to the federal government, which is the lawmaker for the District of Columbia. The only constitutional provision arguably applicable in the Washington cases was the Fifth Amendment to the Constitution, which prohibits the federal government from denying due process of law. Whether the due process clause somehow had the same effect as the Fourteenth Amendment was a difficult question; after all, the Fifth Amendment was not directed specifically at the problem of racial discrimination, as the Fourteenth Amendment was, and the Fourteenth Amendment had a provision, absent from the Fifth, stating explicitly that states could not deny the equal protection of the laws. In addition, because the District of Columbia was part of the federal government rather than a state itself, the property law of the District, including the law dealing with covenants, was federal law that the Supreme Court could define for itself. The District of Columbia cases might avoid the constitutional issues presented in the other cases. When Houston opened his argument by referring to the sociological material, Frankfurter seized on the point to say that "this all goes to the inequities of the case," that is, to the nonconstitutional dimensions of the argument.

Henry Gilligan joined Crooks in representing the white homeowners in Washington. He described Urciolo as a "greedy real estate speculator[ ] posing as [a] friend[ ] of the Negroes." Crooks, responding to Houston's effort to direct the Court's attention to nonconstitutional issues, pointed out that segregation of schools and recreation facilities in the District showed that there was no public policy there against segregation. In rebuttal, Houston said that his opponents had "made his argument" by pointing out that they had gone to the courts ten times to enforce restrictive covenants, and concluded by saying that "racism in the United States must stop" and that "the courts, by making racial unity impossible, are endangering national security."

The oral argument seems to have sharpened the issues in the cases somewhat. To one listener, Houston's argument "combin[ed] intellectual strength with moral force, and . . . communicat[ed] a sense of personal integrity."[31] Frankfurter's questions about the sociological material, and the responses by Marshall and Houston, seem to have established that the material was useful, if at all, only in connection with the nonconstitutional issues in the Washington case. Corrigan's significance had been muddied by the varying approaches the lawyers had taken to it, which was probably beneficial to the NAACP position. Most important, of course, the extended arguments demonstrated how significant everyone involved in the cases believed the issues to be.

The Court issued its opinions in early May. Apparently because they owned houses with restrictive covenants, Justices Stanley Reed, Robert Jackson, and Wiley Rutledge did not participate. The other justices found the cases rather easy.

Chief Justice Vinson told his colleagues that the "letter of the 14th Amend[ment] as interpreted" required the Court to strike down restrictive covenants, and Justice Black said that he "can't see [a] difference between action of legislature & action of courts." Vinson circulated draft opinions in *Shelley* and the District of Columbia case at the end of April and immediately received warm comments. Douglas called them "grand jobs," and Justice Harold Burton, another Truman appointee, congratulated Vinson. "If you can get unanimous action," Burton wrote, "it will be a major contribution to the vitality of the 14th Amendment, the Civil Rights Act, the general subject of interracial justice, and the strength of this Court as the 'living voice of the Constitution' (Bryce)." Frank Murphy, a stalwart liberal, told Vinson, "You will receive many blows" for the decisions but that "with time the cases will make you immortal. It took not only wisdom about the law but also vast courage for a chief justice from Kentucky to hold fast to his beliefs."[32]

Vinson's opinion in *Shelley,* which dealt with the Michigan case as well, was rather turgid, consisting in large part of recitations of facts and holdings in prior cases, interspersed with some largely irrelevant statements of general principle. The opinion began by saying that "basic constitutional issues of obvious importance have been raised." When Vinson reached the point of summarizing *Corrigan,* he said that there the question of the validity of judicial enforcement was not properly before the Court, "as the opinion . . . specifically recognizes." Halfway through the opinion, Vinson turned to the central question, accepting the state-action question as formulated by Marshall and the NAACP lawyers: is judicial enforcement of restrictive covenants state action? Again Vinson ran through the precedents to establish the obvious point that judicial action is state action, drawing on the picketing cases that Marshall had referred to in the oral argument.[33]

In the final quarter of his opinion, Vinson addressed the ultimate issue. He found that "there has been state action in these cases in the full and complete sense of the phrase," because "but for the active intervention of the state courts, supported by the full panoply of state power, petitioners would have been free to occupy the properties in question without restraint." According to Vinson, "the difference between judicial enforcement of the restrictive covenants is the difference . . . between being denied rights of property available to other members of the community and being accorded full enjoyment of those rights on an equal footing." This, he said, was a "clear" case of discrimination. "Because of the race or color of these petitioners they have been denied rights of ownership or occupancy enjoyed as a matter of course by other citizens of different race or color." Vinson rejected the argument that the state courts were not discriminating on the basis of race because they "stand ready to enforce restrictive covenants excluding white persons" as readily as they enforce covenants excluding African-Americans. Relying on *Gaines,* Vinson said that Fourteenth Amendment rights are "personal," which meant that "it is no answer . . . to say that the courts may also be induced to deny white persons rights of ownership and occupancy on grounds of race or color. Equal protection of the laws is not achieved through indiscriminate imposition of inequalities." Vinson concluded his opinion by referring to "the historical context in which the Fourteenth Amendment became part of the Constitution." Its framers, he said, sought to establish "equality in the enjoyment of basic civil and political rights and the preservation of those rights from discriminatory action on the part of the States."

Vinson also wrote the Court's opinion in the District of Columbia cases. His law clerk had suggested the argument that the concept of due process in the Fifth Amendment "is as broad in its scope and applicability to the federal government as the comparable clause of the 14th Amendment in its relation to the states," but Vinson preferred a different route. He found a statutory basis for his decision in the Civil Rights Act of 1866. The act provides that "all citizens of the United States shall have the same right . . . as is enjoyed by white citizens . . . to inherit, purchase, lease, sell, hold, and convey real and personal property." According to Vinson, this statute basically tracked the Fourteenth Amendment. Thus, if judicial enforcement of restrictive covenants violated the Fourteenth Amendment, it also violated the 1866 Civil Rights Act. In addition, Vinson said, such enforcement was contrary to "the public policy of the United States, and as such should be corrected by this Court in the exercise of its supervisory powers over the courts of the District of Columbia." To Vinson, "it is not consistent with the public policy of the United States to permit federal courts in the Nation's capital to exercise general equitable powers to compel action denied the state courts" by the Fourteenth Amendment.[34]

Justice Frankfurter, who was "wary of arguments drawn from" Reconstruction-era civil-rights statutes, wrote a brief concurring opinion in which he said that a federal court of equity, which "is rooted in conscience," should be bound by the same rules that state courts were, when the limits on state courts arose "not for any narrow technical reason, but for considerations that touch rights so basic to our society that, after the Civil War, their protection against invasion by the States was safeguarded by the Constitution."[35]

In the long run, legal scholars have not been generous to Vinson's opinion in *Shelley* even though it tracked a widely admired article published by a respected law professor in 1945.[36] The opinion spends a great deal of time establishing the analytically obvious point that judicial action is state action, and it fails to address the real question, which is whether the courts violate the Constitution when they follow a general rule enforcing covenants in cases where the particular covenant is a racial restriction.

The comments made immediately after the decision focused on its likely consequences. Those who praised the Court's decision routinely noted that it was unlikely to lead soon to changes in housing patterns for, as Loren Miller said, it would be "folly to expect an overnight reversal of social attitudes . . . rooted in custom." African-Americans might be able to buy housing at lower prices as the supply available to them expanded, but discriminatory preferences would still leave many neighborhoods completely white. Observers were more generous in describing the message the decision sent about the Court's willingness to protect human rights. Overall, the decisions were well received.[37]

After *Shelley*, Walter White wrote in his newspaper column, "the fight is not over," because there were "vast interests" attempting to maintain residential segregation. "But we have moved forward a long way through this decision and those who believe in democracy now are on the offensive and have put the enemies of decency on the defensive as they have never been before." For the moment, the NAACP's lawyers pressed their offensive against the federal housing authorities. The FHA continued to take racial concerns into account in appraising properties, approved the financing of housing in the large new suburban development of Levittown even though the houses there were subject to restrictive covenants, and denied approval to interracial projects. The FHA took the position that *Shelley* did not require it to "withdraw its normal protection and benefits from persons who have executed but do not seek judicial enforcement" of restrictive covenants. After meeting with Loren Miller, Hastie, Houston, Bob Ming, and James Nabrit, Marian Perry prepared a long memorandum on FHA practices, which Walter White sent to Harry Truman along with a letter protesting FHA policies. According to Perry, the memorandum and letter "caused some furor in Washington," leading to a meeting between Marshall and Attorney General Clark. Shortly thereafter, the FHA modified its policies somewhat, but the NAACP continued to criticize the agency for failing to follow through on the implications of *Shelley*. Marshall met several times with Solicitor General Perlman, regarded by the NAACP as much more sympathetic than the FHA administrator, and submitted drafts of several regulations, prepared by Perry, including an explicit ban on imposing restrictive covenants during the period of FHA insurance for mortgages.[38]

In August 1949, a year after *Shelley*, Marshall spoke to an FHA conference and again took a hard line. He refused to accept plans that would follow local custom: because segregation was not a permissible option, "there can be no room for a discussion of realities, expediency, or statesmanship." An NAACP staff member said that Marshall was "in rare form" at this meeting "and handed out liberal education all over the place," leaving a government lawyer from Mississippi "closed up like a tongue-tied clam." Late in 1949 the FHA adopted policy changes in line with the NAACP's suggestions, which the NAACP praised while still noting that much remained to be done. As the New York *Times* noted, the policy changes would do little to alter residential segregation maintained "by informal agreement," although its more conservative columnist Arthur Krock thought that the FHA was attempting to impose rigid restraints on the ability of sellers to choose buyers for their property.[39]

As soon as he learned of the Court's decision in *Shelley*, Loren Miller dashed off a "mash note" to Marian Perry "to brag about the fact that in the beginning wasn't nobody but you and me really believed we could restore God to his heaven and sanity to the Constitution (greatest Document ever struck from the minds of men) by overthrowing race restrictive covenants—We told 'em so, huh?" Yet, although the doctrine announced in *Shelley* had enormous potential to undermine all sorts of discriminatory practices by private parties, in employment as well as housing, the decision's actual impact on housing patterns was rather slight. As White and others recognized, those patterns resulted from much more deep-rooted causes than a single Supreme Court decision could reach.[40]

Shelley was important, its doctrine and immediate or even long-run effects on housing patterns apart, for a number of reasons. The NAACP had finally induced

the United States government to intervene on behalf of its challenge to segregation, which certainly lent weight to that challenge. Having entered an NAACP
case once, the government continued to do so in the school segregation cases that
were working their way to the Supreme Court in the late 1940s. In addition, the
sociological material that had been compiled in the restrictive covenant cases
seemed somehow to matter to the outcome. Of course, as Miller told Perry, "ain't
nobody even mentioned [the] sociology in the opinions," and Frankfurter's questions to Marshall at the oral argument suggested that the material did not have any
direct doctrinal impact. Still, the sociological material appeared to have been an
important factor in leading the government to join the case, and it may have led the
justices to take the doctrinal arguments more seriously than they otherwise would
have. In any event, the NAACP's lawyers came to believe, at least partly as a result
of their experience in *Shelley*, that developing a strong sociological case meant a
great deal. Finally, Marshall gained crucial experience in coordinating a large
number of related cases that were destined for the Supreme Court. One lesson he
learned may have been that the NAACP lawyers needed to keep the cases under
tight control if their litigation was to proceed unobstructed by conflicts among the
participating lawyers. Marshall brought this lesson, and the others, to the school
segregation litigation.[41]

7

"Interference with the Effective Choice of the Voters" Challenging the White Primary

African-Americans challenged segregation in court because they knew that legislatures would not take Jim Crow laws off the books. After all, African-Americans were excluded from voting. Challenging disfranchisement in the courts directly attacked one part of the Jim Crow system, and if it succeeded it might provide African-Americans with enough political power to change the rest. Jim Crow's defenders, though, found it easy to accomplish or sustain disfranchisement in ways protected by the state-action doctrine. The NAACP's lawyers had to develop innovative theories to challenge these "private" systems of disfranchisement. In the end they succeeded, but the challenge took so long that the last case reached the Supreme Court at the same time as the direct challenge to segregated education.* Even more, whites maintained political power in the South by means that the legal challenge could not reach, such as physical terror. In voting cases, then, successes were inevitably limited.

During and after the 1890s, Southern legislators adopted two strategies to exclude African-Americans from voting. The first, embodied in Mississippi's 1890 constitution, used poll taxes, literacy tests, and similar devices to define qualifications for voting. These devices did not, in terms, treat African-Americans differently from whites, but they were intended to exclude more African-Americans than whites from voting, and did. Because the Mississippi approach did bar some whites from voting, however, it could be politically controversial, particularly when the approach was aimed at disfranchising whites who supported the Populist and similar parties.[1]

The alternative strategy focused specifically on African-Americans. In some states like Maryland at the turn of the century, vigorous party competition made it politically impossible to propose programs that would disfranchise some whites

---

*As later chapters show, the Court's deliberations in *Brown v. Board of Education* were affected by the concerns the justices expressed in the voting cases.

along with African-Americans: Any party that supported African-American disfranchisement would lose white votes as well. Yet African-Americans were concentrated in the Republican party, and their influence on political outcomes could
be minimized by ensuring that they did not participate in the Democratic party.
The second strategy of exclusion therefore aimed at keeping the Democratic party
white.

The principal method of exclusion was the white primary, that is, the selection
of party candidates in primary elections from which African-Americans were excluded. The white primary posed a legal problem on the border between public and
private discrimination. The problem was public because the white primary was
connected to selecting public officials, but it was private because the party seemed
to be an association of individuals who shared political values.

Although the Supreme Court upheld Mississippi's technique of African-American
disfranchisement, the white primary was more compatible with the political climate in Texas. As part of a Progressive-era effort to reduce political corruption,
Texas adopted primary elections in 1905. The Texas statute initially let each
party's executive committee determine who could vote in the party's primary, but
in the early 1920s, candidates' efforts to attract African-American support led to
agitation for more stringent restrictions. The Texas legislature responded in 1923
by passing a statute explicitly barring African-Americans from Democratic party
primaries.

With substantial numbers of professionals and independent entrepreneurs, the
African-American communities in Houston and El Paso provided the organizational base for a challenge to this statute. L. A. Nixon, an El Paso doctor, agreed to
be the plaintiff in the NAACP's case against the Texas statute. The legal theory of
the challenge was straightforward. Unlike the Mississippi strategy of disfranchisement, which had been upheld because the statute did not in terms treat African-
Americans differently from whites, the Texas white primary law explicitly drew a
line on the basis of race, to the disadvantage of African-Americans. This, the
NAACP lawyers contended, violated the Fourteenth and Fifteenth Amendments.[2]

When Nixon's challenge to the 1923 Texas statute came to the Supreme Court
in 1927, Justice Oliver Wendell Holmes wrote a brief opinion for a unanimous
Court. The Fourteenth Amendment, Holmes said, "was passed . . . with a special intent to protect the blacks from discrimination against them." Texas's statute
"in the teeth of [these] prohibitions" did discriminate on the basis of color, and,
Holmes said, "it is too clear for extended argument that color cannot be made the
basis of a statutory classification" affecting the right to vote.[3]

The key to the Court's analysis, then, was that the Texas legislature itself had
enacted a color line. Texas responded by rewriting its law to authorize each party's
executive committee to define who could vote in the primary. When the Democratic party's executive committee adopted an exclusionary rule, African-
American Texans again challenged the white primary.[4]

The federal district judge in Texas, who, the NAACP's local lawyer said, was
"prejudiced" against the NAACP, ruled against the NAACP. The exclusion, he
said, resulted from state executive committee decisions, not state actions. The

1927 Texas statute gave the committee no greater power to determine the qualifications of party members than they had had before the statute was enacted. The NAACP appealed to the Supreme Court. Two prominent African-American activists from Houston, J. Alston Atkins and Carter Wesley, filed an *amicus* brief. Atkins and Wesley were supported by a vigorous, largely working-class movement in Houston led by Richard Grovey, who ran a barber school and headed a militant African-American political organization. Carter and Wesley's brief forcefully asserted that Texas had violated the *Fifteenth* Amendment. They pressed Walter White to allow one of them to participate in the NAACP's oral argument, but White refused.[5]

The Fourteenth Amendment argument was simple, but the Fifteenth Amendment one was more complicated. That amendment bars states from denying the right to vote on the basis of race. In 1921, the Supreme Court had overturned a conviction for voting fraud in a Michigan primary. Because primary elections were not part of the election process referred to in the Constitution, the Court said, Congress could not make voting fraud in primaries a criminal offense. Although the case did not involve race discrimination, its definition of the election process suggested that barring African-Americans from primaries would not violate the constitutionally protected right to vote. This doctrinal difficulty continued to plague the NAACP's efforts to eliminate white primaries.[6]

The Texans' brief did not acknowledge this doctrinal difficulty. In 1932, the Supreme Court, by a vote of five-to-four, held in *Nixon v. Condon* that the 1927 statute violated the Constitution. Justice Benjamin Cardozo's opinion for the Court began by noting that the result for Nixon was "no different from what it was when his cause was here before." But, Cardozo said, the party officials contended that "identity of result has been attained through essential diversity of method" because the party that excluded Nixon from voting was "merely a voluntary association" which "has inherent power like voluntary associations generally to determine its own membership."[7]

Cardozo was concerned that a broad ruling would have implications for political parties beyond the white primary context. He found "a narrower base" for a decision that Texas, by statute, "lodged the power in a committee, which excluded the petitioner and others of his race, not by virtue of any authority delegated by the party, but by virtue of an authority originating or supposed to originate in the mandate of the law." Cardozo's point was that the party's executive committee, not the party itself, had excluded Nixon, and in doing so the committee was exercising a power the 1927 statute gave it. According to Cardozo, in voluntary associations the power to determine membership would "reside[ ] in the State convention" where "platforms of principles are announced and the tests of party allegiance made known to the world." Yet the state convention had never declared its desire to exclude African-Americans. Cardozo concluded from this that "whatever power of exclusion has been exercised by the members of the committee has come to them, therefore, not as the delegates of the party, but as the delegates of the State." Once he established that the exclusion of African-Americans resulted from state power, of course, the outcome was controlled by the first Nixon case.[8]

White Texans continued to try to bar African-Americans from voting. Two weeks after the decision in *Nixon v. Condon,* the Democratic party's executive committee repealed its exclusionary rule, and shortly thereafter the state convention adopted a resolution making all qualified white citizens eligible for membership. Dr. Nixon was as persistent as the white Democrats, though, and again challenged the exclusion. Strikingly, the same judge described as prejudiced against the NAACP in *Condon* ruled for Nixon this time, on the rather strained ground that although the convention had said that whites *were* eligible to vote in primaries, it had not said that African-Americans were *not* eligible to vote.[9]

At this point the NAACP lost control of the white primary litigation. Wesley and Atkins joined with Richard Grovey in Houston to challenge the convention's resolution. They urged that exclusion of African-Americans from primaries violated the Fifteenth Amendment, because the primary was indeed part of the election process covered by that amendment. This challenge, and an associated Fourteenth Amendment argument, lost decisively when the Supreme Court unanimously rejected Grovey's case in 1935.[10]

Justice Owen Roberts's opinion noted that the Court had never said that an action by the party convention would be state action, and "upon its face" the party's resolution was not state action. Roberts then rejected arguments that would make the exclusion an act of the state. He devoted most of his attention to the argument that the primary election was held "under statutory compulsion" and was heavily regulated by the state. Acknowledging that Texas had "elaborately provided for the expression of party preference as to nominees," Roberts concluded that "it is equally true that the primary is a party primary," and that under state law the party was a voluntary association entitled to determine who its members would be. Roberts also rejected the argument that African-Americans were subjected to "forbidden discrimination" because their exclusion from the primary, in Texas equivalent to the general election, meant that they were barred from selecting members of Congress and the Senate. As Roberts put it, "the argument is that as a negro may not be denied a ballot at a general election on account of his race or color, if exclusion from the primary renders his vote at the general election insignificant and useless, the result is to deny him the suffrage altogether." This, though, confused "the privilege of membership in a party with the right to vote for one who is to hold a public office." The state was not concerned with the former at all, so, to Roberts, Grovey's argument about the practical consequences of the white primary was simply irrelevant.

Grovey v. Townsend led the NAACP to suspend attack on the white primary. The only way to establish state action, it seemed, was to show that primary elections were the real elections, and *Grovey* appeared to foreclose that argument. Marshall toyed with the theory that state action existed because the election judges were state officials. He did not pursue it, largely because he became tired of dealing with squabbling among the leadership of the Texas challengers. As he put it in an exasperated letter to A. Maceo Smith, an NAACP leader in Texas, "I do not quite understand just what is going on in Texas. I doubt that anyone does."[11]

The NAACP's hopes were revived, however, by the Supreme Court's 1941 decision in *United States v. Classic,* and, while the Classic litigation was pending, Marshall deferred any NAACP action. The Civil Liberties Unit of the Justice Department persuaded the Criminal Division to prosecute several Louisiana election officials for denying voters their constitutional rights by altering their votes in a primary election. The case arose out of an investigation aimed at Huey Long's political machine, but the investigation took an unexpected turn when it produced evidence that Classic, a member of the anti-Long reform faction of the Democratic party, had manipulated the vote count to ensure the nomination of Hale Boggs as a candidate for the United States House of Representatives. The government indicted Classic for violating a federal statute making it a crime to deny anyone "any right or privilege . . . secured by the Constitution." It charged that Classic's vote fraud denied eligible voters of their right to have their ballots counted for their preferred candidate. The federal district court dismissed the indictment, relying on the 1921 Supreme Court holding that Congress did not have power to regulate primary elections as the basis for saying that there was no constitutional right to have votes properly counted in primary elections.[12]

The government appealed to the Supreme Court. Over a dissent by the liberal Justices Douglas, Murphy, and Black, who believed that the statute's reference to "rights secured by the Constitution" was too vague to justify a criminal indictment, the Supreme Court allowed the prosecution to go forward.[13] Justice Harlan Fiske Stone laid out the theory underlying his opinion for the Court in a letter to Douglas. Douglas had suggested that "if a primary is a part of the election machinery, it does not make any difference whether the fraudulent count of votes occurs in a party which never elects its candidate or in one which always does." Stone agreed, but noted that "[i]f the primary had no more effect on the election than a Gallup poll, calling it a primary would not bring the votes . . . within the constitutional protection." What mattered, Stone said, was whether the primary was "either by law or in fact influential upon the election." For him, the Constitution guaranteed "the right to participate in the procedure of choice."[14]

Stone's opinion examined Louisiana's extensive regulation of primary elections, which as a practical matter "impose[d] serious restrictions" on candidate choice. He then observed that, according to the indictment's assertions, "the practical operation of the primary in Louisiana is . . . to secure the election of the Democratic primary nominee." Stone concluded that "interference with the right to vote in the Congressional primary . . . is thus, as a matter of law and in fact, an interference with the effective choice of the voters at the only stage of the election procedure when such interference could have any practical effect on the ultimate result." In this way, the primary was "an integral part of the procedure for the popular choice of Congressman."

The question then was whether the Constitution protected the right to choose a member of Congress. Stone said that the right to *vote* in congressional elections was of course guaranteed. The only question was whether the development of the primary election mattered. Stone stressed that "the free choice by the people of representatives in Congress . . . was one of the great purposes of our constitutional scheme of government." What mattered, according to Stone, was "the right to cast a ballot and to have it counted at the general election. . . . Where the state law has made the primary an integral part of the procedure of choice, or where in fact the primary effectively controls the choice, the right of the elector to have his ballot counted at the primary is likewise" protected by the Constitution. Stone explicitly stated that it did not really matter for constitutional purposes whether the primary "invariably, sometimes or never determines the ultimate choice of the representative," but he immediately followed by saying that "we cannot close our eyes to the fact . . . that the practical influence of the choice of candidates at the primary may be so great as to affect profoundly the choice at the general election, even though there is no effective legal prohibition upon the rejection at the election of the choice made at the primary."

As a legal matter, what *Classic* implied for white primary cases was not entirely clear. It was not a case about race discrimination, so the constitutional right at stake was the right to participate in selecting members of Congress. No matter how far this analysis was pushed, therefore, it could not encompass challenges to white primaries for selecting candidates for governor or other state offices. Even more important, Stone's analysis seemed to give state law a central role in defining the constitutionally protected right to participate in primary elections. This could mean that once state law told people they could participate in primaries, their votes had to be fully taken into account; the constitutional guarantee would protect against fooling voters into falsely believing that their votes mattered. If Stone's opinion were read that way, the white primary would survive because there was no deception about the process at all.

Yet, other parts of Stone's opinion suggested that white primaries were unconstitutional. His emphasis on extensive state regulation of the primary and his description of the primary as "an integral part" of the general election process, for example, suggested that the relevant state action consisted of establishing a primary system for selecting candidates. In addition, Stone's ambivalent references to the practical reality that primaries were where members of Congress were chosen plainly implied that Southern white primaries were questionable: if a state could not set up a system for selecting members of Congress that excluded African-Americans openly, it was a short step to the conclusion that it could not set up a system that had the same effect in practice.

Marshall began to coordinate a new challenge to the Texas white primary. Before *Classic*, the NAACP supported a Houston branch case that had been dismissed by the trial judge. After *Classic*, the NAACP decided to begin a different case, where the record could be constructed in light of the Court's analysis in *Classic*. As Marshall described the process, the national office had to consider important issues of "strategy and timing," such as ensuring that the first cases brought involved primary elections for federal rather than state or local offices—which was the reason for abandoning the first Texas case—and developing a substantial body of material to demonstrate the primary's practical significance. Marshall himself rejected the view that the Constitution invalidated only white primaries for federal offices, and he believed that "we will eventually break it down," but in constructing a litigation campaign he had to work with what the Supreme Court had done in

Classic. Because of the NAACP's substantial experience in Texas, it made sense, Marshall concluded, to continue to conduct the campaign there.[15]

First Marshall had to overcome some resentment in Texas over dropping the pending case by "pointing out . . . the true difficulties in the case and the benefits of filing another case." Because the Houston branch was divided by internal dissension, Marshall briefly explored bringing the new case in Dallas. After discovering that the potential plaintiff in Dallas had voted in the 1940 primary, they "were right where we started—out on the street." Marshall returned to Houston and talked with Dr. Lonnie Smith, a dentist who was a Houston branch officer. Marshall checked Smith's story "as best I could," and concluded that Smith, who had tried to vote in the 1940 primary but was denied a ballot, was an appropriate plaintiff. Marshall then spent a couple of days working on the details of the complaint, which was filed in the Texas state courts on November 17, 1941.[16]

To no one's surprise, the Texas courts rejected the NAACP's claims, relying on *Grovey.* Marshall and the NAACP then sought review in the Supreme Court. Marshall approached Herbert Wechsler, an attorney in the solicitor general's office, to see if the government would support the NAACP. Wechsler read *Classic* narrowly, as a case not involving a party's freedom to select its members, and was concerned as well that Department of Justice intervention in Smith's case would cause conflict with the Senate Judiciary Committee. Walter White attempted to persuade Attorney General Francis Biddle to file an *amicus* brief arguing that *Classic* had overruled *Grovey*, but Biddle refused. Given Wechsler's analysis, Biddle concluded, it was not worth the political cost. He told President Roosevelt that "if we intervened here again, the South would not understand why we were continually taking sides." Fred Folsom, an attorney in the Civil Rights Section, did publish an article in the *Columbia Law Review.* He explained that it would be grossly unfair to prosecute Texas officials for maintaining a white primary while *Grovey* remained good law, but otherwise he endorsed the NAACP's position that *Classic* had overruled *Grovey.*[17]

Marshall and Hastie developed the NAACP's case in *Smith.* Milton Konvitz, relying on the most favorable parts of Stone's opinion in *Classic,* urged them to argue that the primary was "an integral part of the procedure of choice as a matter of fact, regardless of the statutory situation." Hastie was more cautious, believing that position "goes far beyond" the holding in *Classic,* and argued instead the "narrow issue" that *Classic* had effectively overruled *Grovey.* The efforts by the lawyers in the national office to control the case again touched sensitive nerves among the Texas members, some of whom wanted to see a local attorney participate in the oral argument. Although Marshall was somewhat impatient at this display of "running off at the mouth," he attempted to accommodate the Texans' concerns by paying the expenses of W. J. Durham, who had helped Marshall prepare the complaint in *Smith,* to come to Washington and assist in writing a reply to the Texas attorney general's brief.[18]

Smith was argued on January 12, 1944. The justices discussed it three days later. According to Justice Felix Frankfurter, the Court voted to overrule *Grovey;* Stone said that he could not "reconcile it with [the] Classic case," and that the Court had before it "more facts . . . on [the] nature of [the] primary than we had in the earlier case," which was enough to overcome concern about overruling a relatively recent decision. Justice Roberts, the author of the Court's opinion in *Grovey,* disagreed. Initially Justices Robert Jackson and Hugo Black also voted against the NAACP's claim. They were concerned that a decision against the white primary would imply that many private associations would find themselves governed by the Constitution. They were persuaded, however, that the decision could cover "not all primaries but this primary."[19]

Within the Court, Frankfurter provoked a discussion of whether "the Court had changed its vie[w]s not on any new facts or any new factors but solely on different notions of policy."[20] Chief Justice Stone ended up designating Justice Reed to write the opinion. Frankfurter tried to get Reed to say that the present justices simply had different views of policy than the justices who decided *Grovey.* When Reed circulated a draft of his opinion, Frankfurter found that its discussion of overruling was inadequate because it was not explicit about the reasons for the Court's "about-face." He wrote Reed that "you are of the opinion that the South can be gently eased into acceptance of our decision . . . if only we are not too explicit. My prophecy is precisely the opposite. . . ." He said that attempting to "screen" the blow would arouse "an added grievance," and insisted that the Court was "absolutely turning about face" from *Grovey.* Under these circumstances, he wrote, the Court's opinion "ought to avoid even the appearance of disingenuousness—of legal pussyfooting and pettyfogging. . . . Lack of candor in a matter of this sort is worse than a wrong, it is a blunder. It is bound to fail since other people are just as bright as we are."[21] Frankfurter prepared a dissent because he "just could not swallow the pussy-footing and petty-fogging of Reed's opinion and especially the uncandid use he was making" of *Classic.* Eventually he concurred in the result, refusing to join Reed's opinion but also not publishing his own.[22]

Meanwhile Roberts was working on a dissent. It had a relatively calm tone, but it irritated Justice Rutledge. Rutledge had told Reed, "I do not believe anyone could have done a more judicial, judicious & statesmanlike job, with your hard problems, than you have done." After receiving Roberts's dissent, Rutledge wrote out, but did not circulate, an opinion expressing his annoyance at statements in various recent opinions that, in Rutledge's view, cast aspersions on the integrity of those who "depart[ed] from accepted bases of judicial action."[23]

Rutledge may have been provoked by the most celebrated phrase in Roberts's dissent. Roberts chided the Court for overruling a unanimous decision, "written with care" only nine years earlier: This "tends to bring adjudications of this tribunal into the same class as a restricted railroad ticket, good for this day and train only." Putting Frankfurter's concern about candor in a more diplomatic way, Roberts said that "[i]f this Court's opinion in the Classic Case discloses its method of overruling earlier decisions, I can only protest that, in fairness, it should rather have adopted the open and frank way of saying what it was doing than, after the event, characterize its past action as overruling Grovey v. Townsend though those less sapient never realized the fact."[24]

Reed's opinion was announced on April 3, 1944. It explicitly overruled *Grovey,* and relied in part on *Classic* to justify that result. "The fusing by the Classic Case of the primary and general elections into a single instrumentality for choice of officers has a definite bearing on the permissibility" of the white primary, Reed wrote. He conceded that *Classic* did not "cut[] directly into the rationale" of *Grovey,* but said that it bore upon *Grovey* "not because exclusion of Negroes from primaries is any more or less state action by reason of the unitary character of the electoral process but because the recognition of the place of the primary in the electoral scheme makes clear that state delegation to a party of the power to fix the qualifications of primary elections is delegation of a state function that may make the party's action the action of the state." Reed concluded that Texas's system of regulating primaries meant that "it endorses, adopts and enforces" discrimination against African-Americans "practiced by a party entrusted by Texas law" with determining the qualifications of participants in the primary. "This," Reed said, "is state action." He concluded his opinion by stressing that "the United States is a constitutional democracy. Its organic law grants to all citizens a right to participate in the choice of elected officials without restriction by any state because of race. This grant to the people of the opportunity for choice is not to be nullified by a state through casting its electoral process in a form which permits a private organization to practice racial discrimination in the election."[25]

As it turned out, Frankfurter's concern that the South would reject a "disingenuous" opinion was misplaced; indeed, the "remarkably calm" reaction in the South might have been less restrained had the Court said more openly that it had simply come to a different view on sound constitutional policy than the *Grovey* Court had. The Atlanta *Constitution* called the opinion "poorly timed," but said that it could not be ignored. Among African-Americans, Hastie praised the decision because it could "galvanize[] democratic forces in the South" that would make the South a leader in American liberalism. The *New Republic* praised the decision but noted that its effects would be limited so long as other restrictions on voting, such as the poll tax, remained in force.[26]

After *Smith,* Marshall proceeded on two fronts. Initially he and the NAACP placed their hopes in the Justice Department, and tried to "hold all decisions in abeyance until I have had a chance to see just where the Department of Justice is going." The NAACP had already spent a great deal of money on white primaries, and it was appropriate "to bring pressure to bear on the Department of Justice" to take over the complex problems of enforcing the Constitution. In theory, once the Court clearly stated that white primaries were unconstitutional, the department could prosecute officials for wilfully denying African-Americans their civil rights. Department officials, however, thought that the "wilfullness" requirement would make it hard to obtain convictions from Southern juries, and they were quite sensitive to the political implications of an aggressive federal campaign against Southern Democrats. The department therefore did not institute any criminal litigation about white primaries.[27]

Criminal prosecutions would have been impeded, in any event, by other actions Southern legislatures took to evade the implications of *Smith v. Allwright.* The Court's decision might invalidate white primaries because they determined election outcomes, or more narrowly because the state regulated the primary process extensively. Acting on the narrower interpretation, South Carolina governor Olin

D. Johnston called a special legislative session that repealed approximately 150 laws relating to primary elections. State officials took the position that *Smith v. Allwright* no longer applied. Because Marshall was recovering from his illness when the South Carolina legislature acted, Robert Carter directed Harold Boulware, the NAACP's chief cooperating attorney in South Carolina, to challenge South Carolina's white primary on the ground that *Smith* invalidated white primaries where they were "tantamount to an election."[28]

Marshall received some minor suggestions on details from Fred Folsom, the Civil Rights Section lawyer who had written about the white primary prior to *Smith*. In the main the theory and the case developed smoothly. One reason was that United States District Judge J. Waties Waring heard the case. Waring, a native of South Carolina, was a dedicated liberal on matters of race. His views were reinforced by his second wife, who had been raised in New York. Waring believed that his state "was backward . . . and that somebody had at last to face the issue," and Marshall called Waring "a tremendous light coming out of the dark."[29]

In July 1947, Waring ruled for the NAACP. Waring specifically emphasized the passage in *Classic* saying that the Constitution came into play "where in fact the primary effectively controls the choice." According to Waring, it was "pure sophistry" to say that the South Carolina Democratic party's "present status" was "materially different" from its status before the repeal of the laws regulating primary elections. He also noted that, as of 1947, South Carolina was the only state with a white primary in the Democratic party. As Waring said, "There was no evasion in the purpose of the Governor and members of the General Assembly and why should there now be evasion of the issue here presented? For too many years the people of this Country, and perhaps particularly of this State, have evaded realistic issues. . . . It is time for South Carolina to rejoin the Union. It is time to fall in step with the other states and to adopt the American way of conducting elections."[30]

The court of appeals affirmed Judge Waring in an opinion by Judge John J. Parker, whose 1930 nomination to the Supreme Court had been rejected after the NAACP and labor unions mobilized substantial public opposition. Parker said that the party's "fundamental error" was to assume that "a political party is a mere private aggregation of individuals, like a country club." Rather, though parties may once have been like private clubs, "with the passage of the years, political parties have become in effect state institutions, governmental agencies though which sovereign power is exercised by the people."[31]

South Carolina was not done, though. The Democratic party's 1948 state convention adopted a new set of membership rules. Only whites could be members, but African-Americans could vote in the primary. Unlike white members, however, African-Americans had to swear that they supported states' rights and segregation and opposed a federal fair employment law. Marshall's advisers gave him several theories to use in a new lawsuit: that the oath unreasonably restricted the right to vote because it referred to such controversial issues, or that the oath's history showed that it was race based. Waring asked Marshall to sift through the complaints against the new rules. Marshall arrived in South Carolina and filed a

lawsuit on July 8, 1948, to block exclusion of African-Americans from the scheduled August primary. Judge Waring held a hearing on July 16, simultaneously with
the Democratic national convention, where Dixiecrats supporting South Carolina
governor Strom Thurmond walked out. At the outset, Judge Waring dismissed
claims against three county chairmen who, defying the convention's rules, continued to enroll African-Americans. "I'm glad to see," he said, "that some of our
citizens realize that this country is an American country; that it is not a country of
persecution."[32]

The only real issue at the hearing was a technical one: did the NAACP wait too
long after the May convention to file a challenge to the August primary? Marshall
argued that newspaper reports indicated that the oath's revision had been under
active consideration, and that it seemed possible that "the good people in the party
would prevail."[33]

Judge Waring, not surprisingly, found the case "narrow" and easy. The prior
South Carolina case showed that the Democratic party was not simply a private
club and necessarily held that African-Americans had to be allowed to participate
in primaries on the same terms as whites. Yet the "loyalty oath" imposed a requirement on African-Americans not imposed on whites. He called the oath "another
attempt to evade the American principle of allowing all persons to freely exercise
the suffrage." For him, requiring potential voters to pledge to support the party
convention's positions was "a flagrant disregard of the rights of Americans to
exercise their own views and opinions in the choice of representatives in their
national government." Waring was as distressed at the idea of an oath to the party
as he was at the discriminatory use of the oath: "[We have not] as yet come to a pass
where a group of party officials, in violation of basic American rights, can prescribe
oaths, methods and a code of thought for voters." According to Waring, because
the Democratic party was performing a public function, it could not discriminate
on the basis of race in any way: "It is time that either the present officials of the
Party, or such as may be in the future chosen, realize that the people of the United
States expect them to follow the American way of elections."[34]

Marshall prepared for the oral argument in the court of appeals by distilling
nine pages of typed memoranda and four pages of notes for the district court
argument down to a single page, in which he stressed that what mattered was that
the primary was "determinative of election within [the] meaning of [the] Constitution," and that the state party had "deliberately flaunted" the prior decision.
Marshall argued that the "law as to primary elections" and the "law as to racial
distinctions in governmental functions" taken together "make the firm basis
for . . . this case." Again Judge Waring's decision was affirmed, with Judge
Parker writing a relatively brief opinion saying that the oath tried "to do by
indirection that which we held . . . they could not do."[35]

The white primary was on its last legs after the South Carolina cases, but in one
part of Texas it staggered on. The Jaybird political association was formed in 1888–
89 in Fort Bend County to challenge African-American political dominance. The
Jaybirds eventually became the main faction in the county's Democratic party. Its
membership had always been limited to white voters, but all registered whites in

the county were automatically members. The Jaybird association ran a primary, usually in May, and selected a candidate to run in the Democratic party primary, usually in July. And the Jaybird candidate ordinarily was unopposed in the Democratic primary and in the general election. The Jaybird case posed in stark form the conflict implicit in the South Carolina cases. Throughout the campaign against the white primary, the judges—if not the NAACP's lawyers—always believed that purely private political associations could discriminate in membership on the basis of race, religion, or anything else. As they saw it, that was what distinguished private associations from each other. The Jaybirds were an almost pure form of private association; unlike the South Carolina Democratic party, the Jaybirds conducted their "preprimary" well before the Supreme Court had cast doubt on the white primary, and the Jaybirds could readily be described as a "faction" or voluntary association within the Democratic party. Yet in practice the Jaybirds' endorsement of a candidate ensured his election.[36]

When the Jaybirds were challenged, Marshall and Houston did not think the case could be won. In the trial court, Judge Thomas Kennerly, who Marshall called "the fatherly type and not by any stretch of the imagination . . . antagonistic to Negro counsel or to the problem" of white primaries, held that *Smith v. Allwright* covered the Jaybirds. The court of appeals reversed. When the case reached the Supreme Court, the justices understood the problem's difficulty. Justice Jackson's law clerk, William Rehnquist, reported that several clerks "began screaming as soon as they saw this that 'Now we can show those damn southerners,' etc." Rehnquist told Jackson that he took "a dim view of this pathological search for discrimination, a la Walter White, Black, [and] Douglas. . . ." He "over-compensate[d]" for his "feeling that the decision is probably right to a lawyer, rather than a crusader," by recommending that Jackson vote to grant review. Despite Rehnquist's recommendation, Jackson voted to deny review. The justices held the case for over a month before they decided by a vote of four to three to grant review; Justice Frankfurter, who had great difficulty with the case, initially wanted to dismiss it because the election had already occurred.[37]

After the case was argued, the justices struggled to develop a theory for reversing the court of appeals. A first vote showed the justices divided five to four, with a majority voting to allow the Jaybird primary. Immediately after that vote, Justice Frankfurter abandoned the majority, perhaps because he could not bring himself to be the decisive vote upholding a white primary. Frankfurter's switch created a narrow majority against the Jaybirds. In the end, only Justice Sherman Minton firmly believed that the Jaybirds were a purely private association. Chief Justice Vinson told his colleagues that, even though the Jaybirds were "no Johnny come lately," he "recognize[d the] implications" if the Court said that the Jaybird primary was not state action. For Justice Black, the Court could not be "helpless when we see the equal protection of laws violated," and suggested that the Court could rely on the fact that Jaybird officials happened to be county officers as well. Like Black, Justice Burton believed that the "Constitution is interested in substance." Justice Clark said that the primary "was the only entrance to the Democratic primary." Justice Reed said that he found the arguments either way "unanswerable," but voted to reverse because the "future of [the] South depends on negro voting." Justice Jackson expressed an ambivalence that characterized much of his confrontation with the question of race and the Constitution, saying that the state could not rig elections, and that the Jaybirds' action "has some nastiness in it," but also that the Constitution did not "deprive groups from associating themselves on color, nationalistic or religious lines." He found the Jaybirds' history of success irrelevant, and suggested that Congress ought to outlaw restrictive primary elections.[38]

Most justices realized that the state action question was legally difficult, and yet most also realized that the Court ought not put the stamp of approval on the Jaybirds' activities. Despite the fact that Vinson, Jackson, and Reed initially voted to affirm the court of appeals, they may well have heaved a sigh of relief when Frankfurter's vote change meant that the Court would not rule in favor of what they all understood to be a white primary.

The Court's difficulties continued as opinions circulated. Justice Black drafted an opinion joined by Justices Douglas and Burton. Explicitly relying on Judge Parker's decisions in the South Carolina cases, Justice Black rejected as "formalistic" the claim that the Jaybirds were "a mere private group." For him, the Constitution prohibited discrimination in "any election in which public issues are decided or public officials selected." The Jaybird election was "the only election that [had] counted" for more than fifty years, and the Democratic primary and general elections had become "no more than the perfunctory ratifiers of the choice that [had] already been made." As a result, the Jaybird primary had "become an integral part, indeed the only effective part, of the elective process that determine[d] who shall rule and govern. . . ." Because the "effect of the whole procedure" was to "strip Negroes of every vestige of influence in selecting the officials who control the local county matters," it violated the Constitution.[39]

Justice Frankfurter was concerned about the remedy this analysis implied. If the Jaybirds were indeed the effective governing party, *Smith v. Allwright* and the South Carolina cases might imply that the association had to enroll African-American members. Frankfurter believed that the Court could rid the county of the Jaybird "stranglehold" by finding that the Jaybirds had effectively "defeat[ed] the law of Texas regulating primaries," and that state election officials could not "aid in this subversion of the State's official scheme." By enjoining the Jaybird preprimary, the federal courts would avoid the details of running a primary or a political faction.

Jackson continued to be plagued by doubt. After Jackson indicated that he might want to dissent, Rehnquist suggested that a dissent should point out that Black's opinion "simply assumes the whole point in issue." Rehnquist continued, using language typical of a Jackson opinion, "Surely the justices of this Court do not sit here to ruthlessly frustrate results which they consider undesirable, regardless of the wording of the Constitution." To Rehnquist, Frankfurter's approach relied on "the rather skimpy support" for state action that flowed from the mere fact that "the county election officials voted in the Jaybird primary!" After all, if *that* was the state action, the remedy should be to enjoin those officials from voting in the election, not to enjoin the election. Rehnquist said that it was important to have "your ideas" stated. These ideas were that "[i]t is about time the Court faced

the fact that the white people on [*sic*] the South don't like the colored people."
Although, Rehnquist wrote, the Constitution bars them from using state action to
"effect[ ] this dislike," it "most assuredly did not appoint the Court as a sociological
watchdog to rear up every time private discrimination raises its admittedly ugly
head." Apparently referring to the battle over the Court during the New Deal,
Rehnquist imputed to Jackson the point that "[l]iberals should be the first to
realize . . . that it does not do to push blindly through towards one constitutional
goal without paying attention to other equally desirable values that are being
trampled on in the process." Jackson drafted a dissent. Echoing a phrase in Rehnquist's memorandum, the draft said that the Court should not read "sociological
views into constitutional law." Then, two weeks later, Jackson drafted a concurring opinion saying that the Jaybirds "appear[ ] in fact to have merged or taken over
the Democratic Party of its locality." Finding neither draft satisfactory, Jackson
joined Justice Clark's opinion two days later.[40]

Clark's opinion found that the Jaybirds were "part and parcel" of the Democratic party, and that the Democratic primary and the general election, though
"nominally open" to African-Americans, involved "empty vote[s] cast after the real
decisions are made." The Jaybirds, as "the decisive power in the county's recognized electoral process," had "take[n] on those attributes of government which
draw the Constitution's safeguards into play." Justice Minton, the only dissenter,
noted acerbically to Jackson that "When the Jaybird opinion comes down, there
may be some question as to which election returns the Court follows! It will be
damn clear they aren't following any law."[41]

Early in the Jaybird litigation, Marshall received an obituary notice for the Jaybird's founder, and wrote the sender that he agreed that "he just couldn't take it."
Yet, although the Jaybird decision concluded the white primary campaign, the
case's impact was both greater and smaller than the justices might have thought as
they worked to decide it. Frankfurter's concern about devising a remedy for a
constitutional violation that was effective yet did not involve the federal courts in
close supervision of local institutions came up again as he thought about the school
desegregation cases; his concerns there affected the decision's timing and, perhaps, its substance.

In addition, Frankfurter's concern about federal judicial supervision of state
elections played an important role in limiting the effectiveness of the overall
litigation against voting discrimination. The alternative to the white primary was
the Mississippi plan, in which apparently neutral rules disfranchised almost all
African-Americans and relatively few whites. Near the turn of the century, the
Supreme Court upheld the Mississippi plan. In *Williams v. Mississippi* it held that
the plan did not violate the Constitution because it did not specifically say that
whites and African-Americans would be treated differently, and because the challengers had not shown that it was administered in a biased way. A few years later,
Giles v. Harris rejected a challenge based on biased administration. Justice Oliver
Wendell Holmes's opinion for the Court had one enduring element. Holmes suggested that, given the depth of feeling about African-American disfranchisement,

the federal courts could not effectively implement a decree purporting to order that African-Americans be allowed to vote.[42]

Holmes put his misgivings in terms of the courts' limited ability to accomplish what the plaintiffs sought. By the late 1940s, the NAACP was in a position to attempt to challenge Mississippi-plan exclusions, but Marshall continued to be met with the argument that "the Federal Court should not have to 'police' the actions of election officials . . . as to each registrant." His initial challenge to "neutral" registration rules succeeded. The effort was relatively novel for the NAACP, however, and a more extensive campaign would have required Marshall and his staff to develop new approaches to voting litigation. The staff of the Legal Defense Fund had other priorities in the late 1940s and early 1950s, and litigation challenges to voting discrimination rather quickly gave way to lobbying efforts that, because of the LDF's tax-exempt status, could not involve the lawyers.

Alabama maintained white supremacy in part through the white primary, but *Smith v. Allwright* made that technique useless. Like many states, Alabama required voter literacy, which excluded disproportionate numbers of African-Americans because of the inadequacies of the state's segregated education system. In 1945, the state's Democratic party, acting through state senator E. C. Boswell, added a requirement that voters not only be able to read a provision of the Constitution but also "understand" it. The proponents knew that the "understanding" requirement would give voter registrars discretion to decide who satisfied the requirement. Its opponents, though, saw that the requirement could be used to perpetuate local political machines, which might want to disfranchise white political opponents as well as all African-Americans. In general, more progressive Democrats, who supported the social welfare programs of the New Deal, believed the Boswell amendment would weaken their position within the state party. Despite a forceful campaign against the Boswell amendment organized by African-Americans, labor union leaders, and other nationally oriented Democrats, Alabama's voters approved it on November 5, 1946, by a margin of approximately 54 percent to 46 percent.[43]

The next day Marshall wrote Bob Ming that a suit challenging the Boswell amendment was "inevitable." Marshall and Motley developed a theory based on *Yick Wo v. Hopkins.* Under *Yick Wo,* biased administration would be unconstitutional, but the NAACP wanted to eliminate the requirement entirely. Challenging biased administration would call for inquiries in each county about how local registrars handled the "understanding" requirement, and such inquiries were beyond the NAACP's capacity in the deep South. The theory Marshall and Motley developed pushed the analysis of *Yick Wo* back one step, and focused on the laws giving registrars discretion. On this theory, unconstitutional discrimination occurred because the legislature gave registrars unconstrained power.[44]

Although the theory was in place and the national office ready to go by September 1947, Marshall, who almost always waited for indications of local enthusiasm before he would begin a lawsuit, found that Alabama's African-Americans were not ready. Part of the difficulty arose from political and organizational rivalry between African-American groups in Birmingham and Mobile. Arthur Shores, the

NAACP's cooperating attorney in Birmingham, could not locate a plaintiff, and had to be "very careful in order not to have it appear that they are trying to stir up litigation." After prodding from Marshall, Shores found a plaintiff, only to discover that the NAACP's proposed lawsuit was preempted by one filed in Mobile in March 1948 and supported by the Chicago branch of the ACLU acting through George Leighton, an African-American Chicago attorney. Leighton offered to co-ordinate this lawsuit with Marshall and the NAACP, but other organizational difficulties intervened. The Mobile suit was nominally sponsored by the Voters and Veterans Association, a local group formed largely in opposition to what its members believed was the excessively cautious approach of the Mobile NAACP branch. Leighton recognized that the VVA lacked the resources to support complex litigation and urged the NAACP national office to ask the Mobile branch to take over, allowing the case to be handled locally rather than from Chicago. Leighton believed that this transfer could occur with no organizational competition.[45]

Leighton's suggestion, however well intentioned, failed to take into account the rules and the internal politics of the NAACP, which required approval by the state conference of branches. The conference was unsympathetic with the VVA, and resisted. Marshall intervened to stop "needless bickering" impeding the lawsuit's progress. Eventually, despite the "deadlock" in Mobile, the attorneys in Chicago and New York worked out an informal agreement to share research. Marshall agreed to drop the NAACP's Birmingham lawsuit and work with Leighton to appeal the Mobile case to the Supreme Court. Unfortunately, the leaders of the VVA did not understand the nature of the working relationship, and directed Leighton to refuse to cooperate. Marshall acknowledged that the VVA, as Leighton's client, had the power to limit Leighton's NAACP contacts, but insisted that the NAACP would continue with its Birmingham lawsuit and would try to file a Supreme Court *amicus* brief, even if the VVA refused to give permission to file.[46]

The trial court in the Mobile case found the Boswell amendment unconstitutional. Speaking through Judge Clarence Mullins, the court—composed of three judges because of a special statute—found that registrars had indeed administered the "understanding" requirement in a discriminatory way, but it went beyond that simple application of *Yick Wo* to accept the theory Marshall and Motley had developed. Judge Mullins wrote that the word "understand" did not "furnish a reasonable standard" but was "so ambiguous, uncertain, and indefinite in meaning" that it gave registrars "arbitrary power to register or to refuse to register whomever they please." He pointed out that controversies among Supreme Court justices demonstrated how difficult it was to determine what a proper "understanding" of the Constitution was. Only after finding that "understand" was unconstitutionally ambiguous did Judge Mullins write about the political context of the Boswell amendment, and when he did he stressed that it was part of an effort "to make the Democratic Party in Alabama the 'White Man's Party'" after *Smith v. Allwright*. This showed that the Boswell amendment, even though it did not mention race directly, was in fact an effort to disfranchise African-Americans. The opinion concluded: "We cannot ignore the impact of the Boswell Amendment upon Negro citizens because it avoids mention of race or color; 'To do this would be to shut our eyes to what all others than we can see and understand.'"[47]

The special statute setting up three-judge courts required that appeals be taken directly to the Supreme Court, which, without hearing oral argument, affirmed the trial court. African-American registration in Alabama did not increase dramatically, however, because the state took Judge Mullins's hint and had the justices of the state's supreme court draft a complex standardized test to determine a voter's "understanding" of the Constitution. As a result, African-Americans could only use the basic *Yick Wo* theory of biased administration, unsuitable for a general challenge to disfranchisement. In addition, internal dissension in Alabama may have discouraged Marshall from pursuing further voting cases. After the Supreme Court decision, Marshall wrote the head of the VVA that they should "bury [their] personal feelings" and cooperate, but he also wrote an indignant letter to Leighton saying that he was shocked to learn that Leighton had criticized the NAACP from the litigation's outset. Leighton wrote a formal reply, which only annoyed Marshall more. Marshall ended the correspondence saying, "I am not interested in personalities," but in "broad general principles." He would not, he said, "use his own personal vindictiveness against the principles for which we are striving." He had been prepared to believe that Leighton was blameless in the conflict but, he concluded, Leighton's letter "has almost completely changed my mind."[48]

By the mid-1950s, the NAACP had won substantially all its challenges to exclusion of African-Americans from voting. Yet, rather little had changed in the actual patterns of voting in the South. African-American registration increased after *Smith v. Allwright,* but the rate of increase had slowed, and the proportion of registered African-Americans remained substantially below the proportion of whites. The most fundamental reason was that exclusion of African-Americans from voting rested on so much more than legal restrictions that the legal challenge could have little effect. The legal challenge did not reach statutes imposing qualifications for voting such as literacy tests or the payment of poll taxes, which were applied even-handedly to African-Americans and whites but which had a much greater impact on African-Americans. And, though the NAACP's legal strategy reached certain types of private discrimination, it did not reach another, perhaps more important type: the use of terror to intimidate African-Americans. Harry Moore, the president of the Florida NAACP conference of branches, organized a large-scale and rather successful voter registration drive in 1950. On Christmas Eve 1951, he and his wife were killed by a bomb exploding at their house; Walter White found that several whites had said that they "thought too many Negroes were getting 'funny ideas' like Harry T. Moore." Marshall concluded that all he could do in similar cases was take them to the FBI.[49] Marshall and the NAACP legal staff had done what they could to increase the level of African-American voting in the South, but they could not do nearly enough to make a substantial difference.

8

"Passing Through a Transition"
Education Cases, 1939–1945

Attacking the separate but equal doctrine of *Plessy v. Ferguson* in education was probably the center of the NAACP's efforts. Achieving voting rights and eliminating kangaroo courts were important, of course, but segregated education was different. Every African-American in the South was subjected to segregated education in grossly inadequate schools. Segregated schools were the central symbol of African-American subordination, a visible and daily demonstration to children as they were growing up that whites did not consider them fit to associate with. Although it was not inevitable that Marshall's triumph came in cases challenging segregated education, it was certainly appropriate.

From 1935 to 1950, the NAACP's lawyers attacked unequal salaries for school teachers and challenged segregated universities. By the late 1940s they were confident that the time had come for a broader attack on segregation. As they saw it, the salary and university cases were successes, and their attachment to the Constitution led them to believe that, once they persuaded the courts that school segregation was unconstitutional, desegregation would also succeed. In the event, their success was limited by others in "Judge and Company." The Supreme Court's justices were unwilling to order immediate desegregation, and the NAACP's opponents evaded the Supreme Court's mandate and, ultimately, simply resisted the Court's interpretation of the Constitution.

Until the mid-1940s, Marshall's education cases dealt primarily with teachers' salaries. They had a number of attractions. African-American teachers provided a relatively large pool of potential plaintiffs; as Marshall's experience showed, if one teacher was fired or became nervous about fighting the school board, another teacher might well step forward. Teachers were found everywhere in the South, and during World War II, the large number of female teachers provided a stable source of potential plaintiffs; in voting or university cases, a male plaintiff might be drafted. Seeking salary increases, the teachers had reasonably strong incentives to make winning the cases their primary concern and to put aside personality conflicts and political differences that could overwhelm the litigation effort in cases,

116

like the white primary cases, with less tangible benefits. Defendants put up less resistance in salary cases, because only money, not the symbolism of segregation, was at stake. And, at least for a while, these were winnable cases; salary differences were gross and sometimes rested on salary schedules explicitly setting lower rates for African-American teachers than for whites.

By 1945, though, salary litigation had become less attractive. The NAACP had won many suits in major cities; continuing the program meant extending it to a multitude of small rural school districts, consuming the organization's resources while providing relatively small payoffs to teachers or the NAACP. The litigation did increase the cost of maintaining a dual system, but not so much that segregation became a severe financial burden; it cost Maryland only $412,000 in 1941 to equalize salaries throughout the state. School boards managed to limit even the financial consequences by switching from race-based payment schedules to "merit" pay systems that "happened" to pay almost all African-American teachers much less than almost all white teachers. If the program of litigating to eliminate Jim Crow was to continue, some other target had to be found. The target turned out to be segregated schools, but Marshall and his colleagues had to prepare the ground.[1]

In 1941 the United States Office of Education reported that it would cost the South about $26 million a year to equalize teachers' salaries, and another $9 million to equalize student-teacher ratios in black and white schools. African-American teachers would get substantial pay raises, but the NAACP had to help organize them for action. Sometimes the cases went smoothly, as most had in Maryland. In Louisville, Kentucky, teachers asked for guidance in early 1938. It took until the middle of the next year to set up the committee of teachers that would handle the case, but after that the case was simple. The city's salary schedule gave African-American teachers 85 percent of what white teachers with equivalent training and responsibilities got. In January 1941, the school board voted to equalize salaries, which occurred in September without a hitch.[2]

Responding to Walter White's concern that the teachers were not doing enough for themselves, Marshall pointed out that their national organization was "just about broke," and he believed that the teachers had given the NAACP "marvelous cooperation" in Maryland. He advised White to stress "that we are passing through a transition in our fight and that during this time we must not only increase our activity . . . but must make plans to meet the other movements by these school boards to circumvent the decisions."[3]

Marshall had another concern. White wanted the teachers' association to "promise to make contributions to the N.A.A.C.P. on condition that we file the case for them." Marshall thought that White's idea was "clearly within the statutes forbidding the solicitation of legal business" and might open the NAACP up to charges of practicing law without a license: "All of the states in the South are convinced that they cannot defeat these cases in court and are looking for any means at all to stop them."[4]

These exchanges identified the themes pervading the salary litigation. Unlike the housing and voting cases, the salary cases rested on a simple legal theory. But school boards attempted to evade their responsibility, developing ingenious substitutes for salary schedules or getting the teachers to accept less than they could win in court. These evasions undermined the teachers' confidence in the NAACP, which Marshall then had to retrieve through personal contacts.

In Norfolk, for example, after the court of appeals ruled in favor of Melvin Alston, P. B. Young, the prominent publisher of the African-American newspaper the *Journal and Guide,* started dealing with the school board. As one observer put it, "The NAACP met with the judge during the day, Mr. P. B. met with white folks at night, unraveled the agreement, and rewrote it to his own satisfaction." Young, a "pragmatic" but "conservative militant," tried to persuade Alston to accept a "settlement" to promote "good race relations." Marshall did not believe Young's explanation that Young was getting the Norfolk authorities to persuade their counterparts elsewhere in Virginia to "straighten out this problem." According to Marshall, Young exploded in anger, saying that the Norfolk teachers had accepted the compromise; Marshall replied by calling Young a liar. Marshall then organized a mass meeting of Norfolk's teachers, but he failed to persuade them to repudiate Young. Marshall called their action "the most disgraceful termination of any case involving Negroes in recent years," and thought about withdrawing from Virginia salary cases entirely. At another meeting a few weeks later, Marshall "took off the gloves," called Young's deal a "backdoor" arrangement, and asked the teachers to appoint a committee to deal with the school board. When Young's son called Marshall a liar, Marshall walked out. After all this turmoil, the teachers came back into the fold, accepting a settlement Marshall prepared. At the conclusion of the episode, Marshall felt compelled to explain in detail why he could not attend a testimonial dinner in Norfolk to offset "discussion . . . that we are 'sore' about the case." Sore Marshall could be, though, at least in private. Writing about a Richmond case, Marshall said, "I personally am sick and tired of having people constantly attempt to use us as a scapegoat when they themselves have brought on the whole situation."[5]

Some of Marshall's passing comments indicate another difficulty: finding local lawyers to work with. He asked the head of the Virginia association of African-American teachers to put his law school classmate Oliver Hill on their program in 1940. The appearance would, Marshall wrote, help Hill build his practice and "would bolster the courage of the teachers to realize that they have an attorney in Virginia on hand at all times for whatever problems which might come up." Marshall asked Roy Wilkins to help him to "continue [Hill's] good will" because, after "tremendous difficulties" with other lawyers, "at last we have one we can work with."[6]

Settlements continued to raise problems. School boards preferred to settle cases by promising to equalize salaries if the teachers dropped their suits. From a lawyer's point of view, this left the teachers with an unenforceable promise. As Marshall wrote, criticizing a teachers' group that had accepted such a promise, "You have agreed that the case is to be dismissed. As soon as this is done the school board can rescind their action on the next day and you will be in the same position you were before the case was filed." Marshall insisted that cases be settled with court orders the boards had to comply with. The second problem with settlements was the time they set for equalizing salaries. Boards had to find the money to raise the salaries, and sometimes had to get voter approval of a tax increase or bond issue. But, Marshall also knew, "the longer this equalization is spread out the more danger there is of future difficulties. It tends to become a continuing irritant. It is much better to get it over once and for all." Marshall strove, usually successfully, to get boards to equalize salaries in no more than two years.[7]

Sometimes the cases simply limped along. Although teachers in Alabama indicated interest in salary cases as early as 1938, the first decree in the state was issued seven years later. It took a couple of years to locate a plaintiff. Although Arthur Shores in Birmingham believed that equalization was "virtually assured," he still had to file a lawsuit in March 1942. The plaintiff was drafted in May and the case then sat around for two more years. Finally, in October 1944, two and a half years after the case began, the court scheduled a pretrial conference. Just before trial in April 1945, the parties settled the case, with equalization scheduled for the fall. Though the litigation was more protracted in Alabama than elsewhere, delay was characteristic. Teachers, unfamiliar with litigation's slow pace, often were confused by it. After all, they had gone into the cases enthusiastically, expecting to see larger paychecks soon. Sometimes they criticized the lawyers for putting up with delays. And sometimes they were correct, at least in that local lawyers felt less urgency about the cases than the teachers, while Marshall, in New York, could do little more than nurse the cases along at long distance. Marshall tried to placate teachers and local lawyers, telling one lawyer that criticism was part of the job of working for "the entire progress of the race."[8]

Marshall was deeply involved in Louisiana salary cases, because he could combine trips to New Orleans with trips to Texas, where the voting cases were being brought. In New Orleans, divisions within the local NAACP branch led the teachers to ask Donald Jones, the editor of a local African-American newspaper, to get the national office to act. Jones thought that "our teachers are on the whole complacent, and some months of pounding will be necessary before they are ready to stiffen for the fight." Marshall responded, as he had replied to White, "we dislike the idea of our taking the initiative." Precisely because he had to rely on local initiative, Marshall found the case developing slowly. In March 1941 he went to New Orleans, and in May a lawsuit was filed. By the end of the year, Marshall was impatient. He wrote the cooperating attorney, A. P. Tureaud, "Just as soon as the local authorities are willing to 'talk turkey,' let me know and I will arrange to come down and close the deal." A month later he wrote Tureaud that the case "has been hanging fire long enough," and asked Tureaud to talk to the trial judge "personally." Tureaud reported that he had prodded Judge Wayne Borah to get the case moving. Still, nothing happened until Tureaud and the teachers offered to settle the case with equalization to occur in two years. The board responded by proposing a five-year schedule. Tureaud, less familiar with salary litigation than Marshall, was inclined to accept the board's proposal, but Marshall found Tureaud's position "alarming." Eventually the board accepted the two-year proposal.[9]

The most important salary case arose in Little Rock. In August 1941, teachers pledged to raise $150 each month to support a lawsuit, and in December they filed a petition with the school board asking for equalization within three years. The teachers were so eager that Marshall tried to restrain them. He recommended that they refrain from filing a lawsuit until they had received contracts for the 1942–43 academic year, but the teachers replied that delay would injure the cause. In late February, when the lawsuit was filed, Marshall was in Little Rock on his way to the Lyons trial in Oklahoma. "Boy," he wrote Roy Wilkins, "these southern teachers have acquired brand new backbones." In September, Marshall returned to Little Rock, this time on his way to the Adams-Bordenave trial in Louisiana, and took depositions of a number of school-board witnesses. In questioning the superintendent, Marshall showed that the board had adopted a race-based "bonus" system: teachers were evaluated and then awarded $3.00 for each point if they were white and half that if they were African-American. He also got the superintendent to admit that the board really was trying to maintain the status quo.[10]

At the depositions, Marshall found that "the other side really means business," and was using "top flight lawyers" who were determined to fight. Their basic strategy was to deny that the board had a salary schedule at all, and to argue that it relied on merit ratings. Their "trump card," to Marshall, was a merit rating sheet for 1941, which showed, as Marshall put it, that all the African-American teachers were "lousy." Still, Marshall thought that he could make some headway by pointing out that new white teachers were paid between $810 and $875, while new African-American teachers were paid almost $200 less. At the conclusion of the five-day trial in October 1943, Marshall called it "one of the hardest cases so far and we are all quite tired of it." Because he had been unable to establish that the school board used a salary schedule, Marshall doubted that the teachers would win. The trial judge did not rule until January 1944, a delay that Marshall called "killing," and then rejected the teachers' claim. According to Milton Konvitz, the judge had "covered his tracks very thoroughly" by relying heavily on how the witnesses appeared as they testified to support his factual determinations.[11]

While the NAACP's appeal was pending, the school board voted to narrow the gaps in salaries, and offered to equalize salaries at the hiring stage while retaining a merit system, including an assessment of "character," afterwards. Marshall replied that he could not even suggest dismissing the case unless the board came up with a satisfactory salary schedule. Although he was "not as confident about the outcome of the case" as one of the local attorneys, Marshall prepared the appeal meticulously. He annotated the trial transcript in detail, pulling together scattered bits of testimony to show that the board really did discriminate in setting salaries. His argument persuaded the court of appeals that the trial judge's factual determinations were "clearly erroneous." The appellate court was most impressed by the "bonus" payments, finding that giving less per point to African-Americans fatally undercut the board's claim that its decisions rested on an unbiased merit pay system.[12]

Marshall had been worried about merit pay systems almost from the beginning. He understood that they could be used "in an effort to circumvent" *Alston,* and that the only way to challenge a merit pay system would be to show that it was almost a salary gerrymander. But even courts that might have been sympathetic to claims of simple discrimination were reluctant to override merit pay systems. If the merit pay system was not a total gerrymander, little could be done. In South Carolina, for example, the state adopted a system under which 90 percent of the white teachers got the highest ratings, compared with only 27 percent of the African-American teachers; the system stayed in place for decades. Even more dramatic, a trial judge in a Tampa case upheld a merit system placing 84 percent of white teachers in the highest group and only 1 percent in the lowest, compared with 80 percent of the African-American teachers in the lowest and only 6 percent in the highest. This, the judge said, resulted from a "fair and conscientious effort" to apply the merit criteria. [13]

The final blow came in a Miami case. Teachers hired a white lawyer who copied the NAACP's pleadings but otherwise did not cooperate with Marshall. The lawyer, according to Marshall, "did not put on any witnesses" but "gave the court a chance to really go to town on rating." The court of appeals, covering the deep South, concluded, "Where all rating is on an individual basis, it is impossible that there should be a class discrimination" except when mistakes were made. Marshall immediately understood that this decision was a "real set back" that would "really hurt." The court's broad language "can be used against us in all of our other cases." [14]

In mid-1943, Marshall wrote a memorandum saying that salary cases were pending in eleven states. The "important" cases he listed were those in Birmingham, Little Rock, Tampa, Palm Beach, Miami, Atlanta, and Dallas. Six months later he reported thirty-one cases pending in twelve states; most were in Maryland, Florida, and Virginia. At the end of 1946, Robert Carter suggested that Walter White say in a speech that "[t]he teachers' salary fight is now about over." And, in a sense, it was. The NAACP had won cases in major cities, and might be able to extend those victories to some other cities. Responding to the decisions, some school boards equalized salaries without litigation. Salaries for African-American teachers increased from about 55 percent of white salaries to about 65 percent. Yet, once school boards understood how to use merit pay systems, the potential for further equalization was limited. In addition, the NAACP's limited resources meant that it had to concentrate on larger cities; rural school boards could continue to discriminate, knowing that they faced a small chance of being sued. Even in Virginia, Marshall had to prod the teachers in 1945 to "make plans to clean up the educational system" once Oliver Hill returned to practice after his military service. The strategy of "compelling local school officials . . . to pay for continued maintenance of the 'luxury' of segregation" in elementary and secondary schools appeared to have reached its limit. Segregated schools themselves had to become the main target. [15]

Marshall and the NAACP pursued salary litigation simultaneously with challenges to segregated universities, all in preparation for the broader attack on segregated education as a whole. Marshall had desegregated the University of Maryland Law School in 1935. Houston followed up by bringing a similar suit in Missouri. Lloyd Gaines, the president of the senior class at Lincoln University in Missouri, wanted to go to law school. He applied to the state university, which offered to give him a scholarship to attend law school in Iowa or elsewhere or to open a law school for African-Americans at Lincoln itself. From a litigator's point a view, the second option opened up a new route to attack the separate but equal doctrine. Houston, intimately familiar with law schools, understood that a state could not create from scratch a new law school that was truly equal to a long-established one. He believed that the claim of equality thus would be easier to challenge here than in elementary or secondary schools. Then, if the cases came out right, the NAACP could use the concept of equality emerging from law school cases to challenge inequality in elementary and secondary schools.[16]

With the plaintiff and the concepts in hand, Houston sued. Marshall suggested that Houston revise his brief to "make [his] legal position perfectly clear" and to "include the necessary social argument." When the case reached the Supreme Court, Houston got his victory. In an opinion by Chief Justice Charles Evans Hughes, the Court adopted the reasoning in the Murray case. Missouri had to provide a legal education for Gaines in one of its own schools. As Maryland had, it could desegregate the state law school. Or, Hughes said, it could open a segregated law school at Lincoln, although a mere promise was not enough; the state had to have a firm timetable so that Gaines could get the legal education he sought for himself.[17]

Missouri took up Hughes's suggestion. Its legislature appropriated $200,000 to expand graduate education at Lincoln. William Taylor, who as dean at Howard had objected to Houston's vision of legal education, was appointed dean of the new Lincoln law school in St. Louis. He hired three teachers and a librarian, and the school was located in a building with a hotel and movie theater. When the school opened in the fall of 1939, less than a year after the Supreme Court's decision, thirty students enrolled. Gaines, however, was not one of them. After spending a year getting a graduate degree at the University of Michigan, Gaines disappeared, and the NAACP was unable to locate him.[18]

From 1939 to 1945, Houston and Marshall struggled to keep the university challenges alive. Again in Missouri, Houston handled Lucille Bluford's case. Bluford, the managing editor of the Kansas City *Call*, wanted to get a graduate journalism degree at the state university. The journalism school there was one of the nation's best, which meant that the state's strategy of opening a new segregated school would be vulnerable to an attack as unequal. Despite valiant efforts, Bluford's lawsuits ended in failure. Bluford applied to the journalism program in August 1939. When she was told that Lincoln did not have a journalism program, Houston filed suit. The state courts dismissed the case, allowing the university authorities to propose to open a segregated journalism program in early 1941, which the courts regarded as the earliest opportunity. This would delay Bluford only two semesters, in their view. Yet by the time the state courts ruled, it was already July 1941, and the university claimed that it could not open a program until January or even September 1942. A program did open in early 1942, and enrolled fourteen students. Houston did not have the opportunity to challenge the program as unequal, though, because the university discovered another way to comply with the Gaines decision: Instead of operating separate programs for whites and African-

Americans, it closed the journalism program for whites, citing reduced demand during the war.[19]

Houston and Marshall continued to have problems with university cases. A case in Georgia with a plaintiff who, Marshall said, "deserves about five medals for having this much courage," nonetheless petered out. Although he would have liked to find a Kentucky case, because the state was "more or less civilized," Marshall decided against helping in the only case to come to the NAACP, because the applicant had graduated from an unaccredited school. One South Carolina case was completely inactive, and the plaintiff in another enlisted in the Army when he found that white employers would not hire him because of his involvement with the NAACP's litigation. Charles Eubanks, the plaintiff in the first Kentucky case the NAACP brought, suffered bouts of depression as the case lingered on; his feeling that the community did not support him was compounded when the Army rejected him and his wife divorced him. When Eubanks filed an affidavit saying that he no longer wanted to continue the case, it was dropped. Pauli Murray wanted to apply to graduate school in North Carolina, but Marshall discouraged her. Because she was a resident of New York, he said, the state might get around *Gaines* by saying that it had no constitutional duty to provide education to nonresidents. Murray suggested that the logic of *Gaines* meant that if North Carolina admitted nonresident whites, it had to admit nonresident African-Americans as well. Marshall, though, believed that this was an extension of *Gaines* that the NAACP should not push yet; he might have been concerned that, in bringing cases for nonresidents, the NAACP would make somewhat more credible the argument that it was a group of "outsiders" trying to disturb harmonious race relations in the South.[20]

By the fall of 1945, Marshall was "more than worried" about the progress of the attack on segregated university education. The cases would be "of tremendous importance" to the branches and were, he said, "the easiest cases to win." Marshall told Walter White, "We have the lawyers ready but we do not have the cases." The lawyers "have done everything they can do without being guilty of litigations," and, Marshall said, the time had come for the rest of the staff "to get our branches to work in this field." A few months later Marshall wrote a woman who had been trying to generate NAACP cases in Atlanta, "What do you think of the idea now being considered of filing cases simultaneously in Maryland, Virginia, Georgia, and Louisiana?" The scope of the challenge, he suggested, would put the "fear of God in the other side." His reversion to the Margold Report's vision of massive coordinated filings suggests that Marshall knew that the litigation needed new directions. The university cases seemed to have stalled, although returning veterans might provide a new source of plaintiffs. The salary cases, though successful, probably had reached the point of diminishing returns. Marshall convened a special legal conference in Atlanta on April 27 and 28, 1946, to discuss the situation.[21]

The discussions were wide ranging. Marshall summarized the first topic, about suing in state courts—which Tureaud said had "little regard for the civil rights of

Negroes"—or federal courts. Marshall concluded that the lawyers should be certain that they had no possibility of winning in the state courts, taking into account the problem of delay, before they tried to use the federal courts.[22]

Then, after hearing reports about pending cases, the lawyers turned to "equal facilities." Their discussion focused on graduate-school cases like *Gaines*—cases where state governments simply did not provide any facilities, much less equal ones. However, the lawyers did not distinguish between universities and secondary schools. Tureaud, for example, mentioned twelve parishes in Louisiana where there were no high schools for African-Americans, and Leon Ransom, though skeptical about using a *Gaines*-type theory in secondary school cases, did suggest that the theory might work "in urban areas where courses are not offered at all in Negro schools."[23]

The lawyers were much more troubled by the more prevalent problem of sheer inequality. First, it was "impossible to get anyone to apply to a white school." Then, Marshall said, even if someone applied, "judges will be uncooperative. . . . Where you sue to compel authorities to make the colored schools equal," he continued, "you get more cooperation." Yet, he said, if the lawsuits sought equalization, "you will get delays." Further complicating the picture was the issue of what sort of relief to seek. Hill proposed seeking injunctions "to restrain school boards from denying to Negroes because of race and color equal educational opportunities." When Ransom objected that this did not openly deal with material inequalities in education, Marshall and Hill replied that the remedy did allow them to "base your prayer on inferior accommodations." Even so, Ransom said, with Marshall's concurrence, that it would be hard to get a judge "to determine standards of equality," and Marshall presciently took the point further in saying that "federal judges will probably not particularize in the injunction in their fear of being forced to police the states." Ransom pressed his point: "[I]f you ask for equality in Negro schools, you would run into the difficulty that the court would not undertake to measure inequality and we would be forced to demand to go into white schools and prove specific inequalities." Marshall, trying to salvage something from the discussion, said that "the question of how to determine equality is a question which we may have to face in the future, but . . . it is not necessary for us to worry about it immediately as a legal problem."[24]

In one sense, the conference, like many that Marshall convened, was inconclusive. The lawyers had thrashed out many important legal questions, but they had not figured out what strategy to use, and their discussion floundered from point to point. In the end, the strategy would turn on how the courts responded to whatever cases the NAACP was able to bring.

In another sense, though, the conference reinvigorated the lawyers. It took place at a time when the lawyers had come to believe that they had played out the string on university and salary cases. According to Marshall, the lawyers ended up by agreeing to file a number of cases "as soon as possible"—university cases in Oklahoma, Texas, Louisiana, Tennessee, and South Carolina, and cases dealing with high schools in Louisiana, Arkansas, Florida, Maryland, and Virginia. Fewer cases than that were in fact filed, as Marshall probably expected from the outset.

The meeting was important as much for the boost it gave the lawyers as for any decisions that were made. Marshall expected that a lawsuit would be filed dealing with the University of Texas law school "within the next few weeks." That case provided the next building block in the challenge to separate but equal in education.[25]

9

To *"Determine the Future Course of Litigation"*
Making the Record on Segregated Universities

In 1945 Heman Marion ("Bill") Sweatt was a mail carrier in Houston. For several years he had been concerned about the postmaster's policy of barring African-Americans from being clerks, which meant that they could never become supervisors. Active in the postal workers' union, Sweatt worked with a local lawyer to develop a complaint against the postmaster. Sweatt's experience with discrimination and his sense that lawyers could help remedy it led him to decide to go to law school. He had graduated from college in 1934, after which he worked as a porter and then for a year as a teacher in Cleburne, Texas. In Houston, Sweatt became active in the NAACP, writing columns for the local African-American newspaper and, in 1944, delivering the principal speech at a rally celebrating National Negro Youth Week.[1]

Sweatt decided to apply to law school just as the NAACP was trying to locate plaintiffs to challenge segregated education in universities. As World War II wound to a close, the NAACP's lawyers began to think about their next steps in the attack on Jim Crow. After quickly deciding to focus on education and transportation, they worried about the implications of different strategies. In 1946 Robert Carter pressed Marshall and Hastie, the more experienced lawyers, to "make an all out attack on segregation," saying that they had "run up against something of a blank wall." According to Carter, Marshall believed that transportation cases should come first, because there "the question of social equality is least likely to be introduced to confuse the court's thinking." Carter and Hastie disagreed with that assessment. Carter thought that the gross inequities of separate but equal could be "best illustrated in a clear and understandable fashion" in school cases. Hastie argued that "any court will have the school problem in mind when it passes on transportation," so the NAACP "might as well look forward to the ultimate attack upon the school situation where inequalities are more glaring and the injury to the community is more apparent." Hastie disagreed with Carter, though, about making "the big legal push against segregation," because he was convinced that the Supreme Court would uphold it. He recommended pursuing the "painfully slow" litigation against segregation in higher education and urged "local attacks on unequal facilities." Marshall decided to put off a final decision until he had to, and concentrated on segregated universities.[2]

No one was enthusiastic about a limited challenge to segregation, though Marshall believed that a wise strategy might be to go somewhat more slowly. The May 1946 lawyers' conference in Atlanta demonstrated substantial support for the all-out attack. When Marshall drafted a policy statement about education cases the next year, he continued to seek to leave things open. The statement called *Sweatt* a "test case" to "determine the future course of litigation." Segregation was unconstitutional, according to Marshall's statement, because "there is no scientific basis for racial classification," because segregation was "intended . . . to set up a system of dual citizenship," and because "it is impossible to have equality in a segregated school system." Merging the approaches advocated by the lawyers in Atlanta, Marshall proposed two forms of attack in elementary and secondary school cases. One would resemble the university cases and seek desegregation; the other would point out inequalities and seek orders requiring that the authorities stop discriminating. The latter, he said, would "keep our position clear" that "we do not consider segregation statutes legal."[3]

Many found Marshall's point about the remedy he would seek in elementary and secondary school cases too subtle. NAACP members in Texas and South Carolina suggested that they could get authorities to upgrade segregated schools and remain within the boundaries of NAACP policy. Even Carter said that Marshall's policy fell "short of the goals you have set." Marshall saw the policy differently. For him, the NAACP should never say to school boards that taking "separate but equal" seriously was enough. He understood that judges and school boards might respond to cases showing inequalities and demanding an end to discrimination by continuing to segregate the schools and attempting to eliminate the grossest forms of discrimination in supplies, buildings, and the like. But, by leaving it to the defendants and the courts to select the response, Marshall believed that his strategy allowed the NAACP to assert that it never "admit[ted] the validity of segregation statutes" and never sought "fair" enforcement of segregation statutes. Rather, it "would be constantly hitting at segregation."[4]

As Marshall saw it, "segregation and discrimination are one"; lawsuits aimed at eliminating discrimination ultimately aimed at segregation itself. The NAACP's Board of Directors clarified the position in 1948, expressing its "unalterabl[e] oppos[ition] to segregation in any form" by stating that it "will not undertake any case or cooperate in any case which recognizes or purports to recognize the validity of segregation statutes," nor would it take part in "any case which has as its direct purpose the establishment of segregated public facilities."[5]

When Sweatt's case arose, the political and intellectual climate in the nation made the South's commitment to segregation increasingly untenable. Gunnar Myrdal's massive study of race relations, *An American Dilemma,* ratified the consensus among liberal intellectuals that segregation was wrong and oppressive. For years the NAACP had been emphasizing the inconsistency Myrdal pointed out between segregation and the nation's commitment to democracy. It repeatedly placed that inconsistency in a larger international framework. In 1939, for example, Marshall wrote that "[a]t the present time all eyes are focussed on democracy in the United States and it seems the fate of democracy depends upon the United States. The true test of democracy is the equality of rights and privileges granted all citizens which is measured by the protection given minority groups." In 1948, referring to segregated lunch counters at Washington's airport, an NAACP activist wrote a federal official, "I know our enemies abroad use such facts to discredit our democratic way of life." President Truman's Committee on Civil Rights referred to "those with competing philosophies" who have "stressed—and shamelessly distorted—our shortcomings," and the Department of Justice brief in the restrictive covenant cases said that segregation caused the United States serious embarrassment in foreign relations.[6]

Carter Wesley, a lawyer and the publisher of the Houston *Informer,* and W. J. Durham, who had been involved in the white primary cases, led the Texas conference of NAACP branches to declare that it wanted to support a lawsuit to desegregate professional education. Wesley's paper helped raise almost $4,000 for the case by October 1945, but finding a plaintiff was more difficult. After interviewing several potential plaintiffs, the lawyers were unsatisfied. Some had weak academic records; another was unenthusiastic about suing, although he said he would apply for a master's degree in law simply to make sure that the NAACP would have at least one plaintiff. By the end of September, Marshall advised the Texans to abandon their search for a law school applicant and to think about attacking elementary or secondary segregation. Fortunately for the course of the litigation, in early October, Sweatt, a friend of Durham, approached Lulu White, a family friend and the NAACP's state director of branches, and told her of his interest in applying to the Texas law school.[7]

Sweatt knew that his application to the law school would be rejected, but he was happy to become a plaintiff. His family divided over his decision. His wife worried about violence and feared that Sweatt would lose his job. One brother thought Sweatt was too old to start a new career and another thought that Texas racism was too strong. Sweatt's father and mother approved, though, and in the end the family stood behind him. Sweatt attempted to deal with his wife's financial concerns by getting Durham and A. Maceo Smith, another lawyer associated with the NAACP, to guarantee that the NAACP would pay the lawsuit's expenses and would pay Sweatt $3,500 a year while the case was pending. A clear violation of legal ethics, this contract got the NAACP and the Legal Defense Fund into trouble in the 1950s.[8]

By February, Wesley had raised $7,200, and the NAACP was ready to proceed. On February 26, 1946, Sweatt went to Austin and attempted to register at the law school. First, he and a delegation from the NAACP met with university officials, including Theophilus Painter, the university president. Painter and his staff indicated their willingness to establish segregated programs for African-Americans, in addition to the existing program of scholarships for education outside Texas. Sweatt said that he could not afford to go out of state for his legal education, which he wanted immediately. He thereupon applied for admission to the law school. Painter withheld action until he could get a formal opinion from the state's attorney general. On March 16, the attorney general upheld the state's "wise and long-continued policy of segregation." Two months later, Sweatt's law-yers filed suit in the state court in Austin, seeking an order requiring the law school to admit him.[9]

The randomness that characterizes all litigation structured Marshall's approach in *Sweatt.* Probably because of the NAACP's strength in Texas, Marshall wanted to use Sweatt's case as the main vehicle to attack segregation in higher education. Before he could, though, other cases came up. In late 1945, before Sweatt applied to law school, Ada Lois Sipuel in Oklahoma asked the NAACP to help her apply to law school there. Roscoe Dunjee worked with Sipuel. The university president told Dunjee that he would put whatever "you feel will get you into court" in the letter rejecting Sipuel's application. Believing, as Marshall put it, that the NAACP could "win this case in Mississippi," Dunjee filed suit for Sipuel a month before Sweatt's case was filed. The complaint's conclusion sought an order direct-ing Sipuel's admission to the law school, although other parts of the complaint suggested that Sipuel would also accept admission to a segregated law school if there was one.[10]

Marshall wanted to try Sipuel's case himself, but he found himself tied up with the trials in Columbia, Tennessee, and then with his illness that summer and fall. In fact, no trial was needed. The trial judge dismissed the case, saying that Sipuel could not challenge the constitutionality of the segregation statute using the pro-cedure she chose. A year later the state supreme court affirmed that decision, finding it fatal to Sipuel's case that she might have been willing to attend a segregated law school in Oklahoma but had failed to demand that the state create one for her. Marshall felt compelled to try to get the United States Supreme Court to review this decision, but he was not happy about it. He would have preferred to take *Sweatt* to the Court first, because there was "practically no record" in *Sipuel.* He was concerned that the Court might use the case to reaffirm rather than extend *Gaines,* and decided that "we must strike out [*sic*] segregation even though we do not have the type of record we want."[11]

Marshall's Supreme Court brief did challenge *Plessy* itself. That did not make all the justices happy, though they agreed that the state courts had to be reversed. Chief Justice Vinson said that the "talk of demand" was "shadow boxing," and Justice Murphy said that he was "opposed to [the] equal but separate doctrine." In contrast, Justice Douglas indicated that Justice Reed was "not in sympathy with what [the] court has been doing in this field," and Justice Jackson, though he believed the case was simple, noted that "every discussion of [the] race problem makes it worse." Vinson drafted a short opinion for the Court, which it issued on January 12, 1948, only four days after the oral argument ended. The opinion relied entirely on *Gaines* and said that the state had to provide Sipuel with a legal education "as soon as it does for applicants of any other group."[12]

The Court's quick action meant that the decision was handed down before second-semester registration. This misled Marshall. The case went back to the Oklahoma supreme court on January 17, still in time for registration. That court, though, found the Supreme Court's citation of *Gaines* significant, and concluded that *Sipuel* meant that it would be enough if the university created a law school for

Sipuel. Two days later they did; the regents created a law school for African-Americans, to occupy three rooms in the state capitol, and staffed by three local white attorneys. This was too much for Marshall to take. Surely the Supreme Court could not have meant that this thrown-together operation satisfied the state's constitutional obligations. He filed a motion in the Supreme Court seeking an order directing that Sipuel be admitted to the existing white law school.[13]

The Court was not ready to take on the separate but equal doctrine. Although his brief did challenge the doctrine, at the oral argument Marshall had been a careful advocate and had refrained from saying much about it, "trying to win his case," as Frankfurter put it, "even on the assumption that the *Gaines* doctrine be accepted." Marshall's cautious argument was enough to get the Supreme Court off the hook. Vinson drafted a short opinion denying Marshall's motion. Justice Frankfurter objected to a sentence saying that the Constitution did not require applicants to demand that a new school be created, because that would "again invite discussion about the issue which Thurgood Marshall skilfully did not explicitly either accept or reject," that is, the validity of segregation itself. Despite Frankfurter's concern that "Thurgood Marshall may use these [statements] as the basis for the claim that we have decided that no separate colored law school . . . will fill the bill," Vinson retained the sentence. He did, however, modify another portion of the opinion in response to objections from Frankfurter and Douglas. Vinson initially wrote that the separate but equal doctrine was not an issue "in the case," but his colleagues corrected him: Saying that the doctrine was not an issue "here" was, Douglas said, "more nearly what Thurgood Marshall conceded." Again Frankfurter was concerned about saying things in a way that did not "invite dispute" by relying on "interpretations" of what Marshall had said.[14]

The Court's opinion said that separate but equal was not an issue before the Supreme Court. Rather, the opinion stated, *Sipuel* decided only that the state courts should not have rejected Sipuel's case for failing to demand that a segregated school be opened. Justices Rutledge and Murphy dissented, with Rutledge writing that Oklahoma had to end its discrimination "at once, not at some later time, near or remote," and that no decent law school could be created "overnight."[15]

As *Sipuel* concluded, Oklahoma produced another case. At the end of January 1948, six African-Americans applied for admission to several graduate programs at the university. After studying the question, the university regents decided *not* to create programs at the state's university for African-Americans. That put them in a completely untenable legal position, and when George McLaurin, who wanted to get a doctoral degree in education, sued, he easily obtained an order directing his admission. The four courses he registered for were rescheduled to meet in a single classroom, which had a small alcove on the side. McLaurin had to sit in the alcove. Marshall thought that this made the case particularly attractive for the NAACP, because the separate arrangements were dramatically "humiliating, degrading, and what have you." By the time the case reached the Supreme Court, the seating arrangements had changed. McLaurin could sit in the classroom, but only in a row reserved for African-Americans, and he was assigned to a separate table in the library. Even with these changes, Marshall thought that *McLaurin* was a good companion to *Sweatt*.[16]

A third preliminary case gave Marshall a chance to develop some supporting theories. In 1946, the legal staff learned that Mexican-American parents had challenged school segregation in Orange County, California. When the school board appealed the decision that segregation was unconstitutional, the NAACP decided to file an *amicus* brief. After using sociological material in the restrictive covenant cases, the lawyers now developed a similar argument about education. Marshall, following William Hastie's advice, developed a ten-page brief relying on previously published materials detailing the harms segregation caused to the education of children. [17]

The preliminary cases moved rather quickly. *Sweatt* did not. In June 1946, the trial judge in Texas denied Sweatt the order he sought, giving the state six months to come up with a "substantially equal" law school. The board of Texas A & M University adopted a resolution saying that it would create a law school for African-Americans on demand. Holding that this satisfied the Constitution, the trial judge dismissed Sweatt's case. That was patently erroneous, as state attorney general Price Daniel conceded when he asked the state court of appeals to send the case back for evidence about what the state had actually done to provide African-Americans a legal education. [18]

Acting on its resolution, Texas A & M hired two African-American attorneys to operate a law school out of their own law offices, but no students applied. Finally, on March 3, 1947, the legislature created Texas State University for Negroes in Houston, supported by an immediate appropriation of $100,000. To get a law school going promptly, though, the state set up a temporary law school in Austin, leasing the basement of a building near the state capitol and ordering a library of respectable size. Three University of Texas law professors were assigned to teach courses there. When the temporary law school opened on March 10, 1947, again there were no students; opposition from the NAACP and the African-American community discouraged enrollment. [19]

Once Texas created a real law school for African-Americans, the context of the litigation changed. *Gaines* was no longer relevant; *Plessy* was. Marshall had to try the question of whether the new law school was equal to the existing one. Supporters occasionally asked Marshall why the principal case involved a law school. He replied, accurately enough, that "it is easier to prove that a law school is unequal than it is to prove a primary school is unequal." He added that states would surely be unable to create medical schools for African-American students, but that it was harder to find qualified applicants and to prove that they were denied admission because of their race. More important than these, though, was the fact that Marshall knew law schools intimately. He understood what made one law school better than another, and his network of acquaintances made it easy for him to find expert witnesses to explain why a new and segregated law school could not possibly be equal to the existing one. Marshall may also have understood that the Justices of the Supreme Court, most of whom, after all, had graduated from law school, would be more comfortable saying that the new law school could not be equal to the old one no matter how elaborate its physical facilities were. [20]

Marshall thought it was "high time" to try the question of equality, and considered the case "wide open" after the court of appeals sent *Sweatt* back for trial. He wanted to experiment with the evidence that might be useful in an all-out attack on segregation. Marshall's principal goal was to construct a record that provided a good basis for evaluating the NAACP's claim that separate facilities could never be equal. Marshall contacted Donald Murray to have him testify that he had not been ostracized when he went to Maryland's law school. Marshall and his friends developed a list of prominent law professors who might testify, although many of the possibilities had some drawbacks: Dean Erwin Griswold of Harvard was too much a symbol of what Texans disliked, Max Radin of the University of California was Jewish, Thomas Emerson of Yale was "on the Reddish side." In the end, Malcolm Sharp of the University of Chicago and Earl Harrison of the University of Pennsylvania were Marshall's expert witnesses about law schools. [21]

In addition, Robert Redfield, an anthropologist, testified that the races were the same in all respects relevant to education. The point was to show that segregation has "no line of reasonableness," in Marshall's terms. In fact, Redfield testified, segregation inhibited education: it prevented students from learning about other groups, and it generated mistrust. Dean Charles Thompson of Howard's education school testified that, "according to any index or criterion for comparing the quality of education, . . . there is great inequality." He also emphasized "the very special problem of the lack of Negro professionals." [22]

Constance Baker Motley called the trial "spectacular." James M. Nabrit, a Texan teaching at Howard Law School, examined the Austin law school's dean Charles McCormick. Nabrit challenged McCormick's assertions of equality by emphasizing the small size of the segregated law school, the lack of extracurricular activities such as a moot court or law journal, and the inadequate library. Marshall himself conducted a less aggressive examination of Helen Hargrave, the librarian of the two law schools. Years later, after he had become Chief Justice of the Texas Supreme Court, Joe Greenhill, Daniel's chief assistant at the trial, recalled that Marshall was "a real pro in examining and cross-examining witnesses," and he and Marshall maintained friendly relations. Greenhill noted that "it is a credit to him that he could be cordial when . . . there was no hotel, restaurant, or restroom open to him on the main street in Austin." [23]

Daniel and Greenhill tried two lines of defense. Daniel suggested that Sweatt was merely the tool of the NAACP and did not really want to attend law school; if he had, Daniel suggested, Sweatt would have gone to the segregated school once it opened. This line was directed more at Daniel's white electorate than at the courts. Daniel and Greenhill also tried to show that the segregated law school was in fact substantially equal to the white one. They turned the low enrollment at the school into an advantage; it contributed, Daniel said, to a low faculty-student ratio. But, Harrison replied, in law schools interaction among students with different views was at least as important as interaction between students and teachers; a school whose faculty-student ratio was low because there were few students could not provide as good an education as one in which the ratio was higher because there were more students. The trial resulted in a record that showed some differences in physical facilities and major differences in the intangible aspects of education. [24]

No one was surprised when the Texas courts rejected Sweatt's claim. As a result of pressure and harassment, Sweatt's longstanding health problems got worse, and he had to be hospitalized for ulcers. He resigned from the postal service and began to work for Carter Wesley in the *Informer*'s circulation department. Marshall called Sweatt a "real good client[ ]," whose only problem was his name; Marshall complained that he had to explain to reporters that Sweatt's first name was not "Herman." Sweatt was a good client because he was a dedicated supporter of the NAACP. He willingly gave interviews stressing his personal desire to go to law school and minimizing the NAACP's role in supporting the litigation; he was not, he said, "an abstract Guinea Pig."[25]

Marshall had to decide how to structure the appeal. He could have focused on the particular facts in the Texas case, emphasizing the small size of the segregated law school and its basement location. Although that would have almost ensured a Supreme Court victory, it might have had few lasting implications. The state, after all, conceded that the Austin law school was temporary. The permanent one opened in Houston in early 1949. Winning the case because the Austin school was unequal might simply initiate another round of litigation, with the Houston school at issue. Hastie did suggest, though, that a narrow holding would help the NAACP in cases involving other kinds of graduate education, where the per capita costs of education were high and demand was limited; it would be far too expensive, Hastie thought, for the Southern states to maintain segregated graduate programs where material resources had to be equal.[26]

Marshall could, instead, have given the case a larger focus, denying that a separate legal education could ever be equal. Here he would stress what the lawyers came to call the "intangible" aspects of legal education: the interaction among students that Harrison had mentioned, the importance of having the range of extracurricular activities that only a relatively large school could maintain, and the like. This approach drew on legal education's special characteristics, with which the justices were familiar. But it confined the challenge to law schools; the "intangibles" that made legal education special might not exist in other programs, including undergraduate education. Finally, as *Sipuel* taught, Marshall had to challenge the separate but equal doctrine itself. In the Texas appellate brief, Marshall "put as much as possible in," allowing him to refine the approach as the appeal proceeded.[27]

A trial on "substantial equality" still had to be held in Sipuel's Oklahoma case. Marshall planned to use that trial to "make an improvement over the Texas case since we have gained our experience there." He took a large group of lawyers and witnesses to Oklahoma in May 1948. The testimony was a more substantial version of what Marshall had put on in Austin. Marshall again extracted concessions from university officials that they really did not believe the segregated school substantially equal to the white one; Charles Bunn of the University of Wisconsin Law School called this examination "a masterpiece," and said that "the ultimate result will show the case was won then and there." Marshall's case was "cheered on" by the faculty at the university's law school, and he got W. Page Keeton, the dean of the state's white law school, to testify on behalf of the NAACP. Dean Griswold of Harvard, who believed that the law school was "an utter fraud," also testified, and was subjected to a ridiculous cross-examination; in his closing argument, Marshall said that it would compound the insult to try to explain away the attorney general's criticisms of Griswold. The Oklahoma trial did not develop new or deeper challenges to segregation, but it increased Marshall's familiarity with the arguments he could use when *Sweatt* reached the Supreme Court.[28]

As usual, Marshall called on his friends to send him their ideas about the legal arguments. He suggested a line of argument that never quite panned out. Marshall concluded from the restrictive covenant decisions that "the going will be easy" if he could establish that there was a civil right not to be segregated in public education, like the civil right not to be discriminated against in purchasing property. Two cases from the 1920s held that states could not prohibit private schools or bar them from teaching German, because the bans violated the "liberty" of parents and teachers. Marshall thought that those cases might be used to show that there was a "liberty" involved in attending public schools without segregation. Today lawyers would say that Marshall was working toward the idea that there was a "fundamental interest" in education. Marshall soon subordinated this argument to a more traditional equality argument, though.[29]

"Getting this whole outline whipped into shape" was a "terrific job." Marshall convened several advisory meetings. After the first, in December 1948, he decided to limit the argument in *Sweatt* and *McLaurin,* concentrating on graduate education rather than the overall evils of segregation. He did plan to use "the high sounding statement" in an earlier case that racial discrimination by the federal government was "odious" to argue that racial discrimination by the states was just as odious. In January 1949 Marshall called another conference, this one designed to generate briefs from friendly groups that might persuade the Supreme Court to hear Sweatt's appeal. Marian Perry coordinated these *amicus* briefs. She encouraged the representative of the Federal Council of Churches to go beyond narrow factual arguments, because it was "appropriate for those charged with the moral leadership of our nation to evaluate those social forces in our society which must enter into" the decision. She also encouraged James Dombrowski of the Southern Conference Educational Fund, an interracial liberal group, to get prominent citizens in Oklahoma to issue a statement "decrying diversion of the efforts of state officials from the function of providing education . . . and pointing out the costs to the taxpayers" of defending *Sipuel* and *McLaurin.*[30]

The most important *amicus* brief was prepared by a group of law professors, headed by Thomas Emerson and John Frank of Yale Law School. It carried the burden of attacking segregation itself, because Marshall's brief had to include an extensive discussion of the question of substantial equality, making it more difficult to develop the argument against *Plessy* in detail. The professors' brief argued that the Fourteenth Amendment was designed to eliminate all forms of segregation, and that *Plessy*'s assumption that legislation could not overcome differences between the races had been undermined by later developments. Indeed, "elimination of patterns of segregation is not only feasible but is rapidly going forward under government sponsorship." The law professors detailed the ways in which the inequality inherent in segregation was exacerbated by "factors peculiar to legal education": the need for specialists in some fields could not be met in a small faculty, the range of courses offered would be smaller, research would be more limited, and extracurricular programs could not be adequate. Perry called the brief "a swell job," and Bob Ming, who was teaching at Chicago's law school, called it "excellent."[31]

Marshall filed the petition for review in *Sweatt* on March 23. In the normal course, the petition might have been considered during the spring, and the case argued in the fall. Instead, the Court sat on the petition for nearly six months; it had already deferred consideration of *McLaurin* for almost that long. The reason for the delay probably was that the justices understood that they were being asked to reconsider and overrule *Plessy v. Ferguson* and needed time to decide how to respond. By the end of the spring, enough justices had voted to bring *Sweatt* up, but they were uncertain about what to do with *McLaurin*. Three justices wanted to affirm the lower court's decision in *McLaurin* holding the separate seating arrangements constitutional. At first, only four justices, the minimum needed to take up a case, wanted to hear *Sweatt*, but in the end they all voted to review both cases.[32]

Before the Court decided to hear *Sweatt* and *McLaurin*, the segregated law school opened in Houston. The leaders of Texas State University tried hard to create a decent law school. They hired Ozie Johnson, a practicing lawyer from Philadelphia, as dean, as well as four faculty members and a librarian. R. O'Hara Lanier, the university's president, wanted Johnson to avoid seeking accreditation, believing that he could use the lack of accreditation to extract money from the legislature to improve the school's program. He was also concerned that accreditation would lead the courts to conclude that the new school was substantially equal to the existing white law school, thus eliminating any incentive the legislature had for investing more in the Houston school. Johnson disagreed, and set to work getting the school accredited. Within a year the American Bar Association had done so.[33]

The Association of American Law Schools was next. Johnson went to Chicago to argue his case at the Association's national meeting. He persuaded the association that the law school satisfied the usual standards. After what Griswold called "quite a time," the executive committee decided against admitting the school to the association while *Sweatt* was pending; it believed that admitting the school would amount to endorsing segregation. Instead, the favorable report of the accreditation committee was filed and action deferred with Johnson's agreement. Johnson decided not to present his case to the members of the association, accepting a letter stating that the school was being denied admission to the association solely because of the pending lawsuit. According to Marshall, President Lanier was about to be fired because of his efforts to improve the university, and Johnson too would be fired, for other reasons. "As expected," Marshall said, "the so-called Negro University has become a mere political football."[34]

Much more significant than developments surrounding Texas's law schools was the arrival of *Henderson v. United States* at the Supreme Court. On May 17, 1942, Elmer Henderson, an African-American employed by the federal Fair Employment Practices Committee, was using the Southern Railway to get from Washington to Birmingham to investigate discrimination in war production. At 5:30 he went to the dining car for dinner. The railroad usually set aside two tables near the kitchen for African-Americans, but if whites filled up the dining car before any African-Americans arrived, the tables were used by whites. When Henderson got to the dining car, it was filled with whites, although one seat at the tables near the kitchen was unoccupied. The dining-car steward offered to serve Henderson at his Pullman seat, but Henderson insisted on eating in the dining car. No seat at a reserved table opened up before dinner ended at 9 P.M. Represented by Belford Lawson, an African-American lawyer and activist in Washington, and with the support of the Alpha Phi Alpha fraternity, Henderson complained to the Interstate Commerce Commission that the railroad's action violated the principle of non-discrimination that the Court had adopted in the Mitchell case in 1941. The commission found that Henderson had indeed been discriminated against, but concluded that the event was "a casual incident brought about by the bad judgment" of the steward, and refused to enter an order prohibiting the railroad's practice. Henderson appealed, and the federal court sent the case back to the commission. In 1946 the railroad changed its rules so that one table with four seats would be reserved for African-Americans; there would be a curtain between that table and the others during meals. The commission then found that this would not violate the Mitchell rule. Henderson again appealed, but this time the lower court held that the railroad's rules were fair.[35]

Although the NAACP had brought some transportation cases, when *Henderson* arose it decided to abandon its cases and file an *amicus* brief there. More important, after some discussions with interested groups, Solicitor General Philip Perlman decided that the government could not defend the commission's decision. He decided that the United States should concede that Henderson was correct and argue that *Plessy* should be overruled, and filed *amicus* briefs supporting the NAACP in *Sweatt* and *McLaurin*.[36]

10

"Replete with Road Markings"
The Supreme Court Deals with
Segregated Universities

Waiting for the Court to decide whether to hear *Sweatt,* Marshall again got the lawyers together to "take stock of the present situation and plan for future legal strategy." Hastie opened the meeting in June 1949 with a discussion of "the changes in the law" during the prior fifteen years. Then Ming discussed *Plessy,* to help "get the theories straightened out" before applying them to actual cases. One issue that had irritated the NAACP's lawyers arose again. Some interest-group representatives, who filed *amicus* briefs, insisted that it was inconsistent to attack segregation itself and yet focus the cases on actual inequalities. The LDF staff thought that there was no such inconsistency, because, as Annette Peyser, the sociologist on the staff, put it, segregation was the disease and inequalities were the symptoms. Peyser thought, however, that the staff had reacted too defensively to outside criticism, and that the long-range interests of the NAACP would be better served by "getting beyond interorganizational jealousies."[1]

In November, the Court announced that it would hear *Sweatt* and scheduled argument for April 4, 1950. On November 14, Robert Carter divided up the research. His plan was comprehensive. Carter himself would develop the argument that the Constitution barred states from "mak[ing] race or color the basis for legislative or governmental classification," because "racial criteria are unreasonable" and "have no relation to the subject matter." He also would argue that *Plessy* was wrongly decided because discrimination was inevitable under the separate but equal doctrine, and because it was used "to maintain Negroes in an inferior color caste status." He proposed historical research on the proposition, strikingly phrased, that "the Fourteenth Amendment was not intended to prohibit segregation in the field of education." Jack Greenberg was to examine whether the courts should presume that classifications based on race were unconstitutional, just as they treated laws affecting free speech rights. Peyser would compile "whatever sociological and psychological findings or conclusions can be drawn" about the way separate but equal actually worked in education. Marshall would develop the argument that the facts in *Sweatt* showed the "inevitability of discrimination under [the] separate but equal formula." He would also show that desegregation had been successful where it had been tried, that it was "beneficial to both the individual and the state," and that it did not lead to "lawlessness." Finally, Marshall and Carter shared the job of demonstrating that *McLaurin*'s facts showed "the real reason" for segregation—"to maintain inferior caste status."[2]

Although Carter said that this was only a sketch of the necessary research, the brief that resulted covered almost the same territory. Marshall asked Dean Griswold for advice and received recommendations that he neither welcomed nor followed. Griswold believed that Marshall was "moving a little too fast," and could make more progress by "inching along," because the cases were "overwhelming" on the question of inequality. Although Griswold agreed that Marshall should show that suggestions the Southern states made about race riots were "just a smoke screen . . . to scare the Court away from the issue here," Griswold suggested that Marshall should try "to make progress in small bits," and should therefore say explicitly that *Sweatt* "does not have anything to do with general education, or with elementary education and education in the high schools." Marshall should say, according to Griswold, "it would be time enough to consider that problem . . . when a case raising that issue gets before the Court." If Marshall obtained a decision "putting Sweatt into the University of Texas Law School, you will have done a very great deal, and perhaps all that you can wisely do at the moment." Griswold believed that "if you tried to argue the entire question now, and lose," the NAACP would suffer "a serious set-back, which might take a generation or more to overcome."[3]

Griswold's concern about losing was understandable. The Supreme Court in 1950 was more conservative on most matters than it had been a few years earlier. Frank Murphy and Wiley Rutledge, probably the Court's most liberal members, died in 1949. Truman named Tom Clark, his attorney general, to replace Murphy, and Sherman Minton, a federal judge who had served with Truman in the Senate, to replace Rutledge. Clark was from Texas, and liberals in the Roosevelt tradition were uncomfortable that a conservative Southern Democrat would sit on the Court. Marshall, though, had developed a good working relationship with Clark, whose views on race were reasonably liberal. Clark drafted the executive order creating Truman's Committee on Civil Rights, and authorized the Justice Department's participation in the restrictive covenant cases. And, as a graduate of the University of Texas Law School, Clark might appreciate the special place its graduates had in the state bar.

As Senator from Indiana, Minton supported Roosevelt's court-packing plan. His experience revealed little about his constitutional views. Chief Justice Vinson, a Kentuckian, was a committed New Deal member of Congress, interested mainly in the Democratic party's economic program, which led him to serve as Truman's secretary of the treasury. Though he definitely was not an enthusiastic supporter of the NAACP's positions, Vinson had written the Court's restrictive covenant opinions. They extended the "state action" doctrine quite far in the service of what the justices clearly believed was the imperative of racial justice. Harold Burton, Truman's first Supreme Court appointee, was a progressive Republican mayor of

Cleveland before his 1940 election to the Senate. His dissent in the Morgan transportation case aside, Burton's opinions "consistently opposed . . . legally mandated discrimination." Griswold's concern about losing, then, was not unreasonable, but he was probably more cautious than necessary. Removed from the struggle, Griswold might have been giving technically sound advice, but he failed to appreciate how important it was by 1950 for Marshall and the NAACP to challenge *Plessy* directly and on every occasion.[4]

Marshall prepared for the oral argument in *Sweatt* by holding a practice session at Howard Law School, where he was peppered with questions the justices might pose. Justice Frankfurter was an aggressive questioner at oral arguments, but one observer who saw Marshall argue a year later described how Marshall used the practice rounds: Marshall, he said, was like a chess grandmaster playing against Frankfurter, a good club player. Frankfurter questioned advocates in his own way, which Marshall could handle; but, in addition, Marshall had to handle questions from other justices. Having faced the hardest questions at the practice rounds, Marshall was poised for the justices.[5]

The arguments began with *Henderson*. J. Howard McGrath, making his first appearance before the Court as attorney general, opened by calling the separate but equal doctrine "a contradiction in terms and an unwarranted departure from the Constitution." He said that separate facilities could never be equal, that "legally enforced segregation necessarily implied inferiority," and that it "was intended to signify Negro inequality." The curtains in the dining car were, according to McGrath, "a ceremonial symbol of a caste system." Dining car segregation was "part of a national pattern of ostracism" that "gravely affected Negro personality." *Plessy* should be overruled; reaffirming it, McGrath said, would strike "a grave blow . . . at democracy." The Court's decision, he concluded, "would either solidify the barriers of prejudice or undermine them and bring them into disrepute."[6]

No one asked McGrath any questions, but the interruptions began during Solicitor General Perlman's argument. Justice Reed got Perlman to say that nothing in the Interstate Commerce Act's legislative history spoke directly to racial separation. Taking up his main theme, Perlman told the justices that they should reconsider *Plessy* because their predecessors "were closer to slavery and the full significance of its effects could not be seen." The view stated by Justice Harlan's dissent in *Plessy* that the Constitution is color blind, Perlman said, "truly reflects the intention of the constitution and truly reflects the rights of all citizens to be treated as equals."

Belford Lawson then "described the rope barriers in the Pullman diner as a badge of inferiority and a remnant of slavery." He praised the government's position as "encouraging all of us who have lived under the iron heel of the proconsul of Jim Crow." Lawson asked the Court to free African-Americans "from the dark night of Jim Crow" by reaching the constitutional question. Although Frankfurter said that Lawson did not have to go "one step further" if the case was controlled by the Mitchell decision, Lawson said that relying on the statute would be a "Pyrrhic victory." If the Court relied on the Commerce Act, Lawson said, the railroad would simply "come up with a new regulation which would take five years to litigate." According to Lawson, the Court had to decide the constitutional question because "colored people all over the world are suspect of democracy in the United States."

The ICC's lawyer had the unhappy task of defending its decision. He tried to argue that "Congress had not intended to forbid segregation" in the Commerce Act because "25 bills to abolish segregation have failed of passage," but Justice Reed replied that "there were more reasons for refusing to pass a bill" than agreement with the railroads' actions. When Charles Clark, representing the railroad, tried to defend segregation itself, he "ran into a barrage of questions." Frankfurter thought it ridiculous to claim, as Clark had, that denying African-Americans service when seats were available in the white section would promote "peace and order." On the constitutional question, Clark argued that "the Fourteenth Amendment could not have been intended to bar segregation because the very Congress which adopted the Amendment in 1868 had also provided for operation of segregated school facilities in the District of Columbia," a point that continued to bedevil the NAACP's lawyers and the justices. The final argument was a "tirade" from Representative Sam Hobbs of Alabama, who excoriated McGrath and Perlman, and said that "Almighty God himself was the author of segregation." Henderson and his supporters, Hobbs said, were "impatient reformers" who "can't wait for the mills of the gods to grind slowly and small."

McLaurin came next. Carter outlined the facts of the case, emphasizing in response to questions that McLaurin was sitting in the same classes as whites, and that all he was complaining of was "the fact that he was assigned segregated facilities": "We are objecting that they are picked out and given certain seats in a certain row. White students are free to sit where they please." Amos Hall, McLaurin's Oklahoma counsel, called the seating arrangements "humiliating." Oklahoma's assistant attorney general made a half-hearted argument supporting the university, calling the university officials "good men doing the best they can under difficult circumstances." When Justice Minton said that when segregation had "broken down" so much, "there isn't much point to segregation," the lawyer replied, "Not possibly on the graduates' level." He was concerned, though, about elementary and secondary schools; segregation in the university would be gone, he said, within a decade, but "it would be much longer" before segregation was eliminated in the lower schools.

Marshall began his argument in *Sweatt* by pointing out that the justices could not use the route they had taken in *Sipuel* to avoid the challenge to *Plessy*. The issue of separate but equal, he said, "was raised right from the beginning of the case." He sarcastically turned the new school in Houston to his advantage. The state courts, Marshall argued, held that the basement school in Austin was substantially equal to the University of Texas Law School: "Since the new Negro law school in Houston was concededly superior to the Austin school, it must be superior to the school for white students." He was "bitter" about the references to violence in the state's brief, and asked the Court "not to be intimidated by vague references to the possibilities of riot by unspecified persons in undesignated places." Marshall said that he was unconcerned with actions students might take:

"We want to remove governmental restriction; if they want to, they can keep their prejudices." He also emphasized that the NAACP had been trying to get the basic question of segregation before the Court "for thirty years," suggesting that it was time for the Court to decide the question. After Joe Greenhill, relying on an extensive discussion of the Fourteenth Amendment's drafting in the state's brief, argued that the Fourteenth Amendment was not intended to bar segregation, Marshall replied that the history of the amendment "afforded arguments for both sides and that it was not possible to make a clear-cut demonstration that the framers . . . intended either to permit or to forbid segregation." Marshall's final point reverted to the possibility of violence. Critics of the NAACP's position had pointed to a recent riot in Washington when a swimming pool was desegregated; Marshall read a letter from the secretary of the interior saying that the pools would reopen without segregation and that he was "confident that there would be no violence."

Marshall's strategy was clear: put the question of segregation directly to the justices, attempt to head off any efforts they might make to confine their decision to the facts, neutralize the apparently adverse legislative history, and treat the risk of violence as both small and irrelevant. His rhetoric matched his strategy: make the moral issues clear by simple and direct statements.

Some of the justices were unhappy with Marshall's strategy, because it placed them in a more difficult position than they desired. On the day argument ended, Justice Jackson wrote Charles Fairman, a law professor in California who had written extensively on Fourteenth Amendment history (though not about segregation). Jackson said that "the argument has not been very enlightening on the points that trouble me." As he saw it, "all parties seemed to vie with each other in enlisting pressure groups and giving the whole thing a general atmosphere of politics." To Jackson, McGrath's appearance underlined the political nature of the question, for he "added nothing except to get into a position to capitalize any advantages for the administration." Jackson was bothered by the fact that "neither side had suggested any logical division" between graduate schools and grade schools. "They all take the position that it is all or none . . . That is the great hope of the one side and the great fear of the other."[7]

Jackson accurately described the way some justices felt about the cases. Some took seriously the government's suggestion that *Plessy* should be overruled. Justice Burton had his law clerks prepare a memorandum on the framing of the Fourteenth Amendment. The clerks told him that the brief of the government "contain[s] as forceful a statement as we have seen of the intangible inequalities which result from even a system which provides equal physical facilities for the separated races."[8] The possibility of overruling *Plessy* pervaded the Court's consideration of the three cases. Some justices went back and forth as they considered the cases. They expressed two related concerns: What did overruling *Plessy* imply about segregated education? And what did overturning segregation in higher education imply about segregation in elementary and secondary schools? Of course the justices knew they could, and undoubtedly would, write opinions that did not directly dispose of the issue in elementary and secondary education. They also knew that the doctrine they articulated and the judgments they reached for themselves would have implications for the broader question.

Chief Justice Vinson believed that the cases put segregation itself at issue. As he saw it, he could not "distinguish professional & elementary schools," and believed that "negroes [were] entitled to enter [a] university without restriction if they are admitted at all."[9] These positions might require Vinson to conclude that segregation in elementary and secondary education was unconstitutional. He was, however, ambivalent about that conclusion, and at the end of his statement he indicated that he "tend[ed] toward" allowing segregation. He could not "conceive that Congress did not have the problem in front of them" when it adopted the Fourteenth Amendment, for discussions of public schools had been "prominent" at the time. He agreed that "as a matter of policy no harm would result from mingling of races," but found that "this is [a] sensitive problem," and could not say that the Civil War "decided that schools shan't be separate." "When we have all this historical background, it is hard for me to say schools should not be separate."[10]

Justice Black told his colleagues that Texas and Oklahoma failed to provide equal facilities: "It is not *equal* to isolate." Elementary schools could be distinguished from professional schools, he suggested: "There is a custom in elementary schools going way back to Civil War days. But you can't set up a law school over night that is equal to [the] old one." He was concerned about extending the holding to elementary schools because there was a "deep seated antagonism to commingling" in the South, which would close its schools "rather than mix races at grade and high school levels." Then, however, Black's tone shifted. As he saw it, the Fourteenth Amendment was not "designed to perpetuate [a] caste system," and segregation was "a hangover from [the] days when [the] negro was a slave." Thus, "if he has to meet the issue there is nothing to make him subscribe to *Plessy*." Segregation, Black said, "was Hitler's creed—he preached what the South believed." Of course, Black conceded, the South "may never accept that view until [the] races amalgamate as they do when they live side by side." Justice Burton interpreted Black as criticizing *Plessy* but not "go[ing] *now* beyond sep[arate] and equal."[11]

Frankfurter and Black had recently divided sharply over the intentions of the drafters of the Fourteenth Amendment regarding the application of the Bill of Rights to the states,[12] and Black's references to Hitler and the Fourteenth Amendment's purposes apparently irritated Frankfurter, who said that it was "futile to talk about what the 14th [Amendment] 'intended,'" that the cases "should be decided aside from any doctrinaire [views] or intentions as we construe them of the 14th Amendment" because "no one knows what was intended," and that it was "absurd to say this is [the] Dred Scott case." Frankfurter found it easy to limit the decision to higher education: law schools had a limited number of good teachers and "intercourse among students is the life of the place." Frankfurter's notes to himself indicate that he thought it important that the record in *Sweatt* was "limited to professional schools," and that "intangibles" and "imponderable inequalities" were important concerns.[13]

Justice Burton thought the effort to limit the decisions' reach would be unavailing, because "we must decide for [the] whole country." He was willing to find unequal facilities, but he preferred "to overthrow [the] *Plessy* doctrine at [the] graduate level."[14] Justice Douglas too "would face *Plessy*" in the railroad case, and overrule it.[15] Stanley Reed, a Southerner, was the only justice to indicate decisively that he would uphold segregation. For him, segregation was like the question of child labor, a matter for legislatures. Although he believed that the facilities in the Texas case were equal, he was willing to remand the case, apparently for additional findings regarding the facilities.[16]

Jackson's letter to Fairman indicated his views. Jackson found it interesting that the cases "show[ed] pretty conclusively that the segregation system is breaking down of its own weight and that a little time will end it in nearly all States." Oklahoma had tried to "save[] face by preserving . . . a sort of token separation which seems to gratify the one race and chafe the other, more for its symbolism than for any real advantage or disadvantage." Finally, Jackson was impressed by the Texas brief, which established to his satisfaction that most proponents of the Fourteenth Amendment did not intend to "interfere with the state school systems on the question of segregation," and that "even those who wanted to see that accomplished acknowledged that it was not accomplished by the Amendment. . . ." For Jackson, this meant that the question for the Court was not whether to "fill gaps or construe the Amendment to include matters which were unconsidered," but was "whether we will construe it to include what was deliberately and intentionally excluded."[17]

At the conference, Jackson said that "these cases [are] fraught with great harm to [the] court & [the] country." For him, "whites as well as blacks are victims of this system," which was "not [a] badge of inferiority today." Rather, as he had said to Fairman, it was becoming too expensive. Jackson, like Vinson, found it impossible to draw a constitutional line between graduate and elementary schools, and insisted that "we owe the South candor" because "it is building several schools for negroes & spending lots of money." This reduced the question to one of pure policy for Jackson: "Is [banning segregation] a wise course?" He was, he said, "fluid enough to join any theory."[18]

Before hearing argument in the cases, Justice Clark's law clerks developed a memorandum attempting "to assure all that your position alone is supported by the present extent of social advancement in the South." According to one clerk, all the justices but Reed agreed that the separate but equal doctrine was untenable, but felt "enormous hesitation" about the wisdom of such a pronouncement. As the clerks saw the Fourteenth Amendment's history, the Constitution "uses big ideas" so that "we have no way of knowing" what its framers would have thought about segregation in its modern settir.. Further, "modern psychology tells us that it is impossible to have segregation with equality." The memorandum the clerks drafted tried to avoid implications for elementary and secondary schools by defining education as skill training, not including general experience and "acquisition of self-confidence."[19]

Clark himself worked on a memorandum explaining his "convictions, based in part upon my experience in Texas." The nearly final uncirculated version of this memorandum stated that "segregated education is unequal education." He found "nothing really conclusive [in the briefs] . . . for or against segregated education

[in] statements in Congress, the legislatures or the press at the time the Amendment was adopted." But "we know that the facilities are in fact unequal throughout the South, and necessarily will remain unequal as long as the whites in the South have the disposition and the political superiority to enforce local segregation." For Clark, "we need no modern psychologist to tell us that 'enforced separation of the two races [*does*] [brackets and emphasis in original] stamp the colored race with a badge of inferiority,' contrary to *Plessy v. Ferguson*. My question, then, is 'how' to reverse, not 'whether' or 'why.'" Clark then noted "fear that a flat overruling of the *Plessy* case would cause subversion or even defiance of our mandates in many communities." Those fears were relevant, and Clark cautioned against holding "today or tomorrow" that swimming pools could not be segregated or that elementary schools had to be desegregated. But, he wrote, "those fears are groundless" as to university segregation, where "the forces of progress in the South" were already apparent. He wanted to confine the ruling to graduate schools but "would not sign an opinion which approved *Plessy*."[20]

The memorandum then struggled to distinguish graduate schools from elementary schools. Clark "recognize[d] that segregated grammar schools may instill racism in young minds at a time and in a manner more destructive of society's fabric than segregated colleges and graduate schools ever will." That, however, was a matter of social equality, not educational equality. For Clark, determining educational equality meant focusing on "the segregated Negro's opportunity to acquire specific skills." Perhaps African-Americans in segregated grammar schools might receive skills in arithmetic and spelling equivalent to those of white students, but it was "obvious that the same cannot be said of graduate schools." For him, "the atmosphere of age and tradition at an established graduate school itself profoundly stimulates its students in achieving professional competence," and "the opportunities for discussion available in a larger school are literally invaluable." He concluded with a question: "How will I vote when the swimming pool and grammar school cases arise? I do not know; that is irrelevant. Should they arise tomorrow I would vote to deny certiorari or dismiss the appeal, so that we would not be compelled to decide the issues."[21]

The memorandum Clark circulated was more restrained in its statement of his misgivings about *Plessy*. The core was Clark's focus on distinguishing elementary from graduate education. He listed seven reasons why educational equality could not be achieved in segregated graduate schools, including the "higher standing" of white schools, the length of time it takes "to establish a professional school of top rank," and the importance of professional networks. Perhaps the memorandum's most striking point is a tension between its opening and closing. At the outset Clark wrote that the states had presented a highly exaggerated picture of the horribles that would ensue if they lost. Clark noted that Oklahoma's concern, in fact, "was the extension of the doctrine to elementary and secondary schools." Clark said that he "would be opposed to such extension at this time and would vote against taking a case involving same. Perhaps at a later date our judicial discretion will lead us to hear such a case." The memorandum's conclusion suggests that this did not mean that Clark accepted elementary and secondary school segregation, but only than he wanted to move one step at a time. After outlining what Clark would do in the pending cases, the memorandum concluded, "If some say this undermines *Plessy* then let it fall as have many Nineteenth Century oracles."[22]

Clark was willing to see *Plessy* fall, but wanted it undermined first. The extension to elementary and secondary education at some time after "today or tomorrow" was not out of the question; indeed, to the extent that he understood that the results he proposed in the university cases would in fact undermine *Plessy*, he welcomed the possibility of a later extension, after the Court exercised its wise discretion to entertain a follow-up case.

By the time the discussions of the three cases ended, it was clear that a firm majority favored finding segregation unconstitutional in the education cases, that nearly all the justices found it difficult to distinguish in principle between higher education and elementary and secondary education, and that though *Plessy* might not be formally overruled, its vitality would be severely impaired by the Court's decisions. The process of drafting opinions proceeded straightforwardly, though with some revealing incidents. Because Chief Justice Vinson initially indicated uncertainty about the outcome, Black assigned the opinions in the university cases to himself. A week later, however, Vinson concluded that he agreed with the majority, and took over the opinions. Vinson's opinions were carefully limited to higher education. When Vinson's draft was circulated, Black told him that it was "written in beautiful style" and hoped that it would "obtain a unanimous approval" because "full court acceptance . . . would add force to our holdings."[23]

Black and Clark encouraged Vinson; Frankfurter restrained him. After discussing the question with Reed, Frankfurter suggested some minor changes. To reduce the implications for elementary and secondary education, Frankfurter suggested that a sentence Reed proposed be changed from "these are handicaps to an effective education" to "these are handicaps to graduate instruction." As in *Sipuel*, Frankfurter wanted to keep the opinions short, for "the shorter the opinion, the more there is an appearance of unexcitement and inevitability about it." He wanted "to accomplish the desired result without needlessly stirring the kind of feelings that are felt even by truly liberal and high-minded Southerners. . . ."[24] Vinson acceded to these and other Frankfurter suggestions, though he noted that he did not agree that his drafts would have stirred up resentment. "I certainly would not want to have anything in the opinion which would stir up" such feelings, but, he wrote Frankfurter, he believed that "the devices used by Oklahoma" and Texas "are in the nature of circumventions."[25]

Frankfurter intervened somewhat more vigorously, though with the same thought, in *Henderson*. Justice Burton drafted an opinion finding that segregated seating violated the Interstate Commerce Act. Burton's draft echoed Attorney General McGrath's argument in calling the curtain between the tables in the dining car "symbolic." Frankfurter objected. "[F]or this Court to indicate objection to the division at tables as being 'symbolic' is to introduce legal objection to separateness as such. 'Symbolic' is the anti-segregation slogan. That is precisely the social objection to segregation, namely, that it represents a symbol of inferiority. We cannot introduce it into an opinion without giving just ground to the notion that we have ruled out segregation as such." Using the term, Frankfurter said, would "open[ ] the door to the very thing which, at least for the moment, we have agreed to keep out—passing on segregation as such—reaching down to primary instruction." Frankfurter did not want to "borrow[ ] future trouble" by "needlessly deciding issues not before the Court . . . particularly when popular passion is involved." Although Douglas thought that mentioning symbolism was important to show that the Court was concerned with segregation itself, Burton removed the word, but did not accept Frankfurter's other suggestions for redrafting the opinion.[26]

The opinions in the three cases were announced on June 5, 1950. *Sweatt* opened by noting that the Court would not decide the "[b]roader issues" urged on it— overruling *Plessy*—and that "much of the excellent research and detailed argument presented" in the briefs was "unnecessary" to the Court's decision. After describing the differences between the law schools in Texas, Vinson's opinion said that the Court could not find "substantial equality in the educational opportunities" they offered. It mentioned such tangible factors as the size of the faculty and the number of courses offered, but called "more important" the "qualities which are incapable of objective measurement but which make for greatness in a law school." These included faculty reputation, "position and influence of the alumni, standing in the community, traditions and prestige." Vinson said pointedly, "It is difficult to believe that one who had a free choice between these law schools would consider the question close." Further, he said, the "practical" aspects of legal practice meant that law schools could not "be effective in isolation from the individuals and institutions with which the law interacts." Finally, calling constitutional rights "personal and present," Vinson said that Sweatt had to be admitted to the University of Texas Law School so that he could obtain "his full constitutional right: legal education equivalent to that offered by the State" to whites.[27]

The *McLaurin* opinion was even shorter. The restrictions the university imposed on McLaurin were not "merely nominal." They "handicapped" him in pursuing his education, because they made it more difficult for him "to study [and] to engage in discussions and exchange views with other students." In response to the suggestion that McLaurin's fellow students might continue to shun him, Vinson replied that there was "a Constitutional difference" between state-imposed restrictions that "prohibit the intellectual commingling of students," and similar decisions by the students themselves. "[A]t the very least, the state will not be depriving [McLaurin] of the opportunity to secure acceptance by his fellow students on his own merits."[28]

Burton's opinion in *Henderson* found the case "largely controlled" by the Court's decision in the Mitchell case. Like Mitchell, Henderson had not been able to get a seat—there in a Pullman car, here in the dining car—that "would have been available to him if he had been white." That in itself was an unreasonable discrimination barred by the Interstate Commerce Act, but the curtains the railroad used "emphasize the artificiality of a difference in treatment which serves only to call attention to a racial classification."[29]

The cases did not overturn the separate but equal doctrine. Their tone suggests that few justices were enthusiastic about distinguishing between higher education and elementary education, and that few indeed would have happily signed an opinion explicitly reaffirming the doctrine. The justices marched to the edge of overruling the doctrine and said, "not yet."

The press and congressional reaction indicated that the Court had prepared the public for a decision explicitly overruling *Plessy*. Arthur Krock of the New York *Times*, rather sympathetic to the South's claims, wrote that the decisions left *Plessy* in "tatters," and that the Court's approach meant that providing facilities that the Court would accept as equal "will impose crushing financial burdens on the community." Other observers also stressed the cost of establishing equal facilities, which missed the point of the Court's emphasis on intangible elements of education. No matter how much it spent, a state could hardly create a school with the "traditions" and community contacts that the Court said were essential to equality. Southern members of Congress of course criticized the decisions, and saw them as foreshadowing "a showdown" on the issue of segregation itself. Virtually everyone who commented on the decisions thought that they jeopardized segregation in elementary and secondary schools.[30]

Writing Marshall on June 6, Dean Griswold said Marshall "came out pretty well in Washington yesterday," and, while noting that Marshall probably "would have liked to have the school decisions go farther," found it "more important that the decisions were unanimous." Howard Jay Graham, a historian of the Fourteenth Amendment, sent Marshall some of his work, saying, "Now that Plessy v. Ferguson is doomed I fervently hope these chapters speed its end." Though Marshall would have welcomed a decision explicitly overruling *Plessy*, he understood that the decisions were "replete with road markings" showing that *Plessy* "has been gutted." For him, "the end is in sight." He sent the publishers of African-American newspapers a letter seeking their financial support for the challenges that were to come now that "we have at last obtained the opening wedge."[31]

Some things remained before launching the next attack on *Plessy*. At the end of June, Marshall convened a meeting of the staff, cooperating lawyers, and lawyers for the interest groups that had supported the NAACP's cases. The lawyers discussed "how far [the June cases] can be used toward the breaking down of governmentally imposed segregation," and finally endorsed the position first urged at the 1946 Atlanta lawyers conference: The NAACP staff would no longer participate in any suit seeking equalization of facilities. That decision ended the ambiguity about whether the NAACP could support complaints alleging that facilities were unequal. Inequality now was relevant only because it was "evidence of the unconstitutionality of segregation." When Marshall learned that Emory Jackson in Alabama had been urging the improvement of five segregated schools, he chastised him mildly. The NAACP, Marshall wrote, must "make it clear to the public that we do not seek Jim Crow education and will not participate in any cases along those lines." He criticized U. Simpson Tate in Texas for suggesting that the NAACP might accept a settlement establishing substantial equality: "This type of position is dangerous. It lends credence to the talk that we are not really fighting against segregation in public education."[32]

Some university cases lingered. In Houston's last substantial trial before his death, he and Marshall cooperated with Donald Murray to desegregate Maryland's nursing program. The court rejected the state's claim that it could satisfy its constitutional obligations, not by creating a separate school—entirely too expensive if each state had to do so—but by cooperating with neighboring states to create regional programs. Southerners supporting segregation found regional programs attractive for obvious financial reasons, yet they also tapped into a strain of liberal Southern thought that saw regional cooperation as a vehicle for economic development. The NAACP, though, believed that "regional education as currently conceived and promoted . . . is unconstitutional, uneconomical, unfair and unnecessary."[33]

Even when Herman Taylor, a North Carolina lawyer, came up with a "well nigh perfect" plaintiff for a medical school case, Marshall said that it was "financially and physically impossible" for the national office to handle any more university cases. By the end of 1950, the LDF was supporting graduate school and law school cases in Louisiana and Virginia, but, according to Marshall, they were "faced with the problem of getting a corps of experts" to do what the law school witnesses had done already.[34]

Lyman Johnson, a civic activist in Kentucky, gave the NAACP its first trial court victory in a university case since the Murray case in 1936. Seeking a doctorate in history, he applied to the University of Kentucky in 1948. The state argued that the programs at Kentucky State, the segregated school, were substantially equal to those at the university. Marshall developed a list of expert witnesses, including John Hope Franklin, then starting his career as a professor of history, to challenge that claim. When the case came to trial, though, the judge had the state put on its witnesses first. Marshall asked the president of the University of Kentucky, "Do you really believe that the educational facilities at Kentucky State are equal to what you have on your campus for white students?" The witness answered honestly, "No." When the state finished its presentation, the judge said, "Why drag this out? The state has won the case for you." Over thirty African-Americans began to attend the university; Johnson himself received several death threats and a number of crosses were burned, although Johnson found little opposition from students or others on the campus.[35]

Finally, Dean Griswold went after John Hervey, who advised the American Bar Association on accrediting law schools. Griswold wrote Karl Llewellyn, then the president of the Association of American Law Schools, criticizing Hervey's testimony in the Oklahoma case that a student at the segregated law school could receive an education equivalent to that available at the University of Oklahoma, and his similar testimony in North Carolina. Griswold had testified in both cases, and expressed "serious doubts" about whether Hervey should both testify and inspect schools for accreditation. Hervey's role in accreditation inevitably "create[d] the impression" the ABA and the AALS "were both in support of" his testimony. Griswold thought that the approval of the newly established schools "came with surprising promptness, and at a time when some of the schools could hardly be regarded as adequate." At a meeting with the AALS's executive committee, Griswold "lost the battle, but . . . may have won the war." The committee, Griswold said, treated his criticisms as a personal attack on Hervey and "got their backs up in defense of their man." He thought Hervey might not testify in any later cases. [36]

Heman Sweatt had a successful career, though not as a lawyer. He registered at the Texas law school in September 1950, where he received a "mixed reception," with some faculty members trying to be friendly to him and others expressing hostility. He became a member of student social committee, but his academic performance was disappointing. He failed several courses, and returned in the fall of 1951 to audit them. He enrolled as a regular student again in the spring, but that was his last semester. The NAACP was slow in sending him the money he had been promised. His ulcers flared up, and he had to have an appendectomy. All these strains contributed to the breakup of his marriage in 1952. After giving up on a legal career, Sweatt got a scholarship to study social work at Atlanta University. He got his degree in 1954 and moved to Cleveland, where he worked for the Urban League. Later he returned to Atlanta and became assistant director of the Urban League's regional office. [37]

11

"A Direct Challenge of the Segregation Statutes"
Making the Record in *Brown*

On Monday, April 23, 1951, Oliver Hill got a telephone call from R. R. Moton High School in Farmville, Virginia. His caller, never identified, told him students were striking to protest conditions there: expanding school enrollments led the school board to put up some leaky and badly heated "temporary" outbuildings made of wood and tarpaper. Barbara Johns, a sixteen-year-old at the school, organized the student strike, working with friends from the school's student council. Johns, born in New York but raised in Farmville, was the niece of Vernon Johns, a fiery preacher whose sermons delivered throughout the South often focused on segregation. Inspired by her uncle, Barbara Johns decided that something had to be done. The school's principal was sympathetic to community efforts to improve the schools, and Johns did not want to implicate him in militant action. She lured him away by placing a call that two high school students were about to be arrested. When he left the school, Johns sent a note in his name to each classroom, calling an assembly. The students and teachers went to the school auditorium and Johns started speaking. When some teachers tried to stop her, she had them escorted out. Johns denounced the school board's failure to provide decent facilities and ended by calling for a strike. The students walked out.[1]

Hill was trying to develop a desegregation case in nearby Pulaski County, and was scheduled to go to the area on Wednesday. After asking that the students write him describing their situation, Hill agreed to meet the students' families on his way to Pulaski County, although he was unsure that Farmville was a good place to bring a lawsuit. Farmville was in Prince Edward County, a "tense" part of Virginia's Southside, and Hill believed that Richmond or Norfolk were better places for the first Virginia desegregation suit. According to Hill, he "had a horror of talking to a group of these kids with no adults around." If the parents did not agree with the students, a lawsuit could not be sustained. And, although students routinely got the attention of recalcitrant school boards by striking, a lawsuit with such a dramatic beginning might be bad public relations; after all, the students were violating the state's compulsory attendance laws.[2]

Hill and his partner Spottswood Robinson met the students at Farmville's First

Baptist Church. The church pastor Leslie Francis Griffin was a civic activist, a supporter of Henry Wallace's 1948 presidential campaign, and president of the local NAACP branch. Like everyone else, he had been caught by surprise when Johns called the student strike. Hill and Robinson expected to meet a small group of students and parents, but when they arrived in Farmville they found the church basement packed with students and only a few parents. At first, Hill and Robinson tried to persuade the students to call off the strike, because they did not believe "in solving our problems by breaking the law." The students insisted on continuing the strike, saying that the jail was not "big enough to hold all our parents."[3]

Hill and Robinson then suggested that the students wait for the Pulaski County case. The students refused, and Hill and Robinson were so impressed with their discipline and dedication that they decided to go ahead. They said they would take the case if the students went back to school. They explained, however, that they would not file a suit simply to eliminate Moton's temporary classrooms. Robinson ended by giving the group thirty days to decide whether they wanted to file a desegregation suit rather than one to equalize the facilities. He was told, though, that the group needed no time to decide; the community had known for a long time that desegregation was a good idea. All that remained was to get the parents on board. The group scheduled a mass meeting for the next evening. Although Hill and Robinson could not attend, they had Lester Banks, the state NAACP's executive secretary, speak. Around two thousand people attended. No serious opposition to filing a desegregation case surfaced.[4]

Hill and Robinson filed the Pulaski County case anyway, on April 30, but it fizzled when their plaintiff died. The students in Farmville returned to school, as Hill and Robinson insisted. Over the next month, Reverend Griffin got signatures on a petition to desegregate the high school. On May 23, a month after the strike began, Robinson filed suit in Richmond, seeking high school desegregation. In June the school board offered to build a new, segregated high school if the plaintiffs withdrew their suit, but the plaintiffs rejected the offer. A few days later, the board fired Moton's principal because, it said, he had not acted vigorously against the student strike. Then the board started to build the new high school anyway. It opened in 1953. But by then it was too late for the board to avoid litigation.[5]

By 1950, the NAACP'S lawyers had made it clear to their constituents that they were ready for the next stage. Many communities were ready. African-Americans, aware of the NAACP's position but acting independently, initiated numerous student strikes to challenge the inequalities of school segregation. After taking the first steps, they approached the NAACP, and, as in Farmville, often enthusiastically agreed to change their focus from equalization to desegregation. As Marshall put it in a 1949 letter to Robinson, "Some of our branches are hell-bent on getting cases started concerning elementary and high school education."[6]

Marshall gradually reached the decision on desegregation rather than equalization before the Court's 1950 opinions, but even toward the end of the 1940s he was willing to devote resources to equalization suits. Attacking segregation directly was a bold step, and not all his constituents were ready for it. Desegregation had some obvious costs. Many believed it would threaten the jobs of African-American teachers. Admittedly, if desegregation occurred, districts would still need teachers for the same total number of students. Despite the fact that, as Marshall told a national radio audience, "Negroes have been disciplining and teaching white children in the homes where they work," many feared that whites would not allow African-Americans to teach their children.[7]

In addition, many African-Americans believed that whites would resist desegregation violently. Their children would have to run the gauntlet, and the educational advantages of desegregation under such conditions were no obviously larger than the educational advantages of forcing the South to invest money to make the segregated schools more nearly equal. Finally, one strand of African-American thought on racial issues was gradualist and accommodationist. According to accommodationist thought, as whites came to understand the inequities of segregation, they would voluntarily modify it, gradually improving conditions. A gradual evolution to integration was, on this view, more likely to stick than desegregation forced on the South through litigation.[8]

No one could fairly dismiss these concerns as unfounded, but Marshall and his staff disagreed with the accommodationists. Using money donated by the Prince Hall Masons, Marshall did hire John W. Davis, former president of West Virginia's segregated college, to work with teachers concerned about jobs. Davis spoke to teachers in the South "to define the tenure and job security problems," "to explain the legal approaches which can be used to thwart any wholesale firing of Negro teachers," and "to enlist the cooperation of teacher groups" in the desegregation effort. He also helped the lawyers prepare legal materials on job security issues.[9]

Perhaps more important, the restrictive covenant cases showed that Marshall and the LDF could control the law's development only if they took the lead. Aggressive communities willing to attack segregation head-on might find their own lawyers, and those lawyers might not be as resourceful as Marshall and the LDF in developing the strongest attacks on segregation. In short, as long as there were communities willing to attack segregation, the exigencies of the litigation campaign required the LDF to be in the lead.

From 1946 to 1950, desegregation cases bubbled up. Some began as equalization suits and stayed that way, while others were converted into direct attacks on segregation. What happened in each case depended as much on local lawyers as on any large strategic decisions made in New York.

In late 1946 families in Lumberton, North Carolina, were so upset about the run-down conditions at African-American schools that the NAACP's youth branch sponsored a student strike, which Marshall called "one of the finest things ever pulled in the NAACP." Herman Taylor, their local lawyer, had been a legal intern at the NAACP's national office. Taylor proceeded cautiously, concerned that aggressive actions might give white lawyers an excuse for excluding him from the bar. The result, though, was that the NAACP's supporters began to complain. Preoccupied with the pending university cases, Marshall responded somewhat testily that "you don't run into court with a legal case overnight" and that he was "sick and tired of people in our branches who wait 81 years to get to the point of bringing legal action to secure their rights and then want the lawyers to prepare the case, file it, have it decided and have everything straightened out in fifteen minutes." By June 1947, the national office treated the case as a simple equalization suit, and the case ended when a new school was built. [10]

In September 1947, 75 percent of the students at the African-American high school in Hearne, Texas, refused to attend school, protesting that they met in classes averaging sixty students while whites went to twenty-seven-person classes. They asked the school board to build a new school. "Terribly impressed with the courage of the 'little Joes' in the South," the national office advised A. Maceo Smith that it preferred to ask for admission to the white schools. Marian Perry wrote Smith that seeking admission was not always possible "in view of the temper of the local community," but recommended that he modify the petition to avoid asking directly for a new school. It should instead protest discrimination and leave it to the school board to decide between building a new school or desegregating. Eventually, under the lawsuit's pressure, the board did improve the school. [11]

Marshall's attention to legal ethics was one source of problems in these cases. Although the national office could "interest itself" in cases initiated locally, it could not "suggest that students institute law suits of any kind," a staff lawyer wrote, "as in our opinion that would be both unethical and illegal." Hill and Robinson retained the letter they received from Barbara Johns to show that she, not they, had taken the initiative in Farmville. Yet, the more the cases were generated by spontaneous local protests, the more difficult it was to ensure that they could be shaped into the challenge to segregation that Marshall and his staff wanted. Somehow they had to take control of cases they did not begin. [12]

In Kansas, Esther Brown, a housewife active in Henry Wallace's Progressive party, prodded the local and national NAACP into action. While driving her maid home, Brown became upset when she saw the run-down condition of the African-American elementary school in South Park. Her speeches to the school board were ignored, and Brown searched for a lawyer to challenge the segregated system. The legal issues were simple, because Kansas statutes permitted segregation only in districts larger than South Park. Several African-American lawyers got involved, though, and began to bicker over controlling the case. Meanwhile, Brown's husband lost his job and a cross was burned on their lawn. From New York, Marshall wanted to take over the case, saying that "we don't like the way it is presently being handled as a one-woman show." Franklin Williams defended Brown, calling her "one of the few militant and out-spoken members of the branch." Brown helped organize a three-week school boycott, during which parents conducted classes for their children. South Park lost the lawsuit and desegregated its schools. [13]

Brown then directed her energy to challenging segregation elsewhere. The Wichita and Topeka branches competed for the honor of leading the challenge. In mid-1947, a member of the Wichita branch wrote the national office describing the conditions in the segregated schools, but nothing developed beyond the circulation of a petition, until schools opened in 1948. Although the Wichita branch was "weak," the president of the parent-teachers association volunteered to be a plaintiff. The state NAACP board voted seven to two to support a Wichita lawsuit, largely because three prominent African-American attorneys lived there and could handle the case. The Wichita branch turned out to be unenthusiastic. African-American teachers, active in the branch, were suspicious of desegregation, and "some officials appear to prefer not to have the active participation of white persons . . . in our conference." When the Wichita branch elected new officers, opponents of litigation seemed to gain a majority, although the well-meaning but "do-nothing" president of the branch stayed on. All this gave the national office "misgivings" about what appeared to an "isolated project" spurred by Brown and a few others.[14]

The Topeka branch, in contrast, had raised $1,000 and come up with a handful of potential plaintiffs in October 1948. They petitioned the school board to end segregation. As usual, getting a lawsuit in shape took longer than anyone expected, but by August 1950, the branch was ready. In February 1951, Elisha Scott and his sons filed suit. The first plaintiff was Oliver Brown, a Kansas City native who worked as a welder for the Santa Fe railway shops. Other plaintiffs were members of the church where Oliver Brown was an assistant pastor. The plaintiffs' grievance against segregation incorporated concern for their children's safety. For example, Brown's daughter Linda had to walk across railroad tracks and the main industrial street in Topeka to get the school bus. More important to the parents, though, was the humiliating fact of segregation itself.[15]

After some confusion, the national office had gotten control of the Kansas litigation. The case Marshall brought in South Carolina was more like the one in Virginia. Local activists got in touch with the national office shortly after they began to organize. In June 1947, James Hinton, president of South Carolina's NAACP conference of branches, addressed students at Allen University in Columbia. Saying that the state's segregated schools were a disgrace, Hinton mentioned the NAACP's interest in finding places where African-American children had to walk to school while whites had buses. Joseph DeLaine, a minister and schoolteacher in rural Clarendon County, was in the audience. DeLaine's students did walk to school. He returned to Clarendon County, which had the highest proportion of African-Americans in the state, and began to organize church members on the bus issue. In July, they petitioned the school board for buses. In March 1948, the NAACP filed a taxpayer's lawsuit in the name of Levi Pearson. Unfortunately, Pearson lived on the boundary between two tax districts, and although his children did attend the schools without bus service, he paid his taxes to the other district. As a result, the court dismissed the lawsuit.[16]

DeLaine continued to worry about segregation. In February 1949, Marshall arranged an unpublicized meeting in South Carolina "to find the exact places where we intend to bring these cases." Marshall met DeLaine and persuaded him that a direct attack on segregation made more sense than a bus lawsuit. Wanting to be sure that the community supported such a challenge, Marshall asked DeLaine and South Carolina NAACP leaders to come up with twenty plaintiffs in Clarendon County. DeLaine organized a series of meetings at local churches, circulated petitions, and got enough signatures. Whites in Clarendon County began to retaliate. The white-owned stores and banks had already denied Pearson credit to purchase fertilizer. Harry Briggs, the first named on the petition, lost his job as an auto mechanic. Other petitioners were fired, and independent farmers "had great trouble getting their cotton ginned that harvest season." DeLaine was fired from his teaching job. Finding itself unable to stem the challenge, though, the school board fired an African-American principal who had alienated the parents, and offered the job first to DeLaine and then to his wife. This attempt to bribe DeLaine failed as well, and an all-out attack on segregation in Clarendon County was filed in November 1949.[17]

Marshall's policy underwent a subtle change as he came to believe that an all-out attack on segregation might succeed. The issue surfaced at the 1946 Atlanta lawyers' conference. Near the end of the conference, discussion turned to bus transportation. Bus cases were hard because requesting only that buses be pro-vided to African-American children as they were provided to whites amounted to attempting to enforce, not overturn, the separate but equal doctrine. Robinson argued that bus cases should be "thrown into our cases as a part of unequal facilities offered." By placing the inadequate bus transportation in its larger con-text, the NAACP's lawsuits could challenge the entire system of segregation.[18]

Marshall understood that Robinson's approach made sense. Initially he made sure that cases were framed to offer school systems a choice of responses. In 1947, Marshall had the NAACP's national office issue a policy statement. After explain-ing why the NAACP was "convinced that segregation statutes violate the Four-teenth Amendment," Marshall proposed two approaches. In one, the lawsuit "directly ask[ed] for admission to the existing facilities previously reserved for white students only." The other "set forth the existing inequalities" and requested an order ending discrimination. Neither approach, he told the branches, "recog-nize[s] the validity of separate school statutes." "This is necessary," he continued, "if we are to keep our position clear which is that we do not consider segregation statutes legal . . . and will continue to challenge them in legal proceedings." Given this policy, Marshall said, "the NAACP cannot take part in any legal proceeding which seeks to enforce segregation statutes [or] which condones seg-regation in public schools."[19]

The NAACP board of directors and its annual conference endorsed this posi-tion in 1948. By 1949, the lawyers formally agreed that every education case "should make a direct challenge of the segregation statutes involved." With that, any ambiguity about the NAACP's position disappeared. The distinction between a direct challenge to segregation and a request that boards stop discriminating was subtle in any event. The final step, merely a formality, was an NAACP board resolution in October 1950, stating that "pleadings in all educational cases . . . should be aimed at obtaining education on a non-segregated basis and . . . no other relief other than that will be acceptable. . . ."[20]

It was no surprise, then, that Robinson could tell Marshall in 1950 that "thus far there have been no known instances in Virginia of Negro groups refusing to go along with us on the policy change." The change, in fact, was less a matter of policy than of litigation strategy, and the NAACP's clients were surely more aware of the policy continuity than of the minor change in the language of the NAACP's legal papers. Robinson and other lawyers, though, "expressed doubt about being able to get many cases" challenging segregation because they did not think that the

NAACP would "get many parents willing to make a test of the segregation laws of their community." They were wrong.[21]

Direct challenges to segregation had one obvious effect on the litigation's shape. In 1913, Congress responded to decisions by conservative judges who blocked states from enforcing their progressive economic regulations. It required that suits seeking to bar states from enforcing their statutes be heard initially not by a single federal judge but by a special panel of three judges. Appeals from these three-judge courts went directly to the Supreme Court. The NAACP's lawyers had a choice in the education litigation's early stages. They could say that school boards maintained unequal facilities and should be required to eliminate the discrimination. This did not challenge the constitutionality of any state statute. The case would be heard by a single federal judge, and appealed to a court of appeals. Alternatively, they could say that the state statutes regulating education were unconstitutional to the extent that they authorized the discrimination. Then the case would be heard by a three-judge court.

As Marshall's legal theory developed, his strategic choices narrowed. Obviously a lawsuit alleging that state segregation statutes were unconstitutional had to be heard by a three-judge court. More subtly, if the lawsuit claimed that segregation inevitably led to discrimination—bad facilities, inadequate transportation, and the like—or that equalizing facilities could not remedy the constitutional violation, it was in effect a challenge to the segregation statute. It too would have be heard by a three-judge court.

Narrowing the strategic choices was mostly insignificant, but there were some modest effects. Most federal judges in the South were unlikely to take bold steps against segregation, and it usually would not matter whether a case was heard by one or three of them. In South Carolina, though, Judge Waring was sympathetic to the NAACP's position, and it might have been attractive to get an initial decision by him in the hope that it would survive court of appeals review.

More generally, routing appeals directly from three-judge courts to the Supreme Court posed some minor risks. Appeals from one-judge courts were time consuming, and the delay gave issues time to develop. Sometimes, by the time the issues reached the Supreme Court, sentiment supporting the NAACP would have developed enough that a favorable Supreme Court decision might not seem so bold. When cases went directly to the Supreme Court, though, the opportunity to build public support was more limited. In the end, the Court itself managed the timing of the cases. It ended up deciding cases filed in 1950 four and five years later, no sooner than it would have if the cases had gone first to a court of appeals.

Marshall had one other important decision to make. He had to persuade the justices that segregation was harmful. The university cases showed harm in two ways. He counted on the justices to understand as lawyers that separate education for lawyers could not be equal, and he presented expert witnesses to testify about how separate professional education ensured inequality. The justices were men of the world as well as lawyers, and Marshall believed they would have some intuitive understanding of the damage that segregation caused young children, just as they understood, without needing expert testimony, that separate legal education had to be unequal. He was less confident, though, about what the justices would think about elementary and secondary education, and wanted to develop expert testimony to help him.

Robert Carter took the lead. He recalled reading a study by Otto Klineberg, a social psychologist at Columbia University, that showed a substantial improvement in the IQ scores of African-American children who moved from segregated schools in the South to unsegregated ones in the North. He called Klineberg to find out what sort of expert testimony might help show damage resulting from segregation. Klineberg told Carter to get in touch with Kenneth Clark, a recent graduate student who had prepared a report on child psychology and segregation for the 1950 White House Midcentury Conference on Youth.[22]

Clark's wife Mamie had begun tests to show how race affected the children's images of themselves, and both Clarks were interested in pursuing the research. The Clarks asked children which of a series of dolls was the nicest doll, which the ugliest, and which was most like them. Typically, they found that African-American children called white dolls nice and dark ones ugly, while saying that the dark dolls were most like them. The Clarks concluded that African-American children had impaired self-images. Carter believed that this evidence would bolster the claim that segregation harmed African-American children. Carter's enthusiasm for this approach was not matched by some of the NAACP's outside advisers, particularly William Coleman, who was quite skeptical about its relevance and had a lawyer's disdain for "soft" evidence from social psychology. One colleague thought Marshall looked at this evidence "with a rather jaundiced eye," but Clark and others thought he was never "negative" about using the evidence. Marshall respected Carter's judgment and was concerned about relying entirely on the justices' intuitions. He and Carter built Clark's testimony into the litigation strategy.[23]

Marshall took charge of the trial in the South Carolina case, *Briggs v. Elliott,* assigned to Judge Waring. The complaint alleged that African-American students did not have equal access to bus transportation, and asked the court to invalidate the "practice of . . . maintaining public schools for Negro children because of their race and color which are in every respect inferior to those maintained for white children." This complaint probably could be handled by a single judge. On November 17, 1950, Judge Waring held a pretrial conference. During the conference, Marshall said that he believed the complaint did raise the basic question of the segregation's constitutionality, perhaps because the phrase "in every respect inferior" implied that segregation could not lead to equal facilities. Judge Waring was skeptical, and said that if the case proceeded along the complaint's lines, he would be inclined to decide only the bus transportation issue. Marshall then asked for permission to amend the complaint to make the challenge to segregation clear. Waring responded that Marshall should dismiss the case and refile a new complaint directly challenging segregation. Marshall was "rather astonished," partly because he did not expect Waring to be so forthright, but partly because under the rules of procedure there was no difference between amending the complaint and filing a new one. For his part, Waring apparently did not think Marshall "militant" enough, and used the pretrial conference to prod Marshall. Marshall did what Waring suggested, and refiled the case on December 22. The case then had to be heard by three judges, and Waring was joined by Judge John Parker of the court of appeals and Judge George Timmerman of the district court.[24]

The court scheduled the trial for May 1951. In January, James Byrnes, former Supreme Court Justice and Cabinet member, was inaugurated as South Carolina's governor. Byrnes was dedicated to maintaining Jim Crow, and his speeches often suggested that South Carolina would "abandon the public school system" rather than eliminate segregation. He knew, though, that even if the Supreme Court allowed segregation to continue, it was likely to insist on serious steps to make the segregated schools substantially equal. Byrnes proposed, and the legislature adopted, the state's first sales tax, to finance a bond issue of over $80 million for school construction and bus purchases. Estimates for equalizing facilities ranged from $40 million to $80 million, and, although nothing in the legislation guaranteed that the funds would be used only for equalization, Byrnes and his supporters clearly hoped that they would be able to improve African-American schools enough to avoid court-ordered desegregation. Some conservative politicians opposed Byrnes's program, but most saw it as essential to segregation's legal defense. Progressives saw the program as an opportunity to improve the "miserable" conditions in South Carolina's schools.[25]

The three-judge court convened on May 28. The courthouse was jammed. Spottswood Robinson, who left for Charleston after filing the complaint in the Prince Edward County case, was afraid that a riot might break out.* Robert McCormick Figg, Clarendon County's lawyer, almost derailed the hearing at the outset. The year before, Clarendon County had spent around $180 for each white child in school and only $43 for each African-American child; many of the schools for African-Americans were little more than shacks, while the white schools were brick-and-mortar structures. Figg acknowledged all this when he read a statement in which the county conceded that the facilities available for African-Americans were unequal, and stated that it would not oppose an order finding inequality and directing the board to eliminate "any discrimination" in connection with the facilities. He suggested that the court "give them a reasonable time to formulate a plan for ending such inequalities," for example, by using the proceeds of the bond issue to build new schools.[26]

Marshall had planned to put on witnesses to show that the facilities in Clarendon County were grossly unequal, and Carter had meticulously lined them up, but Figg's concession made that unnecessary. Marshall simply had one expert witness from Howard's education school describe what he had seen when he inspected the facilities: cracked tables and broken chairs, no lunchrooms or gymnasiums, outdoor toilets. Figg's cross-examination extracted the concession that all the inequalities could be eliminated if the school district simply put more money into the African-American schools, as, according to the board's statement, it planned to.[27]

---

* His fears were heightened when he saw a burly man carrying a coil of rope through the crowd, but he was relieved to discover that the man used the rope to make a passageway for the lawyers and judges.

The next witnesses turned to segregation's psychological effects. Harold McNally, also from Howard, testified that "segregation itself implies a difference, a stigma." Kenneth Clark testified about the doll tests. He relied on the general studies that had attracted Carter's attention, but he also examined sixteen children in Clarendon County. Clark later said that the children were "pretty matter of fact" about taking the tests, even though they were brought to the room with "bodyguards" to ensure that nothing interfered with Clark's work. The children he examined, Clark testified, preferred the white doll. Another witness told the court that desegregation had occurred without violence at West Virginia college. Figg largely ignored the expert witnesses, suggesting primarily they had knew almost nothing about Clarendon County itself.[28]

Marshall ran out of witnesses before the first day's hearing ended. To keep the hearing going, Judge Parker let Figg put on one of his witnesses, "significantly named" Crow, as Judge Waring put it later. E. R. Crow was the director of South Carolina's Educational Finance Commission, established to supervise Byrnes's construction program. Crow explained the program and told the court that "there would be a violent reaction" if the schools were "mixed." "It would eliminate public schools in most if not all of the counties," Crow said. Marshall conducted an aggressive cross-examination. He asked Crow if he believed white parents would "deprive their own children of an education because of this." According to Crow, the problem was that the legislature would not appropriate funds for mixed schools. Turning to the question of violence, Marshall asked whether Crow believed that the people of South Carolina were law-abiding. When Marshall asked whether the people would obey an injunction, Figg objected, and Parker said that the court would "assume that any injunction issued will be obeyed." Marshall concluded the cross-examination by getting Crow to agree that "part" of his reason for fearing that desegregation would have undesirable consequences was that "you have all your life believed in segregation." From a strictly legal point of view, Marshall's questioning did little to undermine Figg's case. It was directed, though, much more at the African-Americans in the audience than at the judges, and that audience loved it. Crow's first name, one listener said, should be "Jim." Another observed that Marshall "sure loves to eat crow."[29]

Carter continued to present expert witnesses on segregation's psychological effects on the second day. They stressed that legal segregation defined African-Americans as inferior, and that segregation in elementary schools "starts the process at a crucial age." Again, Figg's cross-examination aimed at showing that the witnesses were unfamiliar with Clarendon County and the South. Marshall wanted to use Robert Redfield again as a witness, to show that African-American children "do about as well as anybody" if given the opportunity. Redfield, though, had not arrived in Charleston by the morning of May 29. Prodded by Judge Parker to get the case finished, Marshall ended up inserting the testimony Redfield gave in the Texas law school case into the record.[30]

Marshall's closing argument drew on the expert testimony. Legal segregation, he said, gave a "halo of respectability" to the judgment that African-Americans were inferior. The Supreme Court, according to Marshall, had been moving toward saying that "even when facilities are equal, segregation itself is detrimental."

South Carolina ran a system of "exclusion from the group that runs everything." This, Marshall said, "sets up a roadblock in [a child's] mind which prevents his ever feeling he is equal." But, even if the court was not willing to invalidate segregation, the plaintiffs were entitled to immediate relief, because "human rights are now." The only immediate relief possible was a desegregation order. Byrnes' construction program amounted to a promise to borrow some money in July and "build some schools later." Equal facilities would not be available for months at best. "There is no relief . . . except to be permitted to attend existing and superior white schools."[31]

Figg's argument focused on how well established segregation was. He stressed the state's "great progress" in race relations, and quoted the progressive sociologist from North Carolina, Howard Odum, who, Figg said, had told him that "forced mixing" of the races "would destroy 23 years of my work" in improving race relations. Parker pressed Figg to describe the decree he would accept. The difficulty was that Judge Parker did not want to "supervise the administration of the schools," and yet wanted some assurance that the schools Figg promised would indeed be built. Figg suggested that the court could specify that the schools had to be built within some set period, without telling the district exactly how to proceed.[32]

After Figg ended, Parker asked whether the parties planned to file briefs. Sure that the three-judge court would not resolve the separate but equal issue, Marshall filed a rather cursory brief. Judge Waring, at least, found it unsatisfactory, calling it "one of those colorless routine affairs reciting the various decisions which we all know." Waring described Judge Timmerman as a "rigid segregationist," and himself as "an equally rigid anti-segregationist." According to Waring, Judge Parker "just set his feet on Plessy against Ferguson." Waring tried to persuade him that Plessy could be distinguished because it involved transportation, and that the university cases had "in effect" overruled Plessy. Parker, committed to an unimaginative approach to precedent, stood firm.[33]

Parker's opinion was issued on June 23, 1951. Figg's concession, it said, required the court to enter an order directing the school authorities to provide equal facilities.[34] It told them to come back in six months with a report showing what they had done. Then the opinion turned to the broader claim that segregation itself violated the Constitution. Parker called segregation "a matter of legislative policy," emphasizing that "in a country with a great expanse of territory with peoples of widely differing customs and ideas, local self government in local matters is essential to the peace and happiness of the people . . . as well as to the strength and unity of the country as a whole." Parker reviewed the Supreme Court cases, and found that the separate but equal doctrine remained unimpaired. University education, he said, was different from elementary education because of the importance of professional contacts. He also argued that, because the government required parents to send their children to elementary school, it could take into account "the wishes of the parent as to the upbringing of the child and his associates in the formative period of childhood and adolescence." This part of the opinion closed with a scarcely veiled threat: "If public education is to have the support of the people . . . , it must not go contrary to what they deem for the best interests of their children."

The policy arguments for desegregated education, Parker said, depended on "the relationships existing between the races and the tensions likely to be produced" by desegregation. The federal courts, according to Parker, could not make such assessments. Parker concluded by calling it "a late day" to say that segregation was unconstitutional when it had been in place for "more than three-quarters of a century" and had been approved repeatedly by the Supreme Court. If conditions had changed, the legislature should respond. Evoking the progressive response to Supreme Court decisions finding it unconstitutional for legislatures to depart from laissez faire in economic regulation, Parker concluded, "The members of the judiciary have no more right to read their ideas of sociology into the Constitution than their ideas of economics."

Judge Waring wrote a typically impassioned and disjointed dissent. Waring prepared part of his opinion before the defendants conceded inequality, and he criticized them for their "maneuver" designed "to induce this Court to avoid the primary purpose of the suit." For Waring, the Fourteenth Amendment "was intended to do away with discrimination between our citizens," and segregation rested on "sophistry and prejudice." He believed that the Court had come to understand, step by step, that segregation violated the Constitution. Not only was *Plessy* old and outdated, it was, for Waring, merely a "railroad" case. Waring, finally, was impressed with Marshall's expert witnesses, who demonstrated that "the mere fact of segregation, itself, had a deleterious and warping effect upon the minds of children." "Segregation," Waring concluded, "is per se inequality." He was so enamored of the phrase that he pressed Marshall to include it in his Supreme Court brief.[35]

The NAACP'S other school cases proceeded routinely, with only minor variations on the South Carolina case. Clark testified in South Carolina, Virginia, and Delaware, but not in Topeka. There the local Jewish Community Relations Bureau put Carter and Greenberg, who were trying the case, in touch with Hugh Speer, chair of the education department of the University of Kansas City. Speer tried to round up local experts, who would be less vulnerable to the kinds of minor challenges that Figg raised in cross-examining the experts in South Carolina. And, not insignificantly, it would cost less to use local experts; they could arrange to attend the trial more easily, giving the lawyers more flexibility.[36]

The Topeka trial took place in late June 1951, just as Judge Parker issued the court's decision in South Carolina. According to Greenberg, the tangible inequalities were not as great in Kansas as elsewhere. The psychological testimony therefore played a large role in the lawyers' trial strategy, although Walter Huxman, the presiding judge, tried to limit the number of expert witnesses. Preparing one of his witnesses, Greenberg wanted testimony showing "how the frustration and personality damage inflicted upon Negroes hamper them in their education." Following Greenberg's lead that education is "more than [the] course of study[, i]t is the total classroom experience," Speer testified that "education is more than just remembering something. It is concerned with the child's total development." By defining elementary education so broadly, Speer connected the theory of the university cases to elementary schools. "If the colored children are denied the experience in school of associating with white children who make up about 90 percent of our national society," he testified, "then their curriculum is being greatly curtailed." He concluded that no curriculum, in that sense, could be equal under segregation. When the city's school superintendent said that he did not believe the schools should "dictate the social customs of the people," Huxman impatiently said, "The question is what the Fourteenth Amendment warrants and what it doesn't. We don't care what social custom provides."[37]

The three-judge court in Kansas was unanimous. Circuit Judge Huxman, formerly the state's governor, wrote a short, pedestrian opinion. He found the facilities substantially equal, noting in passing that even the NAACP attorneys "did not give [the question of material equality] great emphasis in their presentation." Huxman said that the broader question was "not free from difficulty." Trying to "ascertain the trend" of the Supreme Court's decisions, he found that the 1950 cases did not overrule *Plessy*. However, the court also made an important "finding of fact": segregation, the court found, "has a detrimental effect upon the colored children. The impact is greater when it has the sanction of law. . . . A sense of inferiority affects the motivation of a child to learn." Segregation, therefore, "has a tendency . . . to deprive them of some of the benefits they would receive in a racially integrated school system." Later Huxman would say that he had tried to "wrap[ ] up the decision in such a way that the Supreme Court could no longer duck it."[38]

The Virginia trial took place in February 1952. The school board's lawyers devoted more time to challenging the psychological evidence than any other defendants' lawyers had. According to Kenneth Clark, the board's attorney Justin Moore raised some "significant questions" about his research by getting Clark to concede that his research had not addressed the question of whether the harms he found resulted from segregation established by law rather than from the segregated conditions in the society at large. In addition, Moore located an imposing expert to testify for the board. Henry Garrett, a native of Southside Virginia, taught psychology at Columbia. He had been president of the American Psychological Association, and had been one of the Clarks' dissertation advisers. Garrett believed strongly in segregation, and Clark was unable to convince him not to testify. Much of what Garrett had to say on the stand was a testimonial to segregation, although he offered some technical criticisms of the questionnaires and interviews the NAACP's experts had conducted.[39]

A week after the trial ended, the court ruled against the plaintiffs.[40] Finding the South Carolina decision an "apt and able precedent," the court "refused to decree that segregation be ended incontinently." The judges believed that segregation "has begotten greater opportunities for the Negro," apparently by providing jobs for African-American teachers. In a finding unlike any other, the court said that in seventeen counties and eight cities, the African-American schools were "better" than the white schools. It did find inequality in the Prince Edward

County schools, though. According to the court, "frankness required admission" that the high school buildings were unequal, but the court also found inequality in curricula and bus transportation. It directed the school board to improve the Moton curriculum and to make sure that students there got an equal share of new buses. The tarpaper buildings that provoked the initial student strike, the court said, were about to be replaced by a new high school costing $840,000. No injunction, it concluded, could accomplish more.

As appeals in the South Carolina and Topeka cases were being prepared, NAACP attorneys completed two other cases. Louis Redding, an African-American graduate of Harvard Law School, and Jack Greenberg tried a segregation case in Delaware's state courts. Parents in two Delaware communities complained to Redding about conditions in their schools. High school students in Claymont had to go to Wilmington, nearly an hour away, rather than attend a neighborhood school. The Wilmington high school was inferior to the Claymont one, lacking courses in Spanish and trigonometry, and having a much more limited extracurricular program. Ethel Belton led a group of parents trying to get their children into the Claymont school. In Hockessin, the problem was bus transportation. A school bus taking white children to school passed by Sarah Bulah's house, but the district provided no bus service to the African-American school. Bulah complained to the school authorities, and then to Redding. Redding told her that he would not help "get a Jim Crow bus," but was willing to bring a desegregation suit.[41]

Following the usual pattern, Redding filed the cases in federal court. Delaware's attorney general asked the federal court to refrain from deciding the case until it was heard in state court. Ordinarily, attorneys affiliated with the NAACP would have objected to this procedure, called abstention, because ordinarily they had nothing to gain—and time to lose—by going to state court. Vice chancellor Collins Seitz had ruled against segregated undergraduate education in 1950, though,[*] and Redding did not object to abstention.[42]

By the time of trial in October 1951, the lawyers for both sides knew the steps to the dance, and the trial proceeded uneventfully. Delaware's chancery courts' traditions were more flexible than federal court procedures, and Seitz took some time to inspect the Claymont and Wilmington high schools. He was sympathetic to the plaintiffs' claims from the start. Instead of disparaging the expert witnesses, for example, Seitz noted that two of them had examined "some" children in Delaware and, he said, their findings, "while not at all conclusive . . . gave some support" to his conclusions. In describing one expert's testimony, Seitz said, revealing his views, that the expert had "pointed out that State enforced segregation is important, because it . . . gives legal sanction to the differences."[43]

Seitz's opinion, issued in April 1952, found that "State-imposed segregation in education itself results in the Negro children, as a class, receiving educational

---

[*] In 1950 the Delaware State College for Negroes lost its accreditation. This gave the NAACP its first real chance to try to desegregate an undergraduate program; it would be hard for the state to defend the proposition that an unaccredited school for African-Americans was substantially equal to the accredited state university. Redding and Greenberg filed suit in state court, and won a decision from Seitz. *Parker v. University of Delaware*, 75 A.2d 225 (Del. Ch. 1950).

opportunities which are substantially inferior to those available to white children. . . ." But, Seitz continued, as a lower court judge he could not reject the separate but equal doctrine even though he thought it was wrong, and even though he saw a "trend" against the doctrine "in the wind." On the question of material equality, Seitz found the Claymont high school superior to the Wilmington high school "with respect to teacher training, student-teacher ratio, extra curricular activities, physical plants and esthetic considerations." The schools in Hockessin were similarly unequal. Seitz described the white school as "beautifully situated" and much better maintained than the African-American school.

The final question, then, was what Seitz should do. The defendants said he should direct them to equalize facilities. Seitz disagreed. Once the plaintiffs showed inequality, he said, they were "entitled to have made available . . . the State facilities which have been shown to be superior"—that is, entitled to desegregation. Otherwise, Seitz wrote, the court would be telling them, "Yes, your Constitutional rights are being invaded, but be patient, we will see whether in time they are still being violated."

The state appealed to the state supreme court, which affirmed the desegregation decree in August 1952.[44] It qualified Seitz's analysis slightly by saying that desegregation might not be an appropriate response where "substantial inequality exists only in a few of the many factors entering into the comparison," but it said that the exception was not applicable to either Claymont or Hockessin. Seitz's remedy, the supreme court said, was the only one consistent with the Supreme Court's statement that constitutional rights were "personal and present."

Segregation in the District of Columbia posed distinctive problems. Doctrinally, Washington was different because segregation there resulted from congressional statutes. This raised two problems. The Fourteenth Amendment required states to provide residents the "equal protection of the laws." Whatever that meant exactly, it clearly referred to some sort of equality. The Constitution, though, did not contain language clearly indicating that Congress too was limited by concepts of equality. The best the lawyers could do, as they had in the restrictive covenant case from Washington, was argue that the Fifth Amendment's due process clause imposed equality obligations on Congress. Yet, even if the lawyers cleared the hurdle of the Constitution's language, the hurdle of history remained. Congress segregated schools in Washington at the same time it proposed the Fourteenth Amendment. How could that amendment, not to mention the Fifth Amendment, invalidate a practice its proponents themselves endorsed? In addition, the lawyers in the national office had somewhat less control over Washington cases than they had elsewhere.* Washington's vigorous and talented African-American lawyers were perfectly able to bring segregation cases if the national office lagged.

The students at Browne Junior High School began a strike that led to litigation the NAACP did not control. Browne was seriously overcrowded, and space was

---

*The national office did discourage one peculiar case in the late 1940s, when a white student suggested challenging segregation because the costume design course she wanted to take was offered at one of the African-American schools but not at any white ones. Marian Wynn Perry to files, Jan. 20, 1948, NAACP Papers, Box II-B-136, file: Schools, District of Columbia, Galarza Case, 1947–48.

available at a nearby white school. Acting through Belford Lawson, who had handled a number of discrimination cases independently of the NAACP, their parents sued the school board. Despite a prolonged strike at Browne, the school board stood firm. In February 1948, Gardner Bishop, the moving force behind the litigation, met Houston; to Bishop's surprise, Houston encouraged him. At the time, Houston said that he "was looking for a chance to hit the system" before his son entered it.[45]

Houston decided to challenge inequality in the city's schools, but he did not frame the case as a direct attack on segregation. In 1950, the court of appeals rejected Houston's suit over a vigorous dissent by liberal Judge Henry Edgerton, who said that "segregation is humiliating to Negroes" because it implies "that it is not thought fit to associate" with them. Meanwhile, James Nabrit and other lawyers, whose connection to the LDF national office was by then somewhat closer than Houston's had become, began to think about bringing a direct attack. Carter reported to Marshall that the lawyers did not think they needed "any help" except in drafting a complaint. Still attracted to using inequalities as a basis for the lawsuit, the Washington lawyers wanted "an alternative allegation" that the existing facilities were unequal. Carter promised to draft a sample complaint whose "main thrust" was a direct attack on segregation, using inequalities "as evidence of the unconstitutionality of segregation."[46]

Houston had a heart attack in late 1949. "On the death bed," as Nabrit put it, Houston referred Bishop to Nabrit, who took the case over after the court of appeals rejected the first lawsuit. After the Supreme Court's decisions in the university cases, Nabrit, like Marshall, believed the time had come for a direct attack. At the opening of the school year, eleven African-American students tried to enroll at a new white junior high school. When they were refused, Nabrit filed a desegregation case for them. In April 1951, the district judge rejected the claim, and Nabrit filed an appeal to the court of appeals.[47]

Marshall appealed the South Carolina and Topeka decisions to the Supreme Court in the summer and fall of 1951. Some justices were not happy to get direct challenges to segregation so quickly after the university cases. According to Philip Elman, "the Justices (except for Black and Douglas) were deliberately pursuing a strategy of procrastination." Apparently expecting that when the Court faced the issue it would invalidate segregation, Frankfurter told a group of law clerks that the Court wanted to avoid deciding the cases before the 1952 elections, so that its decision would not become an issue in the fall campaign.[48]

The report Judge Parker sought on the school board's progress was filed on December 21, 1951, as required. According to the report, teachers' salaries had been equalized and bus transportation begun. The board reported that it had spent almost $22,000 for furniture and equipment in African-American schools. The board had adopted a general plan for building new schools, and had advertised for bids on two new African-American schools. Construction of one new school, and remodeling another, was already underway and would be completed by the opening of the 1952–53 school year. The total cost of these projects was over $500,000.[49]

The Supreme Court had not acted on Marshall's appeal when the board submitted its report. Attempting to delay the final decision, the Court sent the case back to the district court for its "views" on the report. Justices Black and Douglas dissented, saying that the facts in the report "are wholly irrelevant to the constitutional questions presented by the appeal."[50]

Black and Douglas were obviously correct, and Judge Parker might have wondered what the Supreme Court's point was. If, as he had already held, segregation itself was not unconstitutional, and the Clarendon County board merely had to make good faith efforts toward equalizing facilities, the report simply nailed down that the board actually was doing something. Judge Parker wrote an opinion for the district court saying that facilities in Clarendon County would indeed be equal by September 1952. Otherwise the opinion reaffirmed the earlier decision. In May, Marshall renewed his appeal to the Supreme Court.[51]

Sending the case back to the district court delayed a decision in the South Carolina case. Handling the Topeka case was somewhat more complicated. When the case came up, the justices decided to defer deciding what to do until they resolved a pending challenge to segregation at the University of Tennessee. They heard the Tennessee case argued in January 1952. When the students challenging segregation were admitted to the university, the Court dismissed the case as moot in early March. Ordinarily, the justices would then decide either to affirm the Topeka decision or to hear oral argument. Instead, the justices continued to defer decision, waiting to see what happened with the South Carolina, Virginia, and District of Columbia cases.[52]

On June 9, 1952, with *Brown* and *Briggs* finally before them, the justices voted to hear the appeals. Argument was set for early October. The strategy of delay, according to Frankfurter, had accomplished one thing. The "outcome" of the cases, he wrote a former law clerk, "at least will not serve as campaign fodder" during the 1952 election season.[53]

That the justices had decided to dispose of the segregation issue became clear over the next few months. When the 1952 term opened in October, the justices voted to hear the NAACP appeal of the Prince Edward County case. More revealingly, they issued an order noting that an appeal from the District of Columbia case was pending in the court of appeals, and invited the plaintiffs to file a petition for Supreme Court review before judgment by the court of appeals—a procedure litigants sometimes try to use for important cases, but which the Court usually frowns on. The invitation to file such a petition meant that the Court was taking control of the litigation. Adding these two cases, though, gave the justices another excuse for delay, and, over Douglas's dissent, the Court postponed the argument until December.[54]

The Topeka school board decided to abolish segregation gradually, and had no interest in trying to persuade the Supreme Court that segregation was constitutional. The Supreme Court, though, was not about to let someone else define the issue. In November, when no one from Kansas filed an appearance in *Brown,* the Court requested the state to "present its views" or at least "to advise this Court whether the State's default shall be construed as a concession of the invalidity of the statute." The state's attorney general promised to appear. The Delaware authorities filed a petition for review in November, following the standard timetable. The Court granted the petition and, despite Delaware's request to allow the case to "take its normal course," ordered the lawyers to prepare for oral argument in December, a few weeks away. The schedule was so accelerated that the parties could not file their briefs before the argument. The Court gave them three weeks after argument to do so. During the Delaware argument, the state's attorney general apologized for being unable to refer to his brief.[55]

According to Justice Clark, the Court wanted "representative cases from different parts of the country."[56] In addition, each case presented a slightly different variant on segregation. *Briggs,* the South Carolina case, had a finding of substantial inequality followed by evidence of progress toward equalization of physical facilities. The Prince Edward County case, also from the heart of the segregated South, had a less credible finding of equality and a record questioning the psychological evidence. *Brown* was a border-state case, with a finding from the lower court that segregation inevitably meant inequality. The Delaware case was not that different from *Brown,* but it came with a state supreme court opinion that separate schools could not be equal. The District of Columbia case raised the question of whether the due process clause of the Fifth Amendment limited the national government in exactly the same way that the equal protection clause of the Fourteenth Amendment limited state governments.

When the lawyers began their arguments in December 1952, control over the segregation issue passed from the NAACP's hands into the control of others in "Judge and Company." In many ways, the NAACP's lawyers were never to regain control.

12

"Behind This Are Certain Facts of Life"
The Law in *Brown*

Oral advocacy before the Supreme Court is a peculiar art. Its point usually is not to persuade undecided justices; rather, it is to inform them about the case. Many justices are better listeners than they are readers, finding it easier to understand an oral argument than a written one. Oral argument, then, often goes over the ground covered in the brief. Of course the style ought to change. Written advocacy has a formal pace and manner, while a good oral argument is more conversational. Many lawyers are intimidated by the Supreme Court setting and the importance of the occasion. Marshall's frequent appearances before the Court, in contrast, made it easy for him to talk with the justices, rather than "make an argument" to them.

Oral arguments also test the waters. Lawyers must decide how to spend their limited time before the Court. They usually will be more comfortable making their easier arguments and ordinarily can present them more clearly in a short time. Yet, precisely because the arguments are easier, lawyers have less to do to bring the justices to see how the argument goes. A lawyer confident that the justices understand the easier arguments might spend the available time in laying out the more difficult ones, knowing that the questioning might be rougher and that the full argument might not get across. The NAACP lawyers in the school segregation cases had the advantage of arguing five cases in succession. If a line of argument did not get across in the first presentation, it might be developed later or abandoned.

Finally, some justices use oral arguments to raise questions that particularly bother them. The point of these questions may be less to get answers from the advocate than to stake out a position with the justice's colleagues; the justices talk to each other using the advocate as an intermediary. The advocate can do little to "answer" these questions, because they are not really questions. At other times a justice's questions show the advocate that the justice is having trouble with the advocate's position, and that the justice's dilemma would be erased if the advocate changed position. Sometimes a justice can extract a concession from an advocate, but more often the lawyer does better to stick with the position. The concession is likely to leave the clients with less than they wanted. By rephrasing their positions, the best advocates can show that the justice's concerns are misplaced or that no possible concession could both satisfy the justice and leave the advocate's clients with even a modest victory.

The oral arguments in the segregation cases served all these functions. A fair amount of the time was spent laying out the arguments in the briefs. Justice Frankfurter was an active questioner, as Marshall and his colleagues had expected. But, it turned out, Frankfurter was seeking concessions they simply could not make. The oral arguments demonstrated to the justices that there was no way out: the Court had to decide whether segregation was constitutional. Forgoing a simpler course, Marshall's team developed factual records closing down the escape hatch that the Court might have used; the Court could not say that the schools were "unequal" in bricks-and-mortar terms. The LDF lawyers had built the cases to force the issue, and Chief Justice Vinson's opinion in *Sweatt* invited a renewed challenge to *Plessy,* but Marshall's innate caution could not have made him entirely comfortable with the argument he had to make.

Under these circumstances, Marshall adopted a powerful rhetorical strategy. Marshall's "supreme self-confidence" meant that the justices' questions would not divert him into dead ends. He assumed that a majority wanted to overrule *Plessy,* though some might be reluctant. Marshall used the oral argument to show them that they could overrule it without violating ordinary legal standards, and, more important, that overruling it was the right thing to do. His argument appealed more to reluctant but sympathetic justices than to skeptical ones.[1]

The oral argument and the Court's deliberations revealed that Marshall's assumption was basically correct, but that "Judge and Company" needed to do more work before the Court would rule against segregation. Three issues turned out to be important. As his comments during the university cases indicated, Justice Jackson wondered whether a decision overruling *Plessy* could be justified as a matter of law rather than politics, and Justice Frankfurter found that question extremely troublesome. As Justice Clark's comments about the university cases showed, the justices decided relatively quickly that if *Plessy* were overruled, the South should be allowed to adjust gradually. Reconciling gradualism with the proposition that constitutional rights were "personal and present," as Vinson had written in *Sweatt,* posed a second difficulty. Finally, the justices wanted a decision overruling *Plessy* to be unanimous; achieving unanimity proved difficult. The justices, led by Frankfurter, adopted a strategy of delay, to give them time to work out the first two problems. One unexpected result was that unanimity became easier to achieve once Earl Warren became Chief Justice.

The justices needed to figure out compromises on the questions of law and politics, and on the issue of remedy. The NAACP's lawyers, though, could hardly urge that the Court should adopt some sort of gradual remedy. Nor could they argue that the Court ought to make a political rather than a legal decision. The most important part of advocacy, then, had to fortify the justices in their decision to overrule *Plessy,* leaving them to work out whatever formulas they found necessary.

Until *Brown,* the argument for rejecting *Plessy* took second place to the argument that universities were not providing equal educational opportunities. Once the argument against *Plessy* became the focus of the cases, it had to be developed in more detail than before. Marshall, described by Spottswood Robinson as a "worrywort" who would "moan and groan" about the difficulties of the arguments, worked almost without stop. At some points the lawyers' conferences would break up at 3 A.M. and Marshall would be back at work at 7 A.M.[2]

The lawyers had several lines to pursue. *Plessy v. Ferguson* involved segregated transportation, not education, and Marshall thought that some justices might find it easier to overturn segregated education if they could say they were not rejecting a square holding by the Supreme Court that segregated education was constitutional. The university cases were easy: The Court assumed that separate but equal would satisfy the Constitution, but found in each that the facilities were not in fact equal. Technically, then, none endorsed the separate but equal doctrine.

Earlier cases were more troublesome. Three years after *Plessy*, the Court rejected a challenge by African-American taxpayers to the use of their taxes to support a white high school in a district that did not maintain a high school for African-Americans.[3] On the surface this looks like a particularly severe application of separate but equal to education. The Court's opinion, though, could be read to say that the plaintiffs had sought the wrong remedy—closing the white high school. Read that way, the case was about remedies, not about segregation. *Gong Lum v. Rice,* decided in 1927, did say that the legality of segregated education "has been many times decided."[4] This too could be distinguished. The case involved a Chinese-American girl whose father challenged her assignment to a school for African-Americans; no one in the case challenged the assumption that segregation of African-Americans was constitutional.

Even more difficult, though, was *Plessy* itself. True, it did not involve education. But, in upholding segregated transportation, the Court squarely endorsed segregated education. The Court cited *Roberts v. City of Boston,* an 1849 case upholding segregation in Massachusetts—under a statute repealed as abolition sentiment grew—to show that segregated education had been held to be "a valid exercise of the legislative power even by courts of states where the political rights of the colored race have been longest and most earnestly enforced." It also said that segregated transportation was no more "obnoxious" than segregated education in the District of Columbia, "the constitutionality of which does not seem to have been questioned." Technically these statements were dicta, and Marshall could indeed argue that the Supreme Court itself had never held that separate but equal was permissible in education. The argument, though, was a difficult one, and it ran against the reality that the courts, and virtually everyone else, acted as if *Plessy* stated a legal rule that applied to education.[5]

The most obvious argument, of course, was that *Plessy* was wrong and should be overruled. That argument had three basic parts. First, the lawyers could argue that *Plessy* misinterpreted the Fourteenth Amendment. The framers of that amendment, the argument would go, intended to prohibit state-sanctioned segregation. This argument, though, was not terribly attractive. When the lawyers were preparing their briefs in 1952, they had relatively little historical research to rely on. Professional historians were still influenced by a school of historians trained by Professor William Dunning of Columbia University. Dunning and his students were quite unsympathetic to the Radical Republicans who, they argued, dominated the era of Reconstruction and imposed a regime of corrupt African-American dominated government on the South. Even if the NAACP's lawyers found statements from Radical Republicans opposing segregation, then, they would be relying on statements from people who were not in good odor in 1952. Worse, Texas's brief in *Sweatt* compiled a fair amount of information indicating that, no matter how "radical" the Republicans were, when they wrote the Fourteenth Amendment they did not seem bothered by school segregation. The most dramatic evidence, of course, was that Congress created segregated schools in the District of Columbia around the time it proposed the Fourteenth Amendment.

If a historical argument about the Fourteenth Amendment was unattractive, still Marshall and his colleagues could make a second one. According to *Plessy,* the Constitution was satisfied when governments separated the races for good reasons; separate but equal was merely one way to show that the government's action was reasonable. But, the lawyers could argue, time had shown that *Plessy* misunderstood equality. In 1944 the Supreme Court, relying on an exaggerated sense of military necessity, upheld the internment of Japanese-Americans in concentration camps.[6] But, significantly for Marshall, it did not rely on a standard of "reasonableness." Justice Black's opinion for the Court said that "all legal restrictions which curtail the civil rights of a single racial group are immediately suspect. . . . [C]ourts must subject them to the most rigid scrutiny." Even if separate but equal was reasonable, as the Court in *Plessy* said, it could not survive the "rigid scrutiny" the Court now understood was necessary in cases involving racial classifications.

Marshall was particularly attracted to a variation of this argument. According to Justice Black, a "pressing public necessity" like war might justify racial classifications, but "racial antagonism never can." Marshall used this observation to show that *Plessy* was wrong because it mistakenly assumed that separate but equal was reasonable. In fact, Marshall liked to argue, segregation was arbitrary and unreasonable precisely because the only "reason" a government could give for segregation was racial antagonism. Marshall made sure the cases had testimony (for example from anthropologist Robert Redfield) that, from a scientific point of view, no differences between the races were relevant to education. More important than the testimony was the culture that had taken hold since *Plessy;* Marshall expected that no lawyer could offer reasons for segregation that did not reduce to racial antagonism. Most important of all, though, were Marshall and his African-American colleagues. When they stood before the Court and argued that African-Americans were no different from whites, their presence alone made the argument.

The third argument that *Plessy* was wrong relied on other parts of the social science evidence. *Plessy* assumed that separate could be equal. Later developments showed this assumption to be wrong. The lawyers could refer to physical inequalities in the schools to demonstrate that schools in a segregated system would never really be equal. South Carolina's building program might produce some new schools, but everyone sophisticated about the South knew that the schools would not be equal no matter what Judge Parker said. Further, Kenneth Clark's testimony showed that separation itself harmed African-American school children.

Some version of the argument that *Plessy* was wrong because it was outdated was the strongest one available. Preparing for the oral argument the lawyers could not know which version would be most attractive to enough justices. As the coordinator who would come to the podium last, and as the most respected advocate on the NAACP team, Marshall had to be ready to try out all the versions to see which seemed most appealing.

The briefs contained few surprises.[7] The brief in *Brown,* for which Carter was primarily responsible, began with the argument that Marshall liked, saying that distinctions based on race were unreasonable and arbitrary because they had no basis in "real differences pertinent to a lawful legislative objective." It then turned to the trial court's finding that segregation "has a detrimental effect." The brief had an appendix signed by thirty-two eminent social scientists on "the effects of segregation and the consequences of desegregation." The appendix summarized recent research on the harms segregation caused. According to the studies, segregation led to "feelings of inferiority and a sense of personal humiliation," which in turn sometimes caused "antisocial and delinquent behavior" or "withdrawal and submissive behavior." As a result, minority-group children had lower educational aspirations which "unnecessarily encumbered" them throughout their lives. Further, the statement said, these harms resulted at least in substantial part from segregation itself, not from "the total society complex of which segregation is one feature," because "enforced segregation gives official recognition and sanction to these other factors . . . and thereby enhances [their] effects." Relying on this statement and the trial court's finding, the NAACP brief said that segregation "places the Negro at a disadvantage in relation to other racial groups in his pursuit of educational opportunities," in violation of the Constitution. The brief was rather low key, as if Marshall and Carter assumed that the justices did not care much about the legal arguments.

Other briefs had a different tone. The brief filed by the American Civil Liberties Union and other liberal interest groups, while containing nothing special about the law, concluded by referring to the ongoing "ideological world conflict in which the practices of our democracy are the subject of close scrutiny abroad." "Our enemies," the brief said, "seize eagerly upon the weaknesses of our democracy and, for propaganda purposes, magnify, exaggerate and distort happenings in the United States." But, the brief continued, segregation dismayed even "the liberal and conservative press abroad"; it illustrated the point by quoting extensively from a number of European anti-Communist publications.

The ACLU brief also addressed the fear that disorder would follow desegregation. University desegregation showed, it said, that "these dire predictions are unfounded." University desegregation in the South had "created no friction or other difficulties," and limited experiences with desegregation in New Mexico, Arizona, Illinois, and Ohio showed that elementary school desegregation could proceed just a- uneventfully.

As in the 1950 cases, the most important brief supporting the NAACP came from the United States government. Although Solicitor General Perlman argued in *Henderson* that *Plessy* should be overruled, when it came to school segregation he balked. According to his assistant Philip Elman, Perlman said, "You can't have little black boys sitting next to little white girls. The country isn't ready for that." When Attorney General McGrath was forced out of office because of scandals in the Internal Revenue Service that seemed to implicate the Justice Department as well, his successor James McGranery clashed with Perlman, who soon resigned. Robert Stern, a long-time deputy in the solicitor general's office, took charge of the office. Stern agreed with Elman that the government should intervene, and easily persuaded McGranery, saying that the government had already told the Court that *Plessy* should be overruled. [8]

Elman called the brief he drafted "the thing I'm proudest of in my legal career." It began with a standard invocation of the importance of the question of segregation to the country as a whole, saying that "racial discriminations imposed by law . . . inevitably tend to undermine the foundations of a society dedicated to freedom, justice, and equality." Like the ACLU brief, Elman's pointed to the international dimensions of the issue: "Racial discrimination furnishes grist for the Communist propaganda mills, and it raises doubts even among friendly nations as to the intensity of our devotion to the democratic faith." The brief then offered the Court nine pages of argument that the records in all five cases showed material inequalities that had to be remedied by desegregation. Frankfurter might at one time have been attracted to that argument, but it was obviously out of place now. In addition, it was undermined by the brief's final and most important section. There Elman, drawing on conversations he had with Frankfurter, made the "entirely unprincipled" argument that desegregation could occur gradually to deal with "the practical difficulties which may be met in making progressive adjustment to a non-segregated system" in states where the "roots" of segregation "go deep in . . . history and traditions." The brief's contribution here was the sketch of a legal argument for the gradualism the justices preferred. [9]

Arriving in Washington a week and a half before the arguments, Marshall set up shop in the Statler Hotel. The lawyers talked the cases over almost incessantly, trying to assure themselves that they knew all the possible lines of argument. Instead of presenting the traditional "trial run" argument at Howard, Marshall shepherded the lawyers through their practice arguments. As each completed his argument, Marshall hovered around, picking up ideas to work into their final preparations. [10]

The Supreme Court chambers were filled, and a line of spectators stretched down the Court's steps, when Robert Carter opened the argument for Oliver Brown. After some preliminaries, Carter said straightforwardly, "we abandon any claim of any constitutional inequality which comes from anything other than the act of segregation itself." The NAACP was not going to give the justices a way to avoid the fundamental question. Carter had nearly finished a basic summary of the argument when the Court broke for lunch. Only Justice Minton had asked a question, seeking clarification of the record. After lunch, though, the Justices began to question Carter vigorously. Justice Reed seemed skeptical about psychological evidence that children in segregated schools found it more difficult to learn. Justice Burton threw Carter an easy question, getting Carter to agree that the NAACP's position was "that there is a great deal more to the educational process even in the elementary schools than what you read in the books." But, Carter said, the trial court "did not feel that it could go in the law beyond physical facilities," which Carter agreed were, on the record in *Brown,* substantially equal.

When Carter developed the argument that *Plessy* was an irrelevant transportation case, Justice Frankfurter jumped in. Wasn't there, he asked, "a large body of adjudications going back" to *Roberts,* upholding school segregation? Carter tried to suggest that the Court had endorsed segregated schools only in passing and when no one had raised any questions about it. Still, Frankfurter replied, the fact was that the Court had assumed that segregation was constitutional, and "the question arises whether, and under what circumstances, this Court should now upset so long a course of decisions." Invoking a theme that concerned him in *Smith v. Allwright,* Frankfurter said that it would not be honest to "chip[ ] away" and distinguish prior cases. Carter had "no hesitancy in saying that the issue of 'separate but equal' should be faced" and overruled. The exchange showed that at least Frankfurter was not happy with the arguments the NAACP lawyers had developed for setting *Plessy* to one side.

Carter tried to make it seem as if the Court actually did not have to do much in *Brown* itself. As he described the precedents, "[t]here is no decision in this Court" upholding segregated education. Even when the Court had used "the language" of separate but equal, Carter said, "the decisions really do not hinge on that." In the narrowest sense that might have been true, but the strategy was ineffective because everyone knew *Brown* was significant, not a modest extension of what the Court had already done. As the exchange continued, Frankfurter again made the basic point that "we are dealing here with . . . not just an episodic piece of legislation in one state."

Frankfurter then shifted ground. Did Kansas have any reason for segregation other than "man's inhumanity to man"? Carter replied that the state's position was that states should be free to segregate or not—hardly responsive to Frankfurter's question, but all the state had offered. According to Carter, this amounted to saying that minority groups would be subject to the "whims" of the majority, which was inconsistent with the intent of the equal protection clause. Frankfurter seized this reference to ask how to find that intent. Frankfurter probably wanted Carter to talk about the amendment's history, but Carter responded by pointing to the Court's decisions, including *Shelley v. Kraemer.* When Frankfurter said that the Court's cases held that classifications were unconstitutional if "there was no rational basis for them," Carter replied that "there is no rational basis for classification based on" race, as, he said, he had been arguing before lunch.

Paul Wilson, representing Kansas, treated his first Supreme Court argument as a professional obligation, not as a part of a crusade to defend a way of life.[11] He began by explaining that the state had initially thought the case raised only a local issue, but that when the Topeka school board decided not to resist Brown's appeal, the attorney general appeared at the Court's request. Wilson outlined Kansas's statutes and answered some questions about how many African-Americans there were in the state and in districts that chose to maintain segregated schools. When Frankfurter asked about desegregation's consequences in Kansas, "and what Kansas would be urging as the most for dealing with those consequences," Wilson replied that, "in perfect candor," the consequences "would probably not be serious." Nor did he defend the state's local option statute vigorously, treating it as a historical accident. When Wilson said that overturning segregation would mean that state legislatures and courts "have been wrong for a period of more than seventy-five years," Justice Burton suggested that he should "recognize it as possible that within seventy-five years the social and economic conditions and the personal relations of the nation may have changed, so that what might have been a valid interpretation . . . seventy-five years ago would not be a valid interpretation . . . today." Wilson agreed, but said that there was nothing in the record to justify that conclusion. Wilson wrapped up his argument by calling insignificant the trial court's finding that segregation had a detrimental effect.

When Carter began his short rebuttal argument by saying that the finding was important, Justice Black was skeptical. What should the Court do, he asked, if some other trial court made a different finding? Carter replied that the Supreme Court itself would "reach its own conclusion." Black, though, was obviously troubled by the possibility that the constitutionality of segregation would turn on findings of "fact" about segregation's impact on children: "If you are going to go on the findings, then you would have different rulings with respect to the places to which this applies."* Carter retreated, saying that he also relied on the theory that racial classifications were arbitrary.

Marshall, of course, had been listening to these exchanges, preparing for his argument in *Briggs*. As he began, he knew that some justices were skeptical about the argument that *Plessy* was irrelevant because it was not an education case, and that the argument that segregation was arbitrary seemed to work reasonably well. Marshall began as Carter had, by emphasizing that the plaintiffs were challenging segregation itself, not inequality in physical facilities, although, Marshall said, it was relevant that segregation "produced these inevitable inequalities in physical facilities." Then Marshall summarized some expert testimony, particularly Redfield's, which established that differences in race had no relation to any legitimate purpose the state might have; that, Marshall said, was enough to invalidate segregation. Marshall's argument was most notable for its conversational and relaxed tone. He used his easy familiarity with the facts to indicate to the justices that he could be counted on to discuss the issues with them as an equal—a visible demonstration, perhaps, that segregation had its costs to the majority as well as to minorities.

Marshall then launched into a discussion of constitutional theory. Quoting Judge Parker's lower court opinion, which said that segregation was "a matter of legislative policy," Marshall scornfully replied, "In each instance where these matters come up in what, if I may say 'sensitive' field . . . , at all times they have this position: The majority of the people wanted the statute; that is how it was

---

*Black returned to this point in the argument in the Delaware case.

passed." For Marshall, the Court had to make "its own independent determination as to whether that statute is valid." Then he returned to the question of whether the Court had to "get to *Plessy v. Ferguson.*" Carter had argued that it did not. The reaction to that argument showed Marshall that he had to present it somewhat differently. He said that "if we lean right on" *Sweatt* and *McLaurin,* they could find a "broader issue," articulated in many other cases, that "distinctions on a racial basis . . . are odious and invidious."

When Vinson suggested that Justice John Marshall Harlan's dissent in *Plessy* regarded segregated education as obviously constitutional, Marshall speculated that things were "in a state of flux" so that Harlan did not know what to say about education. Then Marshall himself said that the majority opinion did rely on the Roberts case. This gave Frankfurter an opening. The Court cited *Roberts,* he said, "at a time when that issue was rampant." Marshall replied, "I do not know about those days," but all *Roberts* could show was that "the legislatures of the states at those times were trying to work out their problems as they best could understand." Those considerations, whatever they were, had no bearing in 1952.[12]

Still, Frankfurter said, "this is not a question to be decided by an abstract starting point of natural law, that you cannot have segregation. If we start with that, of course, we will end with that." Marshall firmly replied, "I do not know of any other proposition, sir, that we could consider that would say that because a person who is as white as snow with blue eyes and blond hair has to be set aside." Marshall's point was that everyone agreed that such a statute would be unconstitutional, and that judgment rested on the "abstract starting point" that Frankfurter said had to be rejected.

Frankfurter did not see Marshall's point. After a brief detour, Frankfurter explained what bothered him about relying on the "abstract" proposition: "Do you really think it helps us not to recognize that behind this are certain facts of life," including differences between states "where there is a vast congregation of Negro population as against the states where there is not." Using a term that Marshall was familiar with, Frankfurter asked, "Can you escape facing those sociological facts, Mr. Marshall?" Frankfurter was hinting that desegregation in the deep South would have to be gradual. Marshall understood what Frankfurter was getting at, and he politely but firmly disagreed. He could not escape that fact, "but if I fail to escape it, I would have to throw completely aside the personal and present rights of those individuals." Frankfurter had not yet developed an answer to that problem, and responded ineffectively that "it does not follow because you cannot make certain classifications, you cannot make some classifications." Marshall repeated that the Court had often recognized the rights here as personal and present.

Marshall then rephrased his argument in a way that, Frankfurter said, he followed: When a classification is attacked as unreasonable, "the least the state has to do is to produce something to defend their statutes." Frankfurter suggested that it was enough that the classification was "imbedded in the conflict of the history of the problem." Marshall replied that the Court had implicitly rejected that argument in the white primary and transportation cases, and "there is no more ingrained rule" than there was in the university cases.

Marshall understood that Frankfurter was worried about what would happen in the South. Marshall tried to ease his fears by referring to the absence of turmoil when universities desegregated. But, he continued, "granting that there is a feeling of race hostility in South Carolina, . . . we cannot have the individual rights subjected to this consideration of what the groups might do." For Marshall, none of this was "significant." Of course, he said, "we are not asking for affirmative relief." All the plaintiffs sought, Marshall said, "is that the state-imposed racial segregation be taken off, and to leave the county school board . . . to work out their own solution of the problem, to assign children on any reasonable basis they want to assign them on."

This was what Frankfurter wanted to hear, and he asked Marshall to spell it out. Marshall said he assumed that school boards would create neighborhood schools. That, though, was *not* what Frankfurter wanted to hear, because it implied that the immediate result of the Court's decision would be that "the children [would] be mixed." Marshall's elaboration did not help: What Marshall wanted was an order barring schools from segregating on the basis of race. Then the schools could draw district lines "on a natural basis." Again Frankfurter objected: "Why would not that inevitably involve—unless you have Negro ghettoes . . . —Negro children saying, 'I want to go to this school instead of that school?'" The only basis for this objection, though, was that Frankfurter thought it important that school districts not have to desegregate immediately, as Marshall suggested next. In South Carolina, he said, "the Negro buildings are scattered around," and in most of the South "there are very few areas that are predominantly one race or the other." All Marshall would concede was that if a court ordered desegregation "in the middle of the year," it could be delayed until the following September, and that the courts could allow time "for the actual enrollment of the children." Obviously, he said, districts "could not do it overnight, and it might take six months to do it one place and two months to do it another place."

Frankfurter's questions had brought gradualism to the surface. His exchange with Marshall showed, however, that Frankfurter did not have a well-worked-out sense of what he meant by gradualism. He seemed troubled by the proposition that the children would be "mixed," although it is difficult to see how even gradual desegregation could avoid some "mixing." Frankfurter wanted Marshall to offer him some way for desegregation to occur gradually. Marshall's response, that his clients simply wanted the government to stop using race as a basis for assigning children to schools, offered instead a minimal definition of desegregation; if he had conceded any more, it is hard to see how he could have won anything. From Frankfurter's point of view, though, gradualism meant more than simply stopping the use of racial classifications. Exactly what it meant, though, remained unclear.

Kansas's defense of segregation was half-hearted. South Carolina's was not. Understanding the importance of the case, South Carolina's governor James Byrnes went to New York to hire John W. Davis to argue the state's case. Davis was the country's most experienced Supreme Court advocate. Born in West Virginia, Davis had been solicitor general under Woodrow Wilson, and was the Democratic candidate for president in 1924. In 1952 he was seventy-nine years old, but despite his age, Davis worked hard on *Briggs*. Although he left West Virginia and the South behind when he moved to New York to head one of Wall Street's most important law firms, defending segregation was a cause in which Davis believed—he did not ask South Carolina for a retainer and ended up donating his services—and he tried to communicate that to the Court. [13]

Davis began late in the afternoon, and gave his opening statement without interruption. Earlier Justice Jackson had mentioned Native Americans, and Davis began by alluding to those questions. If Marshall's position prevailed, he said, it would bar segregation of Native Americans and, even worse, "I am unable to see why a state would have any further right to segregate its pupils on the ground of sex or . . . age or . . . mental capacity." He then outlined the points he would make: that South Carolina's building program eliminated all physical inequalities, that segregation did not violate the Fourteenth Amendment, and that the social scientific evidence was "of slight weight" and in any event "deals entirely with legislative policy, and does not treat on constitutional right." He had time that afternoon to describe only the building program, but he did so quite effectively. The details he offered to support his statement that South Carolina's "surge for educational reform and improvement . . . has not been exceeded in any state" showed that the case could not be resolved by relying on physical inequalities. In this, of course, Davis was simply restating from the defendants' side what Carter and Marshall had already said. Had anyone on the Court been concerned about South Carolina's good faith, though, he would have been satisfied by Davis's powerful statement.

The next morning, Davis started by referring to a fact "of which I think Mr. Marshall should take cognizance when he proceeds to his redistricting program," the fact that there were 2,800 African-American and 295 white students in the Clarendon County district. The statistics were presumably the kind of thing Frankfurter had in mind when he referred to a "vast congregation of Negro population," and Davis played on Frankfurter's concerns by saying that the prospect of putting so few whites among so many African-Americans was one "which one cannot contemplate with entire equanimity." Then Davis turned to "the crux of the case," the constitutionality of segregation. He said he had treated the issue in only five pages in the brief because the Court had dealt with the issue so recently "that it would be a work of supererogation" to go into the question in detail. Davis relied on his strongest argument, the intention of the Fourteenth Amendment's framers. He made the by-now familiar point that the Congress that proposed the amendment also segregated the schools in Washington. Justice Burton asked him whether changed conditions should change the outcome of the constitutional analysis. Davis replied, "Changed conditions may affect policy, but changed conditions cannot broaden the terminology of the Constitution." When Burton said that the Constitution was "a living document that must be interpreted in relation to the facts of the time in which it is interpreted," Davis answered that changed circumstances "may bring things within the scope of the Constitution which were not originally contemplated," but they could not "alter, expand or change the language" of the Constitution.

Frankfurter gently suggested that Davis ought to show that the term "equal" was "less fluid" than the terms of the interstate commerce clause, where the Court had upheld Congress's power to regulate commerce in ways that clearly went well beyond what the framers intended. When Davis could not, Frankfurter helped him out by saying that "history puts a gloss upon 'equal' which does not permit" the Court to find segregation unconstitutional. In relief, Davis returned to his point about the District of Columbia, adding that although Congress was not covered by the Fourteenth Amendment, "it is inconceivable" that Congress would have prohibited the states from segregating their schools just as it was segregating Washington's. Davis next took up the extent of segregation in the states, and the repeated judicial endorsements of segregation. "It would be an interesting, though perhaps entirely useless, undertaking," Davis said, "to enumerate the numbers of men . . . who have declared that segregation is not per se unlawful." He asked, "Is it conceivable that all that body of concurrent opinion . . . misunderstood the constitutional mandate, or was ignorant of the history which gave to the mandate its scope and meaning?"

Having set the stage with an eloquent statement, put in a somewhat old-fashioned rhetorical style, of the historical meaning of the equal protection clause, Davis was in a position to cast doubt on the social scientific testimony, which he regarded as "fluff."[14] He focused on Kenneth Clark because Clark was the only witness who testified on the basis of his examination of Clarendon County itself. Clark found that African-American children in Clarendon County had bad self-images. Davis's main point was that other studies Clark had conducted showed similar results in the North. "What becomes of the blasting influence of segregation" then, Davis asked. Turning to a more general point, Davis referred scornfully to social science as "fragmentary expertise based on an examined presupposition." None of the justices asked Davis any questions here or in the remainder of his argument, suggesting perhaps that they too did not find the social scientific evidence persuasive or relevant.

Davis began his closing statement with a long quotation from W.E.B. Du Bois, the nation's leading African-American intellectual. Over his long career Du Bois had taken a number of positions on the question of segregation, always driven by a determination to make the best of a bad situation. In the 1930s, Du Bois broke with the NAACP when he advocated a form of racial self-pride that other leaders believed inconsistent with their commitment to ending discrimination. During the controversy over Du Bois's position, he noted that ending discrimination would not come free to the African-American community, and Davis quoted Du Bois's discussion of one of the costs: "We shall get a finer, better balance of spirit; an infinitely more capable and rounded personality by putting children in schools where they are wanted . . . than in thrusting them into hells where they are ridiculed and hated." Davis finished by appealing to the justices to leave the question of segregation "to those most immediately affected by it," and to find out "the wishes of the parents, both white and colored, . . . before their children are forced into what may be an unwelcome contact."

Marshall had saved fifteen minutes for rebuttal. Davis had been eloquent; following him, Marshall decided to be matter of fact. Once again he framed his argument using the term "reasonableness." Of course, he said, segregation seemed reasonable to the white majority in South Carolina, but that was not what reasonableness meant. He said it was still "unexplained" why "Negroes are taken out of the main stream of American life in these states." Marshall then made two points about "the feeling of the people in South Carolina." First, "individual rights of minority people are not to be left to even the most mature judgment of the majority." Second, "no matter how great anyone becomes, if he happens to have been born a Negro, . . he is relegated" to a segregated school. Public opinion polls, according to Marshall, had no place before the Supreme Court.

Marshall got into trouble, though, when he tried to rehabilitate the social science testimony. Frankfurter asked, sensibly enough, why the Court could not take judicial notice of the social scientific evidence South Carolina relied on. Marshall replied that it was all right to take judicial notice of serious studies, but that South Carolina was also trying to rely on "a magazine article of a newspaper-man answering another newspaperman," which was out of bounds. Frankfurter suggested that the material was relevant to "the consequences of the proposed remedy." Marshall, again, was unyielding. "Insofar as this is a tough problem, it was tough, but the solution was not to deprive people of their constitutional rights." Nor did Marshall see how the testimony had much bearing on the remedy. He understood, though, what Frankfurter really meant, and continued by saying that the states were "com[ing] to this Court and say[ing] that they could not control their own State." This was too pointed, and Frankfurter said, "[T]hat is not what I have in mind." He meant that the Court should be able to take account misgivings expressed by experts in "finally striking this judgment"—that is, in writing the remedy. After some groping by both Marshall and Frankfurter, Marshall managed to make the point, again, that even those misgivings could not justify denying "present" rights.

Then Marshall touched on the real issue about remedy. "I for one," he said, "do not believe that the people in South Carolina or those southern states are lawless people." Phrasing it this way, Marshall got Frankfurter on his side. He had not heard anyone say, Frankfurter responded, that "South Carolina or Kansas will not obey whatever decree this Court hands down." Yet, of course, that was precisely what concerned Frankfurter. At the least he thought that some decrees had a better chance of being accepted than others; that was why he worried about writing a gradual desegregation decree.

Marshall wound up his argument with a standard summary. Then, when he had finished, Justice Reed asked about the legislative history of segregation in South Carolina. Marshall replied that the lawyers had been unable to find anything useful, because segregation came into existence at a time when there was "terrific objection to public education" and compulsory attendance, and "the three things got wound up together." When Reed said it would be "fair to assume" that segregation was "passed for the purpose of avoiding racial friction," Marshall said, "I think that the people who wrote on it would say that," but, he continued, it was adopted, after all, "right in the middle of the Klan period."

When Reed said that legislatures should be allowed to "weigh as between the disadvantage of the segregated group and the advantage of the maintenance of law and order," Marshall replied that "we have to bear in mind that I know of no Negro legislator in any of these states." No one had to worry about disorder. People "are fighting together and living together. . . [T]hey are working together in other cases." Marshall then said, "in the South where I spent most of my time, you will see white and colored kids going down the road together to school. They separate and go to different schools, and they come out and they play together. I do not see why there would necessarily be any trouble if they went to school together." When Reed said again that balancing interests was for the legislature, Marshall concluded with a short, commonsense statement that "the rights of the minorities . . . have been protected by our Constitution, and the ultimate authority for determining that is this Court. . . . As to whether or not I, as an individual, am being deprived of my right is not legislative, but judicial." In his rebuttal, and after making his main responses, Marshall had seized the opportunity Reed provided to introduce the powerful image of children playing together, only to be separated in schools by force of law.

The Virginia case presented an important variant. The South Carolina trial court found that the state's building program had made the schools equal. The Virginia court, in contrast, found that the schools were not equal but that the state's building program meant that they would soon be equal. If the principle of the university cases applied to elementary schools, though, inequality at the time of trial meant that African-American children were entitled to immediate admission to the white schools. The obvious way to distinguish between universities and elementary schools was that the intangible factors such as reputation, on which the Court had relied in *Sweatt,* were less important in lower schools. But, prodded by Carter, the NAACP's lawyers used sociological evidence to demonstrate that lower schools had "intangible" characteristics equivalent to those in the universities. On the face of things, then, the Virginia case was the place for the justices to explore the significance of the sociological evidence.

They did not. Once again, Frankfurter's concern for remedy dominated the questioning. Frankfurter engaged Spottswood Robinson in a discussion of whether an order directing immediate admission followed directly from *Gaines* and other university cases. Although Robinson was reluctant to rest entirely on *Gaines,* he did agree that it required immediate admission. But, Robinson pointed out, relying on *Gaines* could be disruptive because "as equilibrium is disturbed by the variety of facts . . . in any educational system," segregation might be reestablished. The defendants said they would have a new segregated school in 1953. If the Court relied on *Gaines,* the defendants would be free to resegregate their schools when the new school opened. Frankfurter replied that the Court should not "borrow trouble in 1953 or 1954" if *Gaines* gave it a basis for reversing the trial court. Robinson answered that the real meaning of the university cases was that there "it was pretty nearly impossible to resume segregation at some future time" because of the Court's standards for equality. Robinson seemed troubled by the tenor of Frankfurter's questions, because he used an answer to Justice Reed to say again that "the basis of the decision must be something more than a basis which will permit of a shuttling of pupils back and forth into segregated schools."

As Robinson wound down his argument, Chief Justice Vinson interrupted irritably. Robinson mentioned that the district court had ordered equalization in curricula and transportation, and Vinson's questions seemed to express his belief that that was enough. He asked, "If you did not have the facilities and if you did not have the teachers, how would you take care of them?" Robinson gave the obvious answer, that there were quite enough teachers and space in the county as a whole; after all, desegregation would not increase the number of students, nor decrease the number of teachers, in the system. Vinson's skepticism surely rested on his unstated assumption that white parents would not let African-Americans teach their children. Yet, if he made that assumption explicit, as an opinion might require, Vinson would have to explain why it did not establish an important kind of inequality.

Robinson concluded by returning to the point that constitutional rights were personal and present, this time emphasizing that the courts should not try "to establish or maintain constitutional equality by judicial decree" because then they would be "in the business of supervising the school system . . . indefinitely." That, he said, was "a task for which the Court's machinery is not entirely suited."

Virginia divided its argument between Justin Moore and Lindsay Almond, the state's attorney general. Moore spent most of his time describing Virginia's building and equalization program, although near the end of his time he started to criticize the sociological evidence. Quoting from the testimony of Professor Henry Garrett, Moore said that African-Americans would receive a "better education" in segregated schools "because of this friction that would arise and these eighty years of history in Virginia." This was too much even for Justice Reed, who asked, "What am I to draw from this argument?" Moore was somewhat taken aback, but recovered when Reed explained that he wanted to know what difference it would make if the trial court made different findings of fact. Moore said that the possibility of different fact findings "just illustrates how it really is a policy question."

Reed's question was basically friendly to the state. When Justice Jackson offered another potentially helpful question, though, Moore could not go along. Jackson mentioned section five of the Fourteenth Amendment, which gives Congress the power to enforce the equal protection clause, saying acerbically that "nobody seems to attach any importance" to it. Suppose, though, Congress passed a statute finding segregation "contrary to national policy." Following up the question, Frankfurter tried to help Moore by suggesting that it was one thing for the courts to invalidate segregation "with the momentum and validity that a congressional enactment has," and another for them to invalidate it on their own. Moore would have none of that, because saying that Congress had the power to overturn segregation ran contrary to fundamental premises of states' rights theories. When Moore offered the standard and lame response, "That is another case," Frankfurter replied sarcastically, "That is a good answer." Jackson twisted the knife a bit more. "Apparently," Jackson said, Moore did not "attach any importance to the fact that there is not any Act of Congress." The point here was that if a justice believed Congress could outlaw segregation, and if Moore believed the case was no different merely because there was no such statute, whatever gave Congress authority to overturn segregation gave the courts the same authority, under Moore's theory. Moore could not have been happy to be forced into that position. Even more, as Justice Douglas pointed out a few minutes later, the Court had never held that the Fourteenth Amendment was ineffective "unless Congress acts."

Lindsay Almond gave a political speech. Like Moore he praised the state's equalization program. But he was explicit about "the impact" of a decision invalidating segregation "contrary to the customs, the traditions and the mores of what we might claim to be a great people, established through generations, who themselves are fiercely and irrevocably dedicated to the preservation of the white and colored races." If this threat was not explicit enough, Almond continued by saying that a desegregation decision "would destroy the public school system" because "the people would not vote bond issues through their resentment to it." Further, though this too, Almond said, was "not [said] as a threat," African-American teachers "would not be employed to teach white children in a tax-supported system in Virginia."

In his rebuttal Robinson did not mention the rawness of Almond's argument; that was not his style. After Robinson started a dry recitation of some history of segregation in Virginia, Jackson interrupted to ask about section five. Like Moore, but from the other side, Robinson too said that "the mere fact" of Congress's power would not "encroach upon the jurisdiction of this Court if, as a matter of fact, a violation of the Constitution has been shown."

Justice Reed pointed out a difficulty with the theory to which Jackson seemed attracted: "If segregation is not a denial of equal protection or due process, legislation by Congress could do nothing more except to express congressional views." Reed's point turned on the language of the Constitution. The Fourteenth Amendment's first section said that no state shall deny "the equal protection of the laws," and section five said that "Congress shall have the power to enforce . . . the provisions of this article." However, if a state law did not actually deny equal protection—if a court would not find a constitutional violation—then what provision of the amendment would the statute be "enforcing"? There are ways to deal with this problem,[15] but Reed's question showed that Jackson's approach was not as simple as Jackson hoped. Frankfurter fumbled around trying to rescue Jackson, but he could not. When Reed tried to close the discussion by saying that "the state cannot violate the Fourteenth Amendment," Frankfurter was annoyed: "We do not argue for ten hours a question that is self-evident."

Having watched the justices argue among themselves, Robinson wrapped up his own argument by dealing with equalization. This interested Vinson. He pointed out that Marshall conceded "as a matter of necessity" that if the Court found segregation unconstitutional no matter what, the defendants could have some time to deal with administrative difficulties. Why would the state not have time to complete the building program that, on an equalization theory, would be enough to avoid desegregation? Robinson had a crisp answer. "There is a difference," he said, "between a postponement of a right and a delay which is incidental to affording the remedies we asked for."

Elaborating his idea of "incidental delay," Robinson suggested that if a court

told a person to tear down a house, "the man has got to have a reasonable opportunity to get the house down." Desegregation was, he said, "an administrative
problem initially, at least, for the school authorities to work out." Vinson used
Robinson's argument to make two points. First, the example showed that "you
realize that you have got the rights of other people involved in regard to disloca-
tion." Second, if the Court insisted on real equalization, there would still be
administrative problems to justify some incidental delay.

The Virginia argument made it clear that Vinson was skeptical about immediate desegregation and was attracted to the idea of taking equalization seriously.
Perhaps more important, the discussion of section five showed that a course Jackson might have thought easier—relying on Congress to act, and refusing to do
anything because Congress had not—was theoretically troublesome and unlikely to
satisfy either side politically.

Much of the argument in the Washington case was excruciating. Justice Reed had
asked Robinson the crucial question: Were the due process and equal protection
clauses legally different? Instead of focusing on this important question, though,
most of the argument dealt with minutiae. George E. C. Hayes began by trying to
argue that Congress had never really authorized segregation in the District's
schools. On some theoretical level this was an argument worth making, because if
the justices accepted it they could overturn segregation without holding any federal
statute unconstitutional. A flurry of questions from the justices showed that they
were not buying the theory, and Hayes eventually turned to another topic. Yet,
when Milton Korman got up to argue for the school system, he spent an inordinate
amount of time responding to this argument.

Hayes also developed Marshall's idea that segregation was arbitrary. His concern was the reason for imposing segregation: "to keep him in this place of secondary citizenship." Segregation resulted from "pure racism." Vinson suggested that
Hayes's account was misleading because the Congress that proposed the Fourteenth Amendment could hardly be accused of racism, yet it established segregated
schools in Washington. That, Hayes replied, "was a matter of politics, . . .
giving away this with the idea of pressing this which was the stronger thing"—as
good an answer as anyone was ever to come up with.

Hayes was about to sit down when Justice Frankfurter "violat[ed] my own rule
against posing hypothetical cases" and asked whether the due process clause
barred the government from using any racial classifications under any circumstances, and referred specifically to laws barring marriages between people of
different races. Hayes found the question understandably bothersome, but eventually replied that the Japanese internment case showed that "legislation based upon
race is immediately suspect." Frankfurter was satisfied, because "that simply
means it can be valid" if "great cause" is shown. Hayes agreed, and tried to show
that there was no "public necessity" for segregation. But Justice Black interrupted,
asking whether Hayes thought it necessary "to equate the Fourteenth Amendment
and the Fifth Amendment." Hayes said emphatically not; as he saw it, under the
Fifth Amendment, "you cannot make a quantum with respect to one's liberty," so
that due process could not be satisfied by affording "substantial equality."

James Nabrit followed Hayes, and the discussion of the relation between the Fifth and Fourteenth Amendments continued. Nabrit said that the Reconstruction amendments "removed from the Federal Government any power to impose racial distinctions in dealing with its citizens." Justice Minton noted that this seemed to suggest that the Fourteenth Amendment somehow changed the meaning of the Fifth. Nabrit retreated to the Japanese cases, saying that they required the courts to determine whether there was "some purpose which it is within the competency of this Government to effect" when it tried to classify on the basis of race. When Justice Reed suggested that Congress should determine the purpose, Nabrit disagreed: "Never in the history of this country have the individual liberties of the citizen been entrusted in the hands of the legislators." The Court recessed for the day shortly after this exchange. Nabrit had ended on a high note.

The last day of argument started with the Washington case again, but the drama had gone. As usual, Vinson pressed for factual detail. Reed wondered about the legislative history of segregation in the District. Nabrit returned to Hayes's argument that Congress had not explicitly authorized segregation. Milton Korman, representing the District, gave a pedestrian argument. Incredibly, he quoted with approval from the notorious *Dred Scott* case, endorsing its theory that the Constitution was to be interpreted exactly as it was understood when it was adopted. Nabrit wound up the argument with an appeal to the justices' sense of world politics: "In the heart of the nation's capital, in the capital of democracy, in the capital of the free world, there is no place for a segregated school system. This country cannot afford it, and the Constitution does not permit it, and the statutes of Congress do not authorize it."

Delaware's attorney general Albert Young began the last argument by referring to the "Herculean task" of enlightening the Court after it had already heard eight hours of argument. The argument again focused on remedy. The Delaware courts ordered immediate desegregation. Vinson, the author of *Sweatt,* pointed out that the university cases said the rights involved were "personal and present." Young replied that universities were different from lower schools, though he did not say exactly why. Frankfurter wanted assurance that the Delaware courts had ordered immediate relief because they had to and not because "the equity of the situation require[d]," although Justice Reed pointed out that Chancellor Seitz did say that he would reach the same conclusion "if it be a matter of discretion."

Louis Redding and Jack Greenberg, arguing his first case before the Supreme Court, divided the final argument. Redding got into trouble when he argued that the plaintiffs wanted more than a simple affirmance of the state court decision. He wanted to guarantee that resegregation would not occur if Delaware equalized physical facilities. Frankfurter and Vinson, though, told him sharply that affirming the lower court would give him all he had asked for. Greenberg's argument focused on the issue of delay. In response to a question from Justice Jackson, Greenberg said that the children were entitled to their rights "as quickly as those rights can be made available . . . without regard to the other factors that have been discussed in the other cases." He specifically rejected the position offered by the United States, using an effective example: Consider a child who had spent five years in inferior schools. "To deny him the sixth, seventh and eighth years of equality is to inflict an irreparable injury on him. Those three years cannot be completely recaptured." Greenberg conceded in passing that a court could take the public interest into account, "but there is no showing of any public interest" here. As Frankfurter understood, Greenberg meant to exclude "the whole broad problem" that bothered Frankfurter, though not administrative details. Vinson again asked about details, and Black, this time joined by Frankfurter, raised questions about making constitutional law turn on findings, varying from trial to trial, about psychological effects. With that, the oral arguments ended.

John W. Davis reportedly told a colleague on leaving the arguments that he thought they had won the case five to four or six to three.[16] Only a litigator's optimism could have led him to that conclusion. Davis had been treated with the respect a figure of his stature warranted. He made an eloquent argument, but it was nineteenth-century eloquence used to support a nineteenth-century opinion. Marshall, in contrast, made an argument in the twentieth-century style to defend a twentieth-century position. The fact that the justices did not pester Davis with questions did not signal, as it sometimes does, that they agreed with his position. Only Reed had clearly indicated his inclination to uphold the separate but equal doctrine. Some of Vinson's questions suggested he leaned the same way, but much less strongly, and Vinson's focus on the factual details indicates that he used the argument to work his way into the case, not to explore positions he was inclined to favor or oppose. Jackson tried to get the states to say that the Court should not act until Congress had. When their lawyers would not go along with that suggestion, Jackson pulled back. Jackson might have wanted to pass the buck to Congress, but it would have been dangerous to infer that he too would endorse separate but equal once he had to face up to the issue. Finally, of course, there was Frankfurter. He directed his questions at Marshall and the NAACP lawyers, and expressed skepticism about the breadth of the NAACP position. Listened to carefully, though, the questions indicated that Frankfurter wanted to figure out some way to overturn *Plessy* without ordering immediate desegregation. Davis should not have been encouraged by that.

raises pretty much same issues as Columbia Law essay

"Boldness Is Essential But Wisdom Indispensable"
Inside the Supreme Court

see 209

1952

The justices discussed the segregation cases at their conference on December 13. The Court was divided. Douglas wrote a memorandum to his files on May 17, 1954, the day *Brown* was announced. He stated that "in the original conference, there were only four who voted that segregation in the public schools was unconstitutional": Black, Burton, Minton, and Douglas. According to Douglas, Vinson thought that "the *Plessy* case was right," as did Reed, and Clark "inclined that way." Both Frankfurter and Jackson "expressed the view that segregation in the public schools was probably constitutional." He concluded, "it seemed that if the cases were to be then decided the vote would be five to four in favor of the constitutionality of segregation in the public schools in the States with Frankfurter indicating he would join the four of us when it came to the District of Columbia case." Frankfurter thought that the vote would have been five to four to reverse *Plessy,* with Vinson, Reed, Jackson, and Clark dissenting. Burton and Jackson thought that there would be between two and four dissenters if *Plessy* were reversed.[1]

These speculations written after the decision should be taken cautiously. At the suggestion of Vinson and Jackson, no formal vote was taken,[2] so the justices were inferring from a loosely structured discussion what the ultimate outcome would be. Further, expressions in such a discussion need not indicate firm positions. In the university cases, Vinson said he inclined toward affirming, yet a week later he was confident enough about reversing to start writing the Court's opinions; in the Jaybird primary case, an initial conference vote of five to four to uphold the primary quickly became a vote of eight to one to strike it down. The one sure conclusion is that, at the start, unanimity seemed unlikely.

The justices' political and intellectual circles were hostile to segregation. Most were Democrats friendly with President Harry Truman, who had won reelection in 1948 on a platform with a strong civil rights plank. Truman's Committee on Civil Rights condemned segregation, and Truman ordered the desegregation of the armed forces. The administration urged the Court to overrule *Plessy* in the 1950 railroad case. Granted, the Truman administration's commitments to racial equality were largely political, and it never acted against segregated education. Still, the general atmosphere among the political elite rather strongly favored the NAACP's claims. In theory, they might have favored congressional action. But the justices may have thought, as many liberals did, that even if a congressional majority opposed segregation, it could not get its way because Southerners held strategic leadership positions.

Finally, the ideological rationale for the war against Nazi Germany and the ongoing ideological competition with the Soviet Union made segregation increasingly anomalous. As Marshall put it in a 1954 speech, the desegregation issue had "assumed its most urgent significance" in "the world-wide struggle to stop Communist totalitarianism." Whenever the State Department accused Communist regimes of violations of human rights, Marshall said, they responded "with great ease: 'You tell us of forced labor in Russia—what about the lynchings of Negroes in Alabama? You tell us about undemocratic elections in Bulgaria—what about the poll tax in Mississippi?" Marshall concluded, "the continued existence of racial discrimination here at home seriously negates and jeopardizes the entire meaning of American foreign policy throughout the world." An Australian friend of John W. Davis wrote that "for the . . . good name of the U.S.A. in the world and the absence of hostility of the coloured people of the Far and Middle East, I hope the case goes against you." For Marshall, segregation was wrong because it was unconstitutional and immoral "as much if not more so than [because of] the world picture," but the justices, sophisticated politicians, understood the point. Under these circumstances a majority would have found it extraordinarily difficult to reaffirm separate but equal, and even more difficult to affirm a decision finding separate schools substantially equal.[3]

Yet, some justices who might have voted to overrule *Plessy* were not enthusiastic. If push had come to shove, a majority probably would have overruled *Plessy*. But, as the justices discussed the cases, they discovered that no one was willing to push hard enough. Chief Justice Vinson, whose office gave him some authority to insist on a decision, was quite ambivalent. Frankfurter, who might have taken a leadership role, was ambivalent, not about segregation, but about whether a legally satisfactory opinion overruling *Plessy* could be written. His ambivalence led him to delay a decision.

Justices Jackson and Frankfurter were the key actors inside the Court. Jackson raised questions for which Frankfurter did not have easy answers in 1952. Without those answers, Frankfurter could not bring himself to reject the separate but equal doctrine, as he wanted. And without Frankfurter to take the lead, Vinson, even more ambivalent, was unwilling to press the Court.

Justice Jackson's stance toward African-Americans is difficult to characterize in a phrase. Typically, he came out on the side of the interests they were asserting, though rarely enthusiastically, and sometimes he expressed dismay at the fact, as he saw it, that his colleagues' legal judgment was distorted by sympathy for African-Americans.[4]

Jackson described his views in another letter to Fairman just before the arguments in the university cases.[5] Confessing he was "almost embarrassed to be in doubts about a matter on which nearly everyone here seems, one way or the other, to be fully convinced," Jackson ascribed his doubts to his background, which included attending school "along with a few Negro pupils and never [giving] it a thought." When he first came across "real racial consciousness and antagonism" in Washington, he said, he was "amazed and disappointed at the depth and bitterness of the feeling among the Negroes." His "real concern" was "to see this thing decided wisely rather than to see either side win," but he feared that a wise resolution would result, if at all, only as a "by-product," because "everyone seems under conscious or unconscious emotional commitments of one sort or another." Jackson then referred to "the terrible consequences of racial hatred," and said that he had "no sympathy with racial conceits which underlie segregation policies," but also asserted that "widely held beliefs and attitudes, even if mistaken, are real factors in law and statecraft." Outlining a series of questions he thought Fairman could help him with, Jackson wrote, "I am clear that I would support the constitutionality of almost any Congressional Act that prohibited segregation in education," though as a believer in "the doctrine on which the Roosevelt fight against the old Court was based," he had misgivings about whether the Court was the proper institution to "decide such questions for the Nation." Among the questions he had was, "What, if any, weight should we give to widely and deeply held attitudes whether of the South or of the colored people?" This "would be of no concern if we were applying a clear constitutional or congressional command," but seemed relevant "when we are asked to overrule prior interpretations and initiate a rule that will cut deeply into social customs." Finally, Jackson wondered about the effects of a desegregation decision. He had "seen a good deal of progress in the recognition of Negro rights in the South in the last few years," and thought it "quite possible to move too fast if we have any choice of pace." He mentioned specifically "the identification of left-wingers with this movement to end segregation" as a factor that might promote fascism.[6]

Jackson's ambivalence is apparent. Yet he clearly believed that, as a matter of social policy, segregation was wrong. The letter hints that he was inclined, though not enthusiastically, to overcome his concerns about whether the Court should make that policy. For Jackson, this meant that the segregation cases presented issues of politics rather than law, though he never fully spelled out the nature of the distinction he insisted on drawing. The problem in the segregation context, as Jackson put it to Fairman, was "the scarcity of satisfactory materials for a rational attitude," because the "cryptic words of the Fourteenth Amendment solve nothing" and "three-fourths of a century of judicial interpretation is called in question."[7]

Before the 1952 conference, Jackson asked his law clerks to prepare memoranda on the segregation cases. Both were written in a relatively informal style tracking Jackson's, and the clerks tried to turn phrases as Jackson did. Donald Cronson called his "A Few Expressed Prejudices on the Segregation Cases." It concluded that *"Plessy* was wrong," but that the decision had become embedded in the law, leading to the development "not only [of] rules of law, but ways of life."

Expressing a thought that Jackson had, Cronson wrote that "where a whole way of life has grown up around such a prior error, then I say we are stuck with it" until Congress acts.[8]

Jackson's ambivalence is captured in William Rehnquist's memorandum, captioned "A Random Thought on the Segregation Cases." Its first paragraphs offered a brief survey of constitutional history, clearly resonating with the lessons Jackson learned in the New Deal struggle against the Court. Judicial review, Rehnquist wrote, was justified "on the basis that there are standards to be applied other than the personal predilections of the Justices." Rehnquist took the lesson of history to be that "it was not part of the judicial function to thwart public opinion except in extreme cases." Reaching the segregation cases, Rehnquist wrote, "the Court is . . . being asked to read its own sociological views into the Constitution. Urging a view palpably at variance with precedent and probably with legislative h[is]tory, appellants seek to convince the Court of the moral wrongness of the treatment they are receiving." But, the memo went on, whatever a justice's "individual views on the merits of segregation," it was "not one of those extreme cases." Rather, "if this Court, because its members individually are 'liberal' and dislike segregation, now chooses to strike it down, it differs from the McReynolds court only in the kinds of litigants it favors and the kinds of special claims it protects." In a turn of phrase like Jackson's, Rehnquist wrote, "To the argument made by Thurgood not John Marshall that a majority may not deprive a minority of its constitutional right, the answer must be made that while this is sound in theory, in the long run it is the majority who will determine what the constitutional rights of the minority are." Again history made the point. All the Court's attempts to protect minority rights had failed. "One by one the cases establishing such rights have been sloughed off, and crept silently to rest. If the present Court is unable to profit by this example, it must be prepared to see its work fade in time, too, as embodying only the sentiments of a transient majority of nine men." Rehnquist concluded his memorandum, "I think *Plessy v. Ferguson* was right and should be re-affirmed. If the Fourteenth Amendment did not enact Spencer's *Social Statics,* it just as surely did not enact Myrdahl's [sic] *American Dilemma.*"[9]

With one exception—the statement that *Plessy* should be reaffirmed—this memorandum catches one side of Jackson's ambivalence, stating it more forcefully than Jackson would have, but only because Jackson's expression would have been constrained by his ambivalence in a way Rehnquist's was not.[10] The memorandum certainly is not a transcription of what Jackson said to Rehnquist, but during the discussions in chambers Jackson probably expressed sufficient ambivalence that a law clerk with Rehnquist's inclinations could reasonably expect his employer to sympathize with an argument against overruling *Plessy.*[11] Rehnquist's memorandum in *Terry v. Adams* indicates that he felt no discomfort in criticizing the "liberals" around the Court to Jackson, and its tone suggests that Rehnquist had reason to believe that Jackson would sympathize even if he did not fully agree. Some of Rehnquist's phrases indicate that he was reasonably well in tune with some aspects of Jackson's thinking, and that the *Brown* memorandum, ultimately, was Rehnquist's way of putting in writing that part of Jackson's thinking with which Rehnquist agreed.

By articulating the problem in the segregation cases as one of politics rather than law, Jackson posed a serious problem for Frankfurter. Both accepted the distinction, but Jackson was willing to make a political decision as a Justice of the Supreme Court, while Frankfurter was not. With Jackson asserting that the decision had to be political, and Frankfurter unwilling to make one, what was Frankfurter to do?

Vinson opened the discussion on December 13 with a rambling statement that Douglas disdainfully summarized in two lines. Jackson recorded Vinson's statement in more detail, probably because Vinson touched on themes that gave Jackson concern as well. Vinson began by pointing to the "body of law back of us on separate but equal," and to the fact that Congress had "pass[ed] no statute contrary" to segregation. Indeed, Vinson continued, because segregation in the District of Columbia had been imposed by a Congress including "men . . . who passed [the] amendments," he found it "hard to get away [from] that interpretation," particularly in light of the "long continued acceptance" of segregation in the District. Vinson then mused on congressional power: he thought Congress could abolish segregation in the District but might not do so in the states.[12] Once his mind turned to congressional power, though, Vinson recalled the suggestion Jackson made at the arguments, that the Court should wait for Congress to act. He did "not think much [of that] idea." In the area of the commerce clause, the Court had considered the constitutionality of state laws even if Congress had not acted, and could do so here as well.[13]

Vinson then turned to the state cases. He began with the "idea" that schools must now or in the future be equal. In South Carolina, according to the record, the schools were equal, and Vinson, introducing another recurrent theme, noted that it "took some time to make them equal." The problem was that in the university cases the Court required immediate admission because "we said [the] right was personal." Yet, he continued, applying that doctrine was "more serious when you have large numbers." The Court could not "close our eyes to problems in various parts of the country" or to the "seriousness of [the] problem as to time." In some areas, "the complete abolition of public schools" was possible, and, Vinson said, although some argued "we should not consider this," he could not "throw it all off." He concluded this part of his statement, "Boldness is essential but wisdom indispensable." At the end he reiterated his view that the "situation is very serious and very emotional," and that the prospect of the "abolition of [the] separate school system in [the] South raises serious practical problems."[14]

Nowhere did Vinson commit himself either to reaffirming separate but equal or to overruling *Plessy,* but on balance the tone suggests that he would go along with a majority decision to hold segregation unconstitutional, as he had gone along in the university cases. Certainly as stolid a justice as Vinson would not have said "boldness is essential" if he intended to reaffirm *Plessy.*[15] At the same time, Vinson worried about the consequences of such a decision, and suggested that the Court should concern itself with the period over which desegregation might occur.

Justice Black spoke next. He began by focusing on whether segregation in the District differed from segregation in the states. Picking up on Vinson's commerce clause discussion, Black said he was not sure "Congress is bound by [the] same limitations as [the] States," because "Congress can legislate where states cannot for states are bound by the 14th Amendment."[16] To Black, it was "anomalous if Congress can segregate & [a] state can't." And, he said a bit later, the Court's prior willingness to rule on segregation "cut off" the argument that enforcement of the Fourteenth Amendment was entirely up to Congress; he could not "draw a rational distinction between this case and other cases under the 14th Amendment as respects the self-executing argument."

On the constitutionality of segregation, Black said, "Marshall overestimates [his] case." At this point, though, instead of laying out the case for desegregation, Black mentioned the consequences of holding segregation unconstitutional. He foresaw that there "will be some violence," and South Carolina would go through the "forms" of abolishing public education while other states "would probably take evasive measures while purporting to obey." Black was concerned that resistance to desegregation would place the courts on the "battle front," leading to "law by injunction." Having expressed these concerns, however, Black forcefully stated that he was "driven to" the conclusion that segregation was unconstitutional "with [the] knowledge [that this] means trouble."[17] Segregation rested on the idea of Negro inferiority; one did "not need books" or other sociological evidence "to say that." And, for Black, the Fourteenth Amendment's "basic purpose" was "to protect [against] discrimination" and to abolish "such castes."[18]

Justice Reed "approach[ed the case] from [a] different view," and stated he would uphold the separate but equal doctrine. He emphasized the "constant progress in this field and in the advancement of the interests of the negroes" in areas like transportation, voting, and employment, and believed that the "states should be left to work out the problems for themselves." Yet Reed agreed that the Constitution was "not fixed." For him, though, it changed only "if [a] body of people think [it] unconstitutional." When seventeen states had segregation, the time to say the Constitution had changed had not yet arrived. Reed's belief in racial progress led him to state that we "should allow time for equalizing the opportunity," because "segregation is gradually disappearing." Reed's view that the Constitution was not fixed and his meliorist beliefs opened the way for him to agree to a holding that segregation was unconstitutional, if the opinion stressed how times had changed and the remedy allowed gradual adaptation.

Justice Frankfurter thought segregation in the District raised different questions from segregation in the states, but for Frankfurter segregation in the District was the more questionable. As he saw it, due process made it "intolerable" to have segregation in the District. He referred to "the experiences of colored people here especially [William T.] Coleman, one of his old law clerks." But Frankfurter was more concerned with other issues. He wanted to have the cases reargued, because deferring decision might lead Congress or the newly elected president to act, and "the social gains of having them accomplished with executive action would be enormous." "It is a gain in law administration if it comes not as a pronouncement of coercive law but with the help of the new administration that has promised to change the law here in the District."

Focusing on the political setting, as he saw it, Frankfurter made numerous suggestions. In response to Vinson's concern that the rights at stake were personal, Frankfurter emphasized that "these are equity suits" which "involve imagination in shaping decrees," which could take "problems of enforcement" into account. As in the university cases, he was annoyed at Black's confident invocation of the Fourteenth Amendment's "basic purpose." "How," he asked, "does Black know the purpose" of the amendment? According to Douglas, Frankfurter said he had "read all of [the amendment's] history and he can't say it meant to abolish segregation." For Frankfurter, the proponents of the amendment used "evasive words so as not to stir the issue." Further, Frankfurter "want[ed] to know why what has gone before is wrong." He could not accept a broad rule that "it's unconstitutional to treat a negro differently than a white." The final thought Frankfurter offered was that the Court could not treat segregation as raising "sociological questions."

Frankfurter worked himself into an extremely awkward position. His statement that segregation in the District was intolerable accurately expressed his social policy views. Yet his dismay at Black's confidence about the framers' intent, coupled with his respect for precedent and his disdain for "sociological" arguments in constitutional adjudication, left Frankfurter with no ground on which to rest a conclusion that segregation in the states was unconstitutional. His dilemma led him to urge that the cases be set for reargument.

Frankfurter's reference to equity decrees indicated one route the Court could use to develop a gradual remedy in the face of resistance. For Justice Douglas, though, the cases were simple and the "factor of time" irrelevant. For him, the merits were "not in [the] realm of argument." The Fifth and Fourteenth Amendments barred governments from making "classification on the basis of race." This principle was simple, "though the application of it," Douglas said, may present great difficulties.[19]

Justice Jackson's statement to the conference was a more forceful presentation of Frankfurter's hint that overruling *Plessy* could not be a legal decision. Jackson said he approached the problem "as a lawyer," rather than, presumably, as a politician or a general policy maker. Nothing in the text, the opinions of the courts, or the history of the Fourteenth Amendment "says this is unconstitutional," and he noted that "Marshall's brief starts & ends with sociology." Jackson's ambivalence about the proper policy resolution, so different from Frankfurter's confidence on that question, came out in his statement that "it will be bad for the negroes to be put into white schools." Yet, Jackson continued, although he would not say that "it is unconstitutional to practice segregation tomorrow," he understood that segregation was about to end. He said he would "go along" with a decision against segregation if the Court "g[a]ve them time to get rid of it" by using "equitable remedies that can be shaped to the needs." He suggested that the District of Columbia case be reargued and the relevant congressional committees invited to file briefs and participate in the argument.

Finally, Justice Clark thought the "result must be the same in all the cases." Clark may have had in mind the question about the District of Columbia, but it seems more likely that he meant that the outcome should not turn on trial court findings of fact. In Clark's view, "if we can delay action it will help," and the opinion "should give lower courts the right to withhold relief in light of troubles."

Clark said that he too would "go along" with such an approach, but if the Court tried to impose desegregation immediately "he would say we had led the states on to think segregation is OK and we should let them work it out."[20]

By the end of the conference discussion, all except Reed indicated a willingness to "go along" with a desegregation decision that allowed for gradual compliance, and even Reed's position would allow him to join that result. What stood in the way was not primarily division on the merits, but division over how to justify the result. Black was willing to rely on the framers' intentions; Frankfurter and Jackson disagreed. Douglas, Burton, and Minton thought a simple fundamental principle controlled; Frankfurter disagreed. Frankfurter and Jackson thought it important, and troubling, that opponents of segregation relied on "sociological" rather than legal arguments against the practice; no one else seems to have cared about that.

Overall, the tone of the 1952 discussion suggests that the justices were talking through their concerns about what they knew they were going to do. They drew on personal experience in musing about segregation: Jackson mentioned that they "had segregation in Jamestown [his home town]" but that he was "not conscious of the problem until I came here";[21] Burton "refer[red] to his policies as Mayor of Cleveland in putting colored nurses, etc., in white hospitals"; and Clark, in a statement which, apart from its racism, is quite difficult to figure out, said that Texas "also has the Mexican problem" which was "more serious" because the Mexicans were "more retarded," and mentioned the problem of a "Mexican boy of 15 . . . in a class with a negro girl of 12," when "some negro girls [would] get in trouble." These references capture the personal way the justices understood the problem they were confronting, and the unfocused quality suggests that they were attempting to reconcile themselves to the result they were about to reach.

Douglas believed that if the cases had been decided during the 1952 Term, "there would probably have been many opinions and a wide divergence of views and a result that would have sustained, so far as the States were concerned, segregation of students."[22] So did Frankfurter; three days after *Brown* was announced, he wrote Justice Reed that if the cases had been decided during the 1952 Term, "there would have been four dissenters—Vinson, Reed, Jackson and Clark—and certainly several opinions for the majority view."[23] These conclusions seem seriously overstated. Vinson's statement about "boldness" and "wisdom" indicated that he believed the Court would invalidate segregation. A decision during the 1952 Term might not have been unanimous, but what Douglas and Frankfurter wrote *after* the decision in *Brown* rested on a projection of views expressed in the discussion, without taking into account the ambivalences Frankfurter and Jackson expressed, and without recognizing that once an opinion had been circulated the potential dissenters might have found it acceptable. At the same time, however, some justices were reluctant, and nothing was likely to happen until Jackson and especially Frankfurter signed on. Jackson's position, that overruling *Plessy* was a sociological or political decision and not a judicial one, made it difficult for Frankfurter to come to rest.

The importance of the cases, the difficulties associated with *Terry v. Adams,* and the illnesses of several justices gave Frankfurter his opportunity. At the December discussion, the idea of rearguing the cases had been broached, though then primarily in terms of working out the distinction, if any, between the state cases and the District of Columbia case. As the term approached its end, Frankfurter developed a different approach to reargument. He drafted a set of five questions for the parties to address. The first two asked for argument about the intention of the framers of the Fourteenth Amendment; the third asked, if the historical analysis "do[es] not dispose of the issue, is it within the judicial power, in construing the Amendment, to abolish segregation in public schools?" The last two questions asked the parties to discuss whether an equity court might authorize "gradual adjustment" to a holding that segregation was unconstitutional. As Frankfurter said, some of the questions "give comfort to one side and some to the other," because he wanted to make sure that the questions did not "disclose our minds." He acknowledged that the questions on remedy "may indicate that a decision against segregation has been reached by the Court," but thought that it was "not undesirable that such an adjustment be made in the public mind to such a possibility."[24]

The Court also specifically invited the attorney general to give the Court the government's views. Frankfurter believed this was important because "the new Administration, unlike the old, may have the responsibility of carrying out a decision full of perplexities" and so should "be asked to face that responsibility as part of our process of adjudication."[25] Black objected to the historical questions because he was confident in his assessment of history and thought that inviting reargument on those questions would simply "bring floods of historical contentions" that "would dilute the arguments along broader lines."[26]

According to Alexander Bickel, Frankfurter was "euphoric" about persuading the Court to hear reargument. As Frankfurter presented it to himself and his friends, reargument was essential because the Court would have been sharply divided had a decision been forced during 1953. Writing to Learned Hand in 1954, Frankfurter said that "if the 'great libertarians' had had their way we would have been in the soup."[27] And, in one sense, that is true enough. If *Brown* had been decided in 1953, the Court would have been splintered—not, however, primarily because the "libertarians" had misgauged the positions of their more conservative colleagues, but because Frankfurter himself would not have gone along with the decision, with the effect of reinforcing the reluctance expressed by Clark, Vinson, Reed, and Jackson.

14

"Quietly Ignoring Facts"
Examining History

The order directing reargument did not encourage Marshall; it signalled division in the Court. From the outside, the question was, what sort of division. Although the justices thought it important to invalidate segregation unanimously, Marshall simply wanted to win. Perhaps a majority wanted to bring a minority along, but the reargument order more likely indicated divisions among the justices inclined toward the NAACP.

The questions about remedy were nothing special. Frankfurter's questions at the oral argument indicated his interest in the issue, and Marshall's team had a well-developed position that constitutional rights were personal and present. If some justices were unhappy with that, the lawyers could not accommodate them without giving up a strong position for no obvious gain; the justices could devise whatever compromises they felt comfortable with, but the LDF lawyers did not have to cheer them on.

The questions about history were more threatening. Marshall and his staff were lawyers, not historians. They made offhand references to the Fourteenth Amendment's "purposes" that easily slipped into references to the "intentions" of the amendment's framers, but they never systematically investigated the amendment's origins. They knew, though, that the drafting history would not be favorable. The Texas brief in *Sweatt* and the repeated invocations of Congress's decision to create segregated schools in Washington were enough to show that. What they had to do, then, was neutralize whatever the defenders of segregation came up with, and hope that, as Marshall put it, the justices would see that a "nothin' to nothin' score means we win the ball game."[1]

Marshall assembled a new team of academic specialists to prepare the lawyers for reargument. Social psychologists and sociologists were put aside; historians were drawn in. Through his network of acquaintances, the NAACP commissioned five historians to prepare working papers the lawyers could use to develop their brief. Horace Mann Bond, president of Lincoln University, had written on education history; he was asked to write a paper on the politics of public education during

Reconstruction. C. Vann Woodward, who made his mark with a biography of the populist leader Tom Watson and then turned to a study of the post-Reconstruction South, wrote a less useful paper on how the moral energies of abolitionists and their successors dissipated in the late nineteenth century.   *linked to the Brook*

Three other papers became the center of the NAACP's brief. Howard Jay Graham, a scholarly man whose deafness had forced him into a job at the Los Angeles County Law Library, had written extensively on antislavery constitutional theory. He wrote a paper on the Fourteenth Amendment's intellectual background. Marshall called John Hope Franklin to ask what he was doing. When Franklin replied that he planned to teach at Howard, Marshall replied, "Do you know what else you're going to do? You're going to work for me!" Franklin and Alfred Kelly, chair of the history department at Wayne State University in Detroit, examined the congressional debates over the Fourteenth Amendment and its predecessor, the 1866 Civil Rights Act. Finally, William Coleman worked on the cases on weekends for two years, commuting from Philadelphia part of the time. He coordinated research, performed by a group of his classmates and fellow Supreme Court clerks, into the discussions in the states of the proposed amendment.[2]

As the research dribbled in over the summer of 1953, the initial reactions were discouraged. Coleman said some material would be of "some help to us in explaining away" local requirements for segregated education. Louis Pollak wrote Carter that he was "afraid" that they could not show that the Fourteenth Amendment "was supposed to require integrated education." At best, Pollak said, "If we win, it'll be on the basis that the clause requires an increasingly high standard of achievement as times and mores change." As Franklin later said, the evidence was "not as decisive and clear-cut as we wanted it to be."[3]

The difficulty was clear. Whatever might be said about the amendment's general purposes, virtually every mention of education during the amendment's drafting said that the amendment would not prohibit segregated schools. Occasionally the amendment's opponents would show how terrible the proposal was because it would prohibit segregation, and almost every time that argument was made a supporter responded by saying the amendment would not have that effect. More generally, the amendment's sponsors argued that it would, and should, guarantee civil rights and—for some supporters—political rights, but that it would not, and should not, guarantee what they called social rights. The lines dividing civil, political, and social rights were sometimes blurry, but people routinely treated the right to an education as a social right, dealing with associations among children, rather than as a civil right, dealing with the status of African-Americans in society.[4]

Kelly was quite discouraged by the historical research. John Hope Franklin, in contrast, was more sanguine. In part he regarded the exercise as real historical research, and thought it important to go over the debates systematically in a way no one had done before. In part, too, he may have had a better sense of the roles of lawyers and historians in the enterprise. Kelly seems to have believed that he had to come up with historians' arguments against segregated education. Franklin believed that he simply had to come up with information lawyers would use as they could. The lawyers did not know enough about the history to ask Franklin to shade

his findings; he was "writing on a blank sheet of paper as far as they were concerned." Still, he was pleased when Marshall told him that his working paper
"sounded very much like a lawyer's brief"; as Franklin saw it, his scholarship "did
not suffer" from transforming the information he came up with into "an urgent
plea for justice."[5]

The summer's research culminated in a late September conference, attended
by nearly one hundred lawyers and academics. The program indicated the lawyers'
cast of mind. They wanted to know "what premises helpful and harmful to our
point of view may be drawn from the research," how they could "neutralize[ ] or
minimize[ ]" the harmful material, and "what is the strongest position . . . that
can be taken or must be taken if we are to prevail." The lawyers knew that they
could not answer the Court's historical questions "advantageous[ly]" in the Court's
form. Rather, they had to "go beyond the contemplation and understanding of the
Congress which submitted" the Amendment to the states. As Kelly later put it, the
question was whether the lawyers should use "a generalized or a particularistic
historical approach."[6]

Bob Ming, then teaching at the University of Chicago and about to return to
law practice, forcefully argued that the "particularistic" evidence dealing specifically with education was "so scanty or so unconvincing" that the lawyers could not
base their argument on "the framers' immediate historical intent." He favored
Howard Jay Graham's approach, which stressed "the overall spirit of humanitari-
anism, racial equalitarianism, and social idealism" dominating abolitionists and
their successors. Kelly feared, though, that such an approach would leave the
NAACP vulnerable to the "damning particularism" that the school boards' lawyers
would present and that, through its specificity, might overwhelm the justices'
ability to assess the significance of Graham's more general observations.

Two weeks after the conference, Kelly, Franklin, Ming, and the staff lawyers
got down to reshaping the historians' academic papers into a brief. Over the next
several months, Franklin spent Thursdays through Sundays in New York, and
Kelly spent more long weekends in New York than he had expected. Ming hammered out a first draft, working closely with Kelly. It devoted as little as it could to
the specifics about the framers' views about segregated education. Marshall,
though, concluded that such an approach would "never get past Frankfurter or
Douglas." He asked Kelly to rework the brief.[7]

The central difficulty Kelly confronted was the sequence leading to the Fourteenth Amendment. In 1866, Congress considered a broad civil rights bill that
could have been fairly read to prohibit all forms of segregation. When the bill came
before the House of Representatives, though, John Bingham, a staunch supporter
of equality, objected that the bill was unconstitutional. It was sent back to committee, which eventually reported a narrower bill that could not be read to invalidate
segregated schools. Then, to allay lingering constitutional concerns, Congress
proposed the Fourteenth Amendment to ensure that the narrowed Civil Rights Act
would indeed be constitutional. As Kelly interpreted the events, "The Civil Rights
Act as it passed Congress was specifically rewritten to avoid the embarrassing
question of a congressional attack upon State racial segregation laws . . . [and]
the purpose of the [Fourteenth] amendment was to constitutionalize the Civil

Rights Act." It followed, Kelly believed, that the amendment, constitutionalizing a narrow statute, could not have been intended to invalidate segregation.

Over the next few days, the lawyers and historians, working as "an unusually effective team," worked out an approach that, Marshall believed, would at least give him the tie-score he needed. They used Graham's research to show "how the pre-Civil War views of the radical abolitionists dominated the egalitarian thinking" of the amendment's framers. This had the important rhetorical effect of shifting the burden of explaining things away. Earlier the lawyers worried about how they could "neutralize" statements supporting segregation. But, if the drafters were egalitarians, their occasional statements about segregated education became peripheral. A judge who accepted the framework the NAACP offered would be inclined to ask the states' lawyers to explain why egalitarians sometimes supported segregation, rather than asking Marshall to explain why people who supported segregation nonetheless proposed the amendment.[8]

Next, the lawyers and historians turned the 1866 Civil Rights Act problem around. Bingham objected to the broad initial bill because Congress did not have the power to adopt it. The new argument was that Congress adopted the narrow act because it was convinced it could do no more without amending the Constitution, and proposed the amendment precisely to accomplish the broad antisegregation purposes of the initial civil rights act.

Bond's paper on education history provided a final element, which in the end captured more of what the justices wanted than any discussion of legislative history. The Fourteenth Amendment's drafters wanted to protect civil rights, but did not think that education was a civil right. Bond suggested how to shift education from the category of unprotected social rights into the category of protected civil rights. He emphasized that compulsory public education was "a developing concept" in the 1860s. Although neither Bond nor the NAACP brief put much flesh on the idea, stressing the novelty of public education in the 1860s opened the way to argue that the Fourteenth Amendment's framers did not understand what public education would become, but that in its modern form education satisfied their criteria for civil rights. And, of course, even the most "particularistic" reading showed that the framers did intend to eliminate discrimination in civil rights.

When Kelly helped develop the argument, he felt that he was acting as a lawyer rather than as a historian. "We were using facts, . . . quietly ignoring facts, and above all interpreting facts in a way to do what Marshall said we had to do—'get by those boys down there.'" Seven years later, he conceded that the argument "contains an essential measure of historical truth." And, indeed, the NAACP's interpretation of the events leading to the Fourteenth Amendment's adoption has become the standard one. There are disagreements—some fundamental—and modifications in matters of detail, but the basic structure remains unimpaired. To understand the Fourteenth Amendment, we must understand the general intellectual context in which its supporters lived: their context was strongly egalitarian; they had to compromise during Reconstruction; but when revising the Constitution, they succeeded in persuading their colleagues and the public that the Constitution must incorporate egalitarian premises.[9]

The historical research was the most difficult for Marshall to assimilate, but the Court had asked for more: a discussion of remedy. While the historians were working on the first three questions, Jack Greenberg and David Pinsky, a young graduate of the University of Pennsylvania Law School who had recently joined the NAACP's staff, tried to say something new about that issue. Pinsky correctly inferred that Frankfurter devised the questions. The questions, according to Pinsky, rested on the idea that when plaintiffs asked courts to enjoin ongoing operations, particularly of school boards, the courts could "balance the equities." How could that be reconciled with the idea that constitutional rights were "personal and present"?[10]

First, Pinsky reiterated the point Marshall and Robinson had already made: individual rights were enforceable immediately, but of course school boards could take some short time for administrative "revamp[ing]." The real question was whether longer delays could be justified by "balancing the equities." Pinsky said no. Examining the "balancing" cases, Pinsky concluded that they balanced equities only when property rights rather than constitutional or other personal rights were involved. And, Pinsky added, even when courts balanced, they took account of the nature of the rights; as Greenberg said, because gradual desegregation would do little to help the child already in junior high school, his or her interests had to have great weight.

Greenberg offered an argument somewhat more in tune with the language of balancing and gradualism. He started by pointing out that it was untenable to say that desegregation must occur immediately. The concessions regarding delay to take account of administrative concerns meant, in Greenberg's view, that the NAACP already accepted equitable balancing in principle. Generally, though, a proper balance would lead to rapid desegregation. As Pinsky suggested, there was a public interest in constitutional rights. Further, Greenberg pointed out, the more quickly desegregation occurred, the less the courts would be involved in supervising the details of how school systems were operating. On the other side of the balance, Greenberg said, were only a few factors. School boards actually needed time to transform dual systems into desegregated ones. Alluding to the arguments that Lindsay Almond made, Greenberg said that courts should ignore threats of violent resistance to desegregation and the more subtle threat that desegregation would lead to reduced public support for education.[11]

Greenberg and Pinsky blended their memos into one that accepted the idea of balancing while stressing that it had rarely been done in cases involving personal or constitutional rights. No matter what the formulation, though, the NAACP's position was that desegregation had to occur as rapidly as possible, limited only by the minor impediments arising from administrative difficulties. As Marshall put it, "I am for the gradual approach [but] 91 years since the Emancipation Proclamation has been gradual enough."[12]

The states' briefs relied on the more conventional understanding of the 1866 Civil Rights Act and the Fourteenth Amendment: The statute had a limited effect and certainly did not cover segregated education; the amendment was designed to place in the Constitution, beyond the possibility of repeal, the rights guaranteed by the statute, and no others.

The position of the United States was, once again, more important. Dwight Eisenhower had been president for almost five months when the Court ordered reargument. The order specifically invited the attorney general to participate in the case "if he so desires." The new administration had to decide what to do. Eisenhower was comfortable with segregation, and later said that on "some" racial issues "he was more of a 'states Righter' than the Supreme Court." He had carried four Southern states in 1952, and Republican strategists hoped to build on his victory to erode Democratic strength in the South even more. Southern governors complained to Eisenhower that the Justice Department had gotten into the cases for political reasons. Yet the Republicans were still "the party of Lincoln," with a strong tradition of supporting civil rights. The new attorney general, Herbert Brownell, was a politically active New York lawyer who held conventional Republican views on civil rights; Brownell believed that the states would "work . . . out" desegregation in about a decade. [13]

Ordinarily the solicitor general would develop the Department's position, but the office was unfilled from March 1953 through the middle of February 1954. Brownell brought the issue directly into his office, assigning responsibility to J. Lee Rankin, an assistant attorney general. Eisenhower tried to persuade Brownell not to file anything, saying that for the Department to accept the Court's invitation would invade the Court's authority. Not surprisingly, Brownell replied that doing what the Court asked could hardly count as intruding on its domain. In correspondence with James Byrnes, who had supported him in 1952, Eisenhower expressed skepticism that any building program could really bring about separate but equal schools. [14]

Disagreement over what to say delayed the government's response. Political operatives were unhappy with the strong stand Brownell wanted to take, believing it might alienate the white Southerners they were trying to attract to the Republican party. Because of problems within the administration, Brownell asked the Court to postpone argument from October to December. Over the summer, Elman took charge of writing an enormous brief with an appendix of nearly four hundred pages setting out every quotation relevant to segregation the lawyers could dig up in the legislative history.

In part to satisfy the politicians' concerns, the brief opened by saying it was "an objective non-adversary discussion" of the questions the Court had propounded. [15] Prepared entirely independently of the NAACP's, the government's brief had a strikingly similar structure. Like the NAACP's brief, it began by examining the general background of equal rights thought before and during Reconstruction and then turned to the legislative history. The brief was largely nonargumentative and refrained from drawing strong conclusions. Its tone, and some passing comments, reinforced the NAACP's position. Readers of both briefs would conclude that when a passionate advocate and a dispassionate observer both approached the problem in the same way, the advocate's conclusions were probably right. In addition, the government brief, when it summed up part of the argument, referred

to "the broad scope of the Amendment . . . [to] establish the full constitutional
right of all persons to equality before the law and . . . prohibit legal distinctions
based on race and color." Again, in that setting, the states had to do the hard work
of explaining why their "narrow" views should prevail.

The brief's historical section had an understated but powerful conclusion.
Although the drafters of the Fourteenth Amendment probably did not "specifically" understand that it would abolish racial segregation, they did "understand"
that it "established the broad constitutional principle of full and complete equality
of all persons under the law." They did not think in detail about how that principle
applied to education, although some thought that it would invalidate segregated
schools. As to what happened in the states, the evidence was "too sparse, and the
specific references to education too few," to justify any conclusions at all. But, in
an effective closing, the brief piled quotation upon quotation from Supreme Court
decisions saying it should construe the Constitution expansively, because its provisions "express broad principles of government the essence of which is their vitality
and adaptability to the progressive changes and needs of the nation." If the justices
believed this was an objective, nonadversarial presentation, segregation's defenders were in deep trouble.

The brief contained a relatively short discussion of remedy. It said that equitable balancing was entirely proper, even in cases involving "personal and present"
rights. The brief did note that "plaintiffs could well say that, as individuals whose
constitutional rights have been and are continuing to be violated," balancing decrees providing for desegregation "at some time in the future (perhaps after they
are too old themselves to enjoy the benefits of the Court's decision)" would "afford[ ] them inadequate redress." The government's solution was close to the
NAACP's: The decrees could take into account "the administrative obstacles
involved in making a general transition" from segregated to nonsegregated systems.
A short treatment of "obstacles to integration" mentioned school consolidation,
teacher transfers, and transportation arrangements. On the crucial question, the
relevance of "popular opposition," the brief took the line first laid out in the
ACLU's earlier *amicus* brief: desegregation in New Jersey and, more important,
the desegregation of the armed forces showed that desegregation could be accomplished "without disorder or friction." This was not an entirely satisfactory way of
dealing with what everyone knew was the real problem. Ignoring the threats of
disorder would not make them go away.

Two additional events shaped the Court's actions when it heard the cases reargued. Chief Justice Vinson died of a heart attack on September 8, 1953. Because of
his ambivalence, he had not led the Court to a decision in the segregation cases.
His successor was very different.

Earl Warren was governor of California in 1952, when Eisenhower sought the
Republican nomination. At a crucial moment in the party convention Warren
directed California's delegates to support a motion to seat delegates favoring
Eisenhower over his chief rival Senator Robert Taft. Eisenhower was in debt to
Warren. Almost in passing, while explaining why he was not appointing Warren
attorney general, Eisenhower said he would appoint Warren to the first Supreme

Court vacancy. He did not expect the first appointment to be a new Chief Justice. But, after thinking about the question and having Brownell meet Warren in California, Eisenhower decided to go ahead. On September 30, Eisenhower announced Warren's nomination.[16]

Warren was a vigorous manager, used to directing the complex bureaucracy of California's state government. The Supreme Court, of course, was different, but it too needed a guiding hand that Warren was happy to provide. He was friendly and unpretentious, willing to take on the hard work that each justice had to do. He was resolute in his belief that segregation was unconstitutional. With a leader committed to overturning segregation, the Court was almost ready to decide. Warren was willing to push the Court to the decision it had deferred.

Warren's appointment was a public event. The other significant event occurred within the Court. The Court ordered reargument largely because Frankfurter wanted it, and Frankfurter wanted reargument because he needed time to work out an answer to the problem Jackson raised: How could the Court's decision be legal rather than political? Frankfurter thought the decision would be legal if it rested on solid historical ground. He probably hoped to find out that the Fourteenth Amendment's framers really did intend to make segregation unlawful. At least he wanted to counter claims that the framers intended to allow states to adopt segregated education if they chose, because Jackson seemed to take that position.

While the historians and lawyers were developing their briefs, Frankfurter asked his law clerk, Alexander Bickel, to examine the legislative debates. It was as if Frankfurter was afraid that the NAACP and the government would not come up with what he needed. Perhaps Frankfurter needed something only he and his confidants could come up with—their own answer to the historical questions. Whatever that answer was, it might satisfy Frankfurter that he had done the lawyer's work to support his decision to invalidate segregation.

Just before reargument, Frankfurter sent his colleagues copies of Bickel's long memorandum. As Bickel summarized his conclusions, "little regard was had for language by a Congress not notable for the presence in its membership of very many brilliant men. A blunderbuss was simply aimed in the direction of existing evils in the South, on which all eyes were trained." For Bickel, "it was preposterous to worry about unsegregated schools . . . when hardly a beginning had been made at educating Negroes at all." He found it "impossible to conclude" either that Congress "intended that segregation be abolished" or that they "foresaw it might be, under the language they were adopting." Frankfurter was satisfied that Bickel's research at least neutralized the states' claim, showing that the history was "inconclusive in the sense that the Congress as an enacting body neither manifested that the amendment outlawed segregation . . . nor that it manifested the opposite," and he made that point to his colleagues.[17]

This conclusion broke the ice for Frankfurter. Frankfurter could now put politics aside and think about *Brown* in legal terms. Why Frankfurter found the memorandum satisfying, though, is not obvious. On the face of it, Bickel's conclusion was not sufficient for Frankfurter's purposes: If Congress did not "manifest" an intent to "outlaw segregation," where could the Court find its authority to hold segregation unconstitutional?[18]

Frankfurter did not have to answer. With Warren pushing the Court to a decision, there clearly was a majority to overturn the separate but equal doctrine. Frankfurter might have some misgivings about the Court's ultimate opinion, but he certainly would sign it, particularly because he believed unanimity essential. Yet Frankfurter had to see himself as making important contributions to the decision. The historical questions proved unilluminating. The remedy questions were more promising, and Frankfurter turned away from the merits and focused on them. There, he could exercise his lawyer's abilities in shaping a remedial order.

John W. Davis put the lawyers' problem gracefully when he told the Court at the reargument, "I suppose there are few invitations less welcome in an advocate's life than to be asked to reargue a case on which he has once spent himself." The reargument promised to be particularly difficult for Marshall, for reasons he knew and for some he did not. The Court's questions suggested that the advocates should focus on questions of history and remedy. Marshall was unaccustomed to making arguments that went into the details of legislative history; his strength lay in showing that he was on the side of justice. Further, when reargument took place, the historical argument was less important than the Court's questions suggested. When Frankfurter proposed the questions, Vinson was still chief justice, and Frankfurter could have believed Vinson would have found it important (as Jackson and Frankfurter did) to be sure that the Fourteenth Amendment's framers did not support school segregation. Warren did not have Vinson's misgivings, which Frankfurter thought the historical research would allay. Even more, Bickel's research was enough for Frankfurter; he did not need the oral arguments to explore a problem that had been solved. Marshall and his colleagues, though, could not know that the historical questions the Court had directed to them, and to which they had devoted so much effort, were no longer that important.

In addition, Marshall believed that the historical case he could make was weaker than the moral one. Yet he already had made the moral case as forcefully as he could. If Marshall went over the ground again, not only would he seem to be ignoring what the Court had asked, he would bore the justices by repeating what they already had heard. On the remedy questions, Marshall had said all that he could. The underlying issue was how the Court should respond to the possibility that Southern whites would resist its decision. No one could fairly expect Marshall to tell the justices anything but that they should ignore those implicit threats.

Finally, of course, ten hours is a long time to devote to a single set of cases. Modest variations among the five cases may have justified the length of the first arguments. Nothing anyone could say in the rearguments could justify another ten hours. Because of developments inside the Court, the reargument had little real meaning.

With the Court's permission, Robinson and Marshall presented the Virginia and South Carolina cases first. Robinson spent his time on the historical questions, reciting the conclusions of the NAACP's historical research and supporting his position by quoting parts of the legislative history. After he had gone on for a while, Frankfurter interrupted to ask how important the statements of any particular senator or member of Congress were. Then Frankfurter suggested that all the detailed historical research was largely irrelevant, and that all the Court needed to know were the general purposes of the Fourteenth Amendment. "I grant you we solicited and elicited" the historical research, Frankfurter said, "but I just wondered, now that we have got it, what are we to get out of it?" Robinson fairly might have wondered what was going on. [19]

Marshall stumbled by beginning his argument with a discussion of the Court's cases, not the legislative history. Justice Jackson interrupted: "I do not believe the Court was troubled about its own cases." Marshall persisted with some scattered observations about early civil rights cases and the 1871 Civil Rights Act, and finally managed to make an effective point. The Court's cases acknowledged, Marshall said, that the Fourteenth Amendment did not "enumerate" all the rights it protected; the drafters meant to leave the courts free to do that. The states had the wrong "approach" to interpreting the Constitution. They were asking whether there was "definite material in the debates that shows the intent of Congress to include segregation in public education." But, Marshall said, if the amendment's overall purpose was "to strike down all types of class and caste legislation," the only question was whether segregated education was a form of caste legislation. And, he continued, the university cases showed that the Court had the power to answer that question. He concluded this part by pointing out that everyone agreed the Court could strike down unreasonable classifications, and that his claim was simply that racial segregation was unreasonable.

Marshall's argument was rather unfocused and had a somewhat frenetic quality, quite unlike his assurance at the initial argument. In the end, however, he managed to make a reasonably effective case linking the Fourteenth Amendment's general purposes to the question of judicial power the Court had asked.

Perhaps in deference to his age, the justices let John W. Davis present his argument essentially uninterrupted. He identified several "fallacies" that, he said, infected the NAACP's position. The abolitionist background was irrelevant, Davis said, because the abolitionists wanted to abolish slavery; they said nothing about segregated education. In addition, the NAACP wrongly assumed that Radical Republicans controlled the Congress that submitted the Fourteenth Amendment to the states. Nor should they be allowed to count as an opponent of segregated schools everyone who made general statements favoring racial equality. Then Davis turned to the submission from the United States, which he said reached "rather a lame and impotent conclusion, not calculated to be a great deal of help to the Court." Davis provided a quick review of what Congress had done during Reconstruction, to show that it had never disapproved school segregation even when it could have, and that it supported some segregated schools.

Davis ended by discussing the Court's power to overturn segregation. Here he pinned his argument on precedent. "Somewhere, sometime to every principle comes a moment of repose when it has been so often announced, so confidently relied upon, so long continued, that it passes the limits of judicial discretion and disturbance." The separate but equal doctrine had reached that point. If the schools in Clarendon County were desegregated, Davis asked, "Would that make the children any happier? Would they learn any more quickly? Would their lives be more serene?" Davis concluded, "South Carolina . . . is convinced that the happiness, the progress and the welfare of these children is best promoted in segregated schools. . . . Here is equal education, not promised, not prophesied, but present. Shall it be thrown away on some fancied question of racial prestige?"

Once again Davis had been extraordinarily eloquent. It was, however, the eloquence of an earlier era. The way Davis argued represented a time that had passed. Ironically perhaps, precisely because Davis's eloquence was both so manifest and so old-fashioned, he showed that the position he represented also had become outdated. His argument was an elegy for a social order the Supreme Court could no longer support.

Justin Moore for Prince Edward County, unlike the lawyers before him, tried not to address the Court's questions directly. But, as soon as he mentioned the remedy questions, Frankfurter asked his views. Moore replied, "It really distresses me to face that question," resting as it did on the "unhappy" assumption that he lost the case on the merits. But, pressed, he said that "the courts should be given the broadest possible discretion to act along reasonable lines." The schools should be asked to present a plan for courts to consider. Moore then returned to the historical questions, about which he said nothing interesting. At the end of an otherwise modulated argument, though, Moore let segregation's racist premises slip through. After observing that there were about equal numbers of African-American and white students in Prince Edward County, Moore asked, apparently incredulous at the prospect, "Shall we put one Negro along with every white child in high school when that is the best high school?" By referring to "the best high school," Moore entirely unconsciously demonstrated the impossibility of separate but equal.

Lindsay Almond followed with another stump speech. He asked, "What crime has Virginia committed," and praised "the unfolding evolutionary process of education where from the dark days of the depraved institution of slavery, with the help and the sympathy and the love and the respect of the white people of the South, the colored man has risen . . . to a place of eminence and respect throughout this nation." He ended by disparaging the Reconstruction-era legislatures of the Southern states.

As soon as Marshall came to the podium to respond to the states' arguments, Frankfurter asked him about remedy. Marshall stuck with the position that only administrative problems were relevant, and he could not imagine anything "administrative-wise that would take longer than a year." Marshall used "one of the points that runs throughout the argument on the other side" to shift to the merits. If administrative problems were put to one side, why else might desegregation be difficult? Only, of course, because of prejudice. But, Marshall said, that showed that segregation itself rested on prejudice, which made racial classifications unreasonable. He sarcastically referred to the reliance Davis and Moore had placed on what Marshall called the "horrible number of Negroes in the South" to drive home the point. Then, referring to "the name-calling stage" that Almond had reached, Marshall quoted the respected Senator Carter Glass of Virginia who told the state's constitutional convention, "Discrimination, that is precisely what we propose."

Responding to Davis, Marshall drawled, "I understand them to say that it is just a little feeling on the part of Negroes: They don't like segregation. As Mr. Davis said yesterday, the only thing the Negroes are trying to get is prestige." Marshall snapped, "Exactly right. Ever since the Emancipation Proclamation, the Negro has been trying to get . . . the same status as anybody else regardless of race." Alluding to fears of disorder, Marshall said that he had "more confidence in the people of the South, white and colored, than the lawyers on the other side. I am convinced they are just as lawful as anybody else, and once the law is laid down, that is all there is to it."

Marshall ended with his own brand of eloquence, more effective than Davis's because more contemporary. After saying it was the Court's duty to enforce the Constitution, Marshall said, "I got the feeling yesterday that when you put a white child in a school with a whole lot of colored children, the child would fall apart or something. Everybody knows that is not true." He repeated what he had said a year before about kids playing together and separating only to go to school. "There is some magic to it," he continued. The Court's cases showed that they can vote together, live in the same neighborhoods, even go to college together, "but if they go to elementary and high school the world will fall apart." This, he said, was "the exact same argument that has been made to this Court over and over again."

He ended by talking about reasonableness again. The only way to defend segregation "is to find that for some reason Negroes are inferior to all other human beings." But "nobody will stand in the Court and urge that," yet "the only thing [it] can be is an inherent determination that the people who were formerly kept in slavery . . . shall be kept as near that stage as is possible; and now is the time, we submit, that this Court should make it clear that that is not what our Constitution stands for."

The rest of the reargument was routine. The most important presentation was made by J. Lee Rankin for the government. Rankin put a good light on the government's inconclusive historical analysis by saying that it "clean[ed] out some of the unimportant elements" and left the Court "with the naked problem of what this Amendment means to every American citizen who loves this country and this Constitution." Rankin argued that Congress's actions after 1868 meant that Congress left segregation's constitutionality "in abeyance," and he rejected Reed's reasonable suggestion that Congress's actions actually left the matter to the states. Responding to Jackson's usual question about section five, Rankin replied that the Court had never "waited for Congress to act" in any other situation. It should not matter, Rankin said, that segregation's opponents could not get Congress to act, because that would place their constitutional rights in "the political for[u]m which changes from time to time."

Rankin then took up segregated education in the 1870s, stressing the "far different" status of education then. Both Jackson and Reed were skeptical about his claim that the amendment's drafters were so concerned with general questions about educating freed slaves that they never focused on segregated education in a way that would justify drawing any conclusions about their "intent." They also were uncomfortable with Rankin's claim that the nineteenth-century judges who upheld segregated education had not considered the question in detail. "These men had lived with the thing," Jackson said, and "didn't have to go to books." Reed added that "the very men that sat" in *Plessy* "were thoroughly familiar with all the history." Rankin replied *Plessy* was a transportation case, a distinction Reed was not buying.

Rankin turned in apparent relief to the question of judicial power, saying that "this Court has never seen fit to determine that a man has been denied his constitutional rights and then referred him to Congress to see what type of relief he should be granted." An oddly hostile question from Justice Douglas allowed Rankin to clarify the government's position. It was not, he said, that the history showed segregation was unconstitutional, but only that "some of the conclusions that have been asserted from the history are not borne out." Pressed by Douglas, Rankin finally came out and said what the brief had skirted: "It is the position of the Department of Justice that segregation in public schools cannot be maintained."

After a short lunch break, Rankin resumed on the question of remedy. Again being more precise than the brief, Rankin suggested "a year for the presentation and consideration of a plan . . . with the idea that it might involve the principle of handling the matter with deliberate speed." In response to Justice Jackson's hint that school boards would maintain segregated schools anyway, Rankin said, "We do not assume that . . . our people are not going to try to . . . be in accord with it as rapidly as they can." Jackson, though, did not think "a court can enter a decree on that assumption." If there was resistance, he said, "we have to proceed school district by school district, . . . lawsuit after lawsuit." And what guidance, he asked, would the lower courts have? Jackson's questions acutely identified the difficulty covered up by undefined notions of gradualism, and Rankin lamely said that each case would have to be decided by "the equities of the particular situation." Jackson correctly noted that "a generation of litigation" would occur "if we send it back with no standards."

Frankfurter, gradualism's strongest proponent, offered Rankin a verbal formula that distinguished between "the applicable standard" and "the means by which this standard can be satisfied." In spelling out what this meant, though, Frankfurter inadvertently showed its inadequacy. Frankfurter started his elaboration by saying, "Certainly the fact that local people do not like the result is not any condition that should . . . influence the court." Then he mentioned "whether you actually have a building in which children can go to school, and what distances there are"—precisely the things that Marshall referred to as administrative matters. Frankfurter's distinction differed from Marshall's approach only because Frankfurter really was concerned about local resistance but could not openly say so. His last questions indicated that what he wanted was some solution that would delay desegregation, perhaps for an extended period, to "settle a widespread problem" with some approach that would put the issue to rest and avoid "endless lawsuits of every individual child . . . for the indefinite future." No one had yet come up with such an approach.

Jackson's statements were more candid but hardly more helpful. Consider, he said, a district that had a "pretty good school" for whites and a "pretty poor one" for African-Americans. To desegregate, "you either have to build a new school or you have got to move some white people into the poor school, which would cause a rumpus, or you have to center them all in the good school." The "rumpus," of course, would be caused by white people. And, notably, Jackson's hypothetical case cast doubt on South Carolina's claims that segregation was acceptable because there were no "pretty poor" schools for African-Americans. Rankin said that figuring out what to do had to be left to the school boards under court supervision.

The reargument in the Kansas case did not, as Carter put it, "open[ ] any new avenues,"[20] and the Court took up the Washington case. By this time the justices had almost had enough. No one asked Hayes any questions. Nabrit tried to capture the high moral ground by referring to the "blunt fact" that under segregation, millions of African-Americans "live . . . as second-class citizens, suffering all types of civil disabilities . . . solely because of their race and color." Although Nabrit rapidly got bogged down in details about school board organization in Washington, the argument's tone had changed. Tension had disappeared, and Nabrit was repeatedly interrupted by relaxed laughter at his offhand responses to questions. Frankfurter's questions to Korman, though, were rather hostile, because school board members, Korman's clients, made press statements saying they disagreed with segregation. Frankfurter wondered what Korman was doing if his clients disagreed with his legal position. Korman could say only that the policy of segregation had not been formally changed. Nabrit ended with another powerful statement: "America is a great country . . . and we are not in the position that the animals were in George Orwell's satirical novel *Animal Farm.* . . . Our Constitution has no provision across it that all men are equal, but that white men are more equal than others. . . . Under this Constitution and under the protection of this Court," Nabrit finished, "we believe that we, too, are equal."

The rearguments concluded with a short and uninformative reargument in the Delaware case.[21] It had been an exhausting and, in the end, largely unproductive ten hours. Too much time was spent restating positions already taken in the first argument. Whatever points the historical details showed could not be made effectively in oral argument, and the points that could be made from the broad historical outlines had been made repeatedly. Although Richard Kluger calls Marshall's performance "one of his least creditable performances before the Court," he had done reasonably well under the circumstances.[22] It was not an occasion on which anyone could really shine, except by putting on an oratorical performance like Davis's. That, however, did not suit Marshall's style. Nor was it what the Court wanted.

On December 12, 1953, the justices discussed the cases informally but, at Warren's suggestion, took no votes. After the decisions were announced, Douglas

See 187

wrote that at the conference he could count "a bare majority" in favor of holding segregation unconstitutional, with Reed opposed and Clark, Frankfurter, and Jackson "inclined that way although doubtful." According to Douglas, Frankfurter and Jackson "expressed the hope that the Court would not have to decide these cases but somehow avoid these decisions."[23]

Douglas overstated the opposition to overruling *Plessy*. For Warren, the Court was "now down to [the] point of deciding the issue." As he saw it, *Plessy* rested on the "basic premise that the Negro race is inferior," and he rejected that premise. The Reconstruction amendments, for Warren, "were intended to make equal those who were once slaves," and, although "this view causes trouble perhaps," he did not "see how segregation can be justified in this day and age." Although Warren had not taken part in the earlier discussions, he echoed one of their themes in "recogniz[ing] that [the] time element is important in the deep south," and said that the Court "must act" but "should do it in a tolerant way." This meant considering carefully "the condition in the different states." In dealing with the deep South, "it will take all the wisdom of this Court to dispose of the matter with a minimum of emotion and strife."[24]

Black did not attend the conference because of a family illness, but he sent in a vote to hold segregation unconstitutional. Douglas again called the problem "simple," but acknowledged that "adjustments will have to arise." Burton said the Court "had no choice in the matter but to act." He thought that the Court could "work it out on a judicial basis" and noted the encouraging trend against segregation in restaurants and the armed forces. For Burton, segregation might have been acceptable when the Fourteenth Amendment was adopted because then "life was separate," but "now [segregation] is inadequate preparation for the life today." On the issue of relief, Burton said that he "would go a long way to agree to put off enforcement awhile and to give [the] District Court[s] discretion." Minton noted the discussion's "seriousness," and, like Burton, was encouraged that "so many things [have] broken down the barriers" between the races. For him, the Fourteenth Amendment "was intended to wipe out the badge of slavery" by requiring equal rights; "separate is a lawyer's addition to the language." Minton doubted that holding segregation unconstitutional would cause trouble.[25]

Clark disagreed, saying that "violence will follow in the south." Because this was a "very serious problem" Clark said, "if it is to be abolished it m[ust] be handled very carefully," particularly because "various conditions will require different handling," and the "opinion must indicate that clearly." Clark said he "always thought that the 14th Amend[ment] covered the matter and outlawed segregation," but Congress had been unable to act because "people couldn't vote to integrate here and return home to the south." He once again referred to his experience with segregation, and said that he "does not like the system of segregation and will vote to abolish it," but wanted the remedy to be "carefully worked out."[26]

By the discussion's end, and probably before it began, it was clear that a majority was prepared to hold segregation unconstitutional, and that the justices would be interested in developing a remedy allowing some delay in implementation. Justice Reed reiterated his view that segregation was constitutional because it was "not done on inferiority but on racial differences," for "of course there is no inferior race," although, he said, African-Americans "may be handicapped by lack of opportunity." Rather, segregation "protects people against [the] mixing of races." History and the contemporaneous understanding of the Fourteenth Amendment meant that segregation was constitutionally permissible. Still, even Reed said that the Constitution was "dynamic," and *Plessy* "might not be correct now" because the states had not provided equal facilities to African-Americans. The tone of Reed's comments is not easy to capture, but he seems not to have committed himself to a vigorous fight.[27]

Douglas's notes record Frankfurter as saying that the Fourteenth Amendment "did not abolish segregation when it was adopted," which he probably did say, and that "history in Congress and in this court indicates that *Plessy* is right," which he almost certainly did not say. Clearly, Frankfurter was annoyed by assertions like Warren's that the Fourteenth Amendment was intended to make segregation unconstitutional. At most, he believed, the evidence undermined claims that the amendment's drafters plainly intended to allow segregation. Frankfurter, though, had more serious problems. Jackson continued to assert that a decision invalidating segregation would be political rather than legal, and Frankfurter still had not worked out a response.

Jackson made a rather forceful statement sharpening the issue for him and Frankfurter. Jackson insisted that "this is a political question." The difficulty for segregation's opponents was "to make a judicial basis for a congenial political conclusion," and Jackson doubted it could be done: the Court "can't justify elimination of segregation as a judicial act." For Jackson, the history of the framing, precedents, and custom all supported segregation. Evoking the fight against the pre–New Deal Court, Jackson said, "if we have to decide the question then representative government has failed," and the remedy, leaving matters to the lower courts, was likely to be unsuccessful because some district judges "would put all Board[s] of education in jail" while "others would not give negroes any relief." Under these circumstances, Jackson said, the Court had to consider remedy along with the merits. Seeing a decision against segregation as a political decision, Jackson "personally" did not find the political outcome a problem; "as a political decision, I can go along with it."[28]

Jackson's idea that overruling *Plessy* was a political decision was developed in a draft he prepared during February and March 1954, after it was clear that a majority was committed to overturning segregation. Its introduction alluded to Jackson's early experience in Jamestown, "where Negro pupils were very few," and said that segregation as a social practice was doomed, though his way of putting the point was, as usual, somewhat peculiar: "Whatever we might say today, within a generation it will be outlawed by decision of this Court because of the forces of mortality and replacement which operate upon it." That is, even if by some chance a majority upheld segregation in 1954, eventually new justices would be appointed who would invalidate segregation.[29]

In phrases reminiscent of Rehnquist's earlier memorandum, Jackson stressed the limited power of the Court to "eradicate" the "fears, prides and prejudices" that made segregation an important social practice in the South. Jackson wrote,

"However sympathetic we may be with the resentments of those who are coerced into segregation, we cannot, in considering a recasting of society by judicial fiat, ignore the claims of those who are to be coerced out of it." Those people felt, with "sincerity and passion," that "their blood, lineage and culture are worthy of protection by enforced separatism of races. . . ." These feelings, according to Jackson, were reinforced by "deep resentment" of Reconstruction "and the deep humiliation of carpetbag government imposed by conquest." As a result, Jackson concluded, "the Northern majority of this Court" should not adopt a "self-righteous approach" or be "inconsiderate of the conditions which have brought about and continued this custom."

Jackson then turned to his "lawyer's" analysis, noting how difficult it was to explain how the courts, which were "supposed not to make new law but only to declare existing law," could suddenly overturn a decision of such long standing as *Plessy*. He agreed that the Fourteenth Amendment's "majestic and sweeping generalities" could be read to "require a full and equal racial partnership in all matters within the reach of law," but noted that its drafters did not read it that way. The period of the framing, as Jackson's deprecating mention of carpetbag governments already indicated, "was a passionate, confused and deplorable era." No one thought seriously about segregated education, but there was no reason to think the drafters believed that the amendment prohibited segregated schools, and contemporaneous practice, which included widespread adoption of segregated schooling, was "impossible to reconcile with any understanding" that it did so. Similarly, the courts had accepted segregation. Thus, for Jackson, "I simply cannot find in the conventional material of constitutional interpretation any justification for saying" that segregated education violated the Fourteenth Amendment.

Jackson then mentioned the possibility that Congress might abolish segregation, but he was most concerned with judicial power. Courts were likely to be ineffective in attempting such a "widespread reform of social customs," as indeed separate but equal and its failure showed. That doctrine "has remained an empty pronouncement because the courts have no power to enforce general declarations of law," and the same might be true of a decision overruling *Plessy*. Jackson foresaw litigation extending over "two generations" and eventually "a failure that will bring the court into contempt and the judicial process into discredit." The Court might accomplish something in the border states, where segregation was already fading, but only Congress could effectively deal with segregation "where the practice is really entrenched."

Having said all this about the likely futility of any Supreme Court decision, Jackson somewhat surprisingly asserted that the Court should not leave devising remedies to the district courts. "I will not be a party to thus casting upon the lower courts a burden of continued litigation under circumstances which subject district judges to local pressures and provide them with no standards." His rhetorical strategy became clear in his conclusion. Again in a transformed version of a thought Rehnquist had expressed, Jackson deprecated the Court's ability to enforce its judgment. He insisted that the task not be left to the lower courts, because he wanted to reinforce the proposition that only Congress could effectively act. The emerging gradualist remedy "assumes nothing less than that we must act because our representative system has failed. The premise is not a sound basis for judicial action."

What then was an appropriate premise for overruling *Plessy* if not the failure of the representative branches or the framers' intentions? For Jackson, it was the erroneous "factual assumption" that "there were differences between the Negro and white races, viewed as a whole," sufficient to justify segregation. "Whether these early judges were right or wrong in their times I do not know," Jackson said," but the "spectacular" progress of African-Americans, under adverse circumstances, "enabled [them] to outgrow the system and to overcome the presumptions on which it was based." These changes made educational classifications based solely on race no longer reasonable, even if they once had been. African-Americans now could only "be classified as individuals and not as a race for their learning, aptitude and discipline." This was particularly true, according to Jackson, because of the new importance of public education in modern society. These changed conditions made it appropriate to change constitutional doctrine. "[P]resent-day conditions require us to strike from our books the doctrine of separate-but-equal facilities. . . ."

Jackson's draft shows that he ultimately had resolved his ambivalence by accepting the view that changes in the social position of African-Americans generally, and in the role of public education, justified changes in constitutional doctrine. Yet residues of his ambivalence remained. E. Barrett Prettyman, Jr., one of Jackson's 1954 law clerks, criticized the draft's structure for leaving to "only two out of 23 pages" the affirmative case for overruling *Plessy,* and for saying too much about Jackson's "doubts and fears." Prettyman wrote that the draft opinion made it seem "as if you were ashamed to reach" the conclusion, and that "in a case of this magnitude, the very attitude of the Court is important, and that attitude should be one of faith rather than futility. . . . After all, this is a great country, and its people are great, and they will not tolerate lawlessness if they are convinced it *is* real lawlessness. How can you expect them to be convinced if you are not yourself?"[30]

Prettyman's criticisms were accurate. The draft rather strongly suggested that a decision invalidating segregation was going to be pointless and ultimately damaging to the courts. Even more, Jackson's phrasing near the beginning counterposed the coercion of African-Americans into segregation to the coercion of white Southerners out of it, only to follow the construction with a discussion in which the coercion of whites was the exclusive concern and the coercion of African-Americans went unmentioned except for the "resentments" they felt.

Jackson's draft, taken as a whole, indicates that in the end as in the beginning he believed *Brown* could not be justified as law. Yet the draft also displays a peculiar sense of politics as a justification. The sense in which a decision that would be futile and bring the courts into disrepute is a sound political decision is quite unclear, and in the end Jackson probably could not have sustained the draft's argument. The tension between Jackson's view that *Brown* could indeed be justified, though only as a political decision, and the ambivalence obvious on the surface of his draft concurrence, may have been part of the reason for failing to publish it. The changed conditions on which he relied were fundamentally sociological considerations that Jackson defined as political rather than legal. Jackson did not circulate the draft, though he showed it to Warren and probably Frankfurter, and the opinion Warren wrote in *Brown* contained many of the themes Jackson found congenial.[31]

Warren spent the time between the argument and the spring discussing the case with his more reluctant colleagues. Jackson suffered a heart attack at the end of March, and Warren visited him in the hospital. Warren talked about the case with Reed over lunch. Less by force of argument than by the display of concern for his colleagues, Warren drew them along the path he had marked. Once a majority agreed to invalidate segregation, Warren began to draft an opinion designed to avoid recrimination against the South and to appeal to general readers.

The opinions were released on May 17, 1954. After describing the cases' background, Warren's opinion said that the historical materials were "at best . . . inconclusive."[32] The "most avid proponents" of the Fourteenth Amendment intended it "to remove all legal distinctions"; the opponents wanted it "to have the most limited effect." Beyond that, no one could say "with any degree of certainty." Warren also mentioned changes in "the status of public education." That allowed him to say, after a brief recitation of the Court's prior cases dealing with segregated schools, "we cannot turn the clock back to 1868 . . . or even to 1896. . . . We must consider public education in light of its full development and its present place in American life. . . ." Warren described education as "perhaps the most important function of state and local governments." It was "the very foundation of good citizenship."

With that understanding of education's role, Warren said, the Court had to conclude that segregation deprived children of equal education opportunities. *Sweatt* and *McLaurin* showed that intangible factors mattered, and indeed they "apply with added force to children in grade and high schools." "To separate them from others of similar age and qualifications solely because of their race generates a feeling of inferiority as to their status in the community that may affect their hearts and minds in a way unlikely ever to be undone." Shortly after this statement, Warren included a footnote referring to Kenneth Clark's published work and other psychological and sociological material. Warren later denied that the material was crucial to the Court's decision, and in some sense it clearly was not. The footnote references were asides. And yet, Carter's strategy of introducing the evidence paid off. Something had to bridge the gap between the intangibles of reputation and networking in the university cases and the intangibles in lower schools. Warren's statement about damage to hearts and minds shows that psychological intuitions, if not necessarily the trial court testimony, provided the bridge.

Warren had somewhat more difficulty in disposing of the Washington case. He began by saying that the concepts of equal protection and due process overlapped. His first draft then echoed the themes Marshall hammered at in his arguments. Prior due process cases showed that governments could not "impose arbitrary restraints on access" to public education. Segregation was just such an arbitrary restriction. The final opinion dropped the references to these cases. It relied on the

Japanese internment cases for the proposition that "classifications based solely upon race must be scrutinized with particular care." Following Marshall's approach, the opinion said, "Segregation in public education is not reasonably related to any proper governmental objective," and was arbitrary. What drove the opinion, though, was the statement near its end that, in view of the Court's decision in the state cases, "it would be unthinkable that the . . . Constitution would impose a lesser duty on the Federal Government."[33]

What had the rearguments contributed? The Court's decision to have the cases reargued put the decision off for a year. The postponement came at Frankfurter's urging, and most scholars have supported Philip Elman's claim that Frankfurter adopted a deliberate strategy of delay to give the Court's members time to reach a unanimous decision striking segregation down. That overstates Frankfurter's cleverness. Frankfurter offered varying explanations for what he called his "filibuster" of the cases when they were first argued. He told Elman he wanted to avoid a decision until it was clear that the Court would not be severely divided. After the first argument, Frankfurter suggested a delay until the Eisenhower administration took office because it might act to abolish segregation on its own or at least might support efforts to obtain a judicial determination of segregation's constitutionality. Later still, Frankfurter said he had filibustered "for fear that the case would be decided the other way under Vinson." Some of Frankfurter's statements may have been strategic misrepresentations of his true views; it would have been hard to tell his colleagues that the Court should not decide the cases until it unanimously favored his position, given that some were the potential dissenters. Still, the changing stories suggest that Frankfurter's statements about his strategy cannot be taken at face value.[34]

The Court did need leadership, but the leadership it got from Warren was the result of Vinson's unexpected death. Actually, Frankfurter himself needed the time to put his mind at rest regarding the "legality" of the decision he wanted to reach. He proposed the historical questions, but the answers turned out to be of no interest to anyone but Frankfurter; Warren said at the start that he agreed with Black's interpretation of the history, as did Clark, while the historical material seemed entirely irrelevant to Douglas, Minton, and Burton. The reargument mattered to Frankfurter, though, not because of what anyone said but because he could treat the reargument as *his* contribution to the Court's decision.

What of the oral advocacy at the reargument? According to Elman, "In *Brown* nothing that the lawyers said made a difference. Thurgood Marshall could have stood up there and recited 'Mary had a little lamb,' and the result would have been exactly the same."[35] In one sense, while this view is extraordinarily ungenerous, it is true. Work had to be done in *Brown,* but almost all of it had to be done inside the Court. Someone had to lead reluctant justices like Jackson and, to some extent, Frankfurter to the decision that they wanted to reach, but the leader had to come from within the Court. Frankfurter had to work out a solution to overcome his ambivalence about making a political rather than a legal decision, and Jackson had to overcome his ambivalence about the issue of race itself. In many ways the oral arguments provided them with an opportunity to let off steam—to direct questions with an unfriendly edge at the NAACP's lawyers, so that the justices could then vote to strike segregation down.

The questions had an unfriendly edge because the justices were unhappy at being forced to choose one side or the other of their ambivalences. Yet it was precisely the brilliance of Marshall's strategy that he forced the justices to a choice, believing—correctly, as it turned out—that once he forced them to choose, they could make only one decision. Marshall's colleague from Los Angeles, Loren Miller, provided a far more balanced and astute assessment of Marshall's work than Elman: "An appreciable part of the genius of the NAACP lawyers lay in the acute perception of the depth and direction of [social] changes, and their ability to take them at their flood and translate them into constitutional concepts palatable to Supreme Court justices, who were at once propelled in new directions by social change and architects of that change."[36]

By May 11, Roy Wilkins was impatient. Waiting for the Court to decide the segregation cases, Wilkins drafted two press releases. One "regret[ted] . . . that the Court has not abolished governmentally-imposed segregation" and promised to "continue to press our fight for integration and equality until it is won." Robert Carter, though, was more optimistic. Preparing for the meeting at which Wilkins developed the press releases, Carter told the staff that "we anticipate" a favorable decision. The second press release stated its "delight[ ]" with the Court's opinion invalidating segregation, and expressed confidence that "regardless of technical details, responsible elected officials and community leaders of both races will work together in good faith to carry out the mandate of the court." Among the technical details, though, was what exactly it meant to carry out the Court's mandate. Chief Justice Warren's opinion did not resolve the worrisome issue of gradualism. Instead, it called for a third argument on the two remedy questions the Court had already asked.[37]

15

"When They Produce Reasons for Delay"
Devising the Remedy

The Court's request for a third argument on remedy could not dampen spirits within the NAACP. The argument was unlikely to be helpful, though. Twice the lawyers had laid out the only position they reasonably could take, but the first two arguments made it clear that many justices wanted a more gradual remedy than the NAACP offered. Yet the NAACP position was unassailable on the terms the justices were willing to state in open court. Marshall said the Court should ignore threats of resistance and, taking administrative concerns into account, no more than a year would be needed to desegregate. If the Court ignored the prospect of resistance, Marshall was clearly right. None of the justices was willing to say in public that the remedy ought to take resistance into account. The result was a peculiar sort of oral argument. The justices *said* they agreed with the NAACP's premises, from which the conclusion—quick desegregation—inexorably followed. Yet they persistently rejected that conclusion, sometimes expressing irritation that the lawyers had not gotten the point. Because the justices could not say openly that they expected resistance, however, the argument had people talking at cross-purposes. The real action occurred inside the Court, and the lawyers could do little to influence its outcome.

The reargument took place in April 1955, nearly a year after the Court's initial decision. The reargument was first scheduled for the fall of 1954, but it was postponed. Frankfurter suggested a delay until after the fall elections. More important, Jackson died on October 8, 1954. Warren did not want to decide the remedy issue until the Court was at full strength. Eisenhower nominated John Marshall Harlan, a patrician New York lawyer whose grandfather was the only dissenter in *Plessy v. Ferguson*. Southerners used the nomination to vent their spleen at *Brown*, and delayed Harlan's confirmation until late March 1955.[1]

In the year between the initial decision and the third argument much had happened. In 1953 the board of education in Topeka voted to eliminate segregation. Most children could attend the schools nearest their homes, although African-American children were "given the privilege of attending the nearest Negro school." Nine schools remained completely segregated, largely because of over-crowding; the board did not contemplate sending white children to the previously black schools. Although relatively few African-American children were affected by the plan's first stage, in February 1955 the board voted to complete desegregation. All children were to be assigned to neighborhood schools, and some district bound-aries would be redrawn. Parents could choose to let their children complete their elementary education in the schools they already attended. The initial stages of desegregation aroused little comment in Topeka, and the proposed complete deseg-regation was uncontroversial as well.[2]

In both Delaware and Washington, substantial desegregation occurred before reargument. The named plaintiffs in Delaware were in their third year of attend-ing the schools they applied to. After the Court's decision in *Brown,* the state board of education directed all schools to prepare "tentative plans" for desegregation before October 1, 1954. The Claymont board adopted a complete desegregation plan and started to implement it that fall, but the Hockessin district did nothing before the third argument. Wilmington, the state's largest city, desegregated all its elementary schools. In Washington, Eisenhower met with school board members in May 1954 and pressed them to desegregate the schools. By September, 116 of 158 schools had "bi-racial attendance." Complete desegregation seemed imminent.[3]

Marshall knew he had to answer questions about how difficult desegregation would be. He directed the NAACP's field staff to study West Virginia, Arkansas, and North Carolina. They were specifically directed to see if they could "get from an authoritative source when and how de-segregation was to be effected." A West Virginia superintendent told Margaret Butcher of the NAACP staff that the board had already begun to plan desegregation, and intended to assign children to the school nearest their homes. Substandard schools would be closed, and teachers reassigned. The superintendent expected to complete desegregation in three years, without firing any tenured African-American teachers. Loftus Carson in North Carolina was less optimistic. He was concerned that African-American teachers would offer "the greatest amount of resistance." He thought it important to get the entire community, white as well as African-American, to support complete deseg-regation and to get the African-American community "to make it known to the board that they will not accept anything short of complete integration."[4]

The reports showed that the NAACP staff understood that desegregation was likely to be a long drawn-out process, "doubtless cover[ing] a span of several years." They knew that some parts of the African-American community would be reluc-tant to support desegregation: some teachers, because of concern for their jobs; some parents, because of concern about violence directed at their children; others because of a general conservatism on race relations. This understanding fed into the way the lawyers presented the "immediate" remedy, and in a curious way further distorted the dialogue with the justices. The NAACP knew what "immedi-ate" desegregation meant: School boards would desegregate when prodded by an African-American community with resources to organize itself and with some parents willing to put their children on the line for the principle of desegregation. It meant relatively small steps in the direction of desegregation—larger perhaps, and sooner, in the border states, but small indeed, and delayed for a long time, in the deep South. As a matter of social reality, "immediate" desegregation and gradualism were almost the same.[5]

As the NAACP lawyers saw it, the Court could have its cake and eat it too. Confirming that constitutional rights were personal and present did not conflict with the Court's concerns about abrupt and massive changes in the existing order of things in the South. The Court could announce that desegregation had to occur immediately, subject only to minor administrative delays, and still have gradual desegregation. There was, however, a serious rhetorical tension within this position. The image conveyed by "immediate" desegregation to promote "personal and present" rights was of classrooms filled with equal numbers of white and African-American children in the fall of 1955. The rhetorical image clashed with the social reality the lawyers believed was likely to occur. Most justices were sensitive to the rhetoric and understood less about the reality. They did not know that they had before them a principled way to achieve gradual desegregation.

Justices Black and Douglas persistently tried to press the position Marshall took. Their efforts were ineffective because they were, as Elman put it, "frightening the other Justices" with their candid statements that the deep South would meet desegregation with violent resistance. Black and Douglas meant that, because of resistance, token desegregation was all that would happen even if the Court directed immediate desegregation. Frankfurter continued to be the moving force for an explicitly gradualist remedy. He and most of his colleagues believed they could devise a remedy that would induce the deep South to yield to desegregation step-by-step, without the violent resistance Black and Douglas expected. As Frankfurter and his supporters saw it, resistance to "immediate" desegregation would discredit the Court. As it turned out, the gradualist remedy met the same violent resistance that Black and Douglas forecast.[6]

Frankfurter's first contribution to the gradualist remedy was the reargument questions. The final two questions were directed to remedy. They asked, first, whether a decree must direct the admission of African-American children "forthwith" to the schools of their choice "within the limits set by normal geographic school districting," or whether the Court could permit "an effective gradual adjustment"; and second, whether the Court should formulate detailed decrees, appoint a special master to hear evidence, or remand the cases to the district courts with directions to frame decrees, and if so, under what directions. Black and Douglas were skeptical about these questions, believing they rested on the mistaken view that somehow the Court could solve the looming problem of violent resistance.[7]

Defining a gradualist remedy proved more difficult than agreeing on the principle of gradualism. The Court began to focus on remedy on January 16, 1954, after the second argument. The most notable thing about the discussion was that it occurred at all. The Court had not yet taken a formal vote on the merits, but Warren was confident enough of the ultimate outcome to direct discussion to remedy, apparently believing that the Court could dispose of the cases during the 1953 Term. He was mistaken, because agreement on the terms of a gradualist remedy could not be reached. The justices differed on several questions: whether the remedy should merely ord[...] [...]amed plaintiffs to the schools to which they already so[...] [...] Court chose a broader remedy, it could craft a decree g[...] [...]urt judges sufficient to minimize the risk of violent res[...] [...] Court's opinion should indicate whether lower courts c[...] [...]only the administrative difficulties of merging two syst[...] [...]uth's attitudes toward desegregation. Over the succee[...] [...]lved their differences, though the compromise was not an entirely happy one.

On the day before the January discussion, Frankfurter circulated a memorandum outlining his views on remedy. He began by insisting that a desegregation decree "of necessity would be dramatically different from decrees enforcing merely individual rights," although even in such cases courts do pay attention "to the element of time for obedience." Even more, Frankfurter noted that though the cases formally involved only individual claimants, "the essential subject-matter of the litigation . . . [was] in effect to transform state-wide school systems in nearly a score of States." A mere declaration of unconstitutionality, Frankfurter said, was not "a wand by which these transformations can be accomplished." Even if the states had "the best will in the world," they would face severe administrative difficulties. Frankfurter suspected that "a simple scrambling of the two school systems" would not work, and believed that "spreading the adjustment over time will more effectively accomplish the desired end because more beneficial to the total situation." A mere declaration of unconstitutionality would generate rather than reduce litigation, and yet any decree would necessarily be cast in general terms, "namely, that the inequalities which any segregated school system begets cannot stand and must be terminated as soon as this can be done with due regard to the requirement that school systems not be disrupted and that no substantial lowering of standards over present ones result for any sizeable group." Frankfurter broached the possibility of using a master as a "disinterested digger-out of facts" in cases like these, involving "a social policy with entangling passions." Frankfurter's memorandum apparently presented the Court for the first time with the formulation that desegregation should be accomplished "with all deliberate speed," although Rankin had used the phrase at the reargument.[8]

Frankfurter's memorandum barely kept beneath the surface his concern that the "passions" associated with desegregation might lead to violent resistance. That concern substantially affected the Court's deliberations. Warren opened the discussion on January 16 by saying that the Court should not administer desegregation itself. Rather, it should "turn to the district courts for enforcement," giving them substantial guidance as to "what paths are open to them." Black, speaking next, disagreed. He wanted to leave the issue entirely to the district courts; the more detailed the Supreme Court's guidance was, the more likely the district courts were to govern by injunction. Reed, who had not yet formally agreed to join the majority, nonetheless contributed by saying that the Court should offer "opportunities to adjust" as a "palliative" to the "awful" desegregation decision. Douglas supported using masters, and more generally thought that any decree should incorporate flexibility. Burton and Minton supported some "decentralize[d]" enforcement. Jackson suggested that the remedy question be reargued, and, in a concluding statement, Black agreed. He also insisted, however, that his colleagues not delude themselves into thinking that the decision would be well received in the South even if the Court let the issue of remedy "simmer." Overturning *Plessy,* according to Black, would lead to a "storm over this Court." He indicated that a comprehensive approach to remedy might not be wise; a plethora of individual suits might be better.[9]

The discussion disclosed that the justices' agreement on gradualism concealed fundamental difficulties in defining what it meant. For Black, gradualism meant an open acceptance of token desegregation, achieved by making individual litigants come forward, file suit, and pursue their claims. Because he knew that the actual impact of such an approach would be quite modest, Black believed that violent resistance would be rare. Most of his colleagues, though, thought more could be done while avoiding violence. The Court could move beyond tokenism by directing that the district courts do something, but they had little notion of exactly what. The order directing a third round of argument allowed them to decide the merits but postpone any further action.

Warren directed six law clerks to prepare a report on school desegregation. The law clerks submitted their report in November; they surveyed districting practices and the Southern reaction to the initial decision in *Brown,* and summarized actions to desegregate some schools in border states and threats to abolish public schools elsewhere. Just before the reargument on April 11, 1955, Warren also circulated another, shorter memorandum from the law clerks detailing their recommendations. The clerks agreed that the Court should enter "a simple decree" enjoining the defendants "from determining the admission of the plaintiffs to schools on the basis of a racially segregated school system" and then should remand the cases to the district courts. Five believed that the Court should also formulate "some guides." They argued that the cases were "class suits in fact affecting millions of children." The Court's "general standards" would allow "local judges to point to a superior authority in undertaking [what] will often be unpopular action." The clerks recommended that the decree emphasize the diversity of situations in the South, but insisted that "some degree of judicial control is unavoidable." They also agreed that "whatever may be said for immediate desegregation at all levels of the Southern School systems, such a requirement is impractical." Even moderates, they noted, said that "compliance is unthinkable if the decree does not provide for some gradualism." But, they said, "the mere passage of time without any guidance . . . produces rather than reduces friction. It smacks of indecisiveness, and gives the extremists more time to operate." "Once there is some legal sanction," however, "evasive tactics are cut down and popular acceptance spreads."[10]

Like their employers earlier, the clerks differed on what guidance to give. One would let district courts schedule desegregation in light of "local conditions and sentiment"; the others disagreed, saying that "this would put a premium on local hostility to demonstrate the 'impracticability' of immediate action." Another would accept plans for desegregation within twelve years; the others thought this would increase opposition and "insult those officials who have already begun to desegregate."[11] Instead, they would give school districts one year to deal with planning and administrative matters, and then would insist that the boards take immediate steps toward desegregation. They would allow "grade-a-year" plans if the first step was taken immediately, but they would not have the opinion endorse such a possibility explicitly, because to do so "may encourage gradualism even in communities ready for more speedy action." Their compromise was "that some action of an affirmative and demonstrable nature must be undertaken immediately, but that so long as efforts along these lines are continued in good faith, the states are allowed a reasonable time to carry them out." The law clerks openly discussed problems of resistance and evasion; a Supreme Court opinion could not. [12]

Against this background, the justices considered the briefs and arguments of the parties. Marshall rejected advice that the brief should adopt a "statesmanlike" position and accept gradual desegregation; that was inconsistent with his personal views and with his responsibilities to his clients. There was nothing to be gained by giving up at the start. The brief continued to argue for "desegregation as quickly as prerequisite administrative and mechanical procedures can be completed," which, the brief said, could be done by September 1955. "Each day relief is postponed," the brief said, "is . . . a day of serious and irreparable injury," particularly in light of the Court's statement that segregation affects children's minds and hearts "in a way unlikely ever to be undone." Nor should "local feelings" affect the speed of desegregation. Not only were the "dark and uncertain prophecies" quite "speculative," but minority rights especially needed "protection against local attitudes and patterns of behavior."

The NAACP brief argued against assuming "that gradual as opposed to immediate desegregation is the better, smoother or more 'effective' mode of transition." Indeed, it argued, gradualism might make desegregation more difficult; setting a deadline for desegregation tended to postpone the time when communities got around to dealing with the problem. Finally, the brief distinguished the "balancing equities" cases primarily because they did not involve constitutional rights. Throughout, the brief assumed that desegregation meant "the elimination of race as the criterion of admission to public schools."

Only four states with segregated schools were parties before the Court, and the justices thought it appropriate to invite the other affected states to take part in the argument on remedy. Several Southern attorneys general responded. As responsible public officials, they could not openly say that the people of their states simply would not comply with the Court's decision. Yet the briefs repeatedly referred to "widespread hostility" to integration, the possibility of violent resistance, and the likelihood that whites would reduce their tax support for desegregated public schools. Florida's brief asked for time to persuade the public to swallow the "bitter pill" of desegregation, though it gave little reason to believe that the pill would get any less bitter as time passed. The brief also suggested an elaborate procedure to decide whether to admit an African-American to a previously white school. The child would have to overcome evidence, if it existed, of "such a strong degree of sincere opposition and sustained hostility" to desegregation, and would have to show that he "personally feels that he would be handicapped in his education" by segregation and is "not motivated . . . solely by a desire for the advancement of a racial group on economic, social or political grounds."

Marshall was annoyed by these submissions. The NAACP's reply brief pointed out that applicants would have to satisfy Florida's requirements when they applied to first grade: "Out of the mouths of babes and sucklings," it said, "will have to come a wisdom in self-analysis which surely has never . . . been required" of anyone else. Listening to the oral arguments, Marshall made some notes to prepare for his rebuttal. When the Maryland attorney general said that "thoughtful leaders in Maryland of both races [were] for gradual" desegregation, Marshall noted that Maryland took more than fifteen years after the Gaines case and nearly twenty after the Murray case to abolish out-of-state scholarships. He also noted that Florida and North Carolina were refusing to desegregate their graduate and professional schools nearly five years after *Sweatt* and *McLaurin*. As he saw it, the states had offered "no valid reasons for delay," because they had given "no hope that time will help." At the oral argument, Marshall made a point of saying, "as a Marylander," that he must be "in the thoughtless group," because he opposed "this long, prolonged, gradual business."[13]

The United States again told the Court it could delay desegregation by balancing the equities. Simon Sobeloff, the new solicitor general, shared Elman's and Stern's views. The brief drew on *Brown* to argue that desegregation, like segregation, involved "psychological and emotional factors" that courts could take into account. Eisenhower himself wrote some sentences in the brief, emphasizing that *Brown* had "outlawed a social institution which has existed for a long time in many areas throughout the country."[14] The government argued that "expeditious" compliance with the Constitution also meant devising an "intelligent, orderly, and effective solution" to the problems that might arise during desegregation. After detailing some administrative and fiscal dimensions of desegregation, the brief brought up the existence of "a certain amount of popular hostility." The brief said that the assumption that "responsible officials and citizens will tolerate violations of the Constitution" was unwarranted. Hostility was no reason in itself for delaying desegregation, the brief argued, but it was "relevant in determining the most effective method for ending segregation." For example, sometimes it might be useful to develop programs "not extending for more than a few months" to develop community support for desegregation.

Like almost everyone else involved at this stage, the government's lawyers were caught. Whenever they mentioned time for compliance, they stipulated extremely short periods, entirely consistent with the notion of immediate relief. Yet, the presentation indicated that "more than a few months" was necessary. The government proposed that school boards could delay desegregation if they showed that "their particular program will bring about the total elimination of racial considerations in the admission of pupils . . . as rapidly as local conditions allow." But administrative considerations aside, local conditions could not possibly affect how long it would take to eliminate racial considerations totally; all a board had to do was say, "We no longer use race as a criterion for student assignment." The more the lawyers said about a gradual remedy, the more obvious it was that the Court could not endorse gradualism without simultaneously suggesting its sensitivity to white opposition to desegregation. That, however, was inconsistent with the Court's declaration that segregation was unconstitutional. The solution, it turned out, was to say less rather than more.

The arguments on remedy began with presentations in the cases from Kansas, Delaware, and the District of Columbia. The discussions among the lawyers and the justices were concerned with technical details about meshing the previous dual systems. How many students were involved in one school? How was public education administered? Questions like those constituted almost the entire discussion.

The reason for the focus on detail in the first three cases became apparent once the Court turned to South Carolina and Virginia. The justices knew it would be relatively easy to accomplish whatever they wanted in Kansas or Delaware, whether it was the simple elimination of racial categories in assigning students to particular schools, or full integration. They also knew it would be extremely difficult to accomplish anything at all in South Carolina or Virginia. The NAACP attorneys attempted to capitalize on this by stressing how important it was for the Court to decide that desegregation had to occur, as they put it, "forthwith." The Court should say that schools had to adopt nonracial pupil assignment policies as quickly as was possible in light of the need to coordinate the existing dual administrative systems, but should not allow "the attitude of the people" to affect desegregation's pace. The discussions of details in Kansas, Delaware, and the District of Columbia provided an important rhetorical backdrop: having spent so much time on showing that the administrative details, though important, could readily be handled, the NAACP lawyers could minimize their importance in South Carolina and Virginia as well.

Marshall's oral argument fit into this strategy. His opening argument was restrained and relatively unfocused. By the time Marshall began, the Court had been presented with discussions of administrative details and had been alerted to the problem of "attitudes." Marshall's argument combined pragmatic and principled concerns. He supported a decree ordering desegregation forthwith and specifying a particular date for desegregation, he said, because "when they produce reasons for delay, they are up in the air, they are pretty hard to pin down. And, as a lawyer, it is difficult to meet that type of presentation." Under the separate but equal rule, lawyers knew they had to present evidence about material inequalities in the provision of books, laboratories, and the like. When "attitudes" were offered to justify delay, however, how could a lawyer respond?

Further, "the situation needs a firm hand of government to say, 'We are going to desegregate.' And that's it." It did not matter whether that hand was "executive, legislative, or judicial." Whether for rhetorical purposes or because he was a man of the law, Marshall said that he had "no doubt whatsoever that the people in South Carolina and North Carolina, once the law is made clear, will comply with whatever [the] court does." Many school board members, Marshall said, were "the finest people in the community, and there is nobody more law-abiding." He mentioned the white primary cases and the university cases to show that Southerners.

even in cases that "raised terrific racial feeling,"   ourt's
directives. Almost as an aside, Marshall mentione   "constantly urge" the Court to remember that Afric   ears,
since 1870, been suffering the denial of rights,"   ) the
"faith in our democratic process that gets us throu   le in
the South are no different from anybody else as t

Marshall's argument was characterized by his   Ɪᵉⁿᵗᵃtion. After Justice Frankfurter mentioned the "complexities" arising from the different capital endowments of different school districts, Marshall responded that "assuming throughout each of these states there are terrific complexities, . . . this Court is dealing with whether or not race can be used. That is the only thing that is before this Court." The complexities arising in different areas would have to be worked out locally. "What we want," Marshall told Justice Frankfurter," is the striking down of race."

At this point Marshall turned to an apparently unrelated topic. "Whatever other plan they want to work out, the question is made about the educational level of children." Here Marshall showed that everything articulated as an "attitude" justifying delay could be dealt with as an administrative problem. "They give tests to grade children so what do we think is the solution? Simple. Put the dumb colored children in with the dumb white children, and put the smart colored children with the smart white children—that is no problem." Concern about different educational levels would be met, in Marshall's view, by ordinary application of standards of merit. He returned to this theme in his rebuttal, saying that "there are geniuses in both groups and there are lower ones in both groups, and it has no bearing. No right of an individual can be conditioned as to any average of other people in his racial group or any other group."

Another issue cropped up of particular interest to Justices Black and Douglas. They wondered who would benefit from an order directing desegregation. The cases had been filed as class actions, but the contours of class actions were not as well defined then as they are now. Everyone agreed that a decree would directly benefit only the children in the class named in the complaint; in the Prince Edward County case, for example, the class was defined as high school students. In response to a question from Justice Harlan, Marshall suggested that the relief would be even more restricted. Only the plaintiffs named in the complaint would directly benefit from a decree; other children in the class would have to intervene. Of course, Marshall noted, "I have every faith that the local school board would give [what the decree said] to the whole class. I do not think they will restrict it to the individuals." Even so, his position appeared to be that, if a school board resisted, individual children would have to intervene and get individual orders directing the board to admit each one to a desegregated school.

Marshall ended his initial presentation by returning to the harm that segregation did to children. "This is not a matter of local option," he said, "not a matter that shall be geared down to the local mores and customs of each community in the country." When Justice Reed suggested that a "grade a year" plan might be acceptable, Marshall firmly said that it would not: "You not only destroy completely the rights of the individual pupils, you destroy the rights of the whole class."

Nobody in that class will ever get mixed education." With that, Marshall sat down.

The attorneys for the Southern states followed. Their presentations gave the argument the air of a legislative hearing, as most of them made statements aimed at their constituents, not the justices. The opening argument for South Carolina set the tone. Saying it would be "the understatement of the year" to call *Brown* unpopular in South Carolina, S. E. Rogers refused to state directly that the district would comply with whatever decree the Court issued. "To say we will conform depends on the decree handed down," Rogers said, and he thought it would be "unfair" to tell the Court that "the white people of the district will send their children to the Negro schools." Pressed by Warren, Rogers confirmed that "right now we would not conform."

Robert Figg tried to retrieve the argument. A decree requiring desegregation by the fall "would mean the end of the public school system in the district," because "there are forces at play in this situation over which the trustees have no control." Time was needed to develop "community acceptance" of desegregation. Figg got into trouble trying to explain to Warren how long it would take. First he drew on experiences elsewhere suggesting that a few years would be necessary. Then, however, either caught up in his argument or more candid than before, Figg acknowledged that "this is a school district in which it may well prove impossible to have unsegregated schools in the reasonably foreseeable future." Frankfurter tried to rescue him by suggesting that Clarendon County was "unique," but Figg, again giving an honest rather than a helpful response, said that the county was "typical of others in South Carolina." Elsewhere in the state, he agreed, the problems might be somewhat less severe, but "I do not say that is going to be easy anywhere in South Carolina." He also agreed with Warren that the decree should not "wait until attitudes have changed," but suggested that allowing the lower court to work out a remedy "would advance public acceptance."

A. G. Robertson opened for Virginia with the kind of flat statement that might help at home but could not help in the Court: "We cannot foresee any definite future date when it can be completely solved." He recited Virginia's grievance at being forced to abandon segregation, and although he said that he was "not speaking in defiance or in any ill will," it was hard to avoid hearing those tones in his words. He came close to threatening that the people of Virginia, though they would not "disobey the Court," would use "more difficult and subtle ways" of resistance. Lindsay Almond made a similarly threatening speech, which no justice interrupted. When Almond complained that the Court had not considered the impact of integration on the "hearts and minds" of white children, he gave away the game: The objection was not to an order requiring desegregation "forthwith"; it was to desegregation itself. He closed by evoking the memory of William Jennings Bryan. "Our friends," he said, "sing their siren song entitled, 'The People of the South Are Law-abiding People.' In the next stanza, they urge this Court . . . to press this crown of thorns upon our brow and hold the hemlock up to our lips."

No matter how much they strove to say they were not challenging *Brown* itself, the lawyers presented the Court with what could only be seen as threats of noncompliance. Marshall could hardly restrain himself when he began his rebuttal. His opening argument had been calm, somewhat diffuse, and folksy. Now he was outraged. "To hear from the Lawyer Almond: Not in his lifetime, some other place, it was so for hundreds of years. . . ." Marshall expressed "shock[ ]" at the statements that the governments of Virginia and South Carolina could not enforce the Constitution. Marshall agreed that attitudes in the white community had to be changed, but argued that the most effective way to change attitudes would be "to issue the strongest type of decree." Marshall seemed to be more confident in the good faith of Southern whites than the Southern lawyers were. "Sure, there will be noise here and there," he said, "but we have got to continue."

The representatives from other Southern states then had their say, but the fireworks were over. Florida's attorney general made a measured plea for gradualism, to give the state a chance "to work this out on a local basis." North Carolina's lawyer answered one of Frankfurter's questions by saying that working things out would "take a great deal of time." Frankfurter, apparently irritated that the worst side of the issue of gradualism had again surfaced, responded brusquely, "I am not asking how much." As it turned out, the lawyer took the more extreme position the Court had already heard: "The chance that North Carolina, in the near future, will mingle white and Negro children in her public schools . . . is exceedingly remote."

When Thomas Gentry, the attorney general of Arkansas, implied that there might have to be lawsuits in each of the state's 422 school districts, Justice Douglas was unhappy, but Justice Black used the occasion to explore the possibility of limiting relief to the plaintiffs named in each lawsuit: "What we have," Black said, "is litigation on the part of individuals—a very small number, perhaps a half dozen—that ask to be admitted into certain schools." Why shouldn't the decree direct that these plaintiffs be admitted as they requested, while leaving it to future lawsuits by other plaintiffs to decide whether and how to admit them? Black did not want the Court "to draw some kind of broad plan, which would be in the nature of legislation," but believed that it could "limit itself to the particular lawsuit before it." Frankfurter intervened. If these plaintiffs got orders saying they had to be admitted immediately, every other plaintiff would be entitled to a similar decree. Frankfurter could not see how Black's distinction between a "broad plan" and limited decrees, which would have precedential effect, could be sustained.

The issue came up again during Solicitor General Sobeloff's argument. Sobeloff endorsed Frankfurter's view, noting "the immense importance of [the Court's] declarations in a particular case as a guide to a general treatment of problems in other cases." He then took up the general question of gradualism. Justice Black was skeptical about writing a decree directing action "as soon as feasible," because he could not figure out whether "attitudes of the people" had some bearing on feasibility. Sobeloff offered more guidance than anyone other than Marshall. Every district judge should "call for a plan within 90 days," and then "let the first step be taken as speedily as it can be done without disruption." When pressed, though, Sobeloff softened his stand. The Court should not "tie the hands of the district judge," but should do what it could to "suggest motion, and require motion, and encourage motion" without restricting the district judges' discretion to deal with varying local circumstances.

Shortly before one o'clock on the afternoon of April 15, 1955, Marshall got up to make his last argument in the school segregation cases. First he directed some scornful remarks at statements about how well gradualism would work and how difficult immediate desegregation would be: the university cases, Marshall said, were a better measure of "good faith" than lawyers' representations to the Court. The states repeatedly said "there was no racial hatred involved," but, Marshall said, if the justices looked closely at their arguments, they would see otherwise. "The nicest problem," according to the states, arose when there was a small African-American minority, but "where there are a large number of Negroes involved, and only a small number of white people involved, that is the most horrible situation. . . . And if that is not 'race,' I don't know what race is."

The Court's decision, Marshall continued, "will mean nothing until the time limit is set." There was no "middle ground." No one asked the Court "to postpone the enforcement of a constitutional right . . . until Negroes are involved," Marshall complained. And then, Marshall said, the reason for delay was, "for the sake of the group that has denied you all these rights all of this time." Marshall's tone was almost weary; his argument was as morally compelling as any he made, and he was tired of saying what should have been obvious. His last statement was an appeal to his "faith in our democratic process" that would get us over "problems as tough as these."

On the final day of the argument, Frankfurter sent his colleagues a letter opposing a "bare bones" decree of the sort Black seemed to favor. Such a decree would order the admission of the named plaintiffs and those within the class defined in each law suit without regard to race. Rather, the decree should take "due, even if not detailed, account of considerations relevant to the fashioning of a decree in equity in a situation enmeshed in what are loosely called 'attitudes' as well as physical, financial and administrative conditions. . . ." He did not want the Court to specify a date when desegregation must be accomplished; that, he said, would seem "arbitrary" and would "alienate instead of enlist favorable or educable local sentiment." He also sent along copies of a letter to the New York *Times* by a prominent Southern writer saying that the South was afraid it was being pressured "into a quick reorganization of its whole society." Frankfurter wanted to develop "criteria not too loose to invite evasion, yet with enough 'give' to leave room for variant local problems." Although the Court should not "operate as a super-school board," Frankfurter said, it might emphasize that neighborhood schools could be preserved, and it might specifically note that "spurious" freedom of choice plans could not be tolerated. [15]

Frankfurter's letter, coupled with the law clerks' memorandum and the range of options presented by the parties, indicated that figuring out an appropriate gradualist remedy remained a difficult task. The justices knew that any substantial steps would meet serious resistance in the deep South. Yet they also believed they could not openly mention that concern without encouraging opposition and undermining whatever support there might be for desegregation.

Warren opened the discussion of remedy by saying that he had "no definite opinion." He did want more than a "bare bones" decree. Because he thought the

Court "ought not to turn [the lower courts] loose without guidance," the decree should simply "set forth the considerations which the lower court should keep in mind." These were "administrative problems, fiscal problems, or physical facts," but he "would not intimate that lower courts could take into consideration psychological attitudes," for "if that were allowed, it would defeat the decree."[16]

Black too said he had no fixed views, but thought his "tentative ideas" differed from Warren's. Black "would write a decree and quit" because the "less we say the better." Black understood that "some counties won't have negroes and whites in the same school this generation," and what the Court said was "not going to control [the] destiny of the south," where people "are going to fight this." Because the Court could not settle the problem, it should make a narrow decision. Though Warren said these actions were class suits, Black said he was "not fond of class suits," in part because he was "not sure how many students would want their names in the litigation." Black thought it would be all right "if necessary" to have "700 suits" over segregation.[17]

Black seemed to realize that this might be precisely the answer to the Court's difficulties. If the Court simply ruled in favor of the named plaintiffs, "the administrative difficulty would not be great." Black's fundamental difficulty was that he firmly agreed that *Brown* was correct, and equally firmly anticipated substantial Southern resistance. Like Warren, he believed that "attitudes should not be mentioned in [the] decree but they cannot be ignored," and those attitudes would lead to "deliberate effort[s] to circumvent the decree."[18] Black was telling his colleagues that they need not worry too much about remedial details, because whatever they did would make no difference.[19]

Frankfurter was somewhat more optimistic, believing that the most important thing was to write an "educational" opinion. The Court could thereby acknowledge that the "attitude of the south is a fact to be taken into consideration as much as administrative difficulty." The process, he said, was bound to be slow, "and something should be said about it." He thought desegregation in the border states would be "easy" and "by gradual infiltration" would move into the deep South. Douglas, apparently annoyed by Frankfurter, said the Court should "give a push," but he actually offered a more limited remedy, restricting relief to the named plaintiffs and a few others. Burton disagreed. He said that "it was better to get limited results which are ordered and let them serve as examples than to order something which will not be carried out." He proposed a decree stating that segregation was unconstitutional and enjoining it "as rapidly as possible." He wanted "to decentralize by individual cases." Clark spoke of the "need for slow speed," and, reverting to his origins, said that Texas "is not going to present many acute problems." Minton "doubt[ed] the advisability of writing much," because "big talk in [the] opinion and little words in [the] decree would be bad."[20]

By the discussion's end, it should have been clear that no one really knew what to do. The Court achieved agreement on the merits in large measure because most justices had a vague idea that they could avoid difficulty by allowing desegregation to occur gradually. Justices Black and Douglas insisted that was a vain hope and urged the Court to resolve the question quickly and cleanly. Earlier, Black stressed that a desegregation decision would be "the end of Southern liberalism for the time being," a prediction that, according to Elman, "scar[ed] the shit out of the Justices, especially Frankfurter and Jackson."[21]

Black and Douglas warned their colleagues against a misplaced optimism about what the Court could accomplish. The other justices were unwilling to accept their analysis, but when it came to defining the gradualist remedy in detail, reality appears to have come home. Again Black and Douglas offered a quick solution, granting relief solely to the named plaintiffs, leaving to future litigation additional plaintiffs and other districts. They assumed that, in the near term, only a relatively few courageous individual African-Americans would initiate such litigation, and violence and disruption in the South might be minimized. Their colleagues, in contrast, believed that the courts might actually accomplish something more than the admission of a few African-American students to previously all-white schools, but they did not develop an effective expression of that hope in a remedial decree.

Chief Justice Warren had his law clerks draft a short opinion leaving most of the details to the district courts. Initially, the draft opinion said desegregation should occur "at the earliest practicable date," but Frankfurter prevailed upon Warren to return to the "all deliberate speed" formulation he had presented earlier. That phrase was drawn from a case arising from the separation of West Virginia from Virginia during the Civil War, which represented "the nearest experience this Court has had in trying to get obedience from a state for a decision highly unpalatable to it," and it would educate the public by showing that "we are at the beginning of a process of enforcement."[22] In addition, Warren addressed the question of "attitudes": "[I]t should go without saying that the vitality of these constitutional principles cannot be allowed to yield simply because of disagreement with them."[23] Finally, the draft would have told the district courts to admit with all deliberate speed "the plaintiffs and those similarly situated in their respective school districts who may within such time as may be fixed by the District Court become parties to these cases." This treated the cases as class actions, with relief available to everyone in the class. The final opinion, however, limited the relief to "the parties to these cases." Apparently concerned that what the Court gave with the gradualism of "deliberate speed" it might be taking back by treating the cases as class actions, the Court retreated closer to the Black-Douglas position.[24]

Frankfurter presented the "deliberate speed" formulation as the key to compromise; for him, it allowed his more reluctant colleagues to reject the "immediatism" he associated with Black and Douglas, though he missed the important nuance that they would have accepted immediate but token desegregation. In fact, the precise formulation was merely a form of words that justices who had already accepted gradualism could agree on. According to Bernard Schwartz, Warren "came to believe that it had been a mistake to qualify desegregation enforcement by the 'all deliberate speed' language."[25] With Frankfurter and others, in 1955, Warren believed the Court could soon accomplish something more than token desegregation, if only the Court's opinions demonstrated enough sympathy for the situation of white Southerners and promised a sufficiently gradual process of desegregation.

Black and Douglas, who Frankfurter derided as the "great libertarians," understood the South better. They believed, correctly, that all the Court could accomplish in the short run was a clear statement of fundamental principle. The clearer the statement, perhaps the more effective the long-run educational impact of the Court's decision. But Black and Douglas also believed that only a few African-Americans were likely to be admitted to desegregated public schools in the deep South for many years; there was no reason to appease Southern sentiment through a gradualist decree, and much risk to the courts if they got into the business of government by injunction. They were right.

16

To "Open the Doors of All Schools"
Passive Resistance to *Brown*, 1955–1961

Thurgood Marshall appeared on *Time* magazine's cover on September 19, 1955. His name, the story said, was "indelibly stamped" on *Brown*, and, according to *Time*, "what he decides to do about a thousand practical legal questions will interact powerfully with the decisions and attitudes of other men of similar and quite different and opposite views. The resultant of these forces will determine the pace, the style and the success of an effort to remove from U.S. life a paralyzing sting in its conscience and the ugliest blot upon its good name in the world." The story concluded with a portrait of Marshall at work, "dealing briskly with scores of tactical decisions in the desegregation fight." Marshall was acutely aware "of how far he and his cause had come, and at the same time, he felt a strong sense of how hard and long was the road ahead. He did not want merely to win, but to win in the way that would cause least pain to Negro and white and reflect the most credit on the U.S. Constitution."[1]

Prior to *Brown,* Marshall told an audience of eight hundred NAACP members in Charlottesville, Virginia, "Come hell or high water, we are going to be free by '63. On freedom's 100th anniversary we will be free as we should have been in 1863." Ninety-one years after the Emancipation Proclamation, he said, the time was "definitely right" to achieve democracy in the United States. He rallied his audience to "open the doors of all schools to Negroes . . . in a lawful fashion." Marshall made fun of a statement by Governor James Byrnes of South Carolina comparing the NAACP to the Ku Klux Klan: "How low can you get? When the day comes that we have to make a living selling you bed sheets then the NAACP will close down." Marshall told his listeners, "we have nothing to fear except the belief by anyone that we can't win." He concluded by emphasizing that the Supreme Court cases "do not mark the end of the fight, [because] we have to work constantly to end segregation. We demand freedom and we will take nothing less. As long as there is segregation, we are not free and we are not progressing."[2]

Even before the Supreme Court adopted gradualism, Marshall expected that desegregation—"freedom"—would not be accomplished in a few years. Marshall's speeches insisted that concrete steps be taken toward the goal of complete desegregation by the fall of 1956, but the men of "quite different . . . views" *Time* mentioned would not let desegregation occur easily.[3]

In some places desegregation was almost too easy; lawyers had to do little to prod school boards to comply with *Brown*. Elsewhere desegregation was almost too hard; lawyers in the NAACP's national office in New York could barely keep up with the resistance some Southern school boards and legislatures devised. *Brown* established the fundamental principle; the details of implementation remained, but lawyers centered in New York could contribute only occasionally to working out those details. And because the Court deliberately refrained from intervening substantially in desegregation, the NAACP's lawyers could do little through appellate advocacy at the highest level.

Further, when Southern legislators resisted desegregation, they attacked the NAACP and the LDF. The NAACP was effectively closed in Alabama for a decade, and fighting off attacks in Arkansas, Florida, and Georgia consumed the national organization's attention. NAACP members were important sources of support for desegregation litigation, and NAACP branch meetings in the South switched freely from discussing lobbying to discussing litigation. The more difficult it was for the NAACP to operate in the deep South, the more difficult it was for the LDF lawyers to litigate.

The LDF itself was attacked. Lawyers from the national office and local cooperating attorneys were charged with violating professional ethics; Southern prosecutors said the lawyers stirred up litigation by soliciting plaintiffs and providing financial support for plaintiffs who otherwise would have been satisfied to abandon their lawsuits. These charges raised important questions of free speech law, and the LDF's ultimate success in the Supreme Court made substantial contributions to the First Amendment. Yet the very need to defend against the charges diverted energy from pursuing desegregation.

Finally, changes in the movement against race discrimination began to limit the role lawyers could play. *Brown* invigorated the African-American community throughout the country. Almost immediately afterward, protests against segregated bus systems led to boycotts in Tallahassee and, most prominently, Montgomery, Alabama, where Martin Luther King, Jr., emerged as a new community leader. These protests in turn mobilized political forces for federal legislation to protect voting rights in the South, embodied in the Civil Rights Act of 1957. As the African-American community became more militant, protesters began to "sit in" at segregated lunch counters in February 1960, and conducted "freedom rides" aimed at securing real protection for the already established right to travel on interstate buses.

These new forms of political activity altered what the NAACP's lawyers could do. Because the LDF was a tax-exempt organization, Marshall and his colleagues were barred from lobbying and therefore did not participate in developing the 1957 Civil Rights Act. The act authorized the Department of Justice to sue to enjoin discriminatory administration of voting laws. The Department's resources were far more substantial than LDF's, and the fund's lawyers sensibly waited to see how effective the Department's actions would be.

The bus boycotts and the sit-ins raised new problems of lawyering. After

Brown, it was relatively easy to establish that the Constitution barred cities from requiring bus segregation. Establishing the legal principle and making sure that buses were not segregated, however, were very different matters. Lawyers would most often be called in *after* demonstrations, to defend protesters against criminal charges. The litigation was primarily reactive, and far more difficult to plan and control than the litigation culminating in *Brown.* And the sit-in cases posed an additional difficulty: the state action problem that had consumed so much attention in the 1940s arose in a new form, as protesters objected not to statutes or ordinances requiring segregated lunch counters but to decisions by business owners to maintain segregated facilities.

Even before *Brown II,* some states had taken the initiative. By October 1954, the *Southern School News* reported that Kansas, Missouri, West Virginia, Maryland, and Delaware were "moving toward integration," while South Carolina, Georgia, Mississippi, and Louisiana were "strongly resisting" it. A year later, the paper added Virginia to the states resisting desegregation. It also said that Florida, Tennessee, and North Carolina had adopted the attitude of "wait and see—some more." Texas, Oklahoma, Maryland, Arkansas, and Kentucky had taken some beginning steps to desegregation, and West Virginia, Missouri, and the District of Columbia had achieved substantial desegregation. *Time* magazine provided a somewhat less optimistic "report card" for 1955. Missouri received an A and West Virginia an A minus. The other border states got worse grades—Oklahoma and Kentucky B plus Maryland B minus, Arkansas C plus, and Delaware and Tennessee C.[4]

Even where school boards accepted *Brown,* the decision's impact was not always apparent. Baltimore, for example, had always allowed a form of open enrollment: a white student could attend any white school where there was room, and similarly for African-American students. Immediately after *Brown* the school board adopted nonracial open enrollment. A year later only 4 percent of the African-American students in the system were enrolled in formerly white schools. St. Louis adopted a neighborhood school system, in which two high schools and their attendance areas were essentially all black anyway. The NAACP did not challenge these outcomes, because its leaders believed that *Brown* established the principle that school boards could not take race into account in assigning students to schools; using race, not actual patterns of attendance, in decision making sent the signal to African-Americans that damaged their self-esteem, and the boards in Baltimore and St. Louis did not rely on race at all.

Some border-state school boards needed prodding, and the national staff of the NAACP, including the lawyers, developed a program for the branches. First the branch was to petition the board to adopt a desegregation plan. In September 1954, Marshall asked the branches to send him "specific and detailed information" about what the branches and boards had done and whether petitions to desegregate had been filed. Although this letter urged branches to explain what they *had* done if they had not filed a petition, throughout the 1950s Marshall and the legal staff took the position that further action was up to the parents. He announced that he would not sue "unless there is a complete breakdown of negotiations . . . where individual parents are convinced that negotiations cannot be continued." June Shag-aloff, a social worker on the LDF staff, spoke to meetings to educate parents about the steps they had to take to obtain desegregation, but finding willing parents often meant that NAACP leaders had to go "from house to house" to overcome parents' reluctance to send their children to white schools.[5]

The national office offered no guidelines about what an acceptable desegregation plan was. In the border states, some boards proposed gradual plans to desegregate all the schools within a year. Others offered plans to desegregate the high schools, the junior high schools, and the elementary schools in successive years. Wherever a board adopted these plans, the NAACP's local members accepted it. Only if a school board resisted desegregation entirely, or proposed a manifestly unacceptable plan for desegregation, would litigation become possible. By the late 1950s, the NAACP mounted challenges only to plans that would take twelve years to complete, desegregating one grade a year. These decisions, both national and local, curtailed litigation to clarify *Brown*'s gradualist remedy. Everyone, it seems, was willing to live with a situation in which boards accepted the principle of desegregation, and no one wanted to press hard on the principle's precise meaning. This meant, however, that where boards were relatively adaptable, Marshall and the national legal staff had little to contribute to the desegregation process.

A different set of difficulties arose where boards and legislatures were recalcitrant. University cases in Florida and Alabama may be the most illuminating, because the principle was established in *Sweatt* and *McLaurin* in 1950, and yet resistance, both legal and violent, persisted well into the 1960s. In 1949, the Florida NAACP encouraged Virgil Hawkins, then forty-two years old, to apply to the law school at the University of Florida. Alex Akerman, a white attorney from Orlando, represented Hawkins and five other students who applied for admission to the university's graduate programs in law, engineering, agriculture, and pharmacy. Hawkins had dropped out of high school several times before enrolling in Edward Waters College in Jacksonville, from whose high school he graduated in 1930. He attended Lincoln University in Pennsylvania for two years, but dropped out during the Depression and returned to Florida, where he sold insurance and taught school. When he applied to the law school he was the district manager of the insurance company's office in Gainesville, where the law school was located. The company fired Hawkins when he refused to withdraw his application, and he then became public relations director at Edward Waters College.[6]

The university rejected his application in May 1949. In December it authorized the creation of law, engineering, agriculture, and pharmacy graduate programs at Florida A & M College, the state's land grant college for African-Americans in Tallahassee. Hawkins then asked the Florida Supreme Court to direct the university's governing board to admit him to the University of Florida Law School. A few months after *Sweatt*, the Florida court refused. The Tallahassee law school, it found, might satisfy the state's duty. The decision did seem to indicate that until the Tallahassee school was functioning Hawkins was entitled to attend the school in Gainesville.[7]

Hawkins believed the court's decision entitled him to immediate admission to the University of Florida Law School. After several months of correspondence, the university's board disagreed and again refused to admit him. Hawkins again petitioned the state supreme court. It denied him relief this time because he had not formally reapplied for admission to the Gainesville law school, and because the Tallahassee school would begin operating as soon as he applied.[8]

The Tallahassee school opened in September 1951, with five students and four faculty members. In August 1952, Hawkins tried again, alleging that he had now reapplied to Gainesville and that the Tallahassee school was inadequate. After the state supreme court rejected his claim because the Tallahassee school was operating and was substantially equal to the one in Gainesville, Hawkins went to the United States Supreme Court. By this time the Court expected to resolve the segregation controversy in *Brown* and its companion cases, and it did not act on the petition until a week after *Brown I*. Then it directed the Florida Supreme Court to reconsider its ruling "in light of" *Brown* and "conditions that now prevail."[9]

The state attorney general told the state court that *Brown* was distinguishable from Hawkins's case, largely because *Brown* relied on the psychological damage that segregation did to young children, which was irrelevant in a case involving a mature man like Hawkins. By the time the state supreme court heard Hawkins's case again, *Brown II* had been decided. The state argued that admitting Hawkins would be extremely disruptive. Justice B. K. Roberts, writing for a majority, seized on *Brown II*'s "all deliberate speed" formula to justify further delay. As Roberts interpreted *Brown II*, local circumstances would determine the proper timing of desegregation. The court appointed a judge to survey of attitudes among high school students; one report suggested the survey's purpose was to postpone action on Hawkins's admission until after the 1956 primary elections. Two justices dissented, noting that the "adjustments" necessary to admit Hawkins would not be "major" enough to delay admission. A concurring opinion by Justice Glenn Terrell sounded a strong segregationist note: "Segregation is not a new philosophy. . . . It is and always has been the unvarying law of the animal kingdom . . . [W]hen God created man, he allotted each race to his own continent according to color, Europe to the white man, Asia to the yellow man, Africa to the black man, and America to the red man, but we are now advised that God's plan was in error. . . ." An editorial cartoon in the St. Petersburg *Times* pointed out the difficulties in this formulation by depicting a "red man" saying to Justice Terrell, "Scram, paleface!"[10]

Believing that *Brown II* did not justify delaying his admission, Hawkins again went to the United States Supreme Court. The justices, acutely aware of the attention that *Brown* brought to desegregation, were unhappy at the prospect of another foray into the field. They decided to reverse the state court without hearing argument. Initially, Justice Frankfurter disagreed even though ordering argument would cause "talk" that the Court might retreat from its commitment to desegregation: "Public confidence cannot possibly be hurt and it may be enhanced if we deal with this situation with generous regard for the concern of a State." Alternatively, Frankfurter proposed a "candid and clear" opinion saying that the state supreme court "evidently misapprehended" *Brown*'s meaning. He would have entered an order stating that Hawkins was to be admitted to the law school. Justice Harlan agreed with Frankfurter's "general thesis that we should be scrupulously orthodox," but preferred that the Court issue an order asking Florida to explain why the Court should not issue a directive like Frankfurter's. However, this was clearly too complicated a way of dealing with a problem that, the rest of the Court thought, could be handled more directly.[11]

Justice Reed, whose clerk Roderick Hills wrote a memorandum saying that Florida followed the desegregation rules "with good grace," drafted a brief opinion saying that "deliberate speed" was irrelevant in cases involving professional schools; there was "no reason for delay." Justice Black praised Reed's opinion: "I particularly like the fact that it says very little—the thing needed in this process."[12]

The Court's decision, released on March 12, 1956, crystallized opposition to desegregation in Florida. Although no counties had begun to desegregate in 1955, few school boards had forcefully opposed the possibility and about one-third had appointed study committees. After the Court's decision in *Hawkins*, however, Governor LeRoy Collins pledged to a radio audience that Florida was "as determined as any Southern state to maintain segregation." He convened a conference of public officials to determine how to avoid desegregating the university. The participants adopted new rules for admission to state universities and invited Governor Collins to press President Eisenhower for a meeting with Southern governors on desegregation. In May, the judge appointed by the state supreme court reported that Hawkins's enrollment might cause "serious public discord," and the university's governing board released a study saying that nearly all African-Americans who might enroll in white institutions would have academic difficulty and that revenues from cafeteria sales and alumni contributions might decline significantly if the system was desegregated.[13]

In March 1957 the Florida Supreme Court responded to the United States Supreme Court order. Five judges continued to assert that delay was justified, in light of the reports the court had received. Justice Roberts's opinion for the court praised states' rights as "vital to the preservation of human liberties," and suggested that Hawkins did not really desire to attend law school. As a sop to Hawkins, the opinion said that he could be admitted if he showed that "his admission can be accomplished without doing great public mischief." Justice Terrell wrote a concurring opinion strongly criticizing the Supreme Court for displacing segregation, a practice "as old as the hills," "solely with the writings of Gunnar Myrdal, a Swedish sociologist. What he knew about constitutional law we are not told nor have we been able to learn." Justice Elwyn Thomas, though expressing distaste for the decision by the Supreme Court, dissented because that Court's decision was clear and binding: "It seems to me that if this court expects obedience to its mandates, it must be prepared immediately to obey mandates from a higher court."[14]

Hawkins tried again in the United States Supreme Court. One of Justice Douglas's law clerks called the state court's action a "fantastic instance of defiance," and Chief Justice Warren's clerk said the Florida opinion indicates "in tone if nothing else that the Florida court has tongue in cheek." Justices Brennan,

Harlan, and Frankfurter voted to grant Hawkins's petition, but the Court's majority denied it, indicating that Hawkins might try to get relief from the federal district court. Following that suggestion, Hawkins filed suit, but federal District Judge Dozier DeVane ruled against him. DeVane's decision was then reversed by the court of appeals.[15]

By then, the university authorities had adopted new rules requiring that all applicants to the law school score above 250 points on an admissions test. No test had been used for whites in 1949 when Hawkins initially applied to the law school; Hawkins scored only 200 when he took the examination in 1956. When Hawkins's case came before Judge DeVane again, the judge asked whether Hawkins was willing to reapply. The state indicated it wanted to show that Hawkins had written a bad check, defaulted on a loan, and beaten two children while he was a school teacher, and Hawkins decided to avoid a long inquiry into his qualifications under the 1949 standards and to apply again. Judge DeVane accepted that and issued an injunction against the use of race as a basis for admission. Now, however, Hawkins decided not to pursue his application; he was tired and his wife had asked him not to continue. In August 1958, the first African-American enrolled in the University of Florida Law School. A year later Hawkins enrolled in Boston University, from which he received a master's degree in public relations.[16]

The long story of Virgil Hawkins is an example of one of the methods of resisting desegregation. Using every available procedural technique and inventing ways to distinguish the controlling precedents, state school officials and judges obstructed desegregation while purporting to follow established law. The Supreme Court, concerned not to provoke further resistance, failed to act as forthrightly as it could have. Under these circumstances it was impossible for the NAACP legal staff to develop a coordinated approach that would guarantee the implementation of clearly established rights.

Autherine Lucy's story provides an example of another method of resisting desegregation. Lucy applied for admission to the University of Alabama graduate school in 1952. After her application was denied, she had Arthur Shores file suit in July 1953. The district judge, H. Hobart Grooms, a long-time Birmingham lawyer recently appointed by President Eisenhower to the court, ordered the university to admit her in 1955. The university's trustees, though they did not expect to win the lawsuit, appealed. The court of appeals affirmed Judge Grooms in a brief opinion, and on October 10, 1955, the Supreme Court refused to review that decision. When Lucy applied for admission again, the university rejected the application because enrollment for the first semester's classes ended on October 6. Judge Grooms found the rejection justifiable because it was not based on racial grounds. Lucy then applied for admission to the graduate school for the second semester, and now there was no reason to refuse. When she arrived at the university's campus to register at the end of January 1956, a mob attempted to intimidate her, and she was escorted around the campus by police officers. By Monday, February 6, the mob was nearly out of control, and state police took Lucy off campus to protect her. That evening the university's board of trustees suspended Lucy and expelled one of the mob's leaders.[17]

On Thursday, February 9, Lucy, supported by the NAACP, asked Judge Grooms to hold the university officials in contempt. In addition to saying that her suspension was unjustified, her petition claimed that the officials had conspired with the mob to prevent her from attending school. The judge held a hearing at the end of February. By then it was clear that Lucy's attorneys had no evidence to support the conspiracy claim. Marshall opened the hearing by stating that "we have made as careful an examination as we can make . . . and we are unable to produce any . . . evidence which would support those allegations." He withdrew the claim "in fairness to all concerned."[18]

The subject of the hearing, then, was whether the university's failure to control the mob and its suspension of Lucy amounted to contempt of court. Shores and Marshall divided the examination of the witnesses. In questioning a police officer, Marshall suggested that the police had done little to disperse the crowd. Examining a university dean, Marshall asked, "What can you give us as the reason that that large a group of police could not disperse a crowd of 70 people?" Marshall sarcastically asked a member of the university board of trustees, "As I see it, there is one person that is acting in a completely lawful manner . . . and on the other side there are a large group of people that admittedly are acting in an unlawful manner. That being true, if the Board admittedly excluded Miss Lucy temporarily, what did the Board do to the unlawful group?" The unrepentant trustee replied, "I'm not at all sure that Autherine Lucy and persons accompanying her were not the very cause of the demonstrations. . . [She] came in a Cadillac automobile, she had chauffeurs with her [apparently referring to Shores, who had driven Lucy to the campus]; she walked about on the campus in such a way as to, I suppose, be obnoxious and objectionable and disagreeable." Judge Grooms found that the university had not committed contempt, but ordered Lucy readmitted by March 5. That same evening, however, the board permanently expelled Lucy, because, it said, she made unfounded charges regarding the board's conspiracy with the mob leaders. Judge Grooms found that this expulsion did not violate his injunction because the board invoked proper disciplinary reasons for expulsion, not racial ones.*[19]

The Lucy case combined legal foot-dragging by public officials with violence by obdurate whites. Lawyers accustomed to the courtroom could deal with foot-dragging, but they had no resources to deal with violence. Violence had two effects. First, only lawyers close to the action could have any real impact on fast-moving events. Lawyers centered in New York and with obligations to clients and supporters throughout the country could intervene only sporadically; Marshall's presence gave moral force to the position the local lawyers were taking, but he could hardly participate fully in the litigation. Second, violence projected new legal

---

*When the case ended, Marshall had to explain to Lucy why he was not appealing Judge Grooms' decision. Saying that the question "has given us no end of difficulty," he told her that Judge Grooms' decision did not raise any constitutional questions. Marshall told Lucy that "all good Americans feel endebted to you for all that you have done to bring democracy into practice in Alabama," and that she had "opened" the university and established the fundamental principle of equality. TM to Autherine Lucy Foster, Feb. 15, 1957, Lucy file.1/2/3, Shores Papers.

issues into an already complicated terrain. In *Lucy* the new issues were minor but ultimately fatal to her case: the violence provoked her into making statements that became the basis for her expulsion.

Southern politicians who vigorously disagreed with *Brown* responded in two ways. As politicians, they tried to mobilize opposition. The most visible form this political activity took was the "Southern Manifesto," issued by virtually all the senators and many representatives from the Deep South in 1956. The Manifesto stated that *Brown* was an "unwarranted" abuse of judicial power, embodying the justices' "personal, political and social ideas" rather than constitutional law. It said that its signers would "use all lawful means" to reverse *Brown*. The LDF could not respond directly to these political maneuvers, because it could not engage in political activity without losing its tax exemption, and Marshall meticulously followed the rules.[20]

As the Southern Manifesto said, *Brown*'s opponents also resisted the decision within the law, at least in the sense that they attempted to justify resisting *Brown* with some semblance of legal credibility. Because the Supreme Court had spoken and was generally regarded as having the final say on what the Constitution meant, it was difficult, though not impossible, to resist *Brown* within the law by saying the Court's decision need not be treated as law. It was easier to evade *Brown*'s implications, and for the five years following *Brown II* the NAACP's lawyers found themselves enmeshed in litigation to overcome these legalistic evasions.

Outright defiance, purporting to be within the law, came first. In the fall of 1955, a Virginia lawyer brought the theory of "interposition" to the attention of James Jackson Kilpatrick, the editor of the Richmond *News Leader*, the state's most influential newspaper and one of the South's most important papers. Interposition was a "states' rights" constitutional theory. Developed by Thomas Jefferson and James Madison in the late 1790s and elaborated by John C. Calhoun in the 1830s, the theory of interposition held that the Constitution was created by the states as entities, not by individual American citizens. As a result, the theory contended, each state's legal authority was as great as the national government's. If a state disagreed on constitutional grounds with the national government, it could "interpose" its sovereign power between the national government and its people, thereby effectively nullifying the national action.[21]

Kilpatrick wrote a series of editorials urging the Virginia legislature to adopt an interposition resolution to declare *Brown* "null, void, and of no effect." The legislature adopted a toned-down version in February 1956, and other states in the deep South followed suit with their own resolutions over the next two years. From a legal point of view, these resolutions had no effect whatsoever. Calhoun's theory of the Constitution had not been widely adopted before the Civil War, and the defeat of the South in 1865 meant the theory had no vitality afterward. Lewis F. Powell, later a Supreme Court Justice, wrote a legal memorandum stating that interposition was "simply legal nonsense" that no court would ever adopt; he refrained from publishing the memorandum because he had been told that state officials took the doctrine seriously as "a proper and effective method of protesting against the decision of the Supreme Court." Powell wrote that if he were a federal judge, a lawyer's citation of an interposition resolution "would tend to persuade me the other way." Lindsay Almond, Virginia's attorney general, also thought the state's interposition resolution legally meaningless. Federal Judge Richard Rives, a strong supporter of *Brown* and a leader in the judicial effort to secure desegregation in the deep South, referred in a 1958 opinion to Alabama's interposition resolution as "no more than a protest, an escape valve through which the legislators blew off steam to relieve their tensions." Even Kilpatrick treated interposition primarily as a way to fortify public opposition to *Brown*.[22] In this it resembled the Southern Manifesto, and despite the legalistic form of interposition resolutions, the NAACP lawyers devoted no attention to them.

Far more important from the lawyers' point of view were the legal tactics of evasion rather than resistance. *Brown* held that states could not use race as a basis for assigning students to schools, but it did not say much more. Judge John Parker, writing for the lower court to which *Briggs v. Elliott,* the South Carolina case, had been remanded, said that under *Brown,* "the Constitution . . . does not require integration. It merely forbids discrimination, . . . [that is,] the use of governmental power to enforce segregation."[23] Later Parker's interpretation was criticized as unfaithful to the *Brown*'s promise.[24] Parker's interpretation of *Brown* was certainly plausible; much of the antisegregation argument asserted that it was simply impermissible for governments to make decisions based on race, and that was what Parker took to be *Brown*'s sole holding. The lower courts universally adopted Parker's understanding.[25]

Even Parker's approach, though, left a great deal open, because school boards that did not use race as a basis for assigning students to schools had many alternatives. They might adopt a freedom-of-choice plan, as in Baltimore, or a neighborhood assignment policy, as in St. Louis. For the opponents of *Brown* who desired as little actual desegregation as possible, neither policy was entirely satisfactory. They could not control the outcome of freedom of choice, and in some districts African-Americans might choose to attend previously white schools in greater numbers than they had in Baltimore. Neighborhood assignment policies would be effective, from their point of view, only where there was extensive residential segregation. This characterized many border-state cities but was less common in Deep South cities and did not occur at all in rural districts where any "neighborhood" large enough to support a school would inevitably be large enough to have families of both races.

Further, the most committed opponents of desegregation believed that if even a single school district began to desegregate, the principle would have been established and the "infection," as they saw it, would inevitably spread. As one federal judge put it, the people of Atlanta were willing to accept desegregation in 1960, but "this feeling is not shared by citizens living in the rural areas" because "they do not have the residential patterns that exist in the cities," where neighborhood assignment policies would result in "little mixing." The judge said, "the people in our rural areas have the feeling that if any integration is permitted in Atlanta, . . . it will be but a beginning which will in time spread to their areas."[26] These opponents fought desegregation even where school boards and parents were willing to accept it, and sought to transfer authority from localities, which might yield on the principle, to state governments, where the opponents had greater political power.

The most effective way to control desegregation, for its opponents, was to place student assignment in the hands of school officials, at the state level if necessary. The officials could be expected to employ "neutral" standards to ensure that there would be very little actual desegregation. Until the early 1960s, boards wishing to delay desegregation could use these student assignment policies to minimize desegregation. The result was an ironic vindication of the position of Justices Black and Douglas: the Court adopted "all deliberate speed" because it wanted to encourage lower courts to support plans that promised more than token desegregation, and yet the lower courts, confronted with student assignment policies and other forms of legal evasion and resistance, ended up accepting token desegregation anyway.

In North Carolina, Governor William Umstead responded to *Brown* by appointing an education committee, including three African-American state employees, to recommend legislation. Umstead's successor, Luther Hodges, endorsed the committee's proposals, stating that "the mixing of races forthwith in the public schools . . . should not be attempted." The committee recommended a statute on student assignment, which the legislature adopted. The law directed school boards to determine which school each student should enroll in. They were to consider "the orderly and efficient administration of [the] public schools, the effective instruction of the pupils . . . , and the health, safety, and general welfare of [the] pupils." Most boards required students seeking unusual assignments to complete extensive forms and often to have a personal interview. In addition, the statute set up a system of appeals in cases where applicants were not allowed to enroll in the school they wanted. First the student had to appeal to the school board, which the statute said had to hold a "prompt and fair hearing." The board could overturn the denial if it found that enrollment was "for the best interest of [the] child, and will not interfere with the proper administration of [the] school, or with the proper instruction of the pupils . . . , and will not endanger the health or safety of the children. . . ." If the board affirmed the exclusion, the student could file an appeal in the local state court, and then appeal again to the state supreme court.[27]

African-Americans opposed the student assignment law as a "segregation bill" designed to ensure continued segregation, as it was. Yet, because the statute did not refer to race, the state's attorneys could argue that it was consistent with *Brown*. When the statute was adopted, there already was a case challenging segregation in North Carolina. Herman Taylor, who had been one of the NAACP's cooperating attorneys in North Carolina for many years, had filed an action on behalf of African-Americans in McDowell County, whose children were not allowed to attend the nearby school that whites attended in Old Fort but were required to attend a school fifteen miles away. The complaint, following the model of many filed before *Brown*, asked that a school for African-Americans be established in Old Fort under the separate but equal doctrine, or for a general injunction against discrimination. After *Brown*, federal District Judge Wilson Warlick dismissed the case on the ground that *Brown* made separate but equal relief inappropriate.

The court of appeals reversed the dismissal, saying that the plaintiffs were entitled at least to the injunction against discrimination. But, the court of appeals said, Judge Warlick should consider the implications of the new student assignment law. In particular, the court pointed to the system the law established for applying for admission and appealing to the school board. The court noted the well-established rule that before plaintiffs could get relief from the federal courts for allegedly unconstitutional action, they had to pursue these appeals. This requirement, called "exhaustion of administrative remedies," gave higher officials a chance to correct unconstitutional decisions made by subordinates; if that happened, the federal courts would save some of their own effort, and could avoid making decisions affecting the state government operations. The court of appeals said in the Old Fort case that the exhaustion requirement was "especially applicable" in desegregation cases, because "the federal courts manifestly cannot operate the schools. . . . Interference by injunction with the schools of a state is [a] grave matter . . . and should not be resorted to 'where the asserted federal right may be preserved without it.'"[28]

From a litigator's point of view, the exhaustion requirement had two related effects. First, by increasing the time it took to get anything done, by requiring that applicants complete detailed forms, and by exposing them to hearings at which they might be harassed, the exhaustion requirement inevitably reduced the number of people who would go through the process to the point when litigation could actually begin; many applicants would "exhaust themselves before they exhaust their administrative remedies." Second, even with steadfast applicants the requirement meant that efforts to desegregate the schools could be delayed substantially. The difficulty was compounded when the North Carolina Supreme Court held that each student individually had to apply for admission and then appeal; there were no "class actions" in these cases, the court said, because individual circumstances might vary so much that it would be inappropriate to make broad determinations regarding which students should be allowed to enroll in which schools.[29]

Taylor and his partner Samuel Mitchell believed that the student assignment law amounted to an outright evasion of *Brown* rather than a method of working out gradual desegregation. They wrote the McDowell County school board to find out what steps had been taken to admit African-American children to the Old Fort school. When the board replied that nothing was being done because no students had applied for admission, Taylor and Mitchell revived their suit. Judge Warlick held that the lawsuit could not proceed until the plaintiffs applied for admission and then exhausted their administrative remedies. The plaintiffs then appealed. The court of appeals, in an opinion by Judge Parker, again rejected their claim. The student assignment statute was not unconstitutional "on its face" because it did not mention race at all. The court agreed that the statute might be applied unconstitutionally, for example, if the board pretended to rely on concerns about health and safety but actually made its decisions based on race, but it said it could not consider that question before the administrative remedies had been exhausted: "Somebody must enroll the pupils in the schools. They cannot enroll themselves; and we can think of no one better qualified to undertake the task than the officials of the schools and the school boards." The court "presumed" that the officials "will obey the law, observe the standards prescribed by the legislature, and avoid the discrimination on account of race which the Constitution forbids. Not until they have been applied to and have failed to give relief should the courts be asked to interfere in school administration." Judge Parker conceded that state officials should not engage in "dilatory tactics," but he insisted that plaintiffs at least try to get the school authorities to act before they came to federal court.[30]

The general rule requiring exhaustion of administrative remedies often made sense in the typical case for which it was developed, involving economic regulation of businesses, but even there it rested on the assumption that officials would actually do their best to follow the Constitution. The Supreme Court made that same assumption in endorsing a gradualist remedy, though it said as well that "courts will have to consider whether the action of school authorities constitutes good faith implementation of the governing constitutional principles."[31]

The Supreme Court indulged the presumption of good faith for longer than it should have. Alabama adopted a student assignment law in August 1955. Like the North Carolina statute, it did not refer explicitly to race. The statute said that it would be "disruptive" for school authorities to adopt "any general or arbitrary reallocation of pupils . . . according to any rigid rule of proximity of residence," meaning, of course, that school boards could not adopt a neighborhood assignment policy or any other general approach to desegregation that might actually have more than token impact. It then listed sixteen factors that boards should consider in making individual assignments. These included room and teaching capacity, but also "the adequacy of the pupil's academic preparation," the "scholastic aptitude and relative intelligence or mental energy or ability of the pupil," psychological effects on the student, "the home environment of the pupil," "the possibility of breaches of the peace or ill will or economic retaliation within the community," and "the morals, conduct, health and personal standards of the pupil."[32]

As Robert Carter put it, this statute was "not objectionable" until it was unfairly administered but, he added, it was sure to be used unfairly. It invited school boards to deny admission to any African-American who applied to a previously white school. When four children tried to desegregate the Birmingham schools in 1957, the school board told them to come to the system's guidance center to take placement tests. Instead, their parents, including Reverend Fred Shuttlesworth, one of the leaders of the local African-American community, requested an interview with the superintendent. When that was refused, the children took the tests. Although the student placement statute said applications should be acted on within thirty days, the board did nothing, and in December 1957, two months after the testing, Shuttlesworth and the other parents filed suit.[33]

Defending the suit, the state said that, although the statute was aimed at "eliminat[ing] the absolute requirement of segregation, already a dead letter," it was also designed "to avoid the possibility of the opposite and more offensive compulsion of general racial integration" and to maintain "social order and racial good will." Judge Richard Rives, a native of Montgomery, Alabama, appointed by

President Truman to the court of appeals in 1951, complained that the board's failure to say anything about its inaction placed the court in a difficult position. The court might assume, Judge Rives said, that the board was following the unconstitutional policy of racial segregation, or it could assume that the board relied on one of the many factors stated in the student assignment law. The question then was whether the student assignment law itself was unconstitutional. Shuttlesworth alleged that the student assignment law was part of a package of resistance to desegregation and was designed to be administered to guarantee that no desegregation whatever would occur. Judge Rives said the courts could not examine the Alabama legislature's motivations, and "it is possible for the Act to be applied so as to admit qualified Negro pupils to nonsegregated schools. . . . We cannot say, in advance of its application, that the Alabama Law will not be properly and constitutionally administered." Shuttlesworth objected specifically to the "psychological qualification" and "breach of the peace" factors in the statute, but, Judge Rives said, even though those factors might be impermissible, the board might have relied on educationally and constitutionally permissible reasons for refusing to admit his daughter to a previously white school. He concluded his opinion by emphasizing that the court was dealing with the constitutionality of the law "upon its face," and that later it might be shown to be unconstitutionally applied. [34]

The NAACP national office appealed to the United States Supreme Court, which affirmed Judge Rives without hearing oral argument. The Court's struggles in the case indicate that the justices knew Alabama was evading the mandate of *Brown* and knew they were putting up with that evasion. Initially Justice William J. Brennan drafted a brief opinion quoting the district court's statement that the pupil placement law "furnished the legal machinery for an orderly administration" of the schools. Although Justice Harlan called this "the best way out of a troublesome problem," Chief Justice Warren objected that the quotation might have suggested positive approval of Alabama's statute. Justice Douglas circulated a long memorandum simply laying out the ways in which the Alabama legislature indicated its unwillingness to accept *Brown*. The justices directed Brennan, Black, and Harlan to come up with a better solution. Brennan tried to write a sentence saying that in approving the statute as valid on its face, the Court was merely following precedent, but he became concerned that the Court would then be suggesting it would be impossible to attack the statute's administration later. Finally, the opinion was stripped down to a single sentence, saying that the Court was affirming the lower court "upon the limited grounds on which the District Court rested its decision." The problem was "troublesome," as Harlan put it, because the justices knew that their decision would encourage resistance, as it did. Arthur Krock of the New York *Times* said the Court's action showed how integration "could legally be held to a very small percentage for a long time, . . . if the purpose and result of Negro exclusion were to preserve the moral and adequate educational standards of a public school." [35]

From the justices' point of view, doing anything other than affirming as quietly as possible would have opened up the issue of gradualism they already struggled with. The Court did not want to get involved yet in the actual struggle to obtain real or even token desegregation even in the Deep South. Justice Black's position prevailed in practice, but the Court had forgone the opportunity to make a forth-right statement about the rights of African-Americans. What Frankfurter's "deliberate speed" formula gained the Court and the country remained uncertain.

17

"Civil Rights . . . Civil Wrongs"
Massive Resistance to *Brown*, 1955–1961

Even carefully administered pupil placement laws did not satisfy some opponents of *Brown.* For them, such laws accepted the principle that sometime, somewhere, some African-American child could attend school with white children. Many Southerners could not accept the principle that segregation was wrong, nor the reality of token desegregation. They sponsored another set of devices to overcome *Brown,* the program of "massive resistance."

Massive resistance began as a political campaign in Virginia and then spread; the campaign was most successful in states where rural areas were overrepresented in state legislatures and where entrenched political leaders saw massive resistance as another technique for maintaining their power. And, although massive resistance was primarily a political movement designed to rally white opposition to *Brown,* part of the movement involved enacting statutes, which the NAACP's lawyers had to challenge, to prevent desegregation. The lawyers' challenge to massive resistance took place between late 1955, when massive resistance began, and early 1959, when it became clear that massive resistance was doomed to failure.[1]

The massive resistance statutes were obviously unconstitutional, and the federal courts routinely agreed. Yet combatting massive resistance was time consuming, rather like swatting off a swarm of flies, and the political forces behind massive resistance meant that no desegregation would occur until the last possible moment. As Carter put it in 1956, "What with the . . . utter frustration suffered in efforts to get a fair hearing, and the apparent fact that the white citizens council element now completely dominates the scene and calls the shots everywhere," it was not surprising that he was "somewhat disheartened."[2] Finally, because massive resistance was obviously unconstitutional, no large principles needed to be established in the litigation.

At first, Virginia's leading politicians responded to *Brown* relatively moderately. They seemed resigned to the fact that some desegregation was inevitable. However, there were strong currents of resistance. Twenty state legislators from Virginia's Southside, where the proportion of African-Americans was highest, met in June 1954 and adopted a resolution stating their "unalterable opposition to the principle of integration." A group of political leaders organized the Defenders of State Sovereignty and Individual Liberties in October, to mobilize public opposition to *Brown*. Southside politicians, an important force in Senator Harry Byrd's political organization, insisted that the state stand firm against desegregation anywhere. In contrast, white politicians and their constituents in the Virginia suburbs of Washington, D.C., did not welcome desegregation, but neither did they think that maintaining segregation was the state's highest priority; they could live with desegregation if they had to.[3]

In August 1954, Governor Thomas Stanley appointed an all-white commission to study desegregation; the chair of the commission, state Senator Garland Gray, had also chaired the June meeting of Southside legislators. The Gray Commission released its report in November 1955, after *Brown II*. All things considered, the report was relatively moderate. It proposed that local school boards devise student assignment systems and tacitly assumed that at least some boards would authorize token desegregation. The commission also proposed that the state pay the tuition for children whose parents sent them to private schools to avoid integrated schools, and that school attendance laws be changed so that no child would be required to attend an integrated school. The Virginia Constitution barred the state from giving money to private schools, and a referendum was held in January 1956 for a constitutional convention to amend the state constitution so that the legislature could adopt the tuition grant proposal. The referendum campaign took on a broader significance, however, when Senator Byrd and James Jackson Kilpatrick transformed it into a referendum on whether the legislature should show even greater resistance to *Brown*. The referendum passed by a margin of more than two to one, and politicians took that as a signal to embark on the program of massive resistance.[4]

Stanley convened a special session of the state legislature in August 1956, which adopted a package of laws aimed at *Brown*. Under these laws, the state would obstruct *Brown* in stages. The first step was the creation of a state-wide Pupil Placement Board to assign students to schools. In the unlikely event that the Board assigned an African-American student to a previously white school, or in the somewhat more likely event that some local school board began to desegregate voluntarily, or in the even more likely event that a federal court ordered desegregation, the second step would occur. The state would take charge of the school and close it while the governor investigated. The governor could reopen the school if "the peace and tranquility of the community" would not be disturbed and if no parent objected to desegregation. The local board could then "reclaim" the schools, but if it desegregated the schools, it would be denied all state funds. It could, of course, try to run the schools solely on local money, or it could use tuition grants for parents who sent their children to private schools. Alternatively, the board could give up and turn the schools over to the state government, which would run them as segregated schools.[5]

The legislative movement toward massive resistance occurred as the NAACP tried to secure desegregation through litigation. The pace of litigation was relatively slow. In July 1955, parents in Norfolk petitioned for desegregation. They followed the petition with a letter in April 1956, and filed suit in May. On April 23, the lawyers in the Prince Edward County case asked the federal court to direct that desegregation begin in September. Three days later, a suit was filed in Newport News, and in May, additional actions were begun in Charlottesville and in Arlington County in the suburbs of Washington.[6]

The first hearing in these cases was held on July 12 by Judge John Paul, a seventy-three-year-old Republican appointed by President Herbert Hoover twenty-three years before. At the hearing, Paul rejected the Charlottesville school board's technical defenses, and held that the plaintiffs were entitled to relief. He criticized the state's "policy of calculated delay" and indicated he would order desegregation for September. He issued his formal order in early August, but three weeks later he suspended it, allowing the board time to appeal and, not incidentally, deferring desegregation for at least another year.[7]

The Arlington case came next. In July, Judge Albert Bryan, a Democrat appointed by President Roosevelt, ordered elementary school desegregation for January 1957 and high school desegregation the following September. His opinion indicated that a pupil assignment system would be permissible, and said that, in his view, "compliance with [*Brown*] . . . may well not necessitate such extensive changes in the school system as some anticipate."[8] Supporters of massive resistance, though, could not accept even as small a "change" as token desegregation.

On the last day of 1956, the court of appeals affirmed the decisions in these cases. The court put the new pupil placement law to one side, because it had not been in force when the lawsuits began. Judge Parker noted that the boards' failure to take any steps toward desegregation "was not 'deliberate speed' in complying with the law . . . but was clear manifestation of an attitude of intransigence." The desegregation orders, Judge Parker wrote, were not "harsh or unreasonable," and allowed the boards to adopt reasonable, nonracial standards for student assignment.[9]

The pupil placement law did come under attack in the Norfolk case, which, together with the Newport News case, was heard by Judge Walter Hoffman on November 17. Judge Hoffman had been an active Republican and an early supporter of Eisenhower's candidacy for the party's nomination, and was appointed to the federal court by Eisenhower in 1954. The Norfolk board asked Hoffman to require the plaintiffs to use the placement law's procedures. At the hearing, Judge Hoffman expressed "grave doubts" about the board's argument, saying, "If I had to rule on it today I would throw it out the window." Even more, he severely criticized the state legislature. What it had done, he said, "is not too much a credit to good judgment. . . It is good political maneuvering if you want to get the votes."[10]

It was no surprise, therefore, when he rejected the board's position in January 1957. Reviewing the Gray Commission and the development of massive resistance, Hoffman insisted that he could not assess the pupil placement law's constitutionality in isolation. Plaintiffs could be required to exhaust *adequate* administrative remedies, but the pupil placement law, seen as part of massive resistance, was not adequate. Most dramatic, in Judge Hoffman's view, the law used the term "efficient" in its list of factors the placement board was to consider, and then, throughout the massive resistance package, described segregated schools as "efficient" as well. The pieces of the program, considered together, implied that no African-American student who used the administrative remedies would attend a desegregated school, because the statutes came close to requiring that any school facing desegregation be closed. Pursuing those remedies, then, would be futile. Judge Hoffman concluded that he was "unable to discern any evidence of 'good faith'" in the pupil placement act or any of the massive resistance statutes: "The pattern is plain—the Legislature has adopted procedures to defeat the *Brown* decision."[11]

Oliver Hill and Spottswood Robinson, who handled all these cases, succeeded completely as litigators. Every legal defense against desegregation had failed. The court of appeals affirmed Judge Hoffman's decision in July. It did delay the date the desegregation orders were to take effect in Norfolk and Newport News until the Supreme Court could deal with the cities' appeals. The lawyers for the Charlottesville and Arlington boards tried to piggyback on this delay, arguing that their desegregation orders should be delayed to see what the Court did. Judges Paul and Bryan, for different reasons, each suspended the desegregation orders temporarily. Because the Court would not act on those applications until October, the boards had another year free of desegregation, but it was clear that by the fall of 1958 some desegregation had to occur.[12]

The Norfolk and Charlottesville boards delayed school openings in the fall of 1958, hoping that something would save them from closing. But in September, the governor directed that schools in several districts under desegregation orders be closed. Many parents, both white and African-American, found it difficult to obtain private education, and the education system in Norfolk essentially collapsed. Ironically, the districts where the schools were closed in 1958 were not centers of resistance to desegregation. The Charlottesville board adopted a resolution in January 1959 urging token desegregation. A referendum to reopen the Norfolk schools using local funds only was defeated by a margin of 12,340 to 8,712, smaller than would be expected from an area that strongly supported massive resistance, particularly because the ballot warned that if the referendum passed, parents would have to pay substantial tuition. Public discomfort with school closing as a reality rather than a threat eroded support for massive resistance. On January 19, 1959, the Virginia Supreme Court held that closing the schools violated the state constitution, and on the same day a federal court held the overall program of massive resistance unconstitutional. Massive resistance collapsed, and the state moved easily to accept token desegregation.[13]

That did not mean, however, that the state's schools would soon be integrated. Meeting in February 1959, the LDF's lawyers informed the NAACP that it would have to come up with a large number of plaintiffs if it expected anything other than token desegregation.[14] Notably, litigation successes in Virginia did not result in outcomes substantially different from the one in North Carolina, where the NAACP's position had been rejected. In both states, by the end of the 1950s no more than token desegregation occurred.

In Virginia, the legal challenges to massive resistance proceeded relatively smoothly, though to no great conclusions. Most trial judges opposed massive resistance. Further, the Virginia state conference of NAACP branches was the South's largest, showing that the African-American community was well organized and not easily intimidated by threats of economic or violent reprisal.[15] Elsewhere it was more difficult to defeat massive resistance. By the late 1950s, there were no lawsuits seeking desegregation of the schools in Mississippi and only two in South Carolina; lawsuits were pending in major cities in Georgia, Alabama, Louisiana, Arkansas, and Tennessee; and in Dallas, Houston, and Fort Worth litigation was not being pursued vigorously. Hostility to the legal challenge to segregation was too great in these states, and justified fear of reprisal was widespread.[16]

Even in Virginia, the Prince Edward County case limped along. The case was assigned to Judge C. Sterling Hutcheson, a native of the area who strongly disagreed with *Brown*. On receiving the case to devise a remedy consistent with the "all deliberate speed" formulation, Judge Hutcheson relied on "local" conditions such as the threat of school closings and the "present state of unrest and racial tension" to explain why he refused to set any date for commencing desegregation. Apparently referring to the NAACP, he said that the problems associated with desegregation "cannot be solved by zealous advocates, by an emotional approach, nor by those with selfish interests to advance." The court of appeals reversed him, noting that, although the school board had been enjoined not to rely on race in making student assignments, "more than a year and a half had elapsed . . . , the school year of 1955–56 had come and gone, another school year had been entered, and no steps had been taken to comply with the order. The time had unquestionably come to say plainly to the defendants that they must comply without further delay." Judge Hutcheson then fixed 1965 as the date for compliance; when that decision too was reversed, he resigned from the bench.[17]

In Texas, two segregationist judges did their best to obstruct desegregation in Dallas. Although the case began with a complaint that the schools for African-Americans were overcrowded and unequal to the white schools in their physical facilities, after *Brown* the case proceeded as a desegregation case. Eighty-six year old Judge William Atwell, appointed to the district court by President Warren Harding, dismissed the complaint because the school board had not had enough time to develop a plan. The court of appeals reversed that decision, over a vigorous dissent by Judge Ben Cameron, a strong supporter of segregation whose nomination to the court of appeals in 1955 ironically had been endorsed by the NAACP. When Judge Atwell heard the case again, he indicated he agreed with the dissent. He criticized *Brown* because "the Court based its decision on no law but rather on what the Court regarded as m[o]re authoritative, modern psychological knowledge," and wrote a phrase whose point is clear even though its precise meaning is not: "We have Civil rights for all people under the national Constitution, and I might suggest that if there are Civil rights, there are also Civil wrongs." Judge Atwell again dismissed the suit in December 1956 to give the board "ample time . . . to work out this problem."[18]

The court of appeals reversed him in July 1957, saying that the plaintiffs were entitled to an "all deliberate speed" order. Judge Atwell next entered an order, apparently favorable to the plaintiffs, that he knew would surely be reversed. He directed that the schools be desegregated fully within four months, during the middle of the term. The court of appeals did reverse him at the end of 1957, saying that he had to give the board a reasonable time to prepare for desegregation. One report suggested that this might "presage a softer attitude" toward "all deliberate speed," giving the South time "for a breather." More likely, the court of appeals recognized that Judge Atwell's decision was designed to hinder rather than promote desegregation.[19]

There were no further developments in the case through the 1957–59 school years. To get the school board moving, in May 1959 the plaintiffs requested an order directing immediate desegregation. By 1959, the case had been reassigned to Judge T. Whitfield Davidson, an eighty-two-year-old who had been appointed by President Franklin Roosevelt. Davidson denied the plaintiffs' request and gave the board until April 1960 to develop a desegregation plan. On appeal, the court of appeals sent the case back to Judge Davidson, saying he should require the board to submit a desegregation plan.[20]

In May 1960, the school board presented its plan, which would have desegregated one grade a year, thereby accomplishing full desegregation in twelve years. In an amazing opinion, Judge Davidson disapproved the plan because it imposed too much integration. Judge Davidson's opinion characterized the board's plan as seeking "hasty" integration "by force," and rambled through history with inapposite references to Patrick Henry, Ishmael, Robert E. Lee, John C. Calhoun, the nation's experience with prohibition of alcohol, and—perhaps more relevant—his own family, which had owned "many, many slaves." Judge Davidson suggested that the board adopt a freedom-of-choice plan, setting aside schools that would admit both whites and African-Americans who wanted to attend. He thought there were a few whites in Dallas who were "fairly enthusiastic" about integration, and "some of our Negroes who are being used and are in good faith no doubt plaintiffs in this litigation." A short supplemental opinion provides some clues to what Judge Davidson really thought, and further incoherence. In telling the school board that it could use nonracial grounds for student assignments, he provided two illustrations, a "pampered white boy" who "by reason of his selfish propensities . . . creates disturbance," and "an overgrown Negro boy in an integrated school [who] should be by premature growth inclined to sex and should write verses on the blackboard of an obscene character. . . ." He concluded by saying that, "when exasperated," people should "consider something that's good." He offered the example of Joe Louis, the former heavyweight champion who had recently withdrawn from a project to promote tourism by African-Americans to Cuba—whose purpose, Judge Davidson said, was "not only to bring some money to Cuba, but to give the visitors a touch with the communistic system of government" there—because Louis "was not ready to give up his American citizenship."[21]

Houston offers an apparent contrast to Dallas, yet the differences were superficial. The city maintained the nation's largest segregated system in 1955. While the Supreme Court was considering the segregation cases, Houston NAACP branch members went through black neighborhoods to find parents willing to challenge segregation. A suit was filed in December 1956, on behalf of several plaintiffs, including one who objected to crossing a dangerous set of railroad tracks to get to the segregated school for African-Americans. Although the school board was directed to submit a desegregation plan, in August 1959 it refused to do so. A series of informal negotiations followed, after which the board was ordered to come forward with a plan by June 1960. When it did, the plan called for the voluntary desegregation of one elementary school, one junior high school, and one high school. District Judge Ben Connally, the son of Texas Senator Tom Connally and a Truman appointee to the court, rejected this as a "sham," and ordered grade-a-year desegregation. Twelve African-American children attended previously white schools in the first stage of desegregation in September 1960.[22] Notably, though the Houston litigation met none of the resistance from the trial judge that the Dallas case did, Houston desegregated its schools only a year before Dallas.

When massive resistance collapsed, the federal courts were still willing to accept some student placement plans as constitutional "on their face," and still required students to exhaust their administrative remedies. The task facing litigators seeking substantial desegregation then became even more difficult. They could challenge policies adopted by pupil placement boards that effectively maintained segregation, or particular decisions by school boards to exclude individual students from previously white schools. Doing so, however, meant that they had to show that there were no good reasons to justify the board's decisions. Eventually they might compile enough evidence to show that the pupil placement rules were applied unconstitutionally. Here they would invoke the doctrine of *Yick Wo v. Hopkins,*[23] which meant they would have to show that essentially all African-American applicants were denied admission to previously white schools. Yet in the areas where school boards used pupil placement rules to disguise racial discrimination, relatively few African-American parents were willing to subject their children both to the intrusive inquiries and testing under the pupil placement laws and to the prospect of harassment if they were admitted to white schools. As a result, it would take litigators a long time to accumulate enough evidence to make a powerful showing that the boards were using the rules to evade *Brown.* They could win cases on appeal, or even occasionally in a trial court, but the process was extremely time consuming and a great deal turned on the particular facts of individual cases.

The schools in Greensboro, North Carolina, for example, underwent token desegregation in 1957, when six African-Americans enrolled in previously white schools. Eighteen children applied for transfer the next year, but only two requests were granted. By the fall of 1958, the African-American community had enough of tokenism, and had the LDF file suit. At first the board simply reassigned the students to the same segregated school they had attended. The administrative appeals took the case into the 1958–59 school year, and the parents finally were able to begin their lawsuit in February 1959. In May, before the case came to trial, the school board merged a previously white school with a segregated black school— the two schools had been attached to each other anyway—and assigned all the children of both races to the merged school. The board notified all the parents of the merger. Over the next month the board received applications for reassignment from the parents of every white child assigned to the merged school. In July, the board granted all these applications. Similarly, the board granted the applications of every white teacher in the merged school to transfer elsewhere in the system and replaced them with an African-American principal and teaching staff. The result was that a school that had been all white in 1958–59 became all black the next year, and the plaintiffs were still attending a segregated school. District Judge Edwin Stanley dismissed the case. As he saw it, the plaintiffs applied for admission to the merged school and their applications had been granted. Whatever new complaint they had, he ruled, must be pursued through the administrative remedies. The court of appeals reversed Judge Stanley in November 1960, finding that the school board's tactics should not force the plaintiffs back to square one.[24]

Virginia was nearly as creative. Acting in the Norfolk case in 1959, Judge Hoffman found that the state pupil placement board denied every application by whites or African-Americans to desegregate a school, even where, as in Norfolk, the local board was willing to desegregate. One member of the state board testified that "he could not conceive of any circumstances which would cause him to vote in favor" of an application that would desegregate a school, and other members said, in effect, that "only a 'perfect child' under 'perfect conditions'" could desegregate a school. Judge Hoffman relied on *Yick Wo* to find this an "unconstitutional application of a law which is constitutional on its face." For him, "the melody of massive resistance linger[ed] on" in the state board's actions; he commended the Norfolk board for its "remarkable success" in meeting "the grave problem of racial mixing" since 1958, and hoped that it would "no longer be hampered" in its efforts by the state board.[25] The Norfolk board adopted policies that would desegregate the high schools first, then move downward to the elementary schools. Judge Hoffman and the court of appeals approved this approach as a good-faith effort to desegregate.[26]

Once the courts set aside student assignment policies that blocked desegregation completely, obdurate boards could continue to delay desegregation by making individual determinations. Cases in North Carolina and Virginia illustrate the problems school board tactics posed for the African-Americans' lawyers.

Until the 1959–60 school year, the schools in Durham, North Carolina, were completely segregated. At the end of August 1959, the school board granted applications from seven African-American students to desegregate the city's previously white high school and two of its three previously white junior high schools. It denied more than two hundred other applications. In September, Conrad Pearson asked the board to reconsider its denials. The board refused, because some applicants' parents had not met with it, and because school construction would soon relieve overcrowding. In 1960, the board again granted seven applications for transfer to the previously white schools and denied all others. At that point Pearson filed suit.

Judge Stanley found that Pearson's attempt to obtain reassignment for students whose parents did not attend the board meeting "strongly suggest[ed] a lack of good faith compliance" with the administrative process; the school board's actions in desegregating the high school showed it did not have a "fixed policy" of maintaining "a pattern of total segregation." Of course, the plaintiffs believed, apparently correctly, that the board did have such a policy with respect to elementary schools. But, invoking the *Briggs v. Elliott* approach to desegregation, Judge Stanley said they were not entitled to "a totally integrated school system," only to assignments to schools without regard to race. Having chastised the plaintiffs, Judge Stanley then found that the board had indeed discriminated in the elementary schools, where it maintained separate maps for student assignments based on race. He told the board to develop standards for considering individual applications for transfer, taking into account overcrowded conditions in some schools and the like.[27]

Once a board began to make truly individualized decisions, a pattern might emerge. For example, one case in Alexandria, Virginia, involved seventeen African-Americans denied admission to previously white schools; the board relied on their "academic achievement and mental capacity" and other "factors involving the health and/or well-being of the applicant." Judge Bryan went through what he called the "tedious and tasking" effort to decide whether the applications were properly denied. He compared the applicants' performance with that of whites enrolled in the schools, considering whether the applicants' low performance would have placed them at the bottom of the class (which sometimes would justify denying their applications) or only near the bottom (which sometimes would justify the denial, where the others near the bottom of the class were repeating the grade, and sometimes would not). In the end Judge Bryan overturned eight of the denials and sustained the remaining nine.[28]

The Mecklenburg County board of education in North Carolina, near Charlotte, managed to put off desegregation through the 1960–61 school year by applying the state's student assignment laws. In 1957 and 1958, three African-American families challenged the assignments. Their children were assigned to a segregated school to which they rode a bus, even though they lived much closer to a white school. The board argued that it never made distance the sole determinant of student assignment, and that, because the white school was overcrowded, even some whites who lived near it were bused elsewhere. By the time the case was tried, the county school system had been merged with the desegregated Charlotte system, and perhaps Judge Warlick thought that it was both too late and unnecessary to complain about 1957 and 1958. He praised the members of the school board for their "desire to aid their community else they surely would duck this type of service," and, like Judge Stanley in the Durham case, criticized the plaintiffs for not cooperating with the board. Judge Warlick found that conditions in 1957 and 1958 made it "natural" for the board to approach the problem of desegregation "with extreme caution," and that the board acted in good faith in denying the applications.[29]

School boards could adopt a number of tactics that substantially delayed desegregation or severely limited its scope. If *Briggs v. Elliott* was correct, and *Brown* required not integration but only the elimination of race-based criteria for student assignments, these tactics might well be consistent with *Brown*. But if *Brown* contemplated some real integration, as the Court's interest in gradualism suggested, the tactics were evasions. A fair amount of litigation was necessary to lay the groundwork for cases to clarify *Brown*'s meaning. The lawyers would create records showing that states had used the *Briggs* approach to perpetuate segregation. The LDF could not really develop these cases until the 1960s. The policies school boards used, or the unconstitutional administration under *Yick Wo,* could be identified only through an intensive examination of particular facts. For those who disagreed with *Brown,* a pupil placement law could be administered carefully to produce no more than token desegregation, within the boundaries the federal courts set for gradual desegregation. Unless the Supreme Court intervened, "all deliberate speed" meant token desegregation; for example, only twelve African-American children were enrolled in schools with whites in three of North Carolina's cities in 1957.[30] There was very little Marshall and his staff could do about this situation.

Maneuvering within the parameters set by *Brown* and massive resistance thus yielded basically similar results: long delays before school boards were required to begin desegregation, followed by token desegregation. These results occurred whether the NAACP's lawyers won their lawsuits, as in Virginia, or lost them, as in North Carolina and in the Texas district courts. After *Brown,* the litigation did not involve establishing any great legal principle, but only overcoming a large number of often frivolous technical objections to particular desegregation suits, or objections that went to the heart of *Brown* itself and therefore did not have to be taken terribly seriously by the NAACP's lawyers. Winning the cases, then, accomplished little, at least in the short run.

18

The "Battle Between the Sovereigns"
Violent Resistance to *Brown*, 1955–1961

When *Brown* met violent resistance in Little Rock, Arkansas, the LDF lawyers' deepest feelings about race and the law were drawn into play. Little Rock superintendent Virgil Blossom began planning for desegregation while *Brown* was before the Supreme Court. Over the course of a year, Blossom and his staff developed a plan to desegregate the city's schools in stages. Two schools under construction would open without segregation as high schools, probably in September 1956. A year later the junior high schools would be desegregated, and several years later the plan would spread to the city's elementary schools. In May 1955, the school board modified Blossom's plan: Central High School would be desegregated in September 1957 and the junior highs in 1960, and the date for desegregating elementary schools was left open, though 1963 seemed likely. Students could transfer out of schools where they were part of the minority; as a result, a neighborhood attendance plan would probably end up with some African-Americans attending some previously white schools and no whites attending previously black schools. In making Central High the focus of desegregation, the board selected a school located in a working-class neighborhood while exempting the school under construction in a neighborhood where many white professional and business people lived. Blossom thought preparing a desegregation plan was a routine aspect of his job. In contrast, when the school board announced its plan, it said it was proposing to desegregate the schools only because it had to.[1]

Daisy Bates led the local NAACP branch. Bates, a resident of Little Rock since 1941, published a newspaper for the city's African-American community. Acting with the help of Wiley Branton, the branch filed a petition for desegregation with the school board in August 1954. Branton, the first African-American graduate of Arkansas's law school, practiced law in his home town of Pine Bluff, forty-five miles from Little Rock. The branch watched as the school board's plans developed, and, when its members concluded that the new high school was about to open in 1956 as an all-white school, they filed suit in February 1956 seeking admission to the new school. At the outset, the case was a "routine" desegregation suit, and the LDF national staff had little to do with its first stages; Ulysses Simpson Tate, the regional staff counsel for the Southwest, was informed of the suit's progress but did not attend any preliminary hearings even when Bates urged him to. Tate did attend the trial, though he arrived only the day before it began. The school board defended its action as consistent with "deliberate speed," and the trial court agreed. Marshall argued the unsuccessful appeal, and a few African-Americans were scheduled to enter Central High in September 1957.[2]

The pending desegregation of Little Rock's schools became an important issue in Arkansas's politics in 1956, as Governor Orval Faubus's campaign for reelection focused on the issue after segregationists attacked Faubus for failing to take a strong enough stand. Segregationists proposed several constitutional amendments and statutes to preserve segregation. The voters adopted these proposals when they reelected Faubus in November 1956, and the state's legislators responded by enacting additional prosegregation statutes. In August 1957, Governor Marvin Griffin of Georgia, a strong segregationist, spoke in Little Rock, intensifying white opposition to Central's imminent desegregation. Despite assurances from Blossom that Central's desegregation would not cause violence, Faubus got a state court to issue an injunction against opening Central as a desegregated school. The federal court overturned that injunction, whereupon Governor Faubus mobilized the Arkansas National Guard, telling it to prevent desegregation at Central to prevent rioting and violence.[3]

Bates and the Little Rock branch located about sixty young people interested in desegregating Central High, but the school board agreed to allow only seventeen to attend. By the time school opened on September 3, 1957, only nine were willing to go through the inevitable turmoil. The Department of Justice in Washington tried to negotiate a peaceful solution, urging the students to delay their effort to desegregate Central. By this point the national legal staff had become involved in the case, and Marshall resisted this pressure. The students tried to enroll on September 3, but their efforts were turned back when the National Guard blocked their entry, to the cheers of an extremely hostile crowd. For the next two and a half weeks, Judge Ronald Davies held several hearings on the case.[4] (Davies was a North Dakota judge who had been assigned to the Little Rock case when one local federal judge unexpectedly resigned and the other asked to have the case transferred.)

The national staff provided detailed assistance to Branton through these hearings. When Marshall arrived in Little Rock, he was sanguine. He said that he had been "in touch" with the local situation and that "it looks to me like a matter to be worked out in Arkansas." Although desegregation "takes time," he said, "we're making progress and it's steady." At the hearing's end, Judge Davies ordered the school board to desegregate Central High, and ordered Faubus to stop interfering with desegregation. When Faubus's attorney then walked out, Marshall, incredulous at this disrespect, told Bates, "Now I've really seen everything." Responding to Judge Davies's orders, Faubus withdrew the National Guard.[5]

On Monday, September 23, the nine students returned to Central, where a near-riot broke out. The students did not go to school on Tuesday, and on Thursday President Eisenhower ordered federal troops to Little Rock and took over the state National Guard to protect the students. Each day the students assembled before school at Bates's house, and she was in constant contact with the NAACP's national office. The students attended Central High over the next year under trying circumstances. They had to overcome "daily irritants" within the school such as verbal abuse, destruction of their lockers, and physical jostling. Although none of the harassment inside the school placed the students in serious physical danger, when Minnie Jean Brown, an eleventh grader, was called "nigger bitch," her reply—"white trash"—led to her expulsion.[6]

The Little Rock school board had enough of the turmoil, and in early 1958 it asked Judge Harry Lemley, who had taken the case over from Judge Davies, for permission to discontinue desegregation at Central High and defer all other action until 1960. At a hearing in June Judge Lemley allowed them the two-year delay they sought. Concerned that Judge Lemley's action would prevent any desegregation during the next school year, Branton and the NAACP asked the Supreme Court to review the case immediately, without waiting for the court of appeals to act. The Supreme Court refused the request, as it usually does when lawyers try to get it to decide cases before they have been heard by the court of appeals. Unusually, though, the Court issued an opinion saying, pointedly, that it expected the court of appeals to "recognize the vital importance of the time element in this litigation, and that it will act . . . in ample time to permit arrangements to be made for the next school year."[7]

The court of appeals heard argument in early August, and on August 18 six judges of the court, over a single dissent, reversed Judge Lemley and directed that desegregation proceed as initially approved. However, the court entered a thirty-day stay of this order, which left Judge Lemley's delay in place. At that point, both the Little Rock board and the NAACP went back to the Supreme Court; the board asked the Court to uphold Judge Lemley, and the NAACP asked that the stay be dissolved so that desegregated schools could open on September 2.[8] The Supreme Court was technically not in session when it received these appeals, and several of the justices were out of town. As it had in the past when important cases had to be decided during the summer, the Court convened in what it called a "Special Term" on August 28.[9]

Richard Butler, the school board's attorney, urged the Court to accept Judge Lemley's conclusion that the city needed time "to work in a period of peace and harmony rather than turmoil and strife." Marshall asked the Court to vacate the stay at once so that desegregated schools would open on schedule. Solicitor General J. Lee Rankin, who had been invited to participate, supported Marshall's position, with a brief saying that constitutional rights could not be "suspended or ignored because of the antagonistic acts of others." When the justices met to discuss what to do, Justice Frankfurter had in hand a memorandum rejecting the board's effort to delay: "Whatever sophisticated explanations may be devised to justify such a request, they cannot obscure the essential meaning that law should bow to force." The justices decided they could not immediately order desegregation, but they were, in Frankfurter's words, "fiercely clear" that Judge Lemley was wrong. Instead of granting Marshall's motion, they agreed to hear the board's appeal and set an extremely short schedule. The board had to complete the formal application for review by September 8, and both sides had to file their briefs by September 10.

The Court asked the solicitor general to appear and argue the case as well and set argument for September 11.[10]

Justice Clark voiced some objections to this action. He "adhere[d] steadfastly to my vote [in *Brown*], believing that every American citizen goes first class under the Constitution," but objected to the Court's insistence on a quick decision, which seemed to promise "integration through push button action . . . rather [than] by 'deliberate speed.'" For Clark, "for all practical purposes it makes no difference whether the petitioners enter all integrated schools on Sept. 8th or Oct. 6th, the day we convene our next Term," presumably because the Court, by setting argument for September 12, already made it impossible for the students to enroll in integrated schools on schedule. The majority was vindicated, however, when the school board, learning of the Court's action, delayed opening day until September 15.[11]

Frankfurter took the board's action to confirm his belief that the Court should encourage moderate Southerners. He therefore proposed that Warren open the oral argument by noting the board's decision. That, Frankfurter thought, would support Butler and the board in their struggle against Faubus, and was, in Frankfurter's words, consistent with his long-held view "that the ultimate hope for the peaceful solution of the basic problem largely depends on winning the support of lawyers of the South for the overriding issue of obedience to the Court's decision." The Court's opinion, Frankfurter suggested, should stress "the transcending issue of the Supreme Court as the authoritative organ of what the Constitution requires." In doing so, the justices would "serve as exemplars of understanding and wisdom and magnanimity" to those in the South, particularly in "the younger generation who not only recognize the inevitability of desegregation but want to further the acceptance in action of such inevitability." Alexander Bickel captured Frankfurter's perspective in writing the justice, "for the North to take a high and mighty, you-are-soiled-and-we-are-clean tone would be a frightful mistake. To even appear to be punishing the South for its history is to undermine our own moral position."[12]

Warren saw the situation differently, and rejected Frankfurter's suggestion. For Warren, the school board's efforts to delay desegregation resulted from Faubus's obstructionist tactics, and he believed the Court should criticize Faubus directly, though not by name. Though Frankfurter criticized Warren for acting like "a fighting politician [rather than] a judicial statesman," the Chief Justice's views were more widely shared on the Court.

Butler's brief emphasized the board's good faith effort to begin to desegregate, and the "disastrous" effects the year before. It argued that Judge Lemley's findings about the risk of future violence justified delaying desegregation, and said that it would be particularly unfair to put the board "in the undeserved position of being the sole bastion of Federal authority until it destroys itself." Perhaps the Justice Department might get control of the situation, "but until unlawful force, violence and official state resistance subside," perhaps as the values of the public changed, the delay was justified. The schedule the Court set meant that Marshall and Branton had to prepare their brief without seeing Butler's. It was only twelve pages long, and forcefully stated that "neither overt public resistance, nor the possibility of it," could justify delaying desegregation. Responding to what the lawyers knew would be Butler's plea that the Court should sympathize with the position Faubus put the board in, the brief pointed out that "one state agency, the School Board, seeks to be relieved of its constitutional obligation by pleading the *force majeure* brought to bear by another facet of state power." It was "unthinkable," the brief said, "to solve this problem by further delaying the constitutional rights" of the students. To acquiesce in the argument that "ruffians with or without support from state officials" could impede desegregation "would subvert our entire constitutional framework." "In short," the brief said, the case involved "the very survival of the Rule of Law."[13]

At the oral argument, Butler was peppered with questions, while no one asked Marshall a question and Solicitor General Rankin got only one, indicating that the justices had already decided they were going to uphold the decision that desegregation should occur immediately. Justices Harlan and, especially, Frankfurter used their questions to suggest that the problems in Little Rock occurred because state officials incited opposition to the board's efforts to comply with *Brown* and that before Faubus got involved in the case, "the community . . . [was] if not enthusiastic about it, at least acquiescent" to the idea of gradual desegregation. Near the end of the morning session, Frankfurter "summarized" Butler's argument: "You suggest that the mass of people in Arkansas are law-abiding, are not mobsters; they do not like desegregation, but they may be won to respect for the Constitution as pronounced by the organ charged with the duty of declaring it, and therefore adjusting themselves to it, although they may not like it?"[14]

Warren was more abrupt with Butler. Perhaps responding to the sympathetic tone of Frankfurter's questions, Warren suggested that the board itself failed to do anything "to relieve your community of this feeling." He was particularly skeptical about Butler's suggestion that the Supreme Court might issue an opinion clarifying *Brown,* to lead the people of Arkansas to accept desegregation, but only if the "clarification" went along with Judge Lemley's delay. Butler rather plaintively suggested that someone else—the federal government through Congress in particular—should help his clients out of the hard position that Governor Faubus put them in, but Justice Brennan pointed out that Faubus, like the board itself, was bound to take the Constitution as "the supreme Law of the Land." When Butler said that the school board could not resolve the "head-on collision between the Federal and State Governments," Justice Black said, "there is not any doubt about what the Constitution says about that, is there?"

Marshall began his argument with that point. For him, the "battle between the sovereigns" had been "decided by the Constitution when it was adopted." Then Marshall added another "preliminary" point, that it was "one thing for a politician in a State" to disagree with the Supreme Court, but "it's another thing for a lawyer to stand up in this Court and argue that there is any doubt about it." These two points were at the heart of the controversy. Marshall then elaborated. He read a massive resistance bill, and mentioned others, to show that it was futile to hope that anything good would come from delaying desegregation. He pointed out that, based on what Butler had said, "as of right now the [school board] ha[s] given not the slightest idea of doing anything." To the board's invocation of the problems of desegregation, Marshall responded, "democracy's tough. There's always going to be a measure of difficulty and problems," but, he continued, consider what "these Negro children went through." How could anyone tell them, "All you have done is gone. You fought for what you considered democracy and you lost. And you go back to the segregated school from which you came." The school board expressed concern about disrupting education, Marshall said, but "education is the teaching of the overall citizenship," and "I don't know of any more horrible destruction of principle of citizenship than to tell young children that, those of you who withdrew, rather than go to school with Negroes, . . . Come back, all is forgiven, you win." Marshall said he worried about the white children "who are told, as young people, that the way to get your rights is to violate the law and defy the lawful authorities. . . . I don't worry about those Negro kids' future. They've been struggling with democracy long enough. They know about it."

Marshall then turned briefly to the way gradualism was working. He grudgingly accepted the plan approved by the court of appeals, but could not accept the board's position that this "most gradual of gradual plans can't work." Finally, he restated Warren's point that the board had not pursued other methods of accomplishing desegregation, noting that instead of trying to get the federal government to intervene or attempting to get an injunction against violence, "whenever there was a move against integration of Central High School, each step, each step the School Board made a move to get the Negro kids out of there."

Solicitor General Rankin's argument tracked the United States brief.[15] He emphasized that "the element in this case is lawlessness," and that "there isn't a single policeman who isn't going to watch this Court and what it has to say about this matter that doesn't have to deal with people everyday who don't like the law he is trying to administer and enforce." The board might be in a difficult position, Rankin said, "but I don't think anyone in public office who has tried to do the right thing has ever had an easy time of it." And, like Marshall, Rankin stressed that the board had done nothing to educate the people of Little Rock: "At least they could come forward and say: We'll tell the people that this Supreme Court has spoken; that's the law of the land; it's binding; we've got to do it; the sooner we do it, the better; let's get started on it."

Butler stumbled badly when he tried to respond to Marshall and Rankin. First he hinted that the present board might resign or be forced out of office, and replaced by a more recalcitrant one. Then he launched a genteel attack on the NAACP, calling it "the organization that really sponsored the litigation . . . which prompted this Court, urged this Court to change of doctrine of the law that had been in existence and recognized by this Court for some 58 years." In responding to Rankin, Butler started to argue that the national government was not supreme because, as he put it, "a good many people, not only in the South, have been reading" the Tenth Amendment, which he misquoted as providing that "rights not specifically delegated to the Federal Government shall be reserved to the state or to the people." The amendment actually refers to "powers" not "rights" and does not contain the word "specifically." When Chief Justice Warren interrupted to ask whether Butler really was relying on the Tenth Amendment, Butler retreated.

Marshall's argument did not address the legal details, because the details were, as even Butler conceded, rather clear. Instead, Marshall developed three rhetorical themes, each presented in a down-to-earth way. He undermined Butler's attempt to portray the board as the helpless victim of Faubus's manipulation. If the board really wanted to achieve peaceful desegregation, Marshall pointed out, it could have done much more as the situation developed. The second theme gave a twist to Frankfurter's questions about the educational impact of a decision reiterating *Brown*. Essentially agreeing with the underlying point, Marshall stressed the harmful educational message that a decision in favor of delay would send rather than, as Frankfurter's questions emphasized, the beneficial message a restatement of *Brown* would send. Rankin also developed these themes, in a tone only slightly more formal than Marshall's. Marshall alone, however, introduced the third and perhaps most effective theme. He brought attention back to the African-American students who attended Central High for a year under extremely difficult circumstances. He framed his presentation in terms of how the equitable considerations should be balanced; Butler's discussion of violence and the board's position identified one set of concerns, but Marshall's argument showed what the equities on the other side were.

Immediately after the argument the Court voted unanimously to affirm the court of appeals and vacate its stay so that when the schools opened on September 15, they would be desegregated. Justices Harlan and Frankfurter drafted a three-paragraph order released on September 12; the order said a full opinion would be issued "in due course."[16]

Even before the argument, Warren told Justice William Brennan to begin working on an opinion. Brennan had to juggle three elements in assembling an opinion. First, and least difficult, he had to outline the facts. Warren said that this part of the opinion would be "dry stuff," but thought it important "to emphasize the careful attention given by the Court to following our regular procedures." After proposing to put the case's complex history in an appendix to the opinion, Brennan eventually managed to write a suitable statement of facts. Second, he had to say that disagreement with the Court's decision in *Brown,* no matter how deeply felt and no matter how vigorously or even violently expressed, could not justify refusing to comply with it; if, as the court of appeals held two years before, the school board's desegregation plan was proper within the "deliberate speed" formula, it should go into effect despite disagreement and violent opposition. Third, he had to deal with competing views about what to say about "deliberate speed." Justice Black strenuously argued that the Court should clarify its meaning. The opinion, according to Black, should "anticipate state supported private schools" and indicate that such schools, created to evade *Brown,* were impermissible. More important, the opinion should state specifically that "deliberate speed" meant not only beginning to desegregate but specifying a time when desegregation would be completed as well. Justice Burton disagreed, saying that, at least in the Little Rock case, the only issue was whether the board would start to desegregate, not when it would finish.[17]

Justice Brennan agreed with Black, and his draft contained two sections attempting to define "deliberate speed" more precisely. Because each student had a "personal and present" constitutional right, Brennan wrote, school boards had "to make a prompt start" toward desegregation. They could study the local situation but then had to develop a "detailed plan designed to effectuate complete desegregation." Experience had shown that the time needed for study and planning "need not be long." Then boards "are duty bound to devote every effort towards initiating desegregation and bringing about complete desegregation. . . ." Whether desegregation occurred all at once or in stages, "a prompt commitment to initiate and complete desegregation at specific times is a necessary requirement for compliance with the constitutional principles expressed in *Brown*."[18]

Brennan could not get his colleagues to agree with this part. Frankfurter thought the formulation was too "rigid," and Brennan himself was uneasy at language suggesting that "personal and present" rights could be "delayed for some children so long as the start is made to enforce them for other children." And, in discussing *Brown*, the draft diluted the firm statement, which all on the Court wished to make, that what was wrong in Little Rock was that the governor of the state had stood for outright defiance of the Supreme Court. In the end, Brennan simply dropped the discussion of "deliberate speed."[19]

Justice Harlan prepared a substantial alternative opinion to substitute for the final pages of Brennan's draft, which Brennan accepted. Harlan also made two suggestions designed to emphasize how unified the Court was on desegregation. First, he proposed that the opinion note explicitly that *Brown* had been unanimously decided by justices "of diversified geographical and other backgrounds," and that the three justices who had joined the Court since *Brown* were "at one" with the others "as to the inescapability of that decision." Although Brennan objected that this statement might be "fatal" in suggesting that "the Constitution has only the meaning that can command a majority of the Court as that majority may change with shifting membership," he went along with the views of his colleagues who thought its inclusion a good idea. Second, Harlan proposed that the opinion begin by reciting that it was "an opinion signed by the entire Court." Black and Frankfurter were enthusiastic about the idea, while Douglas thought it "silly" because "it seemed to add nothing in substance." Douglas did note, as a criticism, that the new format would mean that Chief Justice Warren would deliver an opinion that Justice Brennan wrote, but perhaps that made the format attractive to Warren.[20]

The Court's opinion opened with a vigorous statement, drafted by Justice Black, that the case "raise[d] questions of the highest importance to the maintenance of our federal system of government," because it "necessarily involves a claim by the Governor and Legislature . . . that there is no duty on state officials to obey federal court orders resting on this Court's considered interpretation of the United States Constitution." The Court "accepted without reservation" the board's good faith "in dealing with the unfortunate and distressing sequence of events," and accepted also Judge Lemley's findings that education at Central High would continue to suffer "if the conditions which prevailed last year are permitted to continue." But, the opinion said, the difficulties were "directly traceable" to Governor Faubus and the state legislature and their "determination to resist"

Brown. Under these circumstances, delay could not be justified: "The constitutional rights of [the students] are not to be sacrificed or yielded to the violence and disorder which have followed upon the actions of the Governor and Legislature."[21]

After stating that constitutional rights could not be "nullified" either directly or indirectly, the opinion turned to "some basic constitutional propositions" to refute Governor Faubus's premise that he was not bound by *Brown.* Because the Constitution was the "supreme Law of the Land," and because the Supreme Court had the power to "say what the law is," it followed, according to the opinion, that "the federal judiciary is supreme in the exposition of the law of the Constitution." As a result, the Court's interpretation of the Constitution in *Brown* had "binding effect" on state officials like Governor Faubus. "No state legislator or executive or judicial officer can war against the Constitution without violating his undertaking to support it." The opinion concluded by reiterating that segregation "cannot be squared with the [Fourteenth] Amendment's command" of equal protection, and that the principles announced in *Brown* "and the obedience of the States to them . . . are indispensable to the protection of the freedoms guaranteed by our fundamental charter for all of us. Our constitutional ideal of equal justice under law is thus made a living truth."

Just before the Court's decision was released, Justice Frankfurter told his colleagues he planned to write a separate concurring opinion. He wanted to use the separate opinion to appeal to his special audience of right-thinking moderate Southern lawyers. For Warren, Brennan, and Black, the idea of a separate opinion was "a bombshell," and they "spoke very strongly" to dissuade Frankfurter. According to Justice Douglas, even Justice Harlan "spent several hours with Frankfurter trying to get him to alter some phraseology." Frankfurter was "adamant," however, insisting that "it was none of the Court's business what he wrote."[22]

For all the trouble it caused inside the Court, Frankfurter's separate opinion seems completely consistent with the Court's opinion, albeit typically verbose and mildly patronizing. The opinion opened with a declaration that Frankfurter "unreservedly participat[ed]" in the Court's opinion. Frankfurter then praised the Little Rock authorities for their effort to "work[ ] together [and] shar[e] a common effort," to develop "habits of acceptance of the right of colored children to the equal protection of the laws." He forcefully criticized Governor Faubus, saying that "the tragic aspect of [his] disruptive tactic was that the power of the State was used not to sustain law but as an instrument for thwarting law." If this "illegal, forcible interference" were accepted as a justification for delaying desegregation, the "inescapable meaning" would be that "law should bow to force. To yield to such a claim," Frankfurter wrote, "would be to enthrone official lawlessness, and lawlessness if not checked is the precursor of anarchy. . . . Violent resistance to law cannot be made a legal reason for its suspension without loosening the fabric of our society."[23]

Frankfurter then turned to the educational effects of official actions, saying that "local customs . . . are not decreed in heaven," and can "yield . . . to law and education," which can occur through "the fruitful exercise of responsibility of those charged with political official power and from the almost unconsciously transforming actualities of living under law." He acknowledged that desegregation stirred "[d]eep emotions," but said that "[t]hey will not be calmed by letting violence loose." Rather, "[o]nly the constructive use of time will achieve what an advanced civilization demands and the Constitution confirms."

The justices wanted to issue their opinion by the opening day of the Court's term, October 6. As Brennan worked on the opinion, Governor Faubus and the Arkansas legislature responded to the Court's announcement that it had affirmed the court of appeals. They called a special election for Little Rock voters to decide whether the schools should open with desegregation or close down. Faubus announced that if the voters wanted to close the schools, a private corporation would take over the school buildings and open them as "private" segregated schools. The board asked the federal court whether handing the schools over to the new corporation would be constitutional. Because Judge Lemley had retired, the judge hearing the request was John Miller, a former member of Congress and senator who was a close associate of Senator John McClellan. Judge Miller refused to rule on the board's request. When the same request was made by the African-American plaintiffs, Judge Miller said he could not decide the case himself; as a challenge to the constitutionality of a state statute it could be decided only by a three-judge court. [24]

On September 27, the special referendum resulted in a vote of 19,000 to 7,500 to close the city's high schools, and on September 29 the school board signed a lease turning over the high schools to the private corporation. The court of appeals said the lease was invalid, and on November 10 ordered the board to carry out the desegregation plan, but the high schools remained closed until 1959. Judge Miller accepted excuses for delay from the board, which by now was divided between supporters of segregation and members who wanted to get on with the business of education. A badly financed system of private schools limped on, and eventually supporters of desegregation gained a majority on the school board. In 1959 the board assigned three African-American students to Central High and three others to the previously all white Hall High School; despite the fact that Blossom's desegregation plan contemplated some desegregation of junior high schools in 1959 or 1960, none occurred then. [25]

A few years later, the Little Rock scenario of violent resistance was reenacted in New Orleans. Desegregation litigation in New Orleans began early and ended in turmoil. Daniel Ellis Byrd, a member of the NAACP's field staff, met with Earl Bush in late 1950 to discuss a desegregation suit. Bush's employer, an insurance company, gave him permission to bring the lawsuit but, concerned that Bush might go into debt, insisted that the NAACP pay the litigation expenses, which eventually got the NAACP in trouble. After Byrd investigated conditions in New Orleans, Bush filed a desegregation petition with the school board in November 1951, and filed his lawsuit in September 1952. By agreement among the lawyers the lawsuit was left alone until 1956, partly to see what the Supreme Court would do in *Brown* and partly because there were "too few lawyers engaged in the task of dismantling segregation to apply constant, sustained legal pressure everywhere." [26]

In 1956, the school board's regular counsel resigned from the case and was replaced by Gerard Rault, an enthusiastic supporter of segregation. Rault moved to dismiss the action because the plaintiffs had not exhausted their remedies under

Louisiana's 1954 pupil placement act. Judge J. Skelly Wright, a liberal Democrat appointed to the court by President Harry Truman in 1949, found the placement act invalid as part of Louisiana's overall plan for maintaining segregation. Judge Wright did say that "[t]he problem of changing a people's mores, particularly those with an emotional overlay, is not to be taken lightly. It is a problem which will require the utmost patience, understanding, generosity and forebearance from all of us, of whatever race. But the magnitude of the problem may not nullify the principle."[27]

A. P. Tureaud, the NAACP's cooperating attorney in New Orleans, did not push the school board to take immediate action, and the board moved slowly and unwillingly toward adopting a desegregation plan.* When desegregation seemed imminent in 1960, the state legislature responded with a flurry of statutes aimed at taking control of the schools away from the local board. Judge Wright and two colleagues held these statutes unconstitutional. During the hearing, Louisiana's attorney general, Jack Gremillion, vehemently objected to a ruling on some evidence, slammed a book on the table, and stalked out, saying, "I'm not going to stay in this den of iniquity." For this behavior, Gremillion later was held in contempt of court and received a suspended sentence. Meanwhile, white opposition to desegregation grew. The Louisiana legislature convened in an emergency session and adopted new laws to block desegregation; Judge Wright and his colleagues, sitting in essentially continuous session, immediately held the new laws unconstitutional, and eventually Judge Wright took the extraordinary step of barring the state legislature from t⌐k'ng any action that would "interfer[e] with the operation" of New Orleans's sc⌐.⌐ls. When desegregation began in New Orleans, it was accompanied by nearly a year of violence and a white boycott of the schools.[28]

In the years after *Brown,* Marshall continued to travel and make speeches. His tone changed as the prospects for successful desegregation first seemed bright, then faded, then revived with the collapse of massive resistance. Insisting that desegregation occur "at once and firmly" in a 1954 speech, Marshall said that "if the old folks—both colored and white—would leave it alone, the children would settle it themselves." Six months later, he told a Georgia audience that they could not win the battle in the Supreme Court and lose the war in the South. After *Brown II,* Marshall continued to urge that desegregation occur as quickly as possi-

---

* A group of white and African-American parents, centered around the NAACP's branch but not formally acting on its behalf, became impatient in late 1959 and organized meetings at which they developed a program to publicize the inequalities between the African-American and white schools. The parents' group was led by Georg Iggers, a white professor who had been active in the Little Rock NAACP before he took a job in New Orleans. Seeing this effort in part as a challenge to his leadership, Byrd strenuously objected that comparisons might lead to a revival of separate but equal thinking, and that submitting the report to the courts might be considered contempt of court. Byrd wrote that he could not "reconcile this passion to publish a report that can be harmful and [Iggers's] determination to meddle in this case." Somewhat overstating Iggers's intentions and the likely consequences, Byrd thought that "it would be catastrophic for the plaintiffs to be complaining about segregation and the branch complaining about the inequalities in the Negro Schools." Peltason, *Fifty-Eight Lonely Men,* p. 226; Daniel Ellis Byrd to TM, Dec. 11, 1959, A. P. Tureaud Papers, box 11, folder 2, Amistad Research Center, Tulane University.

ble; as each school year ended with only moderately encouraging results, Marshall would set the opening of schools the following September as the "deadline" for integration. For him, delay "hurt[ ] more than it help[ed]" because it gave opponents of desegregation time to organize and divide the community. "It will be just as difficult 20 years from now," he said in 1955, "and you might as well do it and get it over with." By March 1956, he said in a Memphis speech, "We've got the other side licked. It's just a matter of time."[29]

Later that year, Marshall's tone began to shift. At the end of May, he wrote a supporter, "It might be that more [resistance] will awaken good Americans to their responsibility. I say this in all sincerity while still realizing that these statements are still for the most part wishful thinking on my part." To a North Carolina group he said, "there can no longer be any reason for hope of compliance without going to the courts." In August 1956, he was even more downbeat. The NAACP had "lost ground in the area of public opinion" over the prior year, and the hopeful view that "legal action alone would solve the problem" had been "shattered." As the focus of civil rights activity shifted from the courts, Marshall encouraged his listeners to use voting "and other means" of community action. Still, he said, "everyone in the South knows that desegregation is inevitable." Like some opponents of token desegregation, he believed that tokenism meant that "the hole is in the dike." Having run out of "delaying tactics," Marshall said near the end of 1957, the South had fallen back on violence, its "last gimmick." Disgruntled at desegregation's pace, Marshall criticized those who said that African-Americans had been pushing too fast: "I've been trying to figure out what they mean. . . . In this program of action we've been carrying on in the last few years, I'm afraid that we're moving too slowly on it; in fact, we're moving backward." Supporters of massive resistance, he said in 1956, "don't mean go slow. They mean don't go." While the Little Rock desegregation struggle was going on, Marshall thought "there [was] nothing in the world to worry about" regarding the legal issues, and that overall the situation in 1958 was "not either gloomy or bright."[30]

By 1959, Marshall had returned to the theme of seeking "unconditional victory" in the courts. "It will take time to get complete integration, but we are willing to stay in the courts to do it. . . . In a democracy you push for what you want within the law." He called grade-a-year plans legally and morally wrong because they provided no relief to children in some grades and caused problems for families with children in different grades, each attending different schools. Even though massive resistance ended, he said, the civil rights movement was being "slow[ed] down" by tokenism. Still, Marshall would not tolerate a "hard core of permanent resistance," and said that "as long as one Negro in the South comes to us and says, 'I need your help,' he's going to get that help." To the NAACP convention in August 1961, Marshall called tokenism "a step backward." Integration was the right of the African-American, not "some form of charity to be spooned out at the will of the majority."[31]

Nashville's school board adopted a desegregation plan in 1955, as the Little Rock board developed its plan. In Nashville, the schools were to be desegregated one grade at a time, starting with the first grade in 1959. The board redrew attendance zones to minimize desegregation, and its plan allowed white students to transfer freely out of schools attended by African-Americans. The board acknowledged that its plan was designed to "provide the least amount of desegregation over the longest period of time," which was why Coyness Ennix, the school board's only African-American member, voted against it. In the first year of the plan's operation, in fact, only 115 of 1,400 African-American first-graders lived in the attendance zones of previously white schools, and only 55 of 2,000 white first-graders lived in zones for previously black schools. All 55 white students transferred to white schools, and 105 of the African-American students transferred back to black schools. District Judge William Miller, an active Republican who had just been appointed to the court, approved the Nashville plan in 1955. In August, as school was about to open, John Kasper, a segregationist agitator whose speeches against desegregation had provoked a 1956 attack on African-Americans in Clinton, Tennessee, began a similar campaign in Nashville. The schools opened nonetheless on September 8, 1957, with nineteen African-American first-graders attending classes at seven previously white schools. That night a school was bombed. At that point the city's police force, which had been guarding the schools during the day, stopped further demonstrations against desegregation. The mayor obtained an injunction against Kasper, and the schools continued to operate.[32]

The NAACP legal staff believed that grade-a-year plans did not satisfy "deliberate speed." School boards argued that it was easier to change social attitudes by starting with young children and following through. The NAACP's lawyers noted, however, that when it was convenient white officials made the reverse argument. In the colleges in Tennessee, for example, Robert Carter pointed out, officials wanted to start at the graduate level and work down: "Obviously, they said, only the most mature person can be expected to adjust to so great a social change as this. Both of these arguments," Carter concluded, "seem dreamed up mainly for the purpose of procrastination." Z. Alexander Looby and Avon Williams, the NAACP's cooperating attorneys in Nashville, filed an appeal from Judge Miller's order.[33]

The court of appeals decision affirming Judge Miller approved grade-a-year plans. The court's opinion opened with a recitation of the events in Nashville, including Kasper's appearance, and quoted Judge Miller's description of the city as "very nearly approach[ing] . . . a reign of terror among those parents who have children in the public schools." It quoted extensively from the school superintendent, who said that the plan proceeded slowly because it was the best way to "adjust" to the new reality of desegregation, and from other witnesses who described why the grade-a-year plan, by keeping students moving upward together through the system, would be successful. One supporter said she hoped that at the end of twelve years the schools in Nashville would not just be desegregated but would be integrated, as the "feeling" came "from the hearts of people" who became accustomed to schools attended by children of both races.[34]

Judge Thomas McAllister, writing the opinion of the court of appeals, cascaded quotation on quotation, from *Brown II* and the Little Rock case, from courts of appeals and district courts, all designed to show that school boards had a wide range of reasonable choices in planning desegregation. Here, Judge McAllister said, the board acted in good faith, developed a plan that almost all teachers supported, and had a persuasive reason for starting in the first grade, that children there have "no sense of discrimination." The Supreme Court denied the NAACP's application for review; Justices Warren, Douglas, and Brennan wanted the Court to consider whether a desegregation plan could give white students an absolute right to transfer out of schools scheduled to be desegregated.[35]

The court of appeals decision in the Nashville case was both a defeat and a victory for the principles of desegregation. It was a defeat because grade-a-year plans, coupled with residential segregation and transfer policies, ensured that relatively little actual integration would occur. It was a defeat as well, because it left the LDF with essentially nothing to litigate—at least where school boards accepted the principle of desegregation and merely tried to minimize its impact. Yet the Nashville decision was also a victory. It demonstrated that resistance to desegregation was futile—although, given that the court of appeals found acceptable very limited amounts of actual desegregation, resistance might seem unnecessary to all but the most adamant segregationists. The Nashville decision was a victory too, because it showed that the only way to minimize desegregation was to accept *Brown*'s fundamental principle, which proponents of massive resistance refused to do and which even Robert Butler, the Little Rock board's attorney, found difficult in his argument to the Supreme Court. The combination of defeat and victory was an appropriate culmination of the effort from 1955 to 1961 to implement *Brown*.

Litigation aimed at changing important institutions like segregated education has its own rhythm. At first, the lawsuits deal with a large number of issues, because a client's interests can be served by winning on any one of them. The breadth of the lawsuits means that facts in each case must be investigated and presented in some detail, because some facts might be relevant to one issue while others are relevant to another. In the litigation preceding *Brown*, for example, Marshall and the NAACP's lawyers investigated the material conditions at universities and public schools, compiling information on the age of buildings, laboratory quality, gymnasium size, and the like, because their challenge to segregation involved attacking both the premises of "separate but equal" and the facts of inequality in particular cases. A similar intense concentration on facts characterized the post-*Brown* litigation, as the lawyers tried to show that desegregation plans were inadequate or that pupil assignment systems were used to continue segregation.

If the litigation effort begins to succeed, an issue of clarifying principle eventually emerges, as the direct attack on *Plessy* did. The lawsuits will begin to focus almost exclusively on that issue, and the factual variations in particular cases become less important. The process culminates in a case where the factual presentation is carefully shaped to keep the courts from ruling in the client's favor on any ground other than the fundamental one of principle. This can occur, though, only if the Supreme Court cooperates by developing a law that does not obstruct the clarifying principle and then by agreeing to hear the case the lawyers have chosen to be the vehicle for their fundamental challenge.

After *Brown,* the ultimate issue of principle was the meaning of *Brown* itself. Was Judge Parker correct in saying that the Constitution required only that governments refrain from relying on race in making decisions? Or did *Brown* actually stand for the broader implications of Justice Brennan's draft in *Cooper v. Aaron,* that the Constitution required some substantial degree of integration? By 1960, one court of appeals was willing to pursue those implications, holding that it was unconstitutional to apply placement criteria "which produce the result of leaving the previous racial situation existing, just as before. Such an absolute result affords no basis to contend that the imposed segregation has been or is being eliminated."[36] The court then suggested that only an "objective plan" to accomplish some degree of actual desegregation would do. Little progress had been made, however, in developing cases to support a more general application of that theory.

The rhythm of strategic litigation affected the legal work after *Brown.* First, it simply took a great deal of time to prepare cases to shape the ultimate issue of principle. Plaintiffs had to put themselves and their children through the difficulties of attempting to desegregate the schools. Applications had to be made and administrative remedies pursued. After all that, the challenges to the various methods of evasion and resistance could begin. Resolving those challenges in ways that clarified the issue of principle again took time. As Robert Carter put it after the court of appeals upheld North Carolina's administrative exhaustion rule, showing that exhaustion would frustrate desegregation "would need an accumulation of such cases to go behind the law," and that would take "perhaps several years."[37]

Second, aside from the Little Rock case, the Supreme Court was working to a rhythm different from the one the lawyers were working to, and the Court did not give Marshall and his colleagues the opportunity to clarify the meaning of *Brown.* Marshall later said that "the major blame was on us, in not pushing . . . and letting it go by default," but he and his staff had done what they could; success would have required a Supreme Court willing to cooperate with their efforts.[38]

Finally, as Marshall put it in 1960, the Supreme Court did not help the NAACP out by intervening to clarify the meaning of *Brown.* The result was litigation preoccupied with the kinds of time-consuming motions and objections to the admission of evidence that Marshall called "a lot of fast play around second base." By 1960, though, the lawyers in New York were managing from a distance, not playing shortstop.[39]

19

"An Act to Make It Difficult . . . to Assert the Constitutional Rights of Negroes" The Attack on the Lawyers, 1955–1961

In October 1956, Marshall spent more than two weeks at a state court hearing in Tyler, Texas, before state judge Otis Dunagan. Marshall attended the hearing because the judge was considering an effort by the state's attorney general John Ben Shepperd to shut down the NAACP and the LDF. On September 22, 1956, Shepperd obtained a preliminary order from Judge Dunagan barring the NAACP from operating in Texas. A week later he dispatched armed Texas rangers to the homes of state NAACP officials. The rangers seized membership lists and took the NAACP officers to local courthouses. They questioned the officials about their involvement in desegregation litigation, and in particular asked whether NAACP lawyers had persuaded them to get involved. Politics more than evidence led the state to claim that the NAACP was a profit-making enterprise that had not paid its taxes and that the LDF violated law and ethics by seeking out people to start lawsuits and providing them financial support. The hearing Marshall attended was designed to extend the ban for several more months. In closing the state's presentation, Shepperd denounced the NAACP for "dup[ing] and deceiv[ing] not only their own members, but the Negro race as well," for "peddl[ing] false hopes at bargain prices . . . for material gain." The "p" in NAACP meant, Shepperd said, "Pick the Place, Prepare the setting, Procure the Plaintiffs, and Push them forward like Pawns."[1]

Marshall, according to one observer, "seemed to be addressing Negroes" as well as the judge. He rambled through the case, saying that he personally was keeping some names of NAACP members off the record because he was afraid that "someone else might do something with them. *Not*," he said expansively, "the Attorney General." Sarcastically, he criticized the state's complaint for describing race relations in Texas as "harmonious" for a hundred years. All the NAACP had done, according to Marshall, was "nothing worse than getting Texas people to obey the law of the land." He defended the NAACP's activities that the state said were profit-making: "Negroes' faith in American life is supported by the belief they can get justice in the courts. Because of records and printing and briefing, that takes money. Whether they have Christmas seals or pins or rallies or fish fries, it's not only aiding the Negro, it's aiding American democracy."[2]

Although Marshall "did a yeoman's job in the defense," according to W. J. Durham, one of the African-American lawyers from Texas involved in the case, Judge Dunagan found against the LDF. Although he did not bar it completely from operating in Texas, he did order its lawyers to refrain from soliciting clients or providing them financial support. In May 1957, the court held another hearing to decide whether to make the order permanent. Marshall believed that the LDF lawyers should simply accept the injunction. The hearings disclosed that U. Simpson Tate, the NAACP's regional counsel for Texas, had agreed to pay Heman Sweatt $3,500 a year during his lawsuit. Tate also had written to Texas branches urging them to locate potential plaintiffs and to encourage students to apply to segregated colleges and use segregated parks. The contract with Sweatt was a clear violation of the ban on supporting clients, and Tate's other actions were arguable violations. Marshall found this evidence "very damaging" and was extremely annoyed that he had been put in the position of seeming to violate ethical norms. As Roy Wilkins described Marshall's reaction, he found that "laymen had planted booby traps all over the lot. Every time the lawyers saw daylight some exhibit would explode in their faces and they would be buried again."[3]

A permanent injunction was entered in May 1957. Marshall, supported by Durham, felt strongly that the lawyers should lick their wounds and accept the injunction. As they saw it, the injunction merely ordered the lawyers to comply with ethical and statutory requirements, which they ought to do anyway. They believed that they would lose an appeal and that an appeal would direct public attention to a record showing that "the officers of the local branches and some of the state officers came dangerously close to committing" illegal acts. Carter Wesley, a prickly personality who competed with Durham for leadership in the Texas NAACP, wanted to appeal. The national board agreed with Wesley, believing that the NAACP could not appear to concede it had violated the law even where the chances of prevailing on appeal were slim. Durham then tried to withdraw from the case. Wilkins explained that the board agreed with Marshall and Durham on the legal questions, but thought it had to appeal "for the sake of our troops," who might be upset at the implication that the NAACP had been "skating close to the edge" of propriety. Marshall saw the board's action as a direct challenge to his authority over legal strategy and objected that public relations concerns should not override his considered legal judgment. After several months of what Robert Carter described as a "tempest in a teapot," but which Marshall took much more seriously, the board reversed itself and went along with Marshall's recommendation to accept the injunction.[4]

The Texas lawsuit was one of many aimed at paralyzing the NAACP and its lawyers. When the lawsuits ended, none of the states' claims had been upheld. The attack on the NAACP was successful even so, because states managed to keep it on the defensive for several years and diverted a substantial part of the lawyers' energy into defending the NAACP. That defense was of course an essential predicate for the other lawsuits the lawyers wanted to bring, but in taking so much time and energy, the defense reduced the opportunity to pursue more valuable litigation.[5]

The Southern legal attack on the NAACP and the LDF took several forms. The challenge that implicated Marshall directly rested on legal ethics. Ethical norms, backed up in many states by long-established criminal laws, barred lawyers from "stirring up litigation" by persuading people who were otherwise satisfied with their condition to begin lawsuits and from providing financial support to their clients. These ethical requirements rested on a variety of policies: that lawsuits were ordinarily not the best way to solve problems, that if people were satisfied with their arrangements no one else should try to disrupt them, that lawyers could use clients to advance their own rather than the clients' interests.

In many situations the ethical norms made a great deal of sense. Unfortunately for the NAACP and the LDF, much of what their lawyers did resembled these classical ethical violations. Marshall, always quite sensitive to the ethical requirements, repeatedly admonished cooperating attorneys and lay people associated with the NAACP to be extremely cautious in their statements and actions. Writing to A. P. Tureaud, Robert Carter noted that "there is an effort to get all lawyers who have been active" in civil rights litigation, and told Tureaud to be "unduly careful" to get "personal retainers," held "under lock and key," from "everyone that you represent in any cases involving the attack on segregation."[6] As the Texas hearings showed, the people with whom Marshall worked were not always as careful as he would have liked.

More troublesome than these classic violations of professional ethics, which were rare, were efforts by Southern legislatures to expand the definitions of the ethical requirements to encompass the ordinary actions of the NAACP's lawyers. Because these efforts could readily be characterized as attempts to "reform" traditional systems of professional ethics, the NAACP's lawyers had to develop a novel constitutional challenge to the new notions of professional ethics.

Although several Southern states, including Georgia, Mississippi, and South Carolina, adopted these statutes, the most extended struggle took place in Virginia. The fight began with a legislative investigation whose stated purpose was to reform Virginia's regulation of lawyers.[7] In 1956, the Virginia legislature enacted a package of statutes dealing with the NAACP's legal activities. The statutes were known throughout the litigation by their designation as chapters in Virginia's code. Chapters 31 and 32 were registration statutes. Chapter 31 said that no one could solicit funds or spend them to support litigation, unless the person or group was a party to litigation or had a "pecuniary right or liability" in the litigation, or unless the person or group had filed a detailed disclosure form with contributors' names. An organization's officers were liable for the group's violations. Chapter 32 required registration of organizations "whose activities are causing or may cause interracial tension and unrest." Groups that advocated racial integration or that promoted "the passage of legislation . . . in behalf of any race or color" had to register and make broad disclosures of contributors and officers. Chapter 33 modified the state's regulation of attorneys to make it a ground for discipline, including disbarment, for a lawyer to solicit legal business by using an agent in connection with lawsuits in which it was not a party and did not have a pecuniary right. The targets here were the NAACP's cooperating attorneys in Virginia, who received clients through referrals from nonlawyers employed by the NAACP and from the national legal staff. Chapter 35, a so-called barratry statute, made it a misdemeanor for one person to pay another person's litigation expenses, unless the person paying the expenses was a relative or had a pecuniary interest in the litigation's outcome. Finally, chapter 36 prohibited the advocacy of suits against Virginia and giving assistance to such suits.

Marshall, Oliver Hill, Spottswood Robinson, and the rest of the NAACP's lawyers immediately challenged all five statutes in federal court. Virginia's attorney general argued that the three-judge court should not decide the constitutional question because the state's courts had not yet interpreted the statutes. Depending on how the statutes were interpreted, the state said, they might be constitutional, and the federal court should not hold a Virginia statute unconstitutional based on what might turn out to be an erroneous interpretation.

The state's argument relied on a doctrine called "abstention." Although it had some earlier roots, the abstention doctrine came into flower in the 1930s and 1940s. Abstention was one of a number of devices, including the three-judge court provision, aimed at making it more difficult for federal courts to hold state statutes unconstitutional, and liberals supporting progressive reforms were among its major proponents. Justice Frankfurter in particular believed that abstention was an essential element in a legal system that appropriately coordinated federal courts and state legislatures; he believed that abstention helped avoid conflicts between courts and legislatures by deferring rulings on constitutional matters until the meaning of state laws was clarified.[8]

Abstention made sense only if state law was unclear; nothing would be gained, and time would be lost, if the federal courts sent a case to the state courts to clarify the meaning of a statute everyone could understand anyway. The three-judge court in the Virginia case found chapter 33, the antisolicitation statute, and chapter 36, the statute barring advocacy of suits against Virginia, vague and ambiguous. Following the procedure in abstention cases, the court said it would maintain the challenges to those chapters in an inactive status, while giving the NAACP time to get the state courts to interpret them. A majority of the court found, in contrast, that the other statutes were absolutely clear, and invalidated them. After stating that the statutes were part of Virginia's program of massive resistance, Judges Morris Soper and Walter Hoffman held that they violated the NAACP's free-speech rights. Chapter 32's ban on opposing racial legislation went far beyond the permissible bounds of lobbying regulation, they said, while its ban on advocating racial integration was not supported by a significantly strong state interest. The clause referring to activities causing racial conflicts was too vague, and the provision dealing with raising money to support litigation burdened the constitutional right of access to the courts. Further, the majority held that the antibarratry statute violated the equal protection clause because it was aimed at putting the NAACP and the LDF out of business in Virginia, and because it unjustifiably singled out the NAACP's litigation involving race for treatment different from other forms of legal aid litigation.[9]

The NAACP and the LDF immediately filed a state court action seeking declarations that chapters 33 and 36 were either inapplicable to their activities or unconstitutional. Virginia's attorney general Albertis Harrison appealed the decision about the other three chapters to the Supreme Court, arguing that the lower court should have abstained and that the statutes were constitutional. After hearing argument, Chief Justice Warren sympathetically said that the statutes clearly were designed to put the NAACP "out of business."[10]

Unlike Warren, a majority, in an opinion by Justice Harlan, found ambiguities in the statutes, and held that the lower court should have abstained. Chapter 35, for example, might actually narrow rather than expand the traditional prohibition on stirring up litigation, by requiring both a traditional activity and an unjustified payment of expenses. More plausibly, Harlan argued that the NAACP might be found to have a "direct interest" in the litigation it supported "because of the relationship of that organization to its members." The advocacy provision of chapter 32 might be limited to incitement of violence, and the provision dealing with influencing legislation "in any manner" might similarly be narrowed.[11]

Harlan concluded his opinion by adopting a suggestion Justice Clark made. The NAACP was concerned that it would have to stop operating unless the state was barred from enforcing the statute. When the lower court sent chapters 33 and 36 to the state courts, it did so, Judge Soper wrote, on the assumption that state authorities would not act under the statutes until the constitutional questions were resolved. Justice Harlan relied on "similar assurances" made to the Supreme Court about the other three chapters. But, to eliminate any possible wiggle room, Justice Harlan also said that the Court "understood" those assurances to include "the intention . . . never to proceed against [the NAACP] . . . with respect to activities engaged in during the full pendency of this litigation." And, in case the state did not get the message, he pointed out that the lower court had "ample authority . . . to protect [the NAACP] while this case goes forward."[12]

Justice Douglas wrote a dissent that Warren and Brennan joined. Mostly it was a general attack on abstention in civil rights cases as "a delaying tactic," but Douglas also relied on the lower court's discussion of massive resistance in saying, "Where state laws make such an assault as these do on our decisions and a State has spoken defiantly against the constitutional rights of the citizens, reasons for showing deference to local institutions vanish." One reason for the majority's action is suggested in a note from Frankfurter to Douglas, in a futile attempt to keep Douglas from "break[ing] ranks." According to Frankfurter, "the Court having originally adopted gradualism, I think we have to recognize the [reality?]." He wrote that "even those who approve our position *mainly* support gradualism," and said that he had "an idea that there is a chance that the Virginia Supreme Court may actually narrow the statute." He admonished Douglas that "differences *of course* must come sometime, but the longer we postpone public acknowledgement of the differences the stronger we are."[13]

Justice Frankfurter's confidence in abstention was vindicated, though only in part. The Richmond trial court did not narrow chapters 31, 32, and 35, the ones before the Supreme Court, but it did hold them unconstitutional. It upheld chapter 33, the antibarratry statute, and chapter 36. The NAACP and the LDF appealed to the state supreme court, which struck down chapter 36 and upheld chapter 33.

At that point, Marshall and Carter began to pursue different paths. For tactical and technical reasons Marshall took the LDF's case back to the district court that had abstained. In its first decision, the district court made strong findings of fact about the LDF's activities and about the motivation behind the antibarratry statute. In contrast, the state supreme court cast the LDF in an unfavorable light. Marshall believed that the LDF's challenge would be stronger if it could rely on the federal court findings. And, although returning to the district court might delay Supreme Court review, the state had been forced to say it would not enforce the antibarratry statute against the NAACP or the LDF until the case was over; from Marshall's point of view, delay did not matter.

For technical reasons, Marshall was not sure that returning to the district court would actually cause any delay. The Supreme Court can hear cases only after a lower court has made a "final" decision, and it was not clear that the Virginia supreme court's decision was final; the case began in the federal district court and perhaps only a decision by that court would be final. Carter, responsible for the NAACP's case, viewed the case differently. Perhaps because he felt the need to satisfy the NAACP's members by ending the case quickly, he appealed to the Supreme Court.[14]

The case was argued twice. After the first argument in November 1961, the Court voted against the NAACP. Justice Black criticized the statute as "one of a group designed to thwart our segregation decision" but thought the case could be resolved on a "narrow ground." Warren suggested that it was arbitrary for the statute to penalize people who tried to enforce constitutional rights while protecting those who tried to enforce pecuniary rights. They were outvoted, though. Justice Frankfurter seemed offended at the suggestion that the statute was "aimed at Negroes." He "can't imagine," he said, "a worse disservice than to continue being guardians of negroes." In discussing the barratry case, Frankfurter said that "colored people are now people of substance . . . [and] now have responsible positions."* Clark also thought that "to strike this down we would have to discriminate in favor of Negroes," and argued that the NAACP's activities "would have been in violation of [Virginia] law" even before chapter 33 was adopted.[15]

Justice Frankfurter drafted an elaborate opinion upholding chapter 33.** Because the Virginia Supreme Court narrowed chapter 33, Frankfurter argued, the legislature's motivation became irrelevant. A long section examined how the ethi-

---

*By 1962, Frankfurter was annoyed at the course of the Court's decisions in NAACP cases, and defensive about his annoyance. In February, he wrote a note to Justice Black saying that his "convictions" on race issues "have certainly not weakened," but contended that "it will not advance the cause of constitutional equality for Negroes for the Court to be taking short cuts, to discriminate as partisans in favor of Negroes or even to appear to do so." In a note to Alexander Bickel, Frankfurter expressed dismay that the executive branch appeared to have become a "mere adjunct of the NAACP." Frankfurter to Black, Feb. 19, 1962, Frankfurter Papers (HLS), Box 169, folder 4; Frankfurter to Bickel, note on *Bailey v. Patterson* [Dec. 18, 1961], *id.*, Box 206, folder 9.

**One of Frankfurter's law clerks made a futile effort to persuade him that the Virginia court's decision was not final, relying on the disagreement between the factual findings of the federal and the state courts to point out that abstention should not lead litigants to lose the "essential" safeguard of "impartial finding of fact." Frankfurter's draft found the decision final because the NAACP had chosen to submit the entire case to the state courts, taking it completely away from the district court. RH to Frankfurter (with Frankfurter's response), Frankfurter Papers (HLS), Box 164, folder 5.

cal and legal prohibitions against barratry and similar activities aimed at "fomenting litigation" developed, from their Greek roots through the English common law to state laws in the United States in the 1950s. The section was full of references to state attempts to suppress ambulance chasing and similar commercial activities. The point of Frankfurter's discussion never became entirely clear in his draft, though it appears to have been to demonstrate that Virginia's reform was within the range of constitutionally permissible efforts to deal with a problem that had bedeviled the bar for centuries.[16]

Frankfurter appears to have believed that he had shown that chapter 33 was basically constitutional, because he turned in the next section to the NAACP's arguments that it had to be exempted from the statute. For Frankfurter, the state did not have to exempt the NAACP simply because its lawyers were "moved not by financial gain but by public interest." He concluded that the NAACP had "fall[en] short of success" in distinguishing its activities from other arguably "public interest" activities by unions and automobile clubs that other states prohibited. Second, Frankfurter rejected the NAACP's argument that it actually had the same interests as its clients. Invoking his concern for gradualism in school desegregation, Frankfurter wrote that "in a given case it is quite possible that a Negro parent distressed by school conditions might choose to wait with his fellows a longer time for good-faith efforts at improvement . . . than permitted by the centrally determined policy" of the NAACP.

A final section briefly disposed of the NAACP's free-speech claims. Frankfurter earlier pointed out that the Virginia court allowed the NAACP to conduct meetings, inform people generally about their constitutional rights, and contribute money to "needy suitors." Chapter 33, as Frankfurter understood it, merely barred the NAACP from conducting litigation on behalf of others, controlling the strategic decisions made along the way. Frankfurter concluded that Virginia "has here sought protection against abuses in the practice of a profession, and it has done so with due regard for constitutionally protected rights."

Justices Douglas and Black circulated draft dissents stressing the place chapter 33 had in Virginia's program of massive resistance. For Douglas, "the fact that the contrivance used is subtle and indirect is not material to the question" of whether chapter 33 was designed to "penalize the N.A.A.C.P. because it promotes desegregation." Warren joined Black's proposed dissent, which began by saying that chapter 33 "could more accurately be labeled 'An Act to make it difficult and dangerous for the [NAACP] and Virginia lawyers to assert the constitutional rights of Virginia Negroes in state and federal courts.'" Black argued that the statute violated the rights of free speech and petition. Because of the legislature's purpose, the statute directly burdened those rights. And, even if Chapter 33 were treated as a serious effort to regulate legal practice, Black argued, it limited marginal abuses at a substantial cost to free expression. He stressed that Virginia had departed from the traditional norms against stirring up litigation, which required, as Virginia did not, that the offender act maliciously or falsely. Unlike Frankfurter, then, Black found no historical justification for chapter 33, which he described as penalizing "an oppressed group for doing nothing more than banding together to bring meritorious lawsuits to force the stronger groups in society to obey the law and respect the rights of the weak." Black then returned to Virginia's purposes in adopting the regulation, which were to "handicap the activities of the Association" not to regulate real abuses of professional authority. Black found unconvincing Frankfurter's attempt to demonstrate that providing legal aid to poor people, which Virginia exempted from its antibarratry provisions, was different from the NAACP's activities; for Black, both types of activity served the public interest in protecting constitutional rights.

Black concluded his opinion with a description of the noble role lawyers had played on behalf of the oppressed from colonial times on. "The job of lawyers under [the] Constitution," he wrote, "is, not to lead revolutions, but to lead their people in taking advantage of the American methods for correcting injustice." Calling courts "sanctuaries of justice," Black wrote that lawyers must be "wholly free to bring their clients into court" so that problems could be resolved "in an atmosphere of peace." He closed by quoting his opinion in *Chambers v. Florida,* which called courts "havens of refuge," and saying that "courts today, I fear, are a little less havens of refuge than they were before this Virginia law was sustained." Only Warren joined Black's dissent, though, and the dissenters decided to let Justice Brennan try his hand.

Before the justices announced their decision, Justice Charles Whittaker, a member of the majority, retired on April 1. With Whittaker's resignation, the Court appeared to be evenly divided in the case, and on April 2 the Court ordered that the case be reargued in the fall. Four days later Justice Frankfurter suffered a severe stroke, and he resigned from the Court in late August. A five-to-four majority against the NAACP had become a four-to-three majority in its favor. The outcome of the case would turn on who President John Kennedy appointed to replace Whittaker and Frankfurter. For Whittaker's seat Kennedy nominated Byron White, then serving as deputy attorney general. White, who had been an outstanding football player and then a law clerk for Chief Justice Fred Vinson, played a prominent role in Kennedy's presidential campaign. Kennedy nominated Arthur Goldberg, a stalwart liberal, to replace Frankfurter. Goldberg had been the principal lawyer for the United Steelworkers of America and helped greatly when the American Federation of Labor and the Congress of Industrial Organizations merged in 1956. He was Kennedy's secretary of labor when he was nominated.*[17]

When the case was argued again in October 1962, Warren continued to maintain that chapter 33 "discriminates against those who organize to protect civil rights." Black called the statute "nothing but [a] legal contraption to put [the] NAACP out of business." Justice Potter Stewart, who voted to affirm the Virginia court after the first argument, now said that he was "incline[d] to reverse" because he thought it wrong that chapter 33 did not treat constitutional rights as it treated pecuniary ones. Brennan wanted to reverse on free-speech grounds. Justice White said that he did not know where he stood; although the state could not "prevent representation" when the case had been solicited by the NAACP, he was troubled

---

* Frankfurter later criticized the changes in constitutional law that resulted from the appointment of "such wholly inexperienced men as Goldberg and White, without familiarity with . . . the jurisprudence of the Court either as practitioners or scholars or judges." Frankfurter to Bickel, March 18, 1963, Frankfurter Papers (HLS), Box 183, folder 9.

by the degree to which the NAACP actually controlled the litigation, apparently on occasion over the objection of the nominal client. Justice Goldberg found the NAACP's equal protection argument substantial. Only Justices Clark and Harlan firmly reiterated their positions from the preceding term. Harlan called the statute "plainly constitutional," and agreed with Clark that because "financing this activity violates traditional standards," there was "no reason why [the] NAACP is immune from [the] regular rules." Picking up one of Frankfurter's themes, Harlan also said that *Brown* "will never work out if it is left in the federal domain—the states have to do it."[18]

Though they had not settled on a reason, a clear majority of the justices was now prepared to invalidate chapter 33. Warren, believing Brennan best suited to working out a position the majority could agree on, assigned the opinion to him. Before Brennan could get a draft completed, Justice Stewart reconsidered his position and returned to his earlier view that chapter 33 was constitutional. Brennan's draft relied solely on the First Amendment, finding the NAACP's activities in supporting litigation "modes of expression and association." The opinion said that Virginia's attempt to regulate these activities cut too broadly into constitutional rights, an approach that troubled Justice Black because he thought it likely to encourage Virginia to try again. Justice Brennan modified his opinion to make it clear that Virginia could do little to regulate activities like the NAACP's, and Black was satisfied. When Brennan learned that Justice Harlan's proposed dissent would suggest that the Court was creating special rules for the NAACP, Justice Brennan added "a final observation" to his opinion, saying that the fact that the NAACP "happens to be engaged in activities" supporting desegregation "is constitutionally irrelevant" to the First Amendment analysis. "The Constitution protects expression and association without regard to the race, creed, or political or religious affiliation of the members of the group which invokes its shield, or to the truth, popularity, or social utility of the ideas and beliefs which are offered."[19]

In its final version, Brennan's opinion described the NAACP's litigation as "a form of political expression" aimed at achieving equality. "Groups which find themselves unable to achieve their objectives through the ballot frequently turn to the courts." Litigation, Brennan acknowledged, was not identical to classical forms of expression, but the concept of expression had already been expanded to "protect certain forms of orderly group activity." Then the opinion examined Virginia's regulation of the NAACP's litigation considered as political activity protected by the First Amendment. It took the state court to have interpreted chapter 33 to bar "any arrangement by which prospective litigants are advised to seek the assistance of particular attorneys," whether or not the lawyers were under the NAACP's control; Brennan called any "narrower reading" implausible.[20]

As so interpreted, the statute posed "the gravest danger of smothering all discussion looking to the eventual institution of litigation on behalf of the rights of an unpopular minority." It would "prohibit[ ] every cooperative activity that would make advocacy of litigation meaningful." This was, of course, a construction of chapter 33 dramatically different from the one Frankfurter offered, but with that construction the majority's approach was well supported. As Brennan put it, "a vague and broad statute lends itself to selective enforcement against unpopular causes," and included a two-page footnote listing cases that the NAACP had supported to show that "the militant Negro civil rights movement has engendered the intense resentment and opposition of the politically dominant white community of Virginia." Brennan's opinion then rejected Virginia's claim that its regulation was justified as part of its effort to deal with professional conduct. As had Black, Brennan emphasized that chapter 33 modified the common law ban on barratry by eliminating its requirement of malicious intent, and it did not resemble the typical modern modification, which centered on using litigation for private gain. The NAACP, in contrast, "employs constitutionally privileged means of expression to secure constitutionally guaranteed civil rights." In this context there had been no showing of "professionally reprehensible conflicts of interest."[21]

Although the stated doctrine in Brennan's opinion concerned only the First Amendment, in mentioning the hostility to the NAACP in Virginia to illustrate why an overbroad prohibition like chapter 33 was unconstitutional, Brennan provided Harlan with the justification for beginning his dissenting opinion with the observation that so bothered Brennan. The "same basic constitutional standards" applied, Harlan wrote, "whether or not racial problems are involved. No worse setback could befall the great principles established by *Brown* than to give fair-minded persons reason to think otherwise." Harlan's strategy was to minimize chapter 33's impact. As Harlan understood the facts, the NAACP and not the clients determined, "to a considerable extent," the strategic decisions lawyers should make in consultation with clients. In addition, he accepted the state court's findings that the NAACP "does a great deal more than to advocate litigation and to wait for prospective litigants to come forward." The NAACP looked for particular types of plaintiffs, Harlan said, and staff lawyers brought blank forms to meetings to get signatures from prospective clients. Some plaintiffs testified that they never had "personal dealings" with the lawyers in their cases.[22]

By accepting these facts, Harlan presented the NAACP as an organization that had indeed solicited legal business and stirred up litigation. Then Harlan asked whether chapter 33 nonetheless violated the Constitution. He agreed that "litigation is a form of conduct that may be associated with political expression," but invoked his long-standing approach to free-speech questions to say that the state's interest in regulation had to be weighed against the impact on free expression. For Harlan, states had more authority to regulate "speech *plus*" than to regulate pure speech, so the issue for him was whether chapter 33 was justified by a sufficiently important state interest. The interest, of course, was regulating professional ethics, and Harlan disagreed with Brennan's assertion that the ethical concerns were weaker in cases involving public-interest lawyers. Here he adapted several pages from Frankfurter's draft opinion, though he stated his conclusion more crisply. For Harlan, the development of professional ethics reflected a legislative concern "to prevent any interference with the uniquely personal relationship between lawyer and client and to maintain untrammelled by outside influences the responsibility which the lawyer owes to the courts he serves." Yet, Harlan pointed out, a staff lawyer who represented individual litigants necessarily had a dual loyalty, "to his employer and to his client," which might prevent "full compliance" with professional ethics. Harlan also adopted wholesale Frankfurter's discussion of the possibility that an individual litigant's goals might be sacrificed to the NAACP's wider purposes.

As Harlan saw it, the Virginia court interpreted chapter 33 to prohibit "only the solicitation of business for attorneys" controlled by the NAACP, and did not bar the NAACP from advocating litigation or, more important, from directing potential plaintiffs to lawyers not controlled by the NAACP. This narrow ban was, in Harlan's view, clearly justified by the state's interest in regulating lawyers. It was crucial to Harlan's analysis that the ban was narrow rather than broad, and the remainder of his dissent was devoted to explaining that chapter 33 could be made to seem overly broad "only at the price of a strained reading" of the Virginia supreme court decision.[23]

Harlan's dissent relied on the Virginia state court's description of the facts and explicitly rejected the findings made by the three-judge federal court. That might have vindicated Marshall's misgivings about appealing to the Supreme Court had the chance factors of Whittaker's resignation and Frankfurter's stroke not intervened. As it was, the majority and the dissenters were plainly talking past each other. As a matter of constitutional doctrine, the only part of Harlan's analysis with which the majority disagreed was his treatment of the breadth of chapter 33, and, although the point could fairly be argued, Justice Brennan's interpretation of the Virginia supreme court's opinion was not unreasonable. Harlan said that Brennan's interpretation "savors almost of disrespect" for the Virginia court, but in view of the relation between chapter 33 and the program of massive resistance, the attempt that Harlan made to divorce chapter 33 from its origins has an air of unreality; at least it was not unreasonable for the majority to read the state court's opinion with an implicit anxiety about its good faith.

In the barratry case, the Court endorsed the new form of public-interest law practice that Houston, Marshall, and their colleagues had created. They always attempted to observe the standard proprieties of the profession, and they almost always succeeded. But operating a public interest law practice meant that occasionally subordinates would be less attentive to traditional standards. Even more, the demands of a public-interest practice—the contact with people who were not yet clients but might become plaintiffs, the speeches publicizing the organization's willingness to support lawsuits—tested the limits of traditional standards. The barratry case offered the Court and the profession two models of "reform": a transformation of traditional standards that would have restricted the development of public-interest practice, and a transformation that promoted it. The Court chose to promote public-interest practice, giving a stamp of constitutional approval to the kind of lawyering that the Legal Defense Fund developed.

20

"A Mortal Blow from Which They Shall Never Recover"
The Attack on the NAACP, 1955–1961

On June 1, 1956, Alabama's attorney general John Patterson appeared before state judge Walter Jones in Montgomery. Saying that the NAACP violated state law by "doing business" in the state without registering, Patterson asked for an order stopping the NAACP's activities. The business, Patterson said, included supporting Autherine Lucy's attempt to enter the University of Alabama and financing the Montgomery bus boycott, which was then more than six months old. Without giving the NAACP a chance to reply, Judge Jones, an ardent segregationist who said in a subsequent election campaign, "I intend to deal the NAACP . . . a mortal blow from which they shall never recover," immediately issued an order—called a temporary restraining order—barring the NAACP from soliciting memberships or contributions or collecting dues. The NAACP was willing to register; a year later in North Carolina it paid a $500 fine for failing to register and then filed registration papers. Judge Jones, though, said that the NAACP could not even try to register. He and attorney general Patterson wanted something else—NAACP membership lists.[1]

On July 2, the NAACP asked Judge Jones to dissolve his order; he scheduled a hearing for July 17. But on July 5, the state asked the judge to direct the NAACP to produce its records, including membership lists. Four days later, Judge Jones told the NAACP to turn over its membership lists, correspondence files, and financial records. He delayed the already scheduled hearing for a week and then, when the NAACP indicated its willingness to turn over everything but the membership lists and correspondence, held it in contempt of court, fined it $10,000—later increased to $100,000—and refused to dissolve the injunction. This was the opening phase of litigation that kept the NAACP from operating in Alabama from 1956 to 1964. And, notably, Alabama shut down the NAACP despite repeated legal defeats.[2]

Attorneys general in Arkansas and Louisiana, as well as Alabama, claimed that the NAACP was operating a business and tried to force it to register as a business corporation and to pay taxes. They used registration and tax collection suits to try to extract lists of NAACP members. More directly, states relied on statutes aimed at the Ku Klux Klan and used investigative techniques developed to expose the Communist party to get the names of NAACP members. In 1928, early in the Supreme Court's development of free-speech law, the Court held in *Bryant v. Zimmerman* that New York could force the Ku Klux Klan to file membership lists. Without focusing specifically on free speech or association, the Court said that the state's interest in controlling the violent Klan justified the disclosure requirement. Through the 1950s, the Court also allowed inquiries into Communist party membership and activities, though the course of its decisions was quite convoluted. *Bryant* and the Communist cases gave Southern states some legal ground for the attack they mounted on the NAACP.[3]

The NAACP responded by raising important constitutional issues. The constitutional arguments, though, were both novel and difficult, precisely because the attacks were framed in traditional terms. Everyone agreed, for example, that states could require businesses to register and pay taxes, and as a general matter states could ask businesses to disclose information so they could decide how much taxes were due. *Bryant* upheld a statute forcing Klan members to identify themselves, and Southern states argued that its principle applied to their efforts to investigate the NAACP. The interaction between the NAACP's lawyers and the Supreme Court produced major innovations in free-expression law. Yet the outcome was another ambiguous success: the NAACP won all the major battles, even more so than in the school desegregation setting, and yet was severely impaired for many years because of the attacks.

Alabama's attack was the South's most successful. The NAACP believed that its members would lose jobs and be attacked physically if membership were disclosed, and that the Constitution's protection of free speech allowed it to keep the names of its members confidential under those circumstances. After asking Judge Jones to reconsider his ruling, the NAACP asked the state supreme court to suspend the order to produce names until that court could consider the NAACP's constitutional claims. The lawyers argued the motion on July 31, and the state supreme court denied the motion that day. It said it would not intervene until the NAACP followed "the established rule" for obtaining review of contempt judgments, by filing a writ of certiorari. A week later the NAACP did file that writ. On August 13 the state supreme court ruled against the NAACP, saying that the allegations in its application were "insufficient." The NAACP then filed a more detailed application. On December 6, the Alabama supreme court, demonstrating characteristic ingenuity, again ruled against the NAACP. This time it said that the way to challenge the contempt order was through a writ of mandamus, not certiorari. Judge Jones's injunction stayed in force, barring the NAACP from operating, even though no court held a hearing on whether in fact the NAACP had operated without registering or had done anything illegal, and even though the state supreme court had not ruled on the NAACP's constitutional challenge to the disclosure order.

Marshall was willing to turn the membership lists over, concerned "that the NAACP might appear to be advocating a refusal to comply with the law." Carter, who had been appointed general counsel to the NAACP itself, disagreed. As one lawyer familiar with the issue put it, Carter was "younger and less inclined to accommodate himself" to the precedents; in addition, of course, Carter's client was now the NAACP, while Marshall's clients were individuals involved in desegregation litigation. Marshall polled the NAACP's legal committee, and found almost unanimous support for his position; Wilkins polled the NAACP board of directors, and found almost unanimous support for Carter's position. Wilkins went along with his board, and Marshall "washed his hands of the matter."[4]

Carter asked the Supreme Court to review the state supreme court decision. The first hurdle was to get the Court to consider the constitutional claim. Ordinarily, the Supreme Court will not consider claims state courts refuse to decide because the litigant failed to follow state procedural rules. Ordinarily, too, the Alabama court's statement that mandamus was the only way to challenge the contempt order would be enough to keep the Supreme Court out of the case. Here, though, the state supreme court seemed to invite the NAACP to use the writ of certiorari, then apparently rejected the claims as "insufficient," and only at the end came up with the procedural reason for refusing to consider the claim. Carter had no difficulty persuading the Supreme Court to take the case and decide the constitutional questions.

Most of Robert Carter's oral argument laid out the complex procedural history of the case. The questions from the justices focused in addition on the fact that the NAACP never had a chance to present its case against Judge Jones's order. Carter's presentation of the free-expression argument went largely unquestioned. The NAACP's brief argued for a broad constitutional right to anonymity. Carter's oral argument took a narrower path. He said disclosing the names would lead to retaliation, and that, although under some circumstances states could regulate organizations, Alabama had made no plausible argument to show why it needed the names of NAACP members to enforce its corporate registration laws. Carter also argued that *Bryant v. Zimmerman,* the Klan case, involved a subversive organization unlike the NAACP. When Alabama's lawyer got up to argue, the justices expressed skepticism about the need for the members' names, and about the NAACP's inability simply to register once Judge Jones's order had been entered.

When they met to discuss the case the justices had no question about the outcome. Justice Black dismissed the state's procedural argument, saying the state court had issued a "plain invitation to bring the cases up this way." Indeed, the justices considered reversing the Alabama court in an unsigned opinion. They thought of the case as a desegregation case, and they used unsigned opinions in all the post-*Brown* desegregation cases. The task of drafting the opinion was given to Justice John Marshall Harlan, who concluded that a full opinion was necessary. Harlan wrote, "the considerations here are quite different," though he understood that the case had to be handled with the "utmost dispassion." Describing his approach as "orthodox" and "narrow," his draft said that Alabama's attempt to obtain the names violated the Constitution. But, new to the Court, Harlan stepped into a hornet's nest in his description of why it violated the Constitution. The draft relied primarily on the Fourteenth Amendment's due process clause, which, Harlan said, was in this context essentially equivalent to the First Amendment's free speech clause. For years Justices Black and Douglas had been arguing with Justice

Frankfurter over the relation between due process and the Bill of Rights. Black and Douglas argued strenuously that the Fourteenth Amendment made all the guarantees of the Bill of Rights applicable to the states; Frankfurter contended just as strenuously that the states were bound to provide only "due process," which meant for Frankfurter that they sometimes could provide less protection than the free-speech clause provided and sometimes had to provide more.[5]

Douglas immediately responded to Harlan that the draft "unloaded a few very difficult problems" on him. He thought the draft suggested that free-speech protections guaranteed against the states were "watered down by some concept of due process." And, for Douglas, if the only standard were due process, "we are in very deep water in this case," because, he thought, the state could make a "rational judgment for believing that an organization like the NAACP was a source of a lot of trouble, friction, and unrest." But, he said, "once we admit the existence of that kind of test in these racial problems, then I think we are hopelessly lost." Douglas wanted the opinion to be more "absolute" in relying on the First Amendment. The next day Harlan got hit from the other side, by Justice Frankfurter. Frankfurter was "not happy" with the extensive treatment Harlan had given the case. That, he wrote, "blows up the case to undeserved proportions" and gave it "the polemic, passionate appearance which you so rightly are concerned with avoiding." He suggested that the opinion should be redrafted to make the case turn on a general liberty that "includes my right to belong to any organization I please"; such an opinion would avoid "elaborate argumentation that somehow or other what Alabama has done affects free speech." Then Justice Black weighed in, saying that he could not go along with an opinion that did not mention the First Amendment.[6]

Harlan managed to blend Frankfurter's liberty approach with Black and Douglas's free-speech approach by formulating the right as a right of association related to free expression. In doing so, he still had to deal with the interests Alabama asserted, and at a late point proposed to insert a sentence saying that "we cannot blink [at] the fact that strong local sentiment exists" against the NAACP, to show why the interests of the members outweighed the state's interest. Frankfurter, displaying his sensitivity to the South, objected, saying that the sentence "does not add a jot or tittle to the legal argument . . . and gratuitously stirs feelings giving rights to irrelevant controversy." Harlan withdrew the sentence, but by this time the focus on balancing interests had begun to disturb Justice Clark. Clark came to believe that the state's presentation was entirely inadequate, and proposed to send the case back so that the state courts could explain why the state needed NAACP members' names in a registration proceeding. Robert Gorman, one of Clark's law clerks, developed an extensive memorandum arguing that Harlan's opinion was correct, and pointing out that there were "strong policy reasons" against dissents in "these segregation-aftermath cases." Dissents would "create false hopes" and would "multiply the loss of time, money, effort, feelings, and perhaps even life that inevitably will attach to integration in the next half-century." Frankfurter wrote Clark along similar lines, saying that the technical point on which Clark proposed to dissent was not "a good enough starting point for a break in the unanimity of the Court in what is, after all, part of the whole Segregation controversy." For Frankfurter, "the sky is none too bright anyway," and a dissent "would be blown up out of all proportion." On June 30, 1958, the day the decision was announced, Clark withdrew his dissent.[7]

Half of Justice Harlan's opinion for the Court dealt with the procedures in the case, concluding that the NAACP had done what earlier Alabama cases said it should do. The opinion then held that the association could protect its members' names against disclosure even though it was asserting *their* rights, not its own. "To require that [the right of anonymity] be claimed by the members themselves would result in nullification of the right at the very moment of its assertion," Harlan wrote. Then he turned to the free-speech question. "Effective advocacy," he wrote, "is undeniably enhanced by group association." He combined the approaches urged on him, saying that "freedom to engage in association . . . is an inseparable aspect of the 'liberty' assured by the Due Process Clause . . . which embraces freedom of speech." Forcing groups to disclose members' names, he continued, might "constitute as effective a restraint" as other more direct regulations. Because disclosure of NAACP members' names had led to "economic reprisal" and "other manifestations of public hostility," the lower court's order threatened a "substantial restraint" on freedom of association. Finally, Harlan wrote, the state's interest in getting the names was not strong enough. The NAACP was willing to provide enough information about its operations for the state to determine whether it was "doing business" in Alabama, the purpose of the underlying proceeding. Harlan wrote, "we are unable to perceive that disclosure of the names . . . has a substantial bearing" on that question. The Klan case was different, he concluded, because there the state wanted to control violence.[8]

Following its usual course, the Court sent the case back to the Alabama courts, expecting them to proceed with the trial on whether the NAACP should be allowed to register. Instead, the Alabama supreme court defied the order. The NAACP tried to get the state supreme court to send the case back to the Montgomery court in November and December 1958. In February 1959, the court "again affirmed" the contempt decision. It said the Supreme Court had been mistaken in believing that the NAACP had offered to provide everything other than the membership lists and that it was therefore proper to hold the NAACP in contempt. The NAACP again took the case to the Supreme Court, which reversed in an unsigned Harlan opinion. The opinion said that at every earlier point the state's officials stated that, as far as they were concerned, the only issue was whether membership lists had to be produced. The claim that the NAACP had not produced other material, the opinion said, "comes too late." The state supreme court was therefore "foreclosed from re-examining the grounds of our disposition." Once again the Supreme Court sent the case back, again anticipating a trial.[9]

The Supreme Court's decision became legally effective on October 12, 1959, when it denied the state's petition for rehearing. At that point the NAACP had been closed down in Alabama for more than three years, and there had as yet been no inquiry into the underlying case the state had begun. The NAACP tried to get the case sent back to Montgomery; the Alabama supreme court's clerk told the lawyers that "this case will receive attention as soon as practicable." When nothing happened by June 1960, Carter and Arthur Shores began a federal court action to bar the state from enforcing the "temporary" injunction against the NAACP. In

August, federal District Judge Frank Johnson refused the NAACP's request, saying that he wanted to see what the state courts did. The state's delaying tactics thus continued to be effective. The NAACP appealed to the federal court of appeals, claiming that Judge Johnson in effect told them to use state court procedures that were "not merely inadequate [but were] nonexistent." Displaying the generosity in the face of obvious evasion that the Supreme Court itself showed in Florida's *Hawkins* case, a majority of the court of appeals agreed with Judge Johnson, saying that the federal courts "should refrain from determining constitutional questions . . . until the state courts have been afforded a reasonable opportunity to pass upon them."[10]

When the NAACP took the case to the Supreme Court for the third time, Chief Justice Warren observed that it "looks like the state courts are playing fast and loose with the mandate of this court." Justice Harlan called Alabama's behavior "outrageous," and drafted an opinion reversing the court of appeals. Harlan sent around a seven-page opinion saying that Judge Johnson should immediately determine whether the state courts were delaying to prevent a hearing on the underlying constitutional question. Justice Clark objected. In his view, the NAACP's federal claim was not that there was unconstitutional delay but that the "temporary" injunction was unconstitutional; Harlan's proposal, then, did not deal with the case the NAACP presented. "Other litigants," Clark wrote, "are held to the relief sought without benefit of such *sua sponte* action." But, he continued, giving the NAACP the permit it actually wanted would interfere directly with the state court lawsuit. For Clark, Harlan's draft would "result in greater confusion and interminable litigation." He called it "a crude exhibition of power that will prove useless to the NAACP, improper for this Court and harmful to the administration of justice." As far as he could tell, the only result of the case would be "two trials, one federal, one state." "Why do this," he continued, "unless it be to rebuff the State." Clark was willing to require Alabama to act promptly, but not to direct the federal court to go ahead. Justice Harlan responded by scaling down the proposed opinion. It ended up as a single paragraph. Judge Johnson, the Supreme Court said, should hold a trial "unless within a reasonable time, no later than January 2, 1962, the State of Alabama shall have accorded to [the NAACP] an opportunity to be heard on its motion to dissolve" the 1956 injunction.[11]

The state court in Montgomery finally got around to the case in December 1961 and entered a final judgment against the NAACP on December 29, four days before Judge Johnson would have begun the federal hearing. At last, more than five years after it had been forced to stop operating in Alabama, the NAACP thought it had a chance to appeal. The Alabama supreme court, though, continued to play games. It did not decide the NAACP's appeal for another year and then, amazingly, refused to consider the merits. Instead, it said that the NAACP had again failed to comply with its procedural rules. Typically, the document filed in an appeal includes specific "assignments of error." The NAACP's appeal listed twenty-three errors, separately numbered. Its brief supporting the appeal had five sections of "Argument" referring to the assignments of error. The Alabama supreme court found that this violated the court's rules, because each section of "argument" referred to more than one assignment of error and at least one assignment in each section was without merit. The court said that, under its rules, if one assignment in a section lacked merit, it would not consider any others in that section.[12]

The NAACP took the case to the Supreme Court for the fourth time, and by now the justices were fed up. Justice Harlan's opinion called the state court's procedural ruling "wholly unacceptable." Perhaps anticipating that the Court would reject the procedural ruling, Alabama's attorney general asked the Court to send the case back for a decision on the merits. Harlan responded, "while this might be well enough in other circumstances, in view of what has gone before," the Court would reach the merits. At last the NAACP got someone to consider the constitutional questions. Justice Harlan went through the state's eleven allegations against the NAACP. The state said the NAACP could be barred from operating because it had not registered; Harlan responded that the remedy was to register the NAACP, which it had always been willing to do. The state said the NAACP assisted Autherine Lucy; Harlan responded that the Constitution barred the state from "inhibit[ing]" that support. The state said the NAACP supported the "illegal" Montgomery bus boycott; Harlan responded that even if the boycott was illegal—a "doubtful assumption"—permanently barring the NAACP from operating was a clearly excessive reaction. Harlan disposed of the other charges in a single paragraph, finding either that the charges dealt with constitutionally protected activity or that the injunction was an excessive response to whatever wrongs the NAACP might have done or—with respect to the charge that the NAACP conspired to keep the Alabama football team from playing in the Liberty Bowl in Philadelphia—that "by no stretch can it be considered germane."[13]

The NAACP asked, "in view of the history of this case," that the Supreme Court itself allow the NAACP to operate in Alabama, and Justice Brennan urged Harlan to do so. In the end, though, Justice Harlan's opinion, while acknowledging that the Court had the power to enter an order, simply directed the Alabama supreme court to act promptly to vacate the injunction against the NAACP. The opinion concluded, "Should we unhappily be mistaken in our belief that the Supreme Court of Alabama will promptly implement this disposition, leave is given the Association to apply to this Court for further appropriate relief."[14] It was June 1964, nearly eight years after the "temporary" injunction went into effect. The NAACP could operate in Alabama.

The attack on the NAACP caused serious operating difficulties even where the organization remained at work. In September 1956, the NAACP board convened a meeting to deal with the "new situation in [the] South." The committee agreed that branch leaders should be told that they could accept anonymous donations and that they should tell people the NAACP "may be compelled at some future time to disclose" the names of its members. Marshall and the NAACP's membership officers drafted a statement for membership receipts: "Although we will not voluntarily divulge our membership lists, it is possible that in some valid proceedings we might be required by law to produce our membership lists in some states."[15]

The message did not always get through clearly. In late 1955 Louisiana segregationists developed a plan to attack the NAACP by seizing the organization's files and indicting it for failing to disclose members' names. The plan was not carried out, but the state began proceedings under its anti-Klan law to bar the NAACP from doing business in the state and to keep its Louisiana branches from meeting. The responses by the lawyers and by the members moved in different directions. The legal staff invoked a federal statute allowing it to transfer the proceedings to federal court, claiming that the state statute was unconstitutional. The federal statute says explicitly that state courts are not to proceed until the federal courts let them, but the state courts nonetheless entered an injunction against the NAACP.[16]

At that point Daniel Ellis Byrd and Clarence Laws, the staff members who coordinated national and Louisiana branch activities, tried to work around the injunction. They agreed they had to suspend operations by removing the NAACP name from their office's building directory and by transferring the telephone from the organization to Laws personally. Further, Carter told them that the national organization could not employ anyone in Louisiana. However, Byrd, Laws, and anyone from the NAACP could make speeches in Louisiana without violating the ban on "doing business" there, and individuals could still maintain membership. The NAACP could not "meet," but its members could attend meetings organized by other groups, and Laws thought it would be easy to set up new organizations to replace NAACP branches.[17]

Meanwhile the lawyers appealed the injunctions to the state supreme court, arguing that as long as the federal action was proceeding, the state courts could do nothing. In November the state supreme court agreed. However, in a move with some technical justification but that caused additional confusion, it refused to direct the lower court to lift the injunctions. Within two weeks, the NAACP closed down again, this time facing threats of prosecution unless it disclosed its membership lists by December 31, 1956. Carter told Laws, A. P. Tureaud, and Arthur Chapital, the NAACP's cooperating lawyers in New Orleans, that the national office had no policy regarding disclosure of membership lists by branches that were willing to do so. He stressed that "the decision as to whether the membership list must be filed has to be made by the members and not for them."[18]

Chapital was something of a loose cannon, though. Despite Carter's phone calls, Chapital sent the attorney general a membership list for the New Orleans branch, which Carter said was "likely to cause a great deal of personal anguish to many people and give to the N.A.A.C.P. a blackeye." Carter said that "the one factor that the N.A.A.C.P. has held up to its membership . . . during this period of pressure and turmoil was that all of us would stick together to the bitter end to prevent any one of us being harmed by virtue of his being a part of our cause," and chastised Chapital for endangering "this united front." Chapital also wrote a letter of Chief Justice Warren, which Marshall called "a most serious breach of good taste, to say the least." Marshall told Chapital that the Supreme Court "is never to be subjected to letter-writing which could by any stretch of the imagination be interpreted as attempting to influence the judgment of the Court."[19]

Chapital, it turned out, was in tune with the desires of the New Orleans branch members, and by March 1957, several NAACP branches in Louisiana's larger cities were operating after filing membership lists. Statewide membership, though, dropped from more than 12,000 to only 1,700. The NAACP gradually regrouped, reaching a membership of 4,000 by October 1959, when it faced another injunction against operating, this time because it had failed to file affidavits denying that its officers were members of subversive organizations and because some membership lists had not been filed. This injunction came as the fight to desegregate the New Orleans schools was heating up, and it interfered with the NAACP's ability to meet and plan. In February 1960, the three-judge court dealing with New Orleans desegregation held the membership and antisubversive statutes unconstitutional. The state appealed to the Supreme Court.[20]

At first the justices planned to affirm the lower court without an opinion. Warren asked Justice Potter Stewart to look into the case, and Stewart tried to draft a short opinion. He became concerned, however, that Louisiana's case was different from Alabama's and related cases the Court had decided. There the states had been trying to enforce their business registration or tax statutes, and the Court said the names had no bearing. Louisiana, though, purported to be protecting against subversion. Stewart suggested that the Court could still affirm because Louisiana had not shown any reason to believe the NAACP a threat. Instead, the Court ordered argument. After argument, Warren expressed the justices' unanimous view that the antisubversive statute was unconstitutional because "officers can't know [whether] other officers are associated with" subversive organizations, and Justice Harlan reiterated Stewart's point that the state "has shown no need to get anything from [the] NAACP." Justice Douglas wrote a short opinion affirming the lower court, emphasizing that the case came to it at "a preliminary stage." With the facts underlying the case not completely determined, he said, it was proper for the lower court to bar enforcement of statutes whose effect might be "to stifle, penalize, or curb the exercise of First Amendment rights."[21]

During 1957–58, the first year of the Little Rock school crisis, Arkansas attorney general Bruce Bennett became concerned that Governor Faubus was reaping all the political benefits of opposing desegregation. Bennett decided to join the parade by attacking the NAACP. After copying Alabama's tactic of seeking NAACP membership lists in a business registration proceeding, he quickly developed another tactic with different political advantages. In the registration action, Bennett demanded the names of NAACP contributors, but he also asked for a list of state branches. Daisy Bates, as president of the state conference of branches, refused to give the donor list, as Bennett expected, but did list the branches. That list was the heart of what Bennett called his "Southern Plan for Peace." That plan included the unrealistic proposal that Congress withdraw what Bennett called the NAACP's "tax deduction privileges," and a more realistic suggestion that local police use vagrancy laws to arrest "those who come into their community under suspicious circumstances and who appear to be attempting to divide our people."[22]

The most realistic suggestion was that city councils adopt what came to be called "Bennett ordinances" as amendments to city licensing statutes. Businesses, but not charities, usually had to pay modest city taxes to do business. "Bennett ordinances" required all organizations operating to disclose their purposes and a list of members and contributors, supposedly so that city officials could determine whether the organization had to pay the license fee. Bennett decided that he could make political points throughout the state by using the NAACP branch list, and wrote the mayors of every city in which the NAACP had a branch urging them to adopt a "grass-roots" strategy to stop desegregation lawsuits by enacting his ordinances.[23]

Bennett's registration action against the NAACP got nowhere. The state trial judge ordered the NAACP to submit a list of officers only, which Mrs. Bates was willing to do, and to pay the required $350 fee. The state NAACP failed to pay the fee by mistake, and its registration was temporarily suspended, but on correcting the error the NAACP continued to operate. The Little Rock city council was initially more successful. It adopted a Bennett ordinance and on October 15, 1957, the city's mayor wrote Mrs. Bates asking for a membership list; a similar demand was made by the mayor of North Little Rock on Mrs. Birdie Williams, president of the branch there. The cities then filed criminal actions against Bates and Williams for violating the ordinances.[24]

In public statements Mrs. Williams said that people were "afraid to join the NAACP" and that the ordinance would "kill the NAACP" in North Little Rock, and at her trial she testified that she had received threatening telephone calls. Mrs. Bates testified that she lost more than one hundred members "because when I went back for renewals they said, 'Well, we will wait and see what happens in the Bennett Ordinance.'" Inside the organization, the view was more sanguine. Gloster Current of the national staff suggested that Bates "caution" Mrs. Williams, because her public statements "will not serve any public good." The NAACP's national staff officer for Arkansas reported that the lawsuits had "favorably affected" the national NAACP's membership efforts. The ordinances, he said, "have not caused any concern among the members," either because of "increased determination" or "confidence in the legal department that our individual rights will be protected in the courts."[25]

That confidence was vindicated when the case went to the Supreme Court in late 1959 after the Arkansas supreme court, with two justices dissenting, upheld the convictions of Mrs. Bates and Mrs. Williams. Carter argued that the decision in the Alabama case meant that Bennett ordinances were unconstitutional, and the Supreme Court agreed. Warren did not think the "names are essential to accomplishing" the ordinance's purposes, and the Court followed that line of reasoning. Justice Potter Stewart wrote the Court's opinion, saying that "freedom of association for the purpose of advancing ideas and airing grievances" was protected "not only against heavy-handed frontal attack, but also from being stifled by more subtle government interference." Evidence showed that disclosure of NAACP members' names had a "repressive effect." According to Stewart, the question then was whether the cities had a "cogent" interest in obtaining the membership lists. He acknowledged that the interest in collecting taxes was "fundamental," but could not find a "relevant correlation" between the power to collect taxes and the disclosure of names; at most the cities needed to know the NAACP's purposes and activities, which it already had. According to Stewart, without a "controlling justification" for disclosure, the convictions for withholding the membership lists "cannot stand."[26]

A week after the Court's decision, Carter wrote to the NAACP's branches in the South, advising them to "tell everybody . . . that they can now join . . . without fear of public exposure." The Alabama and Bennett ordinance decisions removed the threat of general disclosure of membership, but more focused threats remained. Teachers seemed particularly vulnerable. The "teacher security" program the NAACP developed during the *Brown* litigation worked to protect teachers during desegregation itself; in fact, relatively few teachers lost their jobs because of desegregation, in part because so little desegregation occurred. By the end of 1956, fewer than five hundred teachers had been fired, most in the border states, and nearly all had obtained new teaching positions rather quickly. But if teachers were not put at risk by desegregation itself, they were put at risk by their NAACP membership.[27]

In 1956, South Carolina barred NAACP members from government jobs. Private employers frequently dismissed NAACP members after *Brown,* banks denied credit to members, and landlords evicted them, but South Carolina's statute was a blatant attempt to use public power to coerce the organization's members. The NAACP immediately went to federal court. Over the dissent of Judge Parker, who believed the statute a gross violation of the First Amendment, a majority said it should abstain to give the state courts a chance to interpret the statute. The NAACP took the case to the Supreme Court, but on the day the appeal was filed the South Carolina legislature repealed the statute. It replaced the law barring NAACP members from public jobs with a statute, modeled on one adopted earlier in 1956 by Mississippi, requiring all teachers to declare what organizations they belonged to.[28]

The justices then considered whether they could still deal with the repealed statute. One law clerk hoped the Court could figure out some way to decide the case, because "the southern states would run rampant in repealing and enacting legislation when suits are filed" if the Court dismissed the appeal. Justice Frankfurter initially told his colleagues he wanted to go along with Judge Parker. But, on reflection, he concluded that the case was moot. The new statute did not expressly say that NAACP members would be fired. And, Frankfurter thought, there probably was nothing wrong with a general statute requiring public employees to disclose their memberships, including "pedagogical or professional associations" as well as political ones. He concluded that the Court should not take up this larger issue until a case came up that presented it directly. The Court ended up allowing the NAACP to amend its complaint to challenge the new statute.[29]

Statutes like the amended South Carolina law gave the Court a great deal of trouble. The problem was that, unlike the original South Carolina law, the new one did not single out NAACP membership. And, like Alabama's attempt to obtain membership lists, the new statute was directed at disclosure of membership. Disclosure in itself was less serious than firing, and, as Frankfurter noted, government employers might have an interest in knowing what organizations their employees belonged to—the Ku Klux Klan, the Communist party, or even, as Frankfurter suggested, teachers' groups and other professional associations that might affect the way an employee approached the job. The Court dealt with these more focused disclosure statutes in a Little Rock case, and the setting may have influenced the outcome.

During one of its extraordinary sessions in the midst of the 1958 Little Rock crisis, the Arkansas legislature passed a law like South Carolina's amended statute, requiring teachers to submit affidavits listing all organizations to which they had belonged during the preceding five years. The NAACP wanted to mount an immediate challenge to the statute, but Mrs. Bates had some difficulty locating an attractive plaintiff; teachers, lacking tenure, worried that school boards might refuse to rehire them and offer some other excuse as the reason, not their failure to file the affidavit. Eventually two teachers in Little Rock agreed to file suit, as did a professor at the University of Arkansas. One action began in state court and one in federal court.[30]

Cases involving public employees and the Communist party made the challenge "very difficult," as one of Warren's law clerks put it. In the early 1950s, the Supreme Court decided several cases in which school boards and other public agencies attempted to discover whether their employees were members of the Communist party. Under the Court's rulings, employees had to disclose membership where it might bear on job performance. In the Arkansas cases, both lower courts held that a generalized requirement to disclose all memberships was indeed relevant to job performance. The state supreme court said that private employers typically investigated people they hired, and public employers could do so too. If a teacher was a member of "a nudist colony" or "a drag-racing club," the court said, the membership "might shed light" on the teacher's "fitness to guide young minds in the schoolroom."[31]

When the Supreme Court ruled, Justice Harlan observed that the case involved "an unusual statute that touches constitutional rights whose protection in the context of the racial situation . . . demands the unremitting vigilance of the courts." Warren and Black thought that the statute was "just too broad." Frankfurter observed that the statute might be used to "invade the thought processes of teachers," but he was not willing to assume it would be misused. Harlan agreed that the statute might be misapplied, but he thought there was "no practical way to draw a line," so the state could "go whole hog" in asking questions. Justice Stewart was troubled, though he thought the statute too broad. His comments to his colleagues indicated that he might work out a middle way, which would allow the state to "inquire broadly but in specifics."[32]

Harlan, who dissented with three other justices, implicitly criticized the majority for overlooking "the restraints that attend constitutional adjudication" by treating the case as if it involved racial discrimination. Justice Stewart's opinion for the Court began by agreeing that the case differed from the Alabama and Little Rock registration cases. There, according to Justice Stewart, providing membership lists was completely irrelevant to registering to do business or paying taxes. But, he said, the Court's cases about Communists showed that governments could "investigate the competence and fitness of those whom it hires to teach in its schools." Still, as in the Little Rock case, requiring teachers to disclose all their ties did "impair" free association, particularly when teachers did not have tenure. Justice Stewart also pointed out that the statute did not make the affidavits confidential, but "[e]ven if there were no disclosure to the general public, the pressure upon a teacher to avoid any ties which might displease those who control his professional destiny would be constant and heavy." As Justice Stewart saw the case, the problem was that the statute went too far, requiring disclosure of "every conceivable kind of associational tie," including many which "could have no possible bearing" on the teacher's competence or fitness. This "comprehensive interference with associational freedom goes far beyond what might be justified."[33] The initial South Carolina statute was unconstitutional because it focused too narrowly on the NAACP; the technique used to overcome that objection, broadening the required disclosures, turned out to be equally fatal.

Justice Harlan's dissent agreed with the majority's overall approach, which considered whether the investigation had a "legitimate" purpose and whether the requirement had "substantial relevance." He disagreed with the Court's holding, however, because he could not define a line between a permissibly narrow inquiry into associations and an impermissibly broad one. He agreed that the affidavits would produce a lot of useless information, and that more limited inquiries might be more useful, but could not understand how public officials "can be expected to fix in advance the terms of their enquiry so that it will yield only relevant information." Justice Frankfurter's dissent argued that organization membership was often irrelevant to a teacher's competence, but a teacher might join so many groups that they would drain "his time and energy and interest at the expense of his work."[34]

The teacher-disclosure cases were hard for the Court because they were decided against a background of cases involving Communists. Southern critics of the NAACP routinely called it a subversive organization and attempted to link it to the Communist party. The NAACP adopted a strong anti-Communist resolution in 1950, and though Communists had been influential in some branches through the late 1940s, by the time of the Southern attack on the NAACP there was essentially no Communist influence anywhere in the NAACP.[35] The taint of association with communism was so powerful in the late 1950s, however, that critics continued to try to link the NAACP to communism. One technique was the legislative investigation into relations between the NAACP and the Communist party. Most investigations relied on standard anti-NAACP propaganda statements by professional anti-Communists and prosegregation witnesses. In Florida, though, the legislature's investigation went after membership lists to discover whether the Communists had infiltrated local branches. The NAACP's resistance to disclosure produced yet another important free-speech decision.

The law of legislative investigations was shaped by McCarthy-era investigations of Communism. Witnesses could refuse to answer questions if they invoked their Fifth Amendment right to avoid incriminating themselves, but using the Fifth Amendment was often unattractive. The idea that there were "Fifth Amendment Communists" had taken hold; invoking the Fifth Amendment was often taken to be an admission of wrongdoing because, it seemed, only people who might have actually committed some crime could be afraid of incriminating themselves. Targets of legislative investigations therefore tried to argue that they were protected by the free-speech guarantee of the First Amendment. In the 1950s, though, it was not obvious that they were. In 1951, the Supreme Court upheld prosecutions of Communist party leaders for advocating revolutionary change, rejecting the argument that advocacy alone was protected by the Constitution. The Court's decision meant that legislatures were not absolutely barred from adopting laws directed at some types of subversive speech. Yet if legislatures could enact statutes aimed at subversive speech, surely they could investigate to see whether new legislation was needed. And because the legislature could not know what new laws were needed until it asked people about their activities, it seemed difficult to impose First Amendment limits on legislative investigations. Indeed, the Supreme Court itself held in 1959 that a witness could not rely on the First Amendment to refuse to answer questions.

The Court was sharply divided over the proper response to McCarthy-era investigations, however. Though only a minority believed that free speech imposed sharp limits on investigations, over the course of the 1950s the Court did impose some limits. The legislature had to authorize committee questions clearly, for example, and the witness had to be told why those questions were relevant. The NAACP had to build on these rules to defend itself from attack through investigation. [36]

Although investigating committees were created in Louisiana, Mississippi, Arkansas, and Virginia, [37] Florida's investigation got to the Supreme Court. In 1956, segregationists led the legislature in creating the Florida Legislative Investigation Committee to investigate groups that threatened "the well being and orderly pursuit" of personal and business activities. In early 1957, the committee held hearings in Tallahassee and Miami. NAACP officials were asked to produce membership lists and were questioned about the organization's connection to the *Hawkins* desegregation case. Shortly after the first hearings ended, the legislature extended the life of the committee for two years, but rejected every other part of a package of anti-NAACP proposals segregationists introduced. The extension also modified the committee's mandate, authorizing it to examine the role of Communists in provoking racial agitation. [38]

The committee renewed its investigation of Communist influence in February 1958 using public information. In addition, the committee called two witnesses from Miami who testified that they had belonged to both the Communist party and the NAACP, though neither was a member of the NAACP in 1958. Then the committee turned to Miami NAACP officers. The branch turned its records over to its president, Theodore Gibson, the rector of an Episcopal church. Gibson and Ruth Perry, a white woman who was branch secretary, checked the records to find out whether the committee's witnesses were NAACP members. They decided they would refuse to answer questions about individual members. When Perry made her statement to the committee, one member said that she was "not fit to be a citizen of Florida." The committee asked Gibson to produce the Miami membership list; Gibson refused, called the committee a "Star Chamber," and stalked out of the hearing. [39]

The committee obtained a court order directing Gibson to turn the membership list over. Gibson appealed to the state supreme court, arguing that the Supreme

Court's legislative investigation cases, coupled with its recent Alabama NAACP decision, required a clearer statement by the Florida legislature that the committee could demand the list and a more precise demonstration that there actually was Communist influence on the NAACP. Carter's brief said the committee was really engaged in a "fishing expedition" whose purpose was not to produce legislation but to expose NAACP members to harassment. The committee's counsel responded that it had to be allowed to investigate to determine how to protect the state from subversion.[40]

The state supreme court gave something to both sides, though less to Gibson and the NAACP than to the committee. Gibson did not have to turn over the list, but he did have to bring it to the hearings and consult it when answering questions about whether specific individuals were branch members. Because Florida's purpose was legislation against subversion, Justice Campbell Thornal wrote, the membership information might assist in developing new laws.[41]

Carter asked the United States Supreme Court to review this decision, but the Court refused. Three justices voted to hear the case, one less than necessary for a full hearing. The others apparently believed the case not ready for review because the lower court's order said only that if Gibson did not answer he would be held in contempt. It was not itself a contempt finding. In denying a stay of the Florida court's decision, Frankfurter observed to his colleagues that, "instead of remotely breathing any kind of disregard of this Court's decisions or defiance of this Court, a contrary spirit is manifest" in the opinion.[42]

With a new legislative mandate and the Florida supreme court decision in hand, the committee renewed its inquiry in November 1959. Its hearing carefully followed the script the courts required: the purpose of the investigation, to investigate Communist infiltration, was clearly spelled out; a witness identified fourteen Communists who attended NAACP meetings. Then the committee called Gibson to confirm whether those people were Miami branch members. Gibson was willing to rely on his own memory about members and attendance to answer, but refused to consult the membership lists. In addition, the committee asked Reverend Edward Graham whether he was an NAACP member. Graham, who was not an NAACP officer, also refused to answer, citing his "right to privacy." The committee began contempt proceedings. Gibson testified that membership in the NAACP had dropped since the investigation began, but the judge found that the state's interest in investigating subversion overrode free speech concerns and held Gibson in contempt.[43]

On appeal to the state supreme court, Carter again argued that requiring Gibson to consult the list was equivalent to making him turn it over, which the court had essentially rejected before. The committee's lawyer pointed out that testimony showing that several Communists had attended NAACP meetings was enough to justify asking Gibson to say whether the identified individuals were branch members. Justice Thornal again wrote the court's opinion. Because the committee had no evidence that Graham was a Communist, it could not ask him whether he was an NAACP member, an "organization perfectly legitimate but allegedly unpopular in the community." Gibson, though, did have to consult the membership lists when asked about specific individuals; because the committee had some evidence about them, their protection against intrusions on privacy was smaller, and had to be subordinated to the state's interest in investigating subversion. This time the United States Supreme Court agreed to hear Gibson's appeal.[44]

The Court's recent decisions pointed in opposite directions. It protected NAACP members against disclosure of their names, in the Alabama and Little Rock cases. But those cases did not involve legislative investigations, and the Court's actions in such cases were not encouraging. The decisions limiting the scope of legislative investigations provoked a hostile reaction in Congress, and the Court, perhaps in response, became somewhat more receptive to investigations of Communist activities. When it specifically rejected the absolute free-speech objection to membership inquiries, the Court gave some support to Florida's argument in *Gibson*.[45]

Carter built on the more protective holdings to show they were consistent with the more restrictive ones. The key, he said, was that the restrictive decisions involved investigations of organizations that the investigating committees had good reason to believe were Communist fronts. The legislative investigation cases as a whole, Carter argued, demonstrated that questions about membership were permissible only if the committee showed some "nexus" or connection between the organization's activities and Communist party activities. And the connection had to be more than evidence that some NAACP members were also Communists; Carter argued that there had to be some showing that the activities of the NAACP were Communist-dominated. Carter's argument would have been stronger if Gibson had been unwilling to testify about members entirely. Because he was willing to testify from memory, though, the argument was less than compelling.[46]

After the justices heard argument in December 1961, they divided five to four against the NAACP. Chief Justice Warren said that if the state court decision stands, the Alabama case would be "thwarted" because "all legislatures will let loose on it." Justice Harlan responded that "states must have the power to ferret out communists," and said that "this wasn't an effort to get membership lists wholesale, but to limit them to refreshing recollection" about specific individuals. Frankfurter said that Gibson, the witness, could not be "the judge" of when the legislature had enough information to ask him to examine the membership lists. Clark pointed out that the NAACP itself had passed an anti-Communist resolution, and agreed with Harlan's point about the inquiry's limited scope. In March, Harlan sent around a draft opinion saying that the committee did not have to show "probable cause" to believe that a person was a Communist; a legislative committee was required only to act "responsibly." The Florida committee, guided by the state supreme court, had been responsible; the opinion noted particularly that there was no evidence that the investigation was part of a scheme to destroy the NAACP, and that the organization could not be freed of complying with "a legitimate official inquiry with the same degree of responsibility that is demanded of officials of other organizations."[47]

Gibson, like the Virginia barratry case, did not come out against the NAACP, and for the same reasons: Whittaker's resignation and Frankfurter's stroke. The Court heard the *Gibson* case again at the start of its next term in October 1962. This time the vote was five to four for the NAACP's position. During the justices' discussion of the case, Justice Brennan articulated the new majority's position, saying that the Court "need not find this is [a] campaign to smear [the] NAACP," nor that the investigation's purpose was improper. The tension between the investigation cases and the Alabama case could be resolved, Brennan argued, by saying that "before [the] state can ask [about] NAACP membership, [it] must lay [the] foundation of [Communist party] membership." This was a somewhat weaker version of Carter's "probable cause" argument. Harlan responded that the "purpose of investigation is to investigate," and that "proof need not be adduced of the conclusion before the investigation starts." Justice Clark said that the "quality of proof [was] not as high [as] some investigations," but he believed it sufficient. Even Justice Black, who wanted to provide relatively absolute protection against membership inquiries, noted that Brennan's position "will be very difficult" because he could not find any constitutional provision requiring a "prima facie" case before asking questions. Black thought the Court was "approaching a situation in which the narrow pinpoint positions will no longer be available," and that a broad ruling—for him, a clear First Amendment rule against inquiries into membership—would be necessary. White agreed with Harlan, but because Goldberg agreed with Brennan a majority voted to reverse the contempt citation.[48]

Warren assigned the opinion to Justice Goldberg. His opinion reviewed the NAACP cases protecting members and the Communist cases upholding the legislature's "power adequately to inform itself." Goldberg concluded that there was no real tension, because "[f]reedom and viable government are both, for this purpose, indivisible concepts." The reconciliation lay in the notion of "nexus": where an investigation intruded on sensitive areas of free expression, the government had to show "a substantial relation between the information sought and a subject of overriding and compelling state interest." Following Carter's suggestion, Goldberg distinguished the Communist party cases because they involved inquiries into party membership, and the party was "not an ordinary or legitimate political party, as known in this country." In *Gibson*, Goldberg wrote, the NAACP and not the Communist party was the inquiry's subject, and there was no indication that "the activities or policies" of the NAACP were "either Communist dominated or influenced." The Court had also upheld inquiries into possible Communist fronts, but, Goldberg wrote, only because the questions had been "demonstrated . . . to be essential to fulfillment of a proper governmental purpose." A five-page examination of the facts concluded that they did not show "a substantial connection" between the Miami branch and "Communist *activities*." The analysis of the facts concluded, "The strong associational interest in maintaining the privacy of membership lists of groups engaged in the constitutionally protected free trade in ideas and beliefs may not be substantially infringed upon such a slender showing." Investigations could of course proceed one step at a time, but, Goldberg wrote, each step had to be justified by "an adequate foundation." The Court's opinion ended, "to impose a lesser standard . . . would be inconsistent with the maintenance of those essential conditions basic to the preservation of our democracy."[49]

Justice Harlan's dissent disagreed with the majority's attempt to distinguish between Communist investigations and investigations of Communist infiltration into non-Communist organizations, and reiterated the point that the majority was essentially asking the committee "to prove in advance the very things it is trying to find out." He also argued that Gibson's willingness to testify from memory meant there would be very little additional intrusion on free speech in requiring him to consult the membership lists before answering.[50]

Harlan's dissent clearly had the better of the argument about what the Court's prior cases meant, for some of the cases did involve investigations of non-Communist organizations with not much more evidence of Communist influence than in *Gibson*. Alexander Bickel wrote Frankfurter that the *Gibson* opinion was "quite awful" and was "by way of creating . . . some sort of special constitutional right to be an anonymous Negro." But, despite Harlan's statements that he could find no unfairness in the committee's proceedings but only "a decorous attitude" and "a lawyerlike and considerate demeanor," his analysis and Bickel's criticism failed to place the investigation in its context. Justice Goldberg's opinion was defensible as a technical matter, for it made everything turn on a test of "substantial evidence," which surely could vary from case to case. But, more important, the majority opinion understood that *Gibson* was yet another in the line of cases attempting to discredit the NAACP; decorum might have kept the Court from saying, as Warren had to his colleagues, that this was just another attempt to close down the NAACP in the South, but no opinion that failed somehow to recognize that fact could be defended in the long run. *Gibson* ended legislative investigations of the NAACP in Florida and elsewhere, and the state legislature did not bother to renew the committee again. Although the NAACP suffered some membership losses while the investigation went on, it kept operating, and some Florida affiliates began sit-ins in 1960.[51]

The Court's 1962 decisions in *Gibson* and the Virginia barratry case were the last chapter in the NAACP's response to the South's attack. The years consumed in responding to the attack, and in attempting to implement *Brown,* were years in which Marshall and his staff could do little else. Resistance to segregation succeeded even when the courts rejected the resisters' legal claims. The attack on the NAACP succeeded in the same way, even as the attackers repeatedly were defeated in the courts.

21

"I'd Kind of Outlived My Usefulness"
The Changing Context of Civil
Rights Litigation

Just as the attack on the NAACP took shape, new forces entered the civil rights field. The NAACP's lawyers found it sensible to delay some strategic litigation. They also found that other participants in the civil rights movement changed what the lawyers could do. The lawyers eventually assumed new roles in seeking to guarantee voting rights and access to public transportation and private restaurants, but the path toward these new roles was tortuous. Working out what the lawyers could do took time, and they were sometimes called upon to play roles with which they were not entirely comfortable at the start. By the time of the 1960–61 sit-ins, the time had come for Marshall to move on. As he put it, "I thought I'd kind of outlived my usefulness, in original ideas, in the NAACP hierarchy, what have you."[1]

From a lawyer's point of view, *Brown* doomed all Jim Crow legislation. True, the Court emphasized the special psychological damage segregation did to school children, and lawyers supporting Jim Crow could and did argue that no similar damage occurred when cities maintained segregated parks or buses. The Court's discussion of psychological damage, however, did not play an important part in the constitutional law constructed in *Brown;* it was designed to get around the claim that separate facilities might be equal. No justice really believed that separate facilities could be equal, and the justices rested *Brown* on the underlying legal proposition that government decision making just could not take race into account. That invalidated all Jim Crow legislation. Further, the Court clearly believed, and correctly, that separate schools were segregation's central props. Desegregating schools might be difficult, but the Court expected that desegregating other public facilities would not be hard. Lower courts relied on *Brown* to invalidate segregation in city golf courses, public parks, and other facilities, and the Supreme Court so readily agreed that it simply affirmed them without hearing oral argument.[2]

But if the legal questions about Jim Crow regulations were easy, actually eliminating segregation in public facilities was more difficult. The central event was the Montgomery bus boycott from December 1955 to December 1956. The boycott originated when the community tried to get the city's segregated bus system operated more fairly. The bus operator complied with the city's segregation ordinance by having African-Americans fill up the buses from the back row forward while whites filled them up from the front row backwards. Occasionally, a white got on a full bus, and the driver required the African-American closest to the front to give up his or her seat. At first the community, under the leadership of Jo Ann Robinson and the Negro Women's Political Council, wanted the bus operators simply to direct their drivers to be more courteous, and to adopt rules that, while preserving separate seating, would not require that African-Americans yield seats to whites. The idea of taking action against the company gained strength in the spring of 1955, when a teenager was arrested for violating the bus segregation ordinance. Because the community did not regard the teenager as a suitable plaintiff, her arrest did not produce community action. The December 1 arrest of Rosa Parks, who had been active in the city's NAACP branch, did trigger a boycott. Leading preachers, lawyers, and other activists in Montgomery's African-American community created the Montgomery Improvement Association (MIA) to direct the boycott, and persuaded Martin Luther King, Jr., to head the group.[3]

Because the boycott was an economic action, lawyers had little to do with it as it began. Fred Gray filed an appeal for Mrs. Parks, but the appeal played no role in later events.[4] African-Americans began using taxis instead of buses, but when the city began to enforce an ordinance requiring taxis to charge minimum fares, the community developed a network of volunteer drivers. The police harassed the drivers, but the car pools continued to operate effectively.

In January 1956, the boycott organizers asked the NAACP for legal assistance. Wilkins declined at first, because at that point the MIA was seeking only to make segregation more fair, a position inconsistent with NAACP policy. In mid-January, Gray, King, and E. D. Nixon began discussing challenging segregation itself. Mrs. Parks's conviction might be used for such a challenge, but the state courts controlled when an appeal would be decided. Sustaining the boycott over a long period might be difficult. Instead, Gray filed a federal court action on February 1, 1956, challenging the constitutionality of segregated buses; on the same day, Autherine Lucy registered at the University of Alabama. The lawsuit removed the NAACP's policy objections, and the bombing of King's home on January 30 made it imperative for the NAACP to support him. As a result, in February, the NAACP began to give the Montgomery community its full assistance, arranging for cooperating attorneys in Birmingham to defend them and sending Robert Carter to aid the lawyers representing King.[5]

Legal action proceeded on several fronts. First, there was the federal suit, a three-judge court case that would go directly to the Supreme Court. The course to decision was not completely smooth. The initial complaint named five plaintiffs. The day after the complaint was filed, however, one asked to withdraw, saying that she did not want to be involved and that Gray had tricked her into signing the documents authorizing him to file suit for her.[6]

Also in February, a state grand jury indicted King and more than eighty others for violating a 1921 statute, originally designed to impede labor unions, prohibiting conspiracies to interfere with business. This indictment further unified the African-American community and, ironically, divided the white community's leadership. The city's attorney thought the bus company should seek an injunction against the boycott, rather than having the city bring in the heavy artillery of a criminal indictment. The indictment was particularly troubling because the conspiracy statute might well violate the free expression rights of boycott participants. As a result, the city attorney used King's trial as a test case, rather than as the opening round in a massive effort to destroy the boycott immediately, and after King was convicted chose to suspend further criminal trials until the appellate courts decided King's case.[7]

The legal picture became even more complicated in April. Almost two years earlier, in June 1954, Sarah Mae Flemming boarded a crowded bus in Columbia, South Carolina. When a white passenger got off, Flemming took a seat in the white section of the bus. The driver ordered her to go to the back of the bus. Instead, Flemming tried to get off at the next stop through the front door. The bus driver pushed his elbow into her stomach and told her to use the rear exit. Aided by the NAACP, Flemming sued the bus system for damages, claiming she was injured because the driver was enforcing an unconstitutional ordinance. Judge Timmerman dismissed the complaint, holding the ordinance valid under *Plessy,* which he said was still good law after *Brown.* The NAACP appealed, and in July 1955, the court of appeals, in a brief opinion, reversed, directing Judge Timmerman to consider whether the bus company could be held liable for complying with an ordinance that had not been held unconstitutional when the assault occurred. The bus company appealed to the Supreme Court.[8]

The justices all agreed that the ordinance was unconstitutional, but Chief Justice Warren raised a question about the Court's jurisdiction. Under most circumstances, the Supreme Court can decide cases only after the lower courts have reached a final decision, and Flemming's case was not final because it had been sent back to Judge Timmerman for additional proceedings. The justices decided they could not simply affirm the court of appeals and put *Plessy* to rest. Rather, they dismissed the company's appeal, citing a case invoking the final judgment rule.[9]

The Court announced its decision on April 23, 1956. Many newspapers, failing to understanding the technicalities, reported that the Court "upheld" the court of appeals and thus agreed that Jim Crow bus laws were unconstitutional. Some bus companies, including the parent of Montgomery's bus operators, were relieved that the Court extricated them (or so they believed) from a difficult situation, and decided to ignore Jim Crow requirements. The Montgomery operator directed its drivers to refrain from assigning seats based on race. The city responded by suing the operator in state court, asking the court to declare that the company had to continue to segregate its buses. The company objected, saying that the state court should refrain from acting because of the ongoing federal court litigation involving the same legal questions. Judge Walter Jones of the state trial court ignored that problem. On May 9, he held the Jim Crow laws constitutional and directed the bus company to comply with them.[10]

Two days later, the federal court held a brief hearing on the MIA's challenge. The judges were Richard Rives of the court of appeals and district judges Frank Johnson and Seybourn Lynne. Lynne had been appointed by President Truman. Johnson, a Republican from the northern part of Alabama where the party had remained strong throughout the era of one-party segregationist rule, had been appointed earlier in the year. Two city officials testified that desegregating the buses would lead to violence, a bus company official explained how the seating system worked, and the plaintiffs were questioned about their motives. The city's attorney suggested they were stalking horses for King and the MIA. The three judges promised an early decision.[11]

Before they announced their decision, Judge Jones granted Alabama attorney general Patterson's request to close down the NAACP; among Patterson's reasons was that the NAACP was "organizing, supporting, and financing" the bus boycott. Four days later, on June 5, 1956, the three-judge court struck down the segregation ordinance, with Judge Lynne dissenting. Judge Rives wrote that *Plessy* could not be regarded as good law after *Brown*. On June 19, the court entered an order directing that the city refrain from enforcing Jim Crow, but it suspended the order until the city could appeal to the Supreme Court. The Court had adjourned for the summer, and would not rule on the appeal for several months. The city continued to claim the power to enforce segregated seating on the buses, and the boycott continued as well.[12]

Carter prepared the brief opposing Supreme Court review. Meanwhile, in Montgomery, the city came up with a new tactic: on October 30, the city council told its lawyers to file a state court action to bar the MIA from operating its car pool as an alternative to the city bus system, claiming that the car pool interfered with the bus company's exclusive franchise for a city transit system. The MIA's lawyers, assisted by local NAACP cooperating attorneys, asked Judge Johnson to bar city officials from filing their proposed action, but Judge Johnson refused. He set November 14 for hearing their claim. The city filed its complaint, and state judge Eugene Carter scheduled a hearing for November 13. On that day, the MIA's lawyers futilely argued that Judge Carter should wait until Judge Johnson made his decision the next day. During the state court hearing, word arrived that the Supreme Court affirmed Judge Rives's decision striking down the segregation ordinance, without even hearing argument. One spectator cried out, "God Almighty has spoken from Washington, D.C.!" The next day, Judge Carter did enjoin the operation of the car pool, a ruling that, as a technical matter, was independent of the segregation ordinance's validity. With the ordinance struck down, the MIA had no interest in continuing the boycott. On November 14, MIA leaders called it off, but urged people to stay off the buses until the city began to comply with the Court's ruling. That was delayed when the city asked the Court to rehear the case, but on December 20, the Court's final order reached Montgomery. The bus company then immediately asked Judge Jones to dissolve his May injunction requiring them to continue segregating the buses. With ill grace, Judge Jones denounced the Supreme Court but lifted the injunction. The boycott ended.[13]

The Montgomery bus boycott illuminates the changing context of civil rights litigation. By the time of the boycott, the legal issues raised by Jim Crow ordinances were not difficult, but it took a Supreme Court decision to end bus segregation in Montgomery. Despite the Court's role in the outcome, the most important part of the Montgomery story, to the African-American community and to the nation as a whole, was the boycott itself, not the litigation. The boycott, stimulated by the community's sense that Jim Crow laws were wrong and unconstitutional, provided the context in which a new set of leaders came to the fore. Their emergence was facilitated, too, by the attack on the NAACP. In Alabama, the NAACP simply closed down, and elsewhere its activities were substantially restricted because of the time and energy it took to fight off the attacks.

Perhaps the most dramatic example of the relationship between the attack on the NAACP and the emergence of new leadership occurred in Birmingham. The NAACP was shut down in Alabama on June 1, 1956. Reverend Fred Shuttlesworth and four other ministers called a mass meeting for June 5, and announced the formation of the Alabama Christian Movement for Human Rights. As its name indicates, the group took religion, not law, as the source of its devotion to freedom, and by calling itself a movement it indicated a central concern with action by the African-American community on its own behalf. The ministers' styles, too, differed from the lawyers'. Unsurprisingly, their speeches were attuned to the rhythms of the pulpit rather than the courtroom. These new organizations and their leaders did not disagree with the lawyers' goals; indeed, in one survey the new groups preferred "legalistic" methods to boycotts and direct action. The MIA's initial reluctance to challenge segregation directly does suggest that the new leaders approached segregation's problems differently. The new leaders were in the South, and their only constituents were people in their communities, while the NAACP's leadership had its headquarters in New York and a national constituency. Also, the new leaders tended to be preachers rather than lawyers—even Fred Gray was a part-time minister—and they believed that the differences between legalistic methods and other techniques were smaller than the lawyers thought.[14]

One result, understandably, was a certain amount of personal tension between Marshall and emerging leaders like King. When King said that direct action by students could help desegregate the schools, Marshall said that "desegregation was men's work and should not be entrusted to children." He was also reported to have called King a "first-rate rabble-rouser," and complained about always "saving King's bacon." Yet he understood King's role in the African-American community, and told one caller, "If King's going to jail, I'm going to China."[15]

The lawyers' role changed as the civil rights movement turned increasingly to demonstrations and boycotts. Those activities were planned, of course, but lawyers could contribute little to that planning. Rather, the lawyers responded to what happened after the demonstrations and boycotts began; they reacted to litigation—criminal prosecutions, like those of Parks and King, or attempts to enjoin the civil rights movement—instead of initiating it. Lawyers were still needed, and Marshall remained an important figure in the civil rights movement, but the attack on the

NAACP, the rise of direct action, and the Supreme Court's reluctance to deal with desegregation contributed to a relative decline in litigation's importance to the civil rights movement.

The Montgomery bus boycott and its resolution by the Supreme Court showed how actions by the African-American community could be coupled with actions by supportive public officials to help bring to life the promises of equality implicit in *Brown*. Similar advances were not achieved in the late 1950s in the area of voting rights. The legal context was not as favorable, and the resources available to the African-American community were different. As a result, little was accomplished until 1965.

The cases of the 1940s, culminating in *Terry v. Adams,* established that states could not use devices that effectively excluded people from the vote on account of race. The major target, the white primary, relied explicitly on race. The NAACP also began to challenge, occasionally successfully, techniques like Alabama's Boswell Amendment and its "understanding" clause, which did not refer to race explicitly but which were used to exclude only African-Americans. These techniques would be unconstitutional if they were adopted to exclude African-Americans from voting, or—under the principle of *Yick Wo v. Hopkins*—if they were administered so that white registrants passed easily and African-American registrants routinely failed. Where techniques of exclusion had been adopted recently, establishing discriminatory intent might not be difficult. Most of the techniques, though, were long-standing, and they were unconstitutional only if there was a pattern of discriminatory administration. As in cases involving student assignment laws, proving such a pattern was easy.

As the civil rights movement gathered strength after the Montgomery boycott, however, another line of attack on voting discrimination opened up. Responding to the new political climate, Congress adopted a civil rights act in 1957. President Eisenhower was not an enthusiastic supporter of desegregation, but his attorney general Herbert Brownell came to believe that excluding African-Americans from voting was deeply wrong and, incidentally, that the Republican party could gain some political advantage from sponsoring legislation aimed at securing the right to vote. In the Senate, Democratic majority leader Lyndon Johnson planned to seek the party's nomination for president in 1960 and knew he had to demonstrate that he supported civil rights. The interests of the administration and Johnson converged to produce a civil rights act in 1957, after a protracted struggle against segregationists in the Senate.[16]

During the political battle to enact the 1957 Civil Rights Act, proponents were forced to omit provisions that civil rights advocates regarded as most important, especially one that would have authorized the Justice Department to enforce all constitutional rights, including the rights guaranteed in *Brown*. The NAACP reluctantly supported the watered-down act, which dealt with voting in two ways. It authorized the Justice Department to investigate voting practices and to sue to block the use of registration laws to discriminate. It also created a Civil Rights Commission to investigate discrimination and publicize the results of its inquiries. By making possible a combination of legal action and publicity, the act's supporters hoped the South would feel substantial pressure to eliminate unfair voting practices.[17]

With the Civil Rights Act on the books, civil rights lawyers made a sensible strategic judgment to refrain for a while from making voting a major litigation target. The government's investigative resources, in the Justice Department and the Civil Rights Commission, were obviously more substantial than theirs. If the government's investigations turned up useful information, the government itself might act, or the civil rights lawyers might use the information for their own purposes, including legal action. The government moved slowly, though, and segregationists challenged the 1957 act. They charged that Congress did not have power to displace state registration methods and that the Civil Rights Commission's procedures were unfair. Though the Supreme Court rejected these challenges,[18] the act was ineffective. The method it established for displacing unfair registration procedures simply did not work, and the publicity the Civil Rights Commission could generate had little effect on recalcitrant whites. That lesson was not clear until the 1960s; until then, civil rights lawyers relied on the government.

The Supreme Court's 1950 decision in *Henderson* held that segregation on interstate trains violated federal law, but many railroads in the South continued to operate segregated cars. Although these practices were regularly held illegal in cases brought by individual travelers, the NAACP's lawyers came to believe that a broader challenge was necessary. In addition, no matter what their treatment on the railroads, when African-American travelers arrived at stations in the South they were still forced to use separate waiting rooms, toilet facilities, and restaurants. In 1953, Robert Carter filed a comprehensive complaint with the Interstate Commerce Commission seeking an order directing all carriers in the South to end segregation.[19]

The ICC held its hearing in the case in July 1954, after *Brown*. Most carriers conceded that they segregated their cars, and Carter presented witnesses who showed that the other carriers did so as well. In addition, he had Lester Banks, the secretary of the Virginia NAACP conference of branches, testify about segregation in the Richmond terminal. Carter also brought the terminal restaurant into the complaint. The restaurant refused to serve African-Americans, but claimed it was not covered by the Interstate Commerce Act because it was not providing any services essential to interstate commerce. The ICC agreed with the restaurant's owners and dismissed it from the case. Carter shifted his ground. He agreed that the restaurant might not be covered by the act. Still, he argued, interstate travelers did need restaurant services, and the station operator had to provide them somehow. If the station operator itself ran the restaurant, Carter argued, it could not discriminate, and it should not avoid its duty merely by leasing the restaurant facility to an independent entrepreneur. Attorney General Brownell, acting on the advice of J. Lee Rankin, had the Justice Department support the NAACP. In November 1955, the ICC decided that segregation on trains and in waiting rooms violated the Interstate Commerce Act, but also held that because the restaurant did not provide an essential service to interstate travellers, it was not covered by the act.[20]

The Montgomery bus boycott revitalized a tradition of direct action against segregated transportation. On December 20, 1958, on his way home for the holidays to Selma, Alabama, from Washington, where he was a student at Howard Law School, Bruce Boynton tried to use the restaurant at the Richmond bus depot. Finding the black section overcrowded, Boynton sat down at the counter for whites. When he refused to move, he was arrested for violating Virginia's trespass law, which made it a misdemeanor to stay on someone else's property after being asked to leave unless the defendant had a lawful excuse for remaining. Boynton was represented at his trial by Martin Martin, a partner in the law firm that included Oliver Hill and Spottswood Robinson. The state courts disposed of Boynton's claims without much attention, and the LDF supported his appeal to the Supreme Court.

Boynton's case raised three issues. First, his lawyers could argue that segregation in bus station restaurants violated the Interstate Commerce Act. That would challenge the ICC's ruling. Second, they could argue that bus terminal restaurant segregation interfered with interstate commerce. Finally, and most broadly, they could argue that using state power to enforce the restaurant owner's decision to discriminate was "state action" made unconstitutional by *Shelley v. Kraemer*. Apparently seeking to obtain as broad a ruling as possible, Martin and the NAACP's lawyers mentioned the Interstate Commerce Act claim but deliberately refrained from presenting it in detail. As a result, the trial record was only thirty-four pages long and had no information on the relation between Trailways, the bus station's owner, and the restaurant.[21]

At first Virginia did not file a response to the LDF appeal from the state court decision. When a state fails to respond to an application for review that presents important issues, the Court usually directs its clerk to ask the state's lawyers to file a response. Concerned that the Court might have to decide broad issues about segregation, Justice Frankfurter suggested that when the clerk of the Court requested the response, he also ask that they "deal with the intercorporate relationship" between Trailways and the restaurant operator, as revealed in any documents that the Virginia courts might take into account. That suggestion arose out of the case's technical posture. It was an appeal from a state criminal conviction, and the Supreme Court could not rely on material that, as a matter of state law, the Virginia courts were not allowed to rely on. Virginia's attorneys replied that there were no such documents. Despite the fact that the relationship between Trailways and the restaurant remained obscure, the Supreme Court decided to review Boynton's conviction. In the background was a new upsurge in protest activity: On February 1, 1960, sit-in demonstrations began at the lunch counters of Woolworth's department store in Greensboro, North Carolina.[22]

The Department of Justice gave the Court the information it needed for a relatively narrow ruling, coming up with ICC papers showing that an interstate carrier was a co-owner of the terminal company that operated the Richmond depot. The department then adopted the argument Carter made to the ICC in 1954, that the interstate carrier operating a terminal could not escape its duty to avoid discrimination by leasing a part of its facility to a restaurant owner who then operated segregated counters. The difficulty with this argument was that the ICC documents were not in the record, and that, as Virginia's lawyers pointed out, no exceptions in state law would allow the state courts to rely on this sort of evidence.[23]

After hearing argument in 1960, the justices decided to reverse Boynton's conviction, because the restaurant owner's policy of segregation violated the Interstate Commerce Act. That meant that Boynton had an excuse for staying at the "white" counter, so he could not be convicted for trespass. Justices Clark and Whittaker objected to this result; they agreed that the act barred discrimination in terminals operated by interstate carriers, but argued that the record did not show that the Richmond terminal was covered by the act. Justice Black, writing for the Court, finessed the problem in two ways. First, he said, the statutory issue had been presented to the trial court and was closely related to Boynton's constitutional claim regarding interference with interstate commerce. Second, on the merits, Black argued that the Interstate Commerce Act barred discrimination by carriers in facilities they "controlled." For him, "control" was a practical matter, not a question of the legal relations between carrier and restaurant owner. If the carrier made terminal facilities available to its passengers and the terminal operator "cooperated in this undertaking," the terminal facilities became "an integral part of transportation." The opinion concluded by stressing that it dealt with the facts in Richmond, where the terminal was a regular stop on long-distance routes, and was not holding that "every time a bus stops at a wholly independent roadside restaurant," the restaurant owner could not discriminate.[24]

By deciding *Boynton* on statutory grounds, the Court avoided the more difficult question of "state action." That question was directly presented in cases arising from the sit-ins that began in 1960. The demonstrators typically sat-in at lunch counters operated by stores that operated separate counters for whites and African-Americans. Sometimes city ordinances required segregation, but sometimes it was simply a choice made in light of local social patterns. Participants in the sit-ins were then arrested for trespass, not for violating a Jim Crow ordinance. *Shelley v. Kraemer* held unconstitutional some uses of state power to enforce private discrimination, but *Shelley* was quite controversial among constitutional scholars, and its scope was unclear. Most scholars believed that *Shelley* should be limited to cases in which the state tried to enforce discrimination against buyers and sellers who were willing to ignore race. That, however, did not cover the sit-ins, because there the sellers were the operators of the segregated lunch counters, and unlike the sellers in *Shelley* they wanted the government to back up their desire to discriminate.

Marshall and other leaders of the NAACP were ambivalent about the sit-in tactic at first. There were several reasons. Events moved quickly, and Marshall was out of the country when the first sit-ins occurred. By the time he returned, he had less flexibility than he was accustomed to in structuring a legal response. In Greensboro, where the sit-ins began, local leaders negotiated a moratorium that lasted for a few weeks, but elsewhere arrests occurred from February 8 on. In Atlanta, the students, after being told that the NAACP's local counsel would charge them $5,000, went ahead without legal advice.[25]

In part, too, Marshall and his colleagues were concerned, as they had been in connection with Montgomery, that a new group of leaders might displace them. Robert Carter believed that "in the future Negroes must place emphasis on those type[s] of demonstrations . . . and less on legal suits for striking down racial barriers." He also noted that providing too much support for sit-ins "would tie us to something that some other organization has taken and run with."[26]

Marshall had other concerns as well. In April 1960, he pointed out that the sit-ins spread so rapidly because young people were impatient, "and if you mean, are the young people impatient with me, the answer is yes." Marshall's respect for law also played a part in his reaction. The participants really were violating a law that, unlike a Jim Crow statute, was not itself unconstitutional whenever it was used. And, as was typical of his style, Marshall appreciated the emotional force of the restaurant owners' arguments. When the LDF was first asked to defend the participants, Marshall "stormed around the room proclaiming . . . [that] he was not going to represent a bunch of crazy colored students who violated the sacred property rights of white folks. . . ." He told his staff they better come up with "some powerful arguments" to combat the claims that would be made about private property. He convened a three-day conference of lawyers in March 1960, which concluded that "the use of public force in arrest or conviction of students engaged in peaceful demonstration is in truth state enforcement of private discrimination" and therefore violated the Constitution. In addition, he noted that the police had invoked "public nuisance" laws "in a discriminatory manner." By then the staff and cooperating attorneys were representing over 1,200 students. Marshall announced that "every young person arrested as a result of participation in a peaceful protest against racial segregation will have adequate legal defense," although he understood that "we cannot protect these courageous youngsters from possible violent attack."[27]

There was another front in the attack on the NAACP, and, though the skirmish was minor, it had lasting consequences. Pressed by Southern members of Congress, in 1956 the Internal Revenue Service opened an investigation of the relation between the tax-exempt LDF and the tax-paying NAACP. Formally the organizations were separate, but a number of people served on both boards of directors, and occasionally the LDF gave money to NAACP branches it represented. The meetings with the IRS were "discouraging." The IRS thought the interlocking directorates were a sign that the organizations were not independent, which threatened the tax exemption for the LDF. And, as Marshall told the LDF board, he wondered, "if these corporations are so separate why is it we are defending the NAACP in North Carolina and Louisiana."[28]

Marshall responded to the IRS inquiry by insisting on a further separation of the NAACP and the LDF. The boards were restructured so that no one served on both. Robert Carter left the LDF to become general counsel to the NAACP and took over the defense of the NAACP against the Southern attack. Marshall remained at the head of the LDF.[29] The separation, though induced by the IRS inquiry, served other goals as well. Marshall found it sometimes difficult to coordinate the legal response to Southern attacks with the public relations response; in Texas and Louisiana the members of the NAACP did not always understand the implications of the legal maneuvers in which the legal staff engaged. To some extent, too, the persistent tension between Carter and Marshall began to focus on the problem of coordination with local branches; Marshall tended to see issues as more narrowly legal while Carter tended to take public relations concerns a bit more seriously. The tension between them was not great enough to produce a crisis, but the pressure from the IRS gave them a convenient way to resolve their differences by moving apart without a controversial break.

The separation of the LDF and the NAACP had another effect: it eliminated the formal connection between the LDF and its primary constituency, NAACP members in the South, and reduced their informal ties. The litigants Marshall and the LDF represented in the late 1950s tended to be local NAACP leaders, not the "little Joes" who Marshall found so attractive. According to Motley, Marshall spent less time in direct contact with African-American communities in the South, and was less attentive than he would have been earlier to the changes in attitude that occurred after the Montgomery bus boycott. That too was part of the new context of civil rights litigation.[30]

The constitutional issues raised by the sit-in cases reached the Supreme Court after Marshall left the LDF. His announcement that the staff would provide legal support for the protestors, though, contained an important statement: the fund "must secure financial support far in excess of our anticipated budget." As the civil rights movement grew, so did the demands on the legal staff and the need for financial support. The LDF budget grew from $210,000 in 1952 to $319,500 in 1957, and to $489,540 in 1960. The legal staff remained quite small through the 1950s. Prior to *Brown,* Marshall persuaded the Prince Hall Masons, an African-American fraternal organization, to give him $10,000 a year to hire a recent graduate from law school to help with legal research. Over the course of the decade, Marshall used the Prince Hall funds to pay the salaries of two or three young attorneys each year, to bring into the office the latest thinking in the law schools, and to do research and draft legal memoranda. Though Marshall made it clear that these lawyers were free to stay with the LDF as long as they wished, none remained for more than a few years.[31] *

To the extent that the national office was involved in trial and appellate litigation, the trial work and oral arguments were done by the core staff in place before *Brown:* Marshall, Carter, Greenberg, and Motley. They simply could not provide as strong a guiding hand to the post-*Brown* litigation as Marshall had given to the litigation leading up to *Brown.* There was too much to do, particularly in light of the assault on the NAACP and the LDF.

Marshall's transition from civil rights lawyer to civil rights leader began to take shape early in the 1950s. In 1951, he made a semiofficial trip to Japan and Korea to investigate the courts-martial of African-American soldiers. At first, the Army and State Department obstructed his efforts to obtain the necessary travel documents,

---

* Elwood "Chick" Chisolm was on the staff from 1952 to 1961. Chisolm, who had been at Lincoln University while Marshall was a senior, was a smooth talker and story teller. He had a reputation as a ladies' man, and he provided Marshall with the kind of easy companionship that he found difficult to generate from the more restrained Carter, Greenberg, and Motley.

but Walter White intervened with Truman to get Marshall into Korea, where he spent eight days. Marshall found "Jim Crow practices still persisting in the Army" despite Truman's desegregation orders. One soldier, he discovered, was convicted of not being on duty when he actually was in the army hospital; four others were convicted of misconduct in the presence of the enemy when they were behind the lines on mess duty. Marshall quite properly understood this trip to have a twofold significance: it allowed him to investigate the conditions African-American soldiers were facing, and it showed that he was a public figure whose investigations carried weight.[32]

Walter White divorced his first wife in 1949 and married Poppy Cannon, a white woman from South Africa. White's private life hampered his ability to continue as an effective force in the NAACP's middle-class circles, and he took a leave of absence. During White's leave, Marshall helped run the organization, in a loose triumvirate with Roy Wilkins and Henry Lee Moon, the NAACP's director of publicity. Marshall returned to the legal side when White's leave ended, but his work as a manager was typical. From the early 1950s on, Marshall spent his time on two activities: preparing for *Brown,* which lasted until 1955, and being a fund raiser and manager, which lasted until he left the LDF.[33]

Litigation expenses escalated, and as the civil rights movement turned to demonstrations and sit-ins, the organizations found that they had to post bonds for appeals on behalf of large numbers of defendants. As a result, Marshall found himself increasingly in the role of fund raiser. By 1955, he had abandoned most of his work as a trial lawyer and appellate advocate in the courts of appeals, confining himself to Supreme Court cases and "financial, public relations," and other work. He continued to read the briefs his staff wrote, and occasionally would return a brief with a comment like, "This doesn't hit me." However, because he hired people to work for him whose judgment and ability he rightly trusted, he had little need to supervise their work directly.[34]

The attack on the NAACP and the separation of the LDF from the NAACP meant that small contributions from individual members yielded less and less of the necessary funds. The LDF hired a fund raiser and created a "Committee of 100," people who regularly donated large amounts to the fund; in 1956, the committee's members contributed about half of the LDF's income. Marshall arranged for a grant from the Prince Hall Masons to finance additional staff members, solicited a grant from the Field Foundation, continued to make speeches, and attended cocktail parties to raise funds from liberal supporters of the LDF in New York. He was good at raising money. His personality was attractive and he was a compelling speaker. Years later he laughingly described one cocktail party that he attended after already having "one too many scotches." Deciding that "it would do more damage not to show up," Marshall began his solicitation, "Those of you who don't drink probably suspect that I am drunk; those of you who do drink are certain of it." The event was successful, and Marshall later said that his "only regret was that he was too drunk to remember whatever was so persuasive." What made him persuasive, though, was the ability he demonstrated as an appellate advocate. A "suave and confident" speaker, Marshall spoke "extemporaneously," getting to the heart of the issue he was talking about and making a compelling case in terms his audience, whether judges or potential donors, could immediately appreciate.[35]

Marshall attained his stature because he was a lawyer. By the beginning of the 1960s, his successes, ironically, made it more difficult for him to continue to be a lawyer. The attack on the NAACP and the LDF diverted effort from challenges to segregation to defense against destruction and forced the lawyers to learn and make an entirely new body of law, dealing with free expression. The revitalization of direct action meant that the lawyers were reacting to challenges generated by other civil rights activists rather than developing strategic litigation to undermine discrimination. Perhaps most important, precisely because Marshall was a major figure in the civil rights community, he had to spend his time raising money and inspiring audiences instead of litigating cases. A typical schedule of Marshall's travels, for November 1959, shows him starting the month speaking at an LDF fund-raising luncheon, going to Mississippi to speak to the state conference of branches, then to Washington to speak to the National Council of Negro Women, then to Oklahoma for a testimonial dinner for Roscoe Dunjee, then to Louisiana and South Carolina, ending the month as a delegate to the President's Conference on Education, itself interrupted by a trip to Boston to speak to the New Century Club. In January and February 1960, when the sit-in movement began, he was an official consultant to the conference drafting a constitution for Kenya, another symbol of his role as a civil rights leader.[36]

By 1961, Marshall was considering leaving the LDF. He had two young sons, and believed that his salary was insufficient to raise a family.* Marshall was tired from the speaking and fund raising, and Mrs. Marshall remembers Goody seeing a picture of his father and asking, "What's that man?" But, Marshall's interest in being a lawyer was at least as important as family considerations in leading him to think about changing the direction of his career. He wanted to serve the African-American community of the South; he found that he was spending less time with the people in the South than with his New York "brain trust," and he knew he had changed into a different kind of lawyer. Symbolically, at least, the fact that Marshall was in London for seven weeks helping draft the constitution of Kenya when the first sit-ins occurred suggests his new role. He was, as the New York *Times* put it, a "fighter for his people"—something more than, but different from, a lawyer for his people.[37]

---

*Buster, a heavy smoker, died of lung cancer on February 11, 1955. Marshall married Cecilia Suyatt, a secretary in the NAACP's branch department, on December 17, 1955. Their first son Thurgood Junior ("Goody") was born in August 1956, and their second, John, in July 1958.

Epilogue:
"Power, not Reason"

After serving on the Supreme Court for nearly twenty-four years, Thurgood Marshall retired on June 27, 1991. His last opinion was a dissent in a death penalty case, which opened with the biting sentence, "Power, not reason, is the new currency of this Court's decisionmaking."[1] The Court had overruled two recent decisions barring "victim impact statements" from capital sentencing proceedings. Marshall's most forceful comments were directed at what he regarded as the cavalier way the majority went about its job. For Marshall, "fidelity to precedent is part and parcel of a conception of 'the judiciary as a source of impersonal and reasoned judgments.'" If that conception weakened, the Court's ability to "rein in the forces of democratic politics" by interpreting the Constitution to limit government power would be impaired, because "this Court can legitimately lay claim to compliance with its directives only if the public understands the Court to be implementing 'principles . . . founded in the law rather than in the proclivities of individuals.'"[2]

Why did Marshall care about precedent so much? From 1936 to 1954, he tried first to undermine and then to overrule the precedents that had established the United States system of apartheid. Surely Marshall would not have objected if the Supreme Court simply admitted error at the start.

That oversimplifies Marshall's understanding of constitutional adjudication. Of course advocates would prefer to win as fast as they can. Houston taught Marshall that such a preference was unrealistic in the United States' constitutional system. As a practical matter, precedents had weight, and advocates had to work with and around them. Indeed, for the first ten years of Marshall's work with the NAACP, his strategy accepted the separate but equal doctrine, insisting only that the South comply with it. Not until 1945, when enough precedents had accumulated, did the cases begin to challenge the doctrine itself.

In challenging segregation, Marshall and his colleagues came to understand that the rule of law was both an impediment and an advantage. It was an impediment when the law was unfavorable. But, Marshall learned from Houston, unfavorable law could gradually be converted into favorable law, through a careful litigation strategy pointing out anomalies in doctrine and identifying the inevitable failure of society's efforts to explain why unjust doctrines nonetheless were acceptable.

Once law became favorable, the rule of law was an advantage. Marshall and his colleagues understood that their opponents could work around the law they made, distinguishing the precedents the Court created. The opponents, too, were working with the law's materials. The assertion of power, pure and simple, though, was something else. In the Little Rock case, the force of the rule of law came home. With the law on his side, Marshall insisted that, although lawyers could try to distinguish cases, they could not advise their clients simply to disregard what the Supreme Court had said. Resisting the Supreme Court was out of bounds.

The same theme pervaded Marshall's arguments about the proper remedy in *Brown*. As Marshall repeatedly told the Court, implementing desegregation put the rule of law itself at stake. Delay based on "attitudes" meant that the Court would be implicitly accommodating resistance to its statement of what the Constitution meant. He knew that the Court's decision on remedy in *Brown II* meant that "power, not reason, [was] the . . . currency" of constitutional law. The African-American community had to live with that. Neither the community nor the lawyers, however, had to accept it.

Massive resistance and the Southern attack on the NAACP showed that reason could not readily be divorced from power. Bentham's "Judge and Company" responded to, and created, power as much as they enacted reason into law. Civil rights litigation could transform power, but only within limits that Marshall and his colleagues could never take as final. Marshall's last words on the Supreme Court expressed what he had learned throughout his career: that, although power rather than reason might ordinarily be law's currency, we should always hold as our aspiration the prospect that reason would someday be its currency.

Notes

Prologue

1. W.E.B. Du Bois, *Writings,* from *The Souls of Black Folk* (New York: Viking Press, 1986) (originally published 1903), 364–65.
2. David Wilkins, "Justice as Narrative: Some Personal Reflections on a Master Storyteller," *Harvard Blackletter Journal* (Spring 1989): 68, 73.
3. Ralph Winter, interview with author, New Haven, Connecticut, April 26, 1989.
4. Whitman Knapp, interview with author, New York, July 7, 1989.
5. "Thurgood Marshall Speaks," *Ebony,* May 1979, 176–79.
6. TM, "Reflections on the Bicentennial of the United States Constitution," *Harvard Law Review* 101 (Nov. 1987): 1; also published as "The Constitution's Bicentennial: Commemorating the Wrong Document?" *Vanderbilt Law Review* 40 (Nov. 1987): 1337.
7. 115 F.R.D. 349, 354 (1979); Transcript, WUSA-TV's "Searching for Justice: Three American Stories," Sept. 13, 1987.

Chapter 1

1. On Houston's legal training, see Genna Rae McNeil, *Groundwork: Charles Hamilton Houston and the Struggle for Civil Rights* (Philadelphia: University of Pennsylvania Press, 1983), 46–56.
2. TM, oral history interview with Ed Erwin, Feb. 15, 1977, Columbia Oral History Collection, 18; Houston, "Tentative Findings re Negro Lawyers" (1928), Roscoe Pound Papers, Harvard Law School. See also McNeil, *Groundwork,* 67–68.
3. Oliver Hill, interview with author, Richmond, Virginia, July 13, 1989; Erwin oral history interview, 6, 18, 20; Juan Williams, "Marshall's Law," *The Washington Post Magazine,* Jan. 7, 1990, 17; "Thurgood Marshall Speaks," *Ebony,* May 1979, 176–77.
4. McNeil, *Groundwork,* 65–85; TM, remarks at unveiling ceremony, Howard University Law School, Jan. 23, 1991.
5. Bernard Taper, "A Reporter at Large: A Meeting in Atlanta," *The New Yorker,* March 17, 1956, 84; Tribute to Hon. J. Waties Waring, National Lawyers' Guild Annual Banquet, Feb. 20, 1949, NAACP Papers, Library of Congress, Box II-B-215, file: Voting, South Carolina, Waring, J. Waites [sic] and Elizabeth, 1948–50; TM interview with author, Feb. 2, 1989; Transcript, WUSA-TV's "Thurgood Marshall the Man," Dec. 13,

1987. An observer wrote in 1935 that hostility toward African-Americans in Baltimore's department stores was "more extreme . . . than [in] many cities further south." Ira De. A. Reid, *The Negro Community of Baltimore: A Summary Report of a Social Study* (Baltimore: [Baltimore Urban League], 1935), 40.

6. "The Tension of Change," *Time*, Sept. 19, 1955, 24.

7. "Tension of Change," 24; Taper, "Meeting in Atlanta," 93; Lisa Aldred, *Thurgood Marshall* (New York: Chelsea House Publishers, 1990), 22–26; Williams, "Marshall's Law," 15; Roderick Ryon, "Old West Baltimore," *Maryland Historical Magazine* 77 (March 1982): 54; TM, Erwin oral history interview, 14.

8. TM, Erwin oral history interview, 9; "Tension of Change," 24; Deborah Rhode, notes of conversations with TM, in author's possession. (I have consolidated Rhode's and *Time*'s versions of this story.)

9. Aldred, *Thurgood Marshall*, 33; Erwin oral history interview, 5, 8; "Tension of Change," 24.

10. "Tension of Change," 23, 26; Taper, "Meeting in Atlanta," 82; Hill interview. For a similar reference and a general discussion, not limited to the African-American legal community, see Sanford Levinson, *Constitutional Faith* (Princeton: Princeton University Press, 1988), especially 15 (quoting Rep. Barbara Jordan).

11. Margaret Law Callcott, *The Negro in Maryland Politics, 1870–1912* (Baltimore: Johns Hopkins University Press, 1969), vi–vii, 99–100, 133–37, 157; Cynthia Neverdon-Morton, *Afro-American Women of the South and the Advancement of the Race, 1895–1925* (Knoxville: University of Tennessee Press, 1989), 2; Robert J. Brugger, *Maryland: A Middle Temperament, 1634–1980* (Baltimore: Johns Hopkins University Press, 1988), 420–24.

12. Reid, *Negro Community*, 23–27; Erwin oral history interview, 4–5; Williams, "Marshall's Law," 15.

13. TM, Erwin oral history interview, 6.

14. Reid, *Negro Community of Baltimore*, 11, 15; Brugger, *Maryland*, 451–52, 500–504; Jo Ann Argersinger, *Toward a New Deal in Baltimore: People and Government in the Great Depression* (Chapel Hill: University of North Carolina Press, 1988), especially 33–35, 74–82, 181–96.

15. Houston, "Tentative Findings"; Edwin McDowell, "From Twain, a Letter on Debt to Blacks," New York *Times*, March 14, 1985; TM interview with author, Oct. 18, 1990.

16. Aldred, *Thurgood Marshall*, 44–45; NAACP Papers, Reel 17, file: Marshall, Thurgood, Olive Jones; Robert McGuinn to TM, Sept. 1, 1937, id., Reel 16, file: Marshall, Thurgood, 1937; "Fighter for His People," New York *Times*, Sept. 8, 1962, 11; "Tension of Change," 26; TM to George Crawford, April 23, 1936, NAACP Papers, Reel 16, file: Marshall, Thurgood, Sept. 1935–May 1936; TM to F. O. Reinhard, Oct. 2, 1936, NAACP Papers, Reel 16, file: Marshall, Thurgood, Sept.–Dec. 1936; TM interview with author, Oct. 18, 1990. For a general discussion of the typical practice of African-American lawyers at this time, see Houston, "Tentative Findings," 6–7.

17. Roy Wilkins, with Tom Mathews, *Standing Fast* (New York: Viking Press, 1982), 162; Brugger, *Maryland*, 560; TM to Charles Hamilton Houston, Jan. 21, 1936, NAACP Papers, Reel 14, file: Houston, Charles Hamilton, Jan.–Feb. 1936; Williams, "Marshall's Law," 17; Erwin oral history interview, 13.

18. TM, Erwin oral history interview, 10.

19. White to W.A.C. Hughes, Dec. 5, 1933, NAACP Papers, Reel 17, file: Marshall, Thurgood, University of Maryland, Feb. 1933–Dec. 1934; TM to "Pug" [Conrad Pearson], Dec. 12, 1933, ibid.; TM to Houston, Jan. 1, 1934, ibid.; TM to Houston, March 18, 1935, NAACP Papers, Box I-D-93, file: Cases Supported—University of Maryland, Jan.–April 1935.

20. Edward J. Kuebler, "The Desegregation of the University of Maryland," *Maryland Historical Magazine* 71 (Spring 1976): 37, 39–42; Mark Tushnet, *The NAACP's Legal Strategy Against Segregated Education, 1925–1950* (Chapel Hill: University of North Carolina Press, 1988), 56.

21. For general information on the Garland Fund, see Tushnet, *NAACP's Legal Strategy*, 2–4.

22. Tushnet, *NAACP's Legal Strategy*, 7–8, 13–14.

23. Id., 15–17.

24. Id., 26–28.

25. Id., 29, 34; Houston's notes, June [14], 1935, NAACP Papers, Box I-C-197, file: American Fund for Public Service, 1934–35.

26. Id., 35–36.

27. Tushnet, *NAACP's Legal Strategy*, 56; Houston memorandum of conference with TM and Edward Lovett, May 10, 1935, NAACP Papers, Box I-D-93, file: Cases Supported—University of Maryland, May 1935; Houston to TM, April 15, 1935, NAACP Papers, Reel 17, file: Marshall, Thurgood, University of Maryland Jan.–April 1935; Kuebler, "Desegregation," 42–43; TM, Erwin oral history interview, 12. On the 1889 graduates, see David Bogen, "The First Integration of the University of Maryland School of Law," *Maryland Historical Magazine* 84 (Spring 1989): 39.

28. TM to Prentice Thomas, Jan. 5, 1942, NAACP Papers, Box II-B-1, file: Alpha Phi Alpha contribution; TM to Houston, Aug. 21, 1935, NAACP Papers, Reel 16, file: Marshall, Thurgood, May–Nov. 1935; Houston to TM, Aug. 21, 1935, ibid.; Houston to TM, Aug. 23, 1935, ibid.; TM to Houston, Aug. 21, 1935, NAACP Papers, Box I-D-93, file: Cases Supported—University of Maryland, July–Aug. 1935; Houston to TM, Aug. 24, 1935, ibid.; Draft brief, Oct. 20[?], 1935, NAACP Papers, Box I-D-93, file: Cases Supported—University of Maryland, Oct.–Nov. 1935; Houston to TM, Oct. 8, 1935, ibid.; Draft brief, Oct. 26, 1935, ibid.

29. Tushnet, *NAACP's Legal Strategy*, 56–57; Transcript of oral argument, NAACP Papers, Box I-D-94, file: Cases Supported—University of Maryland, Briefs; Brugger, *Maryland,* 520; Pearson v. Murray, 169 Md. 478, 182 A. 590 (1936).

30. Houston's notes, June [14], 1935, NAACP Papers, Box I-C-197, file: American Fund for Public Service, 1934–35.

31. TM to Houston, May 29, 1935, NAACP Papers, Box I-D-93, file: Cases Supported—University of Maryland, May 1935; Tushnet, *NAACP's Legal Strategy*, 65–66.

32. TM to Houston, Aug. 24, 1935, NAACP Papers, Box I-D-93, file: Cases Supported, University of Maryland, July–Aug, 1935; Tushnet, *NAACP's Legal Strategy*, 65–66.

33. TM to Houston, Sept. 12, 1935, NAACP Papers, Box I-D-45, file: Cases Supported, Baltimore County School Case, March–Dec. 1935; TM to Houston, Feb. 5, 1936, id., file: Cases Supported, Baltimore County School Case, Jan.–Feb. 1936; TM to Houston, Feb. 10, 1935, ibid.; TM to Houston, May 27, 1936, id., file: Cases Supported, Baltimore County School Case, May–June 1936; TM to Houston, July 13, 1936, ibid.; Tushnet, *NAACP's Legal Strategy*, 66.

34. Houston to TM, Sept. 1, 1936, NAACP Papers, Box I-D-45, file: Cases Supported, Baltimore County School Case, Aug.–Sept. 1936; Dean Ransom, Confidential Report, Sept. 20, 1936, ibid.; Williams v. Zimmerman, 172 Md. 563, 192 A. 353 (1937).

35. Wilkins, *Standing Fast,* 161.

36. TM to Houston, Dec. 20, 1935, NAACP Papers, Reel 14, file: Houston, Charles Hamilton, Dec. 1935; TM to Houston, Jan. 14, 1935, NAACP Papers, Box I-D-93, file: Cases Supported, University of Maryland, Jan.–April 1935; TM to Houston, Sept. 9, 1935, id., file: Cases Supported, University of Maryland, Sept. 1935.

37. Houston to White, June 19, 1935, NAACP Papers, Box I-D-93, file: Cases Supported, University of Maryland, June 1935; Houston to White, July 12, 1935, id., file: Cases Supported, University of Maryland, July–Aug. 1935; Houston to Charles Wesley, Dec. 7, 1935, NAACP Papers, Reel 16, file: Marshall, Thurgood, Nov. 1935–Jan. 1936.

38. Houston to TM, Sept. 21, 1935, NAACP Papers, Box I-D-93, file: Cases Supported, University of Maryland, Sept. 1935; TM to Houston, May 25, 1936, NAACP Papers, Reel 14, file: Houston, Charles Hamilton, April–May 1936; TM to Houston, April 23, 1936, ibid.; TM to Leon Ransom, April 22, 1936, id., Reel 16, file: Marshall, Thurgood, Sept. 1935–May 1936; TM to George Crawford, April 23, 1936, ibid.

39. Tushnet, *NAACP's Legal Strategy,* 35.

40. Tushnet, *NAACP's Legal Strategy,* 46; Houston to TM, Sept. 17, 1936, NAACP Papers, Box I-C-200, file: American Fund for Public Service Joint Committee, 1936–37.

41. TM to Houston, Sept. 19, 1936, NAACP Papers, Reel 16, file: Marshall, Thurgood, July–Oct. 1936; Houston to TM, Sept. 28, 1936, ibid.

42. TM to White, Oct. 6, 1936, ibid.; Tushnet, *NAACP's Legal Strategy,* 46–47.

43. TM, Erwin oral history interview, 24–25.

Chapter 2

1. Houston to Leon Ransom et al., Sept. 17, 1936, NAACP Papers, Reel 16, file: Marshall, Thurgood, July–Oct. 1936; Jeremy Bentham, *Works,* vol. 5 (John Bowring ed., 1843), 369, quoted in Paul Freund, *The Supreme Court of the United States: Its Business, Purposes, and Performance* (Cleveland: World Publishing Co., 1961), 146.

2. Tushnet, *The NAACP's Legal Strategy,* 37, 59; John Wennersten, "The Black School Teacher in Maryland, 1930's," *Bulletin of Negro History* (Spring 1976): 370; Robert Brugger, *Maryland,* 520.

3. Tushnet, *NAACP's Legal Strategy,* 59–60; TM to Charles Hamilton Houston, Nov. 15, 1935, NAACP Papers, Box I-D-90, file: Cases Supported, Teachers Salary Cases, Maryland, Montgomery County, 1934–36; TM to Howard Pindell, Jan. 27, 1936, ibid.; TM to Houston and Walter White, Oct. 6, 1936, NAACP Papers, Box I-D-45, file: Cases Supported, Baltimore County School Case, Oct. 1–31, 1936; TM memorandum, Oct. 12, 1936, ibid.; TM to White, Dec. 5, 1936, NAACP Papers, Box I-D-88, file: Cases Supported, Teachers Salary Cases, Maryland, Dec. 1–31, 1936. As late as 1949, Marshall wrote Carl Murphy, "I still feel more than the average responsibility concerning Baltimore." TM to Murphy, Dec. 7, 1949, NAACP Papers, Box II-B-201, file: University of Maryland, 1949.

4. Tushnet, *NAACP's Legal Strategy,* 59–60; Memorandum to County Teachers' Associations: Re: Procedure to equalize teachers' salaries, NAACP Papers, Box I-L-41, file: Teachers Salaries, Calvert County, 1937–39.

5. Tushnet, *NAACP's Legal Strategy,* 60.

6. Tushnet, *NAACP's Legal Strategy,* 60–61; TM to Enolia McMillan, Sept. 1, 1937, NAACP Papers, Box I-L-41, file: Teachers Salaries, Calvert County, 1937–39; TM to McMillan, Jan. 17, 1938, NAACP Papers, Box I-D-89, file: Cases Supported, Teachers Salary Cases, Maryland, Jan.–June 1938; TM to Joint Committee, March [no date], ibid.; Brugger, *Maryland,* 520; TM to Jackson, April 4, 1945, NAACP Papers, Box II-B-37, file: Crime, Jones, Holbrock, and Weldon, 1945–46.

7. TM to White, April 4, 1938, NAACP Papers, Box I-D-89, file: Cases Supported, Teachers Salary Cases, Maryland, Jan.–June 1938; TM to Joint Committee, April 11, 1938,

NAACP Papers, Box I-C-201, file: American Fund for Public Service, Maryland Counties, 1938 (3).

8. TM to William Gibbs, Aug. 22, 1938, NAACP Papers, Box I-C-201, file: American Fund for Public Service, Maryland Counties, 1938 (2); TM to Executive Staff, June 23, 1938, NAACP Papers, Box I-D-89, file: Cases Supported, Teachers Salary Cases, Maryland, Jan.–June 1938; TM to McMillan, May 23, 1938, NAACP Papers, Box I-C-201, file: American Fund for Public Service, Maryland Counties, 1938 (3); TM to Edith Throckmorton, April 21, 1938, id., file: American Fund for Public Service, Maryland Counties, 1938.

9. Tushnet, *NAACP's Legal Strategy*, 61–62.

10. Tushnet, *NAACP's Legal Strategy*, 62–64; TM to William Hastie, Oct. 23, 1939, NAACP Papers, Box I-D-89, file: Cases Supported, Teachers Salary Cases, Anne Arundel County, June–Oct. 1939.

11. TM to Curtis Todd, Aug. 30, 1937, NAACP Papers, Box I-C-198, file: American Fund for Public Service, Educational Campaign, June–Aug. 1937; TM to C. H. Fouse, Dec. 2, 1937, NAACP Papers, Box I-C-198, file: American Fund for Public Service, Educational Campaign, Kentucky Schools, 1937–39; TM to J. W. Nicholson, April 20, 1938, NAACP Papers, Box I-C-197, file: American Fund for Public Service, Alabama Schools, 1937–40; TM to A. Heningburg, Feb. 25, 1938, NAACP Papers, Box I-C-281, file: Discrimination, Teachers Salary, 1937–40; Notes on "Fight for Equal Teachers Salary," undated, ibid.

12. TM to J. L. LeFlore, Sept. 1, 1937, NAACP Papers, Box I-C-197, file: American Fund for Public Service, Alabama Schools, 1937–40; S. D. McGill to TM, Aug. 6, 1937, NAACP Papers, Box I-D-88, file: Cases Supported, Teachers Salary Cases, Gilbert & Highfill, 1937–38; TM to Houston (with Houston's response), ibid.

13. Tushnet, *NAACP's Legal Strategy*, 94–95.

14. TM to White, May 11, 1938, NAACP Papers, Box I-C-197, file: American Fund for Public Service, Alabama Schools, 1937–40; TM to Arthur Shores, May 11, 1938, ibid.; TM to J.W. Nicholson, Sept. 20, 1938, ibid.; TM to W. McKinley Menchan, Oct. 20, 1938, ibid.; TM to White, Aug. 24, 1938, NAACP Papers, Box I-C-281, file: Discrimination, Teachers Salaries, 1937–40; TM to White, Nov. 29, 1938, NAACP Papers, Box I-C-197, file: American Fund for Public Service, Alabama Schools, 1937–40.

15. Tushnet, *NAACP's Legal Strategy*, 77–78; TM to J. M. Tinsley, Aug. 30, 1937, NAACP Papers, Box I-D-91, file: Cases Supported, Teachers Salary Cases, Virginia, 1935–37; TM to Tinsley, Oct. 4, 1937, ibid.; TM to White, Nov. 29, 1937, ibid.; TM to Joint Committee, May 13, 1938, id., file: Cases Supported, Teachers Salary Cases, Virginia, May–Sept. 1938; P. B. Young to TM, Oct. 22, 1938, ibid.; TM to Young, Oct. 31, 1938, ibid.; TM to Joint Committee, June 17, 1939, id., file: Cases Supported, Teachers Salary Cases, Virginia, June–Aug. 1939; Earl Lewis, *In Their Own Interests: Race, Class, and Power in Twentieth-Century Norfolk, Virginia* (Berkeley: University of California Press, 1991), 157–59.

16. Lewis, *In Their Own Interests*, 159–60; Tushnet, *NAACP's Legal Strategy*, 79.

17. TM to Joint Committee, Oct. 30, 1939, NAACP Papers, Box I-D-91, file: Cases Supported, Teachers Salary Cases, Norfolk, Virginia, Oct. 3–31, 1939.

18. TM, Erwin oral history interview, 86–87; Tushnet, *NAACP's Legal Strategy*, 79–80.

19. TM, Erwin oral history interview, 87–88; Tushnet, *NAACP's Legal Strategy*, 80.

20. TM to Lillie Jackson, Aug. 17, 1938, NAACP Papers, Box I-C-197, file: American Fund for Public Service, Feb.–Oct. 1937, 1938.

21. Marshall interview with author, May 23, 1989; Tushnet, *NAACP's Legal Strategy*, 47; White to Houston, May 25, 1939 (with Houston's note), NAACP Papers, Reel 2, file: Houston, Charles Hamilton, 1939.

22. Tushnet, *NAACP's Legal Strategy*, 100; Petition to reconsider tax ruling, 1938, NAACP Papers, Box I-D-91, file: Cases Supported, Teachers Salary Cases, Norfolk, Virginia, Briefs; TM to White and Arthur Spingarn, July 27, 1939, NAACP Papers, Box I-L-38, file: Legal Defense Fund, Establishment of; White to Mr. Turner, May 1, 1940, NAACP Papers, Box II-B-81, file: Inc. Fund, Establishment of, 1940–42.

23. TM to White, Aug. 4, 1939, NAACP Papers, Box I-D-95, file: Cases Supported, University of Missouri, Gaines Case, Miscellaneous Documents (Notes); TM to White, Nov. 22, 1938, NAACP Papers, Box I-D-91, file: Cases Supported, Teachers Salary Cases, Virginia, Jan.–Sept. 1938; TM to Hastie, Dec. 31, 1943, NAACP Papers, Box II-B-96, file: Legal Committee, 1942–43.

24. Franklin Williams, interview with author, New York, Aug. 3, 1989.

25. Allen Thomas to NAACP, Jan. 9, 1942 (with TM's handwritten note), NAACP Papers, Box II-B-58, file: Discharge Requests, 1942; Ralph Jones file, Dec. 19, 1941 (with TM's handwritten notes), NAACP Papers, Box II-B-36, file: J, 1941; TM to Walter Johnson, Sept. 30, 1941, ibid. For Hastie's work as civilian aide, see Philip McGuire, *He, Too, Spoke for Democracy: Judge Hastie, World War II, and the Black Soldier* (New York: Greenwood Press, 1988).

26. These criteria, and a reference to the "legal aid" society, are summarized in Outline of Procedure for Legal Cases, Jan. 1944, NAACP Papers, Box II-B-110, file: Outline of Procedure. See also TM to Hobart LaGrone, Dec. 4, 1945, NAACP Papers, Box II-B-56, file: Crime, Young, Louis, 1945–46 (Marshall "very suspicious" of claims, and says NAACP cannot take case unless defendant is innocent).

27. Franklin Williams to A. J. Simmons, July 3, 1947, NAACP Papers, Box II-B-157, file: Soldier Trouble, C, 1947–48; Edward Dudley to Sidney Redmond, Sept. 28, 1944, NAACP Papers, Box II-B-166, file: R, 1943–44; TM to William T. McKnight, Dec. 21, 1941, NAACP Papers, Box II-B-128, file: Williams, Robert, 1941; TM to Forrest Jackson, Feb. 15, 1944, NAACP Papers, Box II-B-125, file: Rape, Newson, Sidney, Correspondence, 1943–44. For an example in the 1930s of the difficulties that arose from supporting a defendant who was initially thought to be innocent but who turned out to be guilty, see Tushnet, *NAACP's Strategy*, 39–42.

28. Franklin Williams to William A. Stevenson, June 7, 1946, NAACP Papers, Box II-B-18, file: Court Martial, S, 1944–46; Franklin Williams to TM, Nov. 30, 1948, NAACP Papers, Box II-B-153, file: Soldier Trouble, Abston, Dotria, 1948–50; William Hastie to Leslie Perry, Aug. 29, 1944, NAACP Papers, Box II-B-13, file: Court Martial, Foreman, John A., 1943–46; Houston to TM, Sept. 22, 1947, NAACP Papers, Box II-B-124, file: Rape, Mangum, James, 1946–47; TM to Carolyn Moore, Dec. 27, 1944, NAACP Papers, Box II-B-165, file: Soldier Trouble, Oglesby, Joseph, 1944–45; Marian Wynn Perry Yankauer interview with author, North Brookfield, Massachusetts, July 20, 1989.

29. TM to Curtiss Todd, April 4, 1948, NAACP Papers, Box II-B-114, file: Police Brutality, Q, R, 1940–50; Marian Perry to files, Sept. 3, 1947, NAACP Papers, Box II-B-124, file: Rape, Mangum, James, 1946–47; TM to Theodore Spaulding, Oct. 14, 1941, NAACP Papers, Box II-B-12, file: Crime, M, 1941. See also TM to A. Maceo Smith, Feb. 4, 1947, NAACP Papers, Box II-B-50, file: Crime, S, 1947 ("I cannot be a party to any action to have him go from one jurisdiction to another because to do so can easily be charged as obstructing justice, etc.").

30. See James [?] Clark to NAACP, Sept. 4, 1947 (with handwritten note by Perry: "cannot read"), NAACP Papers, Box II-B-119, file: Property, July–Dec. 1947; Franklin Williams to TM, Oct. 25, 1946, NAACP Papers, Box II-B-218, file: Williams, Franklin H., 1945–48; TM to William Burleigh, Dec. 22, 1953, NAACP Papers, Box II-B-36, file:

Crime, Ingram Family, 1953–55; W. D. Lyons to TM, Jan. 7, 1944, NAACP Papers, Box II-B-40, file: Crime, Lyons, W. D., Correspondence, 1944–55; TM to Lyons, Dec. 19, 1944, ibid. On the Ingram case, see Charles H. Martin, "The Civil Rights Congress and Southern Black Defendants," *Georgia Historical Quarterly* 71 (Spring 1987): 25, 34–39.

31. Alice Stovall, interview with author, Wheaton, Maryland, June 11, 1990; TM testimony to Committee on Civil Rights, May 17, 1947, NAACP Papers, Box II-B-8, file: Civil Rights, General, 1944–47; Mileage account, Sept. 8, 1941, NAACP Papers, Box II-A-534, file: Speakers, Marshall, Thurgood, General, Sept.–Dec. 1941; Mileage account, id., file: Speakers, Marshall, Thurgood, General, 1942; Mileage account, Feb. 14, 1944, id., file: Speakers, Marshall, Thurgood, General, 1944.

32. TM to office, Nov. 17, 1941, NAACP Papers, Box II-B-99, file: Marshall, Thurgood, General, 1940–41.

33. TM to office, Jan. 18, 1943, NAACP Papers, Box II-B-99, file: Marshall, Thurgood, General, 1942–43; TM to White, May 5, 1940, NAACP Papers, Box II-A-533, file: Speakers, Marshall, Thurgood, Jan.–June 1940.

34. TM to White, May 14, 1940, NAACP Papers, Box II-A-533, file: Speakers, Marshall, Thurgood, Jan.–June 1940; TM to White, May 22, 1940, ibid.

35. Press release, Dec. 3, 1943, NAACP Papers, Box II-B-5, file: Boilermakers, California, Correspondence, etc., 1943–45; transcript of "America on Guard," broadcast on KSFO, Dec. 4, 1943, ibid.; Clipping, New York *Times*, Feb. 18, 1944, ibid.; James Williams to Wilkins, Dec. 18, 1943, NAACP Papers, Box II-B-6, file: Boilermakers, Providence, Correspondence, 1943–44; Luther Glanton to TM, May 4, 1950, NAACP Papers, Box II-B-124, file: Rape, Mallory, James, 1950; Gloster Current to TM, March 8, 1944, NAACP Papers, Box II-B-74, file: Housing, Detroit, General, 1942–45.

36. For general information on the Port Chicago mutiny, see "Mutiny?" (NAACP pamphlet, 1945), in NAACP Papers, Box II-B-20, file: Court Martial, San Francisco Mutiny, 1944–45; Robert Allen, *The Port Chicago Mutiny* (New York: Warner Books, 1989). The seamen were initially sentenced to fifteen years to life, but all of the sentences were eventually reduced, with the defendants serving about fifteen months; at the end of the war, the Port Chicago defendants were among 1,700 servicemen who were given clemency. Allen, *Port Chicago*, 127, 133–35.

37. TM to office, Oct. 8, 1944, NAACP Papers, Box II-B-20, file: Court Martial, San Francisco Mutiny, 1944–45; TM to office, Oct. 13, 1944, ibid.; C. L. Dellums to White, Oct. 11, 1944, ibid.; TM to Ernest Besig, Feb. 14, 1945, ibid.; TM statement before Judge Advocate General board, April 3, 1945, NAACP Papers, Box II-B-23, file: Court Martial, Yerba Buena Seamen, Correspondence, 1944–46. Marshall also attempted to intervene directly with Secretary of the Navy James Forrestal, who, however, refused to meet with him. Forrestal confirmed the convictions and issued a statement saying that Marshall was satisfied with the conduct of the proceedings. Marshall, who did believe that the military defense attorneys had done the best they could within the limits they faced but who also believed that the prosecutor was "vicious and dumb," was outraged both at the affront Forrestal gave in failing to meet him and at what he called Forrestal's "deliberate attempt to discredit these men by discrediting their attorney." TM to James Forrestal, July 13, 1945, ibid.

38. TM to Mr. Turner, Oct. 7, 1940, NAACP Papers, Box II-B-130, file: Reeves, Frank, 1940–43; Wilkins to White, Oct. 14, 1940, ibid.; TM to White, Oct. 15, 1940, ibid.; Robert Carter, "A Tribute to Justice Thurgood Marshall," *Harvard Law Review*, 105 (Nov. 1991): 33, 37.

39. Prentice Thomas to B. K. Terrell, Feb. 2, 1943, NAACP Papers, Box II-B-172, file: Speakers, Thomas, Prentice, 1942–44; White to Thomas, May 3, 1943, NAACP Papers,

Box II-B-143, file: Thomas, Prentice, 1942–43; Thomas to George Weaver, Aug. 1, 1943, ibid.; Williams interview.

40. Wilkins to TM, Mar. 13, 1942 (with handwritten notes), NAACP Papers, Box II-B-99, file: Marshall, Thurgood, General, 1942–43.

41. Herbert Hill, interview with author, Madison, Wisconsin, Nov. 10, 1990; Robert Carter, interview with author, New York, Dec. 7, 1990; TM to White, Oct. 17, 1947, NAACP Papers, Box II-B-66, file: Discrimination, Theatres, Baltimore, 1947; TM to Gloster Current, Feb. 6, 1947, NAACP Papers, Box II-B-75, file: Housing, General, 1947.

42. Hill interview; Yankauer interview.

43. White to Mrs. Bowman, April 26, 1953, NAACP Papers, Box II-B-83, file: Konvitz, Milton, 1940–44; Konvitz to Wilkins, Sept. 3, 1943, ibid.; Wilkins to Konvitz, Sept. 7, 1943, ibid. For Konvitz's background, see David Danelski, *Rights, Liberties, and Ideals: The Contributions of Milton R. Konvitz* (Littleton, Colo.: Fred B. Rothman, 1983).

44. TM to White, Nov. 1, 1943, NAACP Papers, Box II-B-67, file: Dudley, Edward R., 1943–55. Dudley later served as Borough President of Manhattan, and then was appointed to the New York trial level court.

45. TM to William Hastie, Dec. 18, 1940, NAACP Papers, Box II-B-7, file: Budget, 1940–44; Wilkins to Mary White Ovington, Aug. 27, 1943, NAACP Papers, Box II-B-11, file: Committee of 100, Harold Oram, 1943–44; Anna Caples to TM, April 17, 1947, NAACP Papers, Box II-B-10, file: Committee of 100, General, 1945–50. The figures cited in the text are drawn from the financial reports for 1941 (containing a handwritten note by Walter White), 1942, 1943, and 1944, all in NAACP Papers, Box II-B-72, file: Financial Reports and Statements, 1941–54.

46. Carter interview; Robert L. Carter, interview by John Britton, March 8, 1968, 2, 10, Civil Rights Documentation Project, Moorland-Spingarn Research Center, Howard University; Carter, "Tribute," 37; Motley to Vashti Speller, May 9, 1949, NAACP Papers, Box II-B-120, file: Property, 1949; Z. Alexander Looby, interview by John Britton, Dec. 29, 1967, p. 21, Civil Rights Documentation Project, Moorland-Spingarn Research Center, Howard University.

47. Perry to Ann Fagan Ginger, May 10, 1948, NAACP Papers, Box II-B-72, file: G, 1949; Perry to TM, Oct. 10, 1945, NAACP Papers, Box II-B-111, file: Perry, Marian Wynn, 1945–49; Perry to Wilkins and TM, June 15, 1949, ibid.; Yankauer interview.

48. Williams to J. M. Kaplan, March 17, 1947, NAACP Papers, Box II-B-83, file: K, 1941–48; Harry Bragg to TM, Oct. 20, 1945, NAACP Papers, Box II-B-218, file: Williams, Franklin H., 1945–48; TM to White, Nov. 14, 1945, ibid.; Williams interview; Mrs. Thurgood Marshall, interview with author, Washington, D.C., April 24, 1991. Williams left the national office in 1953 to become regional director for the West.

49. Oral history interview of Constance Baker Motley by Mrs. Walter Gellhorn, March 19, 1977, 170–71, Columbia Oral History Collection; Motley to TM, May 25, 1949, NAACP Papers, Box II-B-101, file: Motley, Constance Baker, 1949–55; Motley to TM and Roy Wilkins, June 20, 1949, ibid.

50. Jonathan Kaufman, *Broken Alliance: The Turbulent Times Between Blacks and Jews in America* (New York: Scribners, 1988), 89–90.

51. TM to Hastie, Sept. 7, 1944, NAACP Papers, Box II-A-299, file: Hastie, William, General, Sept. 1944–45; TM to White, Jan. 31, 1947, NAACP Papers, Box II-B-99, file: Marshall, Thurgood, General, 1947; TM to White, Oct. 13, 1947, ibid.; TM to Committee on Administration, Oct. 27, 1947, ibid.; Committee on Administration minutes, Oct. 27, 1947, ibid.; TM to White, Dec. 4, 1947, ibid.

52. TM to Current, Feb. 6, 1947, NAACP Papers, Box II-B-75, file: Housing, General,

1947; Stovall interview; Gloria Branker, interview with author, Washington, D.C., Jan. 30, 1991.

53. Carter, "Tribute," 37; TM to Leon Ransom et al., July 28, 1939, NAACP Papers, Box II-L-40, file: Ransom, Leon; TM to William Ming, June 3, 1949, NAACP Papers, Box II-B-96, file: Legal Conference, 1949; Williams interview; Coleman interview.

54. Yankauer interview.

55. TM to George E. C. Hayes, June 12, 1950, NAACP Papers, Box II-B-96, file: Legal Conference, 1950; TM to Robert Burrell, Feb. 18, 1941, NAACP Papers, Box II-B-37, file: Crime, Jones, Crawford, 1940–41; TM to Raymond Pace Alexander, April 21, 1943, NAACP Papers, Box II-B-70, file: Extradition, Mattox, Thomas, 1942–43; Alexander to TM [received April 24, 1943], ibid.

56. Constance Baker Motley, interview with author, Chester, Connecticut, Sept. 1, 1989; William L. Coleman, interview with author, Washington, D.C., Oct. 17, 1989; Stovall interview.

57. Yankauer interview; Williams interview; Carter interview. During their discussions, the justices thought that the evidence on the grand jury issue that Marshall argued was "not clear" and was "less compelling" than in other recent cases. A majority was willing to reverse, though, because the confession came after the defendant had been held by the police for an excessive period. Case memorandum, Wiley Rutledge Papers, Library of Congress, Box 175, file: October Term 1948, Cases Memos 601–650 (on *Watts v. Indiana*); Docket sheet, Robert Jackson Papers, Library of Congress, Box 157, file: October Term 1948, Cases No. 610; Conference notes, *Watts v. Indiana*, William O. Douglas Papers, Library of Congress, Box 182, file: Argued Cases, Turner.

58. U.S. Const., art. IV, 2; TM to Loren Miller, Jan. 12, 1950, NAACP Papers, Box II-B-165, file: Soldier Trouble, Middlebrooks, Sylvester, 1946–51. Although Miller prevailed in the trial court, the court of appeals ultimately ruled against the fugitive, on the relatively narrow ground that before he could get a federal court in California to consider whether his initial trial had been unconstitutional, he had to present his claim of unconstitutionality to the Georgia courts. Matter of Middlebrooks, 88 F. Supp. 943 (S.D. Cal. 1950), *rev'd sub nom.*, Ross v. Middlebrooks, 188 F.2d 308 (9th Cir. 1951).

59. Williams interview; Kluger, *Simple Justice*, 438; Marshall interview with author, Feb. 2, 1989.

60. Yankauer interview.

Chapter 3

1. TM to Dewey Fox, Sept. 30, 1947, NAACP Papers, Box II-B-113, file: Police Brutality, Goines, Lester; TM to Hastie and Ransom, July 30, 1941, NAACP Papers, Box II-B-20, file: Extradition, Wellman, William, 1941–43; TM to Netta White, Oct. 18, 1949, NAACP Papers, Box II-B-50, file: Crime, Sellers, Jim, 1949; Yankauer interview; TM to Gloster Current, July 8, 1947, NAACP Papers, Box II-B-99, file: Marshall, Thurgood, General, 1947.

2. Robert Carter to TM, Feb. 28, 1950, NAACP Papers, Box II-B-37, file: Crime, James, O. D., 1950; Ralph Mark Gilbert to White, Dec. 28, 1943, NAACP Papers, Box II-B-37, file: Crime, Jackson, Lonnie, 1943–44; Gilbert to White, Feb. 2, 1944, ibid.; TM note, undated, ibid. In another case, Marshall refrained from writing a letter to a prisoner explaining why the NAACP had declined to handle his case "because it has been our experience that where Negroes are confined in Southern prisons, it is against their interest to receive a letter from us informing them that we cannot help them. It gives the authorities

in these prisons the assurance that these men are without outside assistance and I am sure
you realize what that means to them. At the same time," he noted, "it is hard on the
individual not to hear from us." TM to Samuel Battle, Oct. 1, 1941, NAACP Papers, Box II-
B-49, file: Crime, Robinson, Ernest, 1941–42.

3. TM to Lillie Jackson, April 4, 1949, NAACP Papers, Box II-B-64, file: Discrimination, General, 1949.

4. TM to U. Simpson Tate, Feb. 3, 1950, NAACP Papers, Box II-B-124, file: Rape,
Honeycutt, Edward, 1950. See also TM to Daniel Byrd, Sept. 12, 1947, NAACP Papers,
Box II-B-60, file: Discrimination, Alexandria, LA, 1947 (describing "hearing" TM held to
conciliate dispute over settlement of and fees for suit challenging segregated and unequal
recreational facilities).

5. For details on the Francis case, see Arthur S. Miller, *Death by Installments: The
Ordeal of Willie Francis* (New York: Greenwood Press, 1988).

6. A. P. Tureaud to TM, May 11, 1946, NAACP Papers, Box II-B-32, file: Crime,
Francis, Willie, Correspondence, 1946; Tureaud to Emily Branch (Francis's sister), Aug.
24, 1946, ibid.; Bertrand LeBlanc to NAACP, Jan. 13, 1947, ibid.; White to Legal Department, Jan. 21, 1947, ibid.; White to TM, Jan. 23, 1947, ibid.; Press release, Jan. 17, 1947,
ibid.; TM to White, Jan. 20, 1947, ibid.; White to TM, Jan. 23, 1947, ibid.; White to TM,
Jan. 24, 1947, ibid.

7. Roger Baldwin to Harry Freeman, March 6, 1940, NAACP Papers, Box II-B-126, file:
Rape, Smith, Edgar, 1940; file memorandum, March 31, 1944, NAACP Papers, Box II-B-2,
file: ACLU, 1944–48; TM to Clifford Forster, April 2, 1944, NAACP Papers, Box II-B-20,
file: Court Martial, San Francisco Mutiny, 1944–45; TM's notes, undated, NAACP Papers, Box II-B-23, file: Court Martial, Yerba Buena Seamen, Legal Papers and Notes.

8. White to TM and Reeves, Jan. 13, 1941, NAACP Papers, Box II-B-99, file: Marshall,
Thurgood, General, 1940–41; White to Hastie, Jan. 21, 1942, NAACP Papers, Box II-B-28,
file: Crime, Coleman, Festus, 1941–45; TM to Walter Cordon, Jan. 31, 1944, ibid. On the
Scottsboro case, see Dan Carter, *Scottsboro* (Baton Rouge: Louisiana State University Press,
1969).

9. Yankauer interview; Press release, Jan. 13, 1944, NAACP Papers, Box II-B-30, file:
Crime, Davis, Tee.

10. TM to White, Sept. 4, 1942, NAACP Papers, Box II-B-68, file: Extradition, Gen-
eral, 1942; TM to White, Jan. 23, 1941, NAACP Papers, Box II-54, file: Crime, Waller,
Odell, 1940–41; TM to Lou Pakisar, Dec. 12, 1949, NAACP Papers, Box II-B-202, file:
Universities, Oklahoma, Correspondence, Jan.–May 1948.

11. Roy Wilkins, with Tom Mathews, *Standing Fast* (New York: Viking Press, 1982),
210; TM statement, Sept. 6, 1956, NAACP Papers, Box III-A-76, file: Communism,
General, 1954–63, NAACP Papers, Box II-B-12, file: Communism, Dennis, Eugene; TM
to W. Robert Ming, Aug. 1, 1947; Doxey Wilkerson to TM, Aug. 27, 1947, ibid.

12. Federal Bureau of Investigation, NAACP file 61–3176, Section 7, Sept. 9, 1943; TM
to Theodore Spaulding, June 1, 1949, NAACP Papers, Box II-B-90, file: Labor, Loyalty
Cases—James Kurcher, 1948–50.

13. TM to William Lige, May 2, 1950, NAACP Papers, Box II-B-114, file: Police
Brutality, Pope, Clara, 1950; TM to Milton Brown, Sept. 7, 1948, NAACP Papers, Box II-
B-63, file: Discrimination, General, 1948 (Aug.–Dec.). See also TM to Lillie Jackson, April
28, 1949, NAACP Papers, Box II-B-64, file: Discrimination, General, 1949 (recommending
no greater participation with Civil Rights Congress than filing *amicus* brief in case related to
Baltimore tennis arrests). For a study of the actions of the leading Communist-related group
to support black defendants, see Martin, "The Civil Rights Congress."

14. Yankauer interview. In 1946, Roy Wilkins urged Marshall to pursue a case of police

brutality that had occurred in Freeport, Long Island, "right on the doorstep of the National Office" in "circumstances likely to arouse widespread public indignation and discussion," which the Communists were likely to exploit. Wilkins to TM, March 14, 1946, NAACP Papers, Box II-B-151, file: Soldier Killing, Ferguson, Charles, 1946 (Feb.–Mar.); Williams Report, Feb. 16, 1946, ibid. After investigating the incident, Franklin Williams reported that the case had produced a great deal of misinformation about what the police had done. Williams Report, March 19, 1946, ibid.

15. TM to Margaret Bishop, May 17, 1945, NAACP Papers, Box II-B-61, file: Discrimination, Bars, Hotels, Restaurants, 1945; Outline of Procedure for Legal Cases, Jan. 1944, NAACP Papers, Box II-B-110, file: Outline of Procedure. For the NAACP's efforts to secure antilynching legislation, see Robert Zangrando, *The NAACP Crusade Against Lynching, 1909–1950* (Philadelphia: Temple University Press, 1980).

16. Legal Department Report on Court-Martial Cases, Dec. 1, 1945–June 1, 1946, NAACP Papers, Box II-B-20, file: Court Martial Statistics, 1946; Franklin Williams to TM, Nov. 30, 1948, 153, file: Soldier Trouble, Abston, Dotria, 1948–50.

17. TM to James Forrestal, Jan. 23, 1945, NAACP Papers, Box II-B-195, file: US Navy—Guam, Yerba Buena Court Martial, General, 1944–45; TM to Henry Stimson, May 24, 1945, NAACP Papers, Box II-B-65, file: Discrimination, Redistribution Center, 1944–45. For a brief discussion of the desegregation of VA hospitals in the late 1940s, see E. H. Beardsley, "Good-Bye to Jim Crow: The Desegregation of Southern Hospitals, 1945–1970," *Bulletin of the History of Medicine* 60 (Fall 1986): 367, 371–72.

18. White to James Bennett, Oct. 20, 1943, NAACP Papers, Box II-B-62, file: Discrimination, Bureau of Prisons, 1942–46; TM to White, Oct. 27, 1943, ibid.; TM to Bennett, April 29, 1944, ibid.; White to Harry Truman, Nov. 7, 1945, ibid.; Bennett to White, Nov. 29, 1945, ibid.; White to Bennett, Jan. 3, 1946, ibid.

19. TM to F. B. Ransom, May 1, 1942, NAACP Papers, Box II-B-75, file: Housing, General, 1940–42; TM to Wilkins, Oct. 20, 1941, ibid.

20. White to Board of Directors, June 21, 1944, NAACP Papers, Box II-B-119, file: Property, Property Purchase (NAACP), 1944–45; TM to White, July 5, 1944, ibid. The problem went away when the NAACP's offer to purchase the property was rejected. Hastie to White, Sept. 5, 1944, ibid.

21. Sidney Fine, *Frank Murphy: The Washington Years* (Ann Arbor: University of Michigan Press, 1984), 32; Robert Carr, *Federal Protection of Civil Rights: Quest for a Sword* (Ithaca: Cornell University Press, 1947), 1; Brown v. Mississippi, 297 U.S. 278 (1936); Richard Cortner, A *"Scottsboro" Case in Mississippi: The Supreme Court and* Brown v. Mississippi (Jackson, Miss.: University of Mississippi Press, 1986).

22. TM to Francis Biddle, April 15, 1943, NAACP Papers, Box II-B-151, file: Soldier Killing, Carr, Raymond, 1942–43; Wendell Berge to TM, April 23, 1943, ibid.; TM to Berge, April 26, 1943, ibid.; Berge to Anne Makefield, May 25, 1943, ibid.; TM to Miss Harper, July 14, 1943, ibid.; TM to Berge, July 14, 1943, ibid.

23. John T. Elliff, *The United States Department of Justice and Individual Rights, 1937–1962* (New York: Garland, 1987), 100–01, 163–70.

24. Screws v. United States, 325 U.S. 91 (1945); Carr, *Federal Protection*, 114–15.

25. Perry to A. Maceo Smith, Sept. 7, 1948, NAACP Papers, Box II-B-116, file: Police Brutality, Wills Point, TX, 1947–48; Carr, *Federal Protection*, 124, 138–42, 161–62; Elliff, *Department of Justice*, 142–43, 162–63; T. Vincent Quinn to Perry, Nov. 4, 1947, NAACP Papers, Box II-B-116, file: Police Brutality, Vines, Meb, 1947–48; Perry to TM, Dec. 1, 1947 (with Marshall note), ibid.

26. Chambers v. Florida, 309 U.S. 227, 241 (1940); Canty v. Alabama, 309 U.S. 629 (1940); White v. Texas, 309 U.S. 631 (1940); Ransom to TM, March 12, 1940, NAACP

Papers, Box II-B-27, file: Crime, Canty v. Alabama, 1940–42. The Texas attorney general filed a petition for rehearing in *White,* claiming that it had not had adequate notice of White's effort to have the Supreme Court reopen the case. The Court denied this petition after hearing argument, 310 U.S. 530 (1940).

27. Ransom to TM, June 25, 1943; Konvitz to Ransom, June 29, 1943, both in NAACP Papers, Box II-B-121, file: Ransom, L. A., 1943–46; S. D. McGill to Ransom, May 10, 1940, NAACP Papers, Box II-B-28, file: Crime, Chambers Murder Case, Correspondence, 1940–42; New Orleans *Times-Picayune,* June 11, 1941, NAACP Papers, Box II-B-55, file: Crime, White, Bob, 1941; New York *Daily News,* June 17, 1941, ibid.; Leland Johnson to Konvitz, July 27, 1943, NAACP Papers, Box II-B-123, file: Rape, Hill, Henry Allen, Correspondence, 1941–43. For a later, similar example, see New York *Post,* Feb. 14, 1954, clipping in NAACP Papers, Box II-B-123, file: Rape, Groveland, Florida, 1949–55 (two defendants whose convictions had been reversed by Supreme Court were shot by the sheriff on the way to retrial; one died, the other was convicted).

28. TM to Forrest Jackson, March 22, 1946, NAACP Papers, Box II-B-38, file: Crime, Lewis, James, Correspondence, 1946–47; H. A. Merchant to TM, Dec. 20, 1940, NAACP Papers, Box II-B-122, file: Rape, Burnam, Eugene, 1940–42; Mrs. Burnam to [office], March 28, 1942, ibid.

29. Roy Wilkins to White, Feb. 27, 1942, NAACP Papers, Box II-B-121, file: Ransom, Leon, 1940–42; Ransom to White, April 8, 1942, ibid.; Hill interview; Arthur Shores to TM, Oct. 23, 1950, NAACP Papers, Box II-B-129, file: Residential Segregation, Alabama, Monk v. Birmingham, 1949–51; TM to Shores, Oct. 27, 1950, ibid. (Shores reported that when the posse "finally caught some one," they "riddled him with bullets. He managed to live, however, and is expected to recover.")

30. TM, Memorandum Brief for the Attorney General of the United States, undated, NAACP Papers, Box II-B-9, file: Columbia, TN, Riot, Memos; Stenographer's notes of meeting, March 4, 1946, NAACP Papers, Box II-B-9, file: Columbia, TN, Riot, National Committee for Justice in Columbia, 1946; White press statement, March 25, 1946, ibid., White to branches, March 11, 1946, NAACP Papers, Box II-B-9, file: Columbia, TN, Riot, Cases, 1946–48. Accounts of the incident are in Wilkins, *Standing Fast,* 186–89; Walter White, *A Man Called White: The Autobiography of Walter White* (Bloomington: Indiana University Press, 1970, originally published 1948), 308–21; Wade Hall, *The Rest of the Dream: The Black Odyssey of Lyman Johnson* (Lexington: University Press of Kentucky, 1988), 203–5; Carl T. Rowan, *Dream Makers, Dream Breakers: The World of Justice Thurgood Marshall* (Boston: Little, Brown & Co., 1993), 107–12.

31. Elliff, *The United States Department of Justice,* 216–19; TM to J. Edgar Hoover, May 10, 1946, FBI document 44–1366–128, released under the Freedom of Information Act; Z. Alexander Looby and Maurice Weaver, Work Report, Feb. 26 to April 19, 1946, NAACP Papers, Box II-B-9, Columbia, TN, Riot, Finances, 1946–48; Perry to files, June 19, 1946, NAACP Papers, Box II-A-197, file: Columbia, Tennessee, Riot, Department of Justice, 1946.

32. White to Hastie, July 8, 1946, NAACP Papers, Box II-A-300, file: Hastie, William, General, 1946–49; Catherine Freeland to staff, May 12, 1946, NAACP Papers, Box II-B-99, file: Marshall, Thurgood, General, 1945–46; White to staff, May 12, 1946, ibid.; White to Committee on Administration, May 12, 1946, ibid.; Robert Carter to Mr. Harrington, July 5, 1946, ibid.; Carter to A. T. Walden, Sept. 16, 1946, ibid.; TM to White, Oct. 1, 1946, ibid.; Affidavit of Louis Wright, July 15, 1946, NAACP Papers, Box II-B-9, file: Columbia, TN, Riot, Cases, 1946–48.

33. TM interview, May 23, 1989; Carter to Ransom and Looby, July 18, 1946, NAACP Papers, Box II-A-198, file: Columbia, Tennessee, Riot, Lawyers, Z. Alexander Looby,

1946–47; White to Mrs. Marshall, July 15, 1946, NAACP Papers, Box II-A-197, file: Columbia, Tennessee, Riot, Correspondence, General, July 1946–1947. Ransom's mental condition was beginning to deteriorate at this time. See TM to Daisy Lampkin, Dec. 4, 1946, NAACP Papers, Box II-A-198, file: Columbia, Tennessee, Riot, Lawyers, Leon Ransom, 1946–49; Houston to TM, Jan. 7, 1949, ibid. (calling Ransom "a sick man").

34. Motley to Moon, March 18, 1948, NAACP Papers, Box II-B-9, Columbia, TN, Riot, Cases, 1946–48; Minutes of Executive Committee, National Committee for Justice in Columbia, TN, Oct. 9, 1946, NAACP Papers, Box II-B-9, file: Columbia, TN, Riot, Indictments, 1946–47.

35. Vincent Sheean, "Verdict by Tomorrow Forecast in Trial of Tennessee Negroes," New York *Herald Tribune,* Oct. 3, 1946, 24; Carter to White, Aug. 12, 1946, NAACP Papers, Box II-B-9, file: Columbia, TN, Riot, Finances, 1946–48; Carter to White, Aug. 18, 1946, ibid.; Carter to TM, Aug. 16. 1946, ibid.; TM to White and Carter, Aug. 17, 1946, ibid. The dispute lingered even after the trials were over, with Carter noting that he was "not a little annoyed" at the lawyers' efforts to get more money from the NAACP when their fee of $25 a day was the highest rate the organization had ever paid cooperating attorneys. Z. Alexander Looby to Carter, Aug. 29, 1946, ibid.; Carter to Maurice Weaver, Oct. 26, 1946, ibid.

36. Sheean, "Verdict by Tomorrow"; Motley to Moon, March 18, 1948, NAACP Papers, Box II-B-9, file: Columbia, TN, Riot, Cases, 1946–48; Nashville *Banner,* June 5, 1948, clipping in NAACP Papers, Box II-B-38, file: Crime, Kennedy v. Tennessee, 1947–49. Justices Rutledge, Murphy, and Black voted to hear Kennedy's appeal to the Supreme Court. Jan Palmer, *The Vinson Court Era: The Supreme Court's Conference Votes—Data and Analysis* (New York: AMS Press, 1990), 218.

37. Marshall interview, May 23, 1989; TM to Tom Clark, Dec. 19, 1946, NAACP Papers, Box II-A-197, file: Columbia, Tennessee, Riot, Correspondence, General, July 1946–1947; TM to Theron Caudle, Dec. 4, 1946, ibid.; Gloster Current, Branch Action Letter, Nov. 25, 1946, NAACP Papers, Box II-B-99, file: Marshall, Thurgood, General, 1945–46; Erwin oral history interview, 31–34; Yankauer interview. These accounts of the incident vary in minor details, such as the reason why Looby took over the driving, but they are consistent with respect to the most important aspects. In 1968, Marshall discovered that he was disqualified from sitting as a Supreme Court Justice in a case because he had represented the petitioner twenty years earlier in a case arising out of the Columbia incident. TM to Earl Warren, April 5, 1968, Earl Warren Papers, Library of Congress, Box 356, file: Marshall, Thurgood.

Chapter 4

1. Palko v. Connecticut, 302 U.S. 319 (1937); Adamson v. California, 332 U.S. 46 (1947); Strauder v. West Virginia, 100 U.S. (10 Otto) 303 (1880); *Ex parte* Virginia, 100 U.S. (10 Otto) 339 (1880); Moore v. Dempsey, 261 U.S. 86 (1923); Powell v. Alabama, 287 U.S. 45 (1932). For a review of the Court's decisions in this area prior to 1937, see John Braeman, *Before the Civil Rights Revolution: The Old Court and Individual Rights* (New York: Greenwood Press, 1988), 87–115.

2. C. Jerry Gates to Edward Dudley, April 7, 1945, NAACP Papers, Box II-B-128, file: Rape, Williams, Burnette, 1943–45; Houston to TM, Sept. 22, 1947, NAACP Papers, Box II-B-124, file: Rape, Mangum, James, 1946–47. The Supreme Court discussed and upheld a stringent time limitation in Daniels v. Allen, 344 U.S. 443 (1953).

3. TM to Madeline Brown, March 8, 1943, NAACP Papers, Box II-B-24, file: Crime,

B, 1943. See also TM to Fred Inbau, Oct. 27, 1950, NAACP Papers, Box II-B-50, file: Crime, S, 1950–55.

4. Chambers v. Florida, 309 U.S. 227 (1940).

5. TM to Philadelphia Volunteer Defender Association, July 16, 1940, NAACP Papers, Box II-B-68, file: Extradition, General, 1940; Cassandra Maxwell, Memorandum to Files, May 18, 1940, NAACP Papers, Box II-B-35, file: Crime, Heywood, Benjamin, 1940–41; Carter to Roy Wilkins, May 3, 1947, NAACP Papers, Box II-B-56, file: Crime, D, 1945–47; Neil McMillen, *Dark Journey: Black Mississippians in the Age of Jim Crow* (Urbana: University of Illinois Press, 1989), 286.

6. TM to Roy Wilkins, Jan. 15, 1940, NAACP Papers, Box II-B-25, file: Crime, Baker, John, 1940–43; TM to Joseph Murray, Feb. 2, 1940, ibid.; TM to J. A. Brier, Feb. 8, 1940, ibid.

7. J. M. Hinton to TM, Sept. 24, 1941, NAACP Papers, Box II-B-44, file: Crime, Osborne, Sammie, 1941–42; TM to Hinton, Sept. 26, 1941, ibid.; Hinton to TM, Sept. 28, 1941, ibid.; TM to Hinton, Oct. 24, 1941, ibid.; TM to Miss Bowman, Dec. 17, 1941, ibid.; TM Memorandum for Press Release, July 9, 1942, ibid. The defendant's conviction was reversed because the jury had not been properly instructed about self-defense, but he was convicted at his second trial, and Marshall concluded that there were no constitutional issues in the case that would allow it to be pursued further. Harold Boulware to TM, April 28, 1943, ibid.; TM to file, May 24, 1943, ibid.

8. Marian Wynn Perry to Edward Knott, Aug. 20, 1947, NAACP Papers, Box II-B-128, file: Rape, Tingle, James M., 1947–48.

9. Press release, Nov. 15, 1940, NAACP Papers, Box II-B-54, file: Crime, Waller, Odell, 1940–41; White to TM (with note by TM), June 9, 1941, ibid.; S. D. Redmond to TM, Feb. 15, 1944, NAACP Papers, Box II-B-50, file: Crime, Thornton, George, Correspondence, 1944; TM to S. D. Redmond, Feb. 15, 1944, ibid. For a full account of the Waller case, see Richard B. Sherman, *The Case of Odell Waller and Virginia Justice, 1940–42* (Knoxville: University of Tennessee Press, 1992).

10. Lillie Roberts to TM, Aug. 22, 1944, NAACP Papers, Box II-B-28, file: Crime, Carter, Willie, 1944–46; TM to Forrest Jackson, Sept. 6, 1944, ibid.; Jackson to TM, Sept. 14, 1944, ibid.; TM to Jackson, Sept. 19, 1944, ibid.; Jackson to TM, Sept. 21, 1944, ibid.; Edward Dudley to Will and Temple Carter, Oct. 16, 1944, ibid.; Jackson to Dudley, Nov. 27, 1944, ibid.; Jackson to TM, March 12, 1945, ibid.; TM to Jackson, April 5, 1945, ibid.; Jackson to TM, Aug. 22, 1945, ibid.; TM to Jackson, Aug. 25, 1945, ibid.

11. TM to G. F. Porter, Nov. 3, 1941, NAACP Papers, Box II-B-123, file: Rape, Hill, Henry Allen, Correspondence, 1941–43.

12. TM to Doss Hardin, March 30, 1942, NAACP Papers, Box II-B-123, file: Rape, Hill, Henry Allen, Correspondence, 1941–43; Charles Bracken to TM, June 5, 1942, ibid.; TM to Bracken, June 10, 1942, ibid.; Jackson draft dissent (with note by Black), Hugo Black Papers, Library of Congress, Box 271, file: Supreme Court Case File, October Term 1943, opinions of others, Nos. 319–569; Returns on draft opinion, Harlan Fiske Stone Papers, Library of Congress, Box 67, file: Hill v. Texas; Hill v. Texas, 316 U.S. 400 (1942). Hill was reindicted and again was sentenced to death. Leland Johnson to Milton Konvitz, July 27, 1943, NAACP Papers, Box II-B-123, file: Rape, Hill, Henry Allen, Correspondence, 1941–43.

13. Dallas *Times Herald,* Sept. 16, 1941, NAACP Papers, Box II-B-23, file: Crime, L. C. Akins, 1941–49; Jules F. Mayer to TM, Sept. 25, 1941, ibid.; G. F. Porter to TM, Oct. 20, 1941, ibid.; TM to Porter, Oct. 23, 1941, ibid.; Porter to TM, March 14, 1942, ibid.; A. Maceo Smith to Roy Wilkins, Oct. 15, 1945, ibid.; Porter to Wilkins, Oct. 20, 1945, ibid.; Akins v. State, 167 S.W.2d 758 (Texas Ct. Crim. App. 1943). For additional details on the

Akins case, see George C. Edwards, "White Justice in Dallas," *Nation,* 161 (Sept. 15, 1945), 253–54.

14. Douglas Papers, Box 122, file: Miscellaneous notes (on *Akins*).

15. 325 U.S. 398 (1945) (Justice Wiley Rutledge concurred in the result without joining Reed's opinion, and Chief Justice Stone and Justice Black dissented without opinion); Perry to Wilkins, Nov. 16, 1947, NAACP Papers, Box II-B-23, file: Crime, L. C. Akins, 1941–49. In 1947, when Akins was about to be paroled, the national NAACP office tried but failed to find him a job. Donald Jones to Mrs. Roberta Akins, June 1, 1949, ibid.

16. Lyons v. Oklahoma, 322 U.S. 596 (1944); TM, Memorandum to Office, Jan. 29, 1941, NAACP Papers, Box II-B-39, file: Crime, Lyons, Correspondence, 1940–41. See also NAACP Papers, Box II-B-68, file: Extradition, Burrows, George, 1943–44.

17. TM, Memorandum to office, Jan. 29, 1941, NAACP Papers, Box II-B-39, file: Crime, Lyons, Correspondence, 1940–41. For a description of Dunjee's career, see John Henry Lee Thompson, "The Little Caesar of Civil Rights: Roscoe Dunjee in Oklahoma City, 1915 to 1955," Ph.D. dissertation, Purdue University, 1990.

18. TM, Memorandum to office, Jan. 29, 1941, NAACP Papers, Box II-B-39, file: Crime, Lyons, Correspondence, 1940–41; TM to White, Feb. 2, 1941, ibid.; TM to White, Feb. 5, 1941, ibid.

19. TM to White, Feb. 2, 1941, NAACP Papers, Box II-B-39, file: Crime, Lyons, Correspondence, 1940–41.

20. TM to White, Feb. 2, 1941, NAACP Papers, Box II-B-39, file: Crime, Lyons, Correspondence, 1940–41; Stanley Belden to Roger Baldwin, Feb. 6, 1941, ibid.; Belden to TM (with TM note on copy), March 31, 1941, ibid.

21. Belden to TM, April 26, 1941, NAACP Papers, Box II-B-39, file: Crime, Lyons, Correspondence, 1940–41; TM to Belden, May 7, 1941, ibid.

22. TM to Belden, May 13, 1941, NAACP Papers, Box II-B-39, file: Crime, Lyons v. Oklahoma, Correspondence, 1940–41; TM to Belden, July 29, 1941, ibid.; TM to Belden, Hastie, and Ransom, Aug. 8, 1941, ibid.; Roscoe Dunjee to TM, Aug. 12, 1941, ibid.; Dunjee to TM, Oct. 23, 1942, NAACP Papers, Box II-B-39, file: Crime, Lyons v. Oklahoma, Correspondence, 1942–43; Dunjee to TM, March 27, 1943, ibid.; TM to Dudley and Konvitz, June 25, 1944, NAACP Papers, Box II-B-39, file: Crime, Lyons v. Oklahoma, Correspondence, 1944–52.

23. Conference notes, Douglas Papers, Box 93, file: Argued Cases, No. 433, Lyons v. Oklahoma; Lyons v. Oklahoma, 322 U.S. 596 (1944) (Justice Black joined Murphy's opinion, and Justice Rutledge dissented without opinion; Justice Douglas concurred in the result but not in Reed's opinion).

24. TM to Lyons, Feb. 23, 1945, NAACP Papers, Box II-B-39, file: Crime, Lyons v. Oklahoma, Correspondence, 1944–52; TM to Samuel Latimer [*sic;* Lattimore], Oct. 16, 1952, ibid.; Lattimore to TM, Oct. 28, 1952, ibid. Lyons was pardoned in 1965. Carl Rowan, *Dream Makers, Dream Breakers: The World of Justice Thurgood Marshall* (Boston: Little, Brown & Co., 1993), 97.

25. A. P. Tureaud to Hastie, Aug. 12, 1942, NAACP Papers, Box II-B-153, file: Soldier Trouble, Adams, Richard, Correspondence, May–Sept. 1942; TM to Alexandria Branches, NAACP, Sept. 8, 1942, ibid.; TM to William Ming, Oct. 16, 1942, NAACP Papers, Box II-B-153, file: Soldier Trouble, Adams, Richard, Correspondence, Oct. 1942–March 1943; TM to John Bordenave, Dec. 27, 1944, NAACP Papers, Box II-B-154, file: Soldier Trouble, Adams, Richard, Correspondence, 1944–48; TM to Elmer Newton, April 3, 1945, ibid.; TM interview, May 23, 1989.

26. Adams v. United States, 319 U.S. 312 (1943); A. P. Tureaud to Hastie, Aug. 12, 1942, NAACP Papers, Box II-B-153, file: Soldier Trouble, Adams, Richard, Correspon-

dence, May–Sept. 1942; TM to Alexandria Branches, Sept. 8, 1942, ibid.; TM to Edward Cox, Oct. 14, 1942, NAACP Papers, Box II-B-153, file: Soldier Trouble, Adams, Richard, Correspondence, Oct. 1942–March 1943; TM to office, Jan. 20, 1943, ibid.; A. P. Tureaud, Interview by Robert Wright, Aug. 9, 1969, Civil Rights Documentation Project, Moorland-Spingarn Research Center, Howard University.

27. TM to Louis Redding, Dec. 29, 1942, NAACP Papers, Box II-A-534, file: Speakers, Marshall, Thurgood, General, 1943; TM to Miss Harper, May 6, 1943, NAACP Papers, Box II-B-154, file: Soldier Trouble, Adams, Richard, Correspondence, April–May 1943.

28. John McCloy to TM, May 20, 1943, NAACP Papers, Box II-B-154, file: Soldier Trouble, Adams, Richard, Correspondence, April–May 1943; TM to Myles Hibbler, May 26, 1943, ibid.; TM to Hastie, May 29, 1943, ibid.; Truman Gibson to White, June 18, 1943, NAACP Papers, Box II-B-154, file: Soldier Trouble, Adams, Richard, Correspondence, June–Nov. 1943; TM to White, July 30, 1943, ibid.; Konvitz to Wilkins, May 17, 1944, NAACP Papers, Box II-B-154, file: Soldier Trouble, Adams, Richard, Correspondence, 1944–48; Blanche Holmes to TM, March 28, 1946, ibid.; Fred Rogers to TM, Dec. 5, 1947, ibid.; Transcript, NAACP Papers, Box II-B-155, file: Soldier Trouble, Adams, Richard, Transcript.

29. William Coleman, interview with author, Washington, D.C., Oct. 17, 1989; Spottswood Robinson, "Thurgood Marshall–The Lawyer," *Harvard Civil Rights-Civil Liberties Law Review* 13 (Spring 1978): 234, 235; Joe Greenhill, "Address," *Texas Southern Law Review* 4 (1977): 179, 180. See also J. Skelly Wright, "Thurgood Marshall: A Tribute," *Maryland Law Review* 40 (1981): 398: In a segregation case, counsel had stated that the Southern University Law School was air-conditioned. "Marshall asked the Dean [of Southern University Law School] to describe in detail the building in which Southern was housed. The Dean testified that it was a large wooden frame structure with five floors . . . and that the Law School was on the fifth floor." After Marshall had the dean describe what was on the other floors, Marshall "then asked the witness whether each of the first four floors was air-conditioned like the fifth. The answer as to each floor was 'No.' Feigning surprise at the Dean's answers, Marshall then asked the witness what was immediately above the fifth floor. His answer: 'The roof.' Marshall then suggested to the Dean that the Law School was really housed in the attic of the building. The Dean readily agreed, saying, 'That's why it is air-conditioned.'"

30. "Fighter for His People," New York *Times*, Sept. 8, 1962, 11; Stovall interview; Williams interview.

Chapter 5

1. See Robert McCloskey, *The American Supreme Court* (Chicago: University of Chicago Press, 1960), 165–69; William Leuchtenburg, "The Origins of Franklin D. Roosevelt's 'Court-Packing' Plan," *Supreme Court Review* 1966 (1966): 347; William Leuchtenburg, "FDR's Court-Packing Plan: A Second Life, a Second Death," *Duke Law Journal* 1985 (Summer 1985): 673.

2. Frankfurter to Wiley Rutledge, Jan. 2, 1948, Wiley Rutledge Papers, Library of Congress, Box 157, file: October Term 1947, Case file, Bob-Lo Co. v. Michigan.

3. Frankfurter to Conference, Nov. 11, 1947, Douglas Papers, Box 160, file: Argued Cases, No. 91, Lee v. Mississippi; Conference notes, ibid.

4. Sidney Fine, *Frank Murphy: The Washington Years* (Ann Arbor: University of Michigan Press, 1984), 505–6; Felix Frankfurter to Frank Murphy, Felix Frankfurter Papers, Harvard Law School Library, Box 170, file 14.

5. See Dennis Hutchinson, "The Black-Jackson Feud," *Supreme Court Review* 1988 (1988): 203.

6. Tushnet, *NAACP's Legal Strategy*, 70–71.

7. Missouri ex rel. Gaines v. Canada, 305 U.S. 337 (1938); Tushnet, *NAACP's Legal Strategy*, 73–74.

8. For a thorough study of the challenge to segregated transportation that carries the story through the 1960s, see Catherine A. Barnes, *Journey from Jim Crow: The Desegregation of Southern Transit* (New York: Columbia University Press, 1983).

9. McCabe v. Atchison, Topeka & Santa Fe R. Co, 235 U.S. 151 (1914).

10. Mitchell v. United States, 313 U.S. 80 (1941).

11. Edward Dudley to Spottswood Robinson, March 12, 1945, NAACP Papers, Box II-B-185, file: Transportation, Complaints, 1940–50, H; TM to Harry Phillips, July 20, 1944, NAACP Papers, Box II-B-186, file: Transportation, Complaints, 1940–50, L; TM to Larry Eisenberg, Sept. 6, 1945, NAACP Papers, Box II-B-183, file: Transportation, Complaints, E & F, 1940–55.

12. TM to John LeFlore, Dec. 18, 1940, NAACP Papers, Box II-B-188, file: LeFlore, John L., 1940–50, Correspondence.

13. Spottswood Robinson, interview with author, Aug. 2, 1989; Hill interview; Memorandum, March 24, 1940, NAACP Papers, Box II-B-191, file: Transportation, Murray, Pauli, 1940.

14. Robinson interview. For a description of one of the cases that ended with a conviction for disorderly conduct, see Pauli Murray, *The Autobiography of a Black Activist, Feminist, Lawyer, Priest, and Poet* (Knoxville: University of Tennessee Press, 1989) (originally published as *Song in a Weary Throat: An American Pilgrimage*, 1987), 138–49.

15. Carter to Lillian Falss, Nov. 15, 1945, NAACP Papers, Box II-B-183, file: Transportation, Brown v. Southern R. Co., Correspondence, 1945–50; Robinson interview.

16. Conference notes, William O. Douglas Papers, Library of Congress, Box 122, file: Argued Cases, No. 704, Morgan v. Virginia; Conference notes, March 29, 1946, Wiley Rutledge Papers, Library of Congress, Box 140, file: October Term, 1945, Case memos, 701–750.

17. Morgan v. Virginia, 328 U.S. 373 (1946). Justice Black concurred with a separate opinion, and Justice Rutledge concurred in the result without opinion.

18. Burton memorandum for the Conference, Rutledge Papers, Box 141, file: October Term, 1945, Correspondence, Burton, Harold.

19. Carter to Frank Reeves, NAACP Papers, Box II-B-158, file: Soldier Trouble, D, 1946; TM to Richard Westbrooks, NAACP Papers, Box II-B-186, file: Transportation, General, 1945–46; Carter to Robinson, Sept. 16, 1946, NAACP Papers, Box II-B-186, file: Transportation, Complaints, 1940–50, S; Carter to White, Oct. 20, 1946, NAACP Papers, Box II-B-191, file: Transportation, Morgan v. Virginia, General, 1944–48.

20. Minutes of Nov. 16, 1946, meeting re transportation, Jan. 20, 1947, NAACP Papers, Box II-A-138, file: Board of Directors, National Legal Committee, 1946–49; Carter to T. G. Nutter, Jan. 1, 1947, NAACP Papers, Box II-B-187, file: Transportation, General, 1947; Carter to Joseph S. Freeland, Feb. 4, 1947, NAACP Papers, Box II-B-192, file: Transportation, Whiteside v. Southern Bus Lines, Correspondence, 1946–50; TM to White, Feb. 3, 1947, NAACP Papers, Box II-B-187, file: Transportation, General, 1947.

21. TM to Karl Llewellyn, Dec. 4, 1946, NAACP Papers, Box II-B-186, file: Transportation, Complaints, 1940–50, L.

22. TM to Karl Kuehn, Sept. 18, 1947, NAACP Papers, Box II-B-89, file: Labor, K, 1941–49. For a study of the Boilermakers union and discrimination, see Herbert Hill, *Black*

Labor and the American Legal System (Madison: University of Wisconsin Press, 1985, originally published 1977), 185–208.

23. TM to White and Wilkins, Dec. 22, 1943, NAACP Papers, Box II-B-6, file: Boilermakers, Portland, 1944–45; Press release, Jan. 13, 1944, ibid.; Hill, *Black Labor,* 203–4.

24. James v. Marinship Corp. 25 Cal. 2d 721, 155 P.2d 329 (1944); Boilermakers resolution, May 23, 1946, NAACP Papers, Box II-B-5, file: Boilermakers, California, Correspondence, 1943–45; TM to Herbert Resner, May 27, 1946, ibid.; George Johnson to TM, June 12, 1946, ibid.

25. Steele v. Louisville & N. R. Co., 323 U.S. 192 (1944). On discrimination in the railway unions, see Hill, *Black Labor,* 334–72.

26. TM to Houston, May 31, 1940, NAACP Papers, Box II-B-94, file: Railroad Cases, General, 1940–41; Houston to Frank Reeves, Feb. 25, 1942, NAACP Papers, Box II-B-94, file: Railroad Cases, General, 1942–44.

27. For a discussion of Houston's arguments and their implications, see Karl Klare, "The Quest for Industrial Democracy and the Struggle Against Racism: Perspectives from Labor Law and Civil Rights Law," *Oregon Law Review* 61 (December 1982): 157.

28. Conference notes on *Tunstall,* Douglas Papers, Box 107, file: Argued Cases, no. 37; Steele v. Louisville & N. R. Co., 323 U.S. 192 (1944).

29. For support for Murphy's reading of the majority opinion, see E. Merrick Dodd to Felix Frankfurter, March 19, 1945, Frankfurter Papers, Harvard Law School, box 184.

30. TM to various, Jan. 10, 1945, NAACP Papers, Box II-B-90, file: Labor, Letters to Labor Unions, 1945.

31. Frankfurter to Rutledge, Jan. 2, 1948, Rutledge Papers, Box 157, file: October Term, 1947, case file, Bob-Lo Excursion Co. v. Michigan; Bob-Lo Excursion Co. v. Michigan, 333 U.S. 28 (1948). Justice Douglas concurred, stressing that the case involved a complete exclusion from passage; Justice Jackson, joined by Chief Justice Vinson, dissented. The emphasis on the unique factual setting appears to have originated with Justice Frankfurter. See Conference notes, Dec. 20, 1947, Rutledge Papers, Box 157, file: October Term, 1947, case file, Bob-Lo Excursion Co. v. Michigan.

32. Railway Mail Ass'n v. Corsi, 326 U.S. 88 (1945); Hastie to Orrin Judd, Feb. 13, 1945 NAACP Papers, Box II-B-94, file: Labor, Railway Mail Ass'n v. Corsi, Correspondence, 1943–48; Edward Dudley to Hastie, Feb. 26, 1945, ibid.; Dudley to Hastie, Feb. 23, 1946, ibid.; TM to Joseph LeCount, April 24, 1944, NAACP Papers, Box II-B-6, file: Boilermakers, Portland, 1944–45.

Chapter 6

1. For a discussion of the role of Legal Realism in shaping other aspects of the NAACP's legal strategy, see Tushnet, *NAACP's Legal Strategy,* 117–19.

2. Guinn v. United States, 238 U.S. 347 (1915); Buchanan v. Warley, 245 U.S. 60 (1917).

3. 118 U.S. 356 (1886).

4. Law clerk memorandum (undated), Stanley Reed Papers, Special Collections and Archives, King Library, University of Kentucky, Box 80, file: Smith v. Allwright.

5. Buchanan v. Warley, 245 U.S. 60 (1917). For background on the case, see Kellogg, *NAACP,* 183–87; Clement Vose, *Caucasians Only: The Supreme Court, the NAACP, and the Restrictive Covenant Cases* (Berkeley: University of California Press, 1959), 3–4.

6. Corrigan v. Buckley, 271 U.S. 323 (1926).

7. Margold Report, 121–208, NAACP Papers, Library of Congress, Box I-C-198, file: American Fund for Public Service, Margold Report.

8. This issue has generated a large legal literature. For a relatively early discussion, see Louis Henkin, "*Shelley v. Kraemer:* Notes for a Revised Opinion," *University of Pennsylvania Law Review* 110 (February 1962): 473.

9. TM to Robert Wagner, Aug. 9, 1940, NAACP Papers, Box II-B-71, file: Federal Housing Administration, Dover, Mass., 1940; M. R. Young to David Walsh, Sept. 20, 1940, ibid.; TM to Young, Nov. 4, 1940, ibid.; White to Frederic Morrow, Nov. 8, 1940, ibid.

10. Hansberry v. Lee, 311 U.S. 32 (1940). For a dramatization of the facts of *Hansberry,* see Lorraine Hansberry, *A Raisin in the Sun* (New York: S. French, 1988) (by the purchaser's daughter).

11. TM to Robert Hale, Oct. 28, 1940, NAACP Papers, Box II-B-71, file: Federal Housing Administration, Dover, Mass., 1940; Harlan Fiske Stone Papers, Library of Congress, Box 65, file: Hansberry v. Lee; Cert. memo, William O. Douglas Papers, Library of Congress, Box 50, file: Argued Cases, No. 29.

12. Robinson interview; Robinson to TM, May 19, 1944, NAACP Papers, Box II-B-134, file: Restrictive Covenants, Study of, by Spottswood Robinson, 1944–45; Robinson to TM, Oct. 11, 1945, NAACP Papers, Box II-B-131, file: Restrictive Covenants, Kentucky, 1943–45; TM to Robinson, Dec. 16, 1945, NAACP Papers, Box II-B-134, file: Restrictive Covenants, Study of, by Spottswood Robinson, 1944–45; TM to C. L. Dellums, July 31, 1944, NAACP Papers, Box II-B-129, file: Residential Segregation, General, 1942–53.

13. Vose, *Caucasians Only,* 58–68; Williams interview; TM to National Legal Committee, June 13, 1945, NAACP Papers, Box II-B-131, file: Restrictive Covenants, Chicago Conferences, 1945–46; TM to Loren Miller, June 26, 1945, ibid.; Transcript and statements, July 9–10, 1945, ibid.

14. Robert Weaver, Preliminary Notes on Coordination of Legal and Social Attacks on Race Restrictive Covenants, [1945?], NAACP Papers, Box II-B-131, file: Restrictive Covenants, General, 1943–46; Yankauer interview.

15. TM to Dorothy Height, Nov. 14, 1945, NAACP Papers, Box II-B-130, file: Restrictive Covenants, California, 1940–46; TM to Ruth Weyand, Jan. 20, 1947, NAACP Papers, Box II-B-131, file: Restrictive Covenants, California, 1947–50; Mays v. Burgess, 147 F.2d 869 (D.C. Cir. 1945), *cert. denied,* 325 U.S. 868 (1945); Minutes of Conference on Restrictive Covenants, Howard University, Jan. 26, 194[7?], NAACP Papers, Box II-B-131, file: Restrictive Covenants, General, 1947–50.

16. Vose, *Caucasians Only,* 122–50.

17. Vose, *Caucasians Only,* 74–99; Minutes of Conference on Restrictive Covenants, Howard University, Jan. 26, 194[7?], NAACP Papers, Box II-B-131, file: Restrictive Covenants, General, 1947–50.

18. Vose, *Caucasians Only,* 151–52; Miller to TM, Jan. 29, 1947, NAACP Papers, Box II-B-131, file: Restrictive Covenants, California, 1947–50; Perry to Miller, April 29, 1947, ibid.

19. Vose, *Caucasians Only,* 110–21; Peter Irons, *The Courage of Their Convictions* (New York: Free Press, 1988), 65–68, 75–77.

20. Irons, *Courage,* 68–69.

21. Vose, *Caucasians Only,* 157; TM to David Grant, Aug. 1, 1947, NAACP Papers, Box II-B-134, file: Restrictive Covenants, Shelley v. Kraemer, 1946–48; TM to Grant, Sept. 16, 1947, ibid.; TM to James Bush, Oct. 3, 1947, ibid.; White to Houston, Dec. 19, 1947, NAACP Papers, Box II-B-133, file: Restrictive Covenants, Shelley v. Kraemer, 1947 Nov.–1948, April; Houston to White, Dec. 23, 1947, ibid.; TM to Miller, Oct. 27, 1947, NAACP Papers, Box II-B-134, file: Restrictive Covenants, Sipes v. McGhee, 1947, Sept.–Dec.

22. TM to Houston, Sept. 2, 1947, NAACP Papers, Box II-B-133, file: Restrictive Covenants, Shelley v. Kraemer, Lawyer Conferences, 1947; Minutes of meeting, Sept. 6, 1947, ibid.; Vose, *Caucasians Only,* 161–63.

23. Vose, *Caucasians Only,* 162–63.

24. White to TM, July 1, 1947, NAACP Papers, Box II-B-131, file: Restrictive Covenants, General, 1947–50; White to TM, Sept. 11, 1947, NAACP Papers, Box II-B-133, file: Restrictive Covenants, Shelley v. Kraemer, Lawyer Conferences 1947; Vose, *Caucasians Only,* 163–67.

25. Elliff, *Department of Justice,* 254–57; Vose, *Caucasians Only,* 170, 173; Irons, *Courage,* 69, 70; Michal Belknap, editor, *Civil Rights, The White House, and the Justice Department, 1945–1968* (New York: Garland, 1991), vol. 6: 4–5 (letter from Oscar Chapman to Tom Clark, Sept. 11, 1947); Philip Elman, "The Solicitor General's Office, Justice Frankfurter, and Civil Rights Litigation, 1946–1960: An Oral History," *Harvard Law Review* 100 (February 1987): 817–19; Tom Clark and Philip Perlman, *Prejudice and Property* (Washington, D.C.: Public Affairs Press, 1948) (reprinting the Department of Justice brief).

26. Irons, *Courage,* 71; Report of oral argument, 16 U.S.L.W. 3219 (Jan. 20, 1948) (all further quotations from the oral argument are taken from this report); Elman, "Solicitor General's Office," 819.

27. Elman, "Solicitor General's Office," 820.

28. Irons, *Courage,* 66.

29. Leland Ware, "Invisible Walls: An Examination of the Legal Strategy of the Restrictive Covenant Cases," *Washington University Law Quarterly* 67 (Fall 1989): 737, 760.

30. Francis Allen, "Remembering *Shelley v. Kraemer:* Of Public and Private Worlds," *Washington University Law Quarterly* 67 (Fall 1989): 709, 720.

31. Allen, "Remembering *Shelley,*" 721.

32. Conference notes, William O. Douglas Papers, Library of Congress, Box 122, file: Argued Cases, No. 72, Shelley v. Kraemer; Douglas to Vinson, April 23, 1948 (on return of draft), Fred M. Vinson Papers, Special Collections and Archives, King Library, University of Kentucky, Box 241, file: Restrictive Covenant Cases (folder 2); Burton to Vinson, April 24, 1948 (on return), ibid.; Murphy to Vinson, undated, Vinson Papers, Box 216, file: Subject File, Frank Murphy.

33. 334 U.S. 1 (1948).

34. LFE memorandum, Vinson Papers, Box 241, file: Restrictive Covenant Cases (folder 2); Hurd v. Hodge, 334 U.S. 24 (1948).

35. Frankfurter to Vinson, April 27, 1948, Frankfurter Papers, Harvard Law School, Box 16, file 11.

36. Allen, "Remembering *Shelley,*" 711–12 (citing, among other articles from this period, D. O. McGovney, "Racial Residential Segregation by State Court Enforcement of Restrictive Covenants or Conditions in Deeds is Unconstitutional," *California Law Review* 33 (March 1945): 5).

37. For a summary of comments on the decision, see Vose, *Caucasians Only,* 212–18. For an analysis of Vinson's opinion, see Mark Tushnet, "*Shelley v. Kraemer* and Theories of Equality," *New York Law School Law Review* 33 (1988): 383.

38. Vose, *Caucasians Only,* 214; Loren Miller to White, May 24, 1948, NAACP Papers, Box II-B-71, file: Federal Housing Administration, General, 1940–48; Wilkins to White, June 8, 1948, ibid.; Perry to Ming, Hastie, et al., Jan. 20, 1949, NAACP Papers, Box II-B-71, file: Federal Housing Administration, General, 1949, Jan.–March; White to Harry Truman, Feb. 1, 1949, ibid.; Perry to Miller, Feb. 9, 1949, ibid.; FHA memorandum, Feb. 18, 1949, ibid.; Press release, Feb. 24, 1949, ibid.; Perry to TM, May 24, 1949, NAACP Papers, Box II-B-72, file: Federal Housing Administration, General, April 1949–1955;

Philip Perlman to TM, May 26, 1949, ibid.; TM to Perlman, June 1, 1949, ibid.; Perlman to B. T. Fitzpatrick, June 3, 1949, ibid.

39. TM speech, August 1949, NAACP Papers, Box II-B-72, file: Federal Housing Administration, General, April 1949–1955; FHA press release, Dec. 2, 1949, ibid.; TM to Henry Lee Moon, Dec. 8, 1949, ibid.; TM to Carl Murphy, Dec. 28, 1949, ibid.; Frank Horne to TM, Aug. 9, 1949, Frank Horne Papers, Amistad Research Center, Tulane University, Box 5, folder 16; New York *Times,* Dec. 6, 1949, 30, col. 2 (editorial), col. 5 (Krock, "In the Nation").

40. Miller to Perry, undated, in Yankauer's possession.

41. Ibid.

Chapter 7

1. For general studies of Southern restrictions on voting, see J. Morgan Kousser, *The Shaping of Southern Politics: Suffrage Restriction and the Establishment of the One Party South, 1880–1910* (New Haven: Yale University Press, 1974); Steven Lawson, *Black Ballots: Voting Rights in the South, 1944–1969* (New York: Columbia University Press, 1976).

2. Darlene Clark Hine, *Black Victory: The Rise and Fall of the White Primary in Texas* (Millwood, N.Y.: KTO Press, 1979), 40–48, 56–57, 74–75; Lawson, *Black Ballots,* 24–26.

3. Nixon v. Herndon, 273 U.S. 536 (1927).

4. For a discussion of the NAACP's difficulties in coordinating this case, see Hine, *Black Victory,* 115–20.

5. Hine, *Black Victory,* 129–35; Lawson, *Black Ballots,* 28–30.

6. Newberry v. United States, 256 U.S. 232 (1921).

7. Nixon v. Condon, 286 U.S. 73 (1932).

8. Justice James McReynolds, writing for the four conservative dissenters, rejected Cardozo's argument that the state executive committee was exercising power conferred on it by the state rather than power conferred on it by the party. Like Cardozo, McReynolds was concerned with the implications of a holding that political parties were somehow implicated in state action. To him, "political parties are fruits of voluntary action. . . . White men may organize; blacks may do likewise. A woman's party may exclude males. This much is essential to free government."

9. The state declined to appeal, but the attorney general advised election officials that African-Americans could still be excluded from the primary.

10. Grovey v. Townsend, 295 U.S. 45 (1935).

11. TM to A. A. Lucas et al., June 17, 1940, NAACP Papers, Box II-B-218, file: Wesley, Carter, 1940–41; TM to A. Maceo Smith, Dec. 31, 1943, NAACP Papers, Box II-B-218, file: Wesley, Carter, 1942–45.

12. Lawson, *Black Ballots,* 38–40; TM to Carter Wesley, Nov. 9, 1940, NAACP Papers, Box II-B-218, file: Wesley, Carter, 1940–41; TM to Wesley, May 8, 1941, ibid.; United States v. Classic, 313 U.S. 299 (1941).

13. United States v. Classic, 313 U.S. 299 (1941).

14. Stone to Douglas, April 29, 1941, Stone Papers, Box 74, file: Douglas, William O., 1940–41.

15. Lawson, *Black Ballots,* 38, 41; Hine, *Black Victory,* 208; TM to E. Norman Lacey, Dec. 16, 1941, NAACP Papers, Box II-B-210, file: Voting, Florida Primary, Tampa, 1940–43, 1946, Correspondence; TM to E. L. Bryan, Dec. 24, 1941, ibid.

16. Lawson, *Black Ballots,* 41–42; Hine, *Black Victory,* 198; TM to office, November 17, 1941, NAACP Papers, Box II-B-99, file: Marshall, Thurgood, General, 1940–41.

17. Hine, *Black Victory,* 214; Lawson, *Black Ballots,* 42–43; John T. Elliff, *The United States Department of Justice and Individual Rights, 1937–1962* (New York: Garland Publishers, 1987), 172–73; Fred Folsom, "Federal Elections and the 'White Primary,'" *Columbia Law Review* 43 (Nov.–Dec. 1943): 1026.

18. Hastie to Milton Konvitz, Jul. 13, 1943, NAACP Papers, Box II-A-299, file: Hastie, William, General, July 1943–Aug. 1944; Lawson, *Black Ballots,* 43–44.

19. Lawson, *Black Ballots,* 44; Sidney Fine, *Frank Murphy: The Washington Years* (Ann Arbor: University of Michigan Press, 1984), 392–93; Memorandum on *Smith v. Allwright,* April 10, 1944, Felix Frankfurter Papers, Harvard Law School, box 6, file 17; Conference notes, Douglas Papers, Box 93, file: Argued Cases, No. 51, Smith v. Allwright.

20. Memorandum on *Smith v. Allwright,* April 10, 1944, Felix Frankfurter Papers, Harvard Law School, box 6, file 17. This memorandum contains additional details on the assignment, first of Frankfurter and then of Reed, to write the Court's opinion. It should be noted that Frankfurter's account comes from a file memorandum written by Frankfurter, who often attempted to justify his own actions in this way, and whose account of details and particularly of the emotional tone of conversations must be taken with some skepticism.

21. Ibid.; Frankfurter to Reed, March 15, 1944, Felix Frankfurter Papers, Harvard Law School, box 218, file 14.

22. Felix Frankfurter, Memorandum on *Smith v. Allwright,* April 10, 1944, Felix Frankfurter Papers, Harvard Law School, box 6, file 17; Frankfurter to Stone, March 17, 1944, id., box 172, file 4; Stone to Frankfurter, March 18, 1944, ibid.; Frankfurter to Stone, March 18, 1944, ibid.

23. Rutledge to Reed, April 18, 1944, Stanley Reed Papers, Special Collections and Archives, King Library, University of Kentucky, Box 80, file: Smith v. Allwright; Draft concurring opinion, Wiley Rutledge Papers, Library of Congress, Box 105, file: Smith v. Allwright.

24. Memorandum on *Smith v. Allwright,* April 10, 1944, Felix Frankfurter Papers, Harvard Law School, box 6, file 17.

25. Smith v. Allwright, 321 U.S. 649 (1944).

26. Lawson, *Black Ballots,* 46.

27. TM to A. T. Walden, Sept. 5, 1944, NAACP Papers, Box II-B-211, file: Voting, Georgia, Columbus, 1944–46; Carter to Walter White, July 22, 1946, NAACP Papers, Box II-B-210, file: Voting, Arkansas, 1943–47; TM to Francis Biddle, July 5, 1944, NAACP Papers, Box II-B-212, file: Voting, General, 1944–49; TM to Biddle, July 19, 1944, ibid.; Lawson, *Black Ballots,* 47–50.

28. Elmore v. Rice, 72 F. Supp. 516 (E.D. S.C. 1947); Carter to Boulware, July 10, 1946, NAACP Papers, Box II-B-215, file: Voting, South Carolina, General, 1943–46.

29. Elmore v. Rice, 72 F. Supp. 516 (E.D. S.C. 1947); Tinsley Yarbrough, *A Passion for Justice: J. Waties Waring and Civil Rights* (New York: Oxford University Press, 1987), 68–69; Tribute to Hon. J. Waties Waring, National Lawyers' Guild Annual Banquet, Feb. 20, 1949, NAACP Papers, Box II-B-215, file: Voting, South Carolina, Waring, J. Waites and Elizabeth, 1948–50.

30. Elmore v. Rice, 72 F. Supp. 516 (E.D. S.C. 1947).

31. Rice v. Elmore, 165 F.2d 387 (4th Cir. 1947). For the NAACP's role in the Parker nomination, see Kenneth Goings, *"The NAACP Comes of Age,"* (Urbana: University of Illinois Press, 1990).

32. Yarbrough, *Passion for Justice,* 69–74; TM to James Nabrit et al., June 30, 1948, NAACP Papers, Box II-B-215, file: Voting, South Carolina, General, 1948–50; William Ming to TM, July 1, 1948, ibid.; Konvitz to TM, July 2, 1948, ibid.; Roy Wilkins to White, Aug. 2, 1948, ibid.; TM to Nabrit et al., Nov. 8, 1948, NAACP Papers, Box II-B-213, file:

Voting, South Carolina, Brown v. Baskin, Correspondence, 1944–49; Transcript, July 16, 1948, hearing, NAACP Papers, Box II-B-215, file: Voting, South Carolina, Brown v. Baskin, Legal Papers, 1944–48, July.

33. Transcript, July 16, 1948, hearing, NAACP Papers, Box II-B-215, file: Voting, South Carolina, Brown v. Baskin, Legal Papers, 1944–48, July.

34. Brown v. Baskin, 78 F. Supp. 933 (D. S.C. 1948).

35. Baskin v. Brown, 174 F.2d. 391 (4th Cir. 1949); TM's notes for oral argument, NAACP Papers, Box II-B-214, file: Voting, South Carolina, Brown v. Baskin, Notes.

36. Hine, *Black Victory*, 33–34; Terry v. Adams, 345 U.S. 461 (1953).

37. James M. Nabrit, interview by Vincent Browne, 1968, 11, Civil Rights Documentation Project, Moorland-Spingarn Research Center, Howard University; TM to Mayo Powell, Dec. 19, 1944, NAACP Papers, Box II-B-110, file: P, 1940–46; Rehnquist cert. memo (with Jackson's notes), Jackson Papers, Box 179, file: Terry v. Adams.

38. Conference notes, Tom C. Clark Papers, Tarlton Law Library, University of Texas Law School, Box 149, folder 4; Docket sheet, Jackson Papers, Box 179, file: October Term 1952, Cases No. 52, Terry v. Adams; Mary Frances Berry, *Stability, Security, and Continuity: Mr. Justice Burton and Decision-Making in the Supreme Court 1945–1958* (Westport, Conn.: Greenwood Press, 1978), 126.

39. Terry v. Adams, 345 U.S. 461 (1953).

40. Rehnquist memorandum re: Opinions of Black and Fankfurter in Terry v. Adams, Jackson Papers, Box 179, file: October Term 1952, Cases No. 52, Terry v. Adams; Jackson draft dissent, April 3, 1953, ibid.; Jackson draft concurrence, April 20, 1953, ibid.

41. Minton to Jackson, March 28, 1953, Jackson Papers, Box 16, file: Minton, Sherman.

42. TM to Christia V. Adair, June 2, 1950, NAACP Papers, Box II-B-1, file: A, 1949–50; Williams v. Mississippi, 170 U.S. 213 (1898); Giles v. Harris, 189 U.S. 475 (1903). Holmes also noted that the challengers were seeking to be admitted to the election rolls because, they said, whites who did not meet the statutory qualifications were allowed to vote while African-Americans who did not meet those qualifications were not; Holmes argued that, if that allegation were true, the remedy would be to strike the unqualified whites from registration, not to allow unqualified African-Americans to vote.

43. Lawson, *Black Ballots*, 90–92.

44. TM to Ming, Nov. 6, 1946, NAACP Papers, Box II-B-209, file: Voting, Alabama, Boswell Amendment, General, 1946–49; Motley to Francine Temko, Nov. 12, 1946, ibid.

45. TM to Emory Jackson, Sept. 16, 1947, NAACP Papers, Box II-B-209, file: Voting, Alabama, Boswell Amendment, General, 1946–49; TM to Arthur Shores, Feb. 6, 1948, ibid.; Jackson to TM, Feb. 21, 1948, ibid.; Edward Dudley to Jackson, March 4, 1948, ibid.; Sidney Jones to TM, March 4, 1948, ibid.; Shores to TM, March 8, 1948, ibid.; George Leighton to TM, March 19, 1948, ibid.; Leighton to TM, Aug. 12, 1948, ibid.; Lawson, *Black Ballots*, 94–95.

46. Franklin Williams to Leighton, Aug. 16, 1948, NAACP Papers, Box II-B-209, file: Alabama, Boswell Amendment, General, 1946–49; TM to E. D. Nixon, Oct. 13, 1946, ibid.; TM to John LeFlore, Nov. 13, 1948, ibid.; Carter to LeFlore, Jan. 13, 1949, ibid.; TM to Leighton, Jan. 27, 1948, ibid.; TM to LeFlore, Feb. 23, 1948, ibid.; TM to J. J. Thomas, March 18, 1949, ibid.

47. Davis v. Schnell, 81 F. Supp. 872 (S.D. Ala. 1949).

48. Schnell v. Davis, 336 U.S. 933 (1949); Lawson, *Black Ballots*, 96–97; TM to Thomas, March 1, 1949, NAACP Papers, Box II-B-209, file: Voting, Alabama, Boswell Amendment, General, 1946–49; TM to Leighton, May 27, 1949, ibid.; Leighton to TM, June 28, 1949, ibid.; TM to Leighton, June 30, 1949, ibid.

49. Lawson, *Black Ballots*, 129–34; Perry to Franklin Williams, undated [July 1948],

NAACP Papers, Box II-B-210, file: Voting, Florida, Gadsden County, 1948. For a description of terroristic intimidation of voters in Georgia in 1946, see Patricia Sullivan, "Southern Reformers, the New Deal, and the Movement's Foundation," in Armstead L. Robinson and Patricia Sullivan, eds., *New Directions in Civil Rights Studies* (Charlottesville: University Press of Virginia, 1991), 96.

Chapter 8

1. George Murphy to TM, April 3, 1941, NAACP Papers, Box II-B-136, file: Teachers Salaries, Maryland, Equalization, 1940–41.

2. Report, United States Office of Education, Aug. 4, 1941, NAACP Papers, Box II-B-173, file: Statistics, Education of Negroes, 1941; Tushnet, *NAACP's Legal Strategy*, 90.

3. TM to White, July 23, 1941, NAACP Papers, Box II-B-176, file: Teachers Salaries, General, 1940–41; TM to Murphy, Aug. 16, 1940, NAACP Papers, Box II-B-179, file: Teachers Salaries, Maryland, Mills v. Board of Education, Correspondence, 1940.

4. White to TM (with TM's note), March 18, 1940, NAACP Papers, Box II-B-147, file: Schools, Virginia, Loudoun County, 1940; TM to White, July 23, 1941, NAACP Papers, Box II-B-176, file: Teachers Salaries, General, 1940–41.

5. Henry Lewis Suggs, *P. B. Young, Newspaperman: Race, Politics, and Journalism in the New South, 1910–1962* (Charlottesville: University Press of Virginia, 1988), 161–62; Earl Lewis, *In Their Own Interests: Race, Class, and Power in Twentieth-Century Norfolk, Virginia* (Berkeley: University of California Press, 1991), 163–64; TM to White and Wilkins, Nov. 8, 1940, NAACP Papers, Box II-B-182, file: Teachers Salaries, Virginia, Norfolk, Marshall, Thurgood, 1940–41; TM to Hastie, Ransom, and Hill, Nov. 28, 1940, ibid.; Tushnet, *NAACP's Legal Strategy*, 80; TM to Hastie, Ransom, and White, Feb. 24, 1941, NAACP Papers, Box II-B-100, file: Marshall, Thurgood, Testimonial Dinner at Norfolk, 1941; TM to Ella Baker, May 28, 1942, NAACP Papers, Box II-B-136, file: Schools, Florida, General, 1940–46.

6. TM to L. F. Palmer, Oct. 5, 1940, NAACP Papers, Box II-B-181, file: Teachers Salaries, Virginia, General, 1940–41; TM to Wilkins, April 24, 1940, NAACP Papers, Box II-B-182, file: Teachers Salaries, Virginia, Norfolk, General, 1940.

7. TM to Vernon McDaniel, Aug. 20, 1941, NAACP Papers, Box II-B-175, file: Teachers Salaries, Florida, Escambia County, General, 1940–42; TM to W. Henry Elmore, July 22, 1941, NAACP Papers, Box II-B-180, file: Teachers Salaries, Tennessee, Chattanooga, 1941–42; Tushnet, *NAACP's Legal Strategy*, 98.

8. Tushnet, *NAACP's Legal Strategy*, 93; TM to Amos Hall, June 21, 1947, NAACP Papers, Box II-B-177, file: Teachers Salaries, General, 1947–July 1949.

9. Tushnet, *NAACP's Legal Strategy*, 97–98; Donald Jones to TM, Aug. 10, 1940, NAACP Papers, Box II-B-178, file: Teachers Salaries, Louisiana, New Orleans, 1940–41, General; TM to Jones, Aug. 13, 1940, ibid.; TM to Jones, Feb. 24, 1941, ibid.; TM to Jones, Dec. 1, 1941, ibid.; TM to Tureaud, Jan. 12, 1942, NAACP Papers, Box II-B-178, file: Teachers Salaries, Louisiana, New Orleans, 1942–43, General; TM to Tureaud, July 30, 1942, ibid. At least as alarming was a dispute between the teachers and Tureaud over the size of Tureaud's bill. The teachers were "flabbergasted" at the bill for $3,500. Tureaud, who had graduated from Howard Law School in 1925 and established a struggling practice in New Orleans, had resigned from the NAACP in 1929 when it hired white attorneys to handle a voting rights case, and he seems to have regarded his work with the NAACP as ordinary fee-generating work. The teachers offered him a "donation"—not a fee—and Tureaud told Marshall that he was angry at his treatment. Marshall told Jones and Tureaud

that he could not mediate the dispute because he was not aware of local conditions, but he did urge them to rejoice at their victory rather than to go at each others' throats. In the end, Tureaud accepted a fee of $2,000 for his work. Tushnet, *NAACP's Legal Strategy,* 98–99; Jones to TM, Sept. 7, 1942, NAACP Papers, Box II-B-178, file: Teachers Salaries, Louisiana, New Orleans, 1942–43, General; TM to Jones, Sept. 9, 1942, ibid.; A. P. Tureaud to TM, Nov. 11, 1942, ibid.

10. Scipio Jones to TM, Aug. 12, 1941, NAACP Papers, Box II-B-171, file: Teachers Salaries, Arkansas, Little Rock, Morris v. School Board, 1941–43; J. L.Wilson to TM, Dec. 9, 1941, ibid.; TM to Wilson, Feb. 11, 1942, ibid.; Wilson to TM, Feb. 16, 1942, ibid.; TM to Wilkins, Feb. 28, 1942, ibid.; TM to Jones, Sept. 9, 1942, ibid.; Transcript [of depositions], NAACP Papers, Box II-B-174, file: Teachers Salaries, Arkansas, Little Rock, Transcript.

11. TM to Frank Reeves, Sept. 17, 1942, NAACP Papers, Box II-B-174, file: Teachers Salaries, Arkansas, Little Rock, Morris v. School Board, 1941–43; TM to White, Hastie, and Prentice Thomas, Sept. 19, 1942, ibid.; TM to White and Thomas, Sept. 22, 1942, ibid.; clipping, Arkansas *Gazette,* Oct. 3, 1942, ibid.; TM to White and Thomas, Oct. 3, 1942, ibid.; TM to J. R. Booker, Oct. 1, 1943, ibid.; clipping, Philadelphia *Record,* Jan. 6, 1944, ibid.; Milton Konvitz to Booker and Booker, Jan. 11, 1945, ibid.

12. J. R. Booker to TM, May 18, 1944, NAACP Papers, Box II-B-174, file: Teachers Salaries, Arkansas, Little Rock, Morris v. School Board, 1941–43; TM to Booker, May 20, 1944, ibid.; TM to Myles Hibbler, Feb. 19, 1945, ibid.; Transcript, NAACP Papers, Box II-B-174, file: Teachers Salaries, Arkansas, Little Rock, Drafts, Lists, Memos, 1942–46; Morris v. Williams, 149 F.2d 703 (8th Cir. 1945).

13. Tushnet, *NAACP's Legal Strategy,* 92–93, 96–97; TM to Charles Hyde, Nov. 17, 1941, NAACP Papers, Box II-B-175, file: Teachers Salaries, Florida, Dade County, 1941–43.

14. TM to Office, April 28, 1945, NAACP Papers, Box II-B-177, file: Teachers Salaries, Louisiana, Iberville Parish, Correspondence, 1943–45; Reynolds v. Board of Public Instruction, 148 F.2d 754 (5th Cir. 1945).

15. TM to White, July 15, 1943, NAACP Papers, Box II-B-81, file: Inc. Fund, Cases Pending; List of cases, Jan. 18, 1944, NAACP Papers, Box II-B-176, file: Teachers Salaries, General, 1944–45; Tushnet, *NAACP's Legal Strategy,* 103–04; TM to J. M. Tinsley, December 11, 1945, NAACP Papers, Box II-B-157, file: Soldier Trouble, Clay, Leroy A., 1945; TM to Wilkins, Nov. 27, 1945, NAACP Papers, Box II-B-136, file: Schools, Florida, General, 1940–46.

16. Tushnet, *NAACP's Legal Strategy,* 71.

17. TM to Houston, July 7, 1939, NAACP Papers, Box I-D-95, file: Cases Supported, University of Missouri, Gaines Case, July–Aug. 1939; Missouri *ex rel.* Gaines v. Canada, 305 U.S. 337 (1938).

18. Tushnet, *NAACP's Legal Strategy,* 73–74.

19. Tushnet, *NAACP's Legal Strategy,* 83–85.

20. Tushnet, *NAACP's Legal Strategy,* 86–87; TM to Hastie, April 23, 1940, NAACP Papers, Box II-B-200, file: University of Georgia, 1940–46; TM to Charles Anderson, April 5, 1939, NAACP Papers, Box I-C-198, file: American Fund for Public Service, Educational Campaign, Kentucky Schools, 1937–39; TM to Charles Barley, June 25, 1940, NAACP Papers, Box I-C-202, file: American Fund for Public Service, University of South Carolina, 1938–40; Prentice Thomas to S. A. Burnley, March 24, 1943, NAACP Papers, Box II-B-200, file: University of Kentucky, Eubanks, Correspondence, 1943–45; Charles Eubanks to Thomas, July 7, 1943, ibid.; Houston to Charles Anderson, Jan. 25, 1945, ibid.; Murray, *Autobiography of a Black Activist,* 126.

21. TM to White, Oct. 24, 1945, NAACP Papers, Box II-B-136, file: Schools, General, 1940–46; TM to Grace Hamilton, Jan. 24, 1946, NAACP Papers, Box II-B-137, file: Schools, Georgia, Atlanta, General, 1944–49; TM to [various lawyers], April 1, 1946, NAACP Papers, Box II-B-137, file: Schools, Georgia, Atlanta, Special Lawyers Conference, 1946.

22. TM to James Schwartz, Sept. 26, 1941, NAACP Papers, Box II-B-103, file: National Guard, Minnesota, 1940–44; Digest of Proceedings, NAACP Papers, Box II-B-137, file: Schools, Georgia, Atlanta, Special Lawyers Conference, 1946.

23. Digest of Proceedings, NAACP Papers, Box II-B-137, file: Schools, Georgia, Atlanta, Special Lawyers Conference, 1946.

24. Ibid.

25. TM memorandum to Executive Staff, April 30, 1946, NAACP Papers, Box II-B-136, file: Schools, General, 1940–46.

Chapter 9

1. Michael Gillette, "Heman Marion Sweatt: Civil Rights Plaintiff," in Alwyn Barr and Robert Calvert eds., *Black Leaders: Texans for Their Times* (Austin: Texas State Historical Association, 1981), 161–65.

2. Milton Konvitz to William Standard, May 3, 1944, NAACP Papers, Box II-B-183, file: Transportation, Brown v. Atlantic Coast Line R. Co., 1943–44; Konvitz to Dwight Macdonald, April 21, 1944, NAACP Papers, Box II-B-147, file: Selective Service, Lynn v. Downer, Correspondence, 1943–44; Carter to Hastie, Nov. 15, 1946, NAACP Papers, Box II-A-300, file: Hastie, William, General, 1946–49; Hastie to Carter, Dec. 16, 1946, ibid.; Tushnet, *NAACP's Legal Strategy*, 105–16.

3. Statement of Policy, September 1947, NAACP Papers, Box II-B-67, file: Education, General, 1941–47.

4. Tushnet, *NAACP's Legal Strategy*, 108–09, 111; TM to Wilkins, Oct. 28, 1947, NAACP Papers, Box II-B-137, file: Schools, General, 1947–55.

5. Tushnet, *NAACP's Legal Strategy*, 115; TM, recommended statement by board of directors, June 7, 1948, NAACP Papers, Box II-B-99, file: Marshall, Thurgood, General, 1948–50; TM, Proposed Resolution on Segregation, 1948, National Lawyers Guild Papers, Meiklejohn Civil Liberties Institute.

6. Tushnet, *NAACP's Legal Strategy*, 116–17; David Southern, *Gunnar Myrdal and Black-White Relations: The Use and Abuse of* An American Dilemma (Baton Rouge: Louisiana State University Press, 1987); TM to Grace Corrigan, Dec. 2, 1939, NAACP Papers, Box II-B-144, file: Schools, New Mexico, General, 1940–54; Sadie Alexander to Francis P. Matthews, Nov. 10, 1948, in Michal Belknap, editor, *Civil Rights, the White House, and the Justice Department, 1945–1968* (New York: Garland, 1991), 9: 8–9; Tom Clark and Philip Perlman, *Prejudice and Property*.

7. W. J. Durham, interview by John Britton, May 1, 1970, 4, Civil Rights Documentation Project, Moorland-Spingarn Research Center, Howard University. Sweatt had thought of going back to Michigan for law school, but decided to stay in Texas when his father had a serious heart attack. Gillette, "Sweatt," 159–61.

8. Id., 166–67.

9. Id., 167–69.

10. Gillette, "Sweatt," 172; Roscoe Dunjee to TM, Jan. 15, 1946, NAACP Papers, Box II-B-202, file: Universities, Oklahoma (Correspondence), 1945–46; TM to Dunjee, Feb. 13,

1946, ibid.; Tushnet, *NAACP's Legal Strategy,* 120–21; John Henry Lee Thompson, "Little Caesar of Civil Rights," 138–45.

11. Tushnet, *NAACP's Legal Strategy,* 121; TM to William Ming, Dec. 15, 1947, NAACP Papers, Box II-B-202, file: Universities, Oklahoma (Correspondence), 1947.

12. Conference notes, William O. Douglas Papers, Library of Congress, Box 161, file: Argued Cases, No. 369 (*Sipuel*); Sipuel v. Oklahoma State Regents, 332 U.S. 631 (1948).

13. Tushnet, *NAACP's Legal Strategy,* 121–23. The law school attracted only one student and closed after eighteen months.

14. Frankfurter to Conference, Feb. 13, 1948 (two memos), Fred M. Vinson Papers, Special Collections and Archives, King Library, University of Kentucky, Box 242, file: Sipuel; Douglas to Vinson, undated, ibid.

15. Fisher v. Hurst, 333 U.S. 147 (1948). Sipuel enrolled in the University of Oklahoma Law School in 1949 and graduated in 1951. Tushnet, *NAACP's Legal Strategy,* 123.

16. Tushnet, *NAACP's Legal Strategy,* 125; TM to Hastie, Hill, et al., Oct. 19, 1948, NAACP Papers, Box II-B-202, file: Universities, Oklahoma, Correspondence, Jan.–May 1948.

17. Tushnet, *NAACP's Legal Strategy,* 119–20; Hastie to TM, Oct. 25, 1946, NAACP Papers, Box II-B-136, file: Schools, California, Mendez v. Westminster School Dis., 1946–47.

18. Gillette, "Sweatt," 169.

19. Id., 170–71; Tushnet, *NAACP's Legal Strategy,* 126; Vonciel Jones, "Texas Southern University School of Law—The Beginning," *Texas Southern Law Review* 4 (Special Issue 1977): 197.

20. Minutes of Executive Committee, June 9, 1947, NAACP Papers, Box II-B-99, file: Marshall, Thurgood, General, 1947; G. James Fleming to TM, Oct. 23, 1947, NAACP Papers, Box II-B-137, file: Schools, General, 1947–55; TM to Fleming, Nov. 5, 1947, ibid.

21. TM to W. J. Durham, Dec. 4, 1946, NAACP Papers, Box II-B-205, file: University of Texas, Sweatt v. Painter, Correspondence, Aug.–Dec. 1946; TM to Hastie, April 3, 1947, NAACP Papers, Box II-B-205, file: University of Texas, Sweatt v. Painter, Correspondence, Jan.–June 1947; TM to Donald Murray, April 9, 1947, ibid.; Lloyd Garrison to George Johnson, April 10, 1947, ibid.; William Ming to TM, April 29, 1947, NAACP Papers, Box II-B-137, file: Schools, General, 1947–55.

22. Kluger, *Simple Justice,* 264; Gillette, "Sweatt," 174; Jonathan Entin, "*Sweatt v. Painter,* the End of Segregation, and the Transformation of Education Law," *Review of Litigation* 5 (June 1986): 3, 36–37.

23. Constance Baker Motley to Helen Vance, Jan. 19, 1949, NAACP Papers, Box II-B-205, file: University of Texas, Correspondence, 1949; Entin, "*Sweatt v. Painter,*" 34–36; Gillette, "Sweatt," 173–74; Joe Greenhill, "Address," *Texas Southern Law Review* 4 (Special Issue 1977): 179, 180.

24. Entin, "*Sweatt v. Painter,*" 34–36; Gillette, "Sweatt," 173–74.

25. Gillette, "Sweatt," 175–77; Thurgood Marshall, "Address," *Texas Southern Law Review* 4 (Special Issue 1977): 191.

26. Hastie to TM, April 9, 1947, NAACP Papers, Box II-B-205, file: University of Texas, Sweatt v. Painter, Correspondence, Jan.–June 1947.

27. TM to Charles Thompson, Oct. 4, 1947, NAACP Papers, Box II-B-67, file: Education, General, 1941–47.

28. TM to Hastie, Feb. 18, 1948, NAACP Papers, Box II-B-73, file: H, 1946–48; TM to Roscoe Dunjee, March 39, 1948, NAACP Papers, Box II-B-202, file: Universities, Oklahoma, Correspondence, Jan.–May 1948; Donald Jones to Henry Lee Moon, May 24, 1948,

ibid.; Jones to Moon, May 25, 1948, ibid.; TM to Erwin Griswold, June 7, 1948, ibid.; Charles Bunn to TM, June 8, 1948, ibid.; Erwin Griswold, interview with author, Washington, D.C., June 30, 1989.

29. TM to Hastie, Feb. 18, 1948, NAACP Papers, Box II-B-73, file: H, 1946–48; TM to Ruth Weyand et al., Nov. 2, 1948, NAACP Papers, Box II-B-137, file: Schools, General, 1947–55.

30. TM to Ruth Weyand, et al., Nov. 2, 1948, NAACP Papers, Box II-B-137, file: Schools, General, 1947–55; TM to Spottswood Robinson, Dec. 2, 1948, NAACP Papers, Box II-B-67, file: Education Conference, 1948–49; TM, memorandum, Dec. 15, 1948, ibid.; TM to Friend, Dec. 29, 1948, ibid.; TM to Robinson, Jan. 3, 1949, ibid.; Marian Perry to Carter, Feb. 4, 1949, ibid.; Perry to J. Oscar Lee, Feb. 23, 1949, ibid.; Perry to George L.-P. Weaver, March 15, 1949, ibid.; Perry to Thomas Harris, March 31, 1949, ibid.; Perry to TM, NAACP Papers, Box II-B-56, file: D, 1948–49.

31. Thomas Emerson to John Frank, Feb. 5, 1949, NAACP Papers, Box II-B-146, file: Schools, Texas, General, Jan.–Oct. 1949; Perry to Emerson, May 26, 1949, NAACP Papers, Box II-B-67, file: E, 1948–55; William Ming to TM, March 22, 1949, NAACP Papers, Box II-B-101, file: Ming, William, 1947–49; "Segregation and the Equal Protection Clause: Brief for the Committee of Law Teachers Against Segregation in Legal Education," *Minnesota Law Review* 34 (March 1950): 284.

32. TM to Ming, March 24, 1949, NAACP Papers, Box II-B-62, file: Discrimination—Bars, Hotels, Restaurants, 1948–49; Dennis Hutchinson, "Unanimity and Desegregation: Decisionmaking in the Supreme Court, 1948–1958," *Georgetown Law Journal* 68 (October 1979): 1, 15; Palmer, *The Vinson Court Era,* 264; *Sweatt v. Painter* cert. memo (Larry Tolan), Tom C. Clark Papers, Tarlton Law Library, University of Texas, Box B-142, folder 1.

33. John Frank to Emerson, Feb. 1, 1949, NAACP Papers, Box II-B-146, file: Schools, Texas, General, Jan.–Oct. 1949; TM to Emerson, Feb. 8, 1949, ibid.; Jones, "Texas Southern Law School," 205–6.

34. Jones, "Texas Southern Law School," 206–7; Griswold to TM, Jan. 6, 1950, NAACP Papers, Box II-B-72, file: G, 1950–55; TM to Erwin Griswold, Jan. 10, 1950, ibid.

35. Henderson v. United States, 339 U.S. 816 (1950); Barnes, *Journey From Jim Crow,* 66–71.

36. Tushnet, *NAACP's Legal Strategy,* 130, 193–94; Ming to TM, March 22, 1949, NAACP Papers, Box II-B-101, file: Ming, William, 1947–49; Kluger, *Simple Justice,* 277–78; Philip Elman, "The Solicitor General's Office," 821.

Chapter 10

1. TM to Hastie et al., April 29, 1949, NAACP Papers, Box II-B-96, file: Legal Conference, 1949; TM to Hastie, June 2, 1949, ibid.; Annette Peyser to Carter, June 28, 1949, ibid.

2. Carter to legal staff, Nov. 14, 1949, NAACP Papers, Box II-B-206, file: Universities of Texas and Oklahoma, Correspondence, 1949.

3. Griswold interview; Griswold to TM, March 27, 1950, NAACP Papers, Box II-B-72, file: G, 1950–55.

4. Frances Rudko, *Truman's Court: A Study in Judicial Restraint* (New York: Greenwood Press, 1988), 46–47, 55, 64–65, 88–89; Palmer, *The Vinson Court Era,* 6–14.

5. Gillette, "Sweatt," 178; Abner Mikva, interview with author, Washington, D.C., Dec. 24, 1990.

6. Will Maslow, Summary of Argument, CLSA Reports, NAACP Papers, Box II-B-109,

file: Office Orders & Subscriptions, 1949–50; "Arguments Before the Court," 18 U.S. L.W., April 11, 1950, 3277–81. Quotations that follow are taken from these documents.

7. Robert Jackson to Charles Fairman, April 5, 1950, Robert Jackson Papers, Library of Congress, Box 12, file: Fairman, Charles. Even before the Court voted to hear *Sweatt*, Jackson had written Fairman, saying that he was interested in Fairman's research on the history of the Fourteenth Amendment. Jackson to Fairman, Sept. 30, 1948, ibid.

8. Law clerks' memorandum, March 27, 1950, Harold L. Burton Papers, Library of Congress, Box 210, file: Case #25, Typed Notes, Opinions & Memos.

9. In Clark's notes, these observations are recorded as, "How can you have constitutional provision as to graduate but not as to elementary?" Hutchinson, "Unanimity," 23. Hutchinson interprets this as opposition to desegregation of graduate schools, given Vinson's commitment to segregation of elementary schools. I believe that Vinson was genuinely ambivalent about what to do.

10. Conference notes on *McLaurin*, April 8, 1950, William O. Douglas Papers, Library of Congress, Box 191, file: Argued Cases #34; Conference notes on *Sweatt*, id., file: Argued Cases #44; Hutchinson, "Unanimity," 22–23.

11. Conference notes on *McLaurin*, Douglas Papers; Berry, *Stability, Security, and Continuity*, 120; Hutchinson, "Unanimity," 23.

12. Adamson v. California, 332 U.S. 46 (1947).

13. Conference notes on *Sweatt*, April 8, 1950, Douglas Papers, Box 191, file: Argued Cases #44; Conference notes on *Henderson*, April 8, 1950, Douglas Papers, Box 195, file: *Henderson* Office and Conference Memos; Notes on McLaurin, Frankfurter Papers (HLS), Box 34, folder 3; Hutchinson, "Unanimity," 24.

14. Conference notes on *McLaurin* cert. memo, Stanley Reed Papers, Special Collections, King Library, University of Kentucky, Box 35; Conference notes on *Sweatt*, Douglas Papers, Box 191, file: Argued Cases #44.

15. Conference notes on *Sweatt* cert. memo, Reed Papers, Box 35.

16. Conference notes on *McLaurin* and *Sweatt*, Douglas Papers.

17. Robert Jackson to Charles Fairman, April 5, 1950, Jackson Papers, Library of Congress, Box 12, file: Fairman, Charles.

18. Conference notes on *Henderson*, Douglas Papers, Box 195, file: *Henderson* Office and Conference Memos; Hutchinson, "Unanimity," 24.

19. Cert. memo on *Sweatt v. Painter* and *McLaurin v. Board of Regents* (Larry Tolan), Clark Papers, Box 142, folder 1; PDW and LT to Clark, April 1, 1950, Clark Papers, Tarlton Law Library, University of Texas, Box A2, folder 3.

20. Memorandum, April 1950, Clark Papers, Box A2, folder 3.

21. Ibid.

22. Hutchinson, "Unanimity," 89–90.

23. Black to Vinson, May 18, 1950 (on return), Vinson Papers, Box 262, file: Sweatt v. Painter.

24. Frankfurter to Vinson, May 19, 1950, Felix Frankfurter Papers (HLS), Box 172, folder 10.

25. Vinson to Frankfurter, May 25, 1950, Fred M. Vinson Papers, Special Collections, King Library, University of Kentucky, Box 262, file: McLaurin.

26. Frankfurter to conference, May 31, 1950, Jackson Papers, Box 160, file: OT 1949, Cases #25—Henderson; Frankfurter to Burton, May 26, 1950, Frankfurter Papers (HLS), Box 169, folder 7. Douglas prepared an opinion saying that *Plessy* should be confronted and overruled, but in the end simply concurred in the result. Jackson Papers, Box 160, file: OT 1949, Cases #25—Henderson.

27. Sweatt v. Painter, 339 U.S. 629 (1950).

28. McLaurin v. Oklahoma State Regents, 339 U.S. 637 (1950).

29. Henderson v. United States, 339 U.S. 816 (1950).

30. Tushnet, *NAACP's Legal Strategy*, 132–35.

31. Griswold to TM, June 6, 1950, NAACP Papers, Box II-B-72, file: C, 1950–55; Howard Jay Graham to TM, Oct. 10, 1950, NAACP Papers, Box II-B-109, file: Office Orders & Subscriptions, 1949–50; TM to Charles Bunn, June 12, 1950, NAACP Papers, Box II-B-206, file: University of Texas and Oklahoma, Congratulatory Messages, 1950; TM to Pauli Murray, June 9, 1950, ibid.; TM to [various newspaper publishers], June 7, 1950, NAACP Papers, Box II-B-136, file: Schools, Appeal for Funds, 1950.

32. TM to Walter Gellhorn, June 13, 1950, NAACP Papers, Box II-B-96, file: Legal Conference, 1950; Carter to Oscar Miller, July 7, 1950, NAACP Papers, Box II-B-136, file: Schools, Florida, General, 1943–55; Carter to TM, Nov. 22, 1949, NAACP Papers, Box II-106, file: New York SCAD, Cases "B," 1946–50; TM to Emory Jackson, July 31, 1950, NAACP Papers, Box II-B-136, file: Schools, Alabama, General, 1944–50; TM to U. Simpson Tate, Feb. 7, 1949, NAACP Papers, Box II-B-146, file: Schools, Texas, General, Jan.–Oct. 1949. See also TM to Tate, June 10, 1949, NAACP Papers, Box II-B-64, file: Discrimination, General, 1949; TM to Claudia Nash Thomas, July 23, 1947, NAACP Papers, Box II-B-95, file: Labor, S, 1944–47. These letters, and the one to Tate regarding the schools, show that Marshall was sensitive to the concerns expressed in Atlanta even before the staff decision in 1950, and (perhaps) that he was more vigorous in asserting the position that the NAACP would not seek equalization when less sensitive matters than education were involved.

33. TM to Donald Murray, Jan. 6, 1950, NAACP Papers, Box II-B-201, file: University of Maryland, 1949; TM to Carl Murphy, April 21, 1950, ibid.; McCready v. Byrd, 195 Md. 131, 73 A.2d 8 (1950); John W. Davis to TM, March 7, 1949, NAACP Papers, Box II-B-56, file: D, 1948–49.

34. Herman Taylor to TM, March 30, 1948, NAACP Papers, Box II-B-145, file: Schools, North Carolina, General, 1947–May 1948; TM to Taylor, April 5, 1948, ibid.; Taylor to TM, May 19, 1948, ibid.; Edward Dudley to Kelley Alexander, June 4, 1948, NAACP Papers, Box II-B-145, file: Schools, North Carolina, General, 1948–55; Carter to John Roche, Sept. 27, 1950, NAACP Papers, Box II-B-121, file: R, 1949–55; TM to Griswold, Sept. 7, 1950, NAACP Papers, Box II-B-72, file: G, 1950–55.

35. James Crumlin to TM, March 29, 1948, NAACP Papers, Box II-B-200, file: Kentucky, Johnson v. University of Kentucky, Correspondence, 1948–49; TM to Goodwin Watson, March 31, 1949, ibid.; John Hope Franklin, *Race and History: Selected Essays, 1938–1988* (Baton Rouge: Louisiana State University Press, 1989), 286–87; John Hope Franklin, interview with author (telephone), Nov. 5, 1990; Hall, *The Rest of the Dream,* 154–56.

36. Griswold to Karl Llewellyn, Sept. 6, 1950, NAACP Papers, Box II-B-72, file: G, 1950–55; Griswold to TM, Sept. 23, 1950, ibid.

37. Gillette, "Sweatt," 181–83.

Chapter 11

1. This summary of the events is drawn from Bob Smith, *They Closed Their Schools: Prince Edward County, Virginia, 1951–1964* (Chapel Hill: University of North Carolina Press, 1965), 27, 33–37; Taylor Branch, *Parting the Waters: America in the King Years, 1954–1963* (New York: Simon & Schuster, 1988), 6–21; Kluger, *Simple Justice,* 454–55, 459–60, 467–70.

2. Hill interview; Smith, *They Closed Their Schools,* 44, 47.

3. Robinson interview; Kluger, *Simple Justice,* 462–63, 475–76; Smith, *They Closed Their Schools,* 47–48 (students quoted as saying jail "not big enough for all of us").

4. Robinson interview; Kluger, *Simple Justice,* 475–76.

5. Kluger, *Simple Justice,* 477–78; Smith, *They Closed Their Schools,* 70–72, 103–04.

6. Rowan, *Dream Makers,* 6.

7. Transcript, Youth Wants to Know, Nov. 28, 1954, NAACP Papers, Box II-A-536, file: Speakers, Thurgood Marshall, General, 1952–54.

8. For a brief discussion of these concerns, see Tushnet, *NAACP's Legal Strategy,* 111–13.

9. Press release, May 2, 1952, NAACP Papers, Box II-A-536, file: Speakers, Thurgood Marshall, General, 1952–54; NAACP LDF Monthly Report, January 1955, A. P. Tureaud Papers, Box 14, file 10, Amistad Research Center, Tulane University, New Orleans; NAACP LDF Monthly Report, February 1955, ibid.; Memorandum to staff, July 21, 1955, NAACP Papers, Box II-B-143, file: Schools, Missouri, General, 1944–55.

10. Tushnet, *NAACP's Legal Strategy,* 105–06; Herman Taylor to TM, Oct. 28, 1946, NAACP Papers, Box II-B-145, file: Schools, North Carolina, Lumberton, 1946–49; TM to Gloster Current, Jan. 20, 1947, ibid.; Ruby Hurley to TM, Feb. 5, 1947, ibid.; TM to Hurley, Feb. 6, 1947, ibid.; Carter to Taylor, June 28, 1947, ibid.; Taylor to Carter, April 26, 1949, ibid.

11. Tushnet, *NAACP's Legal Strategy,* p. 106; Perry to A. Maceo Smith, Aug. 19, 1947, NAACP Papers, Box II-B-147, file: Schools, Texas, Jennings v. Board of Trustees, 1947–48; Smith to TM, Sept. 12, 1947, ibid.

12. Edward Dudley to Ella Roberts, Jan. 20, 1948, NAACP Papers, Box II-B-67, file: Education, General, 1948–55; Robinson interview.

13. Kluger, *Simple Justice,* 388–90; Kaufman, *Broken Alliance,* 92–93; Tushnet, *NAACP's Legal Strategy,* 139; Esther Brown to Edward Dudley, Aug. 4, 1948, NAACP Papers, Box II-B-142, file: Schools, Kansas, Webb v. School Board of Merriam, 1948; Brown to Franklin Williams, Aug. 30, 1948, ibid.; Charles Howard, to TM, Aug. 19, 1948, ibid.; TM to Williams, Aug. 23, 1948, ibid.; Williams to TM, Aug. 26, 1948, ibid.; Brown to Williams, Sept. 29, 1948, ibid.

14. Tushnet, *NAACP's Legal Strategy,* 139; Minutes of Kansas State Conference of Branches, Oct. 3, 1948, NAACP Papers, Box II-B-142, file: Schools, Kansas, Webb v. School Board of Merriam, 1948; Brown to Williams, Nov. 28, ibid.; Z. Wetmore to NAACP, June 28, 1947, NAACP Papers, Box II-B-143, file: Schools, Kansas, Wichita, 1945–48; Wetmore to TM, Aug. 7, 1948, ibid.; Williams to TM, Oct. 6, 1948, ibid.; Wetmore to Williams, Nov. 18, 1948, ibid.; Wetmore to Williams, Dec. 24, ibid.; Wetmore to Brown, Jan. 20, 1949, NAACP Papers, Box II-B-143, file: Schools, Kansas, Webb v. School Board of Merriam, Jan.–June 1949; Carter to Williams, Jan. 25, 1949, ibid.; Walter White to Charles Bettis, May 2, 1949, id., file: Schools, Kansas, Wichita, 1949; White to Lucille Black and Williams, May 3, 1949, ibid.; Black to White, May 3, 1949, ibid.

15. Tushnet, *NAACP's Legal Strategy,* 139–40; Charles Scott, Biographical Sketch [of plaintiffs], NAACP Papers, Box II-B-138, file: Schools, Kansas, Topeka, Brown v. Board, Background material, 1945–54.

16. Kluger, *Simple Justice,* 6, 13–18; Tushnet, *NAACP's Legal Strategy,* 138; Barbara Woods, "Modjeska Simkins and the South Carolina Conference of the NAACP, 1939–1957," in Vicki Crawford, Jacqueline Anne Rouse, and Barbara Woods, eds., *Women in the Civil Rights Movement: Trailblazers and Torchbearers, 1941–1965* (Brooklyn: Carlson Publishing Inc., 1990), 108–09.

17. TM to Harold Boulware, Feb. 28, 1949, NAACP Papers, Box II-B-3, file: B, 1948–

49; Kluger, *Simple Justice,* 18–26; Woods, "Modjeska Simkins," 109; Tushnet, *NAACP's Legal Strategy,* 138–39.

18. Digest of Proceedings, April 27, 1946, NAACP Papers, Box II-B-137, file: Schools, Georgia, Atlanta, Special Lawyers Conference, 1946.

19. Action Letter from Department of Branches, Oct. 13, 1947, A. P. Tureaud Papers, Amistad Research Center, New Orleans, Box 9, file 3.

20. Tushnet, *NAACP's Legal Strategy,* 115; Board of Directors Resolution, quoted in Paul Puryear, "The Implementation of the Desegregation Decision in the Federal Courts of Virginia: A Case Study of Legal Resistance to Federal Authority," (Ph.D. dissertation, University of Chicago, 1960), 133.

21. Robinson to TM, Oct. 1, 1950, NAACP Papers, Box II-B-171, file: Speakers, Constance Baker Motley, 1946–1954; A. P. Tureaud to E. A. Johnson, July 15, 1950, Tureaud Papers, Box 10, file 8.

22. Carter interview; Kenneth B. Clark, interview with author, Hastings-on-Hudson, New York, Dec. 6, 1990; Mark Chesler, Joseph Sanders, and Debra Kalmuss, *Social Science in Court: Mobilizing Experts in the School Desegregation Cases* (Madison: University of Wisconsin Press, 1988), 19.

23. Carter interview; Clark interview; Elwood Chisolm, interview by Harold Lewis, Aug. 9, 1967, 24, Civil Rights Documentation Project, Moorland-Spingarn Research Center, Howard University; Chesler, Sanders, and Kalmuss, *Social Science,* 19. The use of social science evidence in discrimination cases was not new. For a discussion of how specific evidence and empirical assumptions that pervaded white culture were used before *Brown,* see Herbert Hovenkamp, "Social Science and Segregation Before *Brown,*" *Duke Law Journal* 85 (June–September 1985), especially 631–32, 636, 659–63.

24. Tinsley E. Yarbrough, *A Passion for Justice: J. Waties Waring and Civil Rights* (New York: Oxford University Press, 1987), 174–75.

25. Id., 177–78, 190–91; Briggs v. Elliott, 98 F. Supp. 529, 547 (E.D. S.C. 1951) (Waring, D. J., dissenting).

26. Kluger, *Simple Justice,* 8; Yarbrough, *Passion for Justice,* 180–81, 184; Robinson interview.

27. Kluger, *Simple Justice,* 335–38; Yarbrough, *Passion for Justice,* 181.

28. Id., 182–83; Clark interview.

29. Yarbrough, *Passion for Justice,* 184–85; Kluger, *Simple Justice,* 361; Briggs v. Elliott, 98 F. Supp. 529, 546 (E.D. S.C. 1951) (Waring, D. J., dissenting).

30. Yarbrough, *Passion for Justice,* 196.

31. Ibid.; Kluger, *Simple Justice,* 363.

32. Id., 187–88.

33. Id., 188–90, 191, 199.

34. Briggs v. Elliott, 98 F. Supp. 529 (E.D. S.C. 1951).

35. Yarbrough, *Passion for Justice,* 201.

36. Chesler, Sanders, and Kalmuss, *Social Science in Court,* 19, n. 20; Kaufman, *Broken Alliance,* 93; Kluger, *Simple Justice,* 411–12.

37. Kluger, *Simple Justice,* 405; Greenberg to W. B. Brookover, June 13, 1951, NAACP Papers, Box II-B-138, file: Schools, Kansas, Topeka, Brown v. Board of Education, Expert Witnesses, 1951; Greenberg, trial memorandum, Oct. 11, 1951, NAACP Papers, Box II-B-139, file: Schools, Kansas, Topeka, Brown v. Board of Education, Legal Papers, 1951–52; Hugh Speer, "The Case of the Century: *Brown v. Board of Education of Topeka,*" *this Constitution,* 14 (Spring 1987).

38. Brown v. Board of Education, 98 F. Supp. 797 (D. Kansas 1951); Speer, "Case of the Century," 27; Kluger, *Simple Justice,* 423–24.

39. Clark interview; Chesler, Sanders, and Kalmuss, *Social Science in Court,* 20, n. 21; Kluger, *Simple Justice,* 482–84, 502–04. For a discussion of the difficulties in the research on which Clark relied, see William Cross, *Shades of Black* (Philadelphia: Temple University Press, 1991).

40. Davis v. County School Board, 103 F. Supp. 337 (E.D. Va. 1952).

41. Kluger, *Simple Justice,* 433–35.

42. Id., 429–32, 435–36.

43. Belton v. Gebhart, 87 A.2d 862, 864 (Del. Ch. 1952).

44. Gebhart v. Belton, 91 A.2d 137 (Del. Sup. Ct. 1952).

45. McNeil, *Groundwork,* 188–89; Kluger, *Simple Justice,* 513–16; Houston to Louis Weiss, Feb. 9, 1948, NAACP Papers, Box II-B-136, file: Schools, District of Columbia, Carr v. Board of Education, 1948–50.

46. Carr v. Corning, 182 F.2d 14 (D.C. Cir. 1950); Kluger, *Simple Justice,* 516–18; Carter to TM, Nov. 28, 1949, NAACP Papers, Box II-B-106, file: New York SCAD, Cases "B," 1946–50.

47. James M. Nabrit, interview by Vincent Browne, 1968, 19–20, Civil Rights Documentation Project, Moorland-Spingarn Research Center, Howard University; McNeil, *Groundwork,* 193; Kluger, *Simple Justice,* 522–23.

48. Elman, "The Solicitor General's Office," 822; Abner Mikva, "The Role of Theorists in Constitutional Cases," *University of Colorado Law Review* 63 (1992): 454–55.

49. Briggs v. Elliott, 103 F. Supp. 920 (E.D. S.C. 1952). Some of these facts were made available to the district court in a supplemental report filed on March 3, 1952.

50. Briggs v. Elliott, 342 U.S. 350 (1952).

51. Briggs v. Elliott, 103 F. Supp. 920 (E.D. S.C. 1952); Hutchinson, "Unanimity and Desegregation," 31, n. 251.

52. Hutchinson, "Unanimity," 31, n. 253; Docket book, *Brown* entry, William O. Douglas Papers, Library of Congress, Box 1154.

53. Frankfurter to Elliot Richardson, Oct. 1, 1952, Frankfurter Papers (HLS), Box 187, folder 10.

54. Hutchinson, "Unanimity," 32, n. 254; Brown v. Board of Education, 344 U.S. 1 (1952).

55. Brown v. Board of Education, 344 U.S. 141 (1952); Kluger, *Simple Justice,* 547–48; Mary Dudziak, "The Limits of Good Faith: Desegregation in Topeka, Kansas, 1950–1956," *Law & History Review* 5 (Fall 1987): 370–71; Bolling v. Sharpe, 344 U.S. 873 (1952).

56. Kluger, *Simple Justice,* 540. Clark also told Kluger that the Court had placed *Brown* first "so that the whole question would not smack of being a purely Southern one." This seems unlikely. Under the Court's internal procedures, *Brown*'s docket number was lower than *Briggs*'s because *Briggs* got its number when the second appeal was filed in May, months after *Brown* was filed.

Chapter 12

1. Mikva interview. Jayme Coleman Williams, "A Rhetorical Analysis of Thurgood Marshall's Arguments Before the Supreme Court in the Public School Segregation Controversy" (Ph.D. diss., Ohio State University, 1959), 162–200, uses the categories of the classical study of rhetoric to examine Marshall's presentation. Williams's more formal analysis appears consistent with mine.

2. Robinson interview.

3. Cumming v. Board of Education, 175 U.S. 528 (1899).

4. 275 U.S. 78 (1927).

5. For materials on and a discussion of the Roberts case, see Leonard Levy and Douglas Jones, *Jim Crow in Boston: The Origin of the Separate But Equal Doctrine* (New York: Da Capo Press, 1974).

6. Korematsu v. United States, 323 U.S. 214 (1944).

7. The briefs are reprinted in Philip Kurland and Gerhard Casper, eds., *Landmark Briefs and Arguments of the Supreme Court of the United States: Constitutional Law,* vol. 49 and 49A (Arlington, Va.: University Press of America, 1975), from which all quotations are taken.

8. Elman, "The Solicitor General's Office," 825–27; Kluger, *Simple Justice,* 558. Kluger's account is drawn from an interview with Elman. I note my skepticism about the dramatic details of Elman's account, though not about the accuracy of the overall picture it gives.

9. Kluger, *Simple Justice,* 559–60; Elman, "Solicitor General's Office," 827–28.

10. Kluger, *Simple Justice,* 561–62.

11. William Harbaugh, *Lawyer's Lawyer: The Life of John W. Davis* (New York: Oxford University Press, 1973), 503–04.

12. The prevailing understanding of the state of the law in 1896 seriously underestimated the degree to which serious arguments had been made, and sometimes adopted, that school segregation was unconstitutional. See J. Morgan Kousser, *Dead End: The Development of Nineteenth-Century Litigation on Racial Discrimination in Schools* (Oxford: Clarendon Press, 1986).

13. Harbaugh, *Lawyer's Lawyer,* 483, 495, 507.

14. Id., 498.

15. See Katzenbach v. Morgan, 384 U.S. 641 (1966).

16. Kluger, *Simple Justice,* 581.

Chapter 13

1. Douglas memorandum for the file, May 17, 1954, William O. Douglas Papers, Library of Congress, Box 1148, file: Segregation Cases; Hutchinson, "Unanimity," 36, n. 284; Berry, *Stability, Security, and Continuity,* 125.

2. According to Douglas, the reason for refraining from voting was "the likelihood that there might be some leaks." Memorandum for the File, May 17, 1954, Douglas Papers, Box 1148, file: Segregation Cases. See also Hutchinson, "Unanimity," 36.

3. TM, Speech to CIO, Dec. 3, 1954, NAACP Papers, Box II-A-536, file: Speakers, Thurgood Marshall, General, 1952–54; Transcript, Youth Wants to Know, Nov. 28, 1954, ibid.; Harbaugh, *Lawyer's Lawyer,* 498.

4. See, e.g., Cassell v. Texas, 339 U.S. 282, 304 (1950), a dissent in which Jackson wrote, "I doubt if any good purpose will be served . . . by identifying the right of the most worthy Negroes to serve on grand juries with the efforts of the the least worthy to defer to escape punishment for crime."

5. Portions of the letter have a formal tone that suggests that Jackson had in mind at least the possibility that the letter would reach an audience beyond Fairman, if only the audience of history.

6. Jackson to Fairman, March 13, 1950, Robert Jackson Papers, Library of Congress, Box 12, file: Fairman, Charles.

7. Ibid.

8. Kluger, *Simple Justice,* 605.

9. Committee on the Judiciary, United States Senate, Hearings on the Nomination of

Justice William Hubbs Rehnquist, Ninety-Ninth Congress, Second Session (1986), 314–15.

10. Jackson may well have said that *Plessy* was correct, meaning that when decided it was consistent with public opinion, but that is different from saying it should be reaffirmed, a view Jackson nowhere else expressed. At most Jackson believed that the Court's institutional role and the force of precedent meant that *Plessy* should not be overruled, a rather different matter.

11. The most extensive analysis arguing that the memorandum expressed Rehnquist's personal views rather than Jackson's is offered by Kluger, *Simple Justice*, 606–9, n. *. Much of that analysis is flawed by Kluger's assumption that Jackson, a "staunch libertarian and humanist," could not have been ambivalent on the issue of segregation. Undoubtedly Rehnquist put the best light on his memorandum when it became a public issue during his nomination hearings nineteen years after the event. I doubt that Jackson asked for memoranda to use as "talking points" at the conference, as Rehnquist said; rather, I believe that Jackson asked his clerks simply to put down on paper the ideas he and they had been batting around in chambers. I have little doubt, too, that the memorandum, while expressing one aspect of Jackson's views, is put in ways that strongly suggest that it expresses all of Rehnquist's. Kluger's more particular arguments are these: (1) "The titles of both memos are strikingly inappropriate" for presentations to Jackson's colleagues, which is true but irrelevant if the memos were to be used to assist Jackson in thinking through the position he would present. (2) "Is it possible that Jackson would have bothered to deliver so crude and elementary a summary of the Court's historic position. . . ." Surely yes; that was the sort of thing Frankfurter did all the time. Further, the law clerks probably believed that the memos they wrote were trial runs for separate opinions, and it would be easier to change the memo into a separate opinion if it already had the historical essay. (3) "Is it possible that Jackson would have disparaged" the Court's history of attempting to protect minorities? Again, surely yes; the view that minorities can be protected only when majorities want to protect them is the kind of irony of which Jackson was fond. (4) "Is it possible that so confident and civilized a man as Robert Jackson would have told his brother Justices anything remotely approaching" the phrases Rehnquist's memorandum uses about being excoriated by liberal colleagues? Here I believe Kluger is right, and the memorandum speaks in Rehnquist's voice rather than Jackson's. But the phrases are peripheral to the main argument, which is precisely the kind of argument Jackson would have made—part of the time.

12. Clark's notes are confusing at this point. They record Vinson as saying, successively, that "Congress would have power for D.C. *or* [emphasis added] the States," and that "[t]hey may try it for D.C. but not States." Hutchinson, "Unanimity," 91. Elsewhere in his notes Clark clearly misrecorded what Black said with respect to this issue, and in light of Vinson's additional statements it seems likely that Vinson tended to believe that Congress had the power to abolish segregation in the states.

13. Notes of Dec. 13, 1952, Conference, Jackson Papers, Box 184, file: O.T. 1953, Segregation Cases.

14. Hutchinson, "Unanimity," 91; Notes of Dec. 13, 1952, Conference, Jackson Papers, Box 184, file: O.T. 1953, Segregation Cases.

15. Kluger, *Simple Justice*, 590–91, reads the evidence to "suggest" that "Vinson was not prepared to overturn segregation," and that Vinson "saw the problem as essentially political and social in nature, not legal." Kluger relies on no additional direct information about Vinson's views; he reports Burton's judgment eighteen months later, a statement by Reed recounting Reed's expectations regarding Vinson's position, a statement that Elman had "heard" that Vinson did not favor overruling *Plessy*, and the inferences Vinson's clerks drew from his request that they prepare a memorandum on problems of enforcing desegregation.

16. Jackson's notes clearly indicate that Black said "not sure Congress is barred by same limitations," while Douglas's, though less clear, suggest that Black said "bound," although the transcription indicates that, after some hesitation, the transcriber concluded that the word was "barred." The meaning of the statement is the same in either case, and my reading of Douglas's handwriting is that Black said "bound."

17. Jackson's notes are "Driven to segregation with knowledge means trouble," but this seems an obvious mistranscription.

18. Except where otherwise indicated, quotations in the remainder of this discussion are taken from Hutchinson, "Unanimity," 91; Notes on Dec. 13, 1952, Conference, Jackson Papers, Box 184, file: O.T. 1953, Segregation Cases; and Notes on Dec. 13, 1952, Conference, Douglas Papers, Box 1149, file: Original Conference Notes re Segregation Cases.

19. Justices Burton and Minton agreed with Douglas on the merits. For Minton, the precedents establishing the "separate but equal" doctrine had been "whittled away," and classifications based on race were invidious. He agreed that "our decree will cause trouble but the race carries trouble with it." Burton believed that "states do not have the choice" of segregation; for him, "separate education is not sufficient for today's problems." Unlike Douglas, however, Burton thought that the decree could give the states "plenty of time" to desegregate.

20. Notes on Dec. 13, 1952, Conference, Douglas Papers, Box 1149, file: Original Conference Notes re Segregation Cases.

21. Hutchinson, "Unanimity," 92, has "[illegible]" for "Jamestown."

22. Memorandum for the File in re Segregation Cases, May 17, 1954, Douglas Papers, Box 1148, file: Segregation Cases.

23. Bernard Schwartz, *Super Chief: Earl Warren and His Supreme Court* (New York: New York University Press, 1983), 72.

24. 345 U.S. 972, 972–73 (1953); Memorandum to the Conference, May 27, 1953, Frankfurter Papers (HLS), Reel 71, file 15.

25. 345 U.S. 972, 972–73 (1953); Frankfurter to Vinson, June 8, 1953, Frankfurter Papers (HLS), Reel 71, file 15.

26. Schwartz, *Super Chief,* 80–81. Douglas agreed with Black.

27. Id., 78, 80–81.

Chapter 14

1. Alfred Kelly, "An Inside View of 'Brown v. Board,'" delivered to the American Historical Association, December 1961, reprinted in Senate Judiciary Committee, 87th Congress, 1st Session, Hearings on the Nomination of Thurgood Marshall.

2. Kelly, "Inside View"; John Hope Franklin, interview with author (telephone), Nov. 5, 1990; Kluger, *Simple Justice,* 621–26; William Coleman to Carter, July 1, 1953, NAACP Papers, Box II-B-141, file: Schools, Kansas, Topeka v. Board, Second reargument, State reports; William L. Coleman, interview with author, Washington, D.C., Oct. 17, 1989.

3. Coleman to Carter, Sept. 14, 1953, NAACP Papers, Box II-B-141, file: Schools, Kansas, Topeka, Brown v. Board, 2d reargument, State reports; Louis Pollak to "Bob" [Carter], Aug. 1, 1953, NAACP Papers, Box II-B-140, file: Schools, Kansas, Topeka, Brown v. Board, 2d reargument, Federal government; Franklin interview.

4. For an examination of the distinction as it developed in the debates, see Mark Tushnet, "The Politics of Equality in Constitutional Law: The Equal Protection Clause, Dr. Du Bois, and Charles Hamilton Houston," in David Thelen, ed., *The Constitution and American Life* (Ithaca: Cornell University Press, 1987), 225–30.

5. Kelly, "Inside View"; Franklin interview; John Hope Franklin, *Race and History: Selected Essays, 1938–1988* (Baton Rouge: Louisiana State University Press, 1989), 306.

6. Conference program, Sept. 25–28, 1953, NAACP Papers, Box II-B-138, file: Schools, Kansas, Topeka, Brown v. Board, Background materials, 1945–54; Report of seminar, Sept. 26, 1953, NAACP Papers, Box II-B-141, file: Schools, Kansas, Topeka, Brown v. Board, Background material, legal issues; Kelly, "Inside View."

7. Franklin, *Race and History,* 286–87; Kelly, "Inside View."

8. Franklin, *Race and History,* 312–13; Kelly, "Inside View."

9. Kelly, "Inside View."

10. David Pinsky, Memorandum, Sept. 4, 1953, NAACP Papers, Box II-B-140, file: Schools, Kansas, Topeka, Brown v. Board, Background material. For a history of "balancing the equities," see Peter Hoffer, *The Law's Conscience: Equitable Constitutionalism in American* (Chapel Hill: University of North Carolina Press, 1990).

11. Jack Greenberg, Memorandum [undated], NAACP Papers, Box II-B-140, file: Schools, Kansas, Topeka, Brown v. Board, 2d reargument, Background material.

12. Transcript, Youth Wants to Know, Nov. 28, 1954, NAACP Papers, Box II-A-536, File: Speakers, Thurgood Marshall, General, 1952–54.

13. Kluger, *Simple Justice,* 650–51; Michael Mayer, "With Much Deliberation and Some Speed: Eisenhower and the *Brown* Decision," *Journal of Southern History* 52 (February 1986): 42, 48; Robert Burk, *The Eisenhower Administration and Black Civil Rights* (Knoxville: University of Tennessee Press, 1984), 135; Pre–Press Conference Briefing, Nov. 14, 1956, in Michal Belknap, ed., *Civil Rights, The White House, and the Justice Department, 1945–1968* (New York: Garland, 1991), 8: 10; Eisenhower Diaries, Nov. 16, 1953, id., 7: 21. For a general discussion of the Eisenhower administration's position on issues of race, see Chester Pach, Jr., and Elmo Richardson, *The Presidency of Dwight D. Eisenhower* (rev. ed.) (Lawrence: University Press of Kansas, 1991), 137–41.

14. Mayer, "With Much Deliberation," 47–50.

15. Burk, *Eisenhower Administration,* 135–36.

16. Mayer, "With Much Deliberation," 51–54.

17. Hutchinson, "Unanimity and Desegregation," 40; Bickel to Frankfurter, Aug. 22, 1953, Frankfurter Papers (HLS), Reel 71, file 15; Notes on Dec. 12, 1953, conference, William O. Douglas Papers, Library of Congress, Box 1149, file: Original Conference Notes re Segregation Cases (transcription).

18. The published version of Bickel's memorandum, Alexander Bickel, "The Original Understanding of the Fourteenth Amendment," *Harvard Law Review* 69 (November 1955): 1, 59–63, argued somewhat tentatively that, because the Constitution was an organic document, it could properly be interpreted to authorize the Court to hold segregation unconstitutional as inconsistent with the ideal of equality it enacted, should future circumstances warrant. In my view, his argument is quite weak, drawing conclusions from what Bickel called "bits and pieces of additional evidence." (p. 61.) (Bickel's strongest phrasing was in the form of a rhetorical question: "[M]ay it not be that the Moderates and the Radicals reached a compromise permitting them to go to the country with language which they could, where necessary, defend against damaging alarms raised by the opposition, but which at the same time was sufficiently elastic to permit reasonable future advances?" Ibid.)

19. Quotations are drawn from Kurland and Casper, eds., *Landmark Briefs and Arguments,* vol. 49A.

20. By 1953, the board of education in Topeka had voted to desegregate. One of the plaintiff children had been admitted to a desegregated school, and the rest would be admitted as soon as possible. Most of the reargument in *Brown* itself dealt with whether the case was moot. The difficulty was that the state still took the position that segregation was

constitutional, and the school board conceivably might revert to a segregated system if the Supreme Court ruled against the NAACP. But, Carter told the Court, that was not likely.

21. The discussion focused on whether the Delaware plaintiffs would be satisfied with an order affirming the Delaware supreme court. Greenberg asked the Supreme Court to make it clear that segregation was unconstitutional. Marshall concluded the arguments by saying that if the Court invalidated segregation in the other cases, he was sure that the Delaware supreme court would modify its decision.

22. Kluger, *Simple Justice,* 669.

23. Memorandum for the File in re Segregation Cases, May 17, 1954, Douglas Papers, Library of Congress, Box 1148, file: Original Conference Notes re Segregation Cases.

24. Notes on Dec. 12, 1953, Conference, Douglas Papers, Box 1149, file: Original Conference Notes re Segregation Cases (transcription); Schwartz, *Super Chief,* 86. The account in Burton's notes of Warren's statements is essentially the same.

25. Kluger, *Simple Justice,* 680; Memorandum for the File in re Segregation Cases, Douglas Papers, Box 1148, file: Segregation Cases; Notes on Dec. 12, 1953, conference, Douglas Papers, Box 1149, file: Original Conference Notes re Segregation Cases (transcription); Notes on Dec. 12, 1953, conference, Harold F. Burton Papers, Library of Congress, Box 337, file: Brown notebook.

26. Memorandum for the File in re Segregation Cases, Douglas Papers, Box 1148, file: Segregation Cases; Notes on Dec. 12, 1953, conference, Douglas Papers, Box 1149, file: Original Conference Notes re Segregation Cases (transcription); Notes on Dec. 12, 1953, conference, Harold F. Burton Papers, Library of Congress, Box 337, file: Brown notebook.

27. Schwartz, *Super Chief,* 87; Notes on Dec. 12, 1953, conference, Burton Papers, Box 337, file: Brown notebook; Notes on Dec. 12, 1953, conference, Douglas Papers, Box 1149, file: Original Conference Notes re Segregation Cases (transcription).

28. Hutchinson, "Unanimity," p. 39; Notes on Dec. 12, 1953, conference, Burton Papers, Box 337, file: Brown notebook; Notes on Dec. 12, 1953, conference, Douglas Papers, Box 1149, file: Original Conference Notes re Segregation Cases (transcription); Schwartz, *Super Chief,* 89.

29. Bernard Schwartz, "Chief Justice Rehnquist, Justice Jackson, and the *Brown* Case," *Supreme Court Review* 1988 (1988): 255–63.

30. Kluger, *Simple Justice,* 691.

31. Schwartz, "Chief Justice Rehnquist," 264.

32. Brown v. Board of Education, 347 U.S. 483 (1954).

33. Hutchinson, "Unanimity," 45–50; Bolling v. Sharpe, 347 U.S. 497 (1954).

34. Notes on April 4, 1954, conference, Douglas Papers, Box 1149, file: Original Conference Notes re Segregation Cases; Elman, "Solicitor General's Office," 822–26, 829.

35. Elman, "Solicitor General's Office," 852.

36. Loren Miller, *The Petitioners* (New York: Pantheon Books, 1966), 261.

37. Roy Wilkins, Suggested Statement for NAACP State and Branch Officers, May 11, 1954, NAACP Papers, Box II-B-142, file: Schools, Kansas, Topeka, Brown v. Board, Statements, 1952–54; Carter to staff, May 6, 1954, NAACP Papers, Box II-A-621, file: Supreme Court, School Cases, Conferences and Meetings, 1953–55.

Chapter 15

1. Hutchinson, "Unanimity," 53–54.

2. Dudziak, "The Limits of Good Faith," 374–80.

3. Mayer, "With Much Deliberation," 62; Brief for Appellants on Further Reargument,

Brown v. Board of Education, in Kurland and Casper, eds., *Landmark Briefs and Arguments,* vol. 49A. Subsequent quotations from the briefs and oral arguments are taken from this volume.

4. Margaret Butcher to TM, Nov. 2, 1954, NAACP Papers, Box II-B-72, file: Field Secretaries' Reports, 1954–55; Loftus Carson, "Tentative Plan to Organize Communities in North Carolina in Action Programs for Desegregation," undated, ibid.

5. Vernon McDaniel, "Activities and Tentative Plans," Oct. 27, 1954, NAACP Papers, Box II-B-72, file: Field Secretaries' Reports, 1954–55.

6. Elman, "Solicitor General's Office," 828.

7. 345 U.S. 972, 972–73 (1953).

8. Frankfurter to Conference, Jan. 15, 1954, Harold Burton Papers, Library of Congress, Box 263, file: Case #1, Notes & Memos (quoted in part in Kluger, *Simple Justice,* 686–87).

9. Schwartz, *Super Chief,* 91–93.

10. Law Clerks' Recommendations for Segregation Decree, Tom C. Clark Papers, Tarlton Law Library, University of Texas, Box A27, folder 5. (Other locations are cited in Hutchinson, "Unanimity," 52, n. 424.)

11. Ibid.

12. Ibid.

13. Handwritten notes, undated, NAACP Papers, Box II-B-140, file: Schools, Kansas, Brown v. Board of Education, 2d Reargument, Background material. Tushnet, *NAACP's Legal Strategy,* 166, erroneously identifies this document as notes taken by Marshall during a preargument conference of the NAACP's lawyers. Examining it in light of the oral argument has made it clear that the document is Marshall's notes taken while listening to the states' arguments.

14. Mayer, "With Much Deliberation," 69.

15. Hutchinson, "Unanimity," 53–54.

16. Unless otherwise noted, statements from this conference are drawn from Conference notes, April 16, 195[5], William O. Douglas Papers, Library of Congress, Box 1149, file: Original Conference Notes re Segregation Cases; and Frankfurter's notes, Frankfurter Papers (HLS), Reel 71, file 15. Reed's notes on the statement regarding "psychological" factors say: "Not an element in case but a basis for moving wisely," but it is unclear whether this records Warren's statement or Reed's sentiment. Notes on Conference Discussion, Stanley Reed Papers, Special Collections, King Library, University of Kentucky, Box 43, file: Brown v. Board of Education.

17. Conference notes, April 16, 195[5], Earl Warren Papers, Library of Congress, Box 574, file: Brown II.

18. Ibid.

19. Reed said that the schools should be directed to admit the named plaintiffs "with all convenient speed," and that he would not set a time limit for desegregation but would leave the details to the district courts.

20. Conference notes, April 16, 195[5], Warren Papers, Box 574, file: Brown II; Schwartz, *Super Chief,* 116–17; Conference notes, April 16, 1955, Harold Burton Papers, Library of Congress, Box 337, Brown notebook; Notes on conference discussion, Reed Papers, Box 43, file: Brown. Clark's definition of "no problems" seems to have accepted as unproblematic the proposition that white people "never will allow white students under [a] colored teacher." Reed's notes suggest he was most concerned about whether the decree or the accompanying opinion would say that segregation was unconstitutional, which perhaps reflects his disagreement not so much with the statement as with Burton's formulation regarding the speed with which desegregation should occur.

21. Kluger, *Simple Justice,* 593–94.

22. Frankfurter to Warren, May 27, 1955, Warren Papers, Box 574, file: Brown II.

23. 349 U.S. 294, 300 (1955).

24. Hutchinson, "Unanimity," 57–58.

25. Schwartz, *Super Chief,* 123.

Chapter 16

1. *Time,* Sept. 19, 1955, 23, 27. *Time* informed the NAACP that it had received forty-seven attacks on its cover story, eight letters alleging a general pro-NAACP bias, and thirty-six commendations. Internal letters reports, Sept. 23 and 30, 1956, NAACP Papers, Box II-B-100, file: Thurgood Marshall, *Time* Cover Story.

2. Report on TM's Speech, March 30, 1954, NAACP Papers, Box II-A-536, file: Speakers, Marshall, Thurgood, General, 1955.

3. See, e.g., *Southern School News,* July 1955 (reporting two TM speeches).

4. *Southern School News,* Oct. 1954, and July 1955; *Time,* Sept. 19, 1955, 25. Robert McKay, "'With All Deliberate Speed': A Study of School Desegregation," *New York University Law Review* 31 (June 1956): 1008, and "'With All Deliberate Speed': Legislative Reaction and Judicial Development 1956–57," *Virginia Law Review* 43 (December 1957): 1205, carry the story forward.

5. "The Supreme Court Order on School Desegregation: What It Means and How to Use It" (NAACP pamphlet including directive to branches on procedures), NAACP Papers, Box II-A-624, file: Supreme Court, School Cases, May 30 Decision, 1955; TM to Branch Presidents, Sept. 17, 1954, Daniel Ellis Byrd Papers, Box 7, Amistad Research Center, Tulane University; *Southern School News,* Sept. 1955 (TM interview); Press release, Feb. 19, 1956, NAACP Papers, Box II-A-95, file: Desegregation, Atlanta Meeting, 1956; June Shagaloff, interview by Robert Martin, Sept. 5, 1968, pp. 10–11, 29–31, Civil Rights Documentation Project, Moorland-Spingarn Research Center, Howard University; Kelly Alexander, interview by Stanley Smith, undated, 9, Civil Rights Documentation Project, Moorland-Spingarn Research Center, Howard University.

6. Whittington B. Johnson, "The Virgil Hawkins Case: A Near Decade of Evading the Inevitable: The Demise of Jim Crow Higher Education in Florida," *Southern University Law Review* 16 (Spring 1989): 55; Darryl Paulson and Paul Hawkes, "Desegregating the University of Florida Law School: Virgil Hawkins v. the Florida Board of Control," *Florida State University Law Review,* 12 (Spring 1984): 59; Algia Cooper, "Brown v. Board of Education and Virgil Darnell Hawkins: Twenty-Eight Years and Six Petitions to Justice," *Journal of Negro History* 64 (Winter 1979): 10. All the *Hawkins* cases have titles that are variants on *Hawkins v. Board of Control.* (During the litigation Hawkins completed his undergraduate training and received a degree from Bethune Cookman College in 1952.)

7. 47 So.2d 608 (Fla. 1950).

8. 53 So.2d 116 (Fla. 1951). Hawkins attempted to get the United States Supreme Court to review the case. The state court had left open the possibility that it would reconsider Hawkins's case after he applied for admission or showed that the facilities at the Tallahassee school were in fact inadequate. This meant that its decision was technically not final, and the Supreme Court refused to take the case. 342 U.S. 877 (1951). Justices Black and Douglas dissented from the Supreme Court's refusal to grant review.

9. 60 So.2d 162 (Fla. 1952); 347 U.S. 971 (1954).

10. 83 So.2d 20 (Fla. 1955); St. Petersburg *Times,* Oct. 21, 1955, A6, col. 3, described in

Paulson and Hawkes, "Desegregating the Univer   53; *Southern School News,* Feb. 1956.

11. 350 U.S. 413 (1956); Frankfurter memo re   *kins v. Board of Control,* Frankfurter Papers (HLS), Box 84, fil   irch 9, 1956, Frankfurter Papers (HLS), Box 169, file 14.

12. RMH memo, Reed Papers, Box 167, file: rn, March 6, 1956, ibid.

13. Paulson and Hawkes, "Desegregating the University of Florida Law School," 63–66.

14. 93 So.2d 354 (Fla. 1957). Justice E. Harris Drew also dissented, saying that further delay would be a denial of Hawkins's constitutional rights as determined by the United States Supreme Court.

15. Johnson, "The Virgil Hawkins Case," 70; Paulson and Hawkes, "Desegregating the University of Florida Law School," 68–70; Memo on #169, Douglas Papers, Box 1186, file: Office Memos; Memo on #169, Warren Papers, Box 182, file: Conference Memos, Oct. Term 1953, ##154–75; 355 U.S. 839 (1957); 253 F.2d 752 (5th Cir. 1958).

16. David Colburn, "Florida's Governors Confront the *Brown* Decision: A Case Study of the Constitutional Politics of School Desegregation, 1954–1970," in James Ely and Kermit Hall, eds., *An Uncertain Tradition: Constitutionalism and the History of the South* (Athens: University of Georgia Press, 1989), 337. In 1965, Hawkins received a law degree from the New England School of Law. In 1976, he applied to the Florida Supreme Court for admission to the bar even though he received his degree from a school that had not yet been accredited. Finding that Hawkins had a "claim on this court's conscience," the court admitted him to the Florida bar. In 1984, Hawkins, then 77 years old, was reprimanded by the Supreme Court and placed on probation for two years, as result of his misconduct in a case where he was the defense attorney. Paulson and Hawkes, "Desegregating the University of Florida Law School," 70–71.

17. A short but comprehensive presentation of the *Lucy* case is Jack Peltason, *Fifty-Eight Lonely Men: Southern Federal Judges and School Desegregation* (Urbana: University of Illinois Press, 1961), 138–42. See also Frank Read and Lucy McGough, *Let Them Be Judged: The Judicial Integration of the Deep South* (Metuchen, N.J.: Scarecrow Press, 1978), 201–06.

18. Transcript, Lucy file, 1/4/1/2, Arthur Shores Papers, Savery Library, Talladega College.

19. Ibid.; Peltason, *Fifty-Eight Lonely Men,* 141–42. (Peltason's quotations from the hearing differ slightly from those in the transcript.)

20. Southern Manifesto, 1 *Race Relations Law Reporter* 435 (1956), from *Congressional Record,* 102(43): 3948, 4004, March 12, 1956.

21. James W. Ely, *The Crisis of Conservative Virginia: The Byrd Organization and the Politics of Massive Resistance* (Knoxville: University of Tennessee Press, 1976), 31; Drew McCoy, *The Last of the Fathers: James Madison and the Republican Legacy* (New York: Cambridge University Press, 1989).

22. Ely, *Crisis of Conservative Virginia,* 40–42; Shuttlesworth v. Birmingham Board of Education, 162 F. Supp. 372 (N.D. Ala. 1958). See also McKay, "School Desegregation," 1017–39, providing a comprehensive legal analysis of interposition.

23. Briggs v. Elliott, 132 F. Supp. 776 (E.D. S.C. 1955).

24. Sometimes his supposedly ungenerous approach was attributed to the fact that the NAACP was a major force behind the failure of Parker's nomination to the Supreme Court by President Herbert Hoover in 1930, and to his hostility toward African-Americans, which led the NAACP to oppose the nomination.

25. Read and McGough, *Let Them Be Judged,* 74, report that several judges commented

in the 1970s that Parker's approach "held us back for years," but state as well that others even in the 1970s regarded the approach as correct.

26. Calhoun v. Latimer, 188 F. Supp. 412 (N.D. Ga. 1960).

27. Wilma Peebles-Wilkins, "Reactions of Segments of the Black Community to the North Carolina Pearsall Plan, 1954–1966," *Phylon* 48(Summer 1987): 112, 113–14; William Chafe, *Civilities and Civil Rights: Greensboro, North Carolina, and the Black Struggle for Civil Rights* (New York: Oxford University Press, 1980), 67–71; N.C. Sess. Laws 1955, c. 366.

28. Carson v. Board of Education, 227 F.2d 789 (4th Cir. 1955).

29. Peltason, *Fifty-Eight Lonely Men,* 80; Joyner v. McDowell County Board of Education, 92 S.E.2d 795 (N.C. 1956).

30. Carson v. Warlick, 238 F.2d 724 (4th Cir. 1956).

31. 349 U.S. 294, 299 (1955).

32. 1955 Acts Ala. 201. Florida adopted a statute modeled on Alabama's. Colburn, "Florida's Governors," 333. For a summary of pupil placement laws, see *Race Relations Law Reporter* 6(913–15).

33. Carter to Henry Moon, Dec. 29, 1958, NAACP Papers, Box III-A-285, file: Schools, Alabama 1956–63. Daniel Meador, "The Constitution and the Assignment of Pupils to Public Schools," *Virginia Law Review* 45 (May 1959): 517, gives a contemporaneous analysis of pupil assignment laws.

34. Meador, "Assignment of Pupils," 528–29; Shuttlesworth v. Birmingham Board of Education, 162 F. Supp. 372 (N.D. Ala. 1958). On Rives, see Read and McGough, *Let Them Be Judged,* 31–38; Bass, *Unlikely Heroes,* 69–74.

35. John Harlan to William Brennan, Nov. 12, 1958, William J. Brennan Papers, Library of Congress, Box 24, file: Shuttlesworth v. Birmingham Board of Education; Douglas, Memorandum to Conference, Nov. 13, 1958, ibid.; Brennan to Black and Harlan, Nov. 17, 1958, ibid.; Shuttlesworth v. Birmingham Board of Education, 358 U.S. 101 (1958); Krock, quoted in Ely, *Crisis of Conservative Virginia,* 128–29.

Chapter 17

1. Numan Bartley, *The Rise of Massive Resistance: Race and Politics in the South During the 1950's* (Baton Rouge: Louisiana State University Press, 1969), 17–20, 320; Ely, *Crisis of Conservative Virginia,* 125–26.

2. Carter to Louis Harris, Aug. 16, 1956, copy from NAACP Papers, in author's possession (my notes are inadequate to let me identify the box and file in which the letter is located).

3. Ely, *Crisis of Conservative Virginia,* 30–31, 36–37; Robbins Gates, *The Making of Massive Resistance: Virginia's Politics of Public School Desegregation, 1954–1956* (Chapel Hill: University of North Carolina Press, 1962), 30–31, 34; Adolph Grundman, "Public School Desegregation in Virginia from 1954 to the Present" (Ph.D. diss., Wayne State University, 1972), 31.

4. Ely, *Crisis of Conservative Virginia,* 38–39.

5. Gates, *Making of Massive Resistance,* 189–90; Ely, *Crisis of Conservative Virginia,* 44–46; *Race Relations Law Reporter* 1 (1091–113). The legislature also declared that it did not consent to suits against state officials running segregated schools; this provision was designed to invoke the Eleventh Amendment of the United States Constitution, which bars people from suing states without their consent.

6. Gates, *Making of Massive Resistance,* 125–26; Paul Puryear, "The Implementation

of the Desegregation Decision in the Federal Courts of Virginia: A Case Study of Legal Resistance to Federal Authority" (Ph.D. diss., University of Chicago, 1960), 148–51.

7. Gates, *Making of Massive Resistance,* 127–28; Ely, *Crisis of Conservative Virginia,* 192; Allen v. School Board, *Race Relations Law Reporter* 1 (886) (W.D. Va. 1956).

8. Thompson v. Arlington County School Board, 144 F. Supp. 238 (E.D. Va. 1956).

9. School Board of Charlottesville v. Allen, 240 F.2d 59 (4th Cir. 1956).

10. Ely, *Crisis of Conservative Virginia,* 190; Puryear, "Implementation," 163.

11. Adkins v. School Board of Newport News, 148 F. Supp. 430 (E.D. Va.), *aff'd,* 246 F.2d 325 (4th Cir. 1957).

12. Grundman, "Public School Desegregation," 182–86.

13. Ely, *Crisis of Conservative Virginia,* 75–80, 88–89; Grundman, "Public School Desegregation," 208.

14. John Morsell to Gloster Current et al., Feb. 27, 1959, NAACP Papers, Box III-A-95, file: Desegregation, General, 1956–59.

15. Grundman, "Public School Desegregation," 4.

16. Jack Peltason, *Fifty-Eight Lonely Men: Southern Federal Judges and School Desegregation* (Urbana: University of Illinois Press, 1961), 99–100. Read and McGough, *Let Them Be Judged,* 617 (Appendix C), has a slightly different count, but the overall picture is similar.

17. Ely, *Crisis of Conservative Virginia,* 195; Davis v. County School Board of Prince Edward County, 149 F. Supp. 431 (E.D. Va.), *rev'd,* 249 F.2d 462 (4th Cir. 1957); Allen v. County School Board of Prince Edward County, 164 F. Supp. 786 (E.D. Va. 1958), *modified,* 266 F.2d 507 (4th Cir. 1959). The Prince Edward County story is brought forward in Jonathan L. Entin, "The Shifting Color Line in Prince Edward County," presented at the annual meeting of the Law and Society Assocation, May 28–31, 1992.

18. Read and McGough, *Let Them Be Judged,* 76–90; Bell v. Rippy, 146 F. Supp. 485 (N.D. Tex. 1956), *rev'd sub nom.* Borders v. Rippy, 247 F.2d 268 (5th Cir. 1957). On Cameron, see Read and McGough, *Let Them Be Judged,* 44–48. For a detailed examination of the stages of the Dallas litigation, see John Spivack, *Race, Civil Rights and the United States Court of Appeals for the Fifth Judicial Circuit* (New York: Garland Publishing Co., 1990), 75–93.

19. Rippy v. Borders, 250 F.2d 690 (5th Cir. 1957).

20. James L. Nabrit, III, interview with author, Washington, D.C., April 23, 1990; Peltason, *Fifty-Eight Lonely Men,* 119; Read and McGough, *Let Them Be Judged,* 85–88.

21. Borders v. Rippy, 184 F. Supp. 402 (N.D. Tex. 1960). The court of appeals ultimately accepted the twelve-year plan, and desegregation began in Dallas in September 1961.

22. Read and McGough, *Let Them Be Judged,* 92–107.

23. 118 U.S. 356 (1886).

24. Chafe, *Civilities and Civil Rights,* 89–90, 103–109; McCoy v. Greensboro City Board of Education, 283 F.2d 667 (4th Cir. 1960).

25. Beckett v. School Board of Norfolk, 185 F. Supp. 459 (E.D. Va. 1959), *aff'd,* Farley v. Turner, 281 F.2d 131 (4th Cir. 1960).

26. Hill v. School Board of Norfolk, 282 F.2d 473 (4th Cir. 1960).

27. Wheeler v. Durham Board of Education, 196 F. Supp. 71 (M.D. N.C. 1961).

28. Jones v. School Board of Alexandria, 179 F. Supp. 280 (E.D. Va. 1959).

29. Morrow v. Mecklenburg County Board of Education, 195 F. Supp. 109 (W.D. N.C. 1961).

30. Robert Crain, *The Politics of School Desegregation: Comparative Case Studies of Community Structure and Policy-Making* (Garden City, N.Y.: Doubleday and Co., 1969), 242.

Chapter 18

1. Tony Freyer, *The Little Rock Crisis: A Constitutional Interpretation* (Westport, Conn.: Greenwood Press, 1984), 16–18. For overview of the Little Rock events, see Bartley, *The Rise of Massive Resistance,* 251–69.

2. Daisy Bates, *The Long Shadow of Little Rock* (1962; reprint, Fayetteville: University of Arkansas Press, 1987), 2–3; Freyer, *Little Rock Crisis,* 42–57, 92; Wiley Branton, interview by James Mosby, Jan. 16, 1969, 16, 20, 27, Civil Rights Documentation Project, Moorland-Spingarn Research Center, Howard University; Washington *Post,* Dec. 17, 1988, B6; Wiley Branton to William Cooper, Aug. 21, 1954, Bates Papers, Box 4, folder 10; Wiley Branton, "Personal Memories of Thurgood Marshall," *Arkansas Law Review* 40 (1987): 665, 668.

3. Raymond Diamond, "Confrontation as Rejoinder to Compromise: Reflections on the Little Rock Desegregation Crisis," *National Black Law Journal* 11 (Summer 1989): 151, 154–57.

4. Branton, "Personal Memories," 669; Diamond, "Confrontation," 157–59; Bates, *Long Shadow,* 82; Terrence Roberts and Ernest Green, statements at symposium at Georgetown University Law Center, Feb. 2, 1989. Overviews of the Eisenhower administration's actions throughout the Little Rock episode are provided in Richard Burks, *The Eisenhower Administration and Black Civil Rights* (Knoxville: University of Tennessee Press, 1984), 174–203, and Chester Pach and Elmo Richardson, *The Presidency of Dwight D. Eisenhower,* rev. ed. (Lawrence: University Press of Kansas, 1991), 150–55.

5. Arkansas *Gazette,* Sept. 7, 1957, 1, col. 5, in Daisy Bates Papers, State Historical Society of Wisconsin, Reel 4; Peltason, *Fifty-Eight Lonely Men,* 172–73; Freyer, *Little Rock Crisis,* 129.

6. Diamond, "Confrontation," 157–59; Roberts and Green, Feb. 2, 1989; Roy Wilkins, with Tom Mathews, *Standing Fast* (New York: Viking Press, 1982), 253–54. Wilkins and Bates state that members of the National Guard stood by while the harassment occurred, but Roberts and Green, two of the students, disagree.

7. Aaron v. Cooper, 357 U.S. 566 (1958). A note from Frankfurter to Alexander Bickel states that there was a "stiff fight" over including this language, and that "some plain talking & an ultimatum to the C.J. became necessary." Frankfurter to Bickel, Aug., 1958 (on copy of court order), Frankfurter Papers (HLS), Box 206, folder 1.

8. Cooper v. Aaron, 358 U.S. 27 (1958).

9. Other Special Terms had been held in 1953, to dissolve a stay of execution that Justice Douglas had issued in the cases of Julius and Ethel Rosenberg, and in 1943, to consider whether military courts could try Nazi saboteurs during World War II. The session was the fifth since 1930. Peltason, *Fifty-Eight Lonely Men,* 187.

10. Brief of United States as *Amicus Curiae,* in Kurland and Casper, eds., *Landmark Briefs and Arguments,* vol. 54; Frankfurter, note on Bickel to Frankfurter, Aug. 21, 1958, Frankfurter Papers (HLS), Box 206, folder 1.

11. Clark draft, Clark Papers, Box A-73, folder 2; Freyer, *Little Rock Crisis,* 150–51. Schwartz, *Super Chief,* 293–94, treats Clark's draft as a proposed dissent from the ultimate decision. The language of the draft, however, seems clearly directed at the expedited schedule, and dating it around August 28 is consistent with another note Frankfurter wrote on the letter from Bickel, that "the special session order . . . has much more than meets the eye," and with Frankfurter's statement in a Sept. 2 letter to Harlan that the school board's action in delaying the opening of schools "saved me the discomfort of writing my reasons for dissenting, had action been taken to change the action the Court took" on August 28. Frankfurter to Harlan, Sept. 2, 1958, Frankfurter Papers (HLS), Box 169, folder 15.

12. Frankfurter to Harlan, Sept. 2, 1958, Frankfurter Papers (HLS), Box 169, folder 15; Schwartz, *Super Chief,* 291–92; Freyer, *Little Rock Crisis,* 151; Bickel to Frankfurter, Sept. 15, 1958, Frankfurter Papers (HLS), Box 183, folder 11.

13. Briefs for Petitioners and Respondents, in Kurland and Casper, eds., *Landmark Briefs and Arguments,* vol. 54.

14. Transcript of Oral Argument, in Kurland and Casper, eds., *Landmark Briefs and Arguments,* vol. 54. All quotations from the oral argument are taken from this volume.

15. J. Lee Rankin to James W. Browning, Sept. 10, 1958, Brennan Papers, Box 14, file: Cooper v. Aaron (declining to file additional brief).

16. Schwartz, *Super Chief,* 293, 295.

17. Notes for conference, Brennan Papers, Box 14, file: Cooper v. Aaron; Conference notes, *Cooper v. Aaron,* Sept. 18, 1958, John Marshall Harlan Papers, Box 57, Seeley G. Mudd Manuscript Library, Princeton University.

18. Draft opinion, Cooper v. Aaron, Warren Papers, Box 584.

19. Notes for conference, Brennan Papers, Box 14, file: Cooper v. Aaron; Schwartz, *Super Chief,* 296–97.

20. Schwartz, *Super Chief,* 299–300; Harlan to Brennan, Sept. 23, 1958, Warren Papers, Box 584, file: Cooper v. Aaron; Memorandum to files re *Cooper v. Aaron,* Oct. 8, 1958, Douglas Papers, Box 1198, file: Cooper v. Aaron.

21. 358 U.S. 1 (1958).

22. Schwartz, *Super Chief,* 302–3; Memorandum to files re *Cooper v. Aaron,* Oct. 8, 1958, Douglas Papers, Box 1198, file: Cooper v. Aaron. Justices Black and Brennan prepared a brief statement that, in their view, Frankfurter's opinion "must not be accepted as any dilution or interpretation of the views expressed" in the Court's opinion. No one else indicated a desire to join that statement, and Justice Harlan circulated a gentle ironic memorandum, which concluded, "I dissent from the action of [Black and Brennan] in filing their separate opinion, believing that it is always a mistake to make a mountain out of a molehill. *Requiescat in pace.*" That was sufficient to get Black and Brennan to withdraw their separate statement.

23. 358 U.S. at 20–26.

24. Freyer, *Little Rock Crisis,* 154–57; Peltason, *Fifty-Eight Lonely Men,* 197–204.

25. Judge Miller applied the exhaustion requirement as a basis for denying admission to other students; the court of appeals reversed him in 1961 because the board had applied different standards to African-Americans seeking admission to white schools than it had to whites seeking transfers. Aaron v. Tucker, 186 F. Supp. 913 (E.D. Ark. 1960), *rev'd,* 287 F.2d 798 (8th Cir. 1961).

26. Read and McGough, *Let Them Be Judged,* 112–17. A detailed review of the legal proceedings is Spivack, *Race, Civil Rights,* 95–121.

27. Bush v. Orleans Parish School Board, 138 F. Supp. 337 (E.D. La. 1956), *aff'd,* 242 F.2d 156 (5th Cir. 1957).

28. Read and McGough, *Let Them Be Judged,* 135. Crain, *Politics of School Desegregation,* 235–322, is a detailed study of the desegregation, resistance, rioting, and boycotts. See also Read and McGough, 111–67, for an overview of the litigation.

29. *Southern School News,* Nov. 4, 1954; Feb. 3, 1955; July 6, 1955; Sept. 1955; Nov. 1955; March 1956.

30. TM to Ralph Harlow, May 29, 1956, Ralph Harlow Papers, Amistad Research Center, New Orleans, Box 2, folder 2; *Southern School News,* June 1956, Aug. 1956, Feb. 1957, Nov. 1957, Feb. 1958, and Aug. 1958; Bernard Taper, "A Reporter at Large—A Meeting in Atlanta," *The New Yorker,* March 17, 1956, 115.

31. *Southern School News,* Feb. 1958, July 1959, Aug. 1959, Oct. 1959, Feb. 1960, and Aug. 1961.

32. Peltason, *Fifty-Eight Lonely Men,* 156–61; Kelley v. Nashville Board of Education, 270 F.2d 209 (6th Cir. 1959).

33. Taper, "Meeting in Atlanta," 117.

34. Kelley v. Nashville Board of Education, 270 F.2d 209 (6th Cir. 1959). The court of appeals also quoted the testimony that expert witnesses Looby and Williams presented. Their position was that a better climate for change would be produced by a less protracted process of desegregation, and that, contrary to the board's assumption, resistance to desegregation did not diminish if the process took a long time. Further, they noted that grade-a-year plans were particularly difficult for families with children in different grades.

35. Ibid.; Brennan Papers, Box 41, file: Kelley v. Nashville Board of Education.

36. Dove v. Parham, 282 F.2d 256 (8th Cir. 1960).

37. *Southern School News,* Feb. 1956.

38. TM, interview with Ed Erwin, 124.

39. *Southern School News,* Feb. 1960.

Chapter 19

1. Peltason, *Fifty-Eight Lonely Men,* 61–62, 69–70; Wilkins, with Mathews, *Standing Fast,* 241–42; Ronnie Dugger, "John Ben Shepperd and the NAACP at Tyler," *Texas Observer,* Oct. 31, 1956, 1, 5.

2. Dugger, "John Ben Shepperd," 1, 5.

3. W. J. Durham to Roy Wilkins, Oct. 24, 1956, NAACP Papers, Box III-A-281, file: Texas Government Actions 1956; Wilkins to Andrew Weinberger, May 6, 1957, id., file: Texas Government Actions, Jan.–May 1957; Wilkins to Carter Wesley, June 10, 1957, ibid.

4. Durham to TM, May 11, 1957, ibid.; Durham to Wilkins, May 16, 1957, ibid.; Wilkins to Lewis Gannett, May 17, 1957, ibid.; Wilkins to Durham, May 31, 1957, ibid.; Carter to Wilkins, June 19, 1957, ibid.; Carter, draft speech for Wilkins, undated [July 1957], id., file: Texas Government Actions, 1956; Wilkins to Boyd Hall, September 23, 1957, id., file: Texas Government Actions, Jan.–May 1957.

5. For overviews of the attacks, written while they were still going on, see Walter Murphy, "The South Counterattacks: The Anti-NAACP Laws," *Western Political Quarterly* 12 (June 1959): 371; 2 *Race Relations Law Reporter* 892–94 (1957); 6 *Race Relations Law Reporter* 917–18 (1961–62); Robert Carter to Telford Taylor, May 16, 1957, copy from NAACP Papers, in author's possession (my notes are inadequate to let me identify the box and file in which the letter is located); McKay, "'With All Deliberate Speed': A Study of School Desegregation," 1056–61; McKay, "'With All Deliberate Speed': Judicial Development 1956–57," 1235–42.

6. Carter to Tureaud, Oct. 15, 1956, A. P. Tureaud Papers, Box 10, folder 28, Amistad Research Center, Tulane University, New Orleans.

7. The first case reaching the Supreme Court arose from a contempt conviction. As part of the investigation, the committee questioned an activist about his efforts to promote desegregation. Chief Justice Warren correctly saw the inquiry as part of a "package of laws . . . to intimidate people," and Justice Potter Stewart said that the inquiry had the "incorrect purpose" of continuing segregation, but the Court reversed the conviction on a narrower ground. It found "an unmistakable cloudiness" about what the committee wanted. Indeed, the Court's opinion quoted from the inquiry to show that both the witness and the committee were "confused" about what the point of the questions was. Docket book,

October Term 1958, #51, William J. Brennan Papers, Library of Congress, Box 408; Scull v. Virginia, 359 U.S. 344 (1959).

8. For discussion of the background of abstention, see Paul Bator, Daniel Meltzer, Paul Mishkin, and David Shapiro, *Hart and Wechsler's The Federal Courts and the Federal System,* 3d ed. (Westbury, N.Y.: Foundation Press, 1988), 1356–57.

9. NAACP v. Patty, 159 F. Supp. 503 (E.D. Va. 1958).

10. Memo on # 127, Earl Warren Papers, Library of Congress, Box 189, file: Conference Memos, October Term 1958, ## 126–150; Frankfurter to Conference, April 14, 1959, Clark Papers, Tarlton Law Library, University of Texas, Box A-82, folder 5. Frankfurter found himself in an uncomfortable position. When the case came up, he initially wanted to affirm the lower court without hearing argument, but once the case was argued, he told his colleagues, he could not reject the views of the four justices who had voted to hear argument, for he shared their understanding of the abstention doctrine. Ironically, Justice Brennan first voted to hear the case on the merits; if he had voted to affirm without hearing argument, there would have been only three votes to bring the case to the Court, and the lower court decision striking down all the statutes would have been affirmed. Docket book, October Term 1958, #127, Brennan Papers, Box 405.

11. Harrison v. NAACP, 360 U.S. 167 (1959).

12. Docket Book, #127, William Brennan Papers, Library of Congress, Box 408; Harrison v. NAACP, 360 U.S. 167 (1959).

13. 360 U.S. at 179–84; Frankfurter to Douglas, In re *Harrison,* undated, William O. Douglas Papers, Library of Congress, Box 1207, file: Harrison v. NAACP. Two weeks later the Supreme Court disposed of a challenge to Arkansas' antibarratry and antisolicitation statutes, adopted during the Little Rock crisis in 1958. In the lower court the state's attorney general contended that the statutes were clear and constitutional, while the NAACP argued that they were clear and unconstitutional. The three-judge district court assumed that the unconstitutionality of the statutes was "obvious," and then, oddly, abstained. Not surprisingly, the Supreme Court reversed that decision, saying that "reference to the state courts . . . should not automatically be made." When the case returned to the lower court, the judges relied on the Virginia abstention case to point out ambiguities in Arkansas's statutes, and abstained again. NAACP v. Bennett, 178 F. Supp. 188 (E.D. Ark.), *vacated,* 360 U.S. 471, *adhered to,* 178 F. Supp. 191 (E.D. Ark. 1959).

14. NAACP v. Button, 371 U.S. 415 (1963).

15. Docket book, October Term 1962, #5, Brennan Papers, Box 409; Conference notes, Nov. 10, 1961, Douglas Papers, Box 1286, file: NAACP v. Gray (Button), Case File, folder 1; Schwartz, *Super Chief,* 450–51.

16. Draft opinion, January 1962, Frankfurter Papers (HLS), Box 164, folder 5.

17. Schwartz, *Super Chief,* 451–52.

18. Conference notes, Oct. 12, 1962, Douglas Papers, Box 1286, File: NAACP v. Gray (Button), Case File, folder 1; Schwartz, *Super Chief,* 451.

19. Stewart to Conference, Oct. 16, 1962, Douglas Papers, Box 1286, file: NAACP v. Gray (Button), Case File, folder 1; Schwartz, *Super Chief,* 451–52.

20. NAACP v. Button, 371 U.S. 415 (1963). Virginia's lawyers had argued that the statute really barred only actual control of litigation by the NAACP, but, according to Brennan, that could not be so; the evidence showed that the NAACP did refer people to nonstaff lawyers, but there was no evidence that these outside lawyers were under the NAACP's control. Nonetheless, the Virginia Supreme Court had found that the NAACP did indeed violate chapter 33, which necessarily meant that general referrals were barred by the statute.

21. Justice White wrote a separate opinion, concurring substantially with Justice Bren-

nan's analysis but expressing concern that the argument that chapter 33 was overbroad would invalidate more narrowly drawn and, to White, constitutionally permissible regulations that barred the NAACP from determining the "day-to-day . . . tactics, strategy, and conduct of litigation."

22. 371 U.S. at 448–70.

23. For Harlan, to the extent that the statute kept the NAACP from directing potential litigants to its own staff attorneys, it was clear enough, and narrow. The only difficulty Justice Brennan had pointed out was that the statute's definition of "agents" might bar the NAACP from directing litigants to "outside" attorneys. Harlan read the passages in the Virginia Supreme Court's decision dealing with "outside" attorneys to refer only to lawyers like Hill and Robinson, who had an extremely close relation to the NAACP.

Chapter 20

1. Peltason, *Fifty-Eight Lonely Men*, 65–67; Carter to Telford Taylor, May 16, 1957, copy from NAACP Papers, in author's possession (my notes are inadequate to let me identify the box and file in which the letter is located).

2. Information about the procedures in the case is taken from Kurland and Casper, eds., *Landmark Briefs and Arguments*, vol. 54.

3. For a discussion of the case law preceding the attack on the NAACP, see Harry Kalven, *A Worthy Tradition: Freedom of Speech in America* (New York: Harper & Row, 1988), 254–58. For an overview of the attack on the NAACP, see Bartley, *The Rise of Massive Resistance*, 214–24.

4. Read and McGough, *Let Them Be Judged*, 49–51; Frank Reeves, interview by Robert Wright, Dec. 28, 1969, p. 15, Civil Rights Documentation Project, Moorland-Spingarn Research Center, Howard University; Carter, "Tribute," 33, 39.

5. Notes, Argued Cases, #91, Box 1185, Douglas Papers; Harlan to Conference, April 22, 1958, Tom C. Clark Papers, Tarlton Law Library, University of Texas, Box A-66, folder 9.

6. Douglas to Harlan, Re: No. 91, April 22, 1958, William O. Douglas Papers, Library of Congress, Box 1184, file: Memoranda by Douglas, OT 1957; Frankfurter to Harlan, April 23, 1958, John Marshall Harlan Papers, Seeley Mudd Manuscript Library, Princeton University, Box 46, file: NAACP v. Alabama; Black to Harlan, May 2, 1958, ibid.

7. Clark draft dissent [undated], Clark Papers, Box A-66, folder 9; Gorman to Clark, ibid.; Frankfurter to Clark, June 25, 1958, ibid.; Clark to Conference, June 30, 1958, ibid.; Schwartz, *Super Chief*, 304–05.

8. NAACP v. Alabama *ex rel.* Patterson, 357 U.S. 449 (1958).

9. 360 U.S. 240 (1959).

10. NAACP v. Gallion, 290 F.2d 337 (5th Cir. 1961).

11. Conference memo, NAACP v. Alabama (Gallion), # 303, Earl Warren Papers, Library of Congress, Box 222, file: Conference memos, October Term 1961, ## 291–305; Notation on cert. memo, NAACP v. Alabama, Harlan Papers, Box 146, file: NAACP v. Alabama; Clark Memorandum to Conference, Oct. 19, 1961, Douglas Papers, Box 1259, file: NAACP v. Alabama.

12. NAACP v. Alabama, 274 Ala. 544, 150 So.2d 677 (1963).

13. NAACP v. Alabama *ex rel.* Flowers, 377 U.S. 288 (1964).

14. Brennan to Harlan, May 25, 1964, Harlan Papers, Box 203, file: NAACP v. Alabama.

15. Memorandum on Suggested Procedure, [Sept. 11 or 12, 1956], NAACP Papers, Box

III-A-278, file: Reprisals, Missouri, St. Louis meeting 1956; Wilkins to Presidents, State Conference of Branches, Sept. 17, 1956, ibid.

16. William McFerrin Stone, "Willie Rainach and the Defense of Segregation in Louisiana, 1954–1959," (Ph.D. diss., Texas Christian University, 1989), 54–56; Carter to Telford Taylor, May 16, 1957, copy from NAACP Papers, in author's possession (my notes are inadequate to let me identify the box and file in which the letter is located).

17. Byrd to TM, April 14, 1956, NAACP Papers, Box III-A-278, file: Reprisals, Louisiana, Government Actions 1956–57; Clarence Laws to Gloster Current, April 5, 1956, ibid.; Laws to Wilkins and TM, May 11, 1956, ibid.; Minutes, June 10, 1956, ibid.; Press release, April 26, 1956 ibid.

18. Walter Murphy, "The South Counterattacks: The Anti-NAACP Laws," *Western Political Quarterly* 12 (June 1959): 371; 376–77; Press releases, Nov. 30, 1956, and Dec. 10, 1956, NAACP Papers, Box III-A-278, file: Reprisals, Louisiana, Government Actions 1956–57; Carter to Laws and Tureaud, Dec. 26, 1956, ibid.

19. Carter to Arthur Chapital, Jan. 2, 1957, NAACP Papers, Box III-A-278, file: Reprisals, Louisiana, Government Actions 1956–57; TM to Chapital, Feb. 15, 1956, A. P. Tureaud Papers, Box 10, folder 27, Amistad Research Center, New Orleans.

20. Current to Henry Lee Moon, March 13, 1957, NAACP Papers, Box III-A-278, file: Reprisals, Louisiana, Government Actions 1956–57; Background information memo, Oct. 14, 1959, id., file: Reprisals, Louisiana, Government Actions 1958–64; Press release, Feb. 11, 1960, ibid.; Byrd to TM, Dec. 11, 1959, Tureaud Papers, Box 11, folder 2.

21. Louisiana *ex rel.* Gremillion v. NAACP, 366 U.S. 293 (1961); Stewart to Conference, Oct. 20, 1960, William J. Brennan Papers, Library of Congress, Box 63, file: Louisiana *ex rel.* Gremillion v. NAACP; Louisiana v. NAACP, Memos, Douglas Papers, Box 1253. Justice Frankfurter wrote a concurring opinion suggesting that the outcome might be different once the lower court held additional hearings.

22. Bruce Bennett to Daisy Bates, Aug. 30, 1957, Daisy Bates Papers, State Historical Society of Wisconsin, Box 6, file 4; Bates to Bennett, Sept. 13, 1957, ibid.; Bennett press release, Oct. 2, 1958, ibid.

23. Bennett to "Dear Mayor," Oct. 9, 1957, ibid.

24. Transcript of conversation among Gloster Current, Clarence Laws, and Daisy Bates, Oct. 11, 1957, Bates Papers, Box 5, file 2; Transcript of conversation among Current, Laws, and Bates, Oct. 16, 1957, ibid.; Transcript of conversation among Current, Laws, Bates, and Christopher Mercer, Feb. 13, 1958, ibid.; Woodrow Mann to Bates, Oct. 15, 1957, Bates Papers, Box 4, file 10.

25. Transcript of conversation among Current, Laws, and Bates, Oct. 16, 1957, Bates Papers, Box 5, file 2; Bates v. Little Rock, 361 U.S. 516, 521–22 nn. 5–7 (1960); Field Secretary's report, Oct. 26, 1957, Bates Papers, Box 4, file 10.

26 Docket book, October Term 1959, #41, Brennan Papers, Box 406; Bates v. Little Rock, 361 U.S. 516 (1960). Justice Black and Douglas objected to Stewart's approach, believing that the right of association was absolutely protected and Brennan observed that Stewart had "unnecessarily emphasized the 'balancing' approach." Stewart tried out a revision that, he believed, should have satisfied them and gained a unanimous decision, but Black was adamant. After checking that his opinion would still have the votes of Warren and Brennan, Stewart returned to his original analysis, and Black and Douglas issued a brief concurring opinion. Brennan to Black, Jan. 1, 1960, Black Papers, Box 340, file: Case file no. 41, October Term 1959; Stewart to Brethren, Jan. 19, 1960, ibid.; Frankfurter to Stewart, Jan. 15, 1960, Frankfurter Papers (HLS), Box 171, folder 8.

27. Carter to Southern N.A.A.C.P Branches, March 3, 1960, Bates Papers, Box 2, file 3; John W. Davis to Daniel E. Byrd, Aug. 16, 1955, Daniel Ellis Byrd Papers,

Amistad Research Center, New Orleans, Box 2, folder 1; *Southern School News,* Nov. 1956.

28. Murphy, "The South Counterattacks," 379–80.

29. Bryan v. Austin, 354 U.S. 933 (1957); HLH [Harry L. Hobson] memorandum, Clark Papers, Box B-163, folder 2; Frankfurter to Conference, June 12, 1957, Frankfurter Papers (HLS), Box 91, folder 5.

30. Shelton v. Tucker, 364 U.S. 479 (1960); Transcript of conversation between Current and Bates, April 9, 1959, Bates Papers, Box 5, file 2.

31. Conference memo, #14—Shelton v. Tucker, Warren Papers, Box 206, file: Conference Memos, October Term 1960, ##14–22; Carr v. Young, 331 S.W.2d 701 (Ark. 1960). The federal decision is Shelton v. McKinley, 174 F. Supp. 351 (E.D. Ark. 1959).

32. Docket book, October Term 1960, #7, Box 407, Brennan Papers.

33. Shelton v. Tucker, 364 U.S. 479 (1960). Black tried to get Stewart to modify his language away from balancing, but Stewart insisted on retaining his statement that there was "no doubt" of the state's ability to investigate fitness and competence. Black to Stewart, Dec. 1, 1960, Black Papers, Box 344, file: October Term, 1960, Conference memoranda; Stewart to Black and Douglas, Dec. 2, 1960, ibid.

34. Shelton v. Tucker, 364 U.S. 479, 490 (Frankfurter, J., dissenting), 496 (Harlan, J., dissenting). Both Harlan and Frankfurter agreed that the statute would be unconstitutional if it were used to discharge teachers "solely because of their membership in unpopular organizations," but the teachers in these cases had challenged the entire statute, not merely its application.

35. On Communists and the NAACP, see Wilson Record, *Race and Radicalism: The NAACP and the Communist Party in Conflict* (Ithaca: Cornell University Press, 1963). On segregationist rhetoric about the NAACP and subversion, see, e.g., Peltason, *Fifty-Eight Lonely Men,* 36–37.

36. Watkins v. United States, 354 U.S. 178 (1957); Sweezy v. New Hampshire, 354 U.S. 234 (1957). For a summary of the law of legislative investigations in the 1950s, see Kalven, *Worthy Tradition,* 459–514.

37. See Bartley, *Rise of Massive Resistance,* 185–87.

38. Steven Lawson, "The Florida Legislative Investigation Committee and the Constitutional Readjustment of Race Relations, 1956–1963," in James Ely and Kermit Hall, eds., *An Uncertain Tradition: Constitutionalism and the History of the South* (Athens: University of Georgia Press, 1989), 299–302.

39. Id., 302–4. Reports to the Federal Bureau of Investigation in 1954 and 1955 found that several members of the Communist party were members of the NAACP, but "they exert no influence or control over the activities of the NAACP chapters in Florida." FBI documents 61–3176–739 (April 22, 1954), 61–3176–894 (April 8, 1955), released under the Freedom of Information Act.

40. Lawson, "Florida Legislative Investigation Committee," 305–07.

41. Gibson v. Florida Legislative Investigation Committee, 108 So.2d 729 (Fla. 1958).

42. Frankfurter to Conference, Feb. 20, 1959, Black Papers, Box 336, file: October Term 1958, Opinions of Other Justices.

43. Lawson, "The Florida Legislative Investigation Committee," 308–11.

44. Gibson v. Florida State Legislative Investigation Committee, 126 So.2d 129 (Fla. 1960).

45. Barenblatt v. United States, 360 U.S. 109 (1959); Uphaus v. Wyman, 360 U.S. 72 (1959). For a discussion of the congressional reaction to the Court's decisions in this area, see Walter Murphy, *Congress and the Court: A Case Study in the American Political Process* (Chicago: University of Chicago Press, 1962).

46. Lawson, "The Florida Legislative Investigation Committee," 312–13.

47. Id., 313–14; Schwartz, *Super Chief,* 452–53; Conference notes, Dec. 8, 1961, Douglas Papers, Box 1287, file: Gibson v. Florida Miscellaneous Memos; Harlan draft, Brennan Papers, Box 76, file: Gibson v. Florida Legislative Investigation Committee.

48. Conference notes, Oct. 12, 1962, Douglas Papers, Box 1287, file: Gibson v. Florida Miscellaneous Memos; Black to Douglas, undated notes, ibid; Clark notes, Clark Papers, Box B-187, folder 8.

49. 372 U.S. 539 (1963). Justices Black and Douglas wrote concurring opinions restating their position that legislative inquiries into membership in lawful political organizations were completely barred by the First Amendment.

50. 372 U.S. at 578–83. Justice White also wrote a dissent criticizing the Court for making it difficult to investigate Communist infiltration of other organizations.

51. Bickel to Frankfurter, April 12, 1963, Frankfurter Papers (HLS), Box 183, folder 9; 372 U.S. at 554; Lawson, "The Florida Legislative Investigation Committee," 315–16.

Chapter 21

1. TM interview by Ed Erwin, 98.

2. Mayor of Baltimore v. Dawson, 350 U.S. 877 (1955) (public beaches); Holmes v. City of Atlanta, 350 U.S. 879 (1955) (golf courses). The one exception, significantly, involved prohibitions on interracial marriages. One of the images latent in white opposition to desegregation was the hulking African-American male student who would sexually assault white girls. That image was directly implicated in cases involving interracial marriage. The Court was presented with a challenge to a ban on interracial marriage in Naim v. Naim, 350 U.S. 891 (1955). It tried to avoid a decision by sending the case back to the state court for clarification of the record. Then, when the state court correctly said that there was nothing that needed to be clarified, the Court simply—and by general agreement lawlessly—refused to hear the case. 350 U.S. 985 (1956). For discussions, see Hutchinson, "Unanimity," 64–66; Alexander Bickel, *The Least Dangerous Branch: The Supreme Court at the Bar of Politics* (Indianapolis: Bobbs Merrill, 1962), 174.

3. The literature on the Montgomery bus boycott is extensive. A useful collection is David Garrow, ed., *The Walking City: The Montgomery Bus Boycott, 1955–1956* (Brooklyn: Carlson Publishing Inc., 1989). See also Catherine Barnes, *Journey from Jim Crow: The Desegregation of Southern Transit* (New York: Columbia University Press, 1983), 108–31; Robert Jerome Glennon, "The Role of Law in the Civil Rights Movement: The Montgomery Bus Boycott, 1955–1957," *Law and History Review* 9 (Spring 1991): 59.

4. After the Supreme Court invalidated Montgomery's segregation ordinance, the Alabama court of appeals affirmed Mrs. Parks's conviction, invoking an extremely technical argument so that it did not have to consider whether the segregation ordinance was unconstitutional. See Glennon, "The Role of Law," 87–88.

5. Glennon, "The Role of Law," 66–69; Barnes, *Journey from Jim Crow,* 115–16; Wilkins, with Mathews, *Standing Fast,* 228.

6. Glennon, "The Role of Law," 69, 71; Thomas Gilliam, "The Montgomery Bus Boycott of 1955–56," in Garrow, ed., *Walking City,* 261–63. A state grand jury soon indicted Gray for malpractice, but the city attorney, most likely for political reasons, declined to pursue the case because, he said, Gray's actions had been taken in connection with a lawsuit in federal court and the state, therefore, could not prosecute him. The city attorney's decision almost certainly had no legal basis; as a general rule states do have the power to invoke ethical standards against lawyers even in connection with at least the out-of-court

actions connected to federal lawsuits. Gray also was harassed by the local draft board. Gray had been entitled to a deferment because he was a part-time minister, but his eligibility for that deferment had expired. When an interview was published that revealed that Gray had not been reclassified, his local board did so, classifying him as immediately eligible for military service. The NAACP intervened with the national head of the Selective Service System, who overturned the local board's decision on procedural grounds. The result was that the board could not reclassify Gray at all, because by the time it got the case again Gray had become too old for immediate service. Gilliam, "Montgomery Bus Boycott," 263–64.

7. Glennon, "The Role of Law," 71–72.

8. Barnes, *Journey from Jim Crow*, 117–18.

9. Id., 118–19. There were some reasons for thinking that, as a technical matter, the Court had erred in the past in applying the final judgment rule to cases like Flemming's, but after receiving memoranda from Justices Reed and Frankfurter, the justices decided not to reconsider those rulings. Memorandum to Conference, Jan. 25, 1956, Frankfurter Papers (HLS), Box 88, folder 10; Memorandum to the Conference re Jurisdiction (by Reed), Jan. 1, 1956, ibid.

10. Barnes, *Journey from Jim Crow*, 119–20; Glennon, "The Role of Law," 74–75; Gilliam, "Montgomery Bus Boycott," 269–71.

11. Glennon, "The Role of Law," 77; Peltason, *Fifty-Eight Lonely Men*, 84; Gilliam, "Montgomery Bus Boycott," 270–71.

12. Glennon, "The Role of Law," 78–81; Gilliam, "Montgomery Bus Boycott," 271.

13. Glennon, "The Role of Law," 81–87.

14. Glenn Eskew, "The Alabama Christian Movement for Human Rights and the Birmingham Struggle for Civil Rights, 1956–1963," in David Garrow, ed., *Birmingham, Alabama, 1956–1963: The Black Struggle for Civil Rights* (Brooklyn: Carlson Publishing Inc., 1989), 14–17, 44; J. Mills Thornton, "First Among Equals: The Montgomery Bus Boycott," in Garrow, ed., *Walking City*, xix–xx.

15. Taylor Branch, *Parting the Waters*, 190, 217; William L. Taylor, interview with author, March 16, 1990, Washington, D.C.; Ralph Temple, interview with author, March 27, 1990, Washington, D.C.

16. For background on the 1957 Civil Rights Act, see Steven Lawson, *Black Ballots: Voting Rights in the South, 1944–1969* (New York: Columbia University Press, 1976), 146–202.

17. Wilkins, with Mathews, *Standing Fast*, 243–46.

18. United States v. Raines, 362 U.S. 17 (1960); Hannah v. Larche, 363 U.S. 420 (1960).

19. Barnes, *Journey from Jim Crow*, 80–87.

20. Id., 94–99.

21. Id., 144–46; John French to Frankfurter, Memorandum re Boynton, Frankfurter Papers (HLS), Box 128, folder 12.

22. Barnes, *Journey from Jim Crow*, 145–46; Frankfurter, Memorandum for the Conference re Boynton, Dec. 9, 1959, Frankfurter Papers (HLS), Box 128, folder 12.

23. Barnes, *Journey from Jim Crow*, 146–47.

24. Boynton v. Virginia, 364 U.S. 454 (1960).

25. Motley interview; Julian Bond, "The Politics of Civil Rights History," 12, in Armstead L. Robinson and Patricia Sullivan, eds., *New Directions in Civil Rights Studies* (Charlottesville: University of Virginia Press, 1991). The LDF's monthly status report first listed sit-in cases in April 1960.

26. Clarence Laws to George Howard, Daisy Bates Papers, Box 2, folder 2; Robert

Weisbrot, *Freedom Bound: A History of America's Civil Rights Movement* (New York: W. W. Norton, 1990), 38.

27. *Southern School News,* April 1960; Derrick Bell, "An Epistolatory Exploration for a Thurgood Marshall Biography." *Harvard Blackletter Journal* (Spring 1989), 55; TM to Friends of the Committee, On: The Student Sit-In Protests, March 31, 1960, Ralph Harlow Papers, Amistad Research Center, Tulane University, Box 2, folder 17.

28. Minutes of Executive Committee, Board of Directors, April 4, 1956, NAACP Papers, Box III-A-173, file: Inc. Fund Meetings, 1956–62.

29. Carter to Finance, Sept. 21, 1956, NAACP Papers, Box III-A-31, file: Staff, Thurgood Marshall, 1956–58. On the separation of the NAACP's legal activities from the LDF, see Rowan, *Dream Makers,* 179–80.

30. Motley interview.

31. Minutes, Dec. 7, 1955, NAACP Papers, Box II-A-400, file: Legal Defense & Educational Fund, Minutes of the Board, 1940–55; Leonard Schroeter interview with author (telephone), July 3, 1990; Taylor interview; Waite Madison interview with author, Washington, D.C., April 24, 1990; Nabrit interview; Irma Robbins Feder interview with author (telephone), May 21, 1990; Washington *Post,* Feb. 25, 1979, C-12; Branker interview; Derrick Bell, interview with author (telephone), Dec. 20, 1990; Herbert Hill, interview with author, Nov. 10, 1990, Madison, Wis.; Norman Amaker, interview with author, Oct. 26, 1990, Chicago. Schroeter, a graduate of Harvard Law School who had participated in a sit-in sponsored by the Congress of Racial Equality in 1946, was hired in 1951 and left in 1953. *See* Thomas Chambers, "Leonard Schroeter," Seattle-King County Bar Association *Bar Bulletin* (Nov. 1989); Victoria Slind-Flor, "A 'Conscience' on the Sidelines," *National Law Journal,* Sept. 3, 1990, 1. Taylor, whose wife's closest friend was the wife of Charles Black, was hired in 1954, worked part-time in the evenings in 1956 through 1958 after he was drafted, and then worked full-time again for a few months. *See also* William L. Taylor, interviewed by John Britton, Aug. 8, 1967, Civil Rights Documentation Project, Moorland-Spingarn Research Center, Howard University. Madison, who graduated from Howard Law School in 1955, worked at the LDF from 1956 to 1957, when he left, planning to move to the West Coast. Feder graduated from Yale Law School in 1956 and worked at the LDF from 1956 to February 1959, after which she moved to Florida. Nabrit's father had been deeply involved in the NAACP's litigation before *Brown;* he graduated from Yale Law School in 1955, went into the Army and then practiced law in Washington with Frank Reeves, another long-time cooperating NAACP lawyer, before joining the LDF staff in 1959, where he remained until 1989.

32. TM interview with author, Aug. 2, 1989; Constance Baker Motley, interviewed by Mrs. Walter Gellhorn, March 19, 1977, 249, Columbia Oral History Collection. For Marshall's report on the investigation, see Draft pamphlet (by Henry Lee Moon), March 12, 1951, NAACP Papers, Box II-B-100, file: Thurgood Marshall, General, 1951–55.

33. Yarbrough, *A Passion for Justice,* 109; Franklin Williams interview; Gloster Current, interview with author (telephone), Jan. 22, 1991; TM to Ogretta Logan, Oct. 9, 1951, NAACP Papers, Box II-A-536, file: Speakers, Thurgood Marshall, General, July–Oct. 1951; TM to James Hinton, June 30, 1953, NAACP Papers, Box II-A-228, file: Desegregation, Schools, Branch Action, South Carolina, 1954–55.

34. TM to Friends of the Committee, On: The Student Sit-In Protests, March 31, 1960, Harlow Papers, Box 2, folder 17; Herbert Haines, *Black Radicals and the Civil Rights Mainstream, 1954–1970* (Knoxville: University of Tennessee Press, 1988), 84; Norman Amaker, interview with author, Chicago, Ill., Oct. 26, 1990.

35. TM to Executive Staff, Nov. 15, 1955, Daniel Ellis Byrd Papers, Box 2, folder 4, Amistad Research Center, Tulane University; Comparative Income Statement, Sept. 1955

and 1956, NAACP Papers, Box III-A-173, file: Financial Material 1956–65; TM to Friend, Jan. 28, 1958, id., Box III-A-172, file: Inc. Fund Conferences; Press release, May 10, 1956, id., Box III-A-173, file: Inc. Fund Contributions; Motley interview; Deborah Rhode, notes on conversations with TM (undated), in author's possession; Pittsburgh *Courier,* Sept. 20, 1958, in Daisy Bates Papers, Reel 5, State Historical Society of Wisconsin; Henry Lee Moon to William Howland, Dec. 29, 1954, NAACP Papers, Box II-A-536, file: Speakers, Thurgood Marshall, General, 1952–54.

36. NAACP LDF Monthly Report, Nov. 1955, A. P. Tureaud Papers, Box 14, folder 12, Amistad Research Center, Tulane University; Senate Judiciary Committee, Hearings on the Nomination of Thurgood Marshall, 89th Cong., 1st Sess., S-1700–2 (1965), 3.

37. Mrs. Thurgood Marshall, interview with author, April 24, 1991, Washington, D.C.; TM, interview by Ed Erwin, Columbia Oral History Collection, 62–67; Williams interview; New York *Times,* Sept. 8, 1962, 11, col. 2.

Epilogue

1. Payne v. Tennessee, 111 S. Ct. 2597, 2619 (1991) (Marshall, J., dissenting).

2. Id. at 2623–24 (Marshall, J., dissenting). For a more detailed analysis of the case, see Mark Tushnet, "Thurgood Marshall and the Rule of Law," *Howard Law Journal* 35 (1991): 7.

Bibliography

There is a substantial literature on the civil rights movement, and a significant literature on that movement's specifically legal aspects. Important monographs include Catherine A. Barnes, *Journey from Jim Crow,* on transportation, Clement Vose, *Caucasians Only,* on restrictive covenants, and Richard Kluger, *Simple Justice,* on *Brown v. Board of Education.* Although this book draws on some material not available to those authors (most notably in some newly available papers from Supreme Court justices and in NAACP papers not available when Vose wrote), its main difference from those works is its emphasis on the way the NAACP's legal activities in different areas interacted, both conceptually and in forcing the organization to structure its activities in particular ways. On one important matter of interpretation, I believe that earlier studies have overestimated the positive contribution Justice Felix Frankfurter made to the outcome in *Brown.*

After my manuscript was complete, two journalistically oriented works on Thurgood Marshall appeared: Carl Rowan, *Dream Makers, Dream Breakers: The World of Justice Thurgood Marshall* (Boston: Little, Brown & Co., 1993); Michael Davis and Hunter Clark, *Thurgood Marshall: Warrior at the Bar, Rebel on the Bench* (Secaucus, N.J.: Carol Publishing Group, 1992). Each has enough minor errors to make me uneasy about altering my judgments about events on which their accounts differ from mine. More important, the authors' purposes and audiences lead them to "humanize" Marshall, for example by emphasizing the dramatic incidents in which he was involved, in ways that in my view make it difficult for readers to appreciate how Marshall was a great *lawyer.*

Manuscript Collections

NAACP-RELATED COLLECTIONS

Manuscript Division, Library of Congress
    NAACP Papers
Amistad Research Center, Tulane University
    Daniel Ellis Byrd Papers
    Ralph Harlow Papers
    Frank Horne Papers
    A. P. Tureaud Papers
Meiklejohn Civil Liberties Institute

National Lawyers Guild Papers
Savery Library, Talladega College
    Arthur Shores Papers
State Historical Society of Wisconsin
    Daisy Bates Papers

SUPREME COURT MANUSCRIPTS

Manuscript Division, Library of Congress
    Hugo Black
    William J. Brennan
    Harold L. Burton
    William O. Douglas
    Robert Jackson
    Harlan Fiske Stone
    Wiley Rutledge
    Earl Warren
Harvard Law School Library
    Felix Frankfurter
    Roscoe Pound
Seeley G. Mudd Manuscript Library, Princeton University
    John Marshall Harlan
Tarlton Law Library, University of Texas Law School
    Tom C. Clark
Special Collections and Archives, King Library, University of Kentucky
    Stanley Reed
    Fred M. Vinson

Interviews

AUTHOR'S INTERVIEWS

Norman Amaker, Chicago, Oct. 26, 1990
Derrick Bell (telephone), Dec. 20, 1990
Gloria Branker, Washington, D.C., Jan. 30, 1991
Robert Carter, New York, Dec. 7, 1990
Kenneth B. Clark, Hastings-on-Hudson, New York, Dec. 6, 1990
William L. Coleman, Washington, D.C., Oct. 17, 1989
Gloster Curent (telephone), Jan. 22, 1991
Irma Robbins Feder (telephone), May 21, 1990
John Hope Franklin (telephone), Nov. 5, 1990
Erwin Griswold, Washington, D.C., June 30, 1989
Oliver Hill, Richmond, Virginia, July 13, 1989
Herbert Hill, Madison, Wis., Nov. 10, 1990
Whitman Knapp, New York, July 7, 1989
Waite Madison, Washington, D.C., April 24, 1990
Thurgood Marshall, Feb. 2, 1989; May 23, 1989; Aug. 2, 1989; Oct. 18, 1990
Mrs. Thurgood Marshall, Washington, D.C., April 24, 1991
Abner Mikva, Washington, D.C., Dec. 24, 1990
Constance Baker Motley, Chester, Conn., Sept. 1, 1989

James L. Nabrit III, Washington, D.C., April 23, 1990
Spottswood Robinson, Washington, D.C., Aug. 2, 1989
Leonard Schroeter (telephone), July 3, 1990
Alice Stovall, Wheaton, Maryland, June 11, 1990
William L. Taylor, Washington, D.C., March 16, 1990
Ralph Temple, Washington, D.C., March 27, 1990
Franklin Williams, New York, Aug. 3, 1989
Ralph Winter, New Haven, April 26, 1989
Marian Wynn Perry Yankauer, North Brookfield, Mass., July 20, 1989

COLUMBIA ORAL HISTORY COLLECTION

Thurgood Marshall, by Ed Erwin, Feb. 15, 1977
Constance Baker Motley, by Mrs. Walter Gellhorn, March 19, 1977

CIVIL RIGHTS DOCUMENTATION PROJECT, MOORLAND-SPINGARN RESEARCH
CENTER, HOWARD UNIVERSITY

Kelly Alexander, by Stanley Smith, undated
Wiley Branton, by James Mosby, Jan. 16, 1969
Robert L. Carter, by John Britton, March 8, 1968
Elwood Chisolm, by Harold Lewis, Aug. 9, 1967
W. J. Durham, by John Britton, May 1, 1970
Z. Alexander Looby, by John Britton, Dec. 29, 1967
James M. Nabrit, by Vincent Browne, 1968
Frank Reeves, by Robert Wright, Dec. 28, 1969
June Shagaloff, by Robert Martin, Sept. 5, 1968
William L. Taylor, by John Britton, Aug. 8, 1967
A. P. Tureaud, by Robert Wright, Aug. 9, 1969

MISCELLANEOUS

Transcript, WUSA-TV's "Searching for Justice: Three American Stories," Sunday, Sept.
    13, 1987.
Transcript, WUSA-TV's "Thurgood Marshall the Man," Sunday, Dec. 13, 1987.

Books and Articles

Aldred, Lisa. *Thurgood Marshall* (New York: Chelsea House Publishers, 1990).
Allen, Francis. "Remembering *Shelley v. Kraemer:* Of Public and Private Worlds," *Washington University Law Quarterly* 67 (Fall 1989): 709.
Allen, Robert. *The Port Chicago Munity* (New York: Warner Books, 1989).
Argersinger, Jo Ann. *Toward a New Deal in Baltimore: People and Government in the Great Depression* (Chapel Hill: University of North Carolina Press, 1988).
Barnes, Catherine A. *Journey from Jim Crow: The Desegregation of Southern Transit* (New York: Columbia University Press, 1983).
Bartley, Numan. *The Rise of Massive Resistance: Race and Politics in the South During the 1950s* (Baton Rouge: Louisiana State University Press, 1969).
Bates, Daisy. *The Long Shadow of Little Rock* (reprint, Fayetteville: University of Arkansas Press, 1987).
Bator, Paul, Daniel Meltzer, Paul Mishkin, and David Shapiro. *Hart and Wechsler's The*

Federal Courts and the Federal System, 3rd ed. (Westbury, N.Y.: Foundation Press, 1988).

Beardsley, E.H.. "Good-Bye to Jim Crow: The Desegregation of Southern Hospitals, 1945–1970," *Bulletin of the History of Medicine* 60 (Fall 1986): 367.

Belknap, Michal, ed. *Civil Rights, The White House, and the Justice Department, 1945–1968* (New York: Garland Publishing Co., 1991).

Bell, Derrick. "An Epistolatory Exploration for a Thurgood Marshall Biography." *Harvard Blackletter Journal* (Spring 1989): 55.

Berry, Mary Frances. *Stability, Security, and Continuity: Mr. Justice Burton and Decision-Making in the Supreme Court 1945–1958* (Westport, Conn.: Greenwood Press, 1978).

Bickel, Alexander. *The Least Dangerous Branch: The Supreme Court at the Bar of Politics* (Indianapolis: Bobbs Merrill, 1962).

———. "The Original Understanding of the Fourteenth Amendment," *Harvard Law Review* 69 (Nov. 1955): 1.

Bogen, David. "The First Integration of the University of Maryland School of Law," *Maryland Historical Magazine* 84 (Spring 1989): 39.

Bond, Julian. "The Politics of Civil Rights History," in *New Directions in Civil Rights Studies,* Armstead L. Robinson and Patricia Sullivan, eds. (Charlottesville: University of Virginia Press, 1991).

Braeman, John. *Before the Civil Rights Revolution: The Old Court and Individual Rights* (New York: Greenwood Press, 1988).

Branch, Taylor. *Parting the Waters: America in the King Years, 1954–1963* (New York: Simon & Schuster, 1988).

Branton, Wiley. "Personal Memories of Thurgood Marshall," *Arkansas Law Review* 40 (1987): 665.

Brugger, Robert. *Maryland: A Middle Temperament, 1634–1980* (Baltimore: Johns Hopkins University Press, 1988).

Burk, Robert. *The Eisenhower Administration and Black Civil Rights* (Knoxville: University of Tennessee Press, 1984).

Callcott, Margaret Law. *The Negro in Maryland Politics, 1870–1912* (Baltimore: John Hopkins University Press, 1969).

Carr, Robert. *Federal Protection of Civil Rights: Quest for a Sword* (Ithaca: Cornell University Press, 1947).

Carter, Dan. *Scottsboro* (Baton Rouge: Louisiana State University Press, 1969).

Carter, Robert. "A Tribute to Justice Thurgood Marshall," *Harvard Law Review* 105 (1991): 33.

Chafe, William. *Civilities and Civil Rights: Greensboro, North Carolina, and the Black Struggle for Civil Rights* (New York: Oxford University Press, 1980).

Chambers, Thomas. "Leonard Schroeter," Seattle-King County Bar Association *Bar Bulletin* (Nov. 1989).

Chesler, Mark, Joseph Sanders, and Debra Kalmuss. *Social Science in Court: Mobilizing Experts in the School Desegregation Cases* (Madison: University of Wisconsin Press, 1988).

Clark, Tom and Philip Perlman. *Prejudice and Property* (Washington, 1948).

Colburn, David. "Florida's Governors Confront the *Brown* Decision: A Case Study of the Constitutional Politics of School Desegregation, 1954–1970," in James Ely and Kermit Hall, eds. *An Uncertain Tradition: Constitutionalism and the History of the South* (Athens: University of Georgia Press, 1989).

Cooper, Algia. "Brown v. Board of Education and Virgil Darnell Hawkins: Twenty-Eight Years and Six Petitions to Justice," *Journal of Negro History* 64 (Winter 1979): 10.

Cortner, Richard. *A "Scottsboro" Case in Mississippi: The Supreme Court and* Brown v. Mississippi (Jackson, Miss.: University of Mississippi Press, 1986).

Crain, Robert. *The Politics of School Desegregation: Comparative Case Studies of Community Structure and Policy-Making* (Garden City, N.Y.: Doubleday & Co., 1969).

Cross, William. *Shades of Black* (Philadelphia: Temple University Press, 1991).

Danelski, David. *Rights, Liberties, and Ideals: The Contributions of Milton R. Konvitz* (Littleton, Co.: Fred B. Rothman, 1983).

Diamond, Raymond. "Confrontation as Rejoinder to Compromise: Reflections on the Little Rock Desegregation Crisis," *National Black Law Journal* 11 (Summer 1989): 151.

Du Bois, W.E.B. *Writings,* from *"The Souls of Black Folk,"* (New York: Viking Press, 1986) (originally published 1903).

Dudziak, Mary. "The Limits of Good Faith: Desegregation in Topeka, Kansas, 1950–1956," *Law & History Review* 5 (Fall 1987): 351.

Dugger, Ronnie. "John Ben Shepperd and the NAACP at Tyler," *Texas Observer,* Oct. 31, 1956.

Edwards, George C. "White Justice in Dallas," *Nation,* 161 (Sept. 15, 1945): 253.

Elliff, John T. *The United States Department of Justice and Individual Rights, 1937–1962* (New York: Garland Publishing Co., 1987).

Elman, Philip. "The Solicitor General's Office, Justice Frankfurter, and Civil Rights Litigation, 1946–1960: An Oral History," *Harvard Law Review* 100 (Feb. 1987): 817.

Ely, James W. *The Crisis of Conservative Virginia: The Byrd Organization and the Politics of Massive Resistance* (Knoxville: University of Tennessee Press, 1976).

Entin, Jonathan L. "The Shifting Color Line in Prince Edward County." Paper presented at the annual meeting of the Law and Society Association, May 28–31, 1992.

———. "*Sweatt v. Painter,* the End of Segregation, and the Transformation of Education Law," *Review of Litigation* 5 (June 1986): 3.

Eskew, Glenn. "The Alabama Christian Movement for Human Rights and the Birmingham Struggle for Civil Rights, 1956–1963," in David Garrow, ed. *Birmingham, Alabama, 1956–1963: The Black Struggle for Civil Rights* (Brooklyn: Carlson Publishing Inc., 1989).

"Fighter for His People," New York *Times,* Sept. 8, 1962.

Fine, Sidney. *Frank Murphy: The Washington Years* (Ann Arbor: University of Michigan Press, 1984).

Folsom, Fred. "Federal Elections and the 'White Primary,'" *Columbia Law Review* 43 (Nov.–Dec. 1943): 1026.

Franklin, John Hope. *Race and History: Selected Essays, 1938–1988* (Baton Rouge: Louissiana State University Press, 1989).

Freund, Paul. *The Supreme Court of the United States: Its Business, Purpose, and Performance* (Cleveland: World Publishing Co., 1961).

Freyer, Tony. *The Little Rock Crisis: A Constitutional Interpretation* (Westport, Conn.: Greenwood Press, 1984).

Garrow, David, ed. *The Walking City: The Montgomery Bus Boycott, 1955–1956* (Brooklyn: Carlson Publishing Inc., 1989).

Gates, Robbins. *The Making of Massive Resistance: Virginia's Politics of Public School Desegregation, 1954–1956* (Chapel Hill: University of North Carolina Press, 1962).

Gillette, Michael. "Heman Marion Sweatt: Civil Rights Plaintiff," in *Black Leaders: Texans for Their Times,* Alwyn Barr and Robert Calvert, eds. (Austin: Texas State Historical Association, 1981).

Gilliam, Thomas. "The Montgomery Bus Boycott of 1955–56," in David Garrow, ed., *The Walking City* (Brooklyn: Carlson Publishing Inc., 1989).

Glennon, Robert Jerome. "The Role of Law in the Civil Rights Movement: The Montgomery Bus Boycott, 1955–1957," *Law and History Review* 9 (Spring 1991): 59.

Goings, Kenneth. *"The NAACP Comes of Age"* (Urbana: University of Illinios Press, 1990).

Greenhill, Joe. "Address," *Texas Southern Law Review* 4 (Special Issue 1977): 179.

Grundman, Adolph. "Public School Desegregation in Virginia from 1954 to the Present." Ph.D. dissertation, Wayne State University, 1972.

Haines, Herbert. *Black Radicals and the Civil Rights Mainstream, 1954–1970* (Knoxville: University of Tennessee Press, 1988).

Hall, Wade. *The Rest of the Dream: The Black Odyssey of Lyman Johnson* (Lexington: University Press of Kentucky, 1988).

Hansberry, Lorraine. *A Raisin in the Sun* (New York: S. French, 1988).

Harbaugh, William. *Lawyer's Lawyer: The Life of John W. Davis* (New York: Oxford University Press, 1973).

Henkin, Louis. *"Shelley v. Kraemer:* Notes for a Revised Opinion," *University of Pennsylvania Law Review* 110 (Feb. 1962): 473.

Hill, Herbert. *Black Labor and the American Legal System* (Madison: University of Wisconsin Press, 1985) (originally published 1977).

Hine, Darlene Clark. *Black Victory: The Rise and Fall of the White Primary in Texas* (Millwood, N.Y.: KTO Press, 1979).

Hoffer, Peter. *The Law's Conscience: Equitable Constitutionalism in America* (Chapel Hill: University of North Carolina Press, 1990).

Hovenkamp, Herbert. "Social Science and Segregation Before *Brown,"* *Duke Law Journal* 1985 (June–Sept. 1985): 624.

Hutchinson, Dennis. "The Black-Jackson Feud," *Supreme Court Review* 1988 (1988): 203.

———. "Unanimity and Desegregation: Decisionmaking in the Supreme Court, 1948–1958," *Georgetown Law Journal* 68 (Oct. 1979): 1.

Irons, Peter. *The Courage of Their Convictions* (New York: Free Press, 1988).

Johnson, Whittington B. "The Virgil Hawkins Case: A Near Decade of Evading the Inevitable: The Demise of Jim Crow Higher Education in Florida," *Southern University Law Review* 16 (Spring 1989): 55.

Jones, Vonciel. "Texas Southern University School of Law—The Beginning," *Texas Southern Law Review* 4 (Special Issue 1977): 197.

Kalven, Harry. *A Worthy Tradition: Freedom of Speech in America* (New York: Haper & Row, 1988).

Kaufman, Jonathan. *Broken Alliance: The Turbulent Times Between Black and Jews in America* (New York: Scribners, 1988).

Kellogg, Charles Flint. *NAACP: A History of the National Association for the Advancement of Colored People, vol. 1: 1909–1920* (Baltimore: Johns Hopkins University Press, 1967).

Kelly, Alfred. "An Inside View of 'Brown v. Board.'" Paper delivered to the American Historical Association, December 1961, and reprinted in Senate Judiciary Committee, 87th Congress, 1st Session, Hearings on the Nomination of Thurgood Marshall.

Klare, Karl. "The Quest for Industrial Democracy the Struggle Against Racism: Perspectives from Labor Law and Civil Rights Law," *Oregon Law Review* 61 (Dec. 1982): 157.

Kluger, Richard. *Simple Justice* (New York: Knopf, 1975).

Kousser, J. Morgan. *Dead End: The Development of Nineteenth-Century Litigation on Racial Discrimination in Schools* (Oxford: Clarendon Press, 1986).

———. *The Shaping of Southern Politics: Suffrage Restriction and the Establishment of the One Party South, 1880–1910* (New Haven: Yale University Press, 1974).

Kuebler, Edward J. "The Desegregation of the University of Maryland," *Maryland Histori-cal Magazine* 71 (Spring 1976): 37.

Lawson, Steven. *Black Ballots: Voting Rights in the South, 1944–1969* (New York: Columbia University Press, 1976).

———. "The Florida Legislative Investigation Committee and the Constitutional Readjust-ment of Race Relations, 1956–1963," in James Ely and Kermit Hall, eds. *An Uncer-tain Tradition: Constitutionalism and the History of the South* (Athens: University of Georgia Press, 1989).

Leuchtenburg, William. "FDR's Court-Packing Plan: A Second Life, a Second Death," *Duke Law Journal* 1985 (Summer 1985): 673.

———. "The Origins of Franklin D. Roosevelt's 'Court-Packing' Plan," *Supreme Court Review* 1966 (1966): 347.

Levinson, Sanford. *Constitutional Faith* (Princeton: Princeton University Press, 1988).

Levy, Leonard and Douglas Jones. *Jim Crow in Boston: The Origin of the Separate But Equal Doctrine* (New York: Da Capo Press, 1974).

Lewis, Earl. *In Their Own Interests: Race, Class, and Power in Twentieth-Century Norfolk, Virginia* (Berkeley: University of California Press, 1991).

Marshall, Thurgood. "Address," *Texas Southern Law Review* 4 (Special Issue 1977): 191.

———. "Reflections on the Bicentennial of the United States Constitution," *Harvard Law Review* 101 (Nov. 1987): 1; also published as "The Constitution's Bicentennial: Commemorating the 'Wrong Document?," *Vanderbilt Law Review* 40 (Nov. 1987): 1337.

Martin, Charles H. "The Civil Rights Congress and Southern Black Defendants," *Georgia Historical Quarterly* 71 (Spring, 1987): 25.

Mayer, Michael. "With Much Deliberation and Some Speed: Eisenhower and the *Brown* Decision," *Journal of Southern History* 52 (Feb. 1986): 42.

McCloskey, Robert. *The American Supreme Court* (Chicago: University of Chicago Press, 1960).

McCoy, Drew. *The Last of the Fathers: James Madison and the Republican Legacy* (New York: Cambridge University Press, 1989).

McDowell, Edwin. "From Twain, a Letter on Debt to Blacks," New York *Times,* March 14, 1985.

McGovney, D.O. "Racial Residential Segregation by State Court Enforcement of Restric-tive Covenants or Conditions in Deeds Is Unconstitutional," *California Law Review* 33 (March 1945): 5.

McGuire, Philip. *He, Too, Spoke for Democracy: Judge Hastie, World War II, and the Black Soldier* (New York: Greenwood Press, 1988).

McKay, Robert. "'With All Deliberate Speed': A Study of School Desegregation," *New York University Law Review* 31 (June 1956): 1008.

———. "'With All Deliberate Speed': Legislative Reaction and Judicial Development 1956–57," *Virginia Law Review* 43 (Dec. 1957): 1205.

McMillen, Neil. *Dark Journey: Black Mississippians in the Age of Jim Crow* (Urbana: Univer-sity of Illinios Press, 1989).

McNeil, Genna Rae. *Groundwork: Charles Hamilton Houston and the Struggle for Civil Rights* (Philadelphia: University of Pennsylvania Press, 1983).

Meador, Daniel. "The Constitution and the Assignment of Pupils to Public Schools," *Virginia Law Review* (May 1959): 517.

Mikva, Abner. "The Role of Theorists in Constitutional Cases," *University of Colorado Law Review* 63 (1992): 451.

Miller, Arthur S. *Death By Installments: The Ordeal of Willie Francis* (New York: Greenwood Press, 1988).

Miller, Loren. *The Petitioners* (New York: Pantheon Books, 1966).

Murphy, Walter. *Congress and the Court: A Case Study in the American Political Process* (Chicago: University of Chicago Press, 1962).

———. "The South Counterattacks: The Anti-NAACP Laws," *Wesyern Political Quarterly* 12 (June 1959): 371.

Murray, Pauli. *The Autobiography of a Black Activist, Feminist, Lawyer, Priest, and Poet* (Knoxville: University of Tennessee Press, 1989) (originally published as *Song in a Weary Throat: An American Pilgrimage*, 1987).

Neverdon-Morton, Cynthia. *Afro-American Women of the South and the Advancement of the Race, 1895–1925* (Knoxville: University of Tennessee Press, 1989).

Pach, Chester Jr., and Elmo Richardson. *The Presidency of Dwight D. Eisenhower*, rev. ed. (Lawrence: University Press of Kansas, 1991).

Palmer, Jan. *The Vinson Court Era: The Supreme Court's Conference Votes—Data and Analysis* (New York: AMS Press, 1990).

Paulson, Darryl and Paul Hawkes. "Desegregating the University of Florida Law School: Virgil Hawkins v. the Florida Board of Control," *Florida State University Law Review,* 12 (Spring 1984): 59.

Peebles-Wilkins, Wilma. "Reactions of Segments of the Black Community to the North Carolina Pearsall Plan, 1954–1966," *Phylon* 48 (Summer 1987): 112.

Peltason, Jack. *Fifty-Eight Lonely Men: Southern Federal Judges and School Desegregation* (Urbana: University of Illinios Press, 1961).

Puryear, Paul. "The Implementation of the Desegregation Decision in the Federal Courts of Virginia: A Case Study of Legal Resistance to Federal Authority." Ph.D. dissertation, University of Chicago, 1960.

Read, Frank and Lucy McGough. *Let Them Be Judged: The Judicial Integration of the Deep South* (Metuchen, N.J.: Scarecrow Press, 1978).

Record, Wilson. *Race and Radicalism: The NAACP and the Communist Party in Conflict* (Ithaca: Cornell University Press, 1963).

Reid, Ira De. A. *The Negro Community of Baltimore: A Summary Report of a Social Study* (Baltimore: [Baltimore Urban League], 1935).

Robinson, Spottswood. "Thurgood Marshall—The Lawyer," *Harvard Civil Rights-Civil Liberties Law Review* 13 (Spring 1978): 234.

Rowan, Carl T. *Dream Makers, Dream Breakers: The World of Justice Thurgood Marshall* (Boston: Little, Brown & Co., 1993).

Rudko, Frances. *Truman's Court: A Study in Judicial Restraint* (New York: Greenwood Press, 1988).

Ryon, Roderick. "Old West Baltimore," *Maryland Historical Magazine* 77 (March 1982): 54.

Schwartz, Bernard. *Super Chief: Earl Warren and His Supreme Court* (New York: New York University Press, 1983).

———. "Chief Justice Rehnquist, Justice Jackson, and the *Brown* Case," *Supreme Court Review* 1988 (1988): 245.

"Segregation and the Equal Protection Clause: Brief for the Committee of Law Teachers Against Segregation in Legal Education," *Minnesota Law Review* 34 (March 1950): 289.

Sherman, Richard B. *The Case of Odell Waller and Virginia Justice, 1940–42* (Knoxville: University of Tennessee Press, 1992).

Slind-Flor, Victoria. "A 'Conscience' on the Sidelines," *National Law Journal,* Sept. 3, 1990.

Smith, Bob. *They Closed Their Schools: Prince Edward County, Virginia, 1951–1964* (Chapel Hill: University of North Carolina Press, 1965).

Southern, David. *Gunnar Myrdal and Black-White Relations: The Use and Abuse of* An American Dilemma (Baton Rouge: Louisiana State University Press, 1987).

Speer, Hugh. "The Case of the Century: *Brown v. Board of Education of Topeka,*" this *Constitution,* 14 (Spring 1987): 24.

Spivack, John. *Race, Civil Rights and the United States Court of Appeals for the Fifth Judicial Circuit* (New York: Garland Publishing Co., 1990).

Stone, William McFerrin. "Willie Rainach and the Defense of Segregation in Louisiana, 1954–1959." Ph.D. dissertation, Texas Christian University, 1989.

Suggs, Henry Lewis. *P. B. Young, Newspaperman: Race, Politics, and Journalism in the New South, 1910–1962* (Charlottesville: University Press of Virginia, 1988).

Sullivan, Patricia. "Southern Reformers, the New Deal, and the Movement's Foundation," in Armstead L. Robinson and Patricia Sullivan, eds. *New Directions in Civil Rights Studies* (Charlottesville: University Press of Virginia, 1991).

Taper, Bernard. "A Reporter at Large: A Meeting in Atlanta," *The New Yorker,* March 17, 1956.

"The Tension of Change," *Time,* Sept. 19, 1955.

Thompson, John Henry Lee. "Little Caesar of Civil Rights: Roscoe Dunjee in Oklahoma City, 1915 to 1955." Ph.D. dissertation, Purdue University, 1990.

Thornton, J. Mills. "First Among Equals: The Montgomery Bus Boycott," in David Garrow, ed. *The Walking City* (Brooklyn: Carlson Publishing Inc., 1989).

"Thurgood Marshall Speaks," *Ebony,* May 1979.

Tushnet, Mark. *The NAACP's Legal Strategy Against Segregated Education, 1925–1950* (Chapel Hill: University of North Carolina Press, 1988).

———. "The Politics of Equality in Constitutional Law: The Equal Protection Clause, Dr. Du Bois, and Charles Hamilton Houston," in David Thelen, ed. *The Constitution and American Life* (Ithaca: Cornell University Press, 1987).

———. "*Shelley v. Kraemer* and Theories of Equality," *New York Law School Law Review* 33 (1988): 383.

———. "Thurgood Marshall and the Rule of Law," *Howard Law Journal* 35 (1992): 7.

Vose, Clement. *Caucasians Only: The Supreme Court, the NAACP, and the Restrictive Covenant Cases* (Berkeley: University of California Press, 1959).

Ware, Leland. "Invisible Walls: An Examination of the Legal Strategy of the Restrictive Covenant Cases," *Washington University Law Quarterly* 67 (Fall 1989): 737.

Weisbrot, Robert. *Freedom Bound: A History of America's Civil Rights Movement* (New York: W. W. Norton & Co., 1990).

Wennersten, John. "The Black School Teacher in Maryland, 1930's," *Bulletin of Negro History* (Spring 1976).

White, Walter. *A Man Called White: The Autobiography of Walter White* (Bloomington: Indiana University Press, 1970) (originally published 1948).

Wilkins, David. "Justice as Narrative: Some Personal Reflections on a Master Storyteller," *Harvard Blackletter Journal* 6 (Spring 1989): 68.

Wilkins, Roy, with Tom Mathews. *Standing Fast* (New York: Viking Press, 1982).

Williams, Jayme Coleman. "A Rhetorical Analysis of Thurgood Marshall's Arguments Before the Supreme Court in the Public School Segregation Controversy." Ph.D. dissertation, Ohio State University, 1959.

Williams, Juan. "Marshall's Law," *The Washington Post Magazine,* Jan. 7, 1990.

Woods, Barbara. "Modjeska Simkins and the South Carolina Conference of the NAACP, 1939–1957," in Vicki Crawford, Jacqueline Anne Rouse, and Barbara Woods, eds.

Women in the Civil Rights Movement: Trailblazers and Torchbearers, 1941–1965 (Brooklyn: Carlson Publishing Inc., 1990).

Wright, J. Skelly. "Thurgood Marshall: A Tribute," *Maryland Law Review* 40 (1981): 398.

Yarbrough, Tinsley. *A Passion for Justice: J. Waties Waring and Civil Rights* (New York: Oxford University Press, 1987).

Zangrando, Robert. *The NAACP Crusade Against Lynching, 1909–1950* (Philadelphia: Temple University Press, 1980).

Table of Cases

Aaron v. Cooper, 357 U.S. 566 (1958),
257–59
Aaron v. Tucker, 186 F. Supp. 913 (E.D.
Ark. 1960), reversed, 287 F.2d 798
(8th Cir. 1961), 361
Adams v. United States, 319 U.S. 312
(1943), 64–66
Adamson v. California, 332 U.S. 46
(1947), 56
Adkins v. School Board of Newport News,
148 F. Supp. 430 (E.D. Va.), af-
firmed, 246 F.2d 325 (4th Cir. 1957),
249–50
Akins v. Texas, 325 U.S. 398 (1945), 60–
61
Allen v. School Board of Charlottesville,
Race Relations Law Reporter 1 (866)
(W.D. Va.), affirmed, 240 F.2d 59
(4th Cir. 1956), 249
Alston v. School Board of Norfolk, 112
F.2d 992 (4th Cir.), cert. denied, 311
U.S. 693 (1940), 24–26, 118
Barenblatt v. United States, 360 U.S. 109
(1959), 298
Bates v. Little Rock, 361 U.S. 516 (1960),
291–92
Beckett v. School Board of Norfolk, 185 F.
Supp. 459 (E.D. Va. 1959), affirmed
sub nom. Farley v. Turner, 281 F.2d
131 (4th Cir. 1960), 254
Bell v. Rippy, 146 F. Supp. 485 (N.D.
Tex. 1956), reversed sub nom. Borders
v. Rippy, 247 F.2d 268 (5th Cir.
1957), on motion for further relief,

250 F.2d 690 (5th Cir. 1957), on re-
mand, 184 F. Supp. 402 (N.D. Tex.
1960), 251–52
Belton v. Gebhart, 87 A.2d 862 (Del.
Ch.), affirmed, 91 A.2d 137 (Del. Sup.
Ct. 1952), decision on merits, 347
U.S. 483 (1954), 163–64, 166–67, 185–
86, 209
Bob-Lo Excursion Co. v. Michigan, 333
U.S. 28 (1948), 79
Bolling v. Sharpe, 347 U.S. 497 (1954),
165, 166–67, 184–85, 209, 214–15
Boynton v. Virginia, 364 U.S. 454 (1960),
308–9
Briggs v. Elliott, 98 F. Supp. 529 (E.D.
S.C. 1951), remanded, 342 U.S. 350
(1952), on remand, 103 F. Supp. 920
(E.D. S.C. 1952), decision on merits,
347 U.S. 483 (1954), on remand, 132
F. Supp. 776 (E.D. S.C. 1955), 154–
55, 157–61, 165–67, 175–81, 205–9,
241, 255, 271, 357–58
Brown v. Baskin, 78 F. Supp. 933 (E. D.
S.C. 1948), affirmed, 174 F.2d 391
(4th Cir. 1949), 108–9
Brown v. Board of Education I, 98 F.
Supp. 797 (D. Kansas 1951), interim
order, 344 U.S. 141 (1952), second interim order, 344 U.S. 1 (1952), decision on merits, 347 U.S. 483 (1954),
153–54, 161–62, 165–67, 173–75, 187,
189–95, 203–4, 209, 209–15
Brown v. Board of Education II, 349 U.S.
294 (1955), 217, 219–22, 224–31, 244

Bryan v. Austin, 354 U.S. 933 (1957), 293

Bryant v. Zimmerman, 278 U.S. 63 (1928), 284, 285

Buchanan v. Warley, 245 U.S. 60 (1917), 81, 83, 84

Bush v. Orleans Parish School Board, 138 F. Supp. 337 (E.D. La. 1956), affirmed, 242 F.2d 156 (5th Cir. 1957), 266–67

Calhoun v. Latimer, 188 F. Supp. 412 (N.D. Ga. 1960), 241

Canty v. Alabama, 309 U.S. 629 (1940), 51

Carr v. Corning, 182 F. 2d 14 (D.C. Cir. 1950), 164–65

Carr v. Young, 331 S.W.2d 701 (Ark. 1960), 366

Carson v. Board of Education, 227 F.2d 789 (4th Cir. 1955), 242–43

Carson v. Warlick, 238 F.2d 724 (4th Cir. 1956), 243–44

Chambers v. Florida, 309 U.S. 227 (1940), 50–51, 57, 68, 70

Civil Rights Cases, 109 U.S. 3 (1883), 75

Cooper v. Aaron, 358 U.S. 1 (1958), 358 U.S. 27 (1958), 259–66

Corrigan v. Buckley, 271 U.S. 323 (1926), 85–86

Cumming v. Board of Education, 175 U.S. 528 (1899), 170

Davis v. County School Board of Prince Edward County, 103 F. Supp. 337 (E.D. Va. 1952), decision on merits, 347 U.S. 483 (1954), 150–51, 162–63, 166–67, 181–84, 204–5, 206

Davis v. County School Board of Prince Edward County, 149 F. Supp. 431 (E.D. Va.), reversed, 249 F.2d 462 (4th Cir. 1957), on remand sub nom. Allen v. County School Board, 164 F. Supp. 786 (E.D. Va. 1958), modified, 266 F.2d 507 (4th Cir. 1959), 251

Davis v. Schnell, 81 F. Supp. 872 (S.D. Ala.), affirmed, 336 U.S. 933 (1949), 113–15

Elmore v. Rice, 72 F. Supp. 516 (E.D. S.C.), affirmed, 165 F.2d 387 (4th Cir. 1947), 108

Fisher [Sipuel] v. Hurst, 333 U.S. 147 (1948), 130

Gayle v. Browder, 352 U.S. 903 (1956), 304

Gibson v. Florida Legislative Investigation Committee, 108 So. 2d 729 (Fla. 1958), cert. denied, 360 U.S. 919 (1959), on contempt finding, 126 So. 2d 129 (Fla. 1960), reversed, 372 U.S. 539 (1963), 296–300

Giles v. Harris, 189 U.S. 475 (1903), 112–13

Gong Lum v. Rice, 275 U.S. 78 (1927), 170

Grovey v. Townsend, 295 U.S. 45 (1935), 102, 105–7

Guinn v. United States, 238 U.S. 347 (1915), 81, 82

Hannah v. Larche, 363 U.S. 420 (1960), 307

Hansberry v. Lee, 311 U.S. 32 (1940), 87

Hawkins v. Board of Control, 47 So. 2d 608 (Fla. 1950), on motion for further relief, 53 So. 2d 116 (Fla. 1951), on motion for further relief, 60 So. 2d 162 (Fla. 1952), remanded, 347 U.S. 971 (1954), on remand, 83 So. 2d 20 (Fla. 1955), remanded, 350 U.S. 413 (1956), on remand, 93 So. 2d 354 (Fla. 1957), cert. denied, 355 U.S. 839 (1957), on motion for injunction, 253 F.2d 752 (5th Cir. 1958), 235–38, 296

Henderson v. United States, 339 U.S. 816 (1950), 135–36, 139–40, 145, 146, 173

Hill v. School Board of Norfolk, 282 F.2d 473 (4th Cir. 1960), 254

Hill v. Texas, 316 U.S. 400 (1942), 59–60, 330

Holmes v. City of Atlanta, 350 U.S. 879 (1955), 301

Hurd v. Hodge, 334 U.S. 24 (1948), 89, 94, 96

James v. Marinship Corp., 25 Cal. 2d 721, 155 P.2d 329 (1944), 76–77

Jones v. School Board of Alexandria, 179 F. Supp. 280 (E.D. Va. 1959), 255

Joyner v. McDowell County Board of Education, 92 S.E.2d 795 (N.C. 1956), 243

Kelley v. Nashville Board of Education, 270 F.2d 209 (6th Cir.), cert. denied, 361 U.S. 924 (1959), 268–70

Korematsu v. United States, 323 U.S. 214 (1944), 171

Lee v. Mississippi, 332 U.S. 742 (1948), 68–69

Louisiana ex rel. Francis v. Resweber, 329 U.S. 459 (1947), 43–44

Louisiana ex rel. Gremillion v. NAACP, 366 U.S. 293 (1961), 291

Lyons v. Oklahoma, 322 U.S. 596 (1944), 61–64

Matter of Middlebrooks, 88 F. Supp. 943 (S.D. Cal. 1950), reversed sub nom. Ross v. Middlebrooks, 188 F.2d 308 (9th Cir. 1951), 39–40, 325

Mayor of Baltimore v. Dawson, 350 U.S. 877 (1955), 301

McCabe v. Atchison, Topeka & Santa Fe R. Co., 235 U.S. 151 (1914), 71

McCoy v. Greensboro City Board of Education, 283 F.2d 667 (4th Cir. 1960), 253–54

McCready v. Byrd, 195 Md. 131, 73 A. 2d 8 (1950), 147–48

McGee v. Sipes, 334 U.S. 1 (1948), 89

McLaurin v. Oklahoma State Regents, 339 U.S. 637 (1950), 130, 134–36, 138, 140, 146

Mills v. Lowndes, 26 F. Supp. 792 (D. Md. 1939), 23

Missouri ex rel. Gaines v. Canada, 305 U.S. 337 (1938), 70, 95, 121–22, 123, 129–30, 181–82

Mitchell v. United States, 313 U.S. 80 (1941), 71–72

Morgan v. Virginia, 328 U.S. 373 (1946), 73–74, 75, 76, 79

Morris v. Williams, 149 F.2d 703 (8th Cir. 1945), 119–20

Morrow v. Mecklenburg County Board of Education, 195 F. Supp. 109 (W.D. N.C. 1961), 255

NAACP v. Alabama, 274 Ala. 544, 150 So. 2d 677 (1963), reversed sub nom. NAACP v. Alabama ex rel. Flowers, 377 U.S. 288 (1964), 288–89

NAACP v. Alabama ex rel. Patterson, 357 U.S. 449 (1958), after remand, 360 U.S. 240 (1959), 283–87

NAACP v. Bennett, 178 F. Supp. 188 (E.D. Ark.), remanded, 360 U.S. 471, on remand, 178 F. Supp. 191 (E.D. Ark. 1959), 363

NAACP v. Button, 371 U.S. 415 (1963), 277–82

NAACP v. Gallion, 290 F.2d 337 (5th Cir.), vacated, 368 U.S. 16 (1961), 287–88

NAACP v. Patty, 159 F. Supp. 503 (E.D. Va. 1958), reversed sub nom. NAACP v. Harrison, 360 U.S. 167 (1959), 275–76

Naim v. Naim, 350 U.S. 891 (1955), after remand, 350 U.S. 985 (1956), 367

Newberry v. United States, 256 U.S. 232 (1921), 101

Nixon v. Condon, 286 U.S. 73 (1932), 100–2

Nixon v. Herndon, 273 U.S. 536 (1927), 100

Palko v. Connecticut, 302 U.S. 319 (1937), 56

Payne v. Tennessee, 111 S. Ct. 2597 (1991), 314–15

Pearson v. Murray, 169 Md. 478, 182 A. 590 (1936), 11, 14–15

Plessy v. Ferguson, 163 U.S. 537 (1896), 12, 71, 76, 83, 135, 136, 137, 139, 141, 144–45, 147, 160, 169–72, 173, 174, 176, 187–88, 189–90, 304, 351

Powell v. Alabama, 287 U.S. 45 (1932), 56

Railway Mail Ass'n v. Corsi, 326 U.S. 88 (1945), 79–80

Reynolds v. Board of Public Instruction, 148 F.2d 754 (5th Cir. 1945), 121

Screws v. United States, 325 U.S. 91 (1945), 49–50

Scull v. Virginia, 359 U.S. 344 (1959), 362–63

Shelley v. Kraemer, 334 U.S. 1 (1948), 89–90, 92–98, 174, 309

Shelton v. Tucker, 364 U.S. 479 (1960), affirming Shelton v. McKinley, 174 F. Supp. 351 (E.D. Ark. 1959), 294–95, 366

Shuttlesworth v. Birmingham Board of Education, 162 F. Supp. 372 (N.D. Ala.), affirmed, 358 U.S. 101 (1958), 244–46

Sipuel v. Oklahoma State Regents, 332 U.S. 631 (1948), 129–30, 133–34

Smith v. Allwright, 321 U.S. 649 (1944), 105–7, 108, 110, 111, 114, 115, 174

South Carolina Electric & Gas Co. v. Flemming, 351 U.S. 901 (1956), 303

Steele v. Louisville & Nashville R. Co., 323 U.S. 192 (1944), 77–79

Strauder v. West Virginia, 100 U.S. (10 Otto) 303 (1880), 56

Sweatt v. Painter, 339 U.S. 629 (1950), 126, 128–29, 131–33, 134–36, 137–38, 140–47, 160, 169, 188–89, 196, 235

Sweezy v. New Hampshire, 354 U.S. 234 (1957), 295–96

Terry v. Adams, 345 U.S. 461 (1953), 109–12, 190, 194, 306

Thompson v. Arlington County School Board, 144 F. Supp. 239 (E.D. Va. 1956), 249

Turner v. Keefe, 50 F. Supp. 647 (S.D. Fla. 1943), 23–24

United States v. Classic, 313 U.S. 299 (1941), 103–7

United States v. Raines, 362 U.S. 17 (1960), 307

Uphaus v. Wyman, 360 U.S. 72 (1959), 298

Watkins v. United States, 354 U.S. 178 (1957), 295–96

Watts v. Indiana, 338 U.S. 49 (1949), 39, 325

Wheeler v. Durham Board of Education, 196 F. Supp. 71 (M.D. N.C. 1961), 254–55

White v. Texas, 309 U.S. 631, rehearing denied, 310 U.S. 530 (1940), 51, 327–28

Williams v. Mississippi, 170 U.S. 213 (1898), 112

Williams v. Zimmerman, 172 Md. 563, 192 A. 353 (1937), 15–17

Yick Wo v. Hopkins, 118 U.S. 356 (1886), 82–83, 113, 115, 253, 254, 255, 306

Index

Abstention, 163, 275, 293

ACLU, 11, 44; brief in school segregation cases, 172

Adams-Bordenave case, 64–66, 120

Akerman, Alex, 235

Akins, L. C., 60

Alabama, attempt to suppress NAACP, 283–89; race discrimination in, 119; University of, desegregation suit against, 238–40; voting discrimination in, 113–15

Alabama Christian Movement for Human Rights, 305

Alabama Supreme Court, in NAACP membership disclosure case, 284, 287–89

Alexander, Raymond Pace, 38

Alexandria, Virginia, desegregation in, 255

"All deliberate speed," meaning of, 263–64; origins of, 230; use in argument, 208

Almond, Lindsay, 182–83, 200, 206, 226, 241

Alpha Phi Alpha (fraternity), 11, 14, 17, 136

Alston, Melvin, 24, 118

American Bar Association, 135

American Civil Liberties Union. *See* ACLU

American Fund for Public Service. *See* Garland Fund

American Jewish Committee, 90, 91

American Veterans Committee, 91

Amicus briefs, by law professors in university cases, 134–35; in restrictive covenant cases, 91; in university cases, 134, 137

Anderson, Charles, 52

Anne Arundel County, Maryland, 21, 23

Antibarratry rules, 274, 275, 276–79; and public interest practice, 282

Arkansas, attempt to suppress NAACP in, 291–92, 294–95; legislature's opposition to desegregation in, 258

Arlington, Virginia, desegregation in, 249, 250

Armed forces, Adams-Bordenave case in, 64–65; courts-martial, 29, 47–48; Port Chicago incident in, 32; race discrimination in, 36, 49

Association of American Law Schools, 7, 135, 148–49

Atkins, J. Alston, 101, 102

Atlanta, Georgia, sit-ins in, 309

Atwell, William, 251–52

Baldwin, Roger, 11–12, 44, 63

Baltimore, Maryland, 21, 43; African-American community of, 8, 9; desegregation in, 234; effects of Depression in, 9; Marshall's recollections of, 7–8, 320; politics of, 9; race discrimination in, 46, 318; segregated schools in, 15–16

Banks, Lester, 151, 307

Bates, Daisy, 257–58, 291–92, 294

Belden, Stanley, 62–63

Belton, Ethel, 163
Bennett, Bruce, 291
Bennett, James, 48
"Bennett ordinances," 291–92
Bickel, Alexander, 195, 203–4, 260, 277, 300
Biddle, Francis, 49, 105
Bingham, John, 198–99
Birmingham, Alabama, school desegregation in, 244–45
Bishop, Gardner, 165
Black, Aline, 24–25
Black, Hugo, 50–51, 56, 103, 106; appointment to Supreme Court, 67–68; assignment of university cases by, 145; on disclosure of teachers' affiliations, 294; in Florida legislative investigation case, 299; on gradualism, 219; in *Hawkins* case, 237; in Jaybird case, 110–11; in Little Rock case, 261, 263, 264; on meaning of "deliberate speed," 263; opinion in *Korematsu* case, 171; questions at *Brown* oral argument, 175, 184, 186; questions at *Brown* remedy argument, 225, 227; in restrictive covenant cases, 95; in Richmond bus terminal case, 309; views at discussion of *Brown*, 191–92; views on free speech, 285–86; views on initial decision in *Briggs* case, 166; views on interstate commerce, 73–74; views in NAACP membership disclosure case, 285; views after reargument in *Brown*, 210; views on remedy in *Brown*, 220–21, 229–30; views on university cases, 142; in Virginia antibarratry case, 277–80
Blair, Sol, 55
Blossom, Virgil, 257, 266
Bluford, Lucille, 122
Boggs, Hale, 103
Boilermakers union, 32, 76–77
Bond, Horace Mann, 196–97, 199
Borah, Wayne, 119
Boswell amendment, in Alabama, 113–15, 306
Boulware, Harold, 108
Boynton, Bruce, 308
Branton, Wiley, 257–58, 259, 260
Brennan, William J., in Alabama student assignment case, 245; in Florida legislative investigation case, 299; in Little Rock case, 261, 263–64; on meaning of "deliberate speed," 263–64; in NAACP membership disclosure case, 289; in Virginia antibarratry case, 279–81
Briggs, Harry, 154
"*Briggs* dictum," 241, 254–55, 271, 357–58
Brooklyn, race discrimination in, 46
Brown, Esther, 153
Brown, Linda, 154
Brown, Minnie Jean, 259
Brown, Oliver, 154
Brown v. Board of Education, 1953 lawyers' conference on, 198; argument on remedy, 217, 224–28; decision to order reargument, 194–95; importance of reargument in, 215–16; oral arguments in, 173–86; reargument on merits, 204–16; reasons for reargument in, 204; Supreme Court deliberations in, 187–95; Supreme Court's discussions after reargument, 209–10
Browne Junior High School, Washington, D.C., 164–65
Brownell, Herbert, 201, 203, 306
Bryan, Albert, 249, 250, 255
Buckley, John, 85
Bulah, Sarah, 163
Bunn, Charles, 133
Burnam, Eugene, 51–52
Burton, Harold, 74; appointment to Supreme Court, 138–39; drafting of *Henderson* opinion, 145–46; in Jaybird case, 110; in Little Rock case, 263; on meaning of "deliberate speed," 263; on overruling *Plessy*, 141; questions at *Brown* oral argument, 174, 175, 178; in restrictive covenant cases, 95; views on initial votes in *Brown*, 187; views after reargument in *Brown*, 210; views on remedy in *Brown*, 220, 229; views on university cases, 142–43
Bush, Earl, 266
Butcher, Margaret, 218
Butler, Richard, 259–63 *passim*
Byrd, Daniel Ellis, 266–67, 290
Byrd, Harry, 248
Byrnes, James, 177, 201, 232; plan to increase school funding, 158, 159; as Supreme Court justice, 69

Calhoun, John C., 240
California, race discrimination in, 32, 77, 89
Cameron, Ben, 251
Cannon, Poppy, 312
Capital punishment, 30, 43–44, 51–52, 59
Cardozo, Benjamin, 101
Carr, Raymond, 49
Carson, Loftus, 218
Carter, Eugene, 304
Carter, Robert, 33, 39, 43, 58, 209; on Alabama student assignment law, 244; argument in *Brown,* 173–74; in Arkansas NAACP membership case, 292; as author of *Brown* brief, 172; at *Briggs* trial, 158–59; at *Brown* trial, 161; in Columbia, Tennessee, trial, 54; on demonstrations, 310; on disclosure of NAACP membership, 293; efforts to obtain trial in Alabama membership disclosure case, 287–88; in Florida legislative investigation case, 297–98; as general counsel to NAACP, 310; hiring of, 35; on legal ethics, 274; on massive resistance statutes, 247; in Montgomery bus boycott litigation, 302, 304; in NAACP membership disclosure case, 284–85; oral argument in *McLaurin,* 140; on pace of desegregation litigation, 271; on race discrimination in transportation, 75; and reaction to *Brown,* 216; relations with Marshall, 311; on resistance to desegregation, 269; role in designing litigation strategy, 157; role in staff, 35; strategy in antibarratry case, 277; on suppression of NAACP in Louisiana, 290; on teachers' salary cases, 121; in transportation cases, 307; in university cases, 137–38; and use of sociological material in *Brown,* 214; views on attacking segregation in 1946, 126; views on disclosure of NAACP membership, 284–85; views on theories of desegregation, 127; views on Washington desegregation cases, 165; in white primary cases, 108
Carter, Willie, 59
Central High School, Little Rock, 257–59, 263, 266

Chapital, Arthur, 290
Chapman, Oscar, 91
Charlottesville, Virginia, desegregation in, 249, 250
Chesnut, Calvin, 23
Chisolm, Elwood, 311
Civil Liberties Unit. *See* Civil Rights Section
Civil Rights Act of 1866, 96, 198–99, 200–1
Civil Rights Act of 1871, 205
Civil Rights Act of 1875, 75
Civil Rights Act of 1957, 233, 306–7
Civil Rights Commission, 306–7
Civil Rights Section, 49, 50, 53, 91, 103
Civil rights statutes, in 1940s, 49–50
Clarendon County, South Carolina, school segregation in, 154–55, 158–59, 165–66
Clark, Charles, 140
Clark, Kenneth, background of, 157; significance of testimony of, 179, 214; testimony by, 159, 161, 162, 172
Clark, Mamie, 157
Clark, Tom, 55; in Alabama membership disclosure case, 288; appointment to Supreme Court, 138; as Attorney General, 91–92, 97; on Court's decision to list *Brown* first, 349; on Court's selection of desegregation cases, 167; in Florida legislative investigation case, 298–99; in Jaybird case, 110, 112; in Little Rock case, 260; in NAACP membership disclosure case, 286–87; in Richmond bus terminal case, 309; views at discussion of *Brown,* 193–94; views after reargument in *Brown,* 210; views on remedy in *Brown,* 229; views on university cases, 143–45; in Virginia antibarratry case, 277, 280; on Virginia regulations of NAACP, 276
Class actions, 87, 243; in *Brown,* 225, 227, 229, 230
Claymont, Delaware, desegregation in, 218; school segregation in, 163–64
Clinton, Tennessee, 269
Coleman, William T., 157, 192, 197
Collins, LeRoy, 237
Columbia University, 35, 36, 157, 162
Columbia, Tennessee, "riot," 52–55, 329

Commerce clause, and race discrimination, 71, 72–73
Committee of 100, 35, 312
Committee on Civil Rights, 91, 128, 138, 187
Communist party, 44–45, 53; investigations of, 284, 296; legal regulation of, 294, 299
Confessions, coerced, 39, 50–51, 57–58, 61–64, 68–69
Connally, Ben, 253
Corrigan, Irene, 85
Court-martial cases, 29–30, 32, 47–48, 49
Court-packing plan, 67
Crimes, against African-Americans, 49
Criminal cases, constitutional limitations in, 56; difficulty of challenging race discrimination in, 56–57; race discrimination in, 39, 42–43, 51–52
Cronson, Donald, memorandum on *Brown*, 189–90
Crooks, James, 93
Crow, E. R., 159
Current, Gloster, 37, 292

Dallas, Texas, desegregation in, 251–52; race discrimination in, 59–61; and voting rights, 105
Daniel, Price, 131, 132
Darrow, Clarence, 7
Davidson, T. Whitfield, 252
Davies, Ronald, 258, 259
Davis, John W. (LDF staff), 152
Davis, John W. (attorney for South Carolina in *Brown*), 188; in *Brown* case, 177–79; reargument in *Brown*, 204, 205–6; views on outcome of *Brown*, 186
Day, William, 84
Death penalty. *See* Capital punishment
Deep South, desegregation in, 251
Defenders of State Sovereignty, 248
DeLaine, Joseph, 154–55
Delaware, desegregation in, 218; race discrimination in, 163–64
Delaware State College for Negroes, 163
Dennis, Eugene, 45
Department of Interior, 91
Department of Justice, 49, 50, 91, 103; position in *Brown*, 172–73, 195, 201–2;

position on remedy in *Brown*, 223–24; in race discrimination cases, 71; in white primary cases, 105, 107
Depression, 9–10, 34
Desegregation, in border states, 234–35; difficulties of litigation to accomplish, 253; in Florida, 237; grade-a-year plans for, 221–22, 269–70; pace of, 233, 234; of public facilities, 301; and student assignment policies, 241–42
Desegregation cases, Supreme Court's decision to decide, 166–67
DeVane, Dozier, 238
Disfranchisement, strategies of, 99–100
District of Columbia. *See* Washington, D.C.
Dombrowski, James, 134
Douglas, William O., on abstention doctrine, 276; in Alabama student assignment case, 245; appointment to Supreme Court, 68; in *Classic* case, 103; on gradualism, 219; in Little Rock case, 265; in Louisiana NAACP membership case, 291; on massive resistance, 276; questions at *Brown* oral argument, 183; questions at *Brown* reargument, 208; questions at *Brown* remedy argument, 225, 227; in restrictive covenant cases, 95; in university desegregation cases, 129–30; views at discussion of *Brown*, 193; views on free speech, 285–86; views on initial decision in *Briggs* case, 166; views on initial votes in *Brown*, 187; views after reargument in *Brown*, 210; views on remedy in *Brown*, 220, 229–30; views on university cases, 143; views on vote in *Brown*, 194; views on vote after reargument in *Brown*, 210; in Virginia antibarratry case, 278; on Virginia regulations of NAACP, 276
Du Bois, W.E.B., 3, 179
Dudley, Edward, 29, 34, 35, 63
Dunagan, Otis, 272–73
Dunjee, Roscoe, 61–63, 129, 313
Dunning, William, 171
Durham, North Carolina, desegregation in, 254
Durham, W. J., 105, 128, 273

Eastern Shore, Maryland, 15, 22
Edgerton, Henry, 165
Edward Waters College, 235
Eisenhower, Dwight, 201, 217, 218, 249;
actions in Little Rock case, 258–59;
and appointment of Earl Warren, 202–
3; participating in writing brief in
Brown, 223; views on civil rights, 306
Elman, Philip, 92, 165, 215, 219, 230; in
Brown, 173; in restrictive covenants
cases, 91; second brief in *Brown*, 201–2
Emerson, Thomas, 132, 134
Employment, race discrimination in, 46,
47, 76–79
Ennix, Coyness, 269
Equal protection clause, and race discrim-
ination, 82–83
Eubanks, Charles, 123
Exhaustion of administrative remedies, de-
fined, 244; as strategy to delay deseg-
regation, 243, 249–50, 253, 266–67,
271
Extradition cases, 39–40, 45

Fairman, Charles, 141
Farmville, Virginia, school segregation in,
150–51
Faubus, Orval, 258, 264–65, 266, 291
Feder, Irma Robbins, 369
Federal Council of Churches, 134
Federal Housing Authority (FHA) 48, 86–
87, 97
Field Foundation, 312
Fifteenth Amendment, 101
Fifth Amendment and race discrimination,
96, 164
Fifth Amendment right against self-
incrimination, 295–96
Figg, Robert M., 158, 159–60, 226
Final judgment rule, 277, 303
Flemming, Sarah Mae, 303
Florida, legislative investigation of
NAACP, 295–300; school desegrega-
tion in, 237; University of, desegrega-
tion suit against, 235–38
Florida A & M College, 235
Florida Legislative Investigation Commit-
tee, 296
Folsom, Fred, 105, 108
Forrestal, James, 48, 323

Fourteenth Amendment, NAACP's interpretation of original intent of, 137,
140; NAACP's research on original intent of, 196, 197–99; original intent of,
170–71, 205; states' interpretation of
original intent of, 200–202; Supreme
Court justices' views of original intent
of, 141, 142, 143
Francis, Willie, 43–44
Frank, John, 134
Frankfurter, Felix, 6; 1954 memorandum
on remedy in *Brown*, 220–21; on abstention doctrine, 275; accounts of Supreme Court deliberations, 338; and
"all deliberate speed" formula, 230; appointment to Supreme Court, 68;
Bickel's historical memorandum to,
203–4; in *Brown*, 169; in *Brown* argument on remedy, 217; on disclosure of
teachers' affiliations, 293–95; in discussion of *Brown*, 188; on draft of *Henderson* opinion, 145–46; on draft of
university cases, 145; in Florida legislative investigation case, 298; on gradualism, 219, 276, 278; in *Hawkins*
case, 236–37; in Jaybird case, 110–11;
in Little Rock case, 259–66 *passim;* on
meaning of "deliberate speed," 264;
and NAACP, 68; in NAACP membership disclosure case, 286–87; in Oklahoma university desegregation case,
130; opinion in restrictive covenants
cases, 96; at oral arguments in general, 139; questions at *Brown* oral arguments, 169, 174–75, 176, 179–86
passim; questions at *Brown* reargument,
205, 206, 208–9; questions at *Brown*
remedy argument, 225, 226, 227;
questions at *Henderson* oral argument,
139–40; and reargument in *Brown*,
215–16; in restrictive covenant cases,
92–94; retirement of, 279, 298; on
rhetoric in Court opinions, 69, 79; in
Richmond bus terminal case, 308; on
timing of desegregation arguments,
165–66; views at discussion of *Brown*,
192–93; views on Florida Supreme
Court, 297; views on free speech,
285–86; views on gradualist remedy in
Brown, 228–29; views on initial votes

Frankfurter, Felix (*Cont.*)
in *Brown*, 187, 194; views on interstate commerce, 74; views of judicial role, 112; views of NAACP, 277; views after reargument in *Brown*, 211; views on Supreme Court and race, 69; views on university cases, 142; in Virginia antibarratry case, 277–79; in white primary cases, 105–6
Franklin, John Hope, 148, 197–98
Freedom rides, 233

Gaines, Lloyd, 70, 121–22
Garland, Charles, 11–12
Garland Fund, 11–13, 15, 19, 70
Garrett, Henry, 162, 182
Gellhorn, Walter, 36
Gentry, Thomas, 227
Gibbs, William, 21, 22
Gibson, Phil, 77
Gibson, Theodore, 296–97
Gilligan, Henry, 94
Glass, Carter, 207
Goldberg, Arthur, appointment to Court, 279; in Florida legislative investigation case, 299–300; in Virginia antibarratry case, 280
Gorman, Robert, 286
Gosnell, William, 11
Gradualism, 206; contrasted with "immediate" desegregation, 218–19; Court's attempt to define, 220–21; Department of Justice position on, 173; in desegregation remedies, 169; difficulties with, 208; discussion by justices in 1954, 219–20; Frankfurter's position on, 177, 193, 208–9, 219–20; LDF's theory of limits on, 200; Marshall's position on, 217, 222–23, 262
Graham, Edward, 297
Graham, Howard Jay, 147, 197, 198, 199
"Grandfather clause" case, 81
Grand juries, race discrimination in, 39, 56–57, 59–61
Gray Commission, 248, 249
Gray, Fred, 302, 305, 367–68
Gray, Garland, 248
Greenberg, Jack, 36–37, 40; at *Brown* trial, 161; at Delaware desegregation case, 163; in university cases, 137; oral argument in *Brown*, 185–86; work on remedy in *Brown*, 200
Greenhill, Joe, 132, 141
Greensboro, North Carolina, desegregation in, 253–54; sit-ins in, 308, 309
Gremillion, Jack, 267
Griffin, Leslie Francis, 151
Griffin, Marvin, 258
Griswold, Erwin, 132, 138; actions in AALS, 135, 148–49; testimony in university cases, 133–34
Grooms, H. Hobart, 238–39
Grovey, Richard, 101, 102

Hall, Amos, 140
Hand, Learned, 195
Hargrave, Helen, 132
Harlan, John Marshall (the first), 176
Harlan, John Marshall, in Alabama student assignment case, 245; appointment to Supreme Court, 217; on disclosure of teachers' affiliations, 294–95; in Florida legislative investigation case, 298–300; in *Hawkins* case, 237; in Little Rock case, 261, 263, 264, 265; in Louisiana NAACP membership case, 291; in NAACP membership disclosure case, 285–87; questions in *Brown* remedy argument, 225; views on Alabama Supreme Court, 288, 289; in Virginia antibarratry case, 280, 281–82; on Virginia regulations of NAACP, 276
Harrison, Albertis, 276
Harrison, Earl, 132
Harvard Law School, 6, 12
Hastie, William, 29, 53, 63, 97; at 1945 restrictive covenants conference, 88; at 1949 conference on school cases, 137; advice on segregation cases, 131; advice in university desegregation cases, 133; as adviser to Marshall, 37, 42; as assistant to Secretary of War, 28; in restrictive covenants cases, 91; and transportation cases, 73, 74, 75; views on attacking segregation in 1946, 126–27; and white primary cases, 105, 107
Hawkins, Virgil, 235, 238, 357
Hayes, George E. C., oral argument in *Brown*, 184, 209

Hearne, Texas, school segregation in, 153
Henderson, Elmer, 135–36
Hervey, John, 148–49
Hill, Oliver, 72, 121, 308; at 1946 Atlanta conference on segregated education, 124; actions against massive resistance, 250; early legal career of, 8, 10, 118; and legal ethics, 153; partnership with Robinson, 72; in Virginia school desegregation case, 150–51
Hills, Roderick, 237
Hinton, James, 59, 154
Hobbs, Sam, 140
Hockessin, Delaware, desegregation in, 218; school segregation in, 163–64
Hocutt, Thomas, 11
Hodges, Luther, 242
Hoffman, Walter, 249–50, 254, 275
Holmes, Oliver Wendell, 100, 112–13
Housing, race discrimination in, 35, 37, 48, 81, 83, 84–86
Houston, Charles Hamilton, 6–7, 37, 45, 97; at 1947 restrictive covenants conference, 91; as adviser to Marshall, 27; on African-American lawyers, 6–7; argument in restrictive covenant cases, 94; on Baltimore lawyers, 10; departure from New York NAACP office, 26; and *Gaines* case, 70, 122; and labor unions, 76, 77–79; on law as social engineering, 6, 16; litigation strategy of, 11, 13, 15; as Marshall's mentor, 11, 14, 15, 16, 17–18, 23–24, 26, 40, 314; in Maryland nursing case, 147–48; as mentor, 7; in *Murray* case, 14; and public interest law, 282; relocation to New York, 13; on restrictive covenants, 88; restrictive covenants case of, 89; role in hiring Margold, 12; role in NAACP, 20; views on Jaybird case, 110; in Washington desegregation cases, 165
Houston, Texas, desegregation in, 252–53; race discrimination in, 126; and voting rights, 105
Howard University Law School, 87; moot court arguments at, 38, 93, 139; NAACP staff graduates of, 33, 34, 35; under Houston, 6–7, 9, 81
Hughes, Charles Evans, 70, 122

Hutcheson, C. Sterling, 251
Huxman, Walter, 161–62

Iggers, Georg, 267
Illinois, race discrimination in, 87
Inc. Fund. *See* NAACP Legal Defense and Educational Fund
Indritz, Phineas, 90–91, 94
Interest groups, and NAACP network, 44–46; reaction to 1950 university cases, 147; in restrictive covenant cases, 90–91
Internal Revenue Service, 27, 310
International Labor Defense, 44, 45, 60
International relations, and segregation, 188
Interposition, theory of, 240–41
Interracial marriages, 44, 367
Interstate commerce, race discrimination in, 79
Interstate Commerce Act, and race discrimination, 71–72, 75, 139–40, 307–9
Interstate Commerce Commission, 71–72, 136, 140, 307–9

Jackson, Emory, 147
Jackson, Forrest, 59
Jackson, Lillie, 10, 19, 43
Jackson, Robert, 60, 94, 106; 1954 heart attack of, 214; appointment to Supreme Court, 69–70; concerns about desegregation cases, 169; death of, 217; in discussion of *Brown*, 187, 188–89; in Jaybird case, 110, 111–12; proposed separate opinion in *Brown*, 211–14; questions at *Brown* oral argument, 182–83, 185; questions at *Brown* reargument, 205, 207–8, 209; and reargument in *Brown*, 215–16; in university desegregation cases, 129; views on desegregation, 188–89; views at discussion of *Brown*, 193; views on initial votes in *Brown*, 187; views after reargument in *Brown*, 211; views on university cases, 141, 143
Japanese-American internment cases, 184–85, 214–15; relation to segregation, 171
"Jaybird" white primary, 109–12
Jim Crow laws, 11, 12, 301; in Maryland, 9; in transportation, 70–71, 73–74

Johns, Barbara, 150–51
Johns, Vernon, 150
Johnson, Frank, 288, 304
Johnson, James Weldon, 12
Johnson, Lyman, 148
Johnson, Lyndon, 306
Johnson, Mordecai, 7
Johnson, Ozie, 135
Johnston, Olin, 107–8
Jones, Donald, 119, 340–41
Jones, Walter, 283, 284, 285, 303–4

Kasper, John, 269
Keeton, W. Page, 133
Kelly, Alfred, 197–99
Kennedy, John, 279
Kennerly, Thomas, 110
Kentucky, race discrimination in, 123,
    148; University of, 148
Kilpatrick, James J., 240–41, 248
King, Martin Luther, Jr., 233, 302–3,
    305
Klineberg, Otto, 157
Kluger, Richard, 5, 209, 351
Konvitz, Milton, 34, 51, 63, 105, 120
Korman, Milton, 184–85, 209
Krock, Arthur, 97, 147, 245
Ku Klux Klan, statutes attacking, 283–84,
    290

Labor unions, race discrimination in, 76–
    80
Lanier, R. O'Hara, 135
Law professors' brief in *Sweatt* case, 134–
    35
Laws, Clarence, 290
Lawson, Belford, 136, 139–40, 165
LDF, attacks on, 233; budget of, 311; and
    cooperating attorneys, 275; creation of,
    27; and legal ethics, 117, 128, 273,
    274; limits on ability to force deseg-
    regation, 233–34; and lobbying, 233;
    separation from NAACP, 310–11; tax-
    exempt status of, 48–49, 113, 240, 310
LeBlanc, Bertrand, 43–44
Legal ethics, and LDF, 117, 128, 273, 274
Legal realism, 6, 81
Legislative investigations, law dealing
    with, 295–96, 298
Leighton, George, 114–15

Lemley, Harry, 259, 260, 261, 264
Liberty Bowl, 289
Lincoln University (Missouri), 70, 121–22
Lincoln University (Pennsylvania), 9, 35,
    36, 235
Literacy tests, 99, 113, 115
Little Rock, Arkansas, and disclosure of
    teachers' affiliations, 294–95; NAACP
    branches in, 292; school closings in,
    266; school desegregation in, 257–66;
    teachers' salary case in, 119–20
Llewellyn, Karl, 148
Long, Huey, 103
Looby, Z. Alexander, 54–55, 269
Louisiana, attempt to suppress NAACP,
    289–91; race discrimination in, 43–44,
    49, 64–66, 119
Louisville, race discrimination in, 81, 84,
    117
Lucy, Autherine, 238–39, 283, 289, 302
Lumberton, North Carolina, school seg-
    regation in, 152–53
Lynne, Seybourn, 304
Lyons, W. D., 61–64, 120

Madison, Waite, 369
Margold, Nathan, 12, 13
Margold Report, 12–13, 86, 123
Marshall, Cecilia Suyatt, 313
Marshall, John, 313
Marshall, Norma, 8
Marshall, Thurgood, and 1945 restrictive
    covenants conference, 88; at 1946 At-
    lanta conference on segregated educa-
    tion, 155; 1946 illness of, 35, 53; and
    1947 restrictive covenants conferences,
    89, 90–91; 1949 conference on school
    cases, 137; 1951 trip to Japan and Ko-
    rea, 311–12; 1960 trip to Kenya, 313; in
    Alabama voting discrimination case,
    113, 115; appearance on *Time* magazine
    cover, 232; as appellate advocate, 139,
    168–69; appointment as Special Coun-
    sel of NAACP, 26; argument in
    Brown, 175–77, 180–81; argument in
    Brown reargument, 204–5; argument
    on remedy in *Brown*, 224–26, 226–28;
    argument in restrictive covenant cases,
    93; on branch activism in segregation
    cases, 151–52; in *Briggs* case, 157–60;

and Columbia, Tennessee, trials, 53–
55, 129; on Constitution, 5; dealings
on FHA discrimination, 87, 97; and
Department of Justice, 49, 50; disagreement with Carter on strategy,
277; early practice in Baltimore, 10,
18–19; early work for NAACP, 17–18;
education of, 9; encounters with violence, 52–55; as fund-raiser, 27, 35,
37, 311–13; in *Gaines* case, 122; hiring
by NAACP, 18–19; and Houston,
Charles Hamilton, 78; initial appeal in
Little Rock case, 258; in Jaybird case,
110; and Kansas school segregation
cases, 153; and labor cases, 32; and labor unions, 76–77, 79; lawsuit against
Baltimore schools, 16–17; and legal
ethics, 117, 128, 273, 274, 282, 290;
in Little Rock case, 258, 259–60; at
Little Rock oral argument, 261–63; in
Lucy case, 239; as manager, 33–34,
36–37; in *Murray* case, 14–15; on
NAACP role in criminal cases, 325–
26; in Oklahoma university desegregation case, 129–30; oral argument in
Sweatt, 140–41; as organizer, 42–43,
59, 63; organizing activities in Maryland, 15–16; on pace of desegregation,
267–68; performance at reargument in
Brown, 209, 215–16; personality of,
38–39, 40–41; planning restrictive covenant cases, 87–90; position on gradualism in *Brown*, 217; preparation for
Brown arguments, 170, 173; reaction to
1950 university cases, 147; reaction to
reargument order in *Brown*, 196; reargument in *Brown*, 205, 206–7; relations with Roger Baldwin, 44; relations
with branches, 46–47; relations with
Carter, 311; relations with Communists, 44–46; relations with cooperating attorneys, 38, 43–44, 88, 90, 98,
118; relations with Martin Luther
King, 305; reliance on international affairs in argument against segregation,
188; reminiscences of Charles Hamilton Houston, 6, 7; retirement from
Supreme Court, 314; role in appealing
desegregation decisions, 165; role in
NAACP, 20, 26, 31–32, 312; role in

NAACP staff, 33; as Second Circuit
judge, 4; on sit-ins, 309–10; in South
Carolina primary case, 108–9; as
speaker, 30, 32; as story teller, 3; on
strategy in antibarratry case, 277; on
strategy in desegregation cases, 155–
57; study of Constitution, 8; style of
argument, 38; style of working, 37–38,
39–40; as Supreme Court Justice, 4; in
teachers' salary cases, 20–26, 31, 117–
19, 119–20; at Texas trial to shut
NAACP, 272–73; in Texas white primary cases, 104–5; theories in university desegregation cases, 123–24, 127,
130, 131–33, 134; and transportation
cases, 72–73, 75–76; as trial lawyer,
61–63, 64–66; trial of *Sipuel* case, 133–
34; trial of *Sweatt* case, 132; trips to
South Carolina on segregation cases,
154; in university cases, 137–38; upbringing of, 7–8; views on attacking
segregation in 1946, 126–27; views on
desegregation strategy, 151–52; views
on disclosure of NAACP membership,
284–85; views on gradual desegregation, 200; views on Jaybird case, 112;
views on pace of desegregation, 232–
33; views on remedy in *Brown*, 222–
23; views on rule of law, 314–15; views
of "separate but equal" doctrine, 72;
views of Heman Sweatt, 133; on white
primary cases, 102
Marshall, Thurgood, Jr., 313
Marshall, Vivian (Buster), 9, 53, 313
Marshall, William, 8
Martin, Martin, 308
Maryland, cost of equalizing teachers' salaries in, 117; politics of, 9; University
of, desegregation case, 11, 14–15
Massive resistance to desegregation, 247–
56, 261; in deep South, 251; in Vir-
ginia, 247–51
McAllister, Thomas, 269–70
McCarthy era, 295–96
McClellan, John, 266
McCormick, Charles, 132
McDowell County, North Carolina, de-
segregation in, 242–43
McGill, S. D., 23–24
McGranery, James, 173

McGrath, J. Howard, 139, 141, 173
McGuinn, Warner, 10
McLaurin, George, 130
McMillan, Enolia Pettigen, 21, 22
McNally, Harold, 159
Mecklenburg County, North Carolina, desegregation in, 255
Medina, Harold, 44–45
Miami, Florida, race discrimination in, 121
Michigan, race discrimination in, 79–80, 89
Miller, John, 266
Miller, Loren, 39–40, 216, 325; in restrictive covenant cases, 89, 90, 93, 96–97, 97–98
Miller, William, 269
Ming, Robert, 97, 113, 135; in 1949 conference on school segregation, 137; in restrictive covenant cases, 91; in school segregation cases, 198
Mink Slide, 53
Minton, Sherman, 110, 140; appointment to Supreme Court, 138; in Jaybird case, 112; questions at *Brown* oral argument, 185; views after reargument in *Brown*, 210; views on remedy in *Brown*, 220, 229
Mississippi, race discrimination in, 51
Mississippi plan of disfranchisement, 99–100, 112–13
Missouri, race discrimination in, 89–90; University of, 70, 121–23
Mitchell, Arthur, 71
Mitchell, Samuel, 243
Mollison, Irving, 88
Montgomery, Alabama, bus boycott, 233, 283, 289, 302–4; effects of, 305
Montgomery County, Maryland, 21, 22, 24
Montgomery Improvement Association, 302, 304, 305
Moon, Henry Lee, 312
Moore, Harry, 115
Moore, Justin, 162, 182–83, 206
Morgan, Irene, 73
Motley, Constance Baker, 36, 113, 132
Mullins, Clarence, 114–15
Murphy, Carl, 10, 16, 21
Murphy, Frank, 61, 69, 103; as Attorney

General, 49; death of, 138; in restrictive covenant cases, 95; in *Steele* case, 79; in university desegregation cases, 129–30
Murray, Donald, 11, 132, 147–48
Murray, Joseph, 58
Murray, Pauli, 123
Myrdal, Gunnar, 127

NAACP, 13, 17; 1947 policy statement on segregation, 155; 1948 resolution on segregation, 127; 1950 resolution on segregation, 155; anti-Communist resolution of 1950, 45; Arkansas branches of, 291–92; attacks on, 233; Baltimore branch of, 10; board's disagreement with Marshall on Texas case, 273; branches of, in general, 42–43; budget for legal cases in 1940s, 34; and civil rights leadership in late 1950s, 305; and Communist party, 295, 298; contribution of Garland Fund to, 12; disclosure of membership in, 284–85; effect of New York location on, 46–47, 326–27; Florida branches of, 296; founding of, 10; fund-raising of, 34; Houston branch of, 252; Kansas branches of, 153–54; legal staff's relations with cooperating attorneys, 58–59; legal staff of, 28, 33–37; Little Rock branch of, 257; Louisiana branches of, 290–91; New Orleans branch of, 267; position on Montgomery bus boycott, 302; relations with branches, 311; response to Southern attack on, 289; separation from LDF, 310–11; studies of desegregation, 218–19; in teachers' salary cases, 117–18, 119; Virginia branches of, 251; in voting discrimination cases, 113–14, 115; in white primary cases, 101–2, 105
NAACP Legal Defense and Educational Fund. *See* LDF
NAACP National Legal Committee, 27, 68
Nabrit, James, 87, 97, 132, 165; oral argument in *Brown*, 185, 209
Nabrit, James M., Jr., 369
Nashville, Tennessee, desegregation in, 268–70

National Association for the Advancement of Colored People. *See* NAACP

National Council of Negro Women, 313

National Guard, in Little Rock, 258

National Lawyers' Guild, 35, 44–45

Negro Women's Political Council (Montgomery), 302

New Deal, 76; and Supreme Court, 67, 112, 189, 190

New Orleans, Louisiana, school desegregation in, 266–67, 291; teachers' salary case in, 119

Newport News, Virginia, desegregation in, 249, 250

New York, race discrimination in, 46, 48

Nice, Harry, 22

Nixon, E. D., 302

Nixon, L. A., 100–102

Norfolk, Virginia, desegregation in, 248–49, 250, 254; teachers' salary case, 24–26, 118

North Carolina, NAACP registration in, 283; NAACP study of desegregation in, 218; race discrimination in, 50, 123, 148; school desegregation in, 242–44, 253–56; University of, 11

O'Dunne, Eugene, 14

Odum, Howard, 160

Ohio, race discrimination in, 40

Oklahoma, University of, desegregation suit against, 129–30, 133–34

Orange County, California, school segregation in, 131

Painter, Theophilus, 128

Parker, John J., "*Briggs* dictum" of, 241, 271, 357–58; in North Carolina student assignment case, 243–44; opinions in *Briggs,* 160, 166; in South Carolina NAACP membership case, 293; in South Carolina voting cases, 108–9, 111; Supreme Court nomination of, 357; and trial in *Briggs,* 158, 159

Parks, Rosa, 302

Patterson, John, 283, 304

Paul, John, 249, 250

Pearson, Conrad, 11, 254

Pearson, Levi, 154

Pennsylvania, race discrimination in, 47

Peonage cases, 45

Perlman, Philip, 91–92, 97, 136, 139, 173

Perry, Marian Wynn, 37, 42, 45, 50, 153; background of, 35, 46; in restrictive covenants cases, 88, 97–98; in university desegregation cases, 134–35

Perry, Ruth, 296

Peyser, Annette, 89, 137

Pinsky, David, 200

Polier, Shad, 90

Pollak, Louis, 197

Poll taxes, 99, 115

Port Chicago incident, 32, 44, 48, 323

Pound, Roscoe, 7

Powell, Lewis F., 240–41

Prettyman, E. Barrett, Jr., 213

Prince Edward County, Virginia, desegregation case in, 162–63, 166; desegregation in, 249, 251; school segregation in, 150–51

Prince George's County, Maryland, 22–23

Prince Hall Masons, 152, 311, 312

Prisons, race discrimination in, 48

Progressive party, 46

Pulaski County, Virginia, school segregation in, 150–51

Race discrimination, in criminal cases, 28–29; in marriage laws, 184; private, 75

Radin, Max, 132

Railroad unions, 76, 77–78

Railroads, segregation in, 36

Rankin, J. Lee, 201, 307; argument in *Brown,* 207–9; in Little Rock case, 259, 261, 262

Ransom, Leon, 42, 51, 58; at 1946 conference on segregated education, 124; assault on, 52; at Columbia, Tennessee, trial, 53, 54

Rape cases, 29, 44, 51, 52, 64–66

Rault, Gerard, 266–67

Redding, Louis, 163; oral argument in *Brown,* 185

Redfield, Robert, 132, 159, 171, 175

Redmond, Sidney D., 59

Redmond, Sidney R., 70

Reed, Stanley, 60–61, 64, 69, 94; appointment to Supreme Court, 68; discussions with Warren about *Brown,* 214;

Reed, Stanley (*Cont.*)
　on drafts of university cases, 145; in
　Hawkins case, 237; at *Henderson* oral
　argument, 139–40; in Jaybird case, 110;
　questions at *Brown* oral argument,
　173–74, 180–81, 182–83, 185; questions
　at *Brown* reargument, 207–8; questions
　at *Brown* remedy argument, 225; on
　race discrimination in interstate com-
　merce, 74; in university desegregation
　cases, 129; views at discussion of
　Brown, 192; views after reargument
　in *Brown,* 210–11; views on remedy in
　Brown, 220; views on university cases,
　143; in white primary cases, 106–7
Reeves, Frank, 33
Rehnquist, William H., in Jaybird case,
　110–12; memorandum on *Brown,* 190,
　351
Republican party, and desegregation, 201
Resistance to desegregation, Black's pre-
　dictions about, 229–30; justices' con-
　cerns about, 176–77, 182, 210, 228;
　Marshall's arguments about, 180; Mar-
　shall's views of, 224–25; as threat in
　Brown, 183; threats of, 222–23, 226–
　27
Restrictive covenant cases, 84–98, 131; ar-
　guments in, 92–94
Restrictive covenants, defined, 81–82, 84;
　1945 conference on, 88; 1947 confer-
　ences on, 89, 90–91
Richmond, Virginia, segregated transpor-
　tation facilities in, 307–8
Rives, Richard, 241, 244–45, 304
Roberts, B. K., 236, 237
Roberts, Owen, 64, 102, 106
Robertson, A. G., 226
Robeson, Paul, 44
Robinson, Jo Ann, 302
Robinson, Spottswood, 72, 308; at 1946
　Atlanta conference on segregated edu-
　cation, 155; actions against massive re-
　sistance, 250; comments on *Briggs*
　trial, 158; and legal ethics, 153; oral
　argument in *Brown,* 181–82, 183–84;
　reargument in *Brown,* 204–5; theories
　in restrictive covenant cases, 87–88;
　and transportation cases, 72–73; on
　Virginia desegregation cases, 155–56;

in Virginia school desegregation case,
　150–51
Rogers, S. E., 226
Roosevelt, Franklin D., 77, 105; impact
　on Supreme Court, 67, 69
Rutledge, Wiley, 69, 79, 94; death of,
　138; in university desegregation cases,
　130; in white primary cases, 106

Sanford, Edward, 85
School closings, in Virginia, 248, 250
Schroeter, Leonard, 369
Scott, Elisha, 154
Scottsboro cases, 44
Screws, Claude, 49–50
Seegers, Gerald, 92
Segregated education, history of judicial
　approval, 170
Segregated elementary and secondary edu-
　cation, challenges to, 15
Segregation, basis of opposition to, 187–88;
　in education, 12; in education, 1946
　conference on, 123–24, 127; in hous-
　ing, 12; and international affairs, 127–
　28, 188; in universities, 116
Segregation in education, importance of,
　116
Seitz, Collins, 163, 185
"Separate but equal" doctrine, 116; argu-
　ments for overruling, 170–72; decision
　to make direct attack on, 155; legal ar-
　guments attacking, 124, 126, 127; ori-
　gins of, 12; overruling of, 164, 303–4;
　relation to salary equalization cases,
　21; in transportation cases, 70, 71–72,
　146–47; in university cases, 129–30,
　131, 139, 140–41
Shagaloff, June, 235
Sharp, Malcolm, 132
Shelley, J. D., 89–90
Shepard, James, 11
Shepperd, John, 272
Shores, Arthur D., 24, 52, 113–14, 119; in
　Lucy case, 238–39; in NAACP mem-
　bership disclosure case, 287–88
Shuttlesworth, Fred, 244, 305
Sipuel, Ada Lois (Fisher), 129
Sit-ins, 233, 300, 301, 308; 1960 confer-
　ence on, 310
Smith, A. Maceo, 102, 128, 153

Smith, L. E. (Lonnie), 31, 105
Sobeloff, Simon, 223, 227
Soper, Morris, 21, 275, 276
South Carolina, attacks on NAACP, 293–94; difficulties of desegregation in, 224; race discrimination in, 45, 58–59, 120–21, 123, 303; school segregation in, 154; voting discrimination in, 108–9
South Park, Kansas, school segregation in, 153
Southern Conference Educational Fund, 134
"Southern Manifesto," 240
Southern Tenant Farmers Union, 45
Speer, Hugh, 161–62
Spingarn, Arthur, 18–19
St. Louis, desegregation in, 234
Stanley, Edwin, 254
Stanley, Thomas, 248
"State action" doctrine, in bus terminal case, 308; defined, 75; in employment discrimination cases, 76, 77–78, 80; in restrictive covenant cases, 81, 82, 83–84, 84–86; in sit-in cases, 234, 309; in voting discrimination cases, 100, 111
State laws against race discrimination, 79–80
Stern, Robert, 173
Stewart, Potter, in Arkansas NAACP membership case, 292; on disclosure of teachers' affiliations, 294–95; in Louisiana NAACP membership case, 291; in Virginia antibarratry case, 279–80
Stimson, Henry, 48
Stone, Harlan Fiske, 60, 69, 73–74; in *Classic* case, 103–4; in *Hansberry* case, 87; in *Steele* case, 78–79; in white primary cases, 105–6
Story, Moorfield, 84
Stovall, Alice, 37
Student assignment laws, in Alabama, 244–45; in North Carolina, 242–44, 253–55; in Virginia, 248–49, 254–55
Sweatt, Heman, 126, 128, 133, 149, 273
Swimming pools, race discrimination in, 40

Tallahassee, Florida, bus boycott, 233
Tampa, Florida, race discrimination in, 121

Tate, Ulysses Simpson, 147, 257–58, 273
Taylor, Herman, 148, 152, 242–43
Taylor, William (educator), 122
Taylor, William L. (NAACP staff), 369
Teachers, attacks on NAACP members as, 293; concerns about desegregation, 151–52, 154; loss of jobs during desegregation, 218, 293
Teachers' salary cases, 13, 20–21, 34, 116–21; in Alabama, 24, 119; in Florida, 23–24; in Little Rock, 119–20; in Louisiana, 119, 340–41; in Maryland, 21–23; and merit pay systems, 120–21; in Miami, 121; in South Carolina, 120–21; in Tampa, 121; in Virginia, 23, 24–26, 121
Teachers' salaries, cost of equalizing, 117
Tennessee, school desegregation in, 268–70; University of, 166
Terrell, Glenn, 236, 237
Texas, attempt to suppress NAACP and LDF, 272–73; school desegregation in, 251–53; white primary cases in, 100–102, 104–7, 109–12
Texas State University for Negroes, 131, 135
Texas, University of, 125; desegregation suit against, 128–29, 131–33; Supreme Court's delay in deciding case against, 135
Thomas, Elwyn, 237
Thomas, Prentice, 33, 52
Thompson, Charles, 132
Thornal, Campbell, 297
Three-judge courts, 114–15, 156, 266, 275, 302
Timmerman, George, 158, 160, 303
Topeka, Kansas, desegregation of schools in, 166, 217–18, 353–54; school segregation in, 154
Transportation, race discrimination in, 126; after *Brown*, 301, 303, 307; early cases challenging, 71–76; and *Henderson* case, 135–36, 139–40
Truman, Harry S, 97; appointments to lower courts, 244–45, 267, 304; appointments to Supreme Court, 69–70, 138–39; and Committee on Civil Rights, 91–92, 187

Tureaud, A. P., 65, 274, 290; at 1946 Atlanta conference on segregated education, 123–24; in New Orleans desegregation case, 267; relations with Marshall, 43, 119, 340

Tyler, Texas, 272

Umstead, William, 242
"Understanding" tests, 113
United Steelworkers of America, 279
Universities, race discrimination in, 121–25
University cases, 11, 13; 1946 conference on, 123–24; 1948 and 1949 conferences on, 134; of 1950, oral arguments in, 139–41; of 1950, reaction to, 147; after 1950, 147–48

Vaughn, George, 90, 92
Veterans, discrimination against African-Americans, 40
Vines, Meb, 50
Vinson, Fred, 279; appointment to Supreme Court, 70; background of, 138; death of, 202; in discussion of *Brown,* 187, 188; drafting opinions in university cases, 145; in Jaybird case, 110; questions at *Brown* oral argument, 176, 182–84, 185–86; in restrictive covenants cases, 93–94, 95–96; in university desegregation cases, 129–30; views at discussion of *Brown,* 191; views on university cases, 142
Virginia, difficulties of desegregation in, 224; efforts to regulate LDF lawyers, 274–82; massive resistance in, 247–51; school desegregation in, 254
Voters and Veterans Association (VVA), 114
Voting, race discrimination in, 81, 82–84
Voting rights, 100; in 1950s, 306–7; effects of litigation on, 115

Wallace, Henry, 46, 151, 153
Waring, J. Waties, 156, 160–61; in *Briggs* case, 157–58; in white primary cases, 108–9
Warlick, Wilson, 242–43, 255
Warren, Earl, in Alabama student assignment case, 245; appointment to Supreme Court, 202–3; in Arkansas NAACP membership case, 292; in *Brown,* 214; on disclosure of teachers' affiliations, 294; in discussion after reargument in *Brown,* 209–10; draft opinion on remedy in *Brown,* 230; in *Flemming* case, 303; in Florida legislative investigation case, 298; law clerks' memorandum on remedy in *Brown,* 221–22; in Little Rock case, 260, 263, 264; at Little Rock oral argument, 261, 262; in Louisiana NAACP membership case, 291; questions in *Brown* remedy argument, 226; views on Alabama Supreme Court, 288; views on desegregation, 203; views after reargument in *Brown,* 210; views on remedy in *Brown,* 220, 228–29; in Virginia antibarratry case, 277, 279–80; on Virginia regulations of NAACP, 276
Washington, D.C., constitutional law applicable to, 94; desegregation in, 218; desegregation case against, 166; race discrimination in, 88, 89; school segregation in, 164–65
Way, Luther, 25–26
Weaver, Maurice, 54
Weaver, Robert, 88, 91
Wechsler, Herbert, 105
Wesley, Carter, 101–2, 128, 133, 273
West Virginia, desegregation in, 218
White, Byron, 279–80; in Florida legislative investigation case, 299
White, Lulu, 128
White primary, creation of, 99–100
White primary cases, 31; reaction to, 107; in Supreme Court, 100–107, 109–11
White, Walter, 45, 48, 62, 75, 87; 1949 divorce of, 312; and Columbia, Tennessee, trial, 53, 54; on FHA discrimination, 97; and Marshall's 1951 trip to Far East, 312; and Marshall's hiring, 18, 19; relations with Marshall, 17, 27, 33, 37, 43–44, 59, 90; on restrictive covenants decision, 96; views of teachers, 117; in white primary cases, 101, 105
Whittaker, Charles, 279, 298, 309
Wichita, Kansas, school segregation in, 153–54

Wilkins, Roy, 34, 48; on legal ethics, 273; and reaction to *Brown,* 216; relations with Marshall, 33, 43, 58, 118, 312; role in Montgomery bus boycott, 302; role in NAACP membership disclosure cases, 285
Willer, Herman, 92
Williams, Avon, 269
Williams, Birdie, 292
Williams, David, 45
Williams, Franklin, 43; background and personality of, 36, 39; in *Brown,* 153; in military cases, 29, 48
Wilmington, Delaware, desegregation in, 218

Wilson, Paul, 174–75
Wirth, Louis, 91
Woodard, Isaac, 50
Woodward, C. Vann, 197
Workers Defense League, 45, 59
World War II, 72, 89, 126; effect of end on NAACP's finances, 34; effect on teachers' salary cases, 116; race relations in military during, 32, 64, 71
Wright, J. Skelly, 267

Yale Law School, 10
Yankauer, Alfred, 88–89
Young, Albert, 185
Young, P. B., 24, 118